THE ENCYCLOPEDIA OF PARENTING THEORY AND RESEARCH

EDITED BY
CHARLES A. SMITH

GREENWOOD PRESS
Westport, Connecticut

Library of Congress Cataloging-in-Publication Data

The encyclopedia of parenting theory and research / edited by
Charles A. Smith.
    p.   cm.
  Includes bibliographical references and index.
  ISBN 0–313–29699–5 (alk. paper)
  1. Child rearing—Encyclopedias. 2. Parenting—Encyclopedias. I.
Smith, Charles A.
  HQ755.8.E526   1999
  649′.1′03—dc21   98–15324

British Library Cataloguing in Publication Data is available.

Library of Congress Catalog Card Number: 98–15324
ISBN: 0–313–29699–5

First published in 1999

Greenwood Press, 88 Post Road West, Westport, CT 06881
An imprint of Greenwood Publishing Group, Inc.

Printed in the United States of America

The paper used in this book complies with the
Permanent Paper Standard issued by the National
Information Standards Organization (Z39.48–1984).

10 9 8 7 6 5 4 3 2

To Sarah and Bill for teaching me the *Important Things* about being a parent

Contents

Preface

The word *parent* is most often used as a referent to a biological relationship with a child. We say, for example, "She is the child's parent." This meaning emphasizes a past, static event. The word *parent*, along with *father* and *mother*, can also mean an act of caring, nurturing, and protecting. This meaning is more dynamic and is based on a relationship that is not necessarily biological. When we say, "That child needs a father," we imply that the child needs a relationship with a man committed to his or her upbringing. The word *parenting* is clearly action oriented. *Parenting* means assuming responsibility for the emotional, social, and physical growth and development of a child. Becoming a parent is relatively easy. Parenting, however, is a skill that is learned and improved over one's lifetime.

The Encyclopedia of Parenting Theory and Research offers 244 entries on a variety of issues that illuminate the nature of the relationship between parents and children. Each of the contributors to the *Encyclopedia* was asked to create an entry of approximately 1,000 words emphasizing only the most important information he or she could find for that entry. Contributors examined the most pertinent research and theory for each term and explored its implications for practitioners and for parents. The *Encyclopedia* is an information-dense book with entries that are readily accessible because of their brevity. Each entry and its associated references provide an excellent launching point for readers interested in studying an issue in more depth. A thorough index enhances the sophistication of the Encyclopedia by guiding readers interested in even more depth.

The Encyclopedia of Parenting Theory and Research provides a comprehensive summary of what we know about parents and parent-child relationships.

Our target audience for the *Encyclopedia* consists of: parent educators, teachers, researchers, health scientists, mental health professionals, community educators, librarians, and others interested in parent-child relationships. In addition, parents seeking a more factual, research-based perspective to understanding parenting should find the material reasonably jargon free and approachable.

If you have suggestions for additional terms in a second edition, should one be undertaken, you can contact me by visiting my website, *The WonderWise Parent* (http://www.ksu.edu/wwparent/).

ACKNOWLEDGMENTS

I would like to thank John Murray, Director of the School of Family Studies and Human Services at Kansas State University for his support and encouragement throughout the arduous process of bringing this effort to publication. The enthusiasm of many of my colleagues, especially Judy Myers-Walls, Wally Goddard, and Jim Ponzetti, was especially important. The professional talents of the editorial staff at Greenwood Press, including Michelle Pini, Norine Mudrick, and Susan Badger, were much appreciated in bringing this work to publication. I would also like to thank George Butler, Associate Editor at Greenwood, for his support and encouragement. Finally, I owe a debt of gratitude to the creators of the Internet, which made rapid communication possible with authors from around the world.

Charles A. Smith

Introduction

Nine categories cluster the *Encyclopedia* terms into groups around shared themes. Each term is listed only once, although most terms could fit into more than one category. These categories are conveniences with fluid boundaries and considerable overlap.

- *Child activity* consists of terms that deal with child behavior.
- *Child outcomes* relate to the effective consequences of parent-child relationships.
- *Child states* involve the relationship between parents and selected child characteristics.
- *Parent behaviors* summarize different types of parental action.
- A *Parent state or context* focuses on parental characteristics or social contexts.
- *External or community factors* examine the forces outside of the parent that influence parenting.
- *System issues* examine the context of parenting within the family as a system.
- *Resources* are available to parents or parent educators.
- *People* consists of historically significant professionals who made a great impact on our understanding of parenting and parent education.

Readers may find it profitable to concentrate their study in these families of terms to take advantage of the overlap and connection between them. For a more detailed and focused review, the reader is advised to make liberal use of the book's extensive index.

Child Activity

Adolescent separation	Mathematics	Resiliency in children
Affectivity, positive and negative	Misbehavior	Self-esteem
Aggression, childhood	Money and children	Separation anxiety
Biting	Narratives, personal	Sex roles
Bullying	Night wakings	Sexuality, adolescent
Chores	Nighttime fears	Shame
Competition	Pain and children	Shyness
Compliance	Peace education	Sports
Crying	Peer influence	Temper tantrums
Eating behaviors, children and	Pets and children	Temperament
Emotion language	Physical activity	Thumb sucking
Fear	Play	Toilet learning
Guilt	Prosocial behavior	Whining
Jealousy	Puberty	

Child Outcomes

Academic achievement	Identity development	Physical fitness
Attachment, secure	Imagination	Playground skills
Conscience	Immunization	Popularity
Cultural competence	Language development	Racial identity
Death, understanding of	Literacy	Religious development
Empathy	Moral development	Social competence
Empowerment	Motor development	Spirituality

Child States

Aids/HIV	Disability, physical	Night terrors
Aids/HIV, adolescent	Eating disorders	Nightmares
Aids/HIV, pediatric	Enuresis	Obesity
ADHD	Failure to thrive	Premature birth
Autism	Fetal Alcohol Syndrome	Runaway children
Cleft lip and palate	Genetic disorders	Sexual offenders, youthful
Colic	Gifted children	Sudden Infant Death Syndrome
Deaf children, parenting	Hospitalization	Substance use, children
Death of a child	Illness, chronic, in children	Suicide in children
Delinquency, juvenile	Munchausen Syndrome by Proxy	Throwaway children
Depression, children	Mental illness, children	Vulnerable Child Syndrome
Disability, learning	Mental retardation	

Parent Behaviors

Abuse, child	Fathering	Problem solving
Acceptance, parental	Floortime	Recognition/ encouragement
Advocacy	Gender socialization	Scaffolding
Authority, parental	Instrumental versus expressive functions	Scapegoating
Breastfeeding	Intuitive parenting	Self-care
Communication	Limit setting	Sex education
Conflict resolution	Listening	Smoking
Consequences, natural and logical	Mothering	Spoiling
Consistency	Mutuality	Synchrony
Control strategies	Nature versus nurture	Substance abuse, parents
Developmentally Appropriate Practice	Nurturance	Television viewing
Discipline	Physical punishment	Touching
Distancing strategies	Prevention	Victim-centered discipline

Parent State or Context

Adolescent parenthood	Custody	Indigenous Peoples parent roles
Adolescent pregnancy	Deaf parents	Infertility
Adoption	Death of a parent	Lesbian mothers
Adult children	Depression in parents	Military families
African American parents	Depression, postpartum	Prison, parents in
Alliance, parenting	Gay fathers	Resiliency in parents
Asian American parents	Grandparenting	
Conflict, interparental	Hispanic/Latino parents	

External or Community Factors

After-school child care	Family support	Sociocultural background
Blaming, parent	Feminism	Socioeconomic status
Child care	Fertilization, in vitro	Stress, parental
Community	Home schooling	Teacher training
Cultural context	Home visitation	Television violence
Domestic labor	Media, mass	Toys
Donor insemination	Poverty	Transition to school
Dual-earner families	Reproductive technology, assisted	Urban parenting
Education, parenting	School	Violence, community
Employment, early maternal	Social context	
Family-school partnerships	Social support, informal	

System Issues

Birth order	Intergenerational parenting	Rules, implicit
Critical periods	Kinship care	Self-fulfilling prophecy
Divorced families	Marital boundaries	Siblings
Family council	Marital interaction	Single parents
Family loyalty	Mediation, parent-child	Standards of care, minimum
Family preservation	Multiples	Stepparents
Family size	Paradigms, parenting	Styles, parenting
Family systems	Reconstituted families	Surrogate motherhood
Family therapy	Rituals	Traditions
Foster parenting	Role strain	Transition to parenthood
Goodness of fit model	Routines	Triangulation

Resources

Cooperative Extension Service	HOME Inventory	Parents without Partners
Dimensions of Temperament Survey	MELD	Psychological testing
Family-centered services	NEPEM	
Head Start	Parents Anonymous	

People

Adler, Alfred	Freud, Anna	Rousseau, Jean Jacques
Brazelton, T. Berry	Ginott, Haim	Skinner, B. F.
Captain Kangaroo (Bob Keeshan)	Locke, John	Spock, Benjamin
Dreikurs, Rudolf	Rogers, Fred	Vygotsky, Lev Semenovich

A

Abuse, child. Since the identification of Battered Child Syndrome by C. Henry Kempe in the 1960s, child abuse and neglect reports in the United States have risen steadily. By the mid-1990s reports reached 2.9 million annually, or approximately 45 children per 1,000. These numbers are only estimates of the actual incidence because child abuse is not always reported, and only about half of all reports are substantiated. Over 1,200 children die each year of maltreatment in the United States. Not all states have child fatality review procedures, however, and estimates of the true number of maltreatment deaths annually have been as high as 5,000.

Public relations campaigns have increased awareness of child abuse, which in turn results in increased reports. By 1967 all states in the United States had passed laws requiring certain professionals to report suspicions of abuse.

The Child Abuse Prevention and Treatment Act (PL# 93-247, passed in 1974) defines child abuse and neglect as the physical or mental injury, sexual abuse or exploitation, negligent treatment, or maltreatment

- of a child under the age of 18
- by a person who is responsible for the child's welfare
- under circumstances that indicate that the child's health or welfare is harmed or threatened.

The act defines sexual abuse as the use, persuasion, or coercion of any child to engage in any sexually explicit conduct for the purpose of producing any visual depiction of such conduct, or the rape, molestation, prostitution, or incestuous pursuit of any child.

Abuse is often divided into three types: physical, emotional, and sexual. Neglect is considered a separate phenomenon and can be divided into physical, medical, and educational.

Death is the most extreme outcome of abuse and neglect and is most likely to occur in children under the age of 1. For infants up to 6 months, child abuse is second only to Sudden Infant Death Syndrome (SIDS) as a cause of death. Other child outcomes are depression, impaired social and moral judgments and skills, lowered self-esteem, and increased violent behavior. Abused children lag behind nonabused children in learning new cognitive and social skills and therefore show delayed academic achievement. In adolescence and adulthood, childhood abuse predicts higher rates of criminality and arrests for violent offenses.

Some children do demonstrate an ability to survive abusive situations. Resilient children are those who respond rapidly to danger, show early maturity, separate their emotions from their situation, and seek out needed information.

Parent factors associated with physical and emotional abuse include being nonbiological parents, having been abused as children, being substance abusers (including alcohol), having a low frustration tolerance, experiencing mental health problems, lacking knowledge of positive parenting, having inappropriate expectations of children, seeing parenting as unpleasant and difficult, being socially isolated, and having an unwanted pregnancy. Child factors that put a child at risk for abuse include being an infant, having a difficult temperament, and being disabled or ill. Family risk factors include marital conflict, domestic violence, single parenthood, ethnic minority status, poor social interaction skills, and ineffective and inconsistent discipline. Environmental and societal factors play an important role, too, such as economic pressure, high stress levels, hierarchical and male-dominated family structures, isolation of families, acceptance of physical control, and low social support for parents.

Factors associated with neglect include social disorganization; high demands on resources (such as large families) or low levels of resources (especially economic); high stress, anxiety, or depression; limited family interaction; poor parenting skills; and inability to access support systems. Sexual abuse factors include family disruption, psychopathology, or illness; history of parent-child problems; substance abuse; and intellectual inadequacies.

A shortcoming with the above research is that the actions of some types of families are likely to come to the attention of authorities, while other families are able to conceal their behaviors. Families who are already involved in social services and those with limited financial resources are especially open to scrutiny.

Programs to prevent abuse and neglect in the United States have taken different routes. Some have targeted adults abused as children and have been based on what researchers have learned about adults who broke the intergenerational cycle. Those mothers were more likely to have received emotional support from a nonabusive adult during childhood, to participate in therapy during any period of their lives, and to have a nonabusive and satisfying relationship with a mate.

A large number of programs labeled as sex abuse *prevention* programs are really *abuse identification* programs. Some of these attempt to screen and identify whether adults should be allowed to work with children. Others teach children to recognize "good and bad touches" and to report bad touches.

Approaches to child abuse/neglect prevention may be *primary* (addressing a large segment of the population and occurring before abuse has begun), *secondary* (directed to families identified as being at risk), or *tertiary* (stopping further abuse after it has occurred). Promising approaches are health care for at-risk populations, home visiting, self-help groups, child care, workplace policies, and parent education programs.

A major issue with child maltreatment is cultural sensitivity. Almost all abuse research has been conducted by European Americans and assumes United States middle-class-parenting standards. A challenge for the future is to define criteria for abuse and neglect that respect cultural differences while protecting children from maltreatment.

References

Hamner, T. J., & Turner, P. H. (1996). *Parenting in contemporary society.* Boston: Allyn & Bacon.

National Center on Child Abuse and Neglect. (1992). *A coordinated response to child abuse and neglect: A basic manual.* DHHS Publication No. ACF 92-30362. Washington, DC: U.S. Department of Health and Human Services.

See also: Conflict resolution; Discipline; Physical punishment; Stress.

JUDITH A. MYERS-WALLS

Academic achievement. Academic achievement refers to the child's performance in an educational setting, generally measured by the child's grade-point average and achievement test scores. Major reviews (Hess & Holloway, 1984; Wentzel, 1994) suggest that parent encouragement, parent involvement, and parenting styles are primary determinants of academic success throughout the school years, from elementary school through college.

Parent encouragement. Positive beliefs and attributions about the child's achievement, high academic aspirations for the child, and academic encouragement are strongly related to the child's academic achievement. Children with parents who have high academic aspirations for them tend to fulfill their parents' expectations and succeed. Parents' high aspirations for their children and parents' support of their children's educational endeavors are important throughout the school years, including college.

Parent involvement. Parent involvement includes participation and interest in their child's school activities, help with homework, and parent-enforced rules regarding homework. Helping children with homework and parent involvement in school activities, including helping in the classroom, attending school assemblies, attending parent/teacher conferences, and involvement in the Parent-Teacher Association, are particularly important for elementary school children. Parents who directly participate in their elementary child's education tend to have children who academically excel. Although direct parent involvement in school activities is extremely important in elementary school, parent involvement may have little relation to the middle or high school student's academic success. Students at this age are more autonomous and care little if their parents participate in activities. The strongest predictors of academic achievement for students in middle school, high school, and college are their parents' aspirations for their achievement and support of their educational efforts.

Parent-enforced rules regarding homework (e.g., homework before television) also have a differential impact at different ages. Parent-enforced rules are positively related to academic success in the elementary years, yet rules regarding homework may have a negative effect on academic achievement for students in middle school and beyond. By this age, children have a developmental need for autonomy and may rebel against rules. It is important, therefore, to establish study habits, with rules enforced by parents, at an early age.

Parenting styles. An authoritative parenting style, characterized by clear expectations, firm rules, responsiveness, and emotional support, is associated with academic achievement (Steinberg et al., 1992). This parenting style is related to the social and emotional adjustment of the child, including self-restraint (compliant, cooperative), a sense of autonomy or self-reliance, and a healthy orientation toward work. These factors may mediate or explain the relation between parenting style and the child's or adolescent's subsequent academic performance (Steinberg et al., 1992; Wentzel, 1994). Children and adolescents who describe their parents as treating them warmly, democratically, and firmly are more likely than their peers to develop a positive attitude toward, and belief about, academic achievement and thus do better in school.

For most children, other parenting styles have a negative relation to grades. These include *authoritarian* parenting, which is high in demandingness (strict control) but low in responsiveness, and *permissive* parenting wherein the parents are tolerant and accepting toward the child's impulses and make few demands on the child. Additionally, DeBaryshe and colleagues (DeBaryshe, Patterson, & Capaldi, 1993) found that ineffective discipline, characterized by inconsistent and punitive parenting practices including nagging, scolding, and expressions of anger, was related to low academic engagement and subsequent low academic achievement.

The results of several recent studies (Steinberg, Dornbusch, & Brown, 1992) suggest that the relation between parenting style and academic achievement may vary depending on the ethnicity of the child. These studies suggest that while low-risk children may benefit from being raised by *authoritative* parents, an *autocratic* parenting style, where parents set rules and enforce them without discussion with their children, may be more beneficial for children in high-risk settings.

Thus, parents' direct involvement in the child's school, particularly in elementary school, and high expectations for, and encouragement of, academic success throughout the school years are predictive of academic success for their children. However, parent involvement must be considered jointly with parenting style. An authoritative parenting style that promotes self-reliance and autonomy is predictive of academic achievement for most children, with the exception of children in high-risk settings.

References

DeBaryshe, B. D., Patterson, G. R., & Capaldi, D. M. (1993). A performance model for academic achievement in early adolescent boys. *Developmental Psychology, 29* (5), 795–804.

Hess, R. D. & Holloway, S. D. (1984). Family and school as educational institutions. In R. D. Parke (Ed.), *Review of child development research* (Vol. 7, pp. 179–222). Chicago: University of Chicago Press.

Steinberg, L. Dornbusch, S. M., & Brown, B. B. (1992). Ethnic differences in adolescent achievement: An ecological perspective. *American Psychologist, 47*, 723–729.

Steinberg, L., Lamborn, S. D., Dornbusch, S. M., Darling, N. (1992). Impact of parenting practices on adolescent achievement: Authoritative parenting, school involvement, and encouragement to succeed. *Child Development, 63*, 1266–1281.

Wentzel, K. R. (1994). Family functioning and academic achievement in middle school: A social-emotional perspective. *Journal of Early Adolescence, 14*, 268–291.

See also: Education, parenting; Family-school partnerships; School; Styles, parenting.

JUDY A. ANDREWS

Acceptance, parental. Parental acceptance is defined as the parents' ability to integrate the child's needs with the parents' own needs. Parents are accepting when they act as if their children's needs are in harmony with their own and when they are responsive to their children's needs. By contrast, rejecting parents act as if their own and their children's needs are in opposition to one another and as if responsiveness to the child's needs implies a thwarting of their own needs.

This definition of acceptance encompasses the interrelated dimensions of sensitivity, responsiveness, and reciprocity (e.g., Ainsworth et al., 1978; Maccoby, 1992; Sroufe, Matas, & Rosenberg, 1981). Parental acceptance integrates and extends beyond previous descriptions by focusing specifically on four aspects of parental behavior critical to children developing control over themselves and their environment:

- *approval* (responsiveness to children's need to feel competent)
- *synchrony* (responsiveness to children's need to be understood)
- *guidance* (responsiveness to children's need to understand their environment)
- *noncoercion* (responsiveness to children's need for choice)

Acceptance does not mean indiscriminate meeting of desires but rather responding to needs in a manner that enables parents to integrate their child's control-related needs with their own need to maintain control.

The Parental Acceptance Coding Scheme (Rothbaum & Schneider-Rosen, 1991) is designed to assess these four aspects of parental behavior in a variety of interactive situations involving parents and their 18- to 48-month-old children. Although the parent's behavior is the focus of assessment in this coding scheme, the child's behavior needs to be considered so as to determine (1) the developmental level at which the child is functioning and (2) the specific needs that are being expressed in the interaction, to which the parent needs to respond. However, ratings of the parent are not based on the child's reactions to the parent's behavior, because this would confound assessments of parent and child. Qualitative and quantitative criteria for evaluating approval, synchrony, guidance, and noncoercion are provided in the manual for the Parental Acceptance Coding Scheme (Rothbaum & Schneider-Rosen, 1991). Scores for these parent behaviors are averaged to determine the overall parental acceptance score.

The overall rating of parental acceptance, which emphasizes the notion of integration of needs, includes five levels. The three anchoring levels can be summarized briefly as follows:

> *Level 1/opponents contending*: The parent fails to meet the child's needs; the parent assumes that one party will win (i.e., his or her needs will be met) and one will lose.
> *Level 3/business partners bargaining*: The parent partially meets the child's needs; there is a sense that the needs of both can be met partially but there is tension along the way.
> *Level 5/companions harmonizing*: The parent works with the child to meet their mutual needs; the parent's major concern is the strengthening of their relationship.

These levels of acceptance may be seen as describing a continuum ranging from extreme incompatibility in need for control (hence, enmity) to extreme compatibility (hence, harmony). At level 1, parents behave as if they perceive their child's need for control as incompatible with their own; thus, they seek control by thwarting or ignoring their child's methods and goals. At level 3, parents behave as if they perceive their child's need for control as partially compatible with their own; thus, they seek control by bargaining over methods and goals. At level 5, parents behave as if they perceive their own and their child's needs as harmonious; thus, they seek control by sharing control with their child because the granting and exercising of control are seen as proper and mutually reinforcing.

Parental acceptance scores have been found to be reliable, to be moderately associated with attachment security (Rosen & Rothbaum, 1993), and to predict longitudinally to low problem behavior scores at home and at school (Rothbaum et al., 1995). Parental acceptance scores have been found to be consistent when mothers are observed interacting with each of their two children; fathers have been found to be consistent in their acceptance of their two children as well (Rosen & Burke, in press). Previous investigators have also found that one or several of the parental behaviors relevant to acceptance predict different aspects of children's social competence, including low aggression, absence of anxious-inhibited and externalizing behaviors and psychosomatic problems, low dependency, helping and altruistic behavior, interpersonal competence, self-esteem, adaptability, constructive play, and intellectual functioning.

These parent-child associations suggest that accepting caregiving behaviors lead to positive social functioning in children. The assumption underlying the definition of parental acceptance is that parents' acceptance of the child will foster reciprocity on the part of the child. Thus, the *opponents contending* (level 1) approach makes it likely that the child will consider methods of control that lead to either winning or losing, while the *companions harmonizing* (level 5) approach makes it likely that the child will be motivated to integrate others' need for control in seeking to satisfy his or her own need for control. This motivation would result from positive feelings toward others for having fulfilled one's own needs, from experiencing the beneficial effects of mutual control, and from perceiving oneself as able to maintain mutuality. The implications for the child's subsequent interactive skills and interpersonal competencies need to be explored in future research.

References

Ainsworth, M. D. S., Blehar, M. C., Waters, E., & Wall, S. (1978). *Patterns of attachment: A psychological study of the Strange Situation.* Hillsdale, NJ: Erlbaum.

Maccoby, E. E. (1992). The role of parents in the socialization of children: An historical overview. *Developmental Psychology, 28,* 1006–1017.

Rosen, K. S., & Burke, P. B. (in press). Multiple attachment relationships within the family: Mothers and fathers with two young children. *Developmental Psychology.*

Rosen, K. S., & Rothbaum, F. (1993). Quality of parental caregiving and security of attachment. *Developmental Psychology, 29,* 358–367.

Rothbaum, F., Rosen, K. S., Pott, M., & Beatty, M. (1995). Early parent-child relationships and later problem behavior: A longitudinal study. *Merrill-Palmer Quarterly, 41,* 133–151.

Rothbaum, F., & Schneider-Rosen, K. (1991). *Parental acceptance scoring manual: A system for assessing interaction between parents and their young children.* Unpublished manuscript, Tufts University and Boston College.

Sroufe, L. A., Matas, L., & Rosenberg, D. M. (1981). *Manual for scoring mother variables in tool use task applicable for two-year-old children.* Unpublished manuscript, University of Minnesota at Minneapolis.

See also: Listening; Synchrony.

KAREN ROSEN AND FRED ROTHBAUM

Adler, Alfred (1820–1937). Alfred Adler was born on February 7, 1870, near Vienna, Austria. He attended the University of Vienna medical school from 1888 to 1894. He specialized first in ophthalmology in 1895, then in internal medicine, and finally in psychiatry.

In 1902 Sigmund Freud invited Adler and three other practicing physicians to join an informal discussion group. Adler was never a student of Freud. They had a nine-year professional relationship ending in 1911. Adler strongly disagreed with Freud's emphasis on sexuality and the unconscious. Freud concentrated on drives, causes of behavior, and problems within the individual. Adler saw the person holistically and behavior as purposeful, developed in response to the human need to find a place in society. He described all problems as social problems. Freud's approach was called psychoanalysis while Adler called his theory *Individual Psychology* to emphasize the whole individual.

Adler was the first to observe the social embeddedness of human beings beginning with the child's need for affection and how this need becomes an essential part of the social feeling. Adler called this "the iron logic of communal life" from which there is no escaping. Mentally healthy individuals must be seen and must see themselves as embedded in a larger society. Adler saw social feeling, also called social interest, as an indicator of mental health and what enables human beings to survive in this world. He viewed all mental health problems as caused by a lack in social interest, courage, and self-confidence. The pampered and rejected child has not sufficiently developed social interest, and good parenting needs to avoid pampering and rejecting children.

Adler emphasized the importance of observing how each child finds a place in the family. He taught about the influence of family values, the home atmosphere, and the style of parenting on the child's developing personality. Adler was the first to describe the significance of birth order, how competition between members develops and interferes with social interest, and the child's early sense of inferiority. The child draws conclusions about that inferiority and what "must" be done in order to overcome it and experience the satisfaction of mastery. All of Adler's teaching underscored the importance of developing courage in the child so that problems will be seen as challenges to overcome, not as excuses for giving up.

In 1904 Adler published *The Physician as Educator.* He suggested that physicians educate teachers and parents to prevent emotional problems from arising in youngsters. His recommendations included:

- Win the child's love.
- Support a child's progress by developing confidence in his or her own strengths. This leads to the courage they need to see their fate as coming from their own strength (pampered, overprotected, weak and sickly, abused, and rejected children can easily lose their self-confidence).
- Under no circumstances should the child be afraid of his or her educator because this fear robs the child of self-confidence and greatly confuses as well.
- Encouragement is preferred over punishment, with correction emphasizing the nature of the mistake and an alternative behavior.
- Offering choices is preferable to demanding blind obedience.

During 1919–1920 Adler established child guidance clinics in Vienna, and by 1934, there were 32. Adler's goal was to end the educational authoritarianism he had personally known and to help all children be seen as unique individuals with specific emotional and intellectual needs. Classroom councils were formed so that students could lead discussions on matters that affected the group, with everyone having the opportunity to voice their opinions and solve problems.

Adler's approach was an optimistic one that helped parents and teachers understand children's behavior. He taught effective methods for guiding them toward productive, other-centered behavior. He wrote in a simple, inclusive language that emphasized the child's inborn capacity for social interest—a connection with others in friendship, community, workplace, and intimacy. Adler did not blame parents; he helped them find solutions.

Adler's younger colleagues were responsible for women teachers being granted equal rights to male colleagues, the provision of free schoolbooks and related materials for all pupils, school libraries for students, educational libraries for teachers, establishing parents' associations in school districts, abolishing corporal punishment in schools, using sociometric methods and insights of group dynamics, discussion and counseling, student-centered teaching, and peer teaching. (Many of these are thought of as new educational methods today.) Adler had a tremendous influence in child guidance and social work.

Professionals from all over the world came to Vienna to study Adler's methods of helping children with emotional problems. He gave courses entitled, "The Difficult Child" and "Problem Children in School." Adler's basic philosophy for running a respectful, cooperative family was the same as for running a classroom and for all of society. These counseling centers were closed with the rise of fascism in 1934.

Adler died on May 28, 1937 while on a speaking engagement in Aberdeen, Scotland. Rudolf Dreikurs, his best-known younger colleague, continued and expanded his work in counseling and parent and teacher education in the United States and in many countries around the world.

For further information, contact: The North American Society for Adlerian Psychology, FAX 312/201-5917.

Books by Adler include: *The Education of Children* (1930), *What Life Should Mean to You* (1931), *and Understanding Human Nature* (1937).

References

Ansbacher, H. L. And Ansbacher, R. R. (Eds.). (1956). *The individual psychology of Alfred Adler.* New York: Basic Books.

Hoffman, E. (1994). *The drive for self.* New York: Addison-Wesley.

See also: Dreikurs, Rudolf.

BETTY LOU BETTNER

Adolescent parenthood. Each year in the United States more than 500,000 young women under age 20 give birth. Nearly three quarters of these young women are unmarried. Although the United State's rate of adolescent parenthood is vastly higher than the rate in any other industrialized country, it has decreased steadily during most of the period since 1960, while the rate of unmarried parenthood has increased steadily (Moore, 1996).

In order for a pregnant adolescent to become an adolescent parent, she must carry the pregnancy to term and maintain custody of the child. Approximately 35% of the pregnancies of adolescents end in abortion and 14% in miscarriages (Moore, 1995). Among those teens who had not planned the pregnancy, those likely to choose abortion are those who have shorter relationships with their partners, do not identify with other young parents, have access to abortion services, had been using contraception, have achieved well in school, and have a mother, partner, and/or best friend who support the abortion choice. Those adolescents who deliver a child and choose adoption (approximately 4% of teen parents) tend to have high academic success and aspirations, have positive experience with adoption, have open adoption available to them, come from families in which single parenting and dependency on public assistance are not seen as normative, come from intact families, have been with their partners for a shorter time, and come from families in which the teen's mother was not a teen parent (Myers-Walls & Myers-Bowman, 1991).

Adolescents who do maintain the pregnancy and custody of the child face a number of challenges. First, health problems are a major concern. Adolescent parents are more likely to have premature and low-birth-weight babies. These infants have higher infant mortality rates, more frequent health problems, and a greater likelihood of developmental difficulties that cause learning problems (Maynard, 1996).

Single parenthood is another complication of adolescent parenthood. An increasing portion of births to teens is a result of premarital sexual activity. There is also a decreasing likelihood that pregnant teens will marry. While the total number of births to teens declined by 25% from 1970 to 1988, the number of nonmarital births to teens increased by two thirds. The majority of these mothers are single at the time of the child's birth, but in addition, those who marry as teens are also very likely to divorce (Congressional Budget Office, 1990).

Teen parents are more likely than other teens to drop out of school, either before the pregnancy or afterward. Teen parents who marry are least likely to finish school (Congressional Budget Office, 1990). Low educational attainment and single parenthood contribute to serious economic risks for teen parents.

A complex combination of factors in the lives of teen parents contributes to risks of poor parenting for their children. Although causality is difficult to track, several factors in the lives of teen parents seem to be associated with increased rates of child abuse and neglect. Some of these factors are poor academic achievement before and after pregnancy, impoverishment because of single parenthood and poor attainment, conflict between parenthood and adolescent developmental stages, and strained relationships with extended family. Children of adolescent parents also have poorer educational attainment themselves, are more likely to run away or be incarcerated, and are more likely to become teen parents themselves (Maynard, 1996).

More generally, the parenting styles of adolescent parents show several troubling characteristics. Compared to older mothers, they have *lower levels of understanding* of children's developmental stages, are *less sensitive* to babies' needs and cues, *play less* with their babies and *vocalize less*, are more *ambivalent about parenthood*, and *use more physical punishment* (Hamner & Turner, 1996).

Although adolescent parents and their children are at increased risk for a variety of negative outcomes, that risk is not evenly spread across all situations. Teen mothers who are able to finish some level of schooling are more likely than others to hold decent jobs and remain independent of public assistance. Those who marry and stay married show better outcomes. For the first five years after delivery or longer, living with the teen's parents is associated with more positive outcomes (Hamner & Turner, 1996).

Living situation is an important predictor of outcomes. Younger teen parents and African American parents are more likely than others to live with their parents. European American teen parents are more likely to marry. Teens who live with their parents are more likely to complete schooling (Congressional Budget Office, 1990). Research has shown that grandparents who assist the teen parents with their role rather than taking over the responsibility facilitate the best outcomes for their grandchildren.

Adolescent parenthood is a life situation that is associated with many risks for the teens, their children, and their parents. It is not an automatic prediction of failure, however. A challenge for researchers and practitioners is to identify interventions that will help teens delay parenthood until they are ready but also to increase protective factors and decrease risk factors for those who do become parents.

References

Congressional Budget Office. (1990). *Sources of support for adolescent mothers.* Washington, DC: Congress of the United States.

Hamner, T. J., & Turner, P. H. (1996). *Parenting in contemporary society.* Boston: Allyn & Bacon.

Maynard, R. A. (1996). *Kids having kids.* New York: Robin Hood Foundation.

Moore, K. A. (1995). *Facts at a glance.* Washington, DC: Child Trends, Inc.

Moore, K. A. (1996). *Facts at a glance.* Washington, DC: Child Trends, Inc.

Myers-Walls, J. A., & Myers-Bowman, K. S. (1991). *Antecedents and correlates of adolescent pregnancy: A teaching model.* Paper presented at the annual meeting of the National Council on Family Relations.

See also: Adolescent pregnancy; Sexuality, adolescent.

JUDITH A. MYERS-WALLS

Adolescent pregnancy. Each year more than 1 million teenage women in the United States become pregnant. In recent years approximately half of those pregnancies have resulted in births and about 30 to 40% in abortions. Almost 55 of every 1000 females aged 15 to 19 delivered a child in 1996 (Moore, 1997).

Many concerned people refer to the "rising rates of adolescent pregnancy." Although the rates are much higher in the United States than in any other industrialized country, they have not been rising. During the last half century, teenage childbearing was highest in 1960 when almost 90 of every 1,000 teen girls ages 15 to 19 gave birth. Since that time the teen birthrate has been decreasing steadily except for a brief increase from 1987 to 1991 (Moore, 1997).

The overall decrease in births to teens appears to be due to a combination of factors, including the legalization of abortion in the 1970s, the introduction of the birth control pill and subsequent methods, AIDS (Acquired Immunodeficiency Syndrome) education that focuses on condom use, and the decrease in early marriages. The decrease is not associated with dropping rates of sexual activity, however; reported sexual activity rates have risen during the same time that birthrates have declined. The percentage of girls who were teenagers in the 1950s and 1960s and had had sex by the age of 18 was around 25%. In contrast, over half of teenage girls in the 1970s had sex by age 18. In 1995, about 40% of both male and female teens reported being sexually active within the last month.

A major reason for the increased concern regarding adolescent pregnancy and parenthood is the increase in nonmarital childbearing. Between 1960 and 1980 the percentage of births to teens that were nonmarital more than tripled from 15% to 48%. By 1994, over three fourths of all births to teens were nonmarital, a fivefold increase. During the same 30-year period, however, nonmarital births to women over 20 increased ninefold.

At the most basic level, adolescent pregnancy is due to two events: sexual intercourse and conception. Research regarding heterosexual activity among teens has identified several factors associated with that sexual activity: forced sexual contact (incest, date/acquaintance rape, or stranger rape), low religiosity, low academic aspirations and achievement, perception of social acceptance of nonmarital sexual activity, early biological maturity in the adolescent girl, and a high level of partner commitment. Several family factors, including low monitoring and control, low levels of support, and family attitudes supporting early sexual activity and parenting, were also significant (Myers-Walls & Myers-Bowman, 1991). In addition, there are stable factors such as racial or ethnic background that are correlated with sexual activity rates.

The factors associated with contraceptive use apply if the teen is not planning a pregnancy. Planned pregnancies account for approximately 14% of pregnancies to teens, and half of those teens are married (Moore, 1995). Teens are likely to use contraception if they have a high acceptance of themselves as sexual beings, if contraceptives are readily available, if the partner relationship is mature, if the teen has a high future orientation and plans, if there is a high level of family support and communication, and if the teens have a realistic understanding of pregnancy risk. These factors predict contraceptive use, but ineffective methods, incorrect use of contraceptives, and/or method failure may cause contraceptors to become pregnant in spite of precautions (Myers-Walls and Myers-Bowman, 1991).

Most of this research has been conducted with adolescent females. There has been a recent surge of interest in the fathers of those babies. Some of them are young, but some reports indicate that only about half of the fathers of babies born to teenage girls are teenagers themselves (Moore, 1996).

The reasons for concern about adolescent pregnancy center on health risks for both the mother and child. Teenage mothers experience higher rates of every risk of pregnancy, labor, and delivery. There is some indication, however, that those risks are not inevitably connected to the mother's young age; there may be stronger associations with the mother's education, income level, and access to resources. There are additional risks for the mother and the child if the mother retains custody and raises the child.

Efforts to prevent adolescent pregnancy using sex education have taken three major directions: programs designed to increase knowledge or change attitudes; programs that provide contraceptives; and life planning approaches that encourage teens to set goals and identify areas of personal strength and direction (National Research Council, 1987). However, two national studies have found no significant increases or decreases in sexual activity after attendance in a sexuality course. A large number of studies, on the other hand, have measured changes in attitudes as a result of courses, usually toward the tolerant or permissive direction (Wies, Rabinowitz, & Ruckstuhl, 1992). An area in which educational efforts have been highly effective is in prenatal education and the prevention of pregnancy and delivery complications.

Continuing dilemmas in the field of adolescent pregnancy include such issues as discouraging too-early sexual activity while still building healthy sexual attitudes (Chilman, 1990), designing prevention and treatment programs that reflect the values and concerns of the broadest range of the population, and providing services to pregnant teens without giving the appearance of rewarding them or condoning their behavior.

References

Chilman, C. (1990). Promoting healthy adolescent sexuality. *Family Relations, 39*, 123–131.

Moore, K. A. (1995). *Facts at a glance*. Washington, DC: Child Trends, Inc.

Moore, K. A. (1996). *Facts at a glance*. Washington, DC: Child Trends, Inc.

Moore, K. A. (1997). *Facts at a glance*. Washington, DC: Child Trends, Inc.

Myers-Walls, J. A., & Myers-Bowman, K. S. (1991). *Antecedents and correlates of adolescent pregnancy: A teaching model*. Paper presented at the Annual Meeting of the National Council on Family Relations.

National Research Council. (1987). *Risking the future: Adolescent sexuality, pregnancy, and childbearing*. Washington, DC: National Academy of Sciences.

Wies, D. L., Rabinowitz, B., & Ruckstuhl, M. F. (1992). Individual changes in sexual attitudes and behavior within college-level human sexuality courses. *Journal of Sex Research, 29* (1), 43–59.

See also: Adolescent parenthood; Sex education; Sexuality, adolescent.

JUDITH A. MYERS-WALLS

Adolescent separation. An underlying theme of adolescence is the acquirement of the ability to separate from parents, both in the physical sense of distance and in the psychological sense of emotional capacity for sustained separateness. As such, *separation* refers to the changes that take place in the parent-child relationship during the period of adolescence. Both psychological research and psychoanalytic thought have examined the separation processes, yet whereas both theoretical and popular views emphasize the disruption in parent-child relationships, research findings indicate that parents continue to serve as significant sources of support and influence for their adolescents (Collins, 1995).

Review of extant research has revealed various indices characterizing the separation process (see Shulman & Seiffge-Krenke, 1997). Approaching adolescence, children have a greater ability to be by themselves and spend longer periods away from their parents. When at home, adolescents tend to stay in their rooms and lock the door. Both the quantity and quality of physical contact with parents change dramatically. Previous elements of close contact such as affectionate touching, embracing, or kissing are greatly reduced in frequency and are replaced by ritualized physical contact such as hugging the parent before departure or upon returning home. This growing *distancing* was particularly documented following the onset of pubertal maturation with both adolescents and parents describing being less close to each other in comparison to prepubertal stages.

The distancing is evident also in the nature of interactions that take place between parents and adolescents. Parental reports of adolescents' willingness to help, and adolescents' helpfulness toward parents in the laboratory, were negatively related to age. Documenting the level of conflict across several domains such as home chores, appearance, or interpersonal relations revealed that conflicts between parents and children occur more frequently in adolescence in comparison to childhood or young adulthood, signifying a growing separation between adolescents and their parents.

Interviewing adolescents about self-generated issues of conflicts and asking them to present the justifications and counterarguments for each conflict showed that while younger children tend to respect parental authority, adolescents tended to question or reject parental authority. Moreover, adolescents tended to perceive and interpret their acts as contingent on personal jurisdiction, regardless of parental preferences. Observations of discussions among father-mother-adolescent triads showed that adolescents tended to interrupt their parents with an increasing frequency. These processes probably lead adolescents to change their views of their parents (Steinberg & Silverberg, 1986). Adolescents were found to perceive their parents as ordinary people, not idealizing them as do younger children.

Taken together, the growing apart between adolescents and their parents is evidenced in three domains. First, adolescents spend increasing amounts of time apart from their parents. Second, adolescents feel that parents are not as close to them as they were in the past. Third, adolescents relinquish their perceptions of parental point of view as well as of parental omnipotence.

Psychoanalytic thinkers perceive of the changes in parent-child relationships, and this penchant for separation, as a result of physiological/sexual maturation. Anna Freud claimed that the ego is overwhelmed by the emergence of sexual instincts. Previously established attachments to parents can reawaken incestuous fixations, and therefore cathexis from parents subsequently takes place. Blos (1967), the best-known psychoanalytic theorist of adolescence, conceptualizes this distancing as the process through which adolescents free themselves from dependencies on parents and dissolve childish libidinal attachments to them. Collins (1995) claims that due to developmental changes, parents and children start to perceive each other differently, and mutual expectations are violated, leading to distancing and conflicts.

However, it should be noted that the separation from parents takes place within the context of closeness. As studies have shown, parents remain important sources of support for their adolescents, even though the salience of peers increases (Youniss & Smollar, 1985). Within the relationship, children and parents have to learn, sometimes painfully, that the adolescent undergoes pubertal, cognitive, and emotional changes. The changes that first lead to perturbations later serve as an impetus for change (Collins, 1995). Through the process of change, adolescents are expected to develop an image of oneself as unique from one's parents, with a separate set of beliefs and values and the capacity to regulate self-esteem. The attainment of freedom from excessive need for parental approval and from excessive guilt or anger in relation to one's parents implies a realistic perception of them. Parents, in turn, are expected to accommodate to the changes in their adolescent and even to serve as a source of support in this process.

When this occurs, adolescents are able to balance their feeling of "being a separate entity" with a sense of closeness to their parents indicating that the parent-child relationship has been transformed into a mature relationship.

References

Blos, P. (1967). The second individuation process of adolescence. *Psychoanalytic Study of the Child, 22,* 162–186.

Collins, W. A. (1995). Relationships and development: Family adaptation to individual change. In S. Shulman (Ed.), *Close relationships and socioemotional development.* Norwood, NJ: Ablex.

Shulman, S., & Seiffge-Krenke, I. (1997). *Fathers and adolescents: Developmental and clinical perspectives.* London: Routledge.

Steinberg, L., & Silverberg, S. (1986). The vicissitudes of autonomy in early adolescence. *Child Development, 57,* 841–851.

Youniss, J., & Smollar, S. (1985). *Adolescent relations with mothers, fathers and friends.* Chicago: University of Chicago Press.

See also: Distancing strategies.

SHMUEL SHULMAN

Adoption. Adoption is the shift of legal rights and responsibilities from one parent or set of parents to another. The adopted child becomes a legal member of the adoptive family, with all of the rights and privileges of a son or daughter.

Adoption has long been seen as a perfect solution to a social problem—a person who is unable or unwilling to care for a biological child places that child with a person or couple who want children but are infertile or otherwise unable to have children of their own. The newly created household is placed at an equal level both legally and socially with families containing only biological children.

However, incongruities do exist. At the core of these differences is that fact that all of the members of the adoption triangle—the birth parents, the child, and the adoptive parents—are all working through a substantial loss. The birth parents face giving the child up for adoption. The child feels the loss of the presence of the birth parents, and the adoptive parents feel loss related to their infertility. In addition, there are few culturally appropriate ways to acknowledge and deal with the losses associated with adoption. For the most part they are ignored, and the feelings experienced by the participants in the adoption process are not validated (Brodzinsky & Schechter, 1990).

There are differences between the experiences of children who grow up adopted and those who are raised in their biological families. Children who have been adopted show a higher rate of emotional and adjustment problems than in the population as a whole. Brodzinsky and Schechter (1990), Hajal and Rosenberg (1991), and Smith and Brodzinsky (1994) reported adopted children as overrepresented in outpatient and residential mental health treatment facilities. Brodzinsky, Schechter, and Henig (1992) concluded that while 85% of adoptions are rated as successful by all involved, adopted children are more likely to require the assistance of the helping professions.

Reactions to being adopted are experienced according to the developmental level of the child.

Infancy (birth–2 years). The attachment process common in infancy can vary for children who have been adopted when there is a poor match in temperament between parents and child or when the baby is colicky or sensitive to changes in environment and routine. This can lead to a disturbance in the development of trust between parent and child that can foreshadow emotional problems later in life. Adoptive parents are advised to acknowledge that differences in temperament are likely to exist and that a poor fit can be overcome when parents are relaxed and calm (Brodzinsky, Schechter, & Henig, 1992).

Toddlerhood and preschool (3–5 years). During this period, most children are told about their adoption, although many may not understand the explanation. "My father's a dentist, my mother's a teacher, and I'm a *dopted,*" says a boy of 5 (Brodzinsky, Schechter, & Henig, 1992, p. 50). Many children at this age enjoy hearing their adoption stories over and over but may worry that they will be returned if they do not behave well enough (Hajal & Rosenberg, 1991).

Middle childhood (6–12 years). As the child begins to have a more accurate picture of what adoption is all about, new issues may begin to surface. Some children may feel that they were rejected by their birth parents and may fear that the adoption occurred because of some failure on their part. This is the stage of life when the grieving process for children begins (Brodzinsky, Schechter, & Henig, 1992).

This grieving process often manifests itself through romantic fantasies about birth parents that develop in an effort to establish a unique identity and internally explain the circumstances surrounding the adoption (Rosenberg & Horner, 1991). The child may decide that his or her "real" parents are better than the adoptive parents who insist on compliance with family rules. The child may visualize the birth parents in a dramatic or heroic way and may create a picture of caring people who would always grant the wishes of their child. Fantasies may also serve the purpose of explaining differences in appearance and temperament from the adoptive family (Brodzinsky, Schechter, & Henig, 1992).

Adolescence. Adolescence is the time when the adopted child develops an identity based on personal experiences, the history of the adoptive family, and actual knowledge and remaining fantasies about the birth family. Values transmitted by the adoptive family may be abandoned in favor of those perceived to have been held by the birth parents, including a possibly accurate perception that the birth parents had been sexually active at a fairly young age (Rosenberg & Horner, 1991).

Adolescents typically are preoccupied with appearance. For children who have been adopted, physical differences from the adoptive family can seem particularly acute. The child may wonder who he or she will grow to look like and feel that there are not family models that will indicate future physical characteristics (Brodzinsky, Schechter, & Henig, 1992).

When asked what percentage of adoptees search for their birth parents, one expert replied, "One hundred percent" (Brodzinsky, Schechter, & Henig, 1992, p. 79). Even if the adoptee does not begin a literal search, virtually all question their origins and wonder what their birth parents are like. Searchers have been found to have come from situations in which they had a poor match (either physically or intellectually) with their adoptive families and where family relationships were unsatisfying (Hoopes, as cited in Brodzinsky & Schechter, 1990).

Adoption is an excellent solution to the social problem of coping with children who cannot be raised in their biological families. Adoption has been found to have better results than foster care, institutionalization, or being raised in a home where parents are unwilling or unable to provide for the needs of their children (Brodzinsky & Schechter, 1990). However, we are neglecting the needs of adopted children when we fail to recognize that their course of development is likely to be different than would be expected for a child raised by his or her biological parents. Adoption can be considered a risk factor, and adopted children may require additional support during their childhood in order to function as productive adults.

References
Brodzinsky, D., & Schechter, M. (1990). *The psychology of adoption.* New York: Oxford University Press.

Brodzinsky, D., Schechter, M., & Henig, R. (1992). *Being adopted: The lifelong search for self.* New York: Doubleday.

Hajal, F., & Rosenberg, E. (1991). The family life cycle in adoptive families. *American Journal of Orthopsychiatry, 61* (1), 78–85.

Rosenberg, E., & Horner, T. (1991). Birthparent romances and identity formation in adopted children. *American Journal of Orthopsychiatry, 61* (1), 70–77.

Smith, D., & Brodzinsky, D. (1994). Stress and coping in adopted children: A developmental study. *Journal of Clinical Child Psychology, 23* (1), 91–99.

See also: Adolescent pregnancy; Attachment, secure; Infertility.

MARTHA YORK

Adult children. Until recently, few researchers and practitioners have addressed the parent-child relationship after the children become adults and leave home. However, most parents will now live for two or more decades after their children leave their home (Suitor et al., 1995). As a result, the parent-child relationship will remain intact well into children's adulthood.

Research indicates that the quality of the relationship between adult children and mature parents generally remains important to both parties. They continue to be impacted by how they relate to each other. For example, strain in the relationship, lack of contact with parents, and perceived lack of parental support are associated with decreased psychological well-being among adult children, and relationship strain and parental dissatisfaction are associated with depression among parents (Umberson, 1992). Moreover, personal problems, such as substance abuse and unemployment among adult children, have a negative impact on the well-being of aging parents (Suitor et al., 1995).

After traversing the adolescent stage of life, which is often characterized by conflict between children and parents, the transition to adulthood generally leads to an improvement in parent-child relationships. As children establish their own households, marry, and become parents, their relationship typically becomes closer (Suitor et al., 1995). Much of this improvement is due to the increased similarity that parents and children experience as they share a common set of life experiences. It is also generally an indicator that children have conformed to parents' expectations of appropriate personal development.

Despite the popular notion that adult children tend to abandon or ignore their parents after reaching adulthood, research clearly demonstrates that most children maintain close relationships with their parents throughout the life of the relationship. Most parents have at least one child living only a few miles from them, and most parents are visited regularly by their children (Bengtson, Rosenthal, & Burton, 1996; Umberson, 1992). Moreover, research indicates that the overwhelming majority of adult children report having an emotionally close relationship with their parents (Lawton, Silverstein, & Bengtson, 1994). Parents, rather than feeling abandoned, report even higher levels of emotional closeness toward their children. Incredibly, the myth that parents are left behind by upwardly mobile children persists despite considerable evidence to the contrary.

The adult child–aging parent relationship tends to be closer among females. Although fathers and sons remain involved in intergenerational relationships, the tendency is for daughters and mothers to have more contact and closer relationships (Bengtson, Rosenthal, & Burton, 1996; Lawton, Silverstein, & Bengtson, 1994).

The relationship between adult children and aging parents does not seem to be negatively impacted by children's divorce, even when they return to live with their parent for a period of time (Suitor et al., 1995). However, the divorce of parents often leads to less frequent contact and less emotional closeness with their children (Umberson, 1992).

At some point after children become adults, parents begin to experience a significant decline in health. This change in health status marks an important change in the relationship, as the relationship shifts from a reciprocal relationship of mutual help and assistance to one where parents become dependent upon their children. The vast majority of help rendered to disabled elderly parents is given by family members (Bengtson, Rosenthal, & Burton, 1996), with the institutionalization of parents occurring only as a last resort and only after an extended period of caregiving by the family. The majority of primary caregivers are daughters rather than sons.

Due to the demands of caregiving, adult children often experience significant physical and emotional distress, with many experiencing increased depression and physical illness (Suitor et al., 1995). Although the burdens of caregiving and the declining health of parents often create stress in the relationship, many caregivers and parents have found that they have maintained or even increased their emotional ties. Indeed, the attachment that parents and children developed in the child's infancy remains remarkably durable throughout the course of the relationship (Pruchno et al., 1994). Even when a parent has been admitted to a nursing home, the attachment ties endure. Until the relationship ends with the death of the parent, the bond between children and parent remains important.

References

Bengtson, V., Rosenthal, C., & Burton, L. (1996). Paradoxes of families and aging. In R. H. Binstock, & L. K. George (Eds.), *Handbook of aging and the social sciences* (pp. 53–282). San Diego, CA: Academic Press.

Lawton, L., Silverstein, M., & Bengtson, V. (1994). Affection, social contact, and geographic distance between adult children and their parents. *Journal of Marriage and the Family, 56* (1), 57–68.

Pruchno, R. A., Peters, N. D., Kleban, M. H., & Burant, C. J. (1994). Attachment among adult children and their institutionalized parents. *Journals of Gerontology: Social Sciences, 49*, S209–S218.

Suitor, J. J., Pillemer, K., Keeton, S., & Robison, J. (1995). Aged parents and aging children: Determinants of relationship quality. In R. Blieszner & V. H. Bedford (Eds.), *Handbook of aging and the family* (pp. 223–242). Westport, CT: Greenwood Press.

Umberson, D. (1992). Relationships between adult children and their parents: Psychological consequences for both generations. *Journal of Marriage and the Family, 54* (3), 664–674.

See also: Family systems; Intergenerational parenting.

RICHARD B. MILLER

Advocacy. A basic parenting function involves advocating for one's children and for the wider community of children and connecting with community agencies. In the National Extension Parent Education Model (Smith et al., 1994), *advocate* is one of the six categories of critical parenting practices. Specifically, the model lists three parent practices in this category: "find, use, and create community resources when needed to benefit one's children and the community of children"; "stimulate social change to create supportive environments for children and families"; and "build relationships with family, neighborhood, and community groups." In a similar way, Alvy (1994) lists "advocating and connecting" as one of his five categories of basic parenting functions and responsibilities.

As families have changed in recent decades, children and families have become involved in agencies and programs outside the family for education, recreation, medical care, financial assistance, legal counsel, social interaction, and employment. Parents who are successful advocates for their children know what the children's needs are, or they know how to find assistance to determine those needs. They also know what services are available in the community, or they know how to locate services. Parents who are advocates may even work to create new services that are needed but do not exist. Children whose parents advocate for them are less likely than other children to have unmet needs or to be offered services that do not fit their needs. Parents who are advocates build threads of connection between home and community by establishing a harmonious and responsive environment for children. As the number of parent advocates increases, the quality of the community environment for children increases.

Authors have identified several skills that parents need in order to be effective advocates for children. Small and Eastman (1991) report that parents are effective advocates if they have self-confidence and an internal locus of control; if they have positive communication and conflict management skills; and if they understand how political, educational, legal, and medical systems operate. In addition, identifying and using high-quality support services seem to be dependent on having information about quality, on adequate resources to be able to use the services, and on the ability to access the services without barriers such as language, transportation, and space limitations (Adams, 1990).

Parents of special-needs children have done pioneering work with advocacy. Because they are dependent on a wide variety of services from outside the family and because their children's needs and abilities are usually quite unique, many parents of special children have developed well-tuned skills in advocacy. Collaborative networks of parents of children with similar needs can help those parents be heard by service providers and government agencies.

Advocacy skills are a critical part of the process of using formal support systems. Parents typically turn to those formal agencies and programs only after their informal support networks have failed to meet their needs. At that point of need, parents with good expressive skills and strong support systems are most likely to enroll in and benefit from programs (Powell, 1986). There may be a significant number of children who are in need of support services and advocacy whose parents are unable or unwilling to fulfill those responsibilities.

Programs to build advocacy skills in parents can take several forms. One approach is to teach parents about quality of services such as child care, medical services, and education and could address how those systems operate. Other programs teach communication and conflict-management skills. Mass media campaigns can be used to encourage parents to become involved in policy issues that impact children in their communities. Home visiting and mentoring programs can help parents learn how services work and can help them learn to negotiate the system. Support groups can help to build collaborations among parents and can give them the strength and direction to establish new, needed programs. Parent advisory boards and parent representation on boards of directors of agencies can be wonderful conduits to allow for parent advocacy. Actually, any program can help to build advocacy skills if it takes an empowerment approach in its organization and helps to support the development of positive self-esteem and an internal locus of control in parents.

References

Adams, G. C. (1990). *Who knows how safe? The status of state efforts to ensure quality child care.* Washington, DC: Children's Defense Fund.

Alvy, K. T. (1994). *Parent training today: A social necessity.* Studio City, CA: Center for the Improvement of Child Care.

Powell, D. R. (1986). Research in review: Parent education and support programs. *Young Children, 45,* 47–53.

Small, S. A., & Eastman, G. (1991). Rearing adolescents in contemporary society: A conceptual framework for understanding the responsibilities and needs of parents. *Family Relations, 40,* 455–462.

Smith, C. A., Cudaback, D., Goddard, H. W., & Myers-Walls, J. A. (1994). *National extension parent education model of critical parenting practices.* Manhattan: Kansas State Research and Extension.

See also: Community; Social support.

JUDITH A. MYERS-WALLS

Affectivity, positive and negative. Affectivity is a stable pattern of exhibiting emotional expressions in various social situations. Parents influence children's affectivity through modeling, coaching, and contingency mechanisms.

Modeling. Strong emotions are common while parenting preschoolers. Parent-child concerns and behaviors are, by definition, often incompatible. A child may want to play a drum, for example, when the parent needs to relax. Yet these concerns and behaviors are often compatible, with resultant positive emotions—a mother may feel joy as her daughter squeals in delight after climbing a tree by herself. In either case, parental emotions are activated.

These patterns of parents' expressiveness implicitly model for the child those emotions that are acceptable in the family—how certain situations evoke specific emotions. For example, a 2-year-old may observe her parent's unease at the approach of a large but friendly dog and thereafter demonstrate fear herself during similar experiences.

Parents also model the manner in which emotions are explicitly displayed. To express fear or wariness, for example, one parent might gasp and exhibit very widened eyes, but another might show much more subtle indicators of wariness.

Parents model the strategies they use to manage their emotions. A parent uneasy about the dog's approach may get up precipitously and whisk the child away from the playground; another equally wary parent may quietly speak to the dog, assess risk, and elect to stay at a safe distance.

Parents also provide an overall affective environment to which the child is exposed. Being immersed in the emotional life of one's family imparts a unique emotional stamp on one's personality (Tomkins, 1991). Parents' habitual emotional expressiveness can become an affective lens that the child then adopts. Children, especially daughters, tend to express emotional profiles similar to their parents in many situations (Denham, 1989; Denham & Grout, 1993).

Coaching influences. Parents who talk about emotions and foster this ability in their children enable their children to separate impulse and behavior, to express optimal patterns of emotions. Emotion language allows for specificity in communicating how to feel, what to say, and what to do in certain emotionally charged situations. Language allows for representing the non-here-and-now; socializers may reminisce about emotional experience or anticipate it, visualizing affective and regulatory possibilities in a noncharged atmosphere.

Mothers who talk more about emotions during such conversations have preschoolers who are happier and less angry during play (Denham et al., 1997). Mothers who repetitively display and discuss their distress have more affectively negative children.

Contingency influences. Parents' behavioral and emotional reactions to their children's emotions may encourage or discourage certain enduring patterns of expressiveness in the children themselves and children's mobilization of emotional resources in situations where they are "on their own." *Rewarding socialization* (Tomkins, 1991) is fostered when caregivers assist the child in maintaining positive affect and reducing negative affect. Important components of rewarding socialization of emotion include aiding the child in attenuating negative affect through strategies that downplay negative experiences and, at the same time, tolerating the child's negative affect as valid and worthy of regard and concern, rather than disgrace.

Parents who are emotional *coaches* in this way have children who show emotional competence on a variety of indices (Denham, 1993; Denham & Grout, 1993). Emerging research shows that rewarding socializers of emotion have kindergartners who were better at handling their own emotions, more popular, rated by teachers and parents as more socially competent, and even more physically relaxed. Amazingly, they also had higher achievement scores by third grade. The payoff for children whose parents are rewarding socializers covers an astounding range of positive outcomes.

In contrast, punitive socialization does not lead to such positive developmental outcomes. Some punitive socializers (or *dismissers*) want to be helpful but ignore or deny their children's experience of emotions, distract them from emotions, which are really a trivial bother, something to let blow over. They do not use emotional moments as a chance to get closer to the child or to help the child learn lessons in emotional competence. Dismissers may also be just too permissive—any alternative a child selects to handle emotions is okay, all upsets are soothed, and even bargaining and bribery are used to stanch the flow of negative emotions. In an even more pernicious way, dismissers may be full of contempt, showing no respect for how the child feels.

References
Denham, S. A. (1989). Maternal affect and toddlers' social-emotional competence. *American Journal of Orthopsychiatry, 59*, 368–376.

Denham, S. A. (1993). Maternal emotional responsiveness and toddlers' social-emotional functioning. *Journal of Child Psychology and Psychiatry, 34*, 715–728.

Denham, S. A., & Grout, L. (1993). Socialization of emotion: Pathway to preschoolers affect regulation. *Journal of Nonverbal Behavior, 17*, 205–227.

Denham, S. A., Mitchell-Copeland, J., Strandberg, K., Auerbach, S., & Blair, K. (1997). Parental contributions to preschoolers' emotional competence: Direct and indirect effects. *Motivation and Emotion, 27*, 65–86.

Tomkins, S. S. (1991). *Affect, imagery, and consciousness, Vol. III. The negative affects: Anger and fear.* New York: Springer.

See also: Conflict resolution; Emotion language; Empathy; Temperament.

SUSANNE A. DENHAM

African American parents. *Parenting* is defined as the process of translating love and care to children and assisting in their growth and development. These tasks include providing for the basic needs of children, such as food, shelter, and clothing. Parents create family life for children, introduce them to the ways of their society, and provide opportunities for the development of competence, mastery, and individuality. *Competent parenting* is the quality of possessing the attributes necessary to achieve tasks associated with raising healthy, well-adjusted children.

Little is known about competent African American parents. Most research studies have focused on the extent to which family structure and poverty explains child outcomes. Available studies have associated low internal control, low academic achievement, juvenile delinquency, early sexual onset, pregnancy, and parenting among African American youth being reared in single, female-headed families. African American parents are often characterized as authoritarian, harsh, demanding, disinterested, and uninvolved in their children's achievements despite having set unrealistically high goals for them to accomplish. Thus to "correct" these patterns, traditional approaches have focused on changing the families that are experiencing problems, rather than requiring change in the more pervasive institutions and practices of society.

Traditional approaches used to study African American families have been criticized in recent years. Concern has been based on the continued use of negative paradigms to explain the socialization process of African American parents. Most studies compare these families to White, middle-class, two-parent families, thus perpetuating a position that African American parents are unable to rear competent children. In an attempt to present a nonpathological view of African American families, some researchers have begun to focus on issues of strength and resiliency (McAdoo, 1995). This approach emphasizes the need to understand how these families survive often-insurmountable circumstances to prepare their children for their adult role in society.

The socialization experience of African American children has been characterized as a *triple quandary* in which the child is taught how to negotiate the mainstream, minority status, and African American experiences. Each of these domains requires its own psychological and behavioral repertoires, which are often at odds with each other in terms of purpose. For example, Thornton and associates (1990) have pointed out that African American parents socialize their children in a broader social environment that is frequently incompatible with having a positive self and group identity. For many African American parents, racial prejudice and discrimination often create obstacles and challenge their ability to accomplish parental goals and expectations.

One of their child-rearing tasks is to socialize their children so that they can survive in a society where racism, prejudice, and discrimination exist. A recent study found that approximately 66% of African American parents convey racial socialization messages to their children (Thornton et al., 1990). Through racial socialization, African American parents teach their children how to (1) survive and cope with prejudice, (2) acquire self-respect and pride, and (3) become aware that life is often not fair. This child-rearing task begins at a very early age and is necessary because it serves as a protective factor when their children are confronted with racism (Jackson, McCullough, & Gurin, 1988).

To extend their parenting capacities, many African Americans connect with social mechanisms that advance their children's chances of success (Harrison et al., 1990; McLoyd, 1990). This process, defined as social capital, is a method by which parents acquire community, friends, extended family, and teachers' involvement to cultivate and promote opportunities for overcoming the odds for upward mobility of their children (Brody, Stoneman, & Flor, 1997; Elder et al., 1995).

Extended family members help African American parents in performing child-rearing tasks, problem solving, and coping with stress. Role flexibility and fluid boundaries in these families provide additional approaches for meeting the needs of children. In addition, religious institutions provide guidance for rearing children and assistance in times of need. For example, when intrafamilial conflict arises, ministers and parishioners are more often sought rather than mental health professionals. Further, attending church has been associated with decreased antisocial behavior in children.

Competent African American parents may be considered rigid and dominant and use pressure in rearing their children. With the problems confronting many African American neighborhoods, parents must be vigilant and proactive and invest enormous energy and ingenuity to ensure a protective community for their children (Elder et al., 1995). Finally, when societies, communities, and parents invest in children, children are better equipped to develop successfully.

References

Bordy, G. H., Stoneman, Z, & Flor, D. (1995). Linking family processes, parental education, and family financial resources to academic competence among rural African American youths living in two-parent families. *Journal of Marriage and the Family*, *57*, 567–579.

Harrison, A. O., Chan, S. Q., Wilson, M. N., Buriel, R., & Pine, C. J. (1990). Family ecologies of ethnic minority children. *Child Development*, *61*, 347–362.

Jackson, J., McCullough, W., & Gurin, G. (1988). Family, socialization environment, and identity development in Black Americans. In H. McAdoo (Ed.), *Black families* (2nd edition, pp. 242–256). Beverly Hills, CA: Sage Publications.

McAdoo, H. P. (1995). African-American families: Strength and realities. In H. I. McCubbin, E. A. Thompson, A. I. Thompson, & J. A. Futrell (Eds.), *Resiliency in ethnic minority families: African-American families* (Vol. 2, pp. 17–30). Madison: The University of Wisconsin System.

McLoyd, V. C. (1990). The impact of economic hardship on black families and children: Psychological distress, parenting, and socioemotional development. *Child Development*, *61*, 311–346.

Murry, V. M. (1997). *Resilient rural African American single-parent families*. Paper presented at the National Council on Family Relations Conference, Crystal City, DC.

Thornton, M., Chatters, L., Taylor, R. J., & Allen, W. R. (1990). Sociodemographic and environmental influences on racial socialization by Black parents. *Child Development*, *61*, 401–409.

See also: Cultural competence; Cultural context; Racial identity.

VELMA MCBRIDE MURRY

After-school child care. After-school child care programs are designed to provide adult supervision and care for children at the end of the regular school day. These programs are operated in schools, YMCAs, child care centers, and community and neighborhood centers. They are similar to preschool child care centers in that they require enrollment and are licensed by states and municipalities. According to the *National Child Care Survey* (Hofferth et al., 1991), 8% of all children ages 5 to 12 years attend after-school programs as their primary child care arrangement during the after-school hours. Use of these programs decreases as children become older: 21% of 5-year-olds attend such programs, whereas only 9% of children ages 6 to 9 years and less than 3% of children ages 10 to 12 years do.

Research on after-school programs has been limited. Early reports indicated positive outcomes for children who attended after-school programs, particularly for low-income children. Greater math and reading achievement, better work habits in school, increases in self-esteem, and better behavioral adjustment have been linked to inner-city children's enrollment in these programs. Middle-class children also have been found to benefit from program attendance, in terms of improved relationships with peers. After-school programs do not uniformly provide positive benefits for children, however. Vandell and Corasaniti (1988) found that school-age children who attended after-school programs in child care centers that primarily served preschoolers fared worse than other children in terms of school classroom sociometric nominations, academic grades, and standardized test scores. These conflicting results point to the importance of the quality of after-school programs and the nature of children's experiences while attending them; program enrollment does not guarantee positive outcomes.

After-school programs vary widely in terms of the number of children enrolled, staff-child ratios, staff experience, staff education, and staff demeanor toward children, as well as the availability of age-appropriate activities and programming flexibility. These program and staff characteristics are linked in numerous ways. Staff behave more positively when they are better educated, staff-child ratios are smaller, and more activities are available that are well suited to children's ages and interests. Programs that offer a greater number of activities are more flexible in allowing children to choose their activities and their playmates. Children's assessments of the psychosocial climate in programs are linked to some of these program and staff characteristics. Program climate is assessed more positively when there are a greater number of developmentally appropriate activities, fewer negative staff-child interactions, and fewer children enrolled. Children's enjoyment of their after-school programs is linked to their perceptions that staff are emotionally supportive and allow children some privacy and opportunities for independent decision making (Rosenthal & Vandell, 1996).

Children's performance in school is associated with their experiences in after-school programs. Pierce, Hamm, and Vandell (in press) found that first-grade boys who participated in flexible programs in which they could choose their own activities were reported by their school classroom teachers to have better social skills with peers. A larger number of available activities in the programs was associated with more emotional and behavior problems and poorer academic grades for boys. These associations were evident when the family's socioeconomic status and parenting practices in the home were taken into account. Similar associations were not found for first-grade girls. It appears that young school-age boys derive social benefits from program flexibility, perhaps because less structure offers more opportunities for sharing and negotiation. Young boys also appear to benefit from having only a few activity options in the after-school hours. Programs that restrict activities may resemble elementary school classrooms and thereby facilitate boy's adjustment at school.

The emotional climate in after-school programs is another important feature of children's experiences. A positive emotional climate, as evidenced by positive staff behavior toward and warm regard for children, is linked to fewer emotional and behavior problems at school, and better reading and math grades for boys but not for girls (Pierce, Hamm, & Vandell, in press). Program staff who are warm and positive may provide a source of emotional support for boys.

The results of recent research provide indications of the particular after-school program characteristics that parents should look for when seeking this type of child care arrangement for their children. In general, high-quality programs have small staff-child ratios. Staff are well educated and behave positively with children. The environment is fun and relaxing. Activities are developmentally appropriate for all children; both younger and older children are given opportunities to pursue things of interest to them.

References

Hofferth, S. L., Brayfield, A., Deich, S., & Holcomb, P. (1991). *National child care survey, 1990.* Washington, DC: Urban Institute Press.

Pierce, K. M., Hamm, J. V., & Vandell, D. L. (in press). Experiences in after-school programs and children's adjustment in first-grade classrooms. *Child Development.*

Rosenthal, R., & Vandell, D. L. (1996). Quality of care at school-aged child care programs: Regulatable features, observed experiences, child perspectives, and parent perspectives. *Child Development, 67,* 2434–2445.

Vandell, D. L., & Corasaniti, M. A. (1988). The relation between third graders' after-school care and social, academic, and emotional functioning. *Child Development, 59,* 868–875.

See also: Child care; Developmentally Appropriate Practices; Family-school partnerships.

KIM M. PIERCE

Aggression, childhood. Aggression involves using hostile, injurious, or destructive behavior to obtain a desired outcome. Childhood (early through middle childhood) aggression is typically expressed through aversive behaviors including, but not limited to, temper tantrums, hitting, fighting, and shouting (Morton, 1987). Aggression is a normal part of childhood, beginning in the second half of the first year of life, increasing during the second year of life, and diminishing by the fourth and fifth years of life. This decline occurs when children gain the ability to express their feelings verbally and obtain their goals using more prosocial methods (Landy & Peters, 1992). If a child's aggression does not diminish by age 6, he or she may have developed patterns of aggressive behavior that will be difficult to change (Eron, Huesmann, & Zelli, 1991).

Interactions between parents and children are a critical factor in the development of aggressive behavior patterns that continue past the preschool years. Research has identified a number of factors that promote or inhibit the development of ongoing aggressive behaviors in children.

Risk factors. Variables that seem to promote aggressive behaviors in children include criminal history or antisocial personality in a parent, parental rejection of the child, weak bonding to caretakers in infancy, highly punitive or abusive parental discipline, lack of parental supervision, and failure to reinforce prosocial behavior (American Psychological Association [APA], 1993). Additionally, coercive patterns of family interaction, in which family members use negative behaviors to control one another, contribute to the development of aggressive behavior patterns in children (Landy & Peters, 1992). Other studies have pointed to parental disharmony and parental modeling as key risk factors (Eron, Huesmann, & Zelli, 1991). If parents positively reinforce the young child's use of aversive or aggressive behaviors and do not model nonviolent social problem solving within the family, the child will be more likely to develop antisocial behavior patterns (APA, 1993).

Lack of parental supervision is a key factor in the development of conduct problems. Lack of appropriate supervision can lead to social and cultural experiences that contribute to the development of aggressive behavior patterns in children and youth. Exposure to violence in the mass media, involvement with antisocial groups, involvement with alcohol and other drugs, and access to firearms have all been implicated in the development of violent behaviors. Numerous studies have associated increased viewing of television violence with greater tolerance of aggressive attitudes and higher levels of aggressive behavior. These effects, however, are mitigated somewhat when parents view programs with children, teach "critical viewing skills," display disapproval of the violence, and encourage children to think about nonviolent alternatives for solving the problems depicted (APA, 1993).

Protective factors. While some children who are exposed to the risk factors listed above develop ongoing aggressive behaviors, many others do not. Recently the research has begun to focus on identifying protective factors that seem to inhibit the development of aggressive behavior patterns in at-risk children. Some of the protective factors identified in the research include appropriate parental supervision, alternate adult caretakers in the family (such as grandparents, aunts, and uncles), and a supportive same-sex model who provides structure (APA, 1993). Clearly, parental behaviors are instrumental in the reduction of childhood aggression. Parents who provide adequate warmth and affection, firm limits rather than punitive discipline, positive reinforcement, and inductive efforts (such as reasoning, explanations of consequence for behavior, and discussion of feeling-behavior relationships) are more successful in helping children develop prosocial problem-solving skills that foster the long-term elimination of aggression (Morton, 1987).

Parental behavior and family relationships are not the only factors that influence the development of aggressive behavior patterns in children. Societal and biological factors can also lead children to exhibit ongoing aggressive behaviors. However, it is within the context of the family that children receive their earliest training regarding appropriate ways to influence the behavior of others and gain desired social outcomes. Further research is needed to pinpoint the ways in which parental behavior and family interactions during the first five years of life lead children to diminish their use of aggression. By better understanding the family variables that inhibit the continuation of aggressive behaviors, researchers and practitioners will be empowered to develop more effective strategies for intervening in the lives of children.

References
American Psychological Association. (1993). *Violence and youth: Psychology's response* (Vol. 1). Washington, DC: Author.

Eron, L. D., Huesmann, L. R., & Zelli, A. (1991). The role of parental variables in the learning of aggression. In D. J. Pepler & K. H. Rubin (Eds.), *The development and treatment of childhood aggression* (pp. 169–188). Hillsdale, NJ: Lawrence Erlbaum.

Landy, S. & Peters, R. D. (1992). Toward an understanding of a developmental paradigm for aggressive conduct problems during the preschool years. In R. D. Peters, R. J. McMahon, & V. L. Quinsey (Eds.), *Aggression and violence throughout the life span* (pp. 1–32). Newbury Park, CA: SAGE Publications.

Morton, T. (1987). Childhood aggression in the context of family interaction. In D. H. Crowell, I. M. Evans, & C. R. O'Donnell (Eds.), *Childhood aggression and violence: Sources of influence, prevention, and control* (pp. 117–158). New York: Plenum Press.

See also: Bullying; Conflict resolution; Violence, community.

KAREN LYNN POFF

AIDS/HIV. In 1982–1983, French scientists isolated a virus—the Human Immunodeficiency Virus (HIV)—responsible for destroying an essential portion of the human immune system. Collectively, the diseases and individual experiences as a result of HIV are referred to as AIDS, an acronym for Acquired Immune Deficiency Syndrome. The letter *A*, acquired, indicates that the virus has been received from someone else. *I*, immune, refers to a protection against disease-causing microorganisms. *D*, deficiency, is a loss of the protection provided by the immune system. *S*, syndrome, is a group of signs and symptoms that together represent AIDS as a human pathology (Stine, 1996).

Description. The body's immune system produces white blood cells (leukocytes), which identify disease-causing elements, referred to as *pathogens* (e.g., bacteria, viruses, or fungi). Once a pathogen has been recognized, white blood cells will envelop and kill it. When HIV infects the body, these viruses attack the body's immune system and weaken natural body defenses. With the immune system in a continually weakened state, the body becomes increasingly vulnerable to opportunistic disease, diseases caused by normally benign microorganisms or viruses that become pathogenic when the immune system is impaired (Stine, 1996).

Diagnosis of HIV. Prior to 1993 an individual would not have been diagnosed with AIDS until presenting an indicator disease such as Kaposi's sarcoma. In 1993 the Centers for Disease Control and Prevention (CDC) proposed new criteria, identifying an individual who is HIV seropositive (having a pathogen or the antibodies for that pathogen in the bloodstream) with AIDS when specified indicator diseases are present and/or if the CD4 cell count is below 200 per cubic millimeter of blood. *CD* refers to cluster differentiating type antigens found on T lymphocytes. Each CD is assigned a number: CD1, CD2, and so on. (Stine, 1996). HIV is diagnosed through blood or saliva tests that detect HIV antibodies.

Other modalities of HIV transmission. In that HIV/AIDS is transmitted through methods other than sexual activity, avoid sharing instruments that could have come in contact with blood (e.g., cuticle scissors or razor blades) and unsafe injection practices ("sharing needles"). Most recently a case has been reported of transmission through "deep" or "french" kissing. Because blood carrying HIV must be transferred, both parties may have had injuries in their mouths (e.g., periodontal disease) that permitted the exchange of blood. This is the first such report recognized by the CDC, and it indicates that it is extremely rare for such to occur.

HIV/AIDS prevention. Prevention requires an interactive involvement of major social systems (i.e., family, educational, religious, and political) promoting values-based interventions that can be adopted by parents and used to facilitate sex education within the family. Unfortunately, society has adopted a "hands-off" philosophy regarding values in sex education curricula. While it is recognized that there are many values-oriented philosophies and the imposition of any one of them would not be ethical, the mere presentation of biological data has had minimal effect in altering attitudes with regard to HIV/AIDS, safer sex practices, or sharing of needles. Attitudes are reflections of values that are incorporated into the standards, expectations, assumptions, and attributions of an individual. As such, values-based decision making seems appropriate for decisions of a sexual nature because of their potential impact on other human beings.

Parents and HIV/AIDS. HIV/AIDS acceptance is the ability to embrace the child/adolescent *and* the illness. The art of acceptance parallels the experience of parents who have children with a permanent disability (e.g., spinal injury, Down Syndrome) or a terminal illness (e.g., cancer). Parents often experience adjustment problems upon learning their child is HIV-positive. Denying the harsh reality of the disease can foster fears stemming from uncertainty as to whether or when the virus will lead to AIDS. This state of "suspended animation" can cause feelings of anxiety, depression and hopelessness, fear of death, guilt, and alienation.

References

Crooks, R., & Bauer, K. (1996). *Our sexuality* (6th ed.). Pacific Grove, CA: Brooks/Cole Publishing Company.
Rathus, S.A., Nevid, J. S., & Fichner-Rathus, L. (1997). *Human sexuality in a world of diversity* (3rd ed.). Boston, MA: Allyn & Bacon.
Stine, G. J. (1996). *Acquired Immune Deficiency Syndrome: Biological, medical, social and legal issues.* Englewood Cliffs, NJ: Prentice Hall.

See also: AIDS/HIV, adolescent; AIDS/HIV, pediatric; Sexuality, adolescence.

D. KIM OPENSHAW

AIDS/HIV, adolescent. To ensure a strong and healthy population of young adults, with whom society can entrust its affairs, Kreiger (1996) indicates that youth should receive two messages: one promoting abstinence and a delay of sexual activity; the other warning against high-risk behaviors. A combined effort of parents, educational, religious, and social systems is encouraged to promote these ideas and to teach teens how to protect themselves.

A significant increase in the rate of sexually transmitted diseases (STDs) is being recorded among adolescents, among which is the human immunodeficiency virus (HIV) that results in AIDS (Acquired Immunodeficiency Syndrome). HIV/AIDS is disproportionate across ethnic groups. Researchers estimate that African American and Hispanic American adolescents are four to five times more likely to be diagnosed with AIDS than white adolescents (DiClemente et al., 1992). African American adolescents account for the greatest number of AIDS cases, with African American female adolescents accounting for 73% and African American males accounting for 48% of new HIV cases reported in 1993 (Centers for Disease Control and Prevention [CDC], 1994). Homeless youth are at special risk of HIV infections because of the prevalence of unsafe sexual practices and shared drug use in this population.

In the *HIV/AIDS Surveillance Report* (CDC, 1994), 558 new AIDS cases were diagnosed among the 13- to 19-year-old age group, and 3,911 new cases were reported among the 20- to 24-year-old population during 1993. It is important to note that since it takes up to 10 years for opportunistic infections related to AIDS to manifest, most of those in the 20- to 24-year-old population were infected either as adolescents or as preadolescents.

Kreiger (1996) has suggested that there are certain factors that place adolescents at greater risk for contracting STDs than other populations. First, adolescents frequently incorporate an attitude of invulnerability or invincibility that heightens the probability that they will engage in risk-taking behaviors, including those of a sexual nature. Because of the degree of naïveté about sexuality among adolescents, they engage in sexually related behaviors without a clear understanding of intimacy or methods of "safer sex." This leads to the second major factor: the practice of "safer sex." The Centers for Disease Control and Prevention (CDC, 1995) found that almost half of high school students who were sexually active did not use condoms the last time they had sex. Neglecting safer sex practices is even truer among teens engaging in sexual activity with multiple partners. In addition, the number of teens engaging in sexual behavior at an earlier age, often with multiple partners, has increased. The 1991 CDC publication, *Premarital Sexual Experience among Adolescent Women in the United States, 1970–1988,* indicates that 77% of girls and 86% of boys will have had sex before they have reached the age of 20. Alcohol and drug use is another contributor not only to the frequency of sex among adolescents but also to their lack of regard for safer sex practices. Finally, teens who are gay, drug users, juvenile offenders, school dropouts, runaways, homeless, or migrant youth are most vulnerable to contracting STDs because of the difficulty in providing preventative information and service delivery.

A comprehensive and accurate understanding of HIV/AIDS opens the avenue for nurturing an unconditional loving relationship with the adolescent who is diagnosed with HIV/AIDS. Only by being informed can one proactively deal with HIV/AIDS in a compassionate, rather than reactive, manner. Parents of infected children should first educate themselves and other family members/neighbors about myths that increase unrealistic fears about the disease. As long as no body fluids are exchanged, there is no risk of contracting AIDS from a person who is HIV infected. Second, parents should establish open communication with their children. Adolescents often experience the same emotions as an adult in the same situation (e.g., fear, sadness, depression, anger, shame, or disbelief). Open communication allows for compassion to be genuinely expressed and received. Third, families with adolescents who are diagnosed with HIV/AIDS experience an increase in responsibilities. Though the potential for rejection is present, an effective support system (e.g., friends, extended family, and social agencies) distributes the responsibilities and provides compassionate service to the family and HIV carrier.

References

Centers for Disease Control and Prevention. (1991). Premarital sexual experience among adolescent women in the United States, 1970–1988. *Morbidity and Mortality Weekly Report, 26,* 246–251.

Centers for Disease Control and Prevention. (1994). *HIV/AIDS Surveillance Report #5.* Washington, DC: Author.

Centers for Disease Control and Prevention. (1995). *Division of STD/HIV Prevention. Annual Report, 1994.* Washington, DC: Author.

DiClemente, R. J., Durbin, M., Siegel, D., Krasnovsky, F., Lazaurs, N., & Comacho, T. (1992). Determinants of condom use among junior high school students in a minority, inner-city school district. *Pediatrics, 89,* 197–201.

Kreiger, L. (1996). *What are adolescents' HIV prevention needs?* Center for AIDS Prevention Studies, University of California at San Francisco.

See also: AIDS/HIV; AIDS/HIV, pediatric; Sex education; Sexuality, adolescent.

D. KIM OPENSHAW

AIDS/HIV, pediatric. Stine (1996) notes that pediatric Acquired Immune Deficiency Syndrome (AIDS) cases (birth through 13 years of age) make up 1.3% of the total number of reported AIDS cases in the United States. At the present this rate for children is similar to the incidence of cancer; however unlike cancer and other diseases resulting in death—which have remained stable over the years—childhood AIDS continues to increase. In fact, AIDS is currently among the 10 leading causes of death in children, with future projections suggesting that it will be among the top 5 within the next couple of years.

Pediatric transmission. Approximately 90% of the pediatric AIDS cases result from children acquiring the human immunodeficiency virus (HIV) from their mothers. Three specific methods involving the mother have been identified. First, transmission can occur while in utero (during gestation). The virus is transmitted to the unborn fetus as it crosses over from the mother through the placenta and enters the fetal bloodstream. Second, during delivery, infants may ingest blood or other maternal fluids that are HIV infected. As many as 50% of the HIV cases contracted from mothers occur during the process of delivery (Kuhn et al., 1994). The third method of HIV transmission from the mother to the newborn is during breastfeeding, where it is suggested that the infant becomes infected through the mother's milk (Van de Perre et al., 1993). In addition to maternal transmission of HIV, the CDC (Centers for Disease Control and Prevention, 1994) has indicated that the virus may also be contracted through hemophilia/coagulation disorder (4%), receipt of blood transfusion, blood components, or tissue (5%), and through undetermined means (1%). As of July 1995, there have been 476,500 reported pediatric AIDS cases in the United States.

Symptoms. Signs and symptoms common to HIV infection in babies and young children include the following: swelling in the lymph glands in the neck, under the arms, and in the diaper area; swollen belly, sometimes with diarrhea; itchy skin rashes; frequent lung infections (pneumonia); frequent ear and sinus infections; problems with gaining weight or growth; inability to do the kinds of things healthy babies do (e.g., sitting alone, crawling, or walking); and crankiness, irritability, and constant crying.

Prognosis. One of the greatest difficulties with the pediatric population is determining which infants truly carry the HIV virus and which are merely carrying the mother's HIV antibodies. Those with the HIV antibody test HIV positive even though they are not infected (false positive). For the most part, infants are more likely to have contracted HIV when the virus can be cultured from the mother's blood, when the mother is in the latent stages of HIV, and/or if the mother's CD4 (T4) counts are low (Stine, 1996). While infants with HIV antibodies, but not infected, may carry antibodies for up to two years, usually these infants will return to seronegativity (no HIV antibody in the serum) within 18 months. Stine (1996) notes that 53% of children reported to the CDC with HIV have died, half of whom died within 9 months after diagnosis.

Preventative treatment. Even before HIV results in AIDS, health problems may occur; thus it is important for parents of infants and children with HIV to learn about how the virus can affect the child's body. In addition to healthy standards of practice such as seeking medical care as soon as a parent knows that a child is HIV-positive, the Agency for Health Care Policy and Research (1994) recommends that parents report unusual physical symptoms immediately to a health care provider. These include fever, cough, fast or difficult breathing, loss of appetite and poor weight gain, white patches or sores in the mouth, diaper rash that will not go away, blood in the diaper or bowel movements, diarrhea, vomiting, and contact with a person who has chicken pox, measles, tuberculosis, or other diseases that can spread.

Medical treatment is, of course, imperative. Children younger than 2 years of age should have their blood tested every two to three months. At 2 years of age, children should have their blood tested yearly until a diagnosis is confirmed or tested negative for HIV. Parents are encouraged to remain up-to-date with methods of treatment applicable to children.

Although by the age of 5 HIV children have learned a lot about living with HIV, their knowledge about the disease tends to be limited. Preschool children seem to be content with minimal information about HIV, and as such, parents can share information with them in short, simple answers to their questions. As the child enters school and can comprehend the nature of the disease, it is important for these children to receive correct information and honest answers. If parents divert the responsibility of communicating with their child to others, it is possible that their children will acquire developmentally inappropriate or distorted information from those who know little or nothing about HIV/AIDS. Finally, a child who is HIV-positive and whose illness is maintained as a secret may suffer emotionally (shame or fear) and/or physically (not get adequate medical treatment) in silence. These children have increased difficulties coping with the disease as it progresses.

Social policy implications. One of the most significant social policy implications involves that of reproductive rights. Reproductive rights, central to a
woman's right to control her body, have not become a public issue since the Supreme Court ruled against sterilization procedures for mentally ill and mentally
disadvantaged (i.e., low IQ) African American women. While the right to continue or terminate a pregnancy continues to be disputed, as more women become
HIV infected and give birth to HIV children, the greater the probability that this
issue will come under the surveillance of the state. Thus, the increased prevalence of pediatric HIV/AIDS has caused the issue of reproductive rights to resur-
face, with these rights taking on new meaning: child-bearing age women may be
among the first to be required to undergo mandatory HIV testing in an attempt to
control the transmission of the virus to infants (Stine, 1996).

References
Agency for Health Care Policy and Research. (1994). *HIV and your child*. Rockville,
    MD: CDC National AIDS Clearinghouse.
Centers for Disease Control and Prevention. (1994). HIV/AIDS Surveillance Mid-Year
    Report. In G. J. Stine, *Acquired Immune Deficiency Syndrome: Biological, medical,
    social and legal issues* (p. 217). Englewood Cliffs, NJ: Prentice Hall, Inc.
Kuhn, L., Stein, Z. A., Thoma, P. A., Singh, T., & Tsai, W. Y. (1994). Maternal-infant
    HIV transmission and circumstances of delivery. *American Journal of Public Health*,
    84, 1110–1115.
Meeks, L., Heit, P., & Burt, J. (1993). *Education for sexuality and HIV/AIDS: Curricu-
    lum and teaching strategies*. Blacklick, OH: Meeks Heit Publishing Company.
Stine, G. J. (1996). *Acquired Immune Deficiency Syndrome: Biological, medical, social
    and legal issues*. Englewood Cliffs, NJ: Prentice-Hall.
Van de Perre, P., Sinonon, A., Hitimana, D., Dabis, F., & Msellati, P. (1993). Infective
    and anti-infective properties of breast milk from HIV-infected women. *Lancet*, *341*,
    914–918.

See also: AIDS/HIV; AIDS/HIV, adolescent; Illness, chronic, in children.

D. KIM OPENSHAW

Alliance, parenting. The parenting alliance, also known as coparenting, refers to the degree to which marital partners work together at the task of child
rearing. A large body of literature has demonstrated that interparental conflict is
associated with the development of behavioral and emotional problems in children. However, researchers who have looked more closely into how interparental conflict affects children tend to emphasize that it is parental disagreements
about child rearing that are most predictive of problems in child development.
Consequently, the parenting alliance plays a central role in current models of the
processes underlying the development of marriage and parenting (see McCale &
Cowen, 1996).

   According to Weissman and Cohen (1985), a good parenting alliance is
demonstrated when parents are equally invested in their child and value one another's involvement, each parent respects the judgment of the other regarding
child-rearing issues, and both parents desire to communicate with the other.

Partners with a strong parenting alliance are able to cooperate on the tasks of child rearing and are therefore better able to meet the needs of their children. At the other extreme are those marital partners who engage in alliances that cross generational boundaries, such as parents who ally with their children rather than with their spouses.

The conceptualization and measurement of parenting alliance. Some researchers assess the degree to which parents match one another by comparing partners' individual ratings of their own behavior, philosophy, or expectations regarding child rearing. Others ask partners to report the extent to which they feel they have a good working relationship with their child's other parent. Yet other researchers observe real-time family interactions in order to assess the extent to which husbands and wives support each other. Effective assessment depends on *triangulating* the perspectives of husbands, wives, and independent observers.

The parenting alliance as a distinct dimension of marriage. Although a weak parenting alliance is associated with interparental conflict and marital dissatisfaction, this correlation does not define a causal link between these variables. The inability to cooperate in parenting may be either a cause or a consequence of marital distress, or alternatively, each may be the result of a third variable that accounts for their relationship. Much still needs to be learned about the mechanisms that link marriage and parenting. However, researchers have established that the parenting alliance is a distinct dimension of the couple relationship, independent of marital happiness or relationship quality.

The origins of the parenting alliance. Gable, Crnic, and Belsky (1994) found that observational ratings of coparenting in couples with toddler-aged sons were not related to similarities between partners in age, education, or even agreement on child-rearing attitudes. Instead, partners who differed from one another on measures of personality traits and interactional style, such as sociability, empathy, comfort with intimacy, or anxiety about relationships demonstrated weak parenting alliances. Specifically, the more that partners' self-reports disagreed regarding their own extroversion, interpersonal sensitivity, and relational style, the more the interaction of the couple in their presence of their child was marked by negative affect and lack of mutual support.

Consequences of the parenting alliance. Given that conflicts over child rearing are related to marital conflicts and child behavioral problems, the lack of a parenting alliance should predict negative outcomes for families and children. Indeed, longitudinal studies have shown that spousal disagreements about parenting preschool children are predictive of marital dissolution 7 years later, as well as psychological and behavioral problems in those children after as long as 15 years (Vaughn, Block, & Block, 1988). On the other hand, children exposed to supportive and unified relationships between their parents may develop positive expectations about others and good skills for interpersonal problem solving. Because the parenting alliance is an aspect of the couple relationship that relates to children rather than the sexual or romantic aspects of marriage, partners may be able to maintain a parenting alliance even in the face of marital dissatisfaction or dissolution. A good parenting alliance, therefore, can act as a buffer against the negative effects of interparental conflict or divorce on children.

Implications for intervention. Gable, Crnic, and Belsky (1994) emphasize the potential preventative value of educating parents about coparenting processes. In addition, they suggest encouraging parents to communicate directly regarding child rearing and their needs for parenting support from one another and to develop conflict resolution skills. Ehrensaft (1990) points out the many impediments to the equal sharing of parenting between men and women, including the fact that financial necessity and traditional socialization push men toward being "breadwinners" and women toward being the "caregivers" in the family. She suggests that partners contract with one another to engage in shared parenting and maintain an active vigilance about sustaining their commitment to maintaining a parenting alliance in the face of the many stressors and forces that will challenge them.

References

Abidin, R. R., & Brunner, J. F. (1995). Development of a parenting alliance inventory. *Journal of Clinical Child Psychology, 24,* 31–40.

Ehrensaft, D. (1990). *Parenting together.* Urbana: University of Illinois Press.

Gable, S., Crnic, K., & Belsky, J. (1994). Coparenting within the family system: Influences on children's development. *Family Relations, 43,* 380–386.

McHale, J. P., & Cowan, P. A. (Eds.). (1996). Understanding how family-level dynamics affect children's development: Studies of two-parent families. *New Directions for Child Development 74,* 5-26.

Vaughn, B. E., Block, J. H., & Block, J. (1988). Parental disagreements on child rearing during early childhood and the psychological characteristics of adolescents. *Child Development, 59,* 1020–1033.

Weissman, S. H., & Cohen, R. S. (1985). The parenting alliance and adolescence. *Adolescent Psychiatry, 12,* 24–45.

See also: Conflict, interparental; Family systems; Marital interaction; Triangulation.

PATRICIA K. KERIG

Asian American parents. Diversity characterizes the Asian Pacific American (APA) population. The APA ethnic mosaic includes Chinese, Japanese, Koreans, Filipino(a)s, Asian Indians, Southeast Asians (Vietnamese, Cambodian, Lao, Hmong, Thai, and others), and those from the Pacific Islands (Samoa, Tonga, and others). APA native languages range from Mandarin and Cantonese to Tagalog, from Japanese to Korean, from Hindi to Vietnamese; adopted languages include French, Spanish, and English. APAs embrace a number of religions and philosophies, including Hinduism, Confucianism, Buddhism, Shinto, Taoism, Islam, Protestantism, and Roman Catholicism. There are major differences in the nature and history of immigration by various APA groups, most notably those related to date of first arrival and circumstances under which migration occurred. APAs, in significant numbers, began residence in the United States as early as the 1830s. Historically, a number of exclusion acts have limited APA immigration; however, recent surges of Asian/Pacific Islander immigration have helped make the APA population one of the fastest growing in the United States. In spite of this diversity, there are significant similarities among

APA ethnic groups that, within the context of the parent-child relationship, bear examination.

APA stereotypes and myths. Among the myths and stereotypes that histori-cally have been so damaging to the APA community is that of the so-called *model minority.* The APA community has been viewed, monolithically, as one that is quiet, industrious, and high achieving. The media has reinforced this im-age. As a result, APAs have been touted as yet another American success story. The APA family has become a model of self-help and solidarity, and in fact, some segments of the APA population have achieved success. However, not all APA groups share the degree of economic, educational, and other forms of prog-ress. For example, some recent Southeast Asian immigrants have experienced profound difficulties in their attempted psychological and economic adjustment to American life. Furthermore, adherence to the myth of a model minority group has led to criticism of non-APA populations (of color) who have not achieved high levels of success and to resulting tensions between and among American ethnic groups. Finally, a dangerous tendency by some Americans to transfer hostility toward Asians (e.g., Vietnamese, as a result of the Vietnam War, or the Japanese, as a consequence of World War II and ongoing business wars) to the APA population has led to increased anti-APA rhetoric and violence (Yama-moto, 1992).

Immigration and intergenerational conflict. Native-born APA parents, like most American parents, face a number of complex family issues. However, for first-generation APA immigrant parents, the resulting clash between traditional Asian values and contemporary Western culture may produce the most formida-ble challenges. To a certain extent these are problems encountered by all immi-grant groups, but they often find unique expression in the APA household. For example, in many traditional APA cultures, family relationships are character-ized by mutual respect and dependence: Not only do children and parents have a lifelong obligation to each other, but the living and deceased have enduring mutual responsibilities. Such shared obligations and duties often run counter to the American emphasis on independence and individualism. Similarly, the filial piety so central to many traditional APA cultures is tested by a number of chal-lenges to parental authority in a contemporary American setting. The extended kinship groups found in APA communities, too, have been subject to change and attempted adaptation. Indicators of this change and adaptation include the geo-graphic dispersion of APAs away from ethnic enclaves (e.g., Chinatowns, Ja-pantowns, Little Manilas); the increase in interracial marriages (more dramatic among some APA groups—Japanese Americans, for example—than among others); and an increase in problems associated with juvenile delinquency and inability to meet the needs of the APA elderly (Mindel, Habenstein, & Wright, 1988).

The APA family and responses to intervention. Traditionally, the APA com-munity has shunned outside intervention. The immediate and extended family, as well as APA social organizations, traditionally has been the locus of problem solving and mediation. Issues ranging from juvenile delinquency to spousal con-flict to care of the elderly have been handled by heads of households rather than by social service agencies. Recently, however, the call by APA families for social service support has been on the increase. APA families, in increasing numbers, have begun to seek the assistance of social workers and therapists. Nevertheless, traditional self-help attitudes of the APA community, the failure of service agencies to fully consider cultural and linguistic differences, and a distrust of outsiders exacerbated by ongoing discrimination and anti-APA violence continue to make intervention difficult. Perhaps, the ideal response to challenge and change remains a combination of self-help and social service support. Like other groups, the APA population will continue to grow, to question traditional values, to encounter challenges to family stability, and ultimately to adapt.

References

Chan, S. (1991). *Asian Americans: An interpretive history*. Boston: Twayne Publishers.

Endo, R., Stanley, S., & Wagner, N. N. (1980). *Asian-Americans: Social and psychological perspectives* (Vol. 2). Ben Lomond, CA: Science and Behavior Books.

Mindel, C. H., Habenstein, R. W., & Wright, R. (Eds.). (1988). *Ethnic families in America: Patterns and variations* (3rd ed.). New York: Elsevier Science Publishing.

Yamamoto, D. Y. (1992). Kindred spirits: The contemporary Asian American family on television. *Amerasia Journal, 18* (2), 35–53.

Ying, Y., & Chao, C. C. (1996). Intergenerational relationship in Iu Mien American families. *Amerasia Journal, 22* (3), 47–64.

See also: Cultural competence; Cultural context; Racial identity.

C. C. HERBISON

Attachment, secure. The theory of John Bowlby (1969) remains enormously influential in the conceptualization and classification of attachments. He proposed that infants enter the world biologically predisposed to attach to caregivers and seek out contact with them. Additionally, Bowlby theorized that the responsiveness of caregivers influences the nature of the child's attachments. Securely attached children have benefited from a responsive caretaker who allows a give-and-take relationship with the child that is both age appropriate and nurturing. *Secure attachment* is considered the optimal attachment form for developmental success beginning in infancy and lasting the life span.

Currently, the most enduring and widely accepted attachment classification scheme is based on Bowlby's theory. Mary Ainsworth devised the *Strange Situation* experimental procedure in the 1970s to measure the nature of children's attachments. Ainsworth's original experiments involved mothers and their youngsters coming into a novel room with a chair and some toys. The procedure involved the baby staying in the room continuously while the mother and a stranger made a series of entrances and exits. The baby's reactions were observed and coded. From this procedure several attachment types emerged: secure, avoidant, and resistant (Ainsworth et al., 1978). Since these initial studies, other researchers, to further illustrate the complexity of child attachment, have added many subtypes.

The securely attached babies were able to comfortably explore the room while their mothers were near but became distressed when their mothers left. Upon mother's return, baby went to her and accepted her comforting. Securely attached babies also actively discriminated between their mothers and the stranger. The stranger was not a "safe base" that could replace or substitute for mother.

These mothers did several things in their interactions that appeared to promote secure attachments. They had more physical contact with their babies. Instead of propping a bottle or handing their babies to someone else for feeding, for example, these mothers fed their babies in their arms. They were also more consistent in responding to cues from their babies. When their baby cried, these mothers reliably responded to the cry. These mothers were consistent in how they approached baby (always comforting rather than alternating between comforting and punitive, for example). Also, these mothers were more often accurate in their interpretation of the cue. They realized when their baby was crying in pain, fussy with sleepiness, or whimpering with fear, for example.

The malleability of children and the indelible impact of environment on even the youngest of children have been clearly established by this research. Long-term studies of children assessed via the Strange Situation reveal the impact and advantages of a secure attachment. Years later, these children were found to be better adjusted in terms of their social skills, intellectual development, self-esteem, freedom from abuse and neglect, and better overall functioning than their resistant and avoidantly attached peers. These children fared better in the face of traumatic events, in academic and occupational realms, in peer and intimate relationships, and in the transition through developmental stages.

Interesting research in other fields have utilized the Strange Situation to assess attachment among different groups. Scholars in the field of research devoted to fathering have found very similar results. Historically, the attachments between fathers and babies have been thought to be less important, if not inconsequential, when compared with those between mothers and babies. Research efforts of Lamb (1978) and others are very conclusive in their findings that babies certainly attach to their fathers, and secure attachments are both formed and beneficial for children. These findings suggest that the nature or quality of the time spent with a child is important.

Other research has investigated the attachment potential between nonrelated care providers and children. This research has tremendous implications for adoptive parents, stepparents, and nonrelated regular care providers. Again, the research has found that a secure attachment between a child and adult is not gender or biologically dependent. Children respond with a secure attachment to the consistent, reliable, and nurturing care provided by any adult on a regular basis. There does not seem to be a limit to how many adults a child can securely attach to except that with too many adults providing care a child may not experience any one of them as consistent or reliable.

An additional body of study supports the assertion that various forms of attachment are cross-cultural (van Ijzendoorn & Kroonenberg, 1988). Children around the world have the capacity to securely attach to caregivers and, in fact, thrive when able to do so. Certainly the "safe base" adult may differ across cultures, but children around the world do form secure attachments to their primary caregivers who are consistent, reliable, and affectionate in their care.

References

Ainsworth, M. D. S., Blehar, M., Waters, E., & Wall, S. (1978). *Patterns of attachment.* Hillsdale, NJ: Erlbaum.

Bowlby, J. (1969). *Attachment and loss: Vol. 1, Attachment.* New York: Praeger.

Lamb, M. E. (1978). Father-infant and mother-infant interaction in the first year of life. *Child Development, 49,* 167–181.

van Ijzendoorn, M., & Kroonenberg, P. M. (1988). Cross-cultural patterns of attachment: A meta-analysis of the Strange Situation. *Child Development, 59,* 147–156.

See also: Conscience; Moral development; Mutuality.

ELISA DOEBLER-IRVINE

Attention Deficit Hyperactivity Disorder (ADHD). Among the disruptive disorders in childhood, behaviors consisting of inattentiveness, impulsivity, hyperactivity, and difficulty responding consistently to consequences result in the most common complaints by parents. Such problems may have multiple causes. Multiple plausible causes, such as genetic, structural, and biochemical abnormalities in the brain, as well as controversial causes, such as diet, candida yeast, and electroencephalograph (EEG) abnormalities, have been suggested as responsible for these childhood problems. The most recent and promising theories suggest that Attention Deficit Hyperactivity Disorder (ADHD) is most accurately described as an impairment of inhibiting behavior and of delaying response. ADHD appears to reflect limited behavior as the result of incompetence and developmental impairment, rather than purposeful noncompliance. It is fair to conclude that a wide range of factors may influence ADHD symptoms and the exact number of children within a population meeting the diagnostic criteria for ADHD. There is no litmus test for ADHD. This diagnosis is confirmed by the intensity, persistence, and clustering of symptom problems, as opposed to the acute presence or absence of certain symptoms.

Children with ADHD associated with a hyperactive-impulsive component are impulsive, easily distracted, overactive, do not play well quietly, talk excessively, have trouble remaining seated, interrupt, and intrude on others. Children with ADHD associated with the inattentive component do not pay attention to details, have trouble sticking to repetitive, effortful, uninteresting activities that are not of their choosing, appear not to listen, are disorganized, lose things, and are forgetful in daily activities. By far the majority of children receiving the ADHD diagnosis demonstrate both sets of symptoms. Increasingly, it is recognized that the impulsive qualities of these children result in lack of attention, poor problem solving, and inability to respond consistently to rewards and punishments. For some, this includes increased risk of related learning, conduct, and emotional problems.

The comorbid problems ADHD children develop, rather than the ADHD symptoms themselves, best predict their life outcome. ADHD in isolation appears to best predict school struggle, social difficulty, and problems meeting expectations within the home setting. However, in and of itself, it does not predict the significant negative, emotional, behavioral, and personality outcomes that have been reported. These outcomes appear to occur when children with ADHD are exposed to high-risk environments, which then increases, in a catalytic way, the development of more serious conduct, emotional, and learning problems.

In the home setting, children with ADHD are often identified by their parents well before entering school. A significant group experience early language problems. Although it has been hypothesized that ADHD symptoms prevent children from achieving their academic potential, the presence of a learning disability often makes children look more inattentive than others. Within the school setting, children with ADHD often become the focus of teachers' negative attention. Their weak performance on intellectual and academic tasks appears to result from the impact of impulsivity and inattention rather than lack of capacity. Over time, however, a lack of follow-through leads to delayed achievement in academic areas requiring practice for proficiency such as spelling, written language, and mathematics.

By adolescence, children with histories of ADHD are often experiencing annoying or withdrawn social problems and likely lower self-esteem. The more glaring symptoms of ADHD, such as hyperactivity, appear to diminish in intensity by adolescence, but the majority of adolescents with histories of ADHD continue to experience a fairly high level of community, family, social, and school problems. The majority of those with ADHD in childhood continue to experience at least some, if not the full syndrome of, problems into adulthood.

Parents should realize that at this time there is no medical, laboratory, or educational test that meets the gold standard for the diagnosis of ADHD. History and current behavior across a number of situations offer the essential data necessary to make the diagnosis. A comprehensive evaluation gathers data concerning children's behavior at home, with friends, and at school and measures academic and intellectual achievement, medical status, and emotional development. Such an assessment lends a careful eye to the evaluation of other childhood problems that may masquerade as, be exacerbated by, or exacerbate symptoms of ADHD.

Treatment of ADHD in the child and adolescent years focuses primarily on management. There is no known cure for these symptoms. It is important for parents to recognize that these problems reflect exaggeration of what is normal behavior resulting from inconsistency of applying skills rather than inability. Very clearly this pattern of difficulty reflects incompetence as opposed to noncompliance. These children know what to do but do not do what they know. Thus, the focus of intervention at home and at school is to increase the ADHD child's ability to do what they know. The most effective short-term interventions for children and adolescents with ADHD reflect the combined use of medical, behavioral, and environmental techniques. Medication appears to reduce the manipulative power of the child's behavior in eliciting certain responses from teachers, parents, and family members. Behavior management increases the salience of behaving in a way more consistent with the environment's expectations. Environmental manipulation (e.g., locking the cabinets) reduces the risk of problems within the natural setting. All of these interventions appear to lead to symptom relief. However, there is only limited data available to suggest that symptom relief is synonymous with long-term outcome. Thus, the course of this group of children appears to be impacted by forces other than treatment of their ADHD symptoms. At the present time it is believed that the forces that affect all children (e.g., resilience factors such as family life) are also powerful contributors to the life outcome for those with ADHD.

A very wide research literature attests to the benefits of stimulants (Ritalin, Dexedrine, Cylert, Desoxyn and Adderall) in reducing key symptoms of ADHD, including motor overactivity, impulsiveness and inattentiveness. Other classes of medicines including antidepressants (Tofranil, Norpramin) and antihypertensives (Catapres, Tenex) have also been reported as successful in reducing ADHD symptoms. Approximately 90% of children in the United States taking medication for ADHD receive Ritalin. In laboratory as well as natural settings, Ritalin has been found to improve time spent on task, work completion, accuracy of work, and general conduct in school; reduce conflicts with peers and siblings; and reduce negative interactions with parents.

Behavior managing interventions have focused on making academic and related tasks more interesting, less repetitive, less effortful, and more of the child's choosing while making payoffs for completing those tasks more immediate, frequent, predictable, and meaningful. Teachers working with ADHD children are urged to be organized and structured, with clear rules, predictable schedule and management of academic materials, transitions, and adherence to rules through the use of a consistently administered reinforcement system.

The consensus for parents of children with ADHD is that they are consistent, predictable, and supportive of their child in daily interactions. Research suggests that the best outcomes for children facing adversity are achieved through the emotionally secure and habitual relationships they develop with their caregivers. Parents of children with ADHD are urged to be educated, learn to manage consequences efficiently; plan, structure, and organize family life; and nurture their relationship with their child. Parents of children with ADHD must recognize that if they approach each day with the sense of hope, encouragement, acceptance, and honesty, they will empower their child. If they approach each day with a sense of despair, discouragement, anger, and blame, they will foster a perception on the child's part of his or her own powerlessness and hopelessness.

References
Goldstein, S., & Goldstein, M. (1992). *Hyperactivity: Why won't my child pay attention?* New York: Wiley.
Goldstein, S., & Goldstein, M. (1997). *Managing attention disorders in children* (2nd ed.). New York: Wiley.
Ingersoll, B. A., & Goldstein, S. (1993). *Attention Deficit Disorder and learning disabilities: Realities, myths and controversial treatments.* New York: Doubleday.
Jones, C. (1992). *Strategies for school age children with ADHD.* San Antonio, TX: Communication Skill Builders, a division of Psychological Corporation.

See also: Disability, learning; Temperament.

SAM GOLDSTEIN

Authority, parental. Parental authority involves both an acceptance of the responsibility to influence a child's behavior and a concomitant investment of power by children in the authority figure. According to this perspective, authority does not reside in a person but in a relationship. Authority emerges out of a relationship in which children view the parent as an attractive model and feel valued and respected. Authority must be legitimized for both parent and child and integrated into the child's emerging sense of justice in order to be effective.

Children draw boundaries regarding what they consider acceptable expressions of authority. Children take into account the type of command, the attributions of the authority figure, and the social setting when making authority judgments.

Type of command. Children as young as 4 years old believe it is appropriate to resist demands to engage in behavior they consider to be morally unacceptable. Demands to engage in certain acts, such as hitting and stealing, do not carry the weight of authority in children's minds (Laupa, Turiel, & Cowan, 1995). Damon (1977) found that children 4 to 10 years of age accepted the legitimacy of parental directives regarding acts such as cleaning one's room but not the legitimacy of directives to steal or hurt someone. When asked to explain, children will justify this position based on considerations for another's welfare, an appeal to fairness, and to pragmatically solving problems (Laupa & Turiel, 1993).

Attributes of the authority figure. Children also make judgments about the legitimacy of the source of authority. Younger children may consider age, appearance, power, and adult status as important indicators of authority. As they grow older they begin to make distinctions between different adults, and peers as well, based on their relative position in a social organization (Laupa, 1994). Grade school–age children recognize that other attributes legitimate authority, such as talents and abilities, prior training, and experience. By early adolescence, children are able to coordinate all these attributes with specific situational factors, and authority is viewed as a shared, consensual relation between parties adopted for the welfare of all (Smetana, 1995).

Parents are also viewed as different from other authority figures with less clearly defined boundaries. The wider authority extended by children to their parents can be seen as coming from parents' special role in child rearing and their power to distribute daily rewards and punishments. Yet children do not view parents as rule makers and enforcers on every issue and and in every social context (Laupa, Turiel, & Cowan, 1995).

Social context. Children also begin to consider the social situation in making judgments about the legitimacy of authority. Each of the three authority attributes—adult status, knowledge (skill or expertise in an area relevant to the command), and social position (social role)—is weighed differently, depending on the social context (Laupa, Turiel, & Cowan, 1995). Elementary school children, for example, would not accept the right of a school principal to set rules for their play in a public park (Laupa & Turiel, 1993). A parent's claim to authority may not be as clear and persuasive within the boundaries of the child's school as within the home. In a study of middle-age children's perceptions of authority, 87% decided that their parents could punish them for a rules transgression at home. Only 60% judged that their parents could punish them for committing the same transgression in a friend's home context (Laupa, Turiel, & Cowan, 1995).

Selman's (1980) investigation of children's perspective-taking abilities revealed a progression in children's ideas about authority issues and parents. Children first view parents as existing primarily to meet children's needs. This purpose is then linked to a unilateral concept of parental authority in which parents love their children and children respond with obedience. In later childhood, the relationship is viewed as more reciprocal, as concepts of emotional support become important. Obedience is no longer viewed as absolute but voluntary. Finally, in early adolescence parents are seen as persons with psychological characteristics. Concepts of mutual respect are more clearly articulated.

One important function of authority is its transfer to the child who is becoming more capable of self-direction. Effective authority is gradually given up in favor of the child's autonomy and self-control. This systematic exchange of authority is a challenge because of the timing problems in making decisions about changing rules and allowing children to make their own choices, especially in matters of social convention. In disputes surrounding family rules, the most frequent justification offered by adolescents, accounting for nearly half of their justifications in interviews and more than a third in family interactions, involves appeals for personal jurisdiction (Smetana, 1995).

References

Damon, W. (1977). *The social world of the child*. San Francisco: Jossey-Bass.

Laupa, M. (1994). "Who's in charge?" Preschool children's concepts of authority. *Early Childhood Research Quarterly, 9*, 1–17.

Laupa, M., & Turiel, E. (1993). Children's concepts of authority and social contexts. *Journal of Educational Psychology, 97* (1), 191–197.

Laupa, M., Turiel, E., & Cowan, P. A. (1995). Obedience to authority in children and adults. In M. Killen & D. Hart (Eds.), *Morality in everyday life: Developmental perspectives* (pp. 131–165). Cambridge: Cambridge University Press.

Selman, R. L. (1980). *The growth of interpersonal understanding: Developmental and clinical analyses*. New York: Academic Press.

Smetana, J. G. (1995). Context, conflict, and restraint. In M. Killen & D. Hart (Eds.), *Morality in everyday life: Developmental perspectives* (pp. 225–255). Cambridge: Cambridge University Press.

See also: Control strategies; Discipline; Limit setting; Physical punishment.

CHARLES A. SMITH

Autism. Autism is the most widely recognized of the pervasive developmental disorders affecting the whole of development from infancy onward. Leo Kanner (1943) was the first to note the characteristics of childhood autism: impairment in reciprocal social interaction, problems in communication and lack of imaginative activity, and a restricted repertoire of interests and activities. Autistic children seem to prefer inanimate objects to human interaction. They seem to be unaware of people. This disruption in social behavior is found in problems in attachment and empathy in social relations, although attachment behaviors that seem normal appear in a subgroup of autistic children. Communication deficits are found in both verbal and nonverbal behaviors. Impairments can range from no speech at all to delays in language acquisition or using language in odd ways. Moreover, about half of autistic children do not develop meaningful, useful speech.

The development of functional speech by the age of 5 is the best predictor of adult outcome (Campbell & Shay, 1995). Echolalic children will repeat what is said to them, sometimes over and over again. Even when autistic children acquire speech, they do not use it effectively for social communication. Impairment in language and communication tends to be the most frequent cause for referral. Autistic children also show a lack of imaginative activity and an absence of pretend play. They may engage in self-stimulatory behavior such as repetitively spinning objects, switching lights on and off, or flapping their hands.

Diagnostic evaluation involves observation and often the administration of a battery of tests designed to assess the child's intellectual abilities, expressive and receptive language skills, social maturation, and emotional responsiveness. About 70% of all autistic children score in the retarded range on measures of intelligence, and this performance is quite stable over time. Since there is heterogeneity within the autistic population itself and since autism shares behavioral characteristics with other disorders, the issue of differential diagnosis becomes very important. Experts today rely on the behavioral criteria described in the fourth edition of the *Diagnostic and Statistical Manual* of the American Psychiatric Association (1994) to make the diagnosis of autism.

Existing studies have put the prevalence of autism between 3.1 and 5.0 per 10,000 live births. One very consistent finding is that autistic boys outnumber autistic girls by about three or four to one. The cause of autism remains unknown. Autism is currently viewed as having a biological cause that has not yet been identified. Biological dysfunction is suggested by the fact that among identical twins both are afflicted in about 86% of cases, while the rate for fraternal twins is about 25%. Moreover, fragile-X chromosome, brain damage, metabolic disturbance, and abnormally high levels of the neurotransmitter serotonin have been found in some autistic children. Still, the exact nature of the cause or causes of autism is unclear. Despite treatment advances, a cure remains elusive. Of the host of treatments that have been tried, behavior therapy appears to be the most effective (Schreibman, 1988). This form of treatment utilizes psychological theories, particularly the principles of operant conditioning, to change behavior. This is a time-consuming treatment producing change that might help children in daily functioning but still leaves them performing out of the range of normal development. Although behavioral techniques have been successful in teaching basic self-care skills, the teaching of language skills has been a disappointment.

Benefits of medication are not consistently obtained, and such treatment is often accompanied with adverse side effects (Campbell & Shay, 1995). Those pharmacological agents receiving the most attention include amphetamines (e.g., Ritalin), neuroleptics (e.g., Mellaril and Haldol), and serotonin inhibitors (e.g., L-Dopa, Pondimin). Megavitamin treatment has also been investigated as a potentially useful intervention. This area of study, however, is hampered by a lack of well-controlled studies, with most reports consisting of individual case descriptions. Classroom instruction for autistic children focuses on a functional curricula, structured classrooms, and transition of the child to less restrictive classroom environments. Families of individuals with autism require specific services in order to maintain individuals with autism in their communities. Family support services such as assistive and adaptive technology, crisis management, counseling and information, estate planning, and employment-related services can be procured at both the state and community-based levels. Intervention at an early age and the involvement of parents in training programs are important for therapeutic success and outcome (Smith, Chung, & Vostanis, 1994).

References

American Psychiatric Association. (1994). *Diagnostic and statistical manual of mental disorders* (4th ed.). Washington, DC: Author.

Campbell, M., & Shay, J. (1995). Pervasive developmental disorders. In H. I. Kaplan & B. J. Sadock (Eds.), *Comprehensive textbook of psychiatry, VI* (Vol. 2, pp. 2277–2293). Baltimore, MD: Williams & Wilkins.

Kanner, L. (1943). Autistic disorder of affective contact. *Nervous child, 8,* 477–479.

Schreibman, L. (1988). *Autism.* Newbury Park, CA: Sage Publications.

Smith, B., Chung, M. C., & Vostanis, P. (1994). The path to care in autism: Is it better now? *Journal of Autism and Developmental Disorder, 23,* 175–183.

See also: Mental illness, children.

STEVEN M. ALESSANDRI

B

Birth order. Birth order refers to the order in which a given child was born into a family. However, there is no generally accepted method or consensus for describing or conceptualizing birth order. Most research in this area has focused on effects associated with being the firstfborn, last-born, middle-born, or only child. Being the only child in a family could be considered an order of birth—and many studies of birth order effects include only children. As family size has shrunk in industrialized and postindustrialized societies, middle children are becoming extinct. Determining a child's birth order becomes particularly complex in blended or stepfamilies. Age-spacing and gender differences have also been hypothesized to interact with and confound birth order effects. Thus, in evaluating research in this area, one must examine carefully just how birth order is being conceptualized in a given study.

Hypotheses about birth order have sprung from two sources: (1) psychological theories of personality and (2) cultural beliefs. Both psychodynamic and family systems models have hypothesized that children in different birth orders find themselves in different patterns or types of relationships with parents. These forces are also thought to interact with the potential effects of sibling rivalry. Another source is cultural beliefs. There are several widespread beliefs within the United States about the effects of birth order on children's personality and development. Baskett (1985) asked a group of adults to rate which of a set of adjective pairs they expected would best describe the typical oldest, youngest, and only child. Adults expected typical oldest children to be outgoing, obedient, secure, and unspoiled. They expected youngest children to be more likeable, disobedient, and not academically inclined. Only children, on the other hand, were most often expected to be spoiled and disliked. In general, adults seem to see oldest children more positively and to have higher expectations for their behavior—whether talking about a hypothetical or their own oldest child (Musun-Miller, 1993).

What do we actually know about birth order effects? Despite a continuing sense both among researchers and the public that birth order is important, the actual data in this area are largely inconclusive. A major review of the literature done in the early 1980s concluded that birth order had not been demonstrated to have a consistent effect upon the personality of the individual (Ernst & Angst, 1983). These authors discuss at length the methodological problems found in many studies of birth order effects. They also found that the correlation often reported between being firstborn and higher IQ scores tends to disappear when other background variables are adequately controlled for in data analyses. Other researchers have also found that the seeming correlation between birth order and intellectual ability may be due to other confounding variables such as sibship size—with children from smaller families typically scoring higher on standardized measures than children from larger families (e.g., Steelman, 1985). The same is true of studies that focus on the common perceptions that firstborn children are overachievers and more likely to attain high occupational status. Birth order may be associated with differences in academic achievement test scores, but it really only explains a very small part of the variance. In fact, the only significant differences in firstborn personality that they found were in studies in which parents were asked to describe their child's personality. Finally, no evidence has been found to support the belief that only or single children are at greater developmental risk (Falbo & Polit, 1986).

Why do people continue to be interested in and hypothesize birth order effects? One factor may be the strongly held cultural beliefs and expectations summarized above. Another may be that the studies Ernst and Angst (1983) included in their review were primarily ones that utilized paper-and-pencil measures rather than observational techniques, and there have been several observational studies that report that parents do treat their children differently based on birth order. Questions about birth order today tend to be posed in terms of identifying patterns of differential treatment by parents that may be more directly linked to differences in personality and other areas of child development. All explanations focus on how being in different ordinal position changes the types of relationships one has with siblings (if present) and especially with parents.

How do parents differentially treat their children based on birth order? Several researchers have reported that parents talk and interact more with and have higher maturity expectations for their firstborn children—at least during infancy and the preschool years. They also interfere and intervene more in young firstborn children's play, and these children may also have closer relationships with their parents (e.g., Ernst & Angst, 1983; Sutton-Smith, 1982). Birth order may be an important variable in the development of a given child within that family depending on parental perception of the importance of birth order and its impact on their differential treatment of children at different ages. These cultural and personal beliefs may be of primary importance in understanding the role that birth order plays in a specific family.

References

Baskett, L. M. (1985). Sibling status effects: Adult expectations. *Developmental Psychology*, *21*, 441–445.

Ernst, C., & Angst, J. (1983). *Birth order: Its influence on personality*. New York: Springer-Verlag.

Falbo, T., & Polit, D. F. (1986). Quantitative review of the only child literature: Research evidence and theory development. *Psychological Bulletin*, *100*, 176–189.

Musun-Miller, L. (1993). Sibling status effects: Parents' perceptions of their own children. *Journal of Genetic Psychology*, *154*, 189–198.

Steelman, L. C. (1985). A tale of two variables: A review of the intellectual consequences of sibship size and birth order. *Review of Educational Research*, *55*, 353–386.

Sutton-Smith, B. (1982). Birth order and sibling status effects. In M. E. Lamb & B. Sutton-Smith (Eds.), *Sibling relationships: Their nature and significance across the life span* (pp. 153–166). Hillsdale, NJ: Lawrence Erlbaum Associates.

See also: Family systems; Siblings.

LINDA MUSUN-MILLER

Biting. Biting is a "hot button" for many parents and caregivers. In fact, some parent educators have reported that adults often express more concern about biting than about hitting or throwing toys, even though all may be examples of aggressive behavior. Parents also seem to feel that biting requires a specialized response.

Most parenting books provide little or no direct information on the topic of biting. Penelope Leach (1989) mentions it briefly, but much of the discussion is dedicated to nursing babies biting the mother's nipple—an important issue to some but a temporary problem and not the primary concern of most parents. Benjamin Spock (1992) spends more time with the topic. His approach is to consider biting a normal behavior but to show concern if it occurs in certain contexts. Rudolf Dreikurs (1964) encourages parents to consider the cause of the misbehavior and stay out of fights if peers or siblings are biting each other. If the child is biting the parent, he suggests that parents do likewise to the child, demonstrating that they should have that "right" if the child does. The Better Homes and Gardens *New Baby Book* (1979) simply explains how to administer first aid to a human bite.

There are several ways in which biting is different from other child actions. First, biting as an eating behavior is vital to life. Clearly, it is not appropriate to teach children never to bite anything. Biting also provides some sense of satisfaction in and of itself when children are teething or needing oral satisfaction. When the action feels good to children, it is especially difficult to convince them that it hurts someone else and that they should not do it.

Another aspect of biting that makes it unique is that very young children can cause pain and/or injury to even a large adult by biting. They are capable of this long before they are able to understand the impact of their actions and before they have developed a repertoire of alternative actions. Finally, biting is a behavior that seems to emerge as a normal stage of development. Almost all children try using biting as one of their first "weapons," usually between the ages of 1 and 2.

As with any form of misbehavior, exploring the reasons for the child's actions can be important for determining responses to eliminate the misbehavior. The previous characteristics suggest some reasons why children might bite:

- It might make their gums or teeth feel good, or they might just like the feeling of biting.
- It may be the only weapon they have available when they are frustrated or angry or may be their "weapon of choice."
- They may be exhibiting a normal developmental behavior.
- They do not understand that biting hurts other people.

There are other reasons why children may bite that are similar to other forms of misbehavior:

- They get attention.
- They are imitating someone else's behavior.
- They are curious about what will happen.

Close observation of a child's biting behavior and monitoring of tooth eruption may help to uncover a child's reasons for biting.

Responses to biting are likely to work if they take into account the child's motivations and needs and if they provide a replacement for the behavior instead of just trying to eliminate it. One approach is to provide the child with something appropriate to bite, such as a teething ring, towel, or washcloth. This substitution may be effective if the child enjoys biting. It also can help provide limits to the behavior by describing when and how biting is appropriate. When the child bites a person, the adult could say, "No, you may not bite people. That hurts. You may bite this instead."

If children are biting because they do not know what else to do when they are angry and frustrated, they could be given other verbal and behavioral alternatives. They might express anger or frustration verbally or walk away from a conflicted situation until people are calm.

Because biting is often a "hot button" for adults, several authors suggest that parents demonstrate a controlled response to it. The child may find it entertaining to see the parent get agitated, even if it means getting in trouble. Biting may be an effective way for a child to get attention. It also could lead parents to actions they would regret later. Therefore, parents would benefit from planning a response to biting before it occurs. A good response might be firmly and calmly reminding the child of the no-biting rule, removing him or her from the situation, and possibly providing something else for the child to bite.

Parents often consider biting the child back to extinguish the behavior as recommended by Dreikurs, a response discouraged by Spock. It would be easy for the parent to injure the child, and it is very difficult to make it clear that biting is not allowed if the parent also does it.

If biting continues beyond toddlerhood, or if it seems to indicate that the child has serious problems with anger or with managing conflict, it may be necessary to get professional help. Just as with any other aggressive behavior, biting can be a signal of a serious disturbance.

References

Better Homes and Gardens. (1979). *New baby book*. Des Moines, IA: Meredith.
Dreikurs, R. (1964). *Children: The challenge*. New York: E.P. Dutton.
Leach, P. (1989). *Your baby & child from birth to age five*. New York: Knopf.
Spock, B. (1992). *Baby and child care*. New York: Dutton.

See also: Aggression, childhood; Discipline; Temper tantrums.

JUDITH A. MYERS-WALLS

Blaming, parent. Parent blaming resides in the general cultural bias in Western industrialized societies toward holding parents responsible for all of their children's outcomes. Parent blaming is almost invariably mother blaming. Ironically, fathers are blamed for being absent, while mothers are often blamed for playing the role for which they were culturally scripted. Mother blaming corresponds with the general tendency in individual-oriented Western cultures to discount systemic explanations in favor of those based on individual-level causation.

Mother blaming originated in the changed views of children that occurred during the early seventeenth century. The eighteenth-century response was the social construction of motherhood as the means to meet these needs (Sommerfeld, 1989). Middle-class women joined religious leaders, educators, and other professionals to promote mothering as women's proper role. By the beginning of the twentieth century, most of this moralizing about the mothering role was directed at lower-class mothers who were engaged in a variety of paid and unpaid work activities for economic survival. Much of the twentieth century saw the growth of professionals who based their conflicting parenting advice on the newly emerging field of psychology. Extrapolations from Freudian theory, rather than the theory itself, contributed to an emphasis in the psychological literature on early mothering as essential for children's psychosexual development.

The tendency for mental health professionals to rely on mother blaming for their diagnoses is documented in a report by Caplan and Hall-McCorquodale (1985) that analyzes the content of 125 articles appearing in major clinical journals in the years of 1970, 1976, and 1982. Two thirds of the 63 coding categories they used (such as attribution of blame, degree to which previous literature cited was critically examined) consisted of activities that could be considered mother blaming. Overall, 72 different types of psychopathology were attributed to poor mothering including poor language development, homosexuality, anorexia nervosa, fetishism, incest, school dropouts, and delinquency. What is striking is the consistency in use of mother blaming across all journals and the relative inattention given to the father role as a source of problems. The tendency to blame mothers more than fathers for negative child outcomes can be seen in the way in which statistics on physical child abuse are uncritically compiled to show higher levels of abuse by mothers than fathers. According to Margolin (1992), the calculation of child physical abuse incidence needs to be adjusted for the greater amount of time that mothers spend on child care.

The large body of research accumulated on maternal employment can be attributed to the mother-blaming bias. This bias was premised on the notion that mothering was a woman's normal role, and thus the vast majority of the research in this area investigated the conditions under which maternal employment could be detrimental to children's development (despite the positive role-modeling effect for daughters). Ironically, during the height of the baby boom era when married women's employment was relatively low, mothers were blamed for doing too much of what they had been exhorted to do by overinvesting in their children, especially sons. The term *momism* was coined to draw attention to male children who might be emotionally incapacitated by their close relationship with their mothers. Such interpretations of the mothering role fit with functionalist analysis of the role strain built into women's roles. Women were to be educated but participate in roles outside the family solely through their child-rearing functions.

The outcome of mother blaming is to further victimize women by not addressing their actual situations of economic and social deprivation. Nowhere is this clearer than in the area of incest for which mothers have been seen as having major responsibility, while the male perpetrator is viewed sympathetically. Some authors suggest that there may be a therapeutic collusion in the tendency for incest victims to direct their anger at their mothers who are situated in their idealized images as all-powerful.

Feminist therapists have initiated workshops to counteract these tendencies toward mother blame at the level of practice. Another antidote is to consider the many ways in which parenting is an ongoing reciprocal process. Ambert (1992) has compiled the ways in which children's temperament and reactions to their involvement in social structures outside families influences parenting.

The consequence of lodging blame in either fathers or mothers is to fall into the "family values" discourse that shifts responsibility from government, business, and industry. Burnham (1996) has documented how, in the early twentieth century, manufacturers of household goods managed to avoid liability for childhood injuries or accidents by blaming mothers. Public solutions such as instituting public health measures and setting manufacturing standards do not solve all parenting problems but broaden the discourse beyond individual-level blame.

References

Ambert, A. (1992). *The effect of children on parents*. Binghamton, NY: Haworth Press.

Burnham, J. C. (1996). Why did the infants and toddlers die? Shifts in Americans' ideas of responsibility for accidents—from blaming mom to engineering. *Journal of Social History*, 29, 817–837.

Caplan, P., & Hall-McCorquodale, I. (1985). Mother-blaming in major clinical journals. *American Journal of Orthopsychiatry*, 55 (3), 345–352.

Margolin, L. (1992). Beyond maternal blame: Physical child abuse as a phenomenon of gender. *Journal of Family Issues*, 13 (3), 410–423.

Sommerfeld, D. P. (1989). The origins of mother-blaming: Historical perspectives on childhood and motherhood. *Infant Mental Health Journal*, 10 (1), 14–24.

See also: Employment, early maternal; Mothering; Social support; Stress.

ELAINE G. PORTER

Brazelton, T. Berry (1918–). Dr. T. Berry Brazelton is a pediatrician, researcher, and author who has made a tremendous impact on the rearing of children in the latter half of this century. He has often been compared to Dr. Benjamin Spock whose writing became influential with parents beginning in the 1940s. Unlike Dr. Spock, however, Berry Brazelton has focused not on the treatment of childhood illnesses but on helping parents understand and guide children through normal developmental crises.

Brazelton was born in 1918 in Waco, Texas. After graduating from Princeton in 1940, he earned a medical degree from Columbia University in 1943 (*Who's Who in America*, 1996). In addition to training in pediatrics, he undertook a residency in child psychiatry. This combination of training in how to recognize and treat mental as well as physical illness gave him a unique insight into children's behavior and development not shared by the typical pediatrician. The marriage of the fields of pediatrics and psychiatry is seen clearly in one of his most recent books, *The Earliest Relationship* (1990), written in collaboration with Bertrand Cramer, a noted infant psychiatrist.

Brazelton's most groundbreaking publication for parents, *Infants and Mothers* (1969), reflected the dual focus of pediatrics and psychiatry. In this book, he translated the concept of temperament (studied by child psychiatrists Chess and Thomas) into terms and examples that made sense to parents. Until this time, advice given to parents by pediatricians and other professionals was given without recognition of individual differences in children. Brazelton painted a vivid picture of three babies from his practice that fit the profile of either a quiet, active, or average baby. He described their development and how their parents coped month by month over the first year. In this pioneering book, Brazelton developed a very effective style and method of communicating to parents that he has used in many subsequent books. He carefully interweaves interesting case material with a professional commentary to convey to parents important medical and behavioral information. The ultimate message of this book for parents is that there is no one correct way to deal with issues such as night waking or crying. The solutions will vary depending on the temperament of the child and the personality of the parent. In helping parents support their child's developing autonomy, Brazelton promotes a problem-solving approach that weighs professional medical and developmental information with an intimate understanding of the child's and parent's own dispositions.

In addition to the combination of pediatrics and psychiatry, Brazelton's work is unique in combining both clinical and research perspectives. Since 1950, he has had his own private pediatric practice that has given him much clinical experience with children and their families. Unlike the advice given to parents by many clinicians, Brazelton's recommendations to parents are informed by research. For example, in his book *Doctor and Child* (1976) he describes descriptive and intervention studies he conducted that demonstrate the effectiveness of his approaches to crying and toilet training. Brazelton's books for parents contain many citations to research and other sources of interest in contrast to many of the parent advice books on the market.

To further his research, in 1972, Brazelton founded the Child Development Unit, a research and training unit for Harvard medical students at Children's Hospital Medical Center in Boston. Through this unit and as professor of pediatrics at Harvard, Brazelton has served as a catalyst for research that has had a great impact on the professional community of pediatricians, psychologists, psychiatrists, nurses, and educators who work with children and their families. In 1974, Brazelton, in collaboration with an interdisciplinary group of professionals at the unit, published the *Neonatal Behavioral Assessment Scale*. This scale was a departure from traditional newborn exams because it did not focus solely on reflexes but rather on behaviors that were controlled at higher levels of the central nervous system. The scale, often referred to as the *Brazelton Scale*, has been used in hundreds of research studies to document the effects of and recovery from events surrounding birth. It has also been shown to be an effective intervention tool with parents as a means of communicating about the baby's strengths and needs. It would be fair to say that until the Brazelton Scale many parents as well as professionals did not know that newborns could see, hear, and interact with their parents at birth.

Brazelton is also unique in a third sense in that he is an excellent communicator. Not only can he speak to and enthrall a live audience; he can make connections with mixed audiences that include parents, physicians, researchers, and students. He can do this while simultaneously interacting on the stage with a mother and her toddler who are relative strangers to him. His familiarity with development and ability to attune to individual children allow him to predict in an uncanny manner how the child will behave in this situation.

Brazelton communicates with his varied audiences through many different media. He is a contributing editor of *Family Circle* magazine and writes a nationally syndicated column on parenting for the *New York Times*. He has broadened his audience by hosting a daily cable TV show called *What Every Baby Knows* on the Lifetime channel. In addition to the many books he has written for parents, he has published many professional journal articles and edited books, often in collaboration with other researchers in related fields. Testimony to his acceptance by the research community is the fact that he served as president of the prestigious Society for Research in Child Development from 1987 to 1990. He is also held in high esteem by the clinical infant psychiatry community as evidenced by his presidency of the National Center for Clinical Infant Programs (Zero to Three) from 1988 to 1991.

References
Brazelton, T. B. (1969). *Infants and mothers*. New York: Delacorte Press.
Brazelton, T. B. (1974). *Neonatal Behavioral Assessment Scale*. London: Spastics International Medical Publications.
Brazelton, T. B. (1976). *Doctor and child*. New York: Delacorte Press.
Brazelton, T. B., & Cramer, B. (1990). *The earliest relationship*. New York: Addison-Wesley.
Who's who in America. (1996). Chicago: Marguis Who's Who, Inc.

See also: Education, parenting.

ANN D. MURRAY

Breastfeeding. Breastfeeding involves providing mother's milk to the infant from the breast. For purposes of research on infant health and development related to feeding method, the *Interagency Group for Action on Breastfeeding* has proposed a schema of breastfeeding definitions to address the "dose" of human milk received by the infant. *Full breastfeeding* is the exclusive or almost exclusive human milk feedings (vitamins, minerals; ritual feedings could be offered infrequently in addition to breastfeeds). *Partial breastfeeding* is subdivided into three levels of intake of human milk: high, medium, and low. *Token breastfeeding* includes minimal, occasional, or irregular breastfeeds.

Infant feeding is the primary caretaking activity in the first weeks of life. Breastfeeding offers both the infant and the mother frequent opportunities for close physical contact, in addition to providing the preferred food for the infant. Mothers report that breastfeeding helps them to develop a close, loving bond with their infant. Women who have bottle-fed and breastfed say that they feel a unique relationship with the child that was breastfed. Research looking at the role of breastfeeding in the development of the maternal-infant relationship neither supports nor refutes these feelings reported by women. However, the physiology of the breastfeeding woman suggests that breastfeeding creates a physiological milieu that would be expected to enhance her feelings of well-being— and therefore the positive feelings about her infant as well as about her breastfeeding experience. When she nurses her infant, electroencephalograph (EEG) patterns change to a relaxation pattern and she experiences a surge of the hormones cholecystokinin (associated with satiety and sedation) and prolactin as well as release of endorphins. Prolactin is associated with maternal behaviors in laboratory animals, and endorphins, which are opioids, are associated with feelings of euphoria.

In addition, there are significant health benefits to the mother. She has decreased risk for development of breast cancer during the premenopausal years, she has decreased risk for osteoporosis, and in the short term, she experiences more rapid recovery during the postpartum period. Further, the family and society at large incur a cost savings related to health care of both mother and infant in addition to the reduced cost of mother's milk feeding versus infant formula feeding.

Benefits to the infant include reduced risk of both acute and chronic illness and optimal neurodevelopmental outcomes. Even short-term, nonexclusive breastfeeding is associated with reduced risk of acute illness; however, the greater the dose, the greater the benefit incurred. In light of this, current recommendations are changing to extend the length of time that breastfeeding is recommended.

Acute illnesses with reduced rates associated with breastfeeding include otitis media, gastroenteritis, meningitis, respiratory diseases of both the upper and lower track, and necrotizing enterocolitis. Chronic illness with reduced risks associated with breastfeeding longer than three to six months include insulin-dependent diabetes mellitus, cancer of childhood (especially lymphoma), and chronic gastrointestinal diseases such as Chrohn's Disease. In particular, premature infants benefit from human milk feedings. Reduction in the incidence of necrotizing enterocolitis, sepsis, and bacteremia are noted. Cognitive outcome in the breastfed premature infant is also superior to the formula-fed infant. Various studies assessing neurodevelopmental status of both preterm and term infants see lower scores on standardized tests in the exclusively formula-fed groups. Additionally, visual development is delayed in the term and preterm formula-fed infant.

In the document *Healthy People 2000* (Soto, Behrens, & Rosemont, 1995), the surgeon general set the goal for breastfeeding initiation at 75% of all mothers delivering infants and the goals for continuing to breastfeed through the first 6 months at 50%. In order to reach these goals, all professionals who interact with childbearing families need to be aware of effective strategies for promotion and support of breastfeeding. The current initiation rate of breastfeeding in the United States is approximately 60%, while those who are still breastfeeding at 6 months is 22%. The acute decline in duration occurs at about 2 weeks postpartum. This indicates a continued need for professional education in the area of lactation and breastfeeding. This should facilitate improved hospital practices to prevent breastfeeding problems, as well as improved postpartum follow-up for the early identification and management of common problems. A national campaign for breastfeeding promotion was launched in 1997 by a coalition of more than 60 governmental and nongovernmental organizations.

In addition to a supportive and knowledgeable health care community, mothers need support from the father of the baby, grandmothers, other family members, and the community to increase her likelihood of breastfeeding success. Reaching these groups is an important element to breastfeeding promotion. Mother-to-mother support is also highly valued. Programs that include peer counseling or provide referrals to support groups have been shown to increase both the incidence and duration of breastfeeding.

Sources of information regarding breastfeeding include the La Leche League International's Center for Breastfeeding Information, Healthy Mothers, Healthy Babies Coalition, the Best Beginnings Program, the Lactation Research Center of Rochester New York, and the International Lactation Consultants' Association.

References

Page-Goertz, S., & McCamman, S. (1996). *Creating breastfeeding friendly environments* (CD-ROM). Overland Park, KS: Best Beginnings Production.

Riordan, J., & Auerbach, K. (1993). *Breastfeeding and human lactation*. Boston: Jones and Bartlett Publishers.

Soto, M. A., Behrens, R., & Rosemont, C. (1995). *Healthy People 2000: Midcourse review*. Washington, DC: National Academy Press.

Spangler, A. (1995). *Breastfeeding: A parent's guide*. Atlanta, GA: Amy Spangler.

See also: Attachment, secure; Eating behavior, children and.

SARAH P. MCCAMMAN

Bullying. Recent studies report levels of bullying in schools as being between 20% and 30% (Whitney & Smith, 1993). Research has shown that bullying can have a devastating effect on the lives of victims, who may suffer loss of confidence, self-esteem, and poor social skills. Also, for the bully, there is an increased likelihood of problems such as involvement in domestic violence, alcohol abuse, and violent crime occurring in later life (Farrington, 1993; Olweus, 1987).

Definition. Bullying is surprisingly hard to define as a phenomenon, depending on an individual's tolerance for aggression. Researchers tend to agree that bullying includes six key elements (Farrington, 1993):

- It is physical, verbal, or psychological attack or intimidation.
- The bully is more powerful, or is perceived to be more powerful than the victim.
- The bully intends to cause fear and/or harm to the victim.
- The act is unprovoked by the victim.
- The act is repeated.
- It produces the desired effect.

Problems can arise from the complexity of this definition—for example, researchers may use one definition while the general populace and media implicitly use or assume another.

How parents fit in. Bullying is a topic of concern and research throughout the world. However, most of the research conducted has been focused on the school environment and upon school-based interventions. Although most bullying does take place in school, there are many factors in a child's life that may affect why they bully or are bullied. School interventions do appear to reduce bullying (Hawkins, Von Cleve, & Catalano, 1991). Unfortunately, there appears to be a "hard core" of bullies who do not respond to programs that attempt to change their behavior.

Some studies have explored the relation between family background and high aggression. Olweus (1980) looked at the home conditions of aggressive children. He found a link between parental negativism and aggression. More recently, Bowers, Smith, and Binney (1994) have explored the family structure of children involved in bullying situations. They found that bullies showed low cohesion with family members generally. Victims of bullies were often raised in an enmeshed family structure. Tremblay et al. (1991) used a parent-training program that attempted to reduce aggression problems within the family before the child reached secondary school.

What parents think. Madsen (1996), in an extensive study of different groups' perceptions of bullying, indicated that parents are not always certain about what to do when dealing with issues of bullying. She concluded that parents need more information on the subject. Some parents regard bullying as a terrible thing, while others consider it only a minor hardship.

When asked what they think about bullying, parents generally express 'provictim' attitudes (Eslea & Smith, 1995). Most are sympathetic to the victim and support school action against the bully. Other parents are sympathetic toward the bully and try to understand their behavior. Consensus between the home and the school should be an important part of reducing bullying. Parents must be confident that school officials will be successful if asked to intervene. Parents will hesitate to report bullying if they fear that the bully will only be aggravated to increase the persecution. Failure to report, however, can create a climate where bullying flourishes.

New research in bullying is focusing upon the parent-child relationship and how this might effect the child's bullying behavior. In a recent review of this area, Smith and Myron-Wilson (in press) have noted how important parental history and attachment relationships can be in influencing a child's bullying behavior. They conclude that parents should become involved in solving school bullying. Parents should recognize that their current and past behavior may be significantly influencing their child's behavior. Future interventions need to take this factor into account.

What parents can do. Parents need to be aware of the fact that many children who are being bullied feel unable to tell anyone (Whitney & Smith, 1993). Parents should encourage children to talk about bullying and be confident and prepared to do something about the bullying (Mellor, 1993). Each child and each situation are different. To tell a child, for example, to "stand up for yourself" might be effective for one child while causing more depression and helplessness in another. Each response should be tailored to fit the specific situation and child.

References

Bowers, L., Smith, P. K., & Binney, V. (1994). Perceived family relationships of bullies, victims, and bully/victims in middle childhood. *Journal of Social and Personal Relationships, 11,* 215–232.

Eslea, M., & Smith, P. K. (1995). *Parental attitudes toward bullying: A new measure.* Paper presented at the BPS Developmental Section annual Conference.

Farrington, D. P. (1993). Understanding and preventing bullying. In M. Tonry & N. Morris (Eds.), *Crime and justice: An annual review of research* (Vol. 17). Chicago: University of Chicago Press.

Hawkins, J. D., Von Cleve, E., & Catalano, R. F. (1991). Reducing early childhood aggression: Results of a primary prevention programme. *Journal of the American Academy of Child & Adolescent Psychiatry, 30,* 208–217.

Madsen, K. C. (1996). *Differing perceptions of bullying.* Unpublished doctoral dissertation, University of Sheffield, Sheffield, England.

Mellor, A. (1993). *Bullying and how to fight it: A guide for families.* Glasgow, Scotland: Scottish Council for Research in Education.

Olweus, D. (1980). Familial and temperamental determinants of aggressive behaviour in adolescent boys: A causal analysis. *Developmental Psychology, 16,* 644–660.

Olweus, D. (1987). Bully/victim problems among school children in Scandanavia. In J. P. Myklebust & R. Ommendsen (Eds.), *Psykogprofesjonen mot ar 2000* (pp. 395-415). Oslo: Universitetsforlaget.

Smith, P. K., & Myron-Wilson, R. (in press). Parenting and school bullying. *Journal of Clinical Child Psychology and Psychiatry, 3* (3), 405-417.

Tremblay, R. E., McCord, J., Boileau, H., & Charlebois, P. (1991). Can disruptive boys be helped to become competent? *Psychiatry, 54* (2), 148-161.

Whitney, I., & Smith, P. K. (1993). A survey of the nature and extent of bullying in junior/middle and secondary schools. *Educational Research, 35* (1), 3-25.

See also: Aggression, childhood; Moral development; Prosocial behavior; Victim-centered discipline.

ROWAN R. MYRON-WILSON

C

Captain Kangaroo (Bob Keeshan) (1927–). Bob Keeshan is widely known for his portrayal of Captain Kangaroo—the star of a children's television program that made its debut on CBS in October 1955. The program continued on CBS for 30 years and is the longest-running children's program on network television. In recent years, *Captain Kangaroo* appeared on PBS for an additional six seasons.

It may seem that Bob Keeshan was born as The Captain, but he came to that role from earlier experiences as *Clarabell the Clown* in one of the first children's television programs, Howdy Doody. In real life, Keeshan was born in Lynbrook, Long Island, New York, on June 27, 1927. He grew up in Forest Hills, New York, and attended Fordham University.

Following his service in the U.S. Marine Corps during World War II, he worked on the Page staff at NBC, where he met Bob Smith who was about to air the *Howdy Doody* children's program in 1948. He played the role of Clarabell the Clown for five years and then left Howdy Doody to start his own local children's television program in New York City. It was there that he captured the attention of CBS—and *Captain Kangaroo* was born in 1955.

The *Captain Kangaroo* program is not only the longest-running program but also the most decorated; having won six Emmy Awards, three Gabriels, and two Peabody Awards, among others. Keeshan has received 19 honorary degrees, including degrees from Dartmouth and Fordham Universities. He has served the public and promoted education at all levels of the educational system, from school board member (West Islip, New York) to college trustee (College of New

Rochelle) to state regent of the Council of Governing Boards of Higher Education in New York State.

Beyond these positions, as a performer and educator, Keeshan has served children and families through his extensive advocacy of children's health and welfare on issues ranging from child care to child abuse and prevention of injury. These advocacy roles have included providing testimony to state and national legislative hearings, as well as serving on the boards of hospitals and the National Committee for the Prevention of Child Abuse. In 1987, he and the former governor of Tennessee, Lamar Alexander, founded Corporate Child Care, Inc. of Nashville. This workplace-based child care program provides services to employees of hospitals, banks, and industrial and service companies, ranging from Prudential Insurance to General Motors and Marriott. In 1990, Keeshan was appointed an Honorary Fellow of the American Academy of Pediatrics in recognition of his outstanding service to children and families.

Bob Keeshan has made a lasting contribution to several generations of children and parents. In 1989, he recorded his thoughts and observations on helping children grow and develop in his book *Growing Up Happy—Captain Kangaroo Tells Yesterday's Children How to Nurture Their Own.* Between 1963 and 1996, he authored eight books for parents and children, among them *Growing Up Happy* and *Books to Grow By.* In 1997, Keeshan turned his hand to writing a children's story, *Itty Bitty Kitty,* a story with a message about self-reliance, a tale with a tail.

The captain, the clown, the advocate, the author—all have a message to share about the importance of childhood and the development of young minds and spirits. Bob Keeshan has been there, done that, and will continue to support children and families.

References
Bendel, P. (1997, April). Bob Keeshan, Captain Kangaroo—celebrities' cats. *Cats Magazine,* pp. 44–46.
Captain Kangaroo/Bob Keeshan, biographical sketch (1997). Keeshan Associates, 40 West 57th Street, New York, NY 10019.
Keeshan, B. (1989). *Growing up happy—Captain Kangaroo tells yesterday's children how to nurture their own.* New York: Berkeley Books.
Keeshan, B. (1997). *Itty bitty kitty.* Minneapolis, MN: Fairview Press.

See also: Prosocial behavior; Television viewing; Television violence.

JOHN P. MURRAY

Child care. With the recent increase in women's employment outside the home, parents are using a variety of arrangements to care for their children. Although parental care is still a common care strategy, child care, regular care of children by individuals other than parents, has become increasingly common. Parents have several options when choosing child care: center care, child care homes, in-home care, and relative care. Center care provides care for larger groups of children in schoollike settings. Centers are generally better equipped, and center caregivers are more highly educated than facilities and caregivers in other types of care. In child care homes (family day care), small groups of mixed-age children are cared for in the provider's home. Parents often prefer this arrangement for young children because they believe it provides a homelike setting with one stable caregiver and relatively few other children. In-home care (nanny care or sitter care) is care provided by a nonrelative in the child's own home. Generally, in-home care is the most expensive form of care and is typically used by affluent professional families. Finally, relative care generally is provided at little or no cost by relatives (typically the child's grandmother or aunt). Relative care is the most common type of care for poor or working-class families.

Quality of care and children's development. Mediocre and poor-quality child care are common in the United States (Galinsky et al., 1994; Helburn et al., 1995; Howes, Phillips, & Whitebook, 1992). The low quality of child care available to parents is worrisome because poor child care quality negatively affects infant, toddler, and preschool children's development. Children in poor-quality infant and toddler care are less compliant and self-regulated, engage in less social pretend play, express less positive affect, are more hostile, and have more difficulty with peers than children in high-quality care (Howes, 1990). Children in high-quality preschool care have better vocabularies and math skills and display more positive affect than children in poor-quality care (Helburn et al., 1995). In addition, the quality of care in preschool positively predicts elementary school behavioral adjustment and academic achievement.

Parents' choice of quality care. Parents may have difficulty recognizing high-quality child care. In a recent study of 100 centers in four states, 90% of the parents rated their children's centers as good, while trained observers rated these same programs as poor or mediocre (Helburn et al., 1995). In addition, parents in families experiencing economic or emotional stress are more likely than affluent or well-functioning families to place their children in low-quality care (Galinsky et al., 1994; Howes, 1990). Consequently, children who are most at risk are placed in lowest-quality care. An important step to improve the quality of care available to children is to educate parents on the dangers of poor-quality care for their children's development and to help parents identify high-quality care (Helburn et al., 1995).

The most important determinants of child care quality are caregiver-child ratios and group sizes, caregiver stability, and caregiver training and attitudes.

Ratios and group sizes. Appropriate caregiver-child ratios and group sizes vary depending on the age of the child. Because infants' developmental needs require almost constant attention, the quality of infant care is highly related to caregiver-infant ratios. Adult-infant ratios of 1:1 increase the probability of sensitive, positive caregiving (NICHD Early Child Care Research Network, 1995). Adult-infant ratios and group sizes are significantly larger in child care centers than in child care homes, which in turn are significantly larger than ratios and group sizes in in-home and relative care. Consequently, sensitive, positive, and involved care for infants is most likely in in-home care and relative care, somewhat less likely in family day care, and least likely in child care centers (NICHD Early Child Care Research Network, 1995).

Because of toddlers' and preschoolers' increasing independence and interest in peers, recommended maximum caregiver-child ratios and group sizes are larger for toddlers and preschoolers. Recommended maximum ratios and group sizes for toddlers are 4 toddlers for each caregiver and a group size of 12. For preschoolers, the recommended maximum ratio is 8 children per caregiver and group sizes of 18 (Howes et al., 1992). Children in care with higher than recommended ratios and group sizes are less likely than children in settings with lower ratios and group sizes to experience positive, sensitive, and stimulating caregiving. Children in settings with small ratios and group sizes are more likely to be emotionally attached to their caregivers, socially competent, and cooperative (Howes et al., 1992) and to have better language and math skills (Helburn et al., 1995).

Stability. Caregiver stability also affects children's adjustment because children need to develop a relationship with one caregiver. Parents should avoid child care settings where a large number of caregivers are responsible for caring for the child or where there are frequent changes of caregivers.

Training and attitudes. Caregiver training and attitudes about child rearing also are important factors for quality care. Caregivers with training in child development and non-authoritarian child-rearing attitudes are more likely than caregivers with no training and authoritarian attitudes to provide sensitive, positive, stimulating care (Helburn et al., 1995; Howes et al., 1992; NICHD Early Child Care Research Network, 1995).

References

Galinsky, E., Howes, C., Kontos, S., & Shinn, M. (1994). *The study of children in family child care and relative care: Highlights of findings.* New York: Families and Work Institute.

Helburn, S., Howes, C., Bryant, D., & Kagan, S., et al. (1995). *Cost, quality, and child outcomes in child care centers: Public report.* Denver, CO: University of Colorado Press.

Howes, C. (1990). Can the age of entry into child care and the quality of child care predict adjustment in kindergarten? *Developmental Psychology, 26,* 292–303.

Howes, C., Phillips, D. A., & Whitebook, M. (1992). Thresholds of quality: Implications for the social development of children in center-based child care. *Child Development, 63,* 449–460.

NICHD Early Child Care Research Network. (1995, April). *The quality of infant child care in the NICHD Study of Early Child Care.* Paper presented at the meeting for the Society of Research in Child Development, Indianapolis, IN.

See also: After-school child care; Developmentally Appropriate Practices; Employment, early maternal; Kinship care.

ANNE DOPKINS STRIGHT

Chores. Chores are household work that parents perceive as necessary for household maintenance. Parents and children alike often view these tasks as unpleasant. Because chores are a form of work, they have an attached economic value, are regarded as useful by a surrounding group (the family), and help to achieve a goal (Goodnow, 1988). Yet chores are distinct from work because they are an integral part of family relationships. Goodnow (1988) suggests that the relational characteristic of chores helps people distinguish between "child" and "servant" and between "helping" and "being responsible" (pp. 6–7). The focus on interpersonal aspects of chores also explains the division of labor within the family and teaches children "about expected relationships with others as well as acquiring the skills called for by the task" (p. 7).

In most families, all family members perform chores but not to the same degree. In general, about 61% of the labor is done by mothers, 14% by fathers, 12% by children, and 2% by other adults in the family (Blair, 1992). The number of chores and the amount of time children spend doing chores are highly influenced by family circumstances. For example, when mothers are employed full-time, the proportion of time that children do chores increases, and youth in rural communities do more chores and participate in more serious household tasks than their urban counterparts (Blair, 1992).

Developmentally, the first chores assigned to young children involve self-care activities, such as making one's bed. By early adolescence, nearly 90% of children are involved in chores necessary for household maintenance (White & Brinkerhoff, 1981b). Middle adolescents do more difficult tasks unaccompanied by parents, and self-care activities become an expected part of everyday life. These changing expectations of chores and how they should be performed suggest that parents expect an increase in self-reliance during adolescence.

The assignment of chores is highly sex-typed. Daughters are most likely to perform traditional female activities, such as meal preparation, washing dishes, cleaning, and ironing.

Sons are most likely to take out the trash, do outdoor maintenance, and help with home repairs. Daughters, more often than sons, spend time doing more chores and do chores dedicated to *family care*, such as taking care of younger siblings (Blair, 1992; Eberly & Montemayor, in press; White & Brinkerhoff, 1981b). Sex-stereotypic task differentiation becomes more pronounced in middle adolescence, during which time daughters are most likely to do in "inside" chores, whereas sons are most likely to do "outside" chores (White & Brinkerhoff, 1981b). Chores dedicated to personal care, such as making one's bed or cleaning up one's room, do not show gender differences. The assignment of chores based on traditional gender roles is most common among blue-collar and working-class families, in single-earner families where the father is the breadwinner, and among families in which parents do not have college degrees (McHale et al., 1990).

The reasons for children's participation in household work often reflect the ideologies and values of parenting. Historically, parents viewed children's chores as a necessary economic contribution to families' welfare. Contemporary views of children as "priceless" and the lack of financial value of adolescent work transformed the meaning of chores from one of economic contribution to a mechanism for socializing responsibility, self-worth, and autonomy (Blair, 1992; Goodnow, 1988). One exception in contemporary society is the substantial contribution of rural youth to the household economy of farm families. In research by White and Brinkerhoff (1981a), parents' reasons for assigning chores were categorized as *developmental* (builds character, develops responsibility), *reciprocal* (obligations, duty to family), *extrinsic* (parents need help), *task learning* (need for learning how), and *residual* (a way to earn money, keep child busy). Parents most often cited developmental (72.4%) as a reason for assigning chores.

For children, the meaning of doing chores is based on the needs of parents. When children were asked why they do chores, about 60% say "to help," 15% emphasized compliance or necessity, and 15% say "to earn money" (Goodnow, 1988).

Chores are embedded in family relationships (Goodnow, 1988). Arguments between parents and adolescents are often about chores (Montemayor, 1983). Yet teens who were found to be helpful toward parents perceived their mothers and fathers as accepting, spent more time with parents, participated in more activities, and reported greater parental influence (Eberly & Montemayor, in press). Parents use a variety of techniques to get their children to do chores, most commonly material rewards (especially money), physical punishment, appeals to moral values, and social reinforcement (Goodnow, 1988). The technique parents use depends on the chore, such as a smile for getting the mail or payment for taking out the trash.

Performing chores is an integral part of being a family. Factors such as gender and age affect the type and number of chores required, as does urban versus rural living, maternal employment, and family composition. Most important, chores are embedded in parent-adolescent relationships. What teens do and how often they perform their chores both reflect and influence the parent-teen relationship.

References

Blair, S. L. (1992). Children's participation in household labor: Child socialization versus the need for household labor. *Journal of Youth and Adolescence, 21*, 241–258.

Eberly, M. B., & Montemayor, R. (In press). Doing good deeds: An examination of adolescents' prosocial behavior in the context of parent-adolescent relationships. *Journal of Adolescent Research.*

Goodnow, J. J. (1988). Children's household work: Its nature and functions. *Psychological Bulletin, 103*, 5–26.

McHale, S. M., Bartko, W. T., Crouter, A. C., & Perry-Jenkins, M. (1990). Children's housework and psychosocial functioning: The mediating effects of parents' sex-role behaviors and attitudes. *Child Development, 61*, 1413–1426.

Montemayor, R. (1983). Parents and adolescents in conflict: All families some of the time and some families all of the time. *Journal of Early Adolescence, 3*, 83–103.

White, L. K., & Brinkerhoff, D. B. (1981a). Children's work in the family: Its significance and meaning. *Journal of Marriage and the Family, 43*, 789–798.

White, L. K., & Brinkerhoff, D. B. (1981b). The sexual division of labor: Evidence from childhood. *Social Forces, 60*, 170–181.

See also: Rules, implicit.

MARY B. EBERLY AND RAYMOND MONTEMAYOR

Cleft lip and palate. Cleft lip and palate (CLP) is a collective term for a subcategory of congenital craniofacial anomalies (CFA) in which oral clefts may occur in various forms and dimensions. The cleft may involve only the lip or the lip and jaw; only the hard and/or soft part of the palate; or both lip, jaw, and palate. In addition, there may be one or more associated congenital malformations. Consequently, research into the psychological effects of oral clefts is characterized by the use of heterogeneous groups, including various subtypes of clefts, comorbid medical conditions, and other craniofacial anomalies. This makes it difficult to determine the exact influence of specific forms of oral clefts.

Many different problems may be associated with CLP. The cleft lip may generate negative feelings about the child's appearance, while the cleft palate puts children and parents at risk with regard to initial feeding difficulties, chronic middle ear problems, and a deviant development of speech. From a medical point of view, an isolated cleft lip constitutes the smallest and most easily remedied problem. Subtypes involving the palate generally require far more extensive and enduring medical care from a large team of specialists.

Although research findings are not fully consistent, at school age the various problems seem to culminate in a slightly increased risk for behavior problems and less desirable self-perceptions in these children. Comorbid medical conditions (i.e., associated malformations) appear to further endanger psychosocial adjustment.

Speltz et al. (1994) identify five domains of variables relevant to the psychosocial development of children with CLP. These include child characteristics, medical factors, quality of the parent-child relationship, parenting skills, and family environment. Family environment includes issues related to parental stress, parental emotional well-being, and social support.

Quality of the parent-child relationship. The first year of life is characterized by many stressors impinging upon the parent-child relationship, such as the parent's emotional reaction to the cleft, worries about early care, and hospitalization experiences. Accordingly, it is not surprising that researchers consistently report lower levels of responsiveness and sensitivity for mothers toward babies with oral clefts. However, up to the present there is no indication that the quality of the attachment relationship of these children is at risk. In accordance with findings for other deviant groups, research shows a normal distribution of secure attachments for children with clefts (Speltz et al., 1997), despite a lack of responsiveness in the mothers (Wasserman et al., 1987). The quality of the relationship seems not even to be seriously disturbed by the repeated events of early hospitalization for surgery on lip and palate (Koomen & Hoeksma, 1993).

Parenting skills. A relatively unresponsive maternal style seems to be characteristic for children with clefts only during the first period after birth. CLP children in the preschool period appear to experience similar parental styles during play interactions to children without clefts. Still, it is in the preschool years that parental responsiveness proves to be of particular importance to CLP children. In a study by Speltz et al. (1993) a less controlling and more child-directed orientation of mothers in a play task proved to be predictive of lower behavior problem and higher self-concept scores of CFA children four years later. A child-directed approach should, however, not be confused with laissez-faire. According to clinicians, some parents of CLP children tend to indulge their child with attention and a large degree of tolerance for behavior in order to compensate for all the unpleasant experiences. Guidance of parents in the preschool period should thus emphasize child-directed interaction skills as well as limit setting and parent-child negotiating.

Parental stress. From clinical sources it is known that the birth of a child with cleft lip and palate may create considerable tension for and between parents. Mothers of infants with CFA have been found to report greater negative recollections of the initial period following birth, higher levels of emotional distress, and greater marital conflict than control group mothers. Moreover, the stress experienced within the relationship with the child appears to be negatively related to the child's social skills and behavioral adjustment.

Parental emotional well-being. In terms of a more general level of emotional functioning, mothers of CFA children do not seem to deviate from the normal population. The co-occurrence of maternal maladjustment with CFA, however, may place a child at greater risk for the development of emotional and behavioral problems.

Social support. Mothers of children with CFA seem to have comparatively small social networks, with a focus on relatives instead of friends. Still, various researchers note that mothers appear to be content with the extent and composition of their social network. Contrary to findings in other risk groups, maternal social support in this particular group does not seem to affect parent and child adjustment. Parental satisfaction with the support from medical professionals might have a more significant impact. The impression from clinical interviews is that families benefit from prompt referral to a well-organized medical team.

Of course the various factors considered here may reinforce each other and interact with child characteristics in ways that further increase the risks of child and parent adjustment problems. Despite numerous risk factors, children with oral clefts and their parents primarily resemble a normal population in terms of psychological functioning. These children and their parents have demonstrated their ability to adapt.

References

Koomen, H. M. Y., & Hoeksma, J. B. (1993). Early hospitalization and disturbances of infant behavior and the mother-infant relationship. *Journal of Child Psychology and Psychiatry, 34,* 917–934.

Speltz, M. L., Greenberg, M. T., Endriga, M. C., & Galbreath, H. (1994). Developmental approach to the psychology of craniofacial anomalies. *Cleft Palate–Craniofacial Journal, 31,* 61–67.

Speltz, M. L., Endriga, M. C., Fischer, P. A., & Mason, C. A. (1997). Early predictors of attachment in infants with cleft lip and/or palate. *Child Development, 68,* 12-25.

Speltz, M. L., Morton, K., Goodell, E. W., & Clarren, S. K. (1993). Psychological functioning of children with craniofacial anomalies and their mothers: Follow-up from late infancy to school entry. *Cleft Palate–Craniofacial Journal, 30,* 482–489.

Wasserman, G. A., Lennon, M. C., Allen, R., & Shilansky, M. (1987). Contributors to attachment in normal and physical handicapped infants. *Journal of the American Academy of Child and Adolescent Psychiatry, 26,* 9–15.

See also: Disability, physical; Language development.

HELMA M. Y. KOOMEN

Colic. Having a child who cries inconsolably is of significant concern to parents. Referred to as *colic*, this condition continues to be an enigma to pediatricians and researchers. There are many hypotheses about the cause of colic, ranging from an allergy to cow's milk to an immature gastrointestinal system. Difficulties with defining the behavioral symptoms of colic are likely to have contributed to the lack of consensus about the origins of this condition. Colic was originally described by Wessel et al. (1954) as occurring in a healthy infant who has "paroxysms of irritability, fussing, or crying lasting for a total of more than three hours a day and occurring on more than three days in any one week." This definition has been more recently extended to include a distinctive pain cry, physical signs of muscle tension, and inconsolability (Lester, 1990). Colic is also known to emerge within the infant's first month of life but to end, sometimes quite abruptly, around the third or fourth month.

Interestingly, one proposed cause of colic has been insensitive parenting. It is believed that parents whose infants develop colic respond inappropriately to the crying of their infants, thereby increasing rather than decreasing their infants' distress. This highly controversial hypothesis is supported by evidence that shows when parents are given instructions on when and how to respond to their infants' cries, crying decreases (Taubman, 1984). While this evidence would indicate that parenting style is related to colic, this study has its limitations. For example, parents who participated in this intervention came to the pediatrician complaining of problematic crying. These parents may have possessed characteristics that led them to differentially interpret the crying of their children as excessive. Because some parents have a low tolerance for infant crying, they may be more likely to refer their infants for colic and overestimate the length of time of their bouts of fussing and crying. Rautava, Helenius, and Lehtonen (1993) examined the prebirth characteristics of families and colic and found that mothers who experienced the most stress were more likely to report their infants as having colic. More recent evidence, however, suggests that parents who refer infants who do not have colic for problematic crying are responding to some qualitative difference in their infants' cry.

The dynamic between the parent and an inconsolable baby may have short- and possibly long-term effects on the parent-child relationship. Some have suggested that infants with colic are at highest risk for child abuse. The few studies that have examined the consequences of having a colicky child indicate that there are no negative outcomes for the parents of colicky infants. Stifter and Braungart (1992) found mothers of colic and noncolic infants to be alike in observed maternal sensitivity at both 5 and 10 months. In another study (St. James Roberts, Conroy, & Wilsher, in press), mothers of colic infants were found to be less sensitive than mothers of noncolic infants at 6 weeks of age, but no differences emerged on maternal interactive behavior at 5 months of age. These studies suggest that maternal behavior may be stressed when colic is at its peak but returns to normal levels when the colic is resolved. They may also explain why no long-term effects of infant colic on the parent-child relationship have been found. Infants who developed colic were no more likely to be insecurely attached than infants who did not have colic (Stifter & Bono, in press). On the contrary, the number of securely attached colic infants was well above the norm found in other studies of noncolic infants.

While there appears to be no negative effect for infant colic on maternal behavior, there is some evidence that mothers are affected personally by their interactions with an inconsolable child (Stifter & Bono, in press). Mothers of infants who had colic rated themselves as less competent than mothers of infants who did not have colic. This finding is not surprising when one considers the intensity and duration of the crying exhibited by colicky infants. The ability to respond with success to an infant's needs is the basis of maternal self-efficacy. When attempts to soothe an infant are met with failure, feelings of incompetence are likely to develop. Mothers also rated themselves as more anxious when separated from their child. This finding may be related to the mother's perception that her child is more vulnerable and in need of her protection. Mothers of colic infants, however, did not appear to allow their personal feelings to influence their interactions with their infants. These feelings were likely resolved once mothers had more experience with a happier, more quiescent infant.

Taken together, research on infant colic suggests that although this is a stressful condition for both child and parent, colic produces no adverse short- or long-term effects on parent behavior or on the parent-child relationship. However, since it is estimated that 15% to 20% of parents consult their pediatrician about problematic crying, it is important that pediatricians and practitioners be attentive to parents who complain about their infants' crying and suggest that parents take occasional breaks from their caretaking responsibilities.

References

Lester, B. M. (1990). Colic for developmentalists. *Infant Mental Health, 11,* 321–333.

Rautava, P., Helenius, H., & Lehtonen, L. (1993). Psychosocial predisposing factors for infantile colic. *British Medical Journal, 307,* 600–604.

Stifter, C. A., & Braungart, J. (1992). Infant colic: A transient condition with no apparent effects. *Journal of Applied Developmental Psychology, 13,* 447–462.

Stifter, C. A., & Bono, M. (in press). The effect of infant colic on maternal self-perceptions and mother-infant attachment. *Child Care, Health and Development.*

St. James Roberts, I., Conroy, S., & Wilsher, K. (in press). Clinical, developmental, and social aspects of infant crying and colic. *Early Development and Parenting.*

Taubman, B. (1984). Clinical trial of the treatment of colic by modification of parent-infant interaction. *Pediatrics, 74,* 998–1003.

Wessel, M., Cobb, J., Jackson, E., Harris, G., & Detwiler, A. (1954). Paroxysmalfussing in infancy, sometimes called "colic." *Pediatrics, 14,* 421–434.

See also: Crying; Self-care; Separation anxiety; Stress.

CYNTHIA STIFTER AND TRACY SPINRAD

Communication. Communication is a symbolic process that involves creating and sharing meanings. Words, or verbal behavior, are the symbols most commonly used to communicate. But the whole spectrum of nonverbal behaviors such as facial expression, eye action, vocal behavior, spatial distance, gestures, touch, movement and posture, appearance, and the use of time and the environmental setting can be used symbolically to convey messages (Burgoon, Hunsaker, & Dawson, 1994; Galvin & Brommel, 1991).

Learning the complex process of communication starts early in the life of an individual, usually within the family context. Infants cry when they need attention and quickly learn that this behavior gives them power to create a shared impact between themselves and those around them. They also learn to discriminate between human speech sounds and other forms of noise in their environment. Young children recognize when certain verbalizations are repeatedly reinforced—thus, the use of language is gradually added to their communication repertoire of sounds and gestures.

Communication is a transactional process. Not just babies but people of all ages have a reciprocal impact on each other when they communicate. The content of the messages, as well as the accompanying nonverbal behaviors, reflects how each person perceives himself or herself in relation to the predicted reactions of the other persons involved. Every communication act is reflective of the relationship between the two who are communicating (Galvin & Brommel, 1991). The nature of a parent and child relationship is embedded in their communication patterns that develop over time. But patterns between two individuals of a family do not happen in isolation from other family members nor from the larger world outside the family. A family needs to be viewed as a system to understand the complexities of its communication behavior.

A family system, just like other social systems, regulates itself by establishing rules and setting goals yet has the characteristics of being ongoing and open to influence from the environment (Broderick, 1993). In any system, the behavior or circumstance of any one member of that system impacts the others. It is no different with the family system and its communication practices.

A parent and child, as do all family members, work out and share symbolic meanings through both verbal and nonverbal communication. Patterns become established. Galvin and Brommel (1991) refer to these patterns as *specific communication codes*. Codes arise out of the family acting as a system and interacting with each other to create shared meanings. For example, a divorced parent may have created a communication code, giving the message both verbally and nonverbally, that the children are not to talk about their absent parent. A boundary has been established. If a family member violates or attempts to change such a code, it not only impacts the parent and the sender of the message, but other family members generally experience consequences as well.

David Olson (1993) defines family communication as the facilitating factor for creating healthy or unhealthy family functioning. Families need to strike a balance between separateness and togetherness in the emotional bonding of family members (family cohesion), depending on the ages and circumstances of family members. They also need to strike a balance between stability and change in leadership and role relationships (family flexibility), again depending on the ages and circumstances of family members.

To make the necessary changes along these two dimensions as children grow and develop, families need to be able to effectively communicate with each other. As a child is moving into adolescence, parents may find that the family cohesion or close emotional bonding to which they had been accustomed is not working. Effective speaking and listening skills, as well as the ability of family members to share personal feelings, give clear messages, stay on the topic, and have high respect and regard for each other, are essential for responding to these family changes (Olson, 1993).

Parents establish internal family communication patterns, but they also teach the general cultural language for interacting and surviving in the outside world. Characteristics such as age, gender, ethnicity, and socioeconomic status are known to influence family communication, both within the family and with systems outside the home (Burgoon, Hunsaker, & Dawson, 1994). For instance, a parent may teach a child to not directly look at an adult when the two are communicating. This is a sign of respect. A parent from a different ethnic heritage may teach a child just the opposite.

Gender differences in communication style also are becoming more widely known. Researchers such as Deborah Tannen (1990, 1996) suggest that men and women grow up in different worlds linguistically. Girls are taught communication codes to reinforce intimacy, and boys are taught communication codes to reinforce independence. The complexity of interpersonal relations reflects these types of demographic differences even within the family context.

The process of learning to communicate continues throughout life. Effective parent-child communication does not remain the same year after year. It keeps changing. As circumstances shift in their lives and the world around them, a parent has to keep relearning effective ways to communicate with a child, and the child continually redefines the means of communication with the parent. Communication, an ongoing process of exchange and interaction, is dynamic and never static (Burgoon, Hunsaker, & Dawson, 1994).

References
Broderick, C. B. (1993). *Understanding family processes: Basics of family systems theory.* Newbury Park, CA: Sage Publications.
Burgoon, M., Hunsaker, F. G., & Dawson, E. J. (1994). *Human communication* (3rd ed.). Thousand Oaks, CA: Sage Publications.
Galvin, K. M., & Brommel, B. J. (1991). *Family communication.* New York: Harper-Collins Publishers.
Olson, D. (1993). Circumplex model of marital and family systems: Assessing family functioning. In F. Walsh (Ed.), *Normal family processes* (2nd ed.). New York: Guilford Press.
Tannen, D. (1990). *You just don't understand: Women and men in conversation.* New York: Ballantine Books.
Tannen, D. (1996). *Gender and discourse.* New York: Oxford University Press.

See also: Cultural context; Family systems; Listening; Synchrony.

CHARLOTTE SHOUP OLSEN

Community. A community consists of separate individuals who are connected by some common thread of interest, proximity, or characteristic. Distinctively, communities vary in a range of individual factors—age, ethnicity, family size—and by the services available, economic conditions, job opportunities, and health and child care options. Within communities, there is commonality—what

Bronfenbrenner, Moen, and Garbarino (1984) term as "interlocking or integrated functional subsystems" (p. 286). Bronfenbrenner and his colleagues offer several definitions of community that focus on three key necessary elements: (1) residence within a delimited area, (2) a set of interlocking economic and social systems serving resident needs, and (3) some feeling of common identity and fate.

Bronfenbrenner (1979) describes four community systems that when visually depicted are concentric circles. The innermost circle is referred to as the *microsystem*. This system represents the most direct day-to-day reality for individuals such as the home. At the second level, *mesosystems* are relationships formed between systems such as the interaction between the home and the school or home and workplace. These systems indirectly affect each other. For example, parents' work can affect their children, and community policies can affect business or the economy. The next highest level is called the *exosystem* representing major institutions in society such as transportation and mass media. Decisions at this level (e.g., television programming) can affect family interactions more indirectly. The outlying *ecosystem* represents broad social systems such as immigration, democracy, or culture.

If there is a clear understanding of the linkages between systems in a community, it becomes apparent that issues of concern to individuals and families cannot be viewed in isolation. Rather, the concerns of individuals are woven into all individual life stages, all types of families, and all of the economic, social, and political ideologies associated with each structure in American society.

Parents, as first teachers, are the front line of influence for children. As children develop and form their opinions of others, family influences are most immediate. Decisions made or events that occur in one setting affect relationships that occur and decisions that are made in other settings. For example, a factory closing affects the local economy in addition to the employees, community service organizations, other employers, and numerous families and individuals. Another example of cross-system community linkages is when a natural disaster (e.g., flood or blizzard) occurs. The effect is felt by multiple families in addition to schools, child care settings, workplaces, and community services. The interdependence of groups creates movement and dynamics within and around communities.

The parent is part of a larger community. Parenting occurs in a community context within various *community support systems* (Bronfenbrenner, 1979; Stevens, Hough, & Nurss, 1993). Parenting involves learning about social networks and community ties that serve as buffers against stressful life transitions (Powell, 1988). As part of a larger community, parents may feel support in one or many areas, or they may feel a total lack of support. Strong communities report networks that connect parents to one another, to services, and to multiple supportive forms of dialogue and discussion.

Supportive family programs can creatively be designed in communities to assure smooth transitions (Bronfenbrenner, 1979). Transitions between community settings (e.g., between jobs, into new school or child care, change of work hours) affect individual well-being and play a major role in affecting direction and rate of development. Disruptive transitions can create or add to parent and child stress and vulnerability (Bronfenbrenner, 1979; Meyers, 1993). Examples include supportive orientation programs designed for parents to ensure effective transitions for families moving from school to school and child care programs designed specifically for parents with rotational work shifts. Such services promote consistency in child care during family transitions while imparting parenting information.

Educational institutions, social agencies, and decision makers who recognize the many layers and players who comprise the community are able to design supportive services and systems to meet family needs. Garbarino (1982) calls for communities to assume comprehensive responsibility for families in order to preserve and protect children while supporting and encouraging parents.

The effect of multifaceted community support on parent-child interactions is critical. With the shift from a service-based economy to an information-based economy, educators and researchers must scrutinize the effectiveness of the methods by which parent education and support programs are delivered in communities to provide optimal nurturing environments for children.

References

Bronfenbrenner, U. (1979). *The ecology of human development: Experiments by nature and design*. Cambridge, MA: Harvard University Press.

Bronfenbrenner, U., Moen, P., & Garbarino, J. (1984). Children, family, and community. In R. Parke (Ed.), *The family: Review of child development research* (Vol. 7, pp. 283–328). New York: Sage Publications.

Garbarino, J. (1982). *Children and families in the social environment*. New York: Aldine Publishing Company.

Meyers, S. A. (1993). Adapting parent education programs to meet the needs of fathers: An ecological perspective. *Family Relations, 42*, 447–452.

Powell, D. R. (Ed.). (1988). *Parent education as early childhood intervention: Emerging directions in theory, research, and practice*. Norwood, NJ: Ablex Publishing.

Stevens, J., Hough, R., & Nurss, J. (1993). The influence of parents in children's development and education. In B. Spodek (Ed.), *Handbook of research on education of young children* (pp. 337–351). New York: Macmillan.

See also: Cultural context; Social context; Social support.

KAREN B. DEBORD

Competition. Competition and cooperation are different strategies for using power to achieve a goal. Both are based on an individual's perspective on the scarcity of what can be achieved and the norms one has about the deservingness of others trying to achieve the goal.

Game theory is often used to establish the motive for competition. In a *zero-sum* game, the benefits achieved by one have to be lost by another (1 minus 1 = 0) (Kohn, 1992). The benefit is perceived as scarce. In a *non-zero-sum* game, the participants believe that there can essentially be more than one winner. Benefits can expand, not contract. Cooperation is focused on increasing the resource pool. Cooperation emphasizes reframing the situation to maximize rewards for all participants, while competition focuses on a more narrow, self-serving view of achievement. With cooperation, participants view each other as partners contributing to maximizing resources for all. With competition, participants view each other as obstacles to individual success. In cooperation the focus is more on the *activity* to achieve a common goal, while in competition the focus is more on *dominance and success* (Pepitone, 1980). Cooperation emphasizes performance while competition emphasizes outcome.

In addition to the perception of goal scarcity, *norms of equity* and *deservingness* can make an impact on how individuals strive to reach a goal. These norms emphasize resource sharing instead of resource hoarding. A person capable of sociocentric thinking and empathy is more likely to cooperate than one who is self-centered (Pepitone, 1980). Social comparison plays an important part in the choice of the strategy.

Both cooperation and competition are linked to cultural views of the relationship between power and achievement. The most significant differences in competition occur not between children of different nations but between children in rural versus urban communities. Urban children have been found to be more competitive than rural children in a variety of studies (McGraw, 1987). The critical factor here is the extent to which the child's cooperation in family activities is vital to the well-being of the family. Rural parents are more likely to involve children in this type of shared activity than urban parents.

The problems associated with competition and the advantages of cooperation have been documented in the research literature (Kohn, 1992). Cooperation promotes higher and more long-term achievement, strengthens self-esteem, and contributes to social relationships. Some research shows that children may become so preoccupied with their competitor's loss that they fail to gain the amount of resources that would have been possible with a more cooperative style.

Although research on how parents contribute to competition and cooperation is woefully inadequate, four tentative conclusions from the research literature can be made:

- Parents contribute to a competitive-selfish style when they create unnecessary scarcity in their relationships with children, especially for resources like parental time and affection.
- Parents contribute to a child's capacity for cooperation by involving them in cooperative activity at an early age in order to establish norms of reciprocity and using power collaboratively.
- Parents contribute to a child's personal accomplishment by emphasizing *intrinsic* (feeling proud, enthusiasm for the effort, recognition of learning) rather than *extrinsic* (money, toys, attention) rewards.
- Parents contribute to competition by consistently comparing their child's abilities to those of others; the pursuit of success is then perceived as a contest between winners and losers.

References

Kohn, A. (1992). *No contest: The case against competition.* Boston: Houghton Mifflin.

McGraw, K. O. (1987). *Developmental psychology.* New York: Harcourt Brace Jovanovich.

Pepitone, E. A. (1980). *Children in cooperation and competition: Toward a developmental social psychology.* Lexington, MA: Lexington Books.

See also: Prosocial behavior; Sports.

CHARLES A. SMITH

Compliance. A person's response to a directive can be categorized as compliant or noncompliant. Children are compliant when they carry out a request or directive within an appropriate amount of time. Noncompliance can be broken down into: *passive noncompliance* (child does not follow request but does not overtly defy the request or show negative affect), *simple refusal* (verbally refuses request without negative affect), *negotiation* (child bargains for a different directive or offers excuses for why the directive should not be complied with), and *direct defiance* (overtly refuses to comply with the request and demonstrates angry, defiant, or negative affect) (Kuczynski et al., 1987). Children will display all of these responses at various times but tend toward noncompliance at certain stages in development such as in the "terrible twos" and in adolescence.

Between the second and third years of life compliance becomes a major issue in the raising of children. At this time children develop the cognitive ability to understand that they are separate from caregivers and have more control of themselves. The ability to use evaluative words and recognize violated rules emerges between 19 and 30 months. Until they have some competency in these prerequisites for self-evaluative emotion (e.g., shame, guilt, pride), children may not be able to repress restricted behaviors in the absence of authority figures (Stipeck, Gralinski, & Kopp, 1990). The beginnings of moral understanding and conscience are seen when children begin restricting behavior in the presence of others, hiding evidence of transgressions, being upset by disapproval, calling attention to transgressions, and/or smiling, joking, or being curious about transgressing rules and norms (Stipeck, Gralinski, & Kopp, 1990). Parents may become upset and interpret some of these behaviors as "deliberately" breaking the rules. However, children at this stage are testing limits and trying to make sense of their surroundings rather than trying to defy authority figures.

During this period of development, children are also working on aspects of autonomy and self-control. Often children test out their newfound autonomy by increasing resistance to parental limit setting and control (Kuczynski et al., 1987). This stage is characterized by the use of "no" in response to parental demands or restrictions. In order to test autonomy the child may reject adult interference. Therefore, compliance is not a good measure of parental effectiveness because noncompliance may reflect the child's development of autonomy, and how he or she expresses noncompliance may reflect social competence. Noncompliance should be conceptualized less as a direct challenge to the parents and more as a self-assertion (Crockenberg & Litman, 1990).

The strategies authority figures use to gain compliance will influence the likelihood of compliance and the types of noncompliance children display. Strategies can be separated into three types: negative control, control, and guidance (Crockenberg & Litman, 1990). *Negative control* is the use of intrusive physical or verbal transactions that convey a negative feeling toward the children (e.g., anger, annoyance, criticism, punishing, spanking, slapping, and threatening). *Control* includes issuing a directive or restriction, offering no choice, and/or offering a reward contingent upon compliance. *Guidance* is a nonintrusive verbal or physical instruction relating to the child's behavior (e.g., suggesting, persuading, verbally assisting, and sitting next to the child). Each type of compliance strategy may have different effects on the child in the long run.

Crockenberg and Litman (1990) studied the effectiveness of maternal use of control strategies. They found that, in general, control combined with guidance elicited a higher frequency of compliance from children, and negative control elicited a higher frequency of defiance from children. The authors of this study suggest that control tempered by guidance gives the child clear information about what is wanted while not threatening the child's autonomy. Conveying respect for the child's autonomy may increase the child's willingness to comply with requests. The child's willingness to cooperate with a caregiver should be enhanced by a parent's willingness to cooperate with the child.

Control can also be viewed in terms of indirect and direct management strategies. *Indirect management* reflects strategies such as suggestions, requests, explanations, distraction, and bargaining. On the other hand, *direct management* strategies consist of commands, reprimands, enforcement (forceful physical guidance, ranging from gentle to rough with child resistance), and stating directly what the child is supposed to do. Indirect strategies correlate with children's employing negotiation strategies, whereas direct strategies correlate with direct defiance. This is consistent with the hypothesis that children's strategies reflect parental models of management (Crockenberg & Litman, 1990; Kuczynski, et al., 1987).

A parent is apt to have a child demonstrating greater compliance and less defiance if he or she introduces indirect management strategies, control, and guidance. Authority figures need to be clear and consistent in what is expected from the child, avoid taking noncompliance as a personal attack, and respect the child's autonomy within the guidelines of the limits that have been set. Utilizing these approaches will not produce a child that always complies with requests but in the long run teaches children how to internalize rules, builds competence, and establishes a relationship wherein negotiation and flexibility are more likely.

References

Crockenberg, S., & Litman, C. (1990). Autonomy as competence in 2-year-olds: Maternal correlates of child defiance, compliance, and self-assertion. *Developmental Psychology, 26,* 961–971.

Kuczynski, L., Kochanska, G., Radke-Yarrow, M., & Girnius-Brown, O. (1987). A developmental interpretation of young children's noncompliance. *Developmental Psychology, 23,* 799–806.

Stipeck, D., Gralinski, J., & Kopp, C. (1990). Self-concept development in the toddler years. *Developmental Psychology, 26,* 972–977.

See also: Authority, parental; Discipline; Limit setting; Misbehavior.

SHANNON DERMER

Conflict, interparental. *Interparental conflict* is a term used to refer to the exposure of children to quarrels between their parents, ranging along a wide continuum from everyday disagreements to physical violence.

Because some disagreements occur in all couple relationships, exposure to interparental conflict is a prevalent source of stress in the lives of children. A large body of research indicates that marital discord has negative effects on the quality of parenting. Such discord is associated with the development of behavioral and emotional problems in children, such as conduct disorders, depression, anxiety, poor peer relationships, low self-esteem, and poor physical health (Reid & Crisafulli, 1990). Although parenting a difficult child may put stress on a marital relationship, the evidence suggests that more often conflictual marital relationships create difficult children. For example, longitudinal studies have shown that measures of the marital relationship taken during pregnancy predict the later development of behavioral and emotional problems in school-aged children (Cowan et al., 1991).

Further work has been devoted to better understanding how it is that exposure to interparental conflict affects child development. Researchers have delineated several dimensions of interparental conflict that might differentially affect children (Grych & Fincham, 1990; Kerig, 1996):

Exposure. Overt interparental conflicts, which children observe or overhear, are associated with more negative effects on child behavior.

Frequency. Children are more likely to be exposed to interparental conflict, and therefore to be affected by it, when parents quarrel more frequently. Consistent with this, studies have confirmed that children whose parents fight more frequently have more symptoms and behavioral problems (Grych & Fincham, 1993).

Intensity. Children are more negatively affected by interparental conflicts that are overtly hostile or physically aggressive. For example, Cummings and his colleagues conducted a series of studies in which children viewed videotapes of angry exchanges between adults (see Cummings & Davies, 1994). Children reported more distress when viewing videotapes that involved physical aggression than verbal aggression, and children who had a history of being exposed to physical aggression in their homes were more distressed by viewing inter-adult anger.

Resolution. Research shows that children are perceptive as to whether their parents have made up after an argument and are more distressed by interparental conflicts that remain unresolved. Children who observe their parents working through their differences in a constructive manner may even gain through learning that conflicts are solvable and may view their parents as models for the development of interpersonal problem-solving skills.

Content. Interparental conflicts that concern the child, or issues related to child rearing, are more likely to be associated with adjustment problems in children.

Child attributions. Grych and Fincham (1990) propose that the effects of interparental conflict on children are mediated by the beliefs that children have about them. In particular, attributions of self-blame and perceived control over their parents' marital problems may lead children to feel more distress.

Child involvement. Children who believe they are responsible for starting or stopping interparental conflicts may be more likely to attempt to intervene during marital quarrels. Intervention in interparental conflicts may place children at risk by making them a party to the quarreling or, in the case of family violence, by making children the targets of abuse as well. Children may also become triangulated in their parents' conflicts, such as by siding with one parent or the other, acting as a "go-between," or acting out in order to divert their parents' attention from their marital stresses.

Conflict between parents has been found to account for the effects of divorce on children, particularly because interparental conflict precedes divorce for as much as two years. However, it is also the case that divorce does not necessarily end the opportunities for conflict between ex-partners, who may continue to have disagreements over such issues as alimony, visitation rights, and child custody.

Research also suggests that parents can act in ways that will buffer children from the impact of interparental conflict. For example, children who are protected from direct exposure to interparental conflict will feel less stressed and fearful than those who observe verbal or physical aggression between their parents. Children also show less distress when parents overtly resolve their quarrels by demonstrating that they have made up with one another after a fight. In addition, children benefit from simple explanations that absolve them from responsibility for causing or controlling parents' marital quarrels. In contrast, parents who abstain from sharing adult-oriented confidences with their children about their marital problems, and refrain from placing their children "in the middle" of their quarrels, are less likely to negatively impact their children's behavioral and emotional development.

References

Cowan, C. P., Cowan, P. A., Heming, G., & Miller, N. B. (1991). Becoming a family: Marriage, parenting, and child development. In P. A. Cowan & E. M. Hetherington (Eds.), *Family transitions* (pp. 79–110). Hillsdale, NJ: Erlbaum.

Cummings, E. M., & Davies, P. (1994). *Children and marital conflict: The impact of family dispute and resolution.* New York: Guilford Press.

Grych, J. H., & Fincham, F. (1990). Marital conflict and children's adjustment: A cognitive-contextual framework. *Psychological Bulletin, 108,* 267–290.

Grych, J. H., & Fincham, F. (1993). Children's appraisals of interparental conflict: Initial investigations of the cognitive-contextual framework. *Child Development, 64,* 215–230.

Kerig, P. K. (1996). Assessing the links between interparental conflict and child adjustment: The Conflicts and Problem-solving Scales. *Journal of Family Psychology, 10,* 454–473.

Reid, W. J, & Crisafulli, A. (1990). Marital discord and child behavior problems: A meta-analysis. *Journal of Abnormal Child Psychology, 18,* 105–117.

See also: Alliance, parenting; Divorced families; Family systems; Triangulation.

PATRICIA K. KERIG

Conflict resolution. In the context of parenting, researchers and practitioners have addressed conflict resolution in several different ways. First, some researchers have studied how parents and children respond to conflict with one another and have attempted to delineate factors that may influence this process. Other researchers and practitioners have focused on teaching parents and children how to work out conflicts in a constructive and positive manner. Finally, recent researchers have discussed parent-child conflict resolution as a natural and potentially beneficial part of children's development.

Descriptive studies of conflict resolution have focused primarily either on families with very young children or on families with adolescents. The work in this area has suggested a number of variables that may influence the manner in which parents and children handle family conflict. These include gender, topic and type of conflict, the child's age, the balance of power between dissenting family members, parental cohort, culture, family structure, socioeconomic status, and parental depression.

Types and topics of conflict. Conflicts between parents and young children have been described in terms of various classifications of initiating actions, parental response, and child response. For example, one coding scheme incorporates all three variables into three types of dispute: *simple disputes*, involving a single prohibition or refusal by either participant; *complex disputes*, involving more than one prohibition or refusal; and *propositional disputes*, involving a propositional statement such as to whom a toy belongs or a philosophical belief (Dunn & Munn, 1987).

Common topics of conflict between parents and young children include caretaking; manners and politeness; possession, rights, and turns; destructiveness or dirt; hurting, aggression, and unkindness; rules of the house; physical space; and independence (Dunn & Munn, 1987). For adolescents, identified topics include regulating behavior; personal style; chores; academic behavior and achievement; interpersonal relationships; and finances (Smetana, Yau, & Hanson, 1991). Conflict resolution appears to vary as a function of the topic of dispute (Dunn & Munn, 1987; Smetana, Yau, & Hanson, 1991).

Conflict responses and resolution styles. Some researchers have characterized parents' responses to conflict with young children in terms of the balance between parental control and child autonomy. For example, conflict resolution styles have been described on a continuum from *negative control* (a high degree of power assertion by the parent) to *control* (parental power assertion is moderate) to *guidance* (low power assertion) (Crockenberg & Litman, 1990). Within different styles, parents may use a variety of tactics such as reasoning, power assertion, silence, acknowledgments of the child's desire, diversion, requests and commands, physically forced compliance, isolation, tangible punishment, verbal punishment, or physical punishment.

Intrusive and power assertive resolution strategies on the part of the parent (e.g., threats, criticism, physical intervention, or anger) have been associated with a child response of defiance and continued conflict. Child compliance appears to be connected with autonomy-granting strategies that combine a clear statement of what the parent wants with an acknowledgment of the child's perspective (Crockenberg & Litman, 1990).

In studies of families with adolescents, the responses to conflict identified by researchers include withdrawal, adolescent giving in, parent giving in, negotiation, standoff, submission, compromise, and unilateral procedures by parent.

Teaching effective conflict resolution. Behavioral interventions that teach parents negotiation and/or communication skills have been successful in reducing conflict in families with adolescents with behavior problems (Foster, 1994). In developing an intervention for parents and adolescents, clinical psychologist Sharon Foster and her colleagues identified four factors that contribute to family conflict. The first two involve deficits in problem solving and in communication skills. The third factor, *cognitive distortion*, refers to irrational beliefs that foster excessive anger or unwillingness to compromise. This includes, for example, unrealistic expectations and attributions around topics such as obedience, perfectionism, ruination, or malicious intent. The fourth factor involves problematic characteristics of the family system itself, such as weak coalitions between parents, triangulation, or excessive disengagement or dependence among family members. Each factor suggests potential family deficits that can in turn be addressed in conflict resolution training (Foster, 1994).

Conflict resolution strategies also often are embedded in general parenting course topics such as discipline, problem solving, and communication skills and reflect the general approach to parenting suggested in the curriculum. A curriculum that emphasizes high parental control, for example, may include behavior modification techniques such as time-out or the use of reinforcement, while lower parental control approaches tend to be oriented toward facilitating a mutual parent-child process rather than toward obtaining a compliant outcome.

Conflict resolution and children's development. The conflict management and resolution process that occurs between parent and child may be a primary learning arena for children's response to conflict with siblings and peers. While preserving their influence over their children, parents also face the challenge of recognizing that parent-child conflict and its resolution are important factors in a child's development toward autonomy (Crockenberg & Litman, 1990; Dunn & Munn, 1987; Kuczynski et al., 1987).

Finally, in most studies, whether of families with adolescents or of families with younger children, researchers have noted the importance of remembering bidirectional influence. Parental strategies may be as much a response to child behavior as child behavior is to parental strategies.

References

Crockenberg, S., & Litman, C. (1990). Autonomy as competence in 2-year-olds: Maternal correlates of child defiance, compliance and self-assertion. *Child Development, 58*, 964–975.

Dunn, J., & Munn, P. (1987). Development of justification in disputes with mother and sibling. *Developmental Psychology, 23*, 791–798.

Foster, S. L. (1994). Assessing and treating parent-adolescent conflict. In M. Hersen, R. M. Eisler, & P. M. Miller (Eds.), *Progress in behavior modification* (Vol. 29). Pacific Grove, CA: Brooks/Cole.

Kuczynski, L., Kochanska, G., Radke-Yarrow, M., & Girnius-Brown, O. (1987). A developmental interpretation of young children's noncompliance. *Developmental Psychology, 23*, 799–806.

Smetana, J. G., Yau, J., & Hanson, S. (1991). Conflict resolution in families with adoles-
    cents. *Journal of Research on Adolescence, 1*, 189–206.

See also: Communication; Mediation, parent-child; Problem solving.

DEBORAH WASSERMAN AND CAROL FORD ARKIN

Conscience. Conscience is a psychological construct that employs the emotional experiences of empathy, shame, guilt, and pride to foster action that is consistent with one's personal standards, rules, and goals. The word *conscience* originates in the Greek word *syneidesis*, the ability to observe and judge oneself. The ethical self-observation in *syneidesis* was attributed to the function of *elenchos* (accusation and conviction). The Latin language united these two emphases in the word *conscientia*. A person with a conscience can recognize the difference between right and wrong, act upon the right, and show restraint to the wrong. Conscience is also the basis for atonement.

Acquisition of conscience. Five cognitive-developmental processes synthesizing emotion with behavior underlie the acquisition of conscience: (1) internalization of standards; (2) recognition of distress in others; (3) compassion toward another's suffering; (4) evaluation of the situation and attribution of personal responsibility; and (5) desire to make amends. Attributions can be global in regard to oneself generally (e.g., child says, "I'm a bad boy!") or specifically ("I was wrong to hit!") (Lewis, 1993).

Although children begin to learn what behavior is expected of them by the end of their first year of life, the most dramatic developmental changes significant for shaping a conscience occur during the second year. By the end of their second year, children are capable of

- differentiating between appropriate and inappropriate behavior,
- following some basic rules, suggesting the ability to make setting limits a part of themselves,
- self-recognition in video and mirrors and the use of personal pronouns,
- showing concern when something is "wrong" (e.g., when toys are in a damaged condition or pictures of people are composed of distorted faces),
- using evaluative words to judge actions of doing harm to others as wrongful or bad,
- showing emotional distress and reparative behavior following acts of wrongdoing,
- expressing a sense of personal blame in response to actions by the self resulting in harm to the other, and
- offering prosocial behavior when they are bystanders to another's distress (Zahn-Waxler & Robinson, 1995).

Each of these skills becomes more elaborated and abstract as children grow older. Children become more capable of regulating their behavior and more effective in taking the perspective of others as they gain more experience and their cognitive skills expand.

Parents and conscience. Discipline is often viewed as a key to nurturing conscience in children. By the end of a child's first year of life, parents begin to exert socialization pressure. They perceive their children as responsible or capable of rudimentary regulation of their actions and start setting limits and expectations for their behavior. During the child's second year of life, parents begin to distinguish in their support and discipline between interpersonal moral transgressions (e.g., hurting others) and transgressions of conventional rules or customs.

Articulating clear and firm expectations regarding appropriate behavior and using victim-centered reasoning in response to a child's misbehavior that causes harm to another are significant for conscience development. Victim-centered reasoning emphasizes the consequences a child's actions have for another person. For example, a father might say, "Look at what you did. See the marks on Sandy's arm? You bit her. Look at her cry. You hurt her." This reaction tends to build a sense of personal responsibility and problem-solving capacity in children. Parental reasoning about such matters is often placed in a spiritual context and supported by others in a shared religious community.

Developing a secure attachment with a caretaker is also critical for the development of conscience. After birth, several specific child behaviors and parental responses need to take place in order for the child to develop normal attachment (Klaus & Kennel, 1976). These goal-oriented child behaviors emerge within a few days of birth and include crying, smiling, clinging, rooting, postural adjustment, and vocalization. Infants who experience a supportive and consistent response by familiar caretakers learn to trust and form attachments. Attachment problems can close important avenues to emotional regulation, including empathy, shame, and guilt, which may lead to disruptive behavioral patterns, especially aggression (Waters et al., 1993). So all of the nurturing, affectionate behaviors that parents offer their children are critical for the emergence of skills that make conscience possible.

Parental contributions, though significant, are not entirely responsible for the growth of conscience. Emerging research shows that a child's temperament interacts with parental socialization practices (Kochanska, 1993). Emotionality and activity level/impulse control are especially important for the development of conscience. Some children feel remorse for their misdeeds more readily than others and are more anxious to please. These children will respond more quickly to parents' efforts to nurture conscience. In addition, some children are more capable of inhibiting forbidden impulses. These children will also respond more readily to parental socialization.

Several parental behaviors appear critical for the development of conscience. Sending clear expectations to children about morality and restitution and encouraging them to reflect on the implications of their behavior for others provide the understanding that is needed. Nurturing a healthy attachment with loving caretakers and providing opportunities for the expression and growth of compassion foster an emotional growth that brings conscience into action.

References

Klaus, M., & Kennel, J. (1976). *Maternal-infant bonding*. St. Louis, MO: C. V. Mosby.

Kochanska, G. (1993). Toward a synthesis of parental socialization and child temperament in early development. *Child Development, 64*, 325–347.

Lewis, M. (1993). Self-conscious emotions: Embarrassment, pride, shame and guilt. In M. Lewis & J. Haviland (Eds.), *Handbook of emotions* (pp. 563–573). New York: Guilford Press.

Waters, E., Posada, G., Crowell, J., & Lay, K. L. (1993). *Is attachment theory ready to contribute to our understanding of disruptive behavior problems? Development and psychopathology* (pp. 215–244). Cambridge: Cambridge University Press.

Zahn-Waxler, C., & Robinson, J. (1995). Empathy and guilt: Early origins of feelings of responsibility. In J. Tangney & K. Fischer (Eds.), *Self-conscious emotions: The psychology of shame, guilt, embarrassment, and pride* (pp. 143–173). New York: Guilford Press.

See also: Empathy; Guilt; Moral development; Shame.

CHARLES A. SMITH

Consequences, natural and logical. Natural and logical consequences constitute a discipline technique that is an alternative to punishment. The use of consequences is aimed at helping children learn from their own actions, rather than learning from punishment administered by the parent. A natural consequence is the naturally occurring result of some behavior. For example, the natural consequence of going out on a snowy day with no mittens is cold hands. Similarly, the natural consequence of leaving a bicycle out in the rain is a rusty bike chain. These consequences can be thought of as a result of the reality of the physical world; the parent is not required to intervene in any way for the child to experience the consequence. A logical consequence can be thought of as the result of the reality of the social world. These consequences are a logical and social result of certain behaviors. For example, the logical consequence of coming home past the dinner hour is eating cold leftovers and washing your own dishes. The logical consequence of painting foul words on the sidewalk is to scrub all the paint away with a scrub brush.

In some cases, natural consequences are too harsh or dangerous to allow a child to experience (e.g., the consequence of crossing the street alone is being struck by an auto), making logical consequences a necessity. When a parent constructs a logical consequence, he or she must be sure it is indeed logical rather than punitive. Doing 25 push-ups because you have not cleaned your room is not a logical consequence. Moreover, consequences must be delivered in a matter-of-fact manner without undue attention to the misbehavior. The consequence simply is—parents need not lecture or berate the child. The consequence speaks for itself.

Using natural and logical consequences rather than punishment is grounded in a "humanistic" philosophy of parenting (Osborne, 1995). Adherents to this philosophy believe that families are small democracies in which parents and children have equal worth and are due equal respect. With these rights comes responsibility to oneself and to the other members of the family. It is from this notion of responsibility to others that the logical consequence arises. Because children function in a social group (the family), they must abide by the rules set by that family. Using natural and logical consequences can remove parents from the position of being the person who administers punishment. Fewer power struggles may result, as well as teaching responsibility to children, the ultimate goal of all discipline techniques.

Natural and logical consequences can be traced to the work of Rudolf Dreikurs (Dreikurs, 1964). Dreikurs was a student of Alfred Adler who followed Adler to the United States. His goal in the United States was to promote Adlerian psychology and build child guidance centers. His vision of these centers followed an educational rather than medical model. Parents needed information and assistance, not therapy or medical treatment in most cases, according to Dreikurs. He believed that the difficulty parents were facing came from the shift in our society from an autocratic society to a democratic one. He hoped to train parents in methods that relied on democratic notions rather than on authoritarian ones (Christensen & Thomas, 1980).

Dreikurian parent education principles have found their way into several more recent parent education resources. Dinkmeyer and McKay (e.g., 1973, 1982), in their various renditions of Systematic Training for Effective Parenting, rely quite heavily on the thinking of Dreikurs and advocate for natural and logical consequences as an alternative to punishment. The Active Parenting program of Michael Popkin also utilizes the notion of natural and logical consequences (Popkin, 1987).

References

Christensen, O. C., & Thomas, C. R. (1980). Dreikurs and the search for equality. In M. J. Fine (Ed.), *Handbook on parent education* (pp. 53–74). Orlando, FL: Academic Press.

Dinkmeyer, D., & McKay, G. (1973). *Raising a responsible child: Practical steps to successful family relationships*. New York: Simon & Schuster.

Dinkmeyer, D., & McKay, G. (1982). *The parents' handbook: Systematic Training for Effective Parenting (STEP)*. Circle Pines, MN: American Guidance Service.

Dreikurs, R. (1964). *Children the challenge*. New York: Hawthorne/Dutton.

Osborne, P. (1995). The parenting experts. In R. D. Day, K. R. Gilbert, B. H. Settles, & W. R. Burr (Eds.), *Research and theory in family science* (pp.320–333). Pacific Grove, CA: Brooks/Cole.

Popkin, M. (1987). *Active parenting*. San Francisco: HarperCollins.

See also: Adler, Alfred; Authority, parental; Consistency; Discipline; Dreikurs, Rudolf; Physical punishment.

BRENDA J. BOYD

Consistency. Discussions regarding effective parenting often include the notion of consistency. Research suggests that consistent parenting practices lead to increased compliance and help children establish trust. Consistency involves having definite beliefs about child rearing and the ability to follow through with those beliefs, through the establishment and enforcement of rules and structure, in a predictable manner. Consistent parenting means establishing clear and concise rules, using regular and anticipated consequences and rewards, and carefully monitoring children. Furthermore, consistent parents agree about child rearing and work as a team.

Research indicates that parental inconsistency is correlated with a greater risk of childhood behavioral disorders among children. Feehan et al. (1991) suggest that inconsistent discipline practices were associated with Attention Deficit

Hyperactivity Disorder, Oppositional Defiant Disorder, and Conduct Disorder. Pehrson (1990) found that the parents reporting the most inconsistency in the sample had children who were diagnosed with an Anxiety Disorder. In addition, Ellwood and Stolberg (1993) found that among divorced families consistency between the parents led to a higher rate of healthy adjustment for both the parents and children. They also found that consistency encouraged greater self-esteem and created a safe environment for the expression of feelings.

Consistent parenting does not carry the expectation of perfection. Parents cannot expect to always do the right thing at the right time. Instead, consistency means that parents have a solid foundation of beliefs, skills, and techniques that they rely upon. Ross (1993) suggests that consistent parents feel a sense of purpose. This sense leads to a philosophy of parenting. She states that without a sense of purpose and an underlying philosophy guiding parental practices, consistency cannot be maintained. Instead, discipline is based solely on a reaction to what is happening at the moment.

Reactive discipline tends to be unpredictable. This unpredictability fosters distrust between parent and child. The child does not trust that the rules and consequences will be the same all the time. Without consistency, the child becomes confused about what behaviors are acceptable. The child then behaves erratically, which the parent may interpret as being irresponsible. Furthermore, without a clear structure, children can develop intense anxiety in the home because they are constantly unsure of the parent's expectations. Clear rules and consistent application of consequences leave little room for doubt—for both the children and the parents.

Inconsistent parenting practices have other disadvantages. According to Gardner (1989), the parent may inadvertently reward problem behavior and punish acceptable behavior. A common example of a parent rewarding problem behavior is telling a child several times to stop a behavior. The reward in this case is the increased attention the child is receiving by being told to stop the behavior. In addition, as the child continues to be disobedient, the parent often times becomes reactive and lashes out through increased anger or other means. Parent educators can help parents to recognize positive and negative consequences and appropriate times to utilize them.

Inconsistent parenting practices may also be a symptom of a larger problem. Other issues such as mental illness, marital conflict, and/or poor social support may all influence one's ability to parent consistently. In these situations, parents will often give in to their children's acting-out behavior. The short-term gain of peace and quiet becomes more important than extinguishing problem behaviors. Educators can help teach parents that expending higher amounts of energy in the beginning to stop unwanted behaviors will actually save them energy in the future.

Interestingly, Feehan et al. (1991) found that inconsistent discipline was more likely to be associated with problem behavior than style of parenting. In other words, whether or not parents were strict or permissive, as long as they were consistent, the behavior problems were not as prevalent. They also found that the combination of permissiveness and inconsistency is perhaps more maladaptive than strictness coupled with inconsistency.

Consistent parenting means that parents consistently agree with each other. When this does not occur, children can play the parents against each other. This can also create distrust between the parents and teach the children how to use manipulation tactics in order to get their needs met. Parental agreement is important in divorced families as well. Similar rules and discipline between households lead to smoother transitions for the children (Ellwood & Stolberg, 1993). When parents differ in their beliefs about child rearing, practitioners can help them to compromise, so they can present themselves as a united front. This can be accomplished with married or divorced families.

Finally, consistent parenting does not mean parents must be inflexible. Successful families adapt to changes in developmental levels. What is important is that parents consistently adhere to the new rules that are brought about by these changes. Parents must also consistently communicate what their expectations are and what defines appropriate behaviors for that developmental level.

References

Ellwood, M. A., & Stolberg, A. L. (1993). The effects of family composition, family health, parenting behavior and environmental stress on children's divorce adjustment. *Journal of Child and Family Studies, 2* (1), 23–36.

Feehan, M., McGee, R., Stanton, W. R., & Silva, P. A. (1991). Strict and inconsistent discipline in childhood: Consequences for adolescent mental health. *British Journal of Clinical Psychology, 30,* 325–331.

Gardner, F. E. M. (1989). Inconsistent parenting: Is there evidence for a link with children's conduct problems? *Journal of Abnormal Child Psychology, 17* (2), 223–233.

Pehrson, K. L. (1990). Parental self-assessment and behavioral problems of preschool children. *Military Medicine, 155* (4), 148–152.

Ross, J. A. (1993). *Practical parenting for the 21st century: The manual you wish had come with your child.* New York: Excalibur Publishing.

See also: Consequences, natural and logical; Discipline; Limit setting.

JAMES M. SEIBOLD

Control strategies. There are many ways that people attempt to control or guide children. Those control strategies have commonly been divided into three broad categories by researchers: coercion, love withdrawal, and induction (Rollins & Thomas, 1979).

Coercion is defined as any attempt to use power to control the child. It might include such power-based techniques as grounding, yelling, punishing, and hitting children. While it is possible to get compliance from children by using coercion, regular use of such a control strategy tends to result in children who lack social ability, are withdrawn, lack spontaneity, are more aggressive, and have an underdeveloped conscience (Maccoby & Martin, 1983).

Love withdrawal is behavior that shows disapproval and suggests that the relationship between the parent and the child cannot be restored until the child changes behavior or makes amends. Love withdrawal might include time-out, lectures, or other guilt-inducing responses to children's behavior. Research has shown mixed results on the effectiveness of love withdrawal in controlling children's behavior. Some researchers have suggested that the regular use of love withdrawal results in children who often feel guilty.

Induction consists of behavior by the parent to elicit voluntary compliance. It includes reasoning with the child and helping the child understand the effects of his or her behavior on others. Parents who use induction generally have children who are more socially competent, responsible, independent, confident, and achievement oriented and have better-developed conscience. It is clear that this gentle and persuasive approach to control is the most effective in developing well-balanced children.

In addition to the three control strategies described above, there are other useful ways of understanding control. For instance, Holden (1983) has studied the behavior of mothers with young children in supermarket settings. He has categorized the control strategies into reactive and proactive. *Reactive* approaches tend to wait until there is trouble and then react with punishment. *Proactive* approaches tend to anticipate problems and needs and act to prevent problems. Not surprisingly, proactive parents have fewer behavior problems with their children than reactive parents do.

In addition to such academic ways of understanding control strategies, there are also very practical approaches. Some parents use distraction to prevent problems by redirecting a child toward acceptable behavior when they are tempted by unacceptable behavior. Some parents use attention and encouragement to keep children pointed toward positive behavior options. Some parents use understanding and caring to build a strong relationship with the child in order to prevent serious problems. Some parents are very skillful at forming alternatives for children so that the children have a choice but the options are acceptable to the parent. Some parents use consistency and natural consequences to help a child discover the lawfulness of their experience. Parents who maintain a positive relationship with their children, appreciate good behavior, plan ahead to prevent problems, allow children a developmentally appropriate amount of freedom, and stay in tune with their children are more likely to have healthy children and to enjoy their relationships with their children.

References

Holden, G. W. (1983). Avoiding conflict: Mothers as tacticians in the supermarket. *Child Development, 54,* 233–240.

Maccoby, E. E., & Martin, J. A. (1983). Socialization in the context of the family: Parent-child interaction. In P. H. Mussen (Ed.), *Handbook of child psychology* (Vol. 4, pp. 1–101). New York: John Wiley.

Rollins, B. C., & Thomas, D. L. (1979). Parental support, power, and control techniques in the socialization of children. In W. R. Burr, R. Hill, F. I. Nye, & I. L. Reiss (Eds.), *Contemporary theories about the family* (Vol. 1, pp. 317–364). New York: Free Press.

See also: Discipline; Limit setting.

H. WALLACE GODDARD

Cooperative Extension Service. The Cooperative Extension Service is a unique partnership established by Congress in 1914. It is a national educational network designed to meet the need for research, knowledge, and educational programs that enable people to make practical decisions (Rasmussen, 1989). This public-funded, *nonformal* (out of school) educational network combines the expertise and resources of federal, state, and local governments. The partnership that supports the Cooperative Extension Service is a collaborative one. It includes the Cooperative State Research, Education and Extension Service (CSREES), an agency in the United States Department of Agriculture, the 105 land-grant universities (in every state and territory), and more than 3,500 county/city offices. The partners share resources and information and act to enhance and achieve goals based on their common interest of developing and conducting nonformal, research-based educational programs. Major program units providing information, educational programs, and support include Agriculture, Community Resource Development, Home Economics/Family Consumer Sciences, and 4-H Youth Development.

Through the county and state offices, staff provide information, educational programs, and technical advice directly to individuals, families, and communities that enable them to be self-reliant and improve their lives through education. Areas of particular interest include Family Development and Resource Management; Nutrition, Diet, and Health; 4-H Youth Development; and Community Resource Development. Families and individuals can access programs and information related to parenting skills, money management and managing other resources, seeking and providing child care, caring for children and dependent elderly, and other areas of interest to improve the well-being of the family.

Extension educators provide volunteers and parents with training, materials, and other opportunities to enhance their skills to encourage and support youth as they learn. Extension educators serve as catalysts, assisting with organizing meetings, agendas, and other assistance to help focus on issues and providing access to expert information from the university and other sources.

A major focus for several years has been a collaborative effort in communities to establish after-school child care. In some communities, extension educators have helped to organize immunization programs in cooperation with health and civic organizations and groups and local government. The Cooperative Extension System (the federal, state, and county partnership) shares resources, exchanges information, and takes actions to enhance the capacity of each partner in the system to achieve their mission to help people improve their lives and communities through educational programs that use scientific knowledge focused on issues and needs.

To provide support to the staff particularly in the areas of children, youth, and families, the Cooperative Extension Service has established five national networks on child care, collaboration building, family resiliency, science and technology literacy, and decisions for health that are linked electronically. The networks provide training, curriculum, and research information. Each network is a collaboration of faculty from departments of several land-grant universities and each ties into family resource research nationwide. For further information, contact your local county extension office (offices are usually listed under local government) or the Cooperative Extension Service at a land-grant university in your state.

Reference
Rasmussen, W. D. (1989). *Taking the university to the people: Seventy-five years of Co-operative Extension*. Ames: Iowa State University Press.

See also: National Extension Parent Education Model (NEPEM).

VIRGINIA GOBELI

Critical periods. The concept of critical periods is intriguing for scientists concerned with development and for parents of young children. Although scientists do not always agree on a strict definition, the critical period concept suggests that organisms are particularly susceptible to environmental stimulation at certain periods of development (Bornstein, 1989). The concept is often used to argue that early influences have greater impact on organisms than later influences and that the effects of early experiences are irreversible.

One of the first proponents of the critical period concept was animal ethologist, Konrad Lorenz (1952), who studied imprinting in animals. Lorenz discovered that after hatching, baby chicks would follow the first moving object that they saw, usually the mother hen. If the mother was not present, other moving objects that were artificially introduced were followed. Lorenz discovered that there was a specific time period during which imprinting occurred and that the early imprinting was permanent because later experiences outside the critical period did not alter the chick's established preferences.

Imprinting is one example that illustrates how experiences during a specified period may be essential for the normal development of an organism. There are also many examples of the deleterious effects of noxious stimulation, especially during prenatal development. A clear example in humans was the thalidomide disaster in the 1960s in Europe, Canada, and Australia (Berk, 1994). When a woman took the sedative thalidomide between the fourth and sixth week of pregnancy, gross deformities of the arms and legs occurred in the fetus. Similarly, exposure to masculine hormones during the sensitive period for the development of external genitalia can result in masculinization of the female fetus (Bornstein, 1989).

The original concept of the critical period as described by Lorenz has been subsequently modified, and the term *sensitive period* is generally preferred today (Bornstein, 1989). The change in terminology reflects the fact that studies have sometimes shown reversibility or modifiability of what were thought to be permanent critical period effects. Also, sensitive periods in mature organisms have been documented. For example, sensitive periods for the initiation of maternal recognition and responsiveness to the young have been documented in adult female rats and goats.

Recent studies have also shown that sensitive periods and the mechanisms for their development vary considerably between species (Bornstein, 1989). For example, some birds must be exposed to the bird song of their species during a sensitive period, while others require no exposure to be able to produce the adult song pattern. Similarly, whereas evidence exists for biochemical mechanisms that mediate maternal responsiveness in some mammals, in humans there is no strong evidence that similar biochemical triggers of maternal bonding exist. Thus, natural selection has resulted in great variability between species in the existence and nature of sensitive periods for the development of behaviors that ensure species survival and reproductive success.

Apart from sensitive periods in human embryological development, there has been much disagreement concerning the existence of sensitive periods postnatally in humans (Berk, 1994). Some of the strongest evidence in humans concerns language development, as suggested by Lenneberg (1967). If deaf and hearing children are not exposed to language before puberty, they will develop vocabulary and consistent word-ordering principles, but they will not develop grammar. Acquisition of a second language is also most successful at 3 to 7 years of age and becomes very difficult after puberty. Studies of children who spent their early years in unstimulating orphanages suggest that lasting damage to social and intellectual development occurs if children are not put in improved environments by at least 2 years of age (Berk, 1994).

Starting Points, an extensive report of the Carnegie Foundation (1994), has called attention to one mechanism by which early experiences can have lasting effects on humans—brain development in the first three years of life. During this period, excess synapses (connections between brain cells) are pruned with the result that the brain is "sculpted" by the child's sensory experiences. The five key findings of the Carnegie Foundation were:

> First, the brain development that takes place before age one is more rapid and extensive than we previously believed.
> Second, brain development is much more vulnerable to environmental influence than we ever suspected.
> Third, the influence of early environment on brain development is long lasting.
> Fourth, the environment affects not only the number of brain cells and number of connections among them, but also the way these connections are "wired."
> Fifth, we have new scientific evidence for the negative impact of early stress on brain function. (pp. 6–7)

These findings suggest the critical importance of the infancy and toddler periods for brain development and the need to support parents and caregivers in the provision of optimal care during this period.

References

Berk, L. (1994). *Child development* (3rd ed.). Needham Heights, MA: Allyn & Bacon.
Bornstein, M. (1989). Sensitive periods in development. *Psychological Bulletin, 105,* 179–197.
Carnegie Corporation. (1994). *Starting Points: Meeting the needs of our youngest children.* New York, NY: Author.
Lenneberg, E. (1967). *Biological foundations of language.* New York: Wiley.
Lorenz, K. (1952). *King Solomon's ring.* New York: Thomas Y. Crowell.

See also: Attachment, secure; Developmentally Appropriate Practice.

ANN D. MURRAY

Crying. Crying is one of the major means by which newborns and preverbal infants communicate their needs to caregivers. Crying is considered by some theorists to be a species-typical behavior that ensures that the infant survives the relatively helpless infancy period (Bell & Ainsworth, 1972). Adults in turn may also be adapted to respond to crying. Studies have found that the typical response to crying by experienced and inexperienced caregivers is to pick up the baby (Gustafson & Deconti, 1990).

Studies have been carried out to document typical amounts of crying and to describe the developmental course of crying during the first year (see Barr et al., 1991 for a review). Despite differences in methodology, many researchers have identified an early peak in crying at about 2 to 3 months of age with babies crying an average of 1.5 to 2.5 hours per day. There is also evidence in some studies that crying peaks in the evening hours during this early period. Following the early peak in crying at 2 to 3 months, the amount of crying gradually diminishes over the first year. Some authors (Barr et al., 1991; Wolke, 1993) claim that crying during the early infancy period (birth to 6 months) is undifferentiated and expressive of the infant's physiological state, whereas later crying (6 to 12+ months) is intended by the infant to communicate specific messages to the caregiver. Evidence to support this position has been provided in a study by Gustafson and her colleagues (Gustafson & Deconti, 1990) who found that before 6 months cries were not coordinated with looks or other gestures to the caregiver. From 6 months on, cries were increasingly combined with other gestures and were directed specifically toward the caregiver.

Some investigators have questioned whether the relatively high level of crying observed in Western cultures is universal or normal in light of studies of hunter-gatherer societies in which crying is said to occur rarely (Barr et al., 1991). In preagricultural societies, infants are carried almost continuously until at least 1 year of age and are fed on demand (approximately four times an hour). Barr and his colleagues closely examined data collected on !Kung San infants of the Kalahari desert and concluded that infants had a similar number of bouts of crying (frequency measure) but that they cried for half as long (duration measure) as Western infants. The reduced duration of crying among !Kung San infants appeared to be related to a pattern of close contact and immediate responses to crying in this culture. When Barr encouraged mothers in a Western culture to carry their infants for three or more additional hours per day, he found that the duration of crying was reduced by half and approximated the level of crying among !Kung San infants. Barr's findings suggest that the frequency of crying is universal and that crying shows a peak across cultures at 2 to 3 months of age. However, the duration of crying is markedly affected by cross-cultural variations in caregiving patterns.

The issue of whether or not to respond to crying infants has been controversial in Western society (Bell & Ainsworth, 1972). Parents have been frequently advised that responding to crying will reinforce crying and result in a "spoiled," demanding baby. However, in a landmark longitudinal study, Bell and Ainsworth found that babies who cried the least by 1 year of age had the most responsive mothers early in the first year. Babies of responsive mothers were also found to have more secure attachments and better communication skills at 12 months of age compared to infants of mothers who delayed responding to their cries. Findings such as these have prompted professionals to advocate responding to crying immediately in the first 6 months when crying appears to be primarily expressive of internal states. Recent studies designed to investigate normal amounts of crying in large samples of Western infants (e.g., Michelsson et al., 1990) have found lower total durations of crying compared with older studies. A widespread reduction in the duration of crying in Western cultures may have resulted from changes in professional advice that discounts the spoiling theory and urges parents to be responsive to crying.

A considerable literature exists on problem crying behavior that is excessive compared to the norm and results in parental exhaustion and desperation (Wolke, 1993). Most recent literature refers to *excessive crying* defined simply as crying that occurs for three or more hours a day on three or more days a week for three or more weeks. Although estimates vary, studies suggest that approximately 10% of infants in Western cultures are thought to cry excessively. Whereas crying typically elicits nurturing responses from parents, excessive crying is stressful for caregivers and is often cited as the major precipitant of child abuse in children under 1 year of age. The term *colic* has been used frequently to refer to problem crying in the first 3 months of life with no other evidence of illness. Although colic implies abdominal distress, studies to date have not identified biological causes for colic, and no single biomedical treatment strategy (drug or dietary treatment) has been found to be effective. Other concepts that may relate to problem crying include difficult temperament and disorders in state regulation, but the boundaries between these concepts are not clear. Wolke (1993) claims that the most effective treatment is an individualized developmental treatment approach targeting parent-infant interactions.

References

Barr, R., Konner, M., Bakeman, R., & Adamson, L. (1991). Crying in !Kung San infants: A test of the cultural specificity hypothesis. *Developmental Medicine and Child Neurology, 33*, 601610.

Bell, S., & Ainsworth, M. (1972). Infant crying and maternal responsiveness. *Child Development, 43*, 1171–1190.

Gustafson, G., & Deconti, K. (1990). Infants' cries in the process of normal development. *Early Child Development and Care, 65*, 45–56.

Michelsson, K., Paajanen, S., Rinne, A., Tervo, H., Kunnamo, I., & Kiminkinen, T. (1990). Mothers' perceptions of and feelings toward their babies' crying. *Early Child Development and Care, 65*, 109–116.

Wolke, D. (1993). The treatment of problem crying behaviour. In I. St. James-Roberts, G. Harris, and D. Messer (Eds.), *Infant crying, feeding and sleeping* (pp. 47–79). New York: Harvester Wheatsheaf.

See also: Attachment, secure; Colic; Temper tantrums.

ANN D. MURRAY

Cultural competence. Cultural competence refers to an individual's values and behavioral patterns that create positive and effective relationships with others from culturally different backgrounds. A culturally competent person exhibits socially adaptive and respectful behavior in cross-cultural settings.

Specific criteria for being culturally competent in cross-cultural settings are defined by Brislin et al. (1986) as:

- good personal adjustment—feelings of well-being and contentment
- good interpersonal relations—sense of mutual respect and comfortable interactions
- task effectiveness—completion of a goal in a satisfactory manner

Becoming culturally competent is a socialization process. *Socialization* is defined as the way in which infants, children, or persons of any age learn about their environment and acquire appropriate physical and social skills for survival and well-being (Eshelman, 1997).

Cultural competence, however, is not necessarily an automatic part of socialization. Children are socialized within a specific culture in which their family and persons around them have a shared sense of beliefs, values, and customs. Culture, a basic concept for understanding social life, influences the socialization goals that a parent has for a child, including the child's adaptive daily behaviors. Children then carry these cultural influences into adulthood (Handel & Whitchurch, 1994).

It is not unusual to think that one's own cultural understandings and practices are preferable to those of others. That is only natural, as they are tied to an individual's social identity.

Gaining cultural competence, therefore, begins with awareness of cultural influences. It starts with a recognition of how one's own cultural knowledge came to be. Persons seek to understand the influence of their culture on personal ways of thinking and patterns of behavior (Dana, 1993). Parents cannot help children with such abstract reasoning unless they have given attention to the process themselves. This reflection requires continuous thinking about micro-influences like family and friends, jobs, and school and macro-influences such as geographical characteristics, social traditions, educational and religious institutions, social class and economic structures, historical and current racial relations, and the political arena.

This type of self-awareness is not easy. It challenges a person to think differently and to analyze the reasons for one's own values and behavior. It pushes a person to be sensitive to cultural differences by studying about others or by having firsthand experiences.

A person begins to accept that it is all right for others to talk differently, act differently, and think differently. This stage of *acceptance*, however, can be preceded by the following three stages: (1) denial of the right for other people to be different (i.e., belief in genocide); (2) defense of own way and malicious belittlement of differences; and (3) minimization or trivialization of differences (Bennett as referenced in Dana, 1993).

Individuals not only have to go through an awareness or consciousness-raising phase to reach the fourth stage of acceptance; they need both a cognitive and an affective understanding of cultural differences, and skills to reinforce culturally appropriate behaviors. Increased cognitive understanding might be gained from reading about others, finding out ways to know the unspoken behavioral guidelines of other cultures, learning about population facts and figures, or examining sources of prejudicial biases. Affective understanding is increased by recognizing the range of emotions that may surface in cross-cultural contact. Skills training involves actual or simulated activities that reinforce culturally appropriate behaviors (Brislin & Yoshida, 1994; Dana, 1993).

Following the acceptance stage is *adaptation,* where a person can empathize with culturally different behaviors and automatically modify behavior and thinking for a successful outcome over time. The final stage, *integration,* is achieved when a person's own identity is immersed in evaluating situations from a cultural perspective.

No longer can one expect to function only in a monocultural environment in our culturally diverse society. Increasingly, individuals are interacting with others from very different cultural backgrounds in child care, school, work, and everyday settings. From a very young age, children observe similarities and differences among people and take in the "spoken and unspoken messages" that others convey (Derman-Sparks & the A.B.C. Task Force, 1989). Only when adults model cultural competence can children learn to get along better and become more respectful of those that may be different from themselves. That is part of becoming socially competent.

References

Brislin, R. W., Cushner, K., Cherrie, C., & Yong, M. (1986). *Intercultural interactions: A practical guide.* Beverly Hills, CA: Sage Publications.

Brislin, R. W., & Yoshida, T. (Eds.). (1994). *Improving intercultural interactions.* Thousand Oaks, CA: Sage Publications.

Dana, R. H. (1993). *Multicultural assessment perspectives for professional psychology.* Boston: Allyn & Bacon.

Derman-Sparks, L., & the A.B.C. Task Force. (1989). *Anti-bias curriculum: Tools for empowering young children.* Washington, DC: National Association for the Education of Young Children.

Eshelman, J. R. (1997). *The family* (8th ed.). Boston: Allyn & Bacon.

Handel, G., & Whitchurch, G. G. (Eds.). (1994). *The psychosocial interior of the family.* New York: Walter de Gruyter.

See also: Community; Cultural context.

CHARLOTTE SHOUP OLSEN

Cultural context. Culture is a collective phenomenon and refers to the patterns of thinking, feeling, and acting shared by those who live within the same social environment. Hofstede (1991) calls these patterns *mental programs* and defines culture as the "collective programming of the mind which distinguishes the members of one group or category of people from another" (p. 5). He identified three broad levels of uniqueness in human mental programming. *Human nature*, which is shared by all humankind, represents the universal level of mental programming (i.e., the human ability to feel anger, joy, or sadness as modified by culture). *Culture* is shared with some, but not all, other people and is learned in the broad social environment in which one grew up and through collected life experiences in the family, neighborhood, school, youth groups, workplace, and living community. Manifestations of cultural differences include symbols, heroes, rituals, norms, and values. Finally, the *personality* of an individual represents the unique level of mental programming that is not shared with any other person and is based on traits that are partly inherited and partly learned.

Research focusing on various constructs attempted to identify specific dimensions that distinguish cultures and differentiates the social behaviors of cultural groups. Reviewing the relevant literature, Rotheram and Phinney (1987) suggested the following four dimensions as central to specifying cultural and subcultural differences. These differences include: "1) an orientation toward group affiliation and interdependence versus an individual orientation emphasizing independence and competition, 2) an active, achievement-oriented style versus a passive, accepting style, 3) authoritarianism and the acceptance of hierarchical relationships versus egalitarianism, and 4) an expressive, overt, personal style of communication versus a restrained, impersonal, and formal style" (p. 22). Parents and children learn patterns of thinking, feeling, and acting that derive from these dimensions. Research findings further documented differences in parental child-rearing practices and children's behavior in terms of these dimensions.

In recent years, there has been an increasing research interest in culture and parenting within several different disciplinary approaches. A theoretical framework has been suggested for studying the ways that a child's microenvironment of daily life is culturally shaped (Super & Harkness, 1986). The *developmental niche* is conceptualized in terms of three components or subsystems, which interact with each other and relate centrally to parents: the physical and social settings of the child's life, culturally regulated customs and practices of child care and child rearing, and the psychology of the caretakers (Super & Harkness, 1986). Research on parenting provides evidence for both universals and cultural variation in parenting.

Several stage models have been proposed to explain the acquisition of ethnic identity and attitudes in children. They suggest that the establishment of ethnic identity follows a developmental, age-related progression in the children's ability to perceive, process, and interpret racial and/or ethnic stimuli (Rotheram & Phinney, 1987). Ethnic identity constitutes a broad concept including many components: ethnic awareness, ethnic self-identification, ethnic attitudes, and ethnic behaviors (Rotheram & Phinney, 1987).

Historically, the child-rearing values, attitudes, and practices of the dominant white, Anglo-Saxon, middle-class structure have been considered to be the norm for optimal child development. The "dominant culture" parenting practices have been used as the standard for comparison of all other parenting practices. The "cultural deprivation" perspective that views differences as deficits has dominated most of the literature regarding various aspects of child development and educational practices regarding school performance and adjustment of minority children.

Although progress has been made in many realms, ethnic and minority parents and children are exposed to, and have to deal with, various problems related to socioeconomic disadvantage. These include differential access to medical care, residential segregation, unsafe neighborhoods, unemployment or underemployment, educational opportunities, and sources of oppression and stress, including discrimination, prejudice, segregation, and subtle forms of racism.

Researchers have emphasized the great variability that occurs between and within different ethnic and minority groups and the different factors affecting their acculturation process. The process of acculturation concerns the family unit as a whole and each family member independently as well and includes experiences that can be positive, negative, or mixed. The degree of family acculturation and the subsequent processes of children's racial and ethnic socialization may be characterized along a continuum ranging from assimilation with the dominant culture to bicultural competence to separation from the mainstream. Degree of acculturation also affects children's school performance and adjustment, academic achievement, and career goals and expectations.

Several researchers dealing with various ethnic groups indicated the importance of various aspects of minority parenting practices as related to their children's ethnic and/or racial socialization and positive developmental outcomes. Minority parents need to teach their children to deal with three different realms of experience: the mainstream culture, their own group culture and heritage, and the minority experience associated with several forms of discrimination, prejudice, and racism. More recently, the concept of bicultural or multicultural competence has become the goal in socializing children of all national/ethnic groups.

References
Hofstede, G. (1991). *Cultures and organizations. Software of the mind*. Berkshire, England: McGraw-Hill.
Rotheram, M. J., & Phinney, J. S. (1987). Definitions and perspectives in the study of children's ethnic socialization. In J. S. Phinney & M. J. Rotherman (Eds.), *Children's ethnic socialization. Pluralism and development* (pp. 10–28). Newbury Park, CA: Sage Publications.
Super, C. M., & Harkness, S. (1986). The developmental niche: A conceptualization at the interface of child and culture. *International Journal of Behavioral Development, 9*, 545–569.

See also: Community; Cultural competence; Social support, informal.

CHRYSE HATZICHRISTOU

Custody. Custody, within the context of divorce, refers to the legal sanctioning and decreeing of guardianship of minor children. Custody decisions proceed in two phases. First, the *determination of guardianship* is made. Once this determination has been decided, an *order describing the guardianship is decreed.*

The initial decision regarding custody of minor children proceeds along a continuum. One of three methods is typically employed. First, parents may decide guardianship of the child, with their recommendation being presented to the court for determination. This is the best alternative and involves minimal conflict. However, this method necessitates that parents (1) have dealt with unresolved marital issues that may subjectively cloud their ability to examine alternatives, (2) keep the best interests of the child in the forefront of the decision-making process, and (3) recognize that although they may be divorced, they remain coparents.

The second method of decision making takes place in a therapeutic (mediation) environment. When parents have reached an impasse, yet are still willing to negotiate the best interests of the child, mediation can provide an environment that minimizes hostility. *Mediation* is a goal-directed process in which parents negotiate an agreement specifying conditions surrounding custody of a minor child (Kelly, 1983). The mediator facilitates the formation of precise guidelines that are consistent with the "best interest of the child." So as to prevent misunderstanding, these guidelines are often included as a part of the divorce decree.

Finally, when parties are unable or unwilling to work harmoniously toward a decision in the interest of the child, the court may order a custody evaluation, requesting that an expert witness (i.e., a clinician trained in evaluation and forensics) examine circumstances and make recommendations on behalf of the child. When an expert witness is requested to help determine guardianship of a minor child, a set of basic guidelines, referred to as the *Best Interests of the Child*, prescribe how the determination should be made.

While it is possible that the parties may accept the decision of the expert, thus eliminating the necessity of a trial, this is not always the case. Should a custody proceed to trial, animosity between the parties will more than likely increase as one parent is pitted against the other in an attempt to prove who is the "best parent" (Gardner, 1982). As the adversarial nature of the decision-making process increases, the well-being of the child, during and after the order is decreed, is significantly decreased (Marlow & Sauber, 1990).

Custody decisions are generally categorized into one of two custodial arrangements, traditional and joint. The traditional definition of custody clarifies guardianship by specifying two parental positions—namely, *custodial* and *noncustodial* parent. The custodial parent typically has the right to determine the child's upbringing (e.g., education, religious training, and health care) unless otherwise specified in the decree (Coogler, 1978). While residence is identified with the custodial parent, visitation is determined within one of three guardianship options:

- An *open arrangement* with regard to visitation permits free access to the child through telephone, writing, or literal time spent with him or her.
- *Limited visitation* arrangements require that the details of when and where the noncustodial parent may have access to the child be specified.
- Due to the lack of desire on the part of the noncustodial parent to visit the child or because of behavior detrimental to the child, the court can order that *no visitation* be granted and may terminate parental rights.

The noncustodial parent has the right and privilege to act in the role of parent as long as he or she fosters a relationship positively affecting the physical, intellectual, emotional, social, and spiritual development of the child. This role is enacted within the context of visitation and decision making on behalf of the child. It should be noted, however, that visitation rights are not absolute and may be denied if the welfare of the child is in jeopardy. The noncustodial parent may participate in decisions pertaining to the child's education and health as decreed by the court.

Joint custody has received considerable attention. A joint custodial arrangement provides for the best interest of the child when parents are free from unresolved marital or personal issues that may complicate the child's development. The basic premise of joint custody involves the sharing of residence, as well as legal and physical responsibility for the child's welfare. While joint custody may appear to be the best alternative for fostering a relationship with both parents, the child may experience a sense of uncertainty and anxiousness as he or she moves back and forth between the two homes (Satten et al., 1980).

References
Coogler, O. J. (1978). *Structured mediation in divorce settlement*. Lexington, MA: Lexington Books.
Gardner, R. A. (1982). *Family evaluation in child custody litigation*. Cresskill, NJ: Creative Therapeutics.
Kelly, J. B. (1983). Mediation & psychotherapy: Distinguishing the differences. *Mediation Quarterly, 1* (1), 33–44.
Marlow, L., & Sauber, S. R. (1990). *Handbook on divorce mediation*. New York: Brunner/Mazel.
Satten, J., Beels, C. C., Boszormenyi-Nagy, I.,Bowen, M., Grunebaum, H. U., Lawrence, M. M., Mendell, D., Nadelson, C., & Paul, N. L. (1980). *New trends in child custody determinations*. Orlando, FL: Harcourt Brace Jovanovich.
Utah Code of Judicial Administration, Rule 4–903.

See also: Conflict, interparental; Divorced families; Reconstituted families.

D. KIM OPENSHAW

D

Deaf children, parenting. Approximately 90% of parents with deaf children have normal hearing and have had little or no experience with deaf people (Meadow-Orlans, 1987). Following the diagnosis, these parents are faced with two difficult realities: (1) the shock of an unexpected disability and (2) the likelihood that they will not share spoken communication with this child. The result may be a sense of loss of control in influencing their child's development. Hearing mothers often experience significant stress following the diagnosis, which may be manifested in counterproductive interaction styles or overprotectiveness. Deaf parents' familiarity with deafness and sign communication makes the experience of rearing a deaf child much less problematic.

Despite available technology, deafness is often not diagnosed until toddlerhood or later. If an infant's early communicative experiences are compromised, other aspects of development (intellectual, social, emotional) may also be at risk. According to Schilling and DeJesus (1993), "A language system is the tool required to work the social development system" (p. 162). Early diagnosis is crucial in assisting both parents and their deaf infants in obtaining needed support and intervention services.

Language and the visual modality. For deaf children, maintaining visual contact is crucial to communication; breaking this contact may terminate the interaction unless there is ongoing tactile contact. (Hearing children can maintain auditory contact and awareness of the partner's continuous presence despite frequently looking away.) Hearing mothers do tend to provide more visual experiences to deaf than to hearing infants during early interactions (Koester, 1995).

However, when the child looks away to explore an object, hearing parents may have more difficulty coordinating their responses to a deaf child. As Swisher (1992) states, "When the child is deaf there is competition between the need to use vision to look at the object and the need to watch signed or lipread comments" (p. 93).

Deaf parents appear to know intuitively how to time their communication with a deaf child to optimize infant attention. By contrast, hearing parents have been found to be more intrusive and didactic, making more overt efforts to guide the infant's role in the interaction.

Social-emotional development. One might expect that deafness would have negative consequences for attachment, due to factors such as poor communication between infant and caregiver, inaccessible vocal feedback, or greater stress in the family. However, Lederberg and Mobley (1990) found no significant differences in attachment classifications of deaf and hearing toddlers. They noted that attachment develops over the first year through numerous caregiver-infant interactions and that many of these involve close physical contact. Therefore, the mother's "body language" or nonvocal responses are often accessible even without vocal reassurances. This may explain the lack of an effect of deafness on the formation of healthy attachments. Deaf children with hearing parents may have less experience developing social problem-solving skills that emerge out of a parent's verbal intervention in child conflict (Meadow-Orlans, 1987).

Educational decisions. Decisions must be made even during infancy about the form of communication to be used with a deaf child. Hearing parents typically choose between the oral approach and some form of visual-gestural (signed) communication. Of course, this decision has implications not just for the deaf child but for the entire family. Studies of deaf children with deaf parents have shown that their acquisition of sign language occurs at about the same rate as spoken language for hearing children. Deaf children exposed primarily to oral language, however, show greater language delays (Schilling & DeJesus, 1993).

The signing proficiency of hearing mothers is also influenced by the number of other adults (family, friends) who learn to sign: Mothers who are not alone in their efforts tend to be more fluent. Even when parental signing is not yet very advanced, the fact that they are using some visual-gestural communication seems to enable their infants to progress to using signs themselves at an appropriate age.

Early intervention programs can be highly effective in enhancing the child's language and social skills, providing needed support for families, and demonstrating models of effective interactions with a deaf child. There is often the added benefit of bringing together parents facing similar dilemmas and decisions and offering valuable support and friendships for both parents and children.

As the deaf child reaches school age, difficult decisions must be made regarding mainstreaming the child or sending the child to a residential school. Deaf adults tend to favor the latter, especially if they themselves were schooled in this way, and often attribute their appreciation of deaf culture to residential school experiences. Hearing parents often describe the decision to send their child to a school for the deaf as very traumatic.

Implications for parents and caregivers. Support from family, friends, and professionals is extremely important for hearing parents with a deaf child, not only during the initial diagnosis but also as the child develops and as new decisions must be made. If visual-gestural communication is chosen, the more people in the child's life who also learn to sign, the better the child's prognosis will be.

Swisher (1992) provides important suggestions for parents or caregivers with a deaf child: Use animated facial expressions and larger signs/gestures than usual, allow sufficient time for the child to look away and explore visually, and wait for the child's attention before communicating.

References

Koester, L. S. (1995). Face-to-face interactions between hearing mothers and their deaf or hearing infants. *Infant Behavior and Development, 18*, 145–153.

Lederberg, A. R., & Mobley, C. E. (1990). The effect of hearing impairment on the quality of attachment and mother-toddler interaction. *Child Development, 62*, 1596–1604.

Meadow-Orlans, K. P. (1987). Understanding deafness: Socialization of children and youth. In P. C. Higgins & J. E. Nash (Eds.), *Understanding deafness socially* (pp. 29–57). Springfield, IL: Thomas.

Schilling, L. S., & DeJesus, E. (1993). Developmental issues in deaf children. *Journal of Pediatric Health Care, 7*, 161–166.

Swisher, M. V. (1992). The role of parents in developing visual turn-taking in their young deaf children. *American Annals of the Deaf, 137* (2), 92–100.

See also: Communication; Deaf parents; Social support, informal.

LYNNE SANFORD KOESTER

Deaf parents. A deaf parent is defined as a parent whose lack of hearing prevents the understanding of speech by the ear alone, with or without using a hearing aid. Although there are different structures of families with deaf parents, they are likely to be composed of both parents being deaf with hearing children. This assumption is based on reported demographics of the deaf population. The Office of Demographic Studies at Gallaudet University estimated that 95% of deaf adults choose deaf spouses, and among this group, 90% of their children are hearing.

Research regarding deaf-parented families and their dynamics, interactions, and child outcome is scarce (Pecora, Despain, & Loveland, 1986). Many people have accepted the common supposition that deaf adults are inferior as parents. Much of the information that is available regarding deaf parents and their relationships with their children is anecdotal or consists of retrospective data gathered from children of deaf adults. Little research has been done that solicits deaf adults' own views and experiences of their parenting role (Jones, Strom, & Daniels, 1989).

For the most part, research involving deaf-parented families can be divided into three themes: (1) the impact of deaf parenting on hearing children's speech and language development; (2) the parenting effectiveness of deaf parents; and (3) deaf parent–hearing children interactions. First, most research on the impact of deaf parents on child outcomes has involved speech and language develop ment of hearing children. Studies often produce contradictory findings due to different methodological approaches and theoretical frameworks guiding the research. However, in general, research has shown that most hearing children of deaf parents experience normal language and speech development (Hoffmeister, 1985). Speech development may be delayed in some children, but manual language or sign language used by the parent positively affects early language and cognitive development. Any delay or deficiency in speech that does exist fades away as these children's cognitive development is normal and often exceeds their language development in the early years. As research has evolved and the negative stereotypes regarding deafness and sign language are being removed, researchers and practitioners emphasize the high quality of interaction. Although the means of communication (oral communication versus manual communication) is different between deaf parents and hearing children, this quality may be just as important for language acquisition as "normal" language exposure (Schiff & Ventry, 1976).

In general, the results of studies using instruments intended for a general audience support a positive view of deaf parents' adaptation to the parenting role, including their effectiveness. However, some have questioned whether these instruments are relative to the experiences of deaf parents, such as communication-related problems in families with deaf parents. Other issues that need to be considered are deaf parents' feelings of competency in terms of raising hearing children and their feelings toward the hearing population. These feelings might be influenced by the positive or negative parenting models they experienced growing up in a hearing family and hearing society (Hoffmeister, 1985). In addition, these feelings and experiences might influence deaf parents' reactions to having hearing children as well as their parental effectiveness.

In studies that have compared family interactions of deaf parents–hearing children and hearing parents–hearing children, few significant differences have been found. However, one common difference that is often cited involves the issue of hearing children interpreting for their deaf parents. Hearing children express negative feelings regarding interpretation including having insufficient skills and knowledge to interpret in many situations, feeling uncomfortable in some situations, and feeling overburdened. Children have also expressed positive feelings that include knowing their parents better than friends do with hearing parents and having experiences that have better prepared them for adulthood. Researchers suggest that deaf parents need to be aware of this unique issue and how their children feel and cope with it. The most recent studies (Jones & Dumas, 1996; Rienzi, 1990) have observed everyday interactions between deaf parents and their hearing children and have compared these data with observations of hearing parents and their hearing children. Findings demonstrate that hearing children of deaf parents have greater influence in decision making, that there is little difference in communication patterns between the two groups of families, that deaf fathers seem to be more authoritarian, and that deaf parents did not dominate decision making as much as hearing parents. In general, results demonstrate the growing evidence that parent-child interactions in deaf- and hearing-parented families are more similar than different.

Future research needs to adopt cultural and ecological perspectives that consider the unique context of deafness and the meaning that parenting has in the deaf community. Differences and challenges that are evident need to be viewed as cultural contrasts and not problematic patterns of parent-child interactions. Current as well as future work will help in the development of parenting programs for deaf adults. Such parenting programs are currently scarce and are mostly limited to informal support groups and family members among the deaf community.

References

Hoffmeister, R. J. (1985). Families with deaf parents: A functional perspective. In S. K. Thurman (Ed.), *Children of handicapped parents: Research and clinical perspectives* (pp. 111–130). Orlando, FL: Academic Press.

Jones, E. G., & Dumas, R. E. (1996). Deaf and hearing parents' interactions with eldest hearing children. *American Annals of the Deaf, 141*, 278–283.

Jones, E., Strom, R., & Daniels, S. (1989). Evaluating the success of deaf parents. *American Annals of the Deaf, 134*, 312–316.

Pecora, P. J., Despain, C. L., & Loveland, E. J. (1986). Adult children of deaf parents: A psychosocial perspective. *Social Casework, 67*, 12–19.

Rienzi, B. M. (1990). Influence and adaptability in families with deaf parents and hearing children. *American Annals of the Deaf, 135*, 402–408.

Schiff, N., & Ventry, I. (1976). Communication problems in hearing children of deaf parents. *Journal of Speech and Hearing Disorders, 40*, 348–356.

See also: Communication; Deaf children, parenting.

BYRAN B. KORTH

Death, understanding of. Talking about death is uncomfortable. Talking to children about death and dying is an upsetting task that may make many parents anxious. Struggling to understand death is an important part of appreciating and understanding life. No one can escape the reality of the final moment in life.

Explaining death. Children are quite perceptive. They become aware when routines are changed. Children less than 1 year of age can recognize changes in an individual's behavior and attitude. They will adapt their behavior according to changes in the environment in which they live.

Questions raised by a child concerning death will vary depending not only on the age of the child but also on the child's concerns and fears. Children may be concerned about what happens to the body when death occurs. They may be confused as to where the body goes after death and why the person appears to be sleeping. Why do we have to die? Does it hurt to die? When explaining death to children, parents should be truthful, factual, and gentle with direct and consistent explanations. The real meaning of children's questions should be understood, and the reply should be clear and direct to prevent misunderstanding.

Fear of the unknown is common to all ages. Fear of the unknown often manifests itself to children who may think they may be the next to die (Dickinson, 1992). Although dying is a natural part of living, children must be reassured that being fearful of death is not a healthy way to live. Other childhood fears may include thoughts such as the dead person will return through nightmares, the dead person is just sleeping and will wake up in the coffin, or the sadness will last forever. Children often fear that life will never be the same. Direct communication can help alleviate children's fears.

Humans have an innate way of self-healing (Smith, 1991). At the onset of any physical damage such as a cut or scrape, the body attempts to repair damage. The mind will also strive for psychological healing when afflicted by sadness, grief, stress, or depression. Children, unlike most adults who have been socialized to doubt their own abilities, are wonderful self-healers. In supportive environments children will ask the necessary questions and process the answers in ways that will facilitate their emotional healing. Children seem to have an inner wisdom about grief and surrounding emotions and an innate ability to direct the learning process (Smith, 1991).

Communication between parent and child. When discussing death with children, adult discomfort originates partly from how society views death and partly because adults feel unprepared to talk about death (Schaefer, 1988). In Western society, individuals typically have a strong association of death with fear and avoid the subject as a topic of conversation. Consequently, most children view death as a taboo topic and find little emotional comfort in the pretense surrounding death.

Opportunities to communicate about the death process will inevitably present themselves as teachable moments. A family pet or a dead animal on the roadside can provide avenues for discussions about dying. Children's books and movies may include themes of death. Children know about death by watching television or hearing about natural disasters and war. Children are naturally curious about death. Although their level of curiosity varies, most children want clear, honest answers to their questions.

First experiences with death. Early childhood memories of death can have an impact on how children handle death and dying issues in the future (Dickinson, 1992). If children remember the death of an important person or even a family pet as a time when feelings were openly expressed and grief was managed positively, then they will find subsequent pain more manageable.

Children do remember details and feelings surrounding significant events. Being punished for crying over a loss may affect the way children respond to loss as adults. Such discouragement distorts what could be a natural healing process. Children must be given opportunities to express grief in their own way and work through loss according to their own emotional schedule.

Reactions to death. Knowing how children perceive death and what feelings they may have will help parents react and respond more positively toward them. Children do experience fear, anger, confusion, sadness, and guilt when dealing with a loss through death. Some children will feel abandoned. Fear of the unknown translates to be a child's fundamental source of anxiety.

Piaget suggests that children between the ages of 3 and 6 see death as reversible (Santrock, 1996). The person will return or wake up from sleeping. Children ages 6 to 9 years begin to understand death as final. Death is unavoidable and you do not return. Older children ages 9 to 12 move toward the grieving process, much like adults do. They are more aware of the emotional impact death has on them and consequently may need more emotional support. Young children faced with the trauma of their own death may accelerate through these stages. Some preschoolers, for example, may give their toys away or try to reassure their parents. Confronting the realities of death and dying is best done in an atmosphere of open communication and positive healing.

References

Dickinson, G. (1992). First childhood death experiences. *Omega, 25* (3), 169–182.
Santrock, J. W. (1996). *Life-span development* (5th. ed., p. 601). Madison, WI: Brown & Benchmark Publishers.
Schaefer, D. (1988). *Communication among children, parents, and funeral directors. Loss, grief, and care.* Binghamton, NY: Haworth Press.
Smith, I. (1991). Preschool children "play" out their grief. In *Death studies.* Washington, DC: Taylor & Francis.

See also: Death of a child; Death of a parent.

CHRISTINE IRISH MOTLEY

Death of a child. Infectious diseases were the scourge of childhood and the primary cause of parental and sibling bereavement at the turn of the century. Over half of all deaths 100 years ago in the United States were of persons 14 years of age and younger. Due to medical breakthroughs and public health advances, childhood mortality rates have dropped dramatically in developed countries during the twentieth century. At least 18 countries today have lower infant mortality rates than does the United States.

When a child dies, parents and siblings experience pronounced distress and trauma. Nothing equals the long-lasting, wrenching pain parents experience at the death of their child, whether an infant or an adult. Often left unnoticed is the grief of the surviving brothers and sisters.

Many persons think grief occurs in stages. Kubler-Ross's (1969) book *On Death and Dying* captured the imagination of much of American society, and many have accepted her description of five stages of emotional responses to terminal illness as a sure understanding of the experience grief elicits. Research has not confirmed these five stages. The stages are best considered helpful rules of thumb rather than identifiers of a universal, invariant, and irreversible sequence of emotions associated with death.

Bereavement influences physiological, emotional, cognitive, behavioral, social, and spiritual responses. For a year or more following a death, bereaved individuals become vulnerable to infection due to reduced lymphocyte production. Trouble getting to sleep or staying asleep is typical in the acute stages of grief; many bereaved persons dream about the person who died. Loss of appetite is not uncommon, particularly in the first few weeks and months following a death.

Emotional responses associated with grief include anger, fear, confusion, loneliness, and depression. The intensity and the duration of feelings that accompany grief not only surprise the bereaved but dismay them, not infrequently making them wonder if they are going crazy. They had thought grief takes less time and is less intense.

Bereaved individuals find concentrating difficult and may be overwhelmed with intrusive thoughts and images of the person who died. Common, ordinary tasks may prove daunting for awhile. Schoolwork will likely suffer.

Just being around other persons may be a painful chore. Both defiance of adults and withdrawal into oneself may occur. Bereaved persons may lash out unpredictably in anger and then feel shame for making an unwarranted attack on an innocent party.

Questions about the meaning of human existence often emerge as bereaved persons grapple with the absurdity of a child's death. Coping with the spiritual manifestations of grief can result in increased empathy and skill in helping others in sorrow and in a transformed understanding of reality.

Family issues emerge and family stability is sorely challenged when a child dies. Overwhelmed with unremitting anguish, parents very likely will be unavailable to comfort one another or to help their grieving children. Fearful that their family will never recover from the pain it feels, children may camouflage their feelings in the hopes of restoring family cheer and security. Parents may misinterpret these reactions as either signs their children are not troubled or signs that they are insensitive.

Individuals seldom experience grief the same as others in their family. Parents may grieve differently than each other and differently than their children. Mothers may be more likely to desire open, public expression of their feelings; fathers may be more likely to pursue private, introspective grief work and think their overwhelming duty is to maintain an atmosphere of calm in a storm of emotion. Such discrepant coping styles may lead to misunderstandings and lead the wife to accuse her husband of being uncaring. Further problems can emerge when grief resolution develops more quickly for some family members than for others; dyssynchrony in grief trajectories can lead to misunderstandings and estrangement.

Parents who participate in self-help and social support groups for the bereaved report reactions that run counter to accepted theories of grief resolution. Rather than detaching emotionally from the child who died, many parents report that they have maintained an ongoing bond with the child (Klass, Silverman, & Nickman, 1996). These parental responses require us to rethink our views of what normal bereavement entails (Klass, 1988). Such rethinking has led Dennis Klass to examine the spiritual transformation that occurs in bereaved parents as they gain solace and resolution in their grief. Klass has noted that many bereaved parents report a sense of communion with the deceased child and a sense of the child's continuing presence in their lives (see Klass, Silverman, & Nickman, 1996). Seldom will they mention these experiences to outsiders because others consider such reports very strange if not pathological. Research into sibling bereavement has begun uncovering the same report of ongoing attachment.

A family climate of cohesion and open communication promotes healing in the aftermath of a child's death. Balk (1981) noted that adolescents did better over time in families marked by emotional closeness and intimate conversation prior to a child's death; however, these adolescents reported an enduring sense of sadness and loneliness surrounding the death. Adolescents in families marked by emotional distance and detached conversation before a child's death reported enduring senses of anger, confusion, and fear. The various forms of support afforded in a family with social, spiritual, cultural, and recreational outlets assist family members, both parents and children, to reach clearer senses of grief resolution.

References

Balk, D. E. (1981). *Sibling death during adolescence: Self concept and bereavement reactions*. Unpublished doctoral dissertation, University of Illinois, Champaign.

Klass, D. (1988). *Parental grief: Solace and resolution*. New York: Springer Publishing Company.

Klass, D., Silverman, P. R., & Nickman, S. L. (Eds.). (1996). *Continuing bonds: New understandings of grief*. Washington, DC: Taylor & Francis.

Kubler-Ross, E. (1969). *On death and dying*. New York: Macmillan.

See also: Death of a parent; Social support, informal.

DAVID E. BALK

Death of a parent. In developed countries, parents expect their children will outlive them. Adult children may take a parent's death very hard, and in the case of some men, the death of their mothers proves most problematic. However, while grief over a parent's death will often be distressing, when the parent dies after a full life there seems less difficulty for adult children to reach resolution to their mourning. Much more problematic for grief resolution and for ongoing development are parental deaths that occurred during the formative years of childhood, adolescence, and young adulthood.

Children with preoperational cognitive skills cannot understand the finality, causality, or universality of death. For 5-year-olds, the death of a parent presents experiences very difficult to assimilate; they may engage in magical thinking about their parent's return and may think they caused the death by getting angry. Older children, adolescents, and adults recognize the finality, causality, and universality of death.

Psychoanalysts have asserted that inability to differentiate self from others prevents children and even adolescents from mourning. Observations, however, indicate that limitations in cognitive development prevent neither young children nor adolescents from grieving. Children and adolescents do engage in grief work, do feel the distress bereavement entails, and do face debilitating consequences should mourning go awry. Descriptions of typical bereavement reactions are given in the entry "Death of a child."

What risks does a youth face following the death of a parent? Some researchers maintained that outcomes were troubling in the first few years after a death and into adulthood; some of these troubling effects involved submissiveness to others, emotional disturbance, sex-role difficulties, and academic or cognitive problems. The sense of financial security a father provided may become a matter of grave concern, as evidenced in the concern of a teenage son over financial matters after his father died.

Silverman and Worden (1992), who completed a carefully designed longitudinal study of children following parental death, concluded that emergent problems depended on how "the surviving parent responds to the child, the availability of social support, and subsequent life circumstances" (p. 93). Evidence indicates that women whose adult life manifested ongoing problems coping with the death of a parent during adolescence had childhoods marked by adjustment problems; one of their problems following the death had been the emotional inaccessibility of their surviving parent.

In short, coping successfully or poorly with parental death cannot be predicted by the death alone and involves an intricate set of influences, among them:

- personal and background factors such as age, self-esteem, temperament, and previous history of coping with loss
- events surrounding the death, such as its sudden or its anticipated nature
- the type of the relationship that existed with the parent who died
- the adaptive tasks the bereaved youth enacts to cope with the crisis of the parent's death
- the quality of support available to the child, either in the family and/or in other social niches

Professionals working with bereaved youth can seek an answer to the question, How did this person cope before his/her parent died? Dramatic differences from behavior prior to the death can signal important unmet needs that the youth is not expressing in words.

In the immediate weeks and months after a death, grieving spouses seldom have the emotional and spiritual strength to help their children cope. Everyone in the home can feel the anguish of everyone else but feel isolated from the other members of the family and fearful of causing anyone more distress. Hopefully, the attachment bonds between the surviving parent and the children will win out and open communication will occur about the death and about how everyone feels.

Attachment theory provides a salient framework for understanding grief reactions following a parent's death. Young children often use parental contact as anchor points to understand their lives. Parents, for example, read them stories, drive them to school, feed them, put them to bed, dress them. The quality of the attachment the child felt to the parent will greatly influence responses to the death.

Adolescents' and young adults' reactions to parental death are also influenced by the attachment bonds formed prior to the death. Surviving parents report that children revisit their attachment to their deceased parent when important milestones occur (e.g., graduation, marriage, giving birth).

Recent research has emphasized that bereaved youth use several strategies to maintain ongoing attachments to deceased parents (Klass, Silverman, & Nickman, 1996). In her study of college females' reactions to fathers' deaths, Tyson-Rawson (1996) said the majority of the young women reported an ongoing attachment to their fathers; the students who showed a clearer sense of grief resolution were the ones who welcomed the continuing presence of their fathers.

One area to which parents and professionals can pay special attention is the stigma children report when others learn about their parent's death. Ironically, given the growth in the number of children in single-parent homes due to divorce, the stigma of parental death may be lessened. However, whereas bereaved youth may "canonize" a deceased parent, children from divorced homes have been known to "demonize" a parent blamed for the divorce.

References
Corr, C. A., & Balk, D. E. (Eds.). (1996). *Handbook of adolescent death and bereavement.* New York: Springer Publishing Company.
Corr, C. A., & Corr, D. M. (Eds.). (1996). *Handbook of childhood death and bereavement.* New York: Springer Publishing Company.
Klass, D., Silverman, P. R., & Nickman, S. L. (Eds.). (1996). *Continuing bonds: New understandings of grief.* Washington, DC: Taylor & Francis.
Silverman, P. R., & Worden, J. W. (1992). Children and parental death. *American Journal of Orthopsychiatry, 62,* 93–104.
Tyson-Rawson, K. J. (1996). Relationship and heritage: Manifestations of ongoing attachment following father death. In D. Klass, P. R. Silverman, & S. L. Nickman (Eds.), *Continuing bonds: New understandings of grief* (pp. 125–145). Washington, DC: Taylor & Francis.

See also: Attachment, secure; Death understanding of; Death of a child; Social support, informal.

DAVID E. BALK

Delinquency, juvenile. *Juvenile* refers to a person *under* the age established by a state to determine when someone is no longer subject to original juvenile court jurisdiction for criminal misconduct. Juvenile delinquency is any action by someone designated a juvenile (nonadult) that brings that individual to the attention of the juvenile court (Kratcoski & Kratcoski, 1996). The state age limit ranges from 15 to 19 years of age, with 17 years of age for a majority of states.

Juveniles (as defined by the individual's state of residence) are subject to arrest for two broad types of offenses: felony and status. *Felony* offenses are criminal behaviors that are unlawful for adults as well (e.g., murder, arson, rape, robbery, etc.). *Status* offenses are inappropriate behaviors applicable only to juveniles (e.g., truancy, incorrigibility, running away from home, alcohol consumption, etc.). The juvenile code in a majority of states differentiates between delinquent (felony) and status offenses, using such categories for the latter as Minors in Need of Supervision (MINS). Seven states make no differentiation between status and delinquent offenses. There is considerable debate now regarding the proper handling of status offenders within the juvenile justice system (Kratcoski & Kratcoski, 1996). Some would remove status offenders from juvenile court jurisdiction. Others would maintain court involvement while excluding them from secure detention.

All states allow juveniles to be tried in criminal courts under certain circumstances as established by the Supreme Court in 1966:

- The seriousness of the alleged offense and the need to protect the community

- Whether the alleged offense was committed in an aggressive, violent, premeditated, or willful manner
- Whether the alleged offense was against persons or against property, greater weight being given to offenses against person, especially if personal injury resulted
- The prosecutive merit of the complaint (that is the likelihood of conviction)
- Whether the juvenile's associates in the alleged offense are adults who will be charged with crimes in the adult court
- The sophistication and maturity of the juvenile as determined by consideration of his or her home, environmental situation, emotional attitude, and pattern of living
- The record and previous history of the juvenile (Kratcoski & Kratcoski, 1996)

A juvenile's case can be transferred to criminal court for trial in one of three ways—judicial waver, prosecutorial descretion, or statutory exclusion from juvenile court jurisdiction. In any State, one, two, or all three transfer mechanisms may be in place (Sickmund, 1994).

In 1993, the Office of Juvenile Justice and Delinquency Prevention (OJJDP) reported an increase in the serious and violent crime rate among juveniles that began during the mid-1980s (Office of Juvenile Justice and Delinquency Prevention [OJJDP], 1993). Juvenile arrests for violent crimes increased 57% from 1983 to 1992. The number of juvenile arrests for murder increased by 128% during this period. In 1998, juvenile arrests accounted for less than 8% of all murder arrests. By 1992, juveniles accounted for 15% (Steiner, 1994). Youth gangs became more violent and economically self-sustaining by providing financial incentives and rewards for their members. A small proportion of offenders commits most of the serious and violent juvenile crimes. Juveniles with five or more police contacts comprise about 18% of delinquents but are responsible for about two thirds of all violent offenses (OJJDP, 1993). Juveniles are frequently the victims of violent juvenile offenders since the rate of juvenile victimization for violent offenses also increased.

In its review of research, the OJJDP (1993) found six behavioral factors that contribute to serious, violent, and chronic juvenile crimes. These include delinquent peer groups, poor school performance, high-crime neighborhoods, weak family attachments, lack of consistent discipline, and physical or sexual abuse. A dysfunctional relationship with parents clearly contributes to delinquency in three of these six factors.

Weak family relationships. In their summary of the research on family influences on delinquency, Wright & Wright (1994) found that children raised in supportive, affectionate, and accepting homes are less likely to become deviant. Rejection by parents puts children at a significant and clear risk for delinquency and drug abuse (Huizinga, Loeber, & Thornberry, 1994). Children who have little or no sense of connection to supportive parents are not likely to internalize a prosocial morality or develop a healthy conscience. This makes them vulnerable to peer pressure.

Inconsistent and inadequate discipline that may be severe and rigid. The deterioration of the parent's authority begins when parents react during the preschool years in such a way to call attention and encourage the child's aggressive behavior. These negative behaviors may bring the child into conflict with school authorities, whose reaction may be to strengthen the child's antisocial self-image. Hirschi (1969) found that the incidence of delinquency increased with the number of hours mothers were employed outside of the home, possibly due to a lack of supervision. Poor parental monitoring and supervision, particularly during middle childhood, may then influence children to become involved with antisocial peers just before the onset of adolescence.

Physical, emotional, and/or sexual abuse. Exposure to violence in the form of witnessing marital discord or of being abused increases the risk of juvenile delinquency. Conflict between parents may increase hostility and provide a poor model for resolving interpersonal problems. A dangerous family environment fosters what Fleischer (quoted in Wright and Wright, 1994, p. 15) calls a "defensive world view." This paradigm is characterized by (1) a feeling of vulnerability and a need to protect oneself; (2) a belief that no one can be trusted; (3) a need to maintain social distance; (4) a willingness to use violence and intimidation to control others; (5) an attraction to others with similar beliefs; (6) an expectation that no one will come to their aid. Being abused or neglected as a child increases the risk of arrest as a juvenile by 53% (Widom, 1992).

The relationship between these three parent-child relationship factors is complex. Additional influences like child temperament and community environment interact with them in ways to increase the risk of delinquency. Most children who are abused, whose families break up, or who experience inconsistencies in discipline do not turn to juvenile delinquency. These factors in the parent-child relationship may put a child at risk for delinquency but do not fully explain why a child engages in this type of behavior.

Children are not passive recipients of parental treatment. Delinquent behavior can create significant stress within a family and influence parental rejection of the child. Biological and genetic factors can make a child predisposed toward aggressive, impulsive, and antisocial behavior. Parents may find themselves rejecting a child who is difficult to manage or avoiding setting limits to purchase a little peace in the home. The result can set into motion an increasing spiral of mutual negation and hostility. Without firm and supportive outside intervention, the relationship may deteriorate. Children who are casualties in this failure of socialization may choose a lifestyle that will bring them into contact with judicial authority.

References

Hirschi, T. (1969). *Causes of delinquency*. Berkeley: University of California Press.

Huizinga, D. H., Loeber, R., & Thornberry, T. P. (1994). *Urban delinquency and substance abuse: Research summary*. Washington, DC: Office Of Juvenile Justice and Delinquency Prevention.

Kratcoski, P. C., & Kratcoksi, L. D. (1996). *Juvenile delinquency*. Upper Saddle River, NJ: Prentice Hall.

Office of Juvenile Justice and Delinquency Prevention. (1993). *Comprehensive strategy for serious, violent, and chronic juvenile offenders: Program summary*. Washington, DC: Author.

Sickmund, M. (1994). *How juveniles get to criminal court*. Washington, DC: Office Of Juvenile Justice and Delinquency Prevention.

Steiner, P. (1994) *Delinquency prevention*. Washington, DC: Office Of Juvenile Justice and Delinquency Prevention.

Widom, C. S. (1992). *The cycle of violence: Research in brief.* Washington, DC: National Institute of Justice.

Wright, K. N., & Wright, K. E. (1994). *Family life, delinquency, and crime: A policy-maker's guide.* Washington, DC: Office Of Juvenile Justice and Delinquency Prevention.

See also: Abuse, child; Misbehavior; Runaway children; Throwaway children.

CHARLES A. SMITH

Depression, postpartum. Postpartum depression is defined as a moderate to severe mood disturbance that is similar to an untreated or outpatient clinical depressive episode. It occurs within 4 to 12 weeks postpartum and is most likely to remit by 6 months postpartum but can last for up to 1 year. When standardized assessments and diagnostic systems are used, prevalence estimates range from 10% to 15%. However, when self-report assessments of depressive symptoms are used, up to 30% of women report at least mild depressive symptom levels during the postpartum period (Whiffen, 1992).

Since depressive symptoms can interfere with daily functioning, including a mother's ability to interact effectively with her child, it is reasonable to expect that early child development would be adversely affected when a mother is depressed. Cross-sectional research has established that mothers experiencing depressive symptoms during the postpartum period and their infants are behaviorally and emotionally distinguishable from nondepressed dyads (Whiffen, 1992). Mothers reporting moderate to high levels of depressive symptoms interact with their babies less and are less positive and less contingently responsive toward their babies than are mothers who report few depressive symptoms. Compared with infants of nondepressed mothers, infants of depressed mothers show fewer positive and more negative facial expressions, make fewer vocalizations, play less, and are more fussy and tense (e.g., Field et al., 1985). Longitudinal studies investigating the association between early maternal depressive symptoms and early child behavioral adjustment have found less direct effects of postpartum depression or depressive symptoms once concurrent levels of maternal depressive symptoms were accounted for (Carro et al., 1993; Phillips & O'Hara, 1991). Postpartum depression is often associated with a history of depression as well as future depressive episodes that are not necessarily linked to the birth of a child (Phillips & O'Hara, 1991; Whiffen, 1992).

It is widely assumed that postpartum depression is uniquely a female experience, most likely hormonal in nature (Whiffen, 1992). However, the prevalence, symptoms, course, and duration of postpartum depression as compared to general depression does not support this conclusion, and the distinction between postpartum and nonpostpartum depression may have little utility (Whiffen, 1992). Although the rate of depression appears elevated in the postpartum period (13% as opposed to 6% in community samples), severity of symptoms has been the only basis in most studies for the distinction between postpartum and nonpostpartum depression, with postpartum depression being less severe (Whiffen, 1992). Moreover, women with a psychiatric history of depression are more likely to develop postpartum depressive symptoms as compared to women without a history of depression. Finally, postpartum depression shares etiological features with nonpostpartum depression including marital discord, low social support, and life stress. Whiffen (1992) argued that postpartum depression may occur due to difficulty adjusting to the major life event of having a child, an event that requires adapting to the role of parent and changes in one's relationships with a partner. Therefore, depressive symptoms may occur during this period, just as they might occur after any other major life event.

The evidence that depressive symptoms during the postpartum period are not a unique response of new mothers suggests that depressive symptoms are at least in part a reaction to the stress of becoming a parent. Therefore, it is plausible that fathers as well as mothers may experience depressive symptoms during this period. Recently, paternal postpartum depression has been studied as an additional risk factor for child maladjustment (Carro et al., 1993). In this study, 13% of fathers experienced mild to moderate depressive symptoms during the first month postpartum. Furthermore, depressive symptoms in fathers during the first month postpartum posed a risk for later child behavioral and emotional outcomes via their impact on mothers' subsequent depressive symptoms. In addition, mothers' and fathers' depressive symptoms interacted to predict higher levels of subsequent child internalizing problems. These data provide the first evidence indicating that fathers' as well as mothers' depressive symptoms during the postpartum period are predictors of later child behavior problems. Thus, until recently the relationship between fatherhood and psychological adjustment may have been overlooked and deserves future research attention, especially given the potential impact on child development (Phares & Compas, 1992).

The implication for prevention and research of postpartum depression and, ultimately, poor child developmental outcomes is the importance of including both husbands and wives in future studies of the emergence of postpartum depressive symptoms. With this in mind, Carro (1997) conducted a study of the emergence of parents' depressive symptoms during the postpartum period. Results indicated postpartum depressive symptoms were marked early on by individuals' and spouses' prepartum marital distress, maladaptive avoidant coping, and depressive symptoms. These findings supported the importance of including couples in research on postpartum depression as well as suggest that treatment and prevention efforts address intrapersonal as well as interpersonal factors.

References
Carro, M.G. (1997). *Depressive symptoms during the pre- and postpartum: Interpersonal models for wives and husbands*. Unpublished doctoral dissertation, University of Vermont, Burlington.
Carro, M. G., Grant, K. E., Gotlib, I. H., & Compas, B. E. (1993). Postpartum depression and child development: An investigation of mothers and fathers as sources of risk and resilience. *Development and Psychopathology, 5,* 567-579.
Field, T. M., Sandberg, D., Garcia, R., Vega-Lahr, N., Goldstein, S., & Guy, L. (1985). Pregnancy problems, postpartum depression, and early mother-infant interactions. *Developmental Psychology, 21,* 1152–1156.
Phares, V., & Compas, B. E. (1992). The role of fathers in child and adolescent psychopathology: Make room for daddy. *Psychological Bulletin, 111,* 387–412.

Phillips, L. C., & O'Hara, M. W. (1991). Prospective study of postpartum depression: 4½-year follow-up of women and children. *Journal of Abnormal Psychology, 100*, 151–155.

Whiffen, V. E. (1992). Is postpartum depression a distinct diagnosis? *Clinical Psychology Review, 12*, 485–508.

See also: Attachment, secure; Depression in parents; Stress.

MICHELLE G. CARRO, IAN H. GOTLIB & BRUCE E. COMPAS

Depression in children. The term *depression*, as used by mental health professionals, refers to a clinical syndrome or cluster of symptoms, with the central feature of pervasive feelings of sadness, irritability, or lack of pleasure. Several other symptoms must also be present, such as suicidal ideation, fatigue, disturbances in sleep or appetite, poor concentration, excessive guilt, feelings of worthlessness or low self-esteem, hopelessness, or social withdrawal.

Four major subtypes of depression have generally been recognized in children: *Manic Depression, or Bipolar Disorder*; *Major Depressive Disorder*; *Dysthymic Disorder*; and *Adjustment Disorder with Depressed Mood* (American Psychiatric Association, 1994). Although Bipolar Disorders often include episodes of major depression and are considered affective disorders like depression, their course and treatment differ from those of major depression and dysthymia, which are referred to as unipolar depressions. Adjustment Disorder with Depressed Mood is an episode involving a reaction of sadness to a stressor that will spontaneously resolve itself. Research with children and adults indicates that Adjustment Disorders are not serious psychiatric disorders and do not have the same course and outcome associated with major depression and dysthymia (Kovacs et al., 1984). Because of the significant differences between unipolar depression and Bipolar and Adjustment Disorders, the latter two disorders will not be discussed in this entry.

Recent research indicates that approximately 20%, or one in five children, will have an episode of depression by the age of 18 years (Lewinsohn et al., 1993). The prevalence of depression, or number of juveniles with the disorder at any one time, changes with age, with rates increasing during adolescence. The prevalence of major depression in preadolescent children has been estimated at less than 3%, with the prevalence of dysthymia possibly being a little higher (Fleming & Offord, 1990). During adolescence, prevalence increases to approximately 3% (Lewinsohn et al., 1993), although here again estimates vary. Rates of depression for males and females also change with adolescence. Prior to adolescence, the rates for girls and boys are similar, but approximately twice the number of adolescent girls as boys will develop the disorder.

From a clinician's perspective, three issues related to depression are of particular interest: risk, identification or diagnosis, and treatment. Parents can play a role in each of these areas.

Risk factors. Although there are no substantiated causes of depression, a number of theories have been proposed. These include biological theories of genetic transmission or neurotransmitter imbalances and environmental or individual factors such as having a depressed parent, life stressors, cognitive style, or social skill deficits. Most experts agree, however, that depression generally results from an interaction of multiple factors (Kazdin, 1990).

Parents can directly or indirectly affect many of these factors. Parents who themselves suffer from depression may have children who are vulnerable to the disorder. In such cases, genetic or environmental factors, or some combination of the two, transmit vulnerability. Environmental factors might include parents modeling depressed emotions or a negative coping style or being less available and responsive to their children.

Life stressors, such as multiple changes in caretakers or residences, parent conflict and divorce, and loss of a family member, may provoke a depressive episode in vulnerable children. Although parents often cannot prevent such events, they can help children cope with stresses by providing additional support during major transitions or losses or seeking professional help at an early stage. Parents who foster negative self-esteem, poor problem-solving skills, self-blaming attributions of failure, and external attributions for success may place their children at greater risk for developing depression.

Identification of depression in children. Parents are frequently the first to identify problems in their children. Compared to hyperactivity, aggressiveness, or other "externalizing" problems, however, depression in children is typically slow to be recognized by parents because many symptoms are internal to the child, such as sad mood or low self-esteem. Often, parents initially seek help because of behavior problems that are secondary to the irritability frequently seen in depressed children. Thus, professionals may not see a depressed child until after the problem has been occurring for a significant period of time.

Treatment of depression in children. Parents generally are the initial "gate-keepers" for access to children's treatment services, and their abilities to negotiate health care services determine the quality of services received. Thus, professionals involved with children should help educate parents regarding best practices for the treatment of depression. Currently, the research suggests that psychotherapy is the treatment of choice for most depressed children and adolescents, with little evidence supporting the use of antidepressants in these age groups (Ambrosini et al., 1993). Furthermore, once a child has been diagnosed as depressed and is in treatment, consistent compliance with treatment is primarily the responsibility of parents. Thus, parents need to be motivated to bring their children to appointments and comply with clinician recommendations. Too often, parents are left out of the "therapeutic loop" after the initial diagnosis and so are uninvolved in their children's treatment and unmotivated to fully support it. Although it is the responsibility of clinicians to involve parents and provide regular feedback, as "educated consumers" of mental health services, parents should also expect and request such services.

References

Ambrosini, P. J., Bianchi, M. D., Rabinovich, H., & Elia, J. (1993). Antidepressant treatments in children and adolescents: I. Affective Disorders. *Journal of the American Academy of Child and Adolescent Psychiatry, 32*, 1–6.

American Psychiatric Association. (1994). *Diagnostic and statistical manual of mental disorders* (4th ed.). Washington, DC: Author.

Fleming, J. E., & Offord, D. R. (1990). Epidemiology of childhood depressive disorders: A critical review. *Journal of the American Academy of Child and Adolescent Psychiatry, 29*, 571–580.

Kazdin, A. E. (1990). Childhood depression. *Journal of Child Psychology and Psychiatry, 31*, 121–160.

Kovacs, M., Feinberg, T. L., Crouse-Novak, M. A., Paulaskas, S.L., & Finkelstein, R. (1984). Depressive disorders in childhood: I. A longitudinal prospective study of characteristics and recovery. *Archives of General Psychiatry, 41*, 643–649.

Lewinsohn, P.M., Hops, H., Roberts, R. E., Seeley, J. R., & Andrews, J.A. (1993). Adolescent psychopathology: I. Prevalence and incidence of depression and other DSM-III-R disorders in high school students. *Journal of Abnormal Psychology, 102*, 133–144.

See also: Attachment, secure; Divorced families; Resiliency in children.

ANDREW G. RENOUF

Depression in parents. Much of what we know regarding depression in parents is unfortunately based on research with mothers only. Thus, there is relatively little information on depression in fathers, with inconclusive research findings regarding the impact of paternal depression on children. Intuitively, one might assume that maternal depression has a greater impact on parenting and children than paternal depression, because mothers are most commonly the primary caretaker. The research indicates, however, that depression in one parent is associated with marital conflict and other family stressors, factors that may compromise both spouses' abilities to parent. It is likely therefore, that depression in either parent has a negative effect on children, with the specific differences in effect of maternal versus paternal depression still to be determined by future research.

At any one time, approximately 8% of mothers have a clinical depression and in the first few months after the birth of a child, this number may be as high as 15%. Rates among fathers, although undetermined, are likely to be lower than those found in mothers because of the generally lower rates in men compared to women and because men do not experience the same postpartum hormonal changes and stressors as women. When one considers both maternal and paternal depression, however, it is likely that more than 1 in every 10 families is affected. This may be a conservative estimate, as investigators in one study found 47% of parents in a randomly selected sample of families belonging to a health maintenance program had a history of major depression or dysthymic disorder (Beardslee et al., 1993). In either case, a significant number of children are likely to be exposed to depression in a parent, making this a serious public health issue because of its impact on parenting and child adjustment. Because of the risk posed to children by parental depression, its identification and effective treatment are essential.

Parenting. Parenting, particularly of young children, requires sustained, effortful behavior; setting aside one's own needs; heightened emotional tone; and tolerance for negative interactions and behaviors. Given the decreased motivation, poor problem-solving skills, flat or depressed affect, and irritability associated with depression, it is not surprising that parenting should be compromised in depressed women (Downey & Coyne, 1990). Depressed mothers, compared to nondepressed mothers, have been shown to have lower rates of behavior and positive affect and to respond more slowly, less consistently, and less contingently to their children's behaviors. Research also indicates that depressed mothers are less able than nondepressed mothers to adaptively resolve conflicts with their children or effectively discipline their children. Furthermore, depressed mothers have been shown to exhibit more hostility, irritability, and rejection in interactions with their children compared to nondepressed mothers and to report feeling less competent as parents.

Child adjustment. Children of depressed parents, compared to normal control children, have been shown to have higher rates of internalizing and externalizing behavior problems, higher rates of psychiatric problems including depression, and poorer school and social functioning (Downey & Coyne, 1990). It has yet to be determined whether these problems are specific to parental depression, versus any psychiatric disorder in a parent, and to what extent depression causes these problems. As mentioned above, depression in parents is associated with marital conflict and high levels of life stressors, both of which are also likely to lead to problems in children. Furthermore, having a child who is depressed or oppositional might contribute to a parent's being depressed. Nevertheless, children with a depressed parent are at significant risk for their own problems.

Identification and treatment. The risk that parental depression poses to children, as well as the suffering of the parent, underscores the importance of identification and treatment of the disorder. Some research suggests, however, that depression is woefully unrecognized in the general population (e.g., Beardslee et al., 1993). Primary care physicians are often in the best position to detect possible depression in parents, although only approximately 40% to 50% of affected patients are correctly diagnosed in primary care settings (Schulberg & Rush, 1994). Identification of depression, whether by primary care physician or others who regularly come in contact with parents, may be facilitated by consultation with or referral to mental health professionals. Even in cases when a physician is experienced with the diagnosis and pharmacological treatment of depression, psychotherapy is likely to be a useful adjunct or viable alternative (Muñoz et al., 1994).

In addition to treating the parents, effective intervention should include measures to aid their children. Interventions aimed at children might include assessments of emotional, behavioral, and relational problems and providing supportive measures. For instance, insuring that the nondepressed parent or other significant adults provide additional positive attention and time to the affected children may help compensate for the depressed parent's withdrawal and/or hostility. Similarly, explaining their parent's illness to children, in age-appropriate language, may help them to cope with their parent's disorder and lessen the guilt and responsibility children often feel for their parent's condition or recovery.

References
Beardslee, W. R., Keller, M. B., Lavori, P. W., Staley, J., & Sacks, N. (1993). The impact of parental affective disorder on depression in offspring: A longitudinal follow-up in

a nonreferred sample. *Journal of the American Academy of Child and Adolescent Psychiatry, 32*, 723–730.

Downey, G., & Coyne, J. C. (1990). Children of depressed parents: An integrative review. *Psychological Bulletin, 108*, 50–76.

Muñoz, R. F., Hollon, S. D., McGrath, E., Rehm, L. P., & Vandenbos, G.R. (1994). On the AHCPR Depression in Primary Care Guidelines: Further considerations for practitioners. *American Psychologist, 49*, 42–61.

Schulberg, H. C., & Rush, A. J. (1994). Clinical practice guidelines for managing major depression in primary care practice: Implications for psychologists. *American Psychologist, 49*, 34–41.

See also: Depression, postpartum; Resiliency in parents; Stress.

ANDREW G. RENOUF

Developmentally Appropriate Practice. Developmentally Appropriate Practice (DAP) refers to a philosophy of early childhood care and education articulated and embraced by the National Association for the Education of Young Children (NAEYC). The premiere professional organization for early educators, NAEYC has virtually changed the landscape of the field of early care and education by articulating a position on best educational practice for young children and educating tens of thousands of early childhood professionals about the importance of implementing this practice. Its greatest impact is in its ability to provide a framework or philosophy around which the sometimes-disparate field of early care and education can gather. The first edition of *Developmentally Appropriate Practice in Early Childhood Programs Serving Children from Birth through Age 8* was published in 1986, followed by an expanded edition in 1987 (Bredekamp, 1987) and revised in 1997 (Bredekamp & Copple, 1997).

DAP is primarily grounded in an understanding of how young children grow and develop. Best practices in early education, according to NAEYC, are both age appropriate and individually appropriate. *Age-appropriate care and education* recognizes the universal and predictable sequences of development, which occur in children between birth and 9 years of age. Thus, the educational environment is designed to match the general, expected level of the children in a group setting, which is often, but not always, age-graded. Consequently, the activities and materials in a classroom will change over the course of time as children develop new skills and ways of understanding. *Individual appropriateness* recognizes that within these general sequences of growth and development all children have a unique pattern of development involving their individual timing of growth, temperament or learning style, family background, and culture.

Additional dimensions of DAP include the notion of teaching the whole child in an integrated, rather than subject segregated, manner. Thus, children's physical, social, and emotional as well as cognitive development are addressed in the DAP classroom by offering activities that address many, if not all, areas of development at one time. Learning is viewed as an interactive process. Young children are believed to learn best when interacting with peers and teachers as well as with concrete, "hands-on" experiences that are central to the curriculum.

DAP is a useful guideline for parents as they select care and education programs for their children under 9 years of age. As parents review programs, they can use the elements of the philosophy engendered in DAP to identify early childhood programs that operate within a best practices rubric. For example, reliance on DAP would inform a parent of a toddler that appropriate practice recognizes the toddler's need to develop a sense of autonomy, and the consequent testing of limits and opposition are seen as healthy. Inappropriate practice can be seen when caregivers engage in power struggles over issues not essential for the safety of the child. A review of DAP would tell parents of 4-year-olds to seek out programs that encourage children to learn through active exploration and interaction with adults and other children, rather than through highly structured teacher-directed lessons.

Under the auspices of the National Academy of Early Childhood Programs, a system of accreditation recognizes child care and education programs that meet the standards originally outlined in the DAP guidelines and the accreditation procedures document (National Association for the Education of Young Children, 1991). Parents who wish to ensure that programming is based in the best practices accepted by the premiere professional organization of the field can look for NAEYC-accredited programs. Programs receiving accreditation have undergone an intensive self-study process and have been observed by a trained validator who has assessed compliance with the criteria set out in the accreditation documentation. Moreover, to maintain accreditation, a program must be reviewed every three years. Consequently, parents can be assured that an accredited program offers a quality that is above the minimum standards prescribed by local child care–licensing regulations. Brochures and other printed materials to help parents select appropriate care and education for their children are available from NAEYC.

References

Bredekamp, S. (Ed.). (1987). *Developmentally Appropriate Practice in early childhood programs serving children from birth through age 8*. Washington, DC: National Association for the Education of Young Children.

Bredekamp, S., & Copple, C. (Eds.). (1997). *Developmentally Appropriate Practice in early childhood programs* (rev. ed.). Washington, DC: NAEYC.

National Association for the Education of Young Children. (1991). *Accreditation criteria and procedures of the National Academy of Early Childhood Programs* (rev. ed.). Washington, DC: Author.

See also: Critical periods.

BRENDA J. BOYD

Dimensions of Temperament Survey–Revised (DOTS–R). The Dimensions of Temperament Survey–Revised (DOTS–R) is a 54-item questionnaire designed to assess temperament across the life span (Windle & Lerner, 1986). This questionnaire is theoretically based on the research of Chess and Thomas (1986), who describe temperament as the "how" rather than the "what" of behavior. Temperament refers to an individual's early appearing and relatively stable behavioral and emotional characteristics. Temperament can influence child and adolescent development, especially through its effect on the quality of parent-child relationships.

The DOTS–R exists in a "child" form that can be completed by a parent, as well as a self-report form that can be completed by older children, adolescents, and adults. Scores from the DOTS–R can be also be used to generate a difficult temperament score (Windle, 1992) similar to the profile outlined by Chess and Thomas. The DOTS–R self-report form has 54 items phrased as statements describing the respondents' behavioral tendencies in general terms—for example, "I can always be distracted by something else, no matter what I may be doing," or "I never seem to stop moving." The respondent marks one of four choices to indicate whether the statement is usually false, more false than true, more true than false, or usually true of himself or herself. Temperament dimensions are scored by summing across the items, with some items reverse scored. The dimensions are: *General Activity Level*; *Sleep Activity Level*; *Approach-Withdrawal*; *Flexibility-Rigidity*; *Positive Quality of Mood*; *Sleep Rhythmicity*; *Eating Rhythmicity*; *Daily Habits Rhythmicity*; *Distractibility*; and *Persistence*. For all but one of the dimensions, a higher score indicates a higher level of the attribute, or in the case of the dichotomized scales, more of the first attribute. For example, a higher score on *Eating Rhythmicity* indicates greater regularity in eating patterns, and a higher score on *Flexibility-Rigidity* indicates greater flexibility. The *Distractibility* dimension is an exception. Higher scores on this scale indicated lower levels of distractibility.

The DOTS–R was developed to provide a reliable and valid means of assessing temperament across various ages, to provide a means of examining temperament longitudinally, and to be able to examine the interaction between temperament and environmental variables. Windle and Lerner (1986) have conducted reliability and validity studies on the DOTS–R. They report internal consistency coefficients for the 10 dimensions between .62 and .89, test-retest stability over a six-week interval from .59 to .75, and moderate to high correlations with other measures of temperament. After factor analysis and pairwise factor comparisons across age groups, items not loading similarly across these groups were deleted, resulting in moderate to high congruence of temperament dimensions for preschool, grade school, and college-aged samples.

Studies using the DOTS–R demonstrate relationships between temperament dimensions and adolescent depression and delinquency (Windle, 1992). Temperament is also associated with greater use of tobacco, alcohol, and marijuana; however, self-regulation and coping skills appear to mediate temperament's association with these behaviors (Wills, DuHamel, & Vaccaro, 1995). Thus, parental support and involvement may serve important protective functions for children and adolescents with a psychosocial vulnerability associated with temperament. Parents' temperaments are also significantly associated with the quality of parent-child relationships, both directly and in interaction with the adolescent's temperament (Kawaguchi et al., 1998). The DOTS–R provides a means to assess parent temperament. Clinicians have used the goodness of fit model of temperament in a more immediate way to help family members understand each other and facilitate adjustment (Chess & Thomas, 1986).

References

Chess, S., & Thomas, A. (1986). *Temperament in clinical practice.* New York: Guilford.

Kawaguchi, M., Welsh, D., Powers, S., & Rostosky, S. S. (1998). Mothers, fathers, sons, and daughters: Temperament, gender, and adolescent-parent relationships. *Merrill-Palmer Quarterly, 44,* 77–96.

Wills, T. A., DuHamel, K., & Vaccaro, D. (1995). Activity and mood temperament as predictors of adolescent substance use: Test of a self-regulation mediational model. *Journal of Personality and Social Psychology, 68,* 901–916.

Windle, M. (1992). Temperament and social support in adolescence: Interrelations with depressive symptoms and delinquent behaviors. *Journal of Youth and Adolescence, 21,* 1–21.

Windle, M., & Lerner, R. M. (1986). Reassessing the dimensions of temperamental individuality across the life span: The revised Dimensions of Temperament Survey (DOTS–R). *Journal of Adolescent Research, 1,* 213–230.

See also: Temperament.

MYRA C. KAWAGUCHI, DEBORAH P. WELSH,
AND SHARON S. ROSTOSKY

Disability, learning. Mearig (1992) states that the National Joint Committee on Learning Disabilities in 1988 developed perhaps the most comprehensive definition of *learning disabilities.* According to this definition, learning disabilities can occur in the areas of listening, speaking, writing, reading, reasoning, or math skills. Furthermore, these disabilities are thought to be the result of neurological problems, although this has not been fully substantiated. Often problems in social relations and self-regulation are also seen with learning disabilities. While learning disabilities can occur with other physical, environmental, and mental handicaps, these handicapping conditions do not cause them.

Children with learning disabilities can experience emotional and social problems that further hinder adaptive functioning. Porter and Rourke (1985) found that learning-disabled children exhibited one of four personality patterns. Almost half the children they studied exhibited no significant emotional difficulties. About 26% demonstrated problems with depression, anxiety, and social withdrawal, and 13% complained of somatic difficulties. Finally, 17% exhibited overactivity, aggressiveness, distractibility, and antisocial behaviors. General problems with self-esteem also can occur in learning-disabled children, even when no other significant emotional problems exist (Mearig, 1992).

The child's disability and emotional state can be quite challenging for parents as well. However, the ability of the parents to adapt to these difficulties will further contribute to the child's level of adjustment. A study by Feagans, Merriwether, and Haldane (1991) found that a *goodness of fit* between the personalities of parents and their children helped determine the children's achievement in school. Children who displayed characteristics that their parents felt were undesirable had more difficulties in school than children who were a better fit with their parents' expectations. Furthermore, learning-disabled children, who were a poor fit in the home, had more difficulties staying on task at school than children who were not learning disabled.

Parents and families of learning-disabled children face many hardships and concerns regarding their children. Waggoner and Wilgosh (1990) interviewed parents of learning-disabled children to ascertain the parents' experiences raising their children. Parents found that they invested a great deal of time in promoting the education of their children. This involvement included advocacy within the school system and time spent helping the child with schoolwork at home. Frustration with the school system was another common theme, as was the need for support from family and community. Finally, parents often reported that they, and the rest of the family, were emotionally and physically taxed by the difficulties of their learning-disabled children.

Parents of learning-disabled children often have difficulties coping with, and understanding, the child's disability. According to Mearig (1992), parents cope with their learning-disabled children in several ways. Often parents themselves suffered from learning disabilities, which can lead to feelings as diverse as frustration, empathy, and guilt. Parents frequently worry about the stigma attached to the learning-disabled child and are concerned about the child's range of career possibilities in the future (Mearig, 1992; Waggoner & Wilgosh, 1990). They may also expect either too little or too much from their children. A study by Lyytinen et al. (1994) demonstrated that mothers of learning-disabled children spent less time and used fewer high-level teaching strategies (e.g., applying concepts rather than using memorization) than mothers of nondisabled children when mothers were asked to teach their child a novel task. Furthermore, mothers of disabled children were generally more authoritarian and less cooperative and displayed less positive emotion than mothers of nondisabled children. In turn, the learning-disabled children learned less of the new material than nondisabled children.

The implications of parent-child relationships in families with learning-disabled children offer several guidelines for teaching, research, and practice. Clinically, parents of learning-disabled children need education, support, and guidance on how best to meet the emotional and educational needs of their youngsters. Learning-disabled children are likely to fare best in homes where parents can accept and cope with the more challenging behaviors their children exhibit. Furthermore, the parents need an understanding of their child's disability so that they can adequately gauge their child's abilities and help the child learn in the most effective manner.

References

Feagans, L. V., Merriwether, A. M., & Haldane, D. (1991). Goodness of fit in the home: Its relationship to school behavior and achievement in children with learning disabilities. *Journal of Learning Disabilities, 24* (7), 413–420.

Lyytinen, P., Rasku-Puttonen, H., Poikkeus, A. M., Laakso, M. L., & Ahonen, T. (1994). Mother-child teaching strategies and learning disabilities. *Journal of Learning Disabilities, 27* (3), 186–192.

Mearig, J. S. (1992). Families with learning-disabled children. In M. E. Procidano & C. B. Fisher (Eds.), *Contemporary families: A handbook for school professionals* (pp. 209–233). New York: Teachers College Press.

Porter, J. E., & Rourke, B. P. (1985). Socioemotional functioning of learning-disabled children: A subtypal analysis of personality patterns. In B. P. Rourke (Ed.), *Neuro-*

psychology of learning disabilities: Essentials of subtype analysis (pp. 257–280). New York: Guilford Press.

Waggoner, K., & Wilgosh, L. (1990). Concerns of families of children with learning disabilities. *Journal of Learning Disabilities*, *23* (2), 97–98, 113.

See also: Academic achievement; Attention Deficit Hyperactivity Disorder; Disability, physical; Family-school partnerships.

SHEILA A. BALOG

Disability, physical. While very little research has focused on parents of children with only physical disabilities, there has been a great deal of research on parents of children with several types of disabilities. In most of these studies, children with physical disabilities are a large subgroup. Additionally, often children with physical disabilities are included in groups described as developmentally delayed or disabled because often other developmental domains (e.g., cognition, communication, sensory) are impacted when children have motoric delays.

With the birth of any child, families adjust to the new child. This is also true with the birth of a child with physical disabilities. However, these families may have more to adjust to, and the adjustment process may take longer. The diagnosis of a physical disability may be made at birth (e.g., spina bifida), or it may be made later when the child has not reached specific motor development milestones (e.g., cerebral palsy). Upon receiving a diagnosis, many families begin a grieving process whereby they mourn the passing of the child that they had expected and come to terms with the child and his or her disabilities. Many models of this grieving process have been proposed. Several are related to Kubler-Ross's (1968) theory of accepting death (i.e., shock, denial, bargaining, anger, guilt, shame, depression, and acceptance). Other theories (Ellis, 1989) focus upon the diagnosis as well as families' growth in response to the diagnosis. While both of these types of theories posit stagelike grieving processes, in actuality there may be backsliding and co-occurrences of stages. Additionally, the mourning process may be more cyclical than the theories suggest; parents seem to deal with these issues and feelings at times of major milestones related to the increased independence of children without disabilities. When a diagnosis is made during late infancy or childhood, parents may also feel some relief that they finally have answers and that their concerns have been validated.

Because of the increased demands of caring for a child with a disability (Erickson & Upshur, 1989), the stresses experienced by parents of children with disabilities and family functioning styles have been studied extensively. There is no consistency in the results of these investigations. While a majority of researchers have found that the parents of children with disabilities report higher levels of child-related stress than parents of children without disabilities, some have found similar levels of child-related stress in the two groups. For parents of children with disabilities, their levels of stress are often in the range where professional help is recommended. There is some evidence that items that reflect characteristics of children with disabilities (e.g., distractibility) are rated as very stressful by parents of children with disabilities. Mothers and fathers, by most accounts, are equally impacted by the presence of a child with disabilities, although they may express the stress differently. There is also evidence that the presence of a disability accounts for a large proportion of the variance in parents' stress ratings. Longitudinal studies have found continuity in parents' ratings of their child-related stress across childhood and adolescence. The stress reported by families follows an inverted "U" function; parents of children with disabilities between 6 and 12 years old reported higher levels of stress than parents of preschoolers and adolescents with disabilities (Orr et al., 1993). Behavior problems were correlated with the high scores for the 6- to 12-year-olds.

The effect of the child's disability on family functioning has also been investigated. While some researchers have found deteriorated family relationships, the majority of studies indicate that families of children with disabilities function similarly to families of children without disabilities (e.g., Dyson, 1993). Parents of children with disabilities do not report higher rates of marital dissatisfaction or maladjustment. There is some evidence that families with children with disabilities emphasize achievement, have strong moral-religious beliefs, value rules and procedures for family life, and participate less in recreational activities than families with normally developing children. These patterns of family functioning appear to be relatively stable. Therefore, even though families of children with disabilities do report experiencing more stress than families of normally developing children, these families are functioning adequately for all family members. An analysis of the accommodations made by families with and without children with disabilities indicates that most families make successful accommodations based upon the individual needs of their members. Physical disability may just be another individual need. Taken together this suggests that these families are resilient and have been capable of adapting their functioning to the limitations imposed by the disability.

Social support is believed to ameliorate the stress felt by families of children with disabilities. Families are often encouraged to access informal (e.g., extended family) or formal (e.g., state agencies) support sources to help them cope with their child with a disability. Families will not access supports if they do not feel that the support source will meet a crucial need. Likewise, internal family coping strategies may be more predictive of family strengths than accessing formal support networks. Thus, accessing social supports may not be a panacea for families with a child with a disability.

References

Dyson, L. L. (1993). Response to the presence of a child with disabilities: Parental stress and family functioning over time. *American Journal on Mental Retardation*, *98*, 207–218.

Ellis, J. B. (1989). Grieving for the loss of the perfect child: Parents of children with handicaps. *Child and Adolescent Social Work*, *4*, 259–270.

Erickson, M., & Upshur, C. (1989). Caretaking burden and social support: Comparisons of mothers of infants with and without disabilities. *American Journal on Mental Retardation*, *94*, 250–258.

Kubler-Ross, E. (1968). *On death and dying*. New York: Macmillan.

Orr, R. R., Cameron, S. J., Dobson, L. A., & Day, D. M. (1993). Age-related changes in stress experienced by families with a child who has developmental delays. *Mental Retardation, 31*, 171-176.

See also: Disability, learning; Social support, informal; Stress.

ABIGAIL BAXTER AND JAMES V. KAHN

Discipline. The word *discipline* is often associated with punishment, training, or obedience. However, the word has its origins in the Latin *disciplina* and *disciplus*, meaning "instruction" and "student." Therefore "to discipline" means to educate or teach, especially in matters of conduct or behavior.

The advice-giving literature for parents and other adults who are in primary care relationships with children is prolific and often confusing. Suggestions for parents about ways to discipline children come primarily from psychology but also draw on the related fields of sociology, history, and anthropology. These related fields underscore the need for recommendations about discipline to be congruent with personal values and to be appropriate for the culture in which the child lives. Within the field of psychology, advocates of behavior management approaches maintain that child behavior persists when it is rewarded and diminishes when the discomfort of a child's actions is reduced. Opponents argue that discipline techniques based on principles of behavior management reduce behavior to a set of actions resulting from stimuli and a system of positive and negative reinforcers, thus failing to recognize the child's intellectual or emotional capabilities. Other social scientists base their concept of effective discipline on social learning theory, maintaining that behavior can be modified by influencing the way children feel and the goals they have for themselves. Finally, there is general consensus that children learn appropriate behavior by observing and imitating the behavior of other people, particularly those for whom they have strong feelings.

The role of the parent educator, social worker, psychologist, or counselor should be to present the choices adults can make among a variety of discipline strategies and to provide information about the consequences of their decisions. For many adults the concept of choice will be new, as many people grow up thinking of parenting as instinctive rather than learned behavior. Using disciplinary techniques they have not experienced will require hard work because they do not come "naturally," particularly because children often respond to change by temporarily increasing their misbehavior.

Discussions about whether or not to spank elicit strong opinions from most adults. While clinicians, practitioners, and researchers are unanimous in their opposition to corporal punishment that is severe, inconsistent, or frequent, there is less agreement about the use of occasional, mild spanking in the context of a generally loving adult-child relationship. Opponents of corporal punishment cite research linking its use with negative outcomes such as increased aggression, delinquency, and psychological maladjustment. Other researchers criticize the methodology of the studies upon which opponents base their recommendations (Rohner, Bourque, & Elordi, 1996) and claim that the apparent negative effects of spanking may in fact be attributed to other complex variables, such as a child's perception of spanking as adult rejection.

As adults make choices among the discipline strategies that are personally and culturally appropriate for them, their parenting will fall into one of three major categories—permissive, authoritative, or authoritarian (Baumrind, 1971, 1991). At this point the weight of the research evidence indicates that the *authoritative* style is most likely to foster the optimal development of children. However, most studies to date have focused on Caucasian or African American children; less is known about the effectiveness of each parenting style with children from other cultures in the United States. For parents who need or want to change, working toward an authoritative style of discipline is most probably a "best buy."

Parenting programs that address discipline as a dimension of child rearing are numerous and are in widespread use across the United States. Analyses of the programs that originate from universities reveal that they usually advocate an authoritative parenting style (Birckmayer, 1995; Pitzer, 1995; Smith, 1993). A common set of principles characterizes most of the popular programs, although areas of emphasis vary and some programs are more comprehensive than others. The following nine areas of agreement about effective discipline can be distilled from a review of these programs:

- Prevent misbehavior by providing for children's needs, developmental level, interests, and goals.
- Set developmentally appropriate rules and limits for behavior.
- Use natural or logical consequences instead of punishments when children misbehave. An adult can modify a natural consequence if it is too severe.
- Practice effective communication skills, by listening, observing, acknowledging efforts, and reflecting feelings.
- Help children find acceptable ways to express strong feelings. When children express feelings or act in ways that are harmful to themselves or others, require them to spend a brief period of time by themselves, in order to regain self-control (time-out). One minute per year of age is a commonly used measure for time-out. (Note: This technique is not recommended for use with children under the age of three.)
- Teach children positive behavior and give them attention when they behave well or try to do the right thing. Ignore misbehavior or allow children to experience the natural or logical consequences of what they have done.
- Restrict the use of discipline strategies to those that foster feelings of competence and self-worth.
- Prevent discipline problems by making the environment appropriate for children, for example, childproofing rooms, offering opportunities for large-muscle activities, or providing a comfortable and quiet place for homework.
- Demonstrate desirable behavior and attitudes. A strong adult model is the most powerful teaching tool of all.

References
Baumrind, D. (1971). Current patterns of parental authority. *Developmental Psychology*, 4, 1–103.
Baumrind, D. (1991). Parenting styles and adolescent development. In R. M. Lerner, A. C. Peterson, & J. Brooks-Gunn (Eds.), *Encyclopedia of adolescence* (Vol. 11, pp. 746–758). New York: Garland.

Birckmayer, J. (1995). *Discipline is NOT a dirty word*. Ithaca, NY: Cornell Cooperative Extension.

Dinkmeyer, D., McKay, G., & Dinkmeyer, J. (1989). *Parenting young children*. Circle Pines, MN: American Guidance Services.

Pitzer, R. (1995). *Positive parenting*. St. Paul, MN: Minnesota Extension Service.

Rohner, R., Bourque, S. L., & Elordi, C. (1996). Children's perceptions of corporal punishment, caretaker acceptance, and psychological adjustment in a poor, biracial southern community. *Journal of Marriage and the Family, 58*, 842–852.

Smith, C. A. (1993). *Responsive discipline*. Manhattan, KS: Kansas State Research and Extension.

Steinberg, L., Mounts, N. S., Lambourn, S. D., and Dornbusch, S. M. (1991). Authoritative parenting and adolescent adjustment across varied ecological niches. *Journal of Research on Adolescence, 1*, 19–36.

See also: Control strategies; Limit setting; Misbehavior; Physical punishment.

JENNIFER BIRCKMAYER

Distancing strategies. Communication between mental health providers, researchers, teachers, and other professionals who interact with families and children can be impeded when the same term is used differently by these professionals. *Distancing strategies* is a construct that has discipline-specific meanings that can cause confusion. For example, distancing behaviors are associated with the diagnosis for Avoidant Personality Disorder (APD) in the *DSM-IV (Diagnostic and Statistical Manual of Mental Disorders*, 4th edition; see Kantor, 1993 for a more extensive discussion). Marriage and family therapists also use the term *distancing strategy* to refer to relationship patterns in which one partner avoids intimacy by attacking or avoiding her or his partner (see Hatfield, 1984 for further discussion). Finally, developmental psychologists discuss distancing strategies as a teaching style that positively influences cognitive development. Although the first two definitions have implications for parent-child relationships (e.g., APD can impair parent-child attachment; intimacy avoidance can lead to triangulation or scapegoating), the third use of the term is especially relevant for parenting.

Irving Sigel has incorporated elements from a variety of theoretical approaches including behavioral genetics, structural development, personal construct theory, and cybernetics with a special focus on representational competence to understand factors that influence children's cognitive development (Sigel, 1986, p. 50). Representational competence, according to Sigel (1986), refers to internalization of experience and competence in three functions: (1) anticipation (planning and predicting), (2) hindsight (recognition and reorganization of past events), and (3) transcendence of the present. Sigel (1978) suggests that representational competence requires conservation of meaning: A photograph of an object and the object maintain a common identity. "The competence to comprehend these representations is what I refer to as representational competence, which means that the child comprehends and hence deals with representations. This type of transformation is exemplified by information represented in pictures which is transformed into words, or words transformed to pictures, or written words transformed to verbal utterances" (Sigel, 1982, p. 53).

Distancing strategies refers to teaching tactics that make "cognitive demands on the person and in so doing serve to separate him or her mentally from the on-going present" (Sigel, 1986, p. 63). These are social behaviors by parents or teachers that create discrepancies and require representational thinking to solve them. These styles occur on a continuum from high to low and include specific strategies as well as processes that the parent encourages. Distancing strategies should match the developmental level of the child and are positively associated with short- and long-term cognitive development (see Sigel, 1986 for a review of his research). Thus, parents and teachers should include these behaviors in their instructional repertoire.

Low-level distancing strategies include description and demonstration such as showing a child a toy and asking her to name it. Developmentally, these are important strategies when children are younger. For example, the best way to teach a child to tie her shoes, a complex task, is to show her. Observation and labeling are also low-level distancing strategies (Sigel, 1986).

Medium-level strategies include asking the child to classify, describe similarities, or make estimations. For example, a parent might ask a child to name a picture of an animal and then identify the sound that particular animal makes. This is a rudimentary form of classification. Other examples of medium-level strategies are: sequence; reproduce; describe similarities or differences; infer similarities or differences; estimating; enumerating; synthesize within classification (Sigel, 1986).

High-level strategies include evaluation and inference of cause-effect (Sigel, 1986). Higher-level strategies promote a form of detachment from the problem that facilitates a more sophisticated thinking process. A parent could describe a situation using a third person to help distance the child from the problem. For example, they might read their children a story and ask them to think of solutions to the fictional person's problem (e.g., Cinderella's conflict with her step-sisters). Other examples of high-level strategies include asking the child to evaluate consequence, competence, affect, or effort; generalize; transform; and plan (Sigel, 1986).

Early experience with distancing strategies provides children with opportunities to differentiate themselves from others so that they can begin to think critically (Sigel, 1986, p. 55). Research suggests that teaching styles that are highly directive and ignore the child's interests and abilities impair linguistic and cognitive competence. Parents and teachers, therefore, should utilize high-level distancing strategies to enhance cognitive development of children. Thus, assessment of academic difficulty should include an evaluation of teaching styles employed by parents and classroom instructors.

References

Hatfield, E. (1984). The dangers of intimacy. In V. J. Derlega (Ed.), *Communication, intimacy and close relationships* (pp. 207–240). Orlando, FL: Academic Press.

Kantor, M. (1993). *Distancing: A guide to avoidance and avoidant personality disorder.* Wesport, CT: Praeger.

Sigel, I. E. (1978). The development of pictorial comprehension. In B. S. Randhawa & W. E. Coffman (Eds.), *Visual learning, thinking, and communication* (pp. 49–65). New York: Academic Press.

Sigel, I. E. (1982). The relationship between parents' distancing strategies and the child's cognitive behavior. In L. M. Laosa & I. E. Sigel (Eds.), *Families as learning environments for children* (pp. 47–86). New York: Plenum.

Sigel, I. E. (1986). Early social experience and the development of representational competence. In W. Fowler (Ed.), *New directions for child development: Early experience and the development of competence* (pp. 49–65). San Francisco: Jossey-Bass.

See also: Academic achievement; Family systems; Nature versus nurture; Problem solving.

RONALD JAY WERNER-WILSON AND MEGAN J. MURPHY

Divorced families. Divorce or marital separation is the most common antecedent of the single-parent household. Extreme variations in the divorce rates and the number of divorced families exist among countries worldwide. The divorce rate has been steadily increased since 1960 in all European, Anglo, and developed countries in which divorce was legal. Comparative data are usually based on the estimates of single-parent families, thus including divorced parents, widowed parents and never-married mothers. The majority of single-parent families are mother headed and are also disproportionately poor. Current estimates of the incidence of single-parent families in the European Union countries range from 5% in Greece to 14% in Denmark and the United Kingdom. The highest current rate of single-parent families in developed countries is found in the United States, where more than 1 million children a year experience parental divorce or separation. Divorce rates differ dramatically according to race, age, education, and socioeconomic status. Studies of divorced families reported more problems in countries where the divorce is less common and thus more stigmatizing.

Divorce should be conceptualized as a long-term multistage process for all family members and is an acknowledged stressor, which is almost universally accompanied by emotional reactions of anger, grief, guilt, and self-doubt. Research findings indicated that a major vulnerability of the single-parent (mother-headed) family is the economic decline with a consequent decline in the standard of living (moving, changing schools for the children, child care placements) and the need for the mother's full-time employment.

The psychological impact of divorce on parents and children can be considered on at least two levels (Emery, 1988): (1) the process of adaptation to change that every family member must go through and (2) the outcomes of this process for each family member's long-term adjustment. Events within families such as marital discord and divorce are often experienced differently by members of the same family. Emotional tasks facing the divorced family include overcoming grief and anger regarding the loss of an intact family unit and renegotiating the relationships altered by family dissolution. The redefinition of roles affects every dyadic relationship in the family system. The redefinition of the dyadic relationship between parents is central and complicated. Because children are a tie between divorced partners, unresolved anger over the marriage can be channeled into disputes about child rearing.

Numerous studies examined the implications of parental divorce for children's development and adjustment. Divorce has been related to increased anxiety, fear, depression, aggressiveness, anger, and conflicts over loyalty to parents. Divorce is also related to shame and other emotional reactions, to poorer social and academic competence ratings and scores, to the increased likelihood of grade retentions and referrals to psychologists, and to broad negative consequences for quality of life in adulthood (Amato & Keith, 1991a, 1991b).

Longitudinal research by Emory (1988), Amato and Keith (1991b), and others on the impact of divorce on children has revealed a long list of mediating factors as key to their adjustment. These include the social-cognitive developmental status of children at the time of separation or divorce, parent and child gender, the length of time since the separation or divorce, the type of custody arrangement and the amount of parent-child contact, economic and social support loss, the level of interparental conflict, the quality of parent-child relationship and discipline, and familial conditions and preparations prior to divorce.

Available findings indicated age-related differences in children's reactions and post-divorce adjustment connected to children's developmental status. Preschoolers' level of cognitive development prevents them from fully understanding the meaning and implications of their parents' divorce and consequent emotional reactions. Due to their cognitive capacities, adolescents have the most complete conception of their parents' separation and the whole process, which possibly facilitates their adjustment. Researchers, though, have underscored the particular difficulties adolescents experience since they have been exposed to the parental conflicts for a long time, and they need to integrate the divorce experience with their developing identity associated with an accelerated independence and greater power of children in divorced families.

Gender differences have been found in the adjustment of younger children to divorce. School-age boys experience more problems than girls in several domains of social-emotional and academic development. Though there is some evidence that a child adjusts better when in the custody of a parent of the same sex, the quality of the parenting environment is most significant. Longitudinal studies concluded that children's and parents' adjustment improves with the passage of time, and most of the families attain a new homeostasis usually within two years after divorce. Although children from divorced families on the average exhibit more psychological and behavioral problems than those in nondivorced families, the vast majority of children in the long run do not show severe or enduring problems.

References

Amato, P. R., & Keith, B. (1991a). Parental divorce and adult well-being: A meta-analysis. *Journal of Marriage and the Family, 53*, 43–58.

Amato, P. R., & Keith, B. (1991b). Parental divorce and the well-being of children: A meta-analysis. *Psychological Bulletin, 110* (1), 26–46.

Emery, R. E. (1988). *Marriage, divorce, and children's adjustment*. Newbury Park, CA: Sage Publications.

Wallerstein, J. S. & Kelly, J. B. (1980). *Surviving the breakup: How children and parents cope with divorce*. New York: Basic Books.

See also: Conflict, interparental; Custody; Single parents.

CHRYSE HATZICHRISTOU

Domestic labor. Domestic labor is the amount and type of time invested in the upkeep of the material household and in the well-being of family members. Most research in this area focuses on why women do the vast majority of household chores and child care. The idea that it is apportioned implies that domestic labor involves more than the allocation of time to different tasks. Couples also may specialize in different tasks, such that women assume the burden of routine child care, while men are responsible for discipline. Other aspects of domestic labor are emotional labor, which includes mood management and attending to relational issues, and household management, which involves identifying necessary tasks, creating standards for their performance, and making sure that they get done.

Women do the vast majority of domestic labor, regardless of social class, employment status, or whether the couple has children. Wives typically do twice as much housework and three times as much child care as husbands, with larger disparities when men are the sole wage earner (Pleck, 1985). Women routinely devote 20 to 30 hours a week more than men to domestic labor, which led Hochschild (1989) to call it the "second shift." Studies have found that household work is shared equally among only 20% of dual-earner couples and 7% of male breadwinner couples. With respect to parenting, the average father devotes little time to child care. In one study, fathers spent the largest amount of time with their children watching television and doing homework, with 10 minutes devoted to each per week, and 17% of fathers engaged in no mutual activities. Research on the transition to parenthood also finds that fathers are less involved in child care than either spouse predicted during pregnancy, although men's contributions are not trivial, given the amount of work to be done when children are young. Despite public recognition of these gender disparities, there is little evidence that men's share of family work has changed much in the last few decades.

Many women do not equate their husband's avoidance of domestic labor with lack of involvement. The reason seems to be that wives value support and emotional availability more than doing chores. That is, husbands are more subjectively involved than in previous generations although they are not directly involved in domestic tasks. A majority of fathers, for example, identify parenthood as the most important part of their lives and are more emotionally connected to their families than their jobs.

If housework is drudgery, women should be resentful of the unfair burden they bear. Indeed, when men are less involved in domestic labor, especially if their wives are employed, women often are unhappy, report more parenting stress, and are less satisfied with the marriage. These adverse effects are more affected by satisfaction with the division of labor than by how tasks are actually shared (Cowan & Cowan, 1988).

Wives' subjective view of domestic labor is critical, because only a minority wish that their husbands would do more chores or child care. In fact, some studies have found that when fathers are more involved in child care, their wives are less satisfied with their roles (Baruch & Barnett, 1986). Although it may seem odd that wives would resist husbands expanding their family role, involved fathers tend to be more critical of the mother's role performance. Also, feminists have recently emphasized the symbolic meaning of housework, suggesting that many women may have an attitude of entitlement and obligation toward domestic labor; it is a way of expressing caring in "their" domain, not subordination. Thus, some women may feel threatened if they believe they are relinquishing key aspects of their role to their husband.

Domestic labor has been fertile ground for developing theories of family functioning (Coverman, 1985). *Relative resource theory*, for instance, asserts that men's greater involvement in paid employment both reduces time allocation to domestic labor and confers greater power in decision making.

The time availability postulate is supported by an inverse relation between the hours men work outside of the home and time spent on domestic labor. Conjugal power also plays a role, to the extent that differences between spouses' incomes and education levels correlate with disparities in task allocation. However, resource theory fails to explain why husbands and wives specialize in different tasks, nor can it accommodate the inequitable division of labor found in dual-earner families where spousal income, education, and time at paid work are comparable. Men in dual-earner families do increase their involvement by a trivial amount (five minutes a day), whereas their wives greatly reduce their time spent on household tasks. Thus, resource theory does not adequately account for dual-earner couples' gender-based conventions in who does what.

From the perspective of *gender socialization* theory, women are socialized to do the emotional work in relationships and to define domesticity as their domain, while men specialize in instrumental roles such as breadwinning (Thompson & Walker, 1989). In terms of family decision making, women's attention to family maintenance may bias them toward accommodation, whereas men's predisposition to be authoritative may lead them to be assertive in task allocation. Thus, wives in dual-earner couples may do more domestic labor because they define it as their domain and because they are at a disadvantage in decision making.

There are two lines of evidence for this explanation. First, domestic tasks remain highly sex-typed in most American families. For instance, wives perform more than 90% of the cooking, washing, cleaning, and diapering of children, whereas husbands do the majority of household repairs, disciplining children, and yardwork. Second, men's earlier caregiving experiences do relate to their involvement in fatherhood. Those who babysat as teens or whose own fathers were highly involved in parenting are more confident in their own child care skills and devote more time to their children. Conversely, men who had an inadequate relationship with their own father often compensate by being more involved with their own children. Although this theory has not been tested adequately, it does make sense that if men grew up in a traditional household, they are likely to have less experience in domestic labor than their wives.

Gender ideology theory emphasizes beliefs and feelings about one's gender, rather than socialization to perform a role. The contemporary feminist critique of the family focuses on cultural forces that sanction women's subordination in decision making and domestic labor. This critique also recognizes the gendered meaning of paid and unpaid work (Ferree, 1990), such that gender ideologies influence role priorities and expectations. Research consistently supports a relation between androgyny or egalitarian attitudes and equitable division of domestic labor. Stated differently, men who adhere to a traditional gender ideology do fewer household chores. These ideologies are both cultural prescriptions and are socialized in the family of origin: Men whose parents held egalitarian sex-role attitudes find the dual-career lifestyle to be less demanding and are bothered less by assuming nontraditional roles. Fathers who are highly involved in child rearing are bucking tradition and so would be expected to have either nontraditional attitudes or an atypical socialization history.

Although much research supports the influence of gender ideologies on the division of domestic labor, the relations often are of small magnitude. This suggests that each theory may explain a small but complementary aspect of domestic labor. Other processes that may be important to involvement in parenting have not yet been examined in detail. For example, men likely vary in motivation and skill when they become fathers. They often want to be involved parents but do not believe that they have the knowledge, competence, or support to do so. Psychological and ecological constraints such as these deserve more attention if we are to grasp why men are not more involved in child rearing.

References

Baruch, G. K., & Barnett, R. C. (1986). Consequences of fathers' participation in family work: Parents' role strain and well-being. *Journal of Personality and Social Psychology, 51*, 983–992.

Coverman, S. (1985). Explaining husbands' participation in domestic labor. *Sociological Quarterly, 26*, 81–97.

Cowan, C. P., & Cowan, P. A. (1988). Who does what when partners become parents: Implications for men, women, and marriage. *Marriage and Family Review, 12* (3/4), 105–131.

Ferree, M. M. (1990). Beyond separate spheres: Feminism and family research. *Journal of Marriage and the Family, 52*, 866–884.

Hochschild, A. (1989). *The second shift*. New York: Avon.

Pleck, J. H. (1985). *Working wives/working husbands*. Beverly Hills, CA: Sage Publications.

Thompson, L., & Walker, A. J. (1989). Gender in families: Women and men in marriage, work, and parenthood. *Journal of Marriage and the Family, 51*, 845–871.

See also: Conflict, interparental; Dual-earner families; Employment, early maternal; Feminism.

DAVID MACPHEE

Donor insemination. There are two main techniques available to assist in conception when male infertility is present: donor insemination (DI), where semen from a donor is inserted into the vagina, and more recently (1994), intracytoplasmic sperm injection (ICSI). ICSI occurs when a single sperm is deposited in the cytoplasm surrounding the nucleus of an egg, harvested, then isolated in a Petri dish. ICSI is used when the quality of the semen is poor. Donors may be anonymous, known (an identified stranger), or personal (chosen by the recipients, such as a friend or family member).

The use of artificial insemination has been known for centuries, but common belief is that it was not until 1790 that John Hunter first used this technique on a human when he inseminated a woman with her husband's sperm. Hummel and Talbert (1989) attribute the innovation of using sperm from a donor to Robert Dickson in 1890. It was not until the early 1970s that widespread attitudinal changes to a number of social and moral issues led to a general acceptance of the procedure. However, for Catholics and other religious groups such as the Orthodox Jewish community, the separation of sexuality from reproduction has been controversial, as has the unclear status of the child.

Because of the confidentiality of donor insemination treatment, social parents are able to register a child's birth recording the mother's husband/partner as father. Several countries have enacted legislation to legitimate this for protection of the donor. For example, the Family Law Reform Act, 1987, Section 27(1) in the United Kingdom; The Status of Children Act, 1985, in New Zealand. These have led to a shift in the definition of family, with the marital link rather than the biological link becoming the method of attributing paternity. This is similar to adoption processes that have recognized parenthood based on emotional links; however, the use of donor gametes (germ cells) has created a situation where biological links can be hidden.

The secrecy that has surrounded donor insemination has made it difficult to study the experiences of parents who conceived by donor insemination. Bush and O'Neill (1985) reviewed literature on the psychological and sociological implications of donor insemination and concluded that parenting after DI was a universally positive experience. This evidence comes not only from responses to questionnaires but also from requests for a second insemination.

There are two important issues for parents of children conceived by donor insemination. First, will the child be told he or she was conceived by means of a donor? Second, will the identity of the donor be disclosed to the child? There are opposing points of view that are reflected in legislation: strict donor anonymity, provision of non-identifying information, or identification of the donor. The rights of children to obtain knowledge of a donor have been emphasized only recently (Daniels & Lalos, 1995).

References

Bush, J. M., & O'Neill, C. J. (1985). *The current practice of artificial insemination by donor (AID), and its psychological and sociological implications: A literature review* (Working Paper No. 25). Hamilton, New Zealand: Population Centre, University of Waikato

Daniels, K., & Lalos, O. (1995). The Swedish insemination act and the availability of donors. *Human reproduction, 10* (7), 1871–1874.

Hummel, W. P., & Talbert, L. M. (1989). Current management of a donor insemination programme. *Fertility and Sterility*, *51* (6), 919–930.

Leeton, J. F. (1980). The development and demand for AID in Australia. In C. Wood, J. Leeton, & G. Kovaks (Eds.), *Artificial insemination by donor*. Melbourne, Australia: Prior Anderson.

See also: Fertilization, in vitro; Infertility.

ANNA RUMBALL AND VIVIENNE ADAIR

Dreikurs, Rudolf (1897–1972). Rudolf Dreikurs, born in Vienna, Austria, on February 8, 1897, was trained as a physician and psychiatrist at the University of Vienna Medical School (1923) and the Psychiatric Clinic. He was drawn to the psychological approach of Alfred Adler, who organized child guidance clinics in the Viennese school systems. Dreikurs was a pioneer in the development of social psychiatry, bringing psychological help to people at all levels of society. He left Austria in 1937 to further develop Adler's work, first in Brazil and then in Chicago.

In Chicago, Dreikurs continued his emphasis on community psychiatry. He worked with families and teachers to help children, based on the Adlerian model that adult health and difficulties have their roots in childhood. His pioneering work reflected his convictions that mental health requires well-developed *social interest* and that social living requires contribution, responsibility, and social equality.

Dreikurs emphasized family dynamics and the influence of siblings in personality development. He asserted that sibling relationships shape the development of each child's personality, especially when siblings are close in age. Children grow up observing the strengths and weaknesses of each sibling. If siblings form an *alliance* they become similar in personality. Otherwise each child develops unique areas of strength and refrains from developing in areas where siblings are strong. Thus, these children actually are competitors and develop opposite personalities.

Adler and Dreikurs believed all behavior is purposeful and intended to move people toward their greater goals of finding a place of significance and belonging. Understanding the goal of a child's misbehavior is a prerequisite to changing it. Toward this end, Dreikurs made one of his most important contributions when he delineated *four mistaken goals* of preadolescent behavior.

The Four Goals are *attention*, *power*, *revenge*, and the display of *inadequacy*. Three issues affect each of these goals. First, the child's behavior is a purposeful attempt to gain a sense of belonging and value. Second, the child feels discouraged about being able to contribute in a way that brings about a feeling of belonging. Third, one can understand the goal by looking at the effect of the child's actions on others.

Dreikurs called the goals "mistaken" because the misbehavior reflects a child's mistaken belief that he or she cannot belong and contribute as an equal member of the family, school, or group and therefore must be "special."

Once parents and teachers recognize the purpose of children's misbehavior, they can change the way they relate to children. It is crucial to encourage children, in order to nurture their sense of competence, connection with others, and ability to contribute to the family or group.

Dreikurs saw that autocratic parents raised either repressed, docile children or rebellious ones; permissive parents raised children who had a sense of entitlement and expectation and were therefore unprepared to meet the demands of everyday life. Children need parents who neither pamper nor domineer but rather respect them as valued family members and competent individuals. These parents understand that children can contribute, share with chores, learn from mistakes, develop a sense of social connectedness, recover from hurts and pains, take responsibility, respect the rights of others, and cooperate.

Encouragement, then, is crucial in raising children to be prepared to meet life's challenges. Adult focus on children's honest efforts (rather than only accomplishments) and positive behavior help them develop the courage necessary to negotiate the tasks of life.

Because a system of rewards and punishments ultimately is discouraging, Dreikurs emphasized children's participation in their surroundings through classroom and family meetings. He also urged adults to rely on logical and natural consequences to help children learn to self-correct misbehavior.

In the United States, Dreikurs introduced a method of public counseling that had been very successful in Vienna. *Open forum family counseling* is a collaboration between family and counselor and involves the community. The parents and then the children are interviewed in front of an audience of other parents. The interview focuses on family composition, birth order, and presenting problem. The counselor explains that the children's behavior is related to one of the Four Goals. Suggestions are made to help correct the children's misbehavior. The family reports back to the group at the next meeting. This exchange emphasizes the commonality of family problems that promotes learning.

Dreikurs' work provides the basis for many parenting programs. His most important parenting contributions (as author and coauthor) are: *Children: The Challenge* (1964), *Psychology in the Classroom* (1968), *Coping with Children's Misbehavior: A Parents Guide* (1972), *Maintaining Sanity in the Classroom* (1984), *A Parent's Guide to Child Discipline* (1984), *Logical Consequences* (1990), and *Discipline without Tears* (1992).

Reference

Terner, J., & Pew, W. L. (1978). *The courage to be imperfect: The life and work of Rudolf Dreikurs*. New York: Hawthorn Books.

See also: Adler, Alfred; Consequences, natural and logical; Discipline.

EDWARD "ABE" ABELSON

Dual-earner families. Today, there are more than 52 million married family units in the United States. Of those, the dual-earner family is the most common, with 60% of all married family units having both spouses working outside the home. These family units are also labeled as dual-income or dual-worker families. For family units with children the rate of two working parents is even higher. Specifically, 70% of the 24.7 million two-parent families in the United States report both spouses working either full- or part-time outside the home (Benokraitis, 1996).

The primary factor related to the increase in dual-earner families over the past 25 years has been the economy. Indeed, in a three-way comparison between married couples with the wife in the labor force, married couples with wife not in the labor force, and female-headed households with no husband present, only those dual-earner families *having the wife in the labor force* have avoided an absolute decrease in family income since 1970 (Cherlin, 1996).

The current median income levels for these groups also helps underscore the problem. For dual-earner families, median income for 1992 was $49,984; for single earner, wife not in labor force, $30,326; and for female household heads, $17,221 (Curran & Renzetti, 1996). Corporate downsizing, global wage competition between workers, and loss of high-paying manufacturing jobs in the United States all suggest there will be a continuing pressure for both spouses to work. Therefore, in the face of this continued pressure, families (and society in general) are required to first assess the effects of dual-earner work on families and then minimize the negative effects.

Having two wage earners affects family relationships in several arenas. These include the quality of the marriage between the spouses, the division of household labor, and of course the quality of child rearing. In terms of the quality of marriage, greater strain occurs to the marriage when either spouse has a job with unsatisfactory working conditions like high demands but low decision-making power, difficulties with coworkers and/or supervisors, low pay, little chance for upward mobility, and few benefits. More important than the work itself, however, are the spouses attitudes toward work. If the marriage partners agree on spousal employment, then less tension and conflict occur in the relationship (Schwartz & Scott, 1994).

With respect to the division of household labor, research consistently finds that husbands still do not make equal contributions to the routine household chores. For example, one typical survey found that women did 77% of the cooking, 66% of the shopping, 75% of the cleaning, and 85% of the laundry (Benokraitis, 1996). Percentages like this result in women's work at home being labeled "the second shift." In contrast, wives who do experience an equitable division of labor at home report higher levels of satisfaction with their marriage, less depression, and less resentment. In fact, the women whose marriages lack equity have said that improvements in this area is one of the most important things that would make their lives better. While a majority of men agree with this position, their behavior continues to lag their attitudes on the subject.

The third arena where relationships are affected by work is the area of child care. Research shows that having both parents work is not automatically damaging to children (Benokraitis, 1996). Instead, what is most important is the *quality* of care given to the children by the parents and outside caregivers.

Children who spend time in quality day care do at least as well and often better in psychosocial development, intelligence, and academic achievement as opposed to children raised at home by both parents (Sullivan & Thompson,

1994). Furthermore, children exposed to quality day care perform equally well in verbal and cognitive skills, creativity, social competence, and cooperation. Quality day care centers are characterized by low child-to-staff ratios, good wages and benefits, and professional development for staff. Children do well both at home and at day care when the environment is responsive, supportive, and consistent. Unfortunately, the supply of quality, affordable child care in the United States does not meet the demand for such services.

To successfully achieve balance among the many role demands, dual-earner families may do the following: (1) emphasize the benefits of their work, (2) set priorities, (3) separate family and work life, (4) set realistic standards for themselves and their children, (5) organize and share domestic responsibilities, (6) provide time to review priorities and household responsibilities with the family, and (7) take some time for leisure activity (Benokraitis, 1996).

References

Benokraitis, N. V. (1996). *Marriages and families: Changes, choices, and constraints* (2nd ed.). Upper Saddle River, NJ: Prentice-Hall.

Schwartz, M. A., & Scott, B. M. (1994). *Marriages and families: Diversity and change.* Englewood Cliffs, NJ: Prentice-Hall.

Cherlin, A. J. (1996). *Public and private families.* New York: McGraw-Hill.

Curran, D. J., & Renzetti, C. M. (1996). *Social problems: Society in crises* (4th ed.). Boston: Allyn & Bacon.

Sullivan, T. J., & Thompson, K. S. (1994). *Introduction to social problems.* New York: Macmillan.

See also: Domestic labor; Employment, early maternal; Socioeconomic status.

WENDY HAMILTON

E

Eating behavior, children and. In their understanding of the true nature of unhealthy eating patterns and attitudes found in children, many underestimate parental influence. Parents, in the name of "good nutrition," often unconsciously overcontrol the when, what, why, and where their children eat. Parents may become overly concerned about food obsessions, body image, or picky eating—identical concerns regarding food expressed by their parents. Food consumption, attitudes about eating, habits, and behaviors are often generational.

The family can affect eating behaviors. The way a family handles food issues can help the child develop either healthy or unhealthy thoughts and behaviors. For instance, a family can actually put the child at risk for future eating problems by overemphasizing slenderness and the need to be a perfect child (Goodman, 1992). Or a family can motivate a child to approach food as having a necessary function in life. Food should be enjoyed but should not be our sole enjoyment. High family self-esteem will help nourish high individual self-esteem. The family can also help a child develop a healthy relationship with food by modeling positive behavior toward food and by expressing accepting attitudes about the diversity of body shapes in our society.

Much of what families know about life and living is passed down through generations, either through knowledge or myth. Myths, rules, and regulations regarding food are indeed intergenerational. Consider the following statements: "If you eat that candy you will ruin your appetite"; "You are not healthy unless you eat meals that are balanced"; "There will be no dessert until your plate is clean and empty." These sentences represent only a few of the food myths passed down from family to family. Although uttered with conscious concern, these myths often precede a child's undesirable eating behaviors. Why should a clean plate deserve a reward (dessert)? Eating now becomes connected with reward, not hunger, which should dictate the eating of food. A particular meal will not make or break one's nutritional health because the body's nutritional demands stretch over a few weeks, not over one day. The nutrients your body receives should be balanced over a two-week time span. How can eating ruin an appetite? Isn't having an appetite a sign of needing something to eat? If left alone, a young child will usually eat when hungry. If a child has been permitted to develop internal clues regarding body hunger, then that child will eat nutritionally and satisfyingly because his or her natural appetite will demand the required foods (Hirschmann & Zzaphirooulous, 1993). Parents must become aware of lingering food myths and must be willing to examine their personal family structure for both restrictive and traditional reasons used to exert control over the child and food. A personal examination of such questions as "Why do I eat?" "When do I usually eat?" "How do I describe my eating patterns?" and "What are my views regarding overweight individuals?" can often provide insight into one's food attitudes and feelings. Connecting feelings with eating is often the beginning step in understanding one's relationship with food.

Emotions and eating. Through practical experience working with second-grade students, the author has found 7- and 8-year-olds to be knowledgeable about nutrition. They eagerly relate the six basic nutrients and the major food groups. They know about fat grams and dieting but have not made the connection between emotions and eating. Children have difficulty fully comprehending the abstract concept partly because of developmental factors but largely due to environmental factors. They are perhaps too young to understand the abstraction, yet they are not too young to observe parental behavior or to hear value-laden commentary from siblings. Children learn about emotional eating from their families.

A growing concern. There is a growing concern about the escalating obesity rate of children in the United States. The number of overweight youth has doubled in the past 25 years from 5% to 11% of Americans ages 6 to 17 ("National Center for Health Statistics, CDC," 1995). There is also concern about the adolescent and adult populations in regard to poor daily nutritional practices. It is believed that approximately 20% of women between the ages of 12 and 30 are currently suffering from an eating disorder, specifically compulsive overeating, anorexia nervosa, or bulimia. Approximately 5% to 10% of all persons diagnosed having an eating disorder are male (Goodman, 1992).

In addition to comprehensive nutrition curricula that exist, a multidisciplinary approach to providing information about developing healthy childhood eating behavior is needed. Children should be educated about eating behaviors at an early age. Education from parents, the community, and the school is essential if a child is to develop a lifelong healthy relationship with food.

References

Goodman, L. (1992). *Is your child dying to be thin?* Pittsburg, PA: Dorrance Publishing Co.

Hirschmann, J., & Zzaphirooulous, L. (1993). *Preventing childhood eating problems.* Carlsbad, CA: Gurze Books.

National Center for Health Statistics, CDC. (1995, October 16). *U.S. News & World Report* (pp. 23-25).

See also: Eating disorders.

CHRISTINE IRISH MOTLEY

Eating disorders. *Anorexia nervosa* and *bulimia nervosa* are the most commonly known eating disorders. However, eating disorders may be better considered along a continuum of eating and body image problems. Serious problems with eating and body image can develop without ever meeting the diagnostic criteria (American Psychiatric Association, 1994). Within the class of eating and body image problems there is also considerable overlap in causative factors and symptomatology. Additionally, those suffering from an eating disorder often vacillate between the variously recognized diagnoses of anorexia, bulimia, and *binge eating disorder* (Schlundt & Johnson, 1990).

Anorexia nervosa involves self-imposed starvation resulting in a dramatic weight loss. The starvation is usually motivated by an intense fear of fat and overconcern with one's own body shape and size. Individuals with *anorexia* may limit daily food intake to 500 calories and exercise daily. Without intervention, *anorexia* is fatal. A body simply cannot live without adequate nutrition and hydration.

Bulimia nervosa is similar to anorexia with regard to the fear of fat and excessive concern with body shape and size. However, the crucial difference lies in the occurrence of frequent binge episodes. Binges involve eating more, in a discrete period of time, than would most other people under the same circumstances. Following a binge, those with bulimia purge using inappropriate compensatory mechanisms such as vomiting, fasting, laxative and diuretic abuse, or excessive exercise.

The diagnostic category binge eating disorder (BED) has been proposed and is being considered for inclusion in the next revision of the American Psychiatric Association's *Diagnostic and Statistical Manual* (DSM). BED is quite similar to bulimia in that bingeing is a primary symptom. However, BED does not involve purging, and this population usually suffers from obesity as well. As many as 30% of those frequenting weight loss clinics may suffer from BED.

A number of commonalties thread through these three disorders. Chief among them is a relationship with food and eating colored by simultaneous love and hate and a fear of losing control. A preoccupation with food, eating, and feeding is very common among those suffering from eating disorders. Additionally, this population appears to suffer from a lack (or impairment) of *interoceptive awareness*. Interoceptive awareness is the ability to accurately identify one's own internal physiological and emotional states (Bruch, 1978). For example, many individuals with bulimia have difficulty distinguishing between anxiety, hunger, and satiation.

An additional similarity is an increasing social isolation and set of behaviors and emotions that serve to perpetuate the eating disorder itself. Initially, the adjustments in eating are made in an effort to solve a problem, and it is only over time that the adjustments turn into problems. For example, most cases of anorexia begin with a self-imposed diet designed to "take off a few pounds." It is only after the individual begins to find the hunger comforting and the compliments exhilarating that the diet becomes increasingly restrictive and medically dangerous. At this point, however, the anorexic behaviors are viewed through a set of cognitive distortions that present the eating disorder as a salvation or method of keeping things from getting worse.

Historically, mothers have been blamed for being overinvolved and domineering, while fathers have been criticized for being passive and uninvolved. In reality, though, many of these studies are unreliable indicators of the family's global functioning, as they have been done during a crisis profoundly affecting daily functioning and patterns of interaction. It is more accurate to consider these as studies of families changed by their struggles with eating disorders rather than as perpetually dysfunctional families that happened to have a single member with an eating disorder.

Regardless of whether parenting becomes troubled before or after the eating disorder develops, intervention aimed at the parental subsystem can be useful. Useful primary prevention strategies include: avoiding power struggles over food, allowing children choices in what they eat within a structured context, and modeling self-acceptance and healthy eating habits. Also, during early childhood, parents can facilitate their child's interoceptive awareness by waiting to respond until he or she provides cues. Parents may make the mistake of responding to their children's needs before children have the chance to experience identifying and responding to their own internal cues. For example, a father might regularly check his infant's diapers and change them before the infant recognizes discomfort and has the chance to express it.

In the midst of an eating disorder, most parents become profoundly frightened for the health and life of their child, power struggles often dominate, and secrecy and anger abound. Under these stressful conditions, caring parents can become overwhelmed, inconsistent, and unable to view the situation objectively. In order to cope, they may also become disengaged and appear uninterested or oblivious. All of these can promote distance in familial relationships and serve to entrench the eating disorder in the family system. Parents would be more effective by responding to their child's struggle proactively while maintaining some degree of differentiation.

Establishing clarity of responsibility and limits around the child's eating and body is an important first step. In part, this should be determined by the child's age. However, the effects of starvation and malnutrition on the brain should also be considered. Research suggests that a starving brain is impaired, just as are other organs. In fact, in many cases of semistarvation, the individual becomes unable to think without cognitive distortions or magical thinking and has occasional psychotic symptoms (Keys et al., 1950). These individuals can certainly benefit from a parent's well-timed intervention. Many fine self-help books are available for family members and parents affected by their child's eating disorder and can aid in directing parents attention and behavior (e.g., see Siegel, Brisman and Weinshel, 1988).

References

American Psychiatric Association. (1994). *The diagnostic and statistical manual of mental disorders* (4th edition). Washington, DC: Author.

Bruch, H. (1978). *The golden cage: The enigma of anorexia nervosa.* New York: Random House.

Keys, A., Brozek, J., Henschel, A., Michelson, O., & Taylor, H. (1950). *The biology of human starvation.* Minneapolis: University of Minnesota Press.

Schlundt, D. G. & Johnson, W. G. (1990). *Eating disorders: Assessment and treatment.* Boston: Allyn & Bacon.

Siegel, M., Brisman, J., & Weinshel, M. (1988). *Surviving an eating disorder: Strategies for families and friends.* New York: Harper & Row.

See also: Eating behavior, children and; Mental illness, children.

ELISA DOEBLER-IRVINE

Education, parenting. Parenting education consists of programs, services, and resources offered to parents and caregivers that are designed to support and empower them or increase their capacity and confidence in raising healthy children.

The use of the word *parenting* is preferred over the word *parent* in an effort to be inclusive of those individuals who are not biological or legal parents but nonetheless carry the responsibility of raising a child. The use of the word *education* is employed to acknowledge that this exercise is, most commonly, a learning activity. There are some who prefer the word *support* instead, in part as a negative reaction to the more didactic and expert-driven programs but also, more positively, as an asset-based affirmation. These concerns are of some merit, but most educators would themselves reject the negatives and embrace the positives as hallmarks of current educational theory and practice.

The additional advantage of this definition is that it supports the now nearly complete consensus that the skills of good parenting are not as much intuitive as they are learned.

Within the realm of family support theory, parenting education should be seen as one strategy among many (e.g., child care, job training, health care services), although most would say it is the central strategy.

Alternative names for the same basic activity include *family life education, parent support, parent education,* and *family support.*

References

Carter, N. (1996). *See how we grow: A report on the status of parenting education in the United States.* Philadelphia: Pew Charitable Trusts.

Kagan, S., & Weissbourd, B. (1994). *Putting families first.* San Francisco: Jossey-Bass.

See also: Family support.

NICK CARTER

Emotion language. Emotion language is any discourse that conveys the name of an emotion, the nature of experiencing it, and its causes and consequences. This type of communication is a powerful tool, allowing children to state their feelings, to understand feedback about them, and to process causal links between events and emotions, thus enabling the choice of a coping response. Young children's ability to use and understand emotion-descriptive adjectives is substantial (Ridgeway & Kuczaj, 1985). Toddlers begin to employ this emotion language to influence others to meet their own emotional needs (e.g., to obtain comfort, support, or attention; to express pleasure or affection; to maintain a happy state; or to anticipate, achieve, or avoid other affective states; see Brown & Dunn, 1991). By 3 years, over 75% of children use terms for feeling good, happy, sad, afraid, angry, loving, mean, and surprised. By the end of the preschool period, over 75% of 6-year-olds also used terms for feeling comfortable, excited, upset, glad, unhappy, relaxed, bored, lonely, annoyed, disappointed, shy, pleased, worried, calm, embarrassed, hating, nervous, and cheerful.

Young children do not construct this vocabulary of emotion in a nonsocial vacuum; they have conversations about emotions with parents, grandparents, and siblings. Dunn and associates have specified naturally occurring conversations about feelings with mothers and their 18- to 36-month-old children (e.g., Brown & Dunn, 1991, 1992). Parental verbalizations about emotions assist children in learning about expression and causes of emotion and understanding of emotions. Individual differences in mothers' usage of emotion language in its various functions may give children unique understandings about emotion.

By the time toddlers reach 18 months, both mothers and children discuss the causes of emotions, particularly the toddlers' own. They use emotion language that fulfills a variety of other functions as well (e.g., socialization, guiding behavior, questioning). Mothers change their feeling state language as their preschoolers mature: They refer to others' thoughts, feelings, and desires, and their use of emotion language to control behavior decreases.

Children are not passive participants in such conversations, of course, and developmental changes can be discerned in the content and context of young children's emotion language with mother. Between 24 and 36 months, children make more frequent reference to feeling states and use such language more often in reflective discussions, especially about the causes and consequences of emotions, and in order to manipulate the feelings and behaviors of others. Similarly, 3- and 4-year-olds and their mothers used an average of six emotion terms in discussing eight photos of infants expressing peak emotional expressions (Denham, Cook, & Zoller, 1992).

Stable individual differences in family emotion language also appear, with maternal emotion utterances at 18 months related to the child's emotion utterances at 24 months. Brown and Dunn (1992) and Denham, Cook, and Zoller (1992) found that children who talked to mother or siblings about feelings had family members who also conversed about emotions at both 33 and 47 months.

From 33 to 47 months, conversations about feelings between mothers and children decrease, whereas those between siblings increase, paralleling the increased ability of the young sibling to engage in such conversation independent of mother (Brown & Dunn, 1992). Older siblings are very different interaction partners than mothers, affording the preschooler with a new set of experiences around the developmental task of using emotion language, different from talking with mother, both in respect to whose feelings are discussed and the context of the feelings considered. Siblings talk more about their own feelings than do mothers, perhaps pushing their young brother or sister to take their perspective. Siblings also engage their younger brothers and sisters in more emotion talk centered on themes of play and humor.

Siblings' emotion conversations also serve somewhat different functions than those with mother. Older siblings use sibling-centered emotion language most often during the mother's absence, or during conflict or play. Such language allows the older siblings to regulate interaction and construct shared meanings about their world. For example, the older sibling might say, "You'd better stop before you make me mad!" to regulate interaction, or "It made me cry, too, when I hit my head before. Do you need Mommy?" to construct shared meanings about mutual caregiving.

Parent-led conversations about the names, causes, and consequences of different emotions may aid the child's active attempts to link expressions, situations, and words into coherent, predictable schema about emotional experience. Parents' openness to discuss emotions also heightens their children's awareness of emotion within interaction, motivating them to attend to and process such emotional information.

The naturalistic study of children's conversations about emotions has added much to knowledge of their understanding of emotion. Conversations about parents' own, and their children's, emotions are associated with preschoolers' developing social cognition of emotions. Individual differences in mothers' usage of emotion language and in usage of its various functions may teach children to use emotion language in specific ways. Both total emotion language and specific function usage predict children's concurrent and later understanding of emotion (Denham, Cook, & Zoller, 1992, Denham, Zoller, & Couchoud, 1994; Dunn et al., 1991).

References

Brown, J., & Dunn, J. (1991). "You can cry, mum": The social and developmental implications of talk about internal states. *British Journal of Developmental Psychology, 9*, 237–256.

Brown, J., & Dunn, J. (1992). Talk with your mother or your sibling? Developmental changes in early family conversations about feelings. *Child Development, 63*, 336–349.

Denham, S. A., Cook, M. C., & Zoller, D. (1992). "Baby looks very sad": Discussions about emotions between mother and preschooler. *British Journal of Developmental Psychology, 10*, 301–315.

Denham, S. A., Zoller, D., & Couchoud, E. A. (1994). Socialization of preschoolers' understanding of emotion. *Developmental Psychology, 30*, 928–936.

Dunn, J., Brown, J. R., Slomkowski, C., Tesla, C., & Youngblade, L. (1991). Young children's understanding of other people's feelings and beliefs: Individual differences and their antecedents. *Child Development, 62* 1352–1366.

Ridgeway, D., & Kuczaj, S. (1985). Acquisition of emotion-descriptive language: Receptive and productive vocabulary norms for ages 18 months to 6 years. *Developmental Psychology, 21*, 901-908.

See also: Affectivity, positive and negative; Empathy.

SUSANNE A. DENHAM

Empathy. Empathy is an emotional reaction to the comprehension of another's emotional state or condition that is the same or very similar to the other's state or condition. Thus, if a girl sees her mother crying and reacts by feeling sad, this is empathy. Empathy involves the recognition and understanding of another's emotional state (or what the other person is likely to be feeling, given the situation) and the emotional experience of the other person's emotional state (see Eisenberg & Strayer, 1987).

In most situations, particularly after the first couple years of life, empathy is likely to turn into either sympathy or personal distress (or both). *Sympathy* is an emotional reaction based on the apprehension of another's emotional state or condition, a reaction that involves feelings of sorrow, compassion, or concern for the other person(s) rather than feeling the same emotion as the other individual. So if the little girl who sees her mother crying feels sorry for her mother (rather than only sadness), she is sympathizing. Sympathy involves an other-orientation and the motivation to assist the needy or distressed person, whereas empathy by itself does not. Sympathy may stem not only from empathy but also from cognitively putting oneself in another's situation or accessing from memory information about how the other person must feel.

Personal distress, which often is confused with empathy or sympathy, is an aversive, self-focused emotional reaction to another's emotional state or condition such as anxiety, discomfort, or worry. Thus, if her mother's crying makes a girl feel uncomfortable or distressed for herself, and the child is focused on her own unpleasant emotions, she is experiencing personal distress. Personal distress leads to the egoistic motive of alleviating one's own distress, although people experiencing personal distress may help another if that is the easiest way to eliminate their own distress (e.g., if the girl cannot ignore or leave her sad mother). Unfortunately, in real life and in much of the existing research, it is difficult to differentiate among empathy, sympathy, and personal distress.

Children exhibit empathy and personal distress between 12 to 18 months of age. By 2 to 3 years of age, as children learn to differentiate their own internal states from those of others, they seem capable of experiencing sympathy for another person, as well as empathy and personal distress. It is not clear whether empathy, sympathy, and personal distress increase in quantity after the preschool years (see Eisenberg & Fabes, 1998).

In studies of twins, there is some evidence that genetic factors partially account for individual differences in empathy-related responding. However, there also is considerable evidence that socializers influence the development of empathy-related responding in a variety of ways.

In specific, children with a secure attachment to their parent, and who experience supportive parenting, appear to be more empathic, although the findings are not always consistent. In addition, parents' self-reported sympathy and cognitive perspective-taking have been associated with same-sex elementary school children's sympathy and low levels of personal distress reactions. Supportive, empathic caretakers are likely to model and encourage the capacity for empathy in children. However, parental warmth in isolation may be insufficient to foster empathy in children. Parental practices that involve some discipline or restrictiveness may foster empathy and sympathy. For example, mothers' and fathers' demands for responsible behavior have been associated with elementary school children's self-reported empathy (see Eisenberg, 1992; Eisenberg & Fabes, 1998; Hunt, 1990).

Parents also may subtly model or communicate acceptance of children's emotional responses through their own expression of emotion or their acceptance of others' emotional reactions in everyday life. In homes where negative emotions such as sympathy and apologizing are expressed frequently, children, particularly girls, seem to learn to express empathy and sympathy and to be relatively uninhibited in doing so. In contrast, the expression of hostile or aggressive emotions (e.g., anger) in the home has been associated with low levels of sympathy in boys and girls.

In addition, parental attitudes regarding the expression of emotion appear to affect children's empathy-related responding. Parents who emphasize controlling the experience or expression of negative emotions such as sadness or anxiety tend to have sons prone to experience personal distress rather than sympathy. In contrast, boys seem to be prone to sympathy if their parents discuss ways to deal instrumentally with situations that cause the child's negative emotion (i.e., taking care of the problem). Mothers' discussions in which they link the child's own experience to that of a needy person in an empathy-inducing context (e.g., "Remember when you fell and had to go to the hospital?") have been associated with high levels of children's empathy-related responding of all types. In contrast, mothers' reports to their children of feeling sad or sympathetic in an empathy-inducing context have been associated with boys' self-reported sympathy. Furthermore, mothers who report reinforcing elementary school children's sympathetic and prosocial reactions to needy or distressed people tend to have daughters who are prone to empathy or sympathy and are helpful and sons who are relatively sensitive in their helping behavior (see Eisenberg & Fabes, 1998).

In summary, a number of parental characteristics and behaviors have been linked with the development of empathy, sympathy, or personal distress. However, there is, as yet, little research on this topic, so conclusions from the few existing studies must be viewed as tentative until more research is available.

References

Cohen, A. (1990). *The brighter side of human nature: Altruism and empathy in everyday life*. New York: Basic Books.

Eisenberg, N. (1992). *The caring child*. Cambridge: Harvard University Press.

Eisenberg, N., & Fabes, R. A. (1998). Prosocial development. In W. Damon (Series Ed.) & N. Eisenberg (Vol. Ed.), *Handbook of child psychology: Vol. 3. Social, emotional, and personality development* (5th ed., pp. 701-778). New York: Wiley.

Eisenberg, N., & Strayer, J. (1987). *Empathy and its development*. Cambridge: Cambridge University Press.

Hunt, M. (1990). *The compassionate beast*. New York: William Morrow and Company.

See also: Conscience; Prosocial behavior; Victim-centered discipline.

NANCY EISENBERG

Employment, early maternal. Recent years have seen a phenomenal rise in the number of two-earner and single-parent households, with corresponding increases in the labor force participation rates of mothers of young children. In the United States today, nearly two thirds of mothers of preschoolers are in the paid labor force, more than double the rate of just two decades earlier. This dramatic movement of mothers out of the home and into the labor force suggests a crucial question: What, if any, are the effects of early maternal employment on child well-being?

Effects on child behavior and social development. In terms of effects on child behavioral outcomes, the research literature is somewhat equivocal. Some researchers find that early maternal employment has negative implications for child social and behavioral outcomes, while others argue that the effects of maternal employment on child behavior, if any, are minimal.

There are at least three mechanisms through which maternal employment might produce variations in the social or cognitive development of young children. Perhaps the most obvious are the possible effects of *substitute forms of child care* during the first year of life. Alternate forms of care—particularly when they are of low quality—may be responsible for impairing social development or creating undesirable behavior patterns such as aggression and noncompliance.

Second, the *amount of time the mother is away* from the child during infancy may be a crucial factor affecting social development and the quality of the child's family environment in at least two ways. Belsky (1988), for example, has argued that full-time maternal employment during infancy may be a risk factor for developmental difficulties.

Many clinical studies indicate that children who had nonmaternal care experiences as infants tend to be less compliant with their parents and more aggressive with their peers. Clarke-Stewart (1989), however, suggests that these findings may simply reflect the fact that children in substitute care arrangements are more aggressive simply because they have not had time to develop the appropriate social skills necessary to be assertive and independent in socially acceptable ways.

While these first two mechanisms may produce negative outcomes, a third possible mechanism whereby maternal employment might have positive effects on the well-being of children is the economic consequence of such employment. One could reasonably expect that, all things being equal, mothers with higher incomes would be more likely to be able to find high-quality alternative care for their children, as well as better provide goods and services to enhance the child's environment.

Many of these processes interact with each other and with other factors. The effects of maternal employment are probably different for boys as compared to girls, and effects are probably different for families of differing socioeconomic status.

Effects on child cognitive development. The empirical literature on the effects of early maternal employment on child cognitive outcomes is quite extensive and includes research conducted by psychologists, educators, sociologists, and economists. Results of these studies have been mixed, although none finds across-the-board negative effects. Some studies, especially those of children from disadvantaged families, suggest that early maternal employment may enhance cognitive development.

While most studies suggest that there is no net effect of early maternal employment on child cognitive development, several studies have suggested that early maternal employment may interact with other factors to produce effects on cognitive ability. Differential effects of maternal employment on child cognitive outcomes—by ethnicity, gender, and other factors—were observed more than two decades ago (see Hoffman, 1974 for a review) and in a recent study (Greenstein, 1995). Parcel and Menaghan (1994) argued that early maternal employment has negative effects on child cognition only for mothers with poor job prospects. Greenstein (1995) concluded that while the effects of maternal employment seem to differ by ethnicity and gender of the child, there was no pattern of negative effects of maternal employment on cognitive ability of young children and some evidence that the additional income from the mother's employment may facilitate cognitive development.

References

Belsky, J. (1988). The "effects" of day care reconsidered. *Early Childhood Research Quarterly, 3*, 235–72.

Clarke-Stewart, K. A. (1989). Infant day care: Maligned or malignant? *American Psychologist, 44,* 266–73.

Greenstein, T. N. (1995). Are the "most advantaged" children truly disadvantaged by maternal employment? Effects on cognitive outcomes. *Journal of Family Issues, 16* (1), 149–69.

Hoffman, L. W. (1974). Effects of maternal employment on the child: A review of research. *Developmental Psychology, 10*, 204–228.

Parcel, T. L., & Menaghan, E. G. (1994). Early parental work, family social capital, and early childhood outcomes. *American Journal of Sociology, 99*, 972–1009.

See also: Domestic labor; Dual-earner families.

THEODORE N. GREENSTEIN

Empowerment. Empowerment is accomplished through creating opportunities for families to acquire the knowledge and skills necessary to become stronger and better able to manage and negotiate the many demands and forces that impinge upon the family. An empowered individual meets these demands and forces in ways that promote well-being for the family and its individual members (Dunst, Trivette, & Deal, 1988).

Empowerment is a relatively new concept that has emerged to describe a style of working with parents and families. Empowerment is not a new technique that clinicians have recently discovered and added to their arsenal.

Empowerment is a capability that all persons have, not something that professionals give to parents. More accurately, empowerment is something parents do for themselves, sometimes even without the help of professionals. Empowerment is not something that professionals can do to or for others. Consequently, the responsibility of professionals working with parents is to help them recognize the knowledge and skills that will lead to their becoming empowered. Often individuals become empowered through enabling. *Enabling* is providing or creating opportunities for individuals to develop and employ their competencies. Some of the knowledge and skills that empowered parents develop include access and control over needed resources, decision making and problem-solving abilities, and instrumental behaviors needed to interact effectively with others to procure resources.

An empowering perspective views people as competent individuals or as individuals who have the ability to become competent. The failure to behave competently is interpreted as being due to social systems that fail to create opportunities for an individual to display his or her competence (lack of enabling experiences) rather than to individual deficits. Individuals who are empowered attribute changes to their own actions and thus develop the sense of control necessary to manage individual and family affairs. Empowerment allows individuals to take a proactive stance. Empowerment is accepting of individual differences and focuses on individual strengths as a way of supporting and strengthening individual functioning. Finally, true empowerment changes professionals' roles. The goal of empowerment is to allow parents to access resources and solve problems rather than depending on professionals for this help. Thus, the professional does not solve parents' problems; instead, he or she helps the parents develop the ability to solve the problem without the professional.

In order to help parents become empowered, there must be a specification of needs, aspirations, and projects by the individual, not the professional. Next, there is an identification of intrafamily strengths and capabilities and an identification of sources of support and resources for meeting needs and achieving projects. The professional takes a proactive role in helping families meet their needs by using identified strengths and resources.

A typical empowering approach may be to identify, through needs-based assessment procedures (e.g., questionnaire, interview), needs, aspirations, projects, and strategies that the family considers important enough to work on by devoting their time and energy toward developing a solution. The professional then helps the family identify strengths and capabilities that emphasize what they do well and determine their strengths that may increase the likelihood of mobilizing resources to meet the identified needs. A map of families' personal and social networks can be used to identify existing sources of support and resources and untapped but potential sources of aid and assistance. The professional may provide information and opinions in response to family requests or requests of members of the family's network, in addition to acting as a clearinghouse for information about community resources or different types of services. The professional may also create opportunities for families to become skilled at obtaining resources and support (enabling), make the family aware of unutilized resources and sources of support, help them mobilize support and access resources, or link the family to others with new or alternative perspectives on meeting needs. Additionally, when there are negative encounters with social networks, professionals may work directly with different individuals or agencies to promote cooperation. They may provide families with knowledge and skills to protect the rights of parents and children, negotiate effectively with policy makers, and create opportunities to influence the establishment of policies on behalf of children and families.

Professionals are more likely to develop empowered individuals when the professional is positive and proactive, waits for help to be requested, allows decision making to be done by families, and promotes the family's use of natural support networks while neither replacing nor supplanting them with professional networks. Responsible professionals convey a sense of cooperation and joint responsibility (partnership) for meeting needs and solving problems and promote the families' acquisition of effective behaviors that decrease the need for help. Likewise, the aid and assistance professionals give families will be more effective if they do not infer deviance or undue variations in the family, are congruent with families' appraisal of problems or needs, and can be reciprocated, and the possibility of "repaying" the professional is sanctioned and approved but not expected. Finally, when response costs do not outweigh benefits, the family experiences immediate success in solving a problem or meeting a need, and the parent perceives improvement and sees himself or herself as responsible for producing the change, empowerment is likely to occur.

References

Dunst, C. J., Trivette, C. M., & Deal, A. G. (1988). *Enabling and empowering families: Principles and guidelines for practice.* Cambridge, MA: Brookline.

See also: Family support; Social support, informal.

ABIGAIL BAXTER AND JAMES V. KAHN

Enuresis. Bed-wetting, or nocturnal enuresis, refers to involuntary urinating while sleeping. To meet criteria for a diagnosis, the child must have reached a chronological or developmentally equivalent age of 5 years, and the bed-wetting must occur at least twice per week for at least three consecutive months (American Psychiatric Association, 1994). Bed-wetting can be secondary to medical conditions including disorders of the nervous system, the spinal cord, and the bladder and may be secondary to a variety of chronic illnesses including diabetes and sickle cell disease. Further, bed-wetting can be the result of an untoward effect of various pharmacological agents. It has been estimated that at least 5% of children and adolescents experience some form of nocturnal enuresis, with the disorder occurring twice as frequently for males as for females (Walker, 1995). Approximately 85% of all reported cases of bed-wetting are classified as primary (i.e., it has been a lifelong problem). Secondary enuresis ensues for a period of at least one year following successful toilet training, most commonly occurs between the ages of 5 and 8 years, and is often associated with a psychosocial stressor (e.g., birth of sibling, loss of loved one, sexual abuse).

Bed-wetting occurs more frequently among lower socioeconomic classes, in families with many siblings, and in families with mothers who have fewer years of schooling (Walker, 1995). Interestingly, the prevalence of enuresis has been found to be independent of the child's intelligence. Some cultural differences pertaining to enuresis have been found that are suspected to be a function of the differential emphasis placed upon toilet training (de Jonge, 1973). However, there are no studies available to determine whether enuresis is associated with time or intensity of the toilet training process (for review, see Walker, 1995). There is some anecdotal evidence to suggest that children who are bed-wetters also have sleep disturbances; that is, they are difficult to arouse during sleep. These reports have not been substantiated in the literature, and additional sleep studies of children with nocturnal enuresis are warranted.

Regarding a biological etiology, there is some evidence of a maturational delay of the nervous system. One investigation found children with enuresis to be characterized by hormonal deficiencies and poor muscular control (Houts, 1991). However, the most compelling biological evidence lies in genetics. Evidence suggests that bed-wetting is familial (Walker, 1995), although no specific transmission has been identified.

There are available to the practicing physician three types of medication for the management of enuresis, namely, tricyclic antidepressants (e.g., imipramine), antidiuretics (e.g. desmopressin acetate [DDAVP]), and antispasmodics. Each of these agents is partially successful in managing bed-wetting while the child is receiving the active substance. However, due to potential untoward effects and the frequency of relapse following the cessation of pharmacotherapy, medication alone may be inappropriate as the sole treatment modality.

Rooted in the clinical folklore of the disorder has been the notion that bed-wetting is associated with childhood depression and hostility toward the child's mother. More recently, however, these myths have been refuted. Whereas there is a higher incidence of enuresis among children with emotional disturbances, the majority of children diagnosed with enuresis do not have adjustment difficulties (Walker, 1995). The lore that bed-wetting is a precursor to aggression, particularly when it co-occurs with other conduct-related symptoms, has not been supported. There is a learning model that has been developed to explain enuresis, suggesting that genetic and maturational factors place children at risk for bed-wetting and that enuresis is caused by a delay in mastering urinary functioning (for review, see Walker, 1995). This model offers parents hope in that it has direct and positive treatment implications.

The behavioral therapies that are based on the learning model are particularly promising. These include the urine-alarm, retention control training, waking schedules, self-monitoring, and positive reinforcement schedules for appropriate toileting (for review, see Walker, 1995). The urine-alarm procedure employs a urine sensing device that attaches to the child's clothing or bed sheets (Doleys, 1985). An alarm is sounded upon the onset of voiding. Once awakened, the child appropriately toilets and returns to bed. Thus, the child learns to inhibit voiding and to sleep through the night; alternatively, bladder distension will begin to cue the child to awaken and void in the bathroom. Over the past 50 years, research has overwhelmingly supported the efficacy of the urine-alarm, and the device has been available for consumer purchase in the retail market (Doleys, 1985; Walker, 1995). Finally, a multifaceted learning-based program is the dry-bed training technique developed by Azrin and Besalel (1979). This procedure involves positive practice (i.e., having the child drink a great deal of fluid and void), parental positive reinforcement for appropriate urination, retention control training, nighttime awakening, and full-cleanliness training (i.e., when wetting the bed, the child is required to change wet sheets and pajamas, and then bathe). Although it has been empirically supported (for review, see Doleys, 1985; Walker, 1995), this program requires additional demands on caretakers.

The use of family therapy in conjunction with a behavioral program may have particular promise in managing enuresis, particularly when there are associated adjustment difficulties with bed-wetting or other life stressors. Children whose parents sustained a divorce or separation may have an increased risk for enuresis due to the stressors associated with the change in their families (Jarvelin et al., 1990). Moreover, as Walker (1995) has suggested, children's and their families' concerns about the enuresis and the subsequent accommodations that must be made may exacerbate the problem and contribute to further adjustment difficulties. Thus, efforts at improving family dynamics and communication skills as well as encouraging parents and caretakers to be supportive and active collaborators with the child in managing the enuresis are of prime importance.

References

American Psychiatric Association. (1994). *Diagnostic and statistical manual of mental disorders* (4th ed.). Washington, DC: Author.

Azrin, N. H. & Besalel, V. A. (1979). *Parent's guide to bedwetting control: A step-by-step method.* New York: Simon & Schuster.

de Jonge, G. A. (1973). Epidemiology of enuresis: A survey of the literature. In I. Kolvin, R. C. MacKeith, & S. R. Meadow (Eds.), *Bladder control and enuresis* (pp. 39–46). Philadelphia: J. B. Lippincott.

Doleys, D. M. (1985). Enuresis and encopresis. In P. H. Bornstein & A. E. Kazdin (Eds.), *Handbook of child behavior therapy* (pp. 412–440). Homewood, IL: Dorsey Press.

Houts, A. C. (1991). Nocturnal enuresis as a biobehavioral problem. *Behavior Therapy, 22,* 133–151.

Jarvelin, M. R., Moilanen, I., Vikevainen-Tervonen, L, & Huttunen, N. P. (1990). Life changes and protective capacities in enuretic and non-enuretic children. *Journal of Child Psychology and Psychiatry and Allied Disciplines, 31,* 763–774.

Walker, C. E. (1995). Elimination disorders: Enuresis and encopresis. In M. C. Roberts (Ed.), *Handbook of pediatric psychology* (2nd ed., pp. 537–557). New York: Guilford Press.

See also: Disability, physical; Night wakings; Resiliency in children.

LINDSEY L. COHEN AND RONALD T. BROWN

F

Failure to thrive. Failure to thrive (FTT) affects numerous children during infancy and early childhood. The term FTT is utilized to represent growth failure in infants and children, but in the past, clinicians and researchers lacked agreement on a clear definition for FTT. In 1984 the National Institute on Mental Health conference on FTT agreed to base the definition of FTT according to the National Health Center for Health Statistics (NHCHS) norms. Presently, the criteria used most frequently considers a child as FTT if their weight is below the 5th percentile on the NHCHS growth charts or if a deceleration occurs in the rate of weight gain of at least two standard deviations on the NHCHS charts from birth to the present (Drotar, 1985).

FTT is not a diagnosis but rather a symptom with varying degrees of effects related to malnutrition and developmental delays. It is estimated that prevalence rates range from 1% to 5% of all pediatric infant hospital admissions and from 3.5% to 14% of the infants in ambulatory care settings (Benoit, 1993).

For some time, the traditional definition considered the etiological dichotomy of *organic* versus *nonorganic*. More recently, clinicians and researchers consider that dichotomy misleading and prefer to consider organic (physical) and nonorganic (psychosocial) contributors along a continuum. This continuum examines factors from three areas: (1) organic, (2) nonorganic, and (3) mixed (Powell, 1988). Thus, FTT is not synonymous with a feeding disorder, even though nonorganic failure to thrive (NOFTT) is classified under the FD category in the DSM IV (Ramsey, 1995).

With the absence of a clear organic base, the use of the term *nonorganic failure to thrive* pervades much of the literature on FTT. The identification of an organic base associated with FTT does not necessarily preclude psychosocial factors. Weight loss due to psychosocial factors may possibly make the child more susceptible to physical disorders (Bithoney & Dubowitz, 1985). Due to these ambiguities, further information under this term will continue to utilize the term FTT but will reflect research and information pertaining to what is considered NOFTT or FTT without apparent organic explanation.

Clinical impressions and research provide a basis for descriptions of infant characteristics typical of male and female FTT children. In the area of biological risks, low birth weight, perinatal problems and prematurity have often been considered as contributing to FTT in infants. Studies in this area are conflicting and do not support this conclusion. However, some research congruency exists to suggest that FTT infants are more prone to recurrent infections and recover slower and that most have motor, cognitive, and psychosocial developmental delays (Benoit, 1993). Specifically, most exhibit less motor activity, facial expression, and appropriate gaze and respond less to stimulation. These specific behaviors seem to contribute to parent-child interactional problems during times of eating, sleeping, and elimination. During feeding times more feeding difficulties occur since these infants may eat less regular meals or skimpier meals and in general respond less to food (Heffer & Kelly, 1994).

Maternal characteristics are sometimes described in clinical impressions as contributing to FTT. The list of problem areas includes depression, anger, and inability to stimulate their child, addictions, social isolation, and psychopathology. In spite of these claims, empirically valid research has found little evidence of maternal psychopathology or of any differences in the psychological characteristics between mothers of FTT children and those with thriving children. However, a few stringent studies do imply a link between mothers' early experiences and FTT. Mothers who had negative memories of childhood—such as feeling unloved, unhappy memories, and frequent beatings—were associated with infant FTT children (Boddy & Skuse, 1994). Literature reviews do indicate observable behavioral differences between mothers of FTT children and those of thriving children in the areas of sensitivity and communication. Specifically, the maternal behavior of FTT children at mealtime was rated as more indifferent and anxious, and showed more negative affect, and the mothers were less likely to give instructions, communicate, or socialize. In a another study, FTT and control infants were equally likely to sleep through feedings, but the maternal response to the sleep was different. The FTT mothers were less likely to awaken their child for feedings than the mothers of thriving children (Boddy & Skuse, 1994).

Parents and children do not interact in isolation. Psychosocial factors are often considered as contributors. Families with FTT children tend to be isolated, see their relatives less, and dislike their neighborhoods. Also, these families seem to experience more physical violence resulting from arguments and more problematic relationships. These associations do not imply a causal relationship but rather the possibility that FTT is influenced by psychosocial stress (Boddy & Skuse, 1994; Heffer & Kelly, 1994).

Given the many associations between organic and nonorganic contributors and the wide variety of child-specific, family, and psychosocial variables that may influence FTT, treatment and the assessment of these factors ought to be approached with a multidisciplinary team. For example, the assessment should include an evaluation of specific child behaviors and affects with family and nonfamily members, the child's developmental status, a family history (health, marital status, and satisfaction), parental knowledge and cognitions about children, and their psychosocial conditions. In addition, it is critical that one evaluate parent-child interactions in feeding and nonfeeding situations through direct observations.

Interventions can then be developed from this individualized assessment. With this approach, it is likely that the treatment will be a complex process with multiple and specific problem-solving interventions (Heffer & Kelly, 1994).

Few well-done, controlled treatment outcome studies exist with regard to physical, emotional, behavioral, and intellectual changes (Benoit, 1993). Those available indicate little positive impact on developmental outcomes, while others suggest moderate gains. In addition, research on the parenting process with FTT children is needed to evaluate parental response and parental ideas or cognitive processes during parent-child interactions. Future research will hopefully address the methodological fallacies and make an impact on the prevention and treatment of FTT children.

References

Benoit, D. (1993). Failure to thrive and feeding disorders. In C. H. Zeanah (Ed.), *Handbook of infant mental health* (pp. 317–331). New York: Guilford Press.

Bithoney, W. G., & Dubowitz, H. (1985). Organic concomitants of nonorganic failure to thrive: Implications for research and practice. In D. Drotar (Ed.), *New directions in failure to thrive: Implications for research and practice* (pp. 47–68). New York: Plenum Press.

Boddy, J. M., & Skuse, D. H. (1994). Annotation: The process of parenting in failure to thrive. *Journal of Child Psychiatry and Allied Disciplines*, 35 (3), 401–424.

Drotar, D. (1985). Summary of discussion at NIMH conference: "New directions in failure to thrive research: Implications for prevention." In D. Drotar (Ed.), *New directions in failure to thrive: Implications for research and practice* (pp. 369–375). New York: Plenum Press.

Heffer, R. W., & Kelly, M. L. (1994). Nonorganic failure to thrive: Developmental outcomes and psychosocial assessment and intervention issues. *Research on Developmental Disabilities*, 15 (4), 247–268.

Powell, G. F. (1988). Nonorganic failure to thrive in infancy: An update on nutrition, behavior and growth. *Journal of the American College of Nutrition*, 7, 345–353.

Ramsey, M. (1995). Feeding disorder and failure to thrive. *Child and Adolescent Psychiatric Clinics of North America*, 4 (3), 605-616.

See also: Attachment, secure; Social support, informal; Stress.

FAYE SPRUNGER KOOP

Family-centered services. The term *family-centered* has been widely used to characterize a preferred way of delivering essential human services to children and their families. Alarmed at the poor health and well-being status of many children in the United States, many parents, professionals, and policy makers believe that family-centered services result in better outcomes for children and families. Family-centered services are different than *child-centered* services that have historically been the dominant professional approach. In child-centered services, the individual child is the focus of attention. The professionals (e.g., doctors, nurses, social workers, psychologists, teachers) work directly with the child, with minimal attention to the child's family. In contrast, family-centered practice views the child within the context of the family, so that the family, rather than the child, becomes the focus of attention.

Definition. Family-centered service delivery, across professional disciplines and settings, recognizes the centrality of the family in the lives of individuals. It is guided by fully informed choices made by the family and focuses upon the strengths and capabilities of these families (Allen & Petr, 1996).

Recognizing the family as the unit of attention. Many families have objected to the child-centered model of service delivery because the parent and family role is minimized. In family-centered approaches, the professional communicates clearly that the family is the most important source of support and influence in a child's life. Children's needs and behaviors affect and are affected by other family members. The boundaries of the family are not limited to the nuclear family but include extended family, friends, neighbors, and whomever the child and parents include in their circle of support.

Maximizing informed choice and decision making for families. In child-centered service, not only is the child the unit of attention, but the professional is the expert about the child and the child's needs. The professional knows best what to do and makes the decisions about the care of the child. In child-centered service, the parents can feel that they are working for the professional to achieve the professional's goals. In family-centered practice, the professional recognizes the central responsibility and authority of parents to make informed decisions about their child. The professional works for the family, providing the parents with all the information they need to make decisions and exploring all options. Family involvement and decision making can extend to the organizational level through membership on committees and governing boards. Although the family's choices are limited by ethical and legal considerations (e.g., parents cannot choose to physically or sexually abuse their children), family-centered services are designed to support and encourage the right of the family to make decisions for itself.

Recognizing the strengths and capacities of families. Too often, professionals have unduly blamed and criticized parents of children with special needs. Professionals have usually been trained to identify problems and deficiencies in children and their families rather than strengths (Saleebey, 1992). Children and families are often measured against white, middle-class norms so that the unique strengths and capabilities of diverse cultures are overlooked. Family-centered professionals are guided by a respect for the child and family's positive attributes, talents, resources, and aspirations.

To date, standards for family-centered service have not been widely or universally accepted. Researchers at the Beach Center on Families and Disability at the University of Kansas have developed the *Family-Centered Behavior Scale* (FCBS) that can be used by researchers and programs to evaluate the level of family-centeredness demonstrated by professional staff (Allen, Petr, & Brown, 1995). The above three elements of family-centered practice are operationalized into 26 behaviors. Parents of children rate professionals on each of the 26 items according to how often the professional exhibits the behavior. A companion instrument (FCBS-I) asks the parent to rate the importance of each of the 26 behaviors. Both scales include Spanish translations. Organizations interested in improving their level of family centeredness can use the scales to target areas of strength and improvement for their staff.

Tools such as the FCBS are necessary to test the belief that family-centered services produce better outcomes for children and families. By measuring the level of family-centered practice, researchers can study whether higher levels of family centeredness were associated with better outcomes. For example, does a higher level of family centeredness improve immunization rates among preschool children? Do family-centered approaches in special education improve students' academic performance? Does a family-centered approach in child abuse result in fewer instances of abuse or fewer children that must be removed from their families?

References

Allen, R. I., & Petr, C. G. (1996). Toward developing standards and measurements for family-centered practice in family support programs. In G. H. S. Singer, L. E. Powers, & A. L. Olson (Eds.), *Redefining family support: Innovations in public-private partnerships* (pp. 57–85). Baltimore, MD: Paul H. Brookes.

Allen, R. I., Petr, C. G., & Brown, B. F. C. (1995). *Family-Centered Behavior Scale and user's manual*. Lawrence, KS: Beach Center on Families and Disability, Life Span Institute, University of Kansas.

Saleebey, D. (Ed.). (1992). *The strengths perspective in social work practice*. New York: Longman.

See also: Family preservation; Family support.

CHRISTOPHER G. PETR

Family council. Given the moral crisis of our times, finding effective ways parents can enhance moral reasoning in their children and adults is a crucial task (Stanley, 1978). Experiences that enhance moral reasoning include situations that encourage cognitive restructuring, role-taking opportunities, participation in groups perceived as fair or just, and exposure to the views of others different from one's own. As a young person grows both in awareness that others' viewpoints and feelings are different from one's own and in the capacity to see one's own behavior from others' perspectives, so too does the young person's moral development grow (Stanley, 1978).

From a review of four computer databases over the past 6 to 30 years (1967–1996), two studies were found with empirical evidence of positive family changes as a result of participating in parent-training programs that included family meetings (Stanley, 1978; Wantz & Recor, 1984). Parents who participated in a 6 weekly 2-hour *Systematic Training for Effective Parenting* (STEP) program (Dinkmeyer & McKay, 1989) reported their children's behavior improved significantly. Changes in parents and adolescents were even more impressive in an experimental-control group study in which two groups participated in 10 weekly 2.5-hour sessions on using conflict resolution and family meetings. Parents in both experimental groups significantly increased their egalitarian attitudes toward family decision making. Families improved their effectiveness in collective decision making. The group that included both parents and adolescents showed greater improvements on most variables measured. Families became more democratic in the ways they established rules and resolved conflicts. They improved their communication, were more effective in solving problems, and increased their egalitarian family relationships. Finally, adolescents who participated in the training significantly improved their scores in moral reasoning, and the results continued for at least nine months afterward (Stanley, 1978).

An excellent way for families to enhance moral reasoning and anger management skills is to communicate openly and reduce anger and conflict via regular family meetings. Regular family meetings are safe opportunities where everyone is free to say what they think and feel as they cooperate in making decisions, solving problems, recognizing good things happening in the family, setting up rules and distributing chores fairly, settling conflicts, and pointing out individual strengths.

When a family is ready, they can begin planning more formal meetings. This forces them to set aside time to be together and to look at their lives and what is working and what is not. Begin with an attitude of openness and acceptance rather than one of dominance or control. Be flexible. The meeting place and length can vary. At first, plan fun activities that involve all household members.

As soon as children can use words, they can participate. Especially with young children (e.g., ages 2 to 6), it is important to keep the family meeting as short as 10 to 20 minutes, gradually increasing the time. With older children, decide ahead how much time to spend, depending on the agenda. Many families find it valuable to schedule meetings for the same time and place weekly or every other week. The key is to design the meetings to fit the family. Intergenerational families with adult children sometimes find it more useful to have monthly family meetings with their length determined by the complexity of the topics to be discussed. By holding family meetings regularly, it is easier to keep them balanced with both celebrating happy times and solving family problems. Discussing one or two problems per meeting is usually a good limit to set.

For 9 practical steps for successful family meetings, see Fetsch and Jacobson (1996) and Slagle (1985):

- Meet at a regularly scheduled time.
- Rotate meeting responsibilities.
- Encourage all family members to participate.
- Discuss one topic and solve one problem at a time.
- Use I-messages and problem-solving steps.
- Summarize the discussion to keep the family on track and to focus the discussion on one issue at a time.

- Make decisions by consensus. Once an agreement appears to acceptable to many, check to see if consensus has been reached.
- If things get too hot to handle, anyone can call for a break.
- End with something that is fun and that affirms family members.

The key to successful family meetings is to be flexible and to use what works to help your family ride the ups and downs of family living and to maintain your family's resiliency or ability to bounce back after experiencing a stressful event. Families that know how to adapt well to inevitable changes tend to have higher marital and family satisfaction levels.

References

Dinkmeyer, D., & McKay, G. D. (1989). *The parent's handbook: Systematic Training for Effective Parenting.* Circle Pines, MN: American Guidance Service.

Fetsch, R. J., & Jacobson, B. (1996). *Manage anger through family meetings* (Fact Sheet no. 10.249). Fort Collins: Colorado State University Cooperative Extension.

Slagle, R. (1985). *A family meeting handbook: Achieving family harmony happily.* Sebastpol, CA: Family Relations Foundation.

Stanley, S. F. (1978). Family education to enhance the moral atmosphere of the family and the moral development of adolescents. *Journal of Counseling Psychology, 25* (2), 110–118.

Wantz, R. A., & Recor, R. D. (1984). Simultaneous parent-child group intervention. *Elementary School Guidance and Counseling, 19* (2), 126–131.

See also: Communication; Conflict resolution; Family loyalty; Family systems.

ROBERT J. FETSCH

Family loyalty. Family loyalty can be defined as a member's response to external coercion, conscious recognition of interest in membership, consciously recognized feelings of obligation, and unconsciously binding obligation to belong (Boszormenyi-Nagy & Ulrich, 1981). It is the responsibility of parents to pass on trustworthiness to their children. This transmission begins early in life and is carried on through adulthood. The child is then linked to the parents by this trustworthiness and seeks to repay it, which creates a legacy to which both the parent and child must respond.

In order to be a loyal member of a family, one has to internalize its expectations and attitudes (Boszormenyi-Nagy & Sparks, 1973). Family loyalty commitments are like invisible but strong fibers that hold family relationships together (Boszormenyi-Nagy & Sparks, 1973). Parent and child are held together by these invisible loyalties. Parents try to impart their own normative values to the child. The child for his or her part has to eventually balance the past, present, and future give and take of the family loyalty commitments (Boszormenyi-Nagy & Sparks, 1973).

These loyalty commitments are keep in an invisible merit ledger. The merit ledger is an accounting of the give and take of the parent-child relationship in which the child is an unmatched partner in the relationship (Boszormenyi-Nagy & Krasner, 1986). Emotional indebtedness then accompanies the merit ledger for both parent and child. Family loyalty and the emotional indebtedness that accompanies it have important parent-child relationship implications.

Parent-child ledgers. Early in life the child is an unequal partner who cannot be expected to reciprocate the give and take of the parent-child relationship. Parents are obligated to provide love, care, nurturing, security, protection, and discipline (Hardgrave & Anderson, 1992). However, the child's only obligation is to grow and learn (Hardgrave & Anderson, 1992). Healthy parent-child interaction raises the level of loyalty and trust in the relationship (Boszormenyi-Nagy & Krasner, 1986). As the child gets older, he or she may be expected to repay or balance the loyalty account. The expectation of the parents may stem from their own emotional indebtedness from childhood, and the parenting they received. However, no child can repay or balance the loyalty account if the parent expects to be repaid in kind for what he or she has given the child (Boszormenyi-Nagy & Krasner, 1986).

Split loyalty. Split loyalty may occur when divorcing parents vie for the affection and love of their child at the expense of the other parent. Children who find themselves in this situation are torn between parents and often find themselves in a no-win situation. This no-win situation may result in dysfunctional behavior by the child who sees no way out without being disloyal to one of the parents. The loyalty of the child toward both parents is of central and vital interest and must be respected (van Heusden & van den Eernbeemt, 1987). Therefore, parents should work to remain in a position of trustworthiness with respect to the child (van Heusden & van den Eernbeemt, 1987).

Achieving healthy balance. One task of parents is to enable their children to become competent healthy adults. The task of becoming an adult should be viewed as being balanced against the loyalty obligations of the maturing child toward the nuclear family (Boszormenyi-Nagy & Sparks, 1973). In other words, the child has to balance old and new loyalties and negotiate with parents regarding his or her loyalty obligations. Goldenthal (1996) put forth the premise that "those who undervalue their ability to give, or who feels that others undervalue it, may experience self-doubt, low self-esteem, depression, and related psychological distress. Those who feel they are giving too much are often chronically angry, and seen by others as self-focused and over entitled" (p. 27). Parents and children benefit from relationships that have a fair balance between giving and receiving loyalty (Goldenthal, 1996). Successful parents have been able to balance their own past loyalty obligations to their parents as well as their child.

References

Boszormenyi-Nagy, I., & Krasner, B. R. (1986). *Between give and take.* New York: Brunner/Mazel.

Boszormenyi-Nagy, I., & Sparks, G. (1973). *Invisible loyalties.* New York: Harper & Row.

Boszormenyi-Nagy, I., & Ulrich, D. N. (1981). Contextual family therapy. In A. S. Gurman & D. P. Kniskern (Eds.), *Handbook of family therapy* (pp. 159–186). New York: Harper & Row.

Goldenthal, P. (1996). *Doing contextual therapy.* New York: W. W. Norton & Company.

Hardgrave, T. D., & Anderson, W. T. (1992). *Finishing well.* New York: Brunner/Mazel.

van Heusden, A., & van den Eernbeemt, E. (1987). *Balance in motion.* New York: Brunner/Mazel.

See also: Family systems.

RICK L. PETERSON

Family preservation. Family preservation refers both to a specific type of service that aims to prevent the out-of-home placement of children and a philosophical approach to providing a continuum of services to children and their families. Family preservation philosophy emphasizes the importance of the family to a child and the sanctity and rights of the family to be together. Families are also viewed as a potential source of strength, and that respect, empathy, and collaboration toward the family promote effective use of services.

Public Law 96-272, the *Adoption Assistance and Child Welfare Act of 1980,* is considered the impetus for many of the changes in the child welfare system, resulting in the current practice of family preservation. Providing the framework for the permanency planning for children in our society, PL 96-272 renewed the emphasis of the child welfare system on strengthening families as a means for providing protection for children. A direct result of the increasing numbers of children entering foster care and experiencing multiple placements while the family deteriorated, these mandates focused on resolving the problem with the family intact, to ensure that children are not unnecessarily removed from their families and that parents are given the opportunity to correct the difficulties that led to the involvement of social control agents.

In an effort to reduce unnecessary placements and preserve and strengthen the family unit as an alternative means for protecting children, the child welfare system has experienced the evolution of family-centered services. Family preservation is now a professional service with a system of values, theories, and interventions. Family preservation services involve delivery of services in the family's natural environment, are generally time limited (four weeks to six months), and are flexible in delivery time in order to accommodate the schedule of the family. They are also intensely delivered (8 to 20 hours a week) and are strength based in their focus on assessment and intervention (Nelson, Landsman, & Deutelbaum, 1990).

Problems such as substance abuse, homelessness, single-contributor households, the lure of the underground economy, and insufficient education and training have not been responsive to traditional interventions. Although it would seem that such complex issues would not be amenable to intense, short-term therapy, three controlled studies suggest that the family preservation approach to family intervention is an effective alternative to out-of-home placements (see Szykula & Fleischman, 1985).

Family preservation is generally considered an approach that emphasizes maintaining the integrity of the family unit, resolving problems with the family intact. Family preservation interventions have been shown to reduce out-of-home placements of children between 70% and 95%, while ensuring safety of family members (Nelson, Landsman, & Deutelbaum, 1990). Further, length of placements outside of the home has been shown to be drastically reduced when interventions with the family are employed (Schwartz, AuClaire, & Harris, 1991).

There are times, however, when it is not in the best interest of the child or a family member for the family to continue as an intact unit, and placement outside of the home becomes necessary. There are also times when it is not possible for the child to return to the family environment. Family preservation philosophy allows for nontraditional family arrangements that promote the maintenance of family relationships without actual in-home placement. Some parents and children can maintain a more positive, effective relationship when they are not residing under the same roof. Alternative arrangements can include relative placement, long-term foster care, open adoption, or independent living. Emphasis is placed on the quality of the parent-child relationship and the acknowledgment of the family connections important to the child.

The majority of attributes of the family preservation philosophy center around the common theme of respect and empowerment of the client family. The philosophical belief that children are better off with their biological families has been credited as the most influential construct related to positive outcomes (Nelson, Landsman, & Deutelbaum, 1990). Bailey and McWilliam (1990) found that offering choices of services to families and respecting their decisions resulted in more active involvement in services.

References
Bailey, D. B., & McWilliam, R. A. (1990). Normalizing early intervention. *Topics in Early Childhood, 10*, 33–45.
Gordon, D. A., Arbuthnot, J., Gustafson, K. E., & McGreen, P. (1988). Home-based behavioral-systems family therapy with disadvantaged juvenile delinquents. *American Journal of Family Therapy, 6*, 243–255.
Nelson, K. E., Landsman, M. J., & Deutelbaum, W. (1990). Three models of family-centered placement prevention services. *Child Welfare, 49*, 3–21.
Schwartz, I. M., AuClaire, P., & Harris, L. J. (1991). Family preservation services as an alternative to the out-of-home placement of adolescents: The Hennepin County experience. In D. E. Biegel & K. Wells (Eds.), *Family preservation services: Research and evaluation* (pp. 33–46). Newbury Park, CA: Sage Publications.
Szykula, S., & Fleischman, M. (1985). Reducing out of home placements of abused children: Three controlled field studies. *Child Abuse and Neglect, 9*, 277–283.

See also: Custody; Empowerment; Family-centered services.

                                                                VICKY PRIMER

Family-school partnerships. Reciprocal communication and shared planning and decision making where families and educators contribute, listen, and understand the needs of each other are characteristics of family-school partnerships. While parents have many opportunities for involvement, including volunteering, providing home support for learning, and engaging in decision making at school, viewing their involvement as essential is an important characteristic for a partnership. Christenson and Buerkle (in press) argue that parents are essential—not merely desirable—for optimal child outcomes. Optimal student performance depends on students' in-school and out-of-school time, teacher and parent support for student learning, and a consistent message about the value of education from schools and families.

Dunst et al. (1992) found that a partnership develops over time as trust, caring, honesty, flexibility, shared responsibility, two-way communication, empathy, and the disclosure of information develop. Furthermore, the efforts of those involved are complementary, joint, and reciprocal. As interaction between parents and professionals increases, so do opportunities for the display of factors that characterize partnerships. Thus, the nature of the relationship progresses from being coordinated or cooperative to being a partnership. According to Swap (1993), elements of the family-school partnerships are based on reciprocity: two-way communication, enhancing learning at home and school, providing mutual support, and making joint decisions.

Parents across educational and income levels and ethnic groups want their children to succeed in school, need better information from educators about ways to help, and want to be partners in their children's education. While most teachers and administrators want to involve parents, they do not know how to build effective partnerships (Epstein, 1995).

Comer and colleagues established the first School Development Program in 1968 (Comer & Haynes, 1991). The essential piece of this program, the School Planning and Management Team, is shared governance between parents and educators to set school policies and practices. The goals of this team focus on improving student achievement, school climate, staff development, and community relations. Team members represent adult stakeholders in the student's life, allowing members a sense of community and ownership of program outcomes.

Weiss and Edwards (1992) developed climate-building activities to connect families and schools for the benefit of student's education. The activities are designed to overcome three major barriers that inhibit family-school partnerships: infrequent opportunities for sharing information between home and school; cultural, social, economic, and racial differences between school staff and families that create either real or assumed barriers; and a limited conception of roles parents can fill. A cooperative process of planning and problem solving among school staff, parents, and students is used to assess current family-school interactions, set goals for improvement, and identify specific activities to build trust and improve school climate. Their approach is unique in that it involves students in all aspects of the program.

Epstein (1995) developed a framework for developing comprehensive family-school partnership programs in grades K–12 that combines six elements: parenting, communicating, volunteering, home learning activities, shared decision making and governance, and community support. Parenting skills classes, language translators to assist families at conferences, opportunities for parents to volunteer, providing grade-appropriate information for learning activities at home, offering parents positions on governing bodies, and connecting with community programs illustrate that parent involvement in education occurs at school and at home in a partnership model.

There is no one way to create successful partnership programs. The focus of programs is to improve learning outcomes and opportunities for students. Successful programs are long term, comprehensive, and well planned and consider the talents and strengths of individuals at a particular school. Furthermore, effective programs recognize and value the effects home and school have on student development.

References

Christenson, S. L., & Buerkle, K. (in press). Families as educational partners for children's school success: Suggestions for school psychologists. In C. R. Reynolds & T. B. Gutkin (Eds.), *Handbook of school psychology.* New York: Wiley.

Comer, J. P., & Haynes, N. M. (1991). Parent involvement in schools: An ecological approach. *Elementary School Journal, 91* (3), 271–278.

Dunst, C. J., Johanson, C., Rounds, T., Trivette, C. M., & Hamby, D. (1992). Characteristics of parent-professional partnerships. In S. L. Christenson & J. C. Conoley (Eds.), *Home-school collaboration: Enhancing children's academic and social competence* (pp. 157–174). Silver Spring, MD: National Association of School Psychologists.

Epstein, J. L. (1995). School/family/community partnerships: Caring for the children we share. *Phi Delta Kappan, 76,* 701–712.

Swap, S. M. (1993). *Developing home-school partnerships: From concepts to practice.* New York: Teachers College Press.

Weiss, H. M., & Edwards, M. E. (1992). The family school collaboration project: Systemic interventions for school improvement. In S. L. Christenson & J. C. Conoley (Eds.), *Home-school collaboration: Enhancing children's academic and social competence* (pp. 215–243). Silver Spring, MD: National Association of School Psychologists.

See also: Academic achievement; Family support; Home schooling; Teacher training.

TARA THOMAS SCHLUESCHE, JUANITA LARAMIE, AND
SANDRA L. CHRISTENSON

Family size. Family size in developing countries such as India is often the result of joint families, kinship members living together in the same household. In Western industrialized countries, *family size* refers to the number of children in a family. It was frequently studied during the baby boom era in Canada and the United States when a woman's lifetime fertility was around 3.5 and the emphasis was on predicting fertility levels. As women's lifetime fertility dropped to below replacement (below 2 children) in developed countries, the range in the number of children per family is much more restricted than in the past and is reflected in the significant body of research directed now at the effects of being an only child.

On the basis of their meta-analysis of 141 studies, Polit and Falbo (1987) concluded that there were no personality differences between onlies and children with siblings in the areas of character, personal control, personal adjustment, sociability, and relations with parents. The notions of personality maladjustment that formed the hypotheses of most studies were based on stereotypes of only children from a high-fertility era. Like children from small families, only children were thought to benefit from close personal interactions with their parents who were substitutes for the sociability provided through sibling interaction. Extending Polit and Falbo's analysis to the effects of number of siblings on affiliative tendencies, Blake, Richardson and Bhattacharya (1991) analyzed two United States national data sets. Their findings confirm that only children are not less able to get along with peers than those from larger families.

Family size effects on child outcomes covary with a number of other possibly confounding fertility-related variables. Families with more children have less space between children and contain a higher number of later-born children. Mother's age could also be higher, although this was more the case before the 1980s when women's age at first birth began rising. In any cross-sectional sample, younger mothers might not have completed their childbearing. Larger family sizes are more likely to contain unwanted children than those that are smaller. Finally, socioeconomic status (SES) is negatively associated with family size and, thus, acts as a confounding variable. Socioeconomic status acts as a contextual variable, so most of the effects of family size are specific to lower-income groups.

The most frequently studied effects of family size on child outcomes are IQ and achievement levels, both of which are highly associated with SES. Only children and children from small families have been found to be more advantaged in being more achievement oriented than those from larger families. Although some of this relationship is due to the higher social class background of small families, Blake (1989) found that children from small families had superior academic achievement even with social class effects removed. Despite the pervasiveness of this finding, there has been little research on its basis in parent-child origins.

Parental effects on achievement have more often been theorized about than studied directly. The *confluence* model indirectly implicates parenting in the process. This model emphasizes how each child successively reduces the overall intellectual milieu available to the children in their families. Each child receives fewer interactions with more skilled and knowledgeable adults and more interactions with siblings who have had less mental development.

The *resource dilution* model is another variant of a model built on scarcity of resources. This model adds consideration of financial resources and access to parents. Downey (1995) found an interaction effect between parental and financial resources to show that the value of economic resources such as books was less if interpersonal resources were not there in the form of parental attention to reading. There was also a threshold effect for parenting to the effect that parenting resources were diluted only after a certain number of children. Downey cautions that such findings might not hold for extended family systems.

Considerations of reciprocal effects of children on parents indicate that the marital relationship is negatively affected with increasing family size which, in turn, may influence parent-child relationships. The classic study by Bossard and Boll (1956) shows parents responding to the organizational demands of a large number of children. Apparently, parents with many children are more punitive and more emotionally distant from their children than are those with smaller numbers of children. Parents tend to be more authoritarian. These types of interactions may set the stage for the pattern of abuse that tends to be found more frequently for children in larger families, but low income could be an important confounding variable in this relationship.

References

Blake, J. (1989). *Family size and achievement*. Berkeley: University of California Press.

Blake, J., Richardson, B., & Bhattacharya, J. (1991). Number of siblings and sociability. *Journal of Marriage and the Family*, *53* (2), 271–283.

Bossard, J., & Boll, E. (1956). *The large family system*. Philadelphia: University of Philadelphia.

Downey, D. (1995). When bigger is not better: Family size, parental resources, and children's educational performance. *American Sociological Review*, *60*, 746–761.

Polit, D. F., & Falbo, T. (1987). Only children and personality development: A quantitative analysis. *Journal of Marriage and the Family*, *49* (2), 309–325.

See also: Birth order; Family systems; Siblings.

ELAINE G. PORTER

Family support. Family support programs are designed to foster the well-being of children at risk of less than optimal development by attending to the needs of the family as a whole. Such programs are often termed "two-generation" programs because their focus encompasses parents as well as children.

Since their grassroots beginnings in the 1970s, family support programs have varied markedly in their activities and goals. Still, most family support proponents subscribe to a common set of assumptions and principles (compiled from Kagan et al., 1987; Weiss & Jacobs, 1988; Weissbourd, 1993):

- Families need to be viewed in context; they are embedded in an ecological system of extended family, friends, acquaintances, and community.
- All families have strengths.
- All families need support; it is a myth that any family can "do it alone."
- Parents who are receiving adequate support become empowered to manage their lives and their environment.
- Primary responsibility for children belongs to their parents, who are the most important people in their children's lives.
- Most parents want to be good parents; if they fail to do so, it is because of shortcomings in their own development.
- Parents need child development information in order to respond appropriately to their children.
- Parents, as well as professionals, have expertise to share.

Principles of program design include the following emphases:

- Programs ought to be family focused rather than child focused, treating families as a whole and attending to the developmental needs of both parents and children.
- Programs ought to be controlled at the community level and ought to reflect the culture and values of the community.
- The programmatic emphases should be on prevention, not on crisis intervention, and on health and well-being, not on deficits.
- Programs ought to be open to any parent who wishes to participate, regardless of "need."
- Peer support networks should be nurtured and facilitated.

- Professionals and parents ought to collaborate; the role of professionals should be to do things *with*, not *to*, families.
- Parents should be encouraged to participate in defining their needs and deciding on the content of programs.

Family support programs vary in their format and activities. Home visits are one means of delivering services. Another means is bringing groups of parents together in any number of settings. In some communities, a *full-service* family resource center offers a wide range of activities, including drop-in programs and toy and book libraries. A given family support program may use only one of these formats, or it may use some combination of the three. Typical program activities include parent education, developmental screening for children, vocational development activities for parents, and facilitation of the use of community resources (Epstein, Larner, & Halpern, 1995; Weissbourd, 1993).

The format, activities, and goals of a family support program depend on the characteristics of the families it serves and on the nature of the sponsor. Sponsors have been as varied as parents' cooperatives, charitable and service organizations, foundations, or government agencies. In recent years, several states have initiated family support programs for their residents, with programs being administered by state social service departments or by state departments of education. In other states, family support principles have been incorporated into reforms of the way human services are delivered (Epstein, Larner, & Halpern, 1995; Weiss, 1989; Weissbourd, 1993).

Along with the growth of the family support movement have come concerns that the approach will be "oversold." Proponents point out that family support programs are not a substitute for such basic needs as income assistance or affordable housing (Weissbourd, 1993), and they are inadequate if a family needs skilled clinical intervention (Epstein, Larner, & Halpern, 1995).

Nevertheless, human service programs that respect the primacy of the family and recognize its responsibility have broad political appeal (Weiss, 1989). Perhaps as a result, the family support movement has spread from the local to the state and national levels as evidenced by federal legislation in recent years (PL 99–457 in 1986; PL 100–485 in 1988; PL 101–501 in 1990; and PL 103–66 in 1993). On the state level, the tenets of family support appear to be effecting a fundamental change in the relationship between families and the tax-supported institutions they turn to for aid (Weiss, 1989). In sum, the family support movement has staged a quiet revolution (Kagan et al., 1987).

References

Epstein, A. S., Larner, M., & Halpern, R. (1995). *A guide to developing community-based family support programs.* Ypsilanti, MI: High/Scope Press.

Kagan, S. L., Powell, D. R., Weissbourd, B., & Zigler, E. F. (Eds.). (1987). *America's family support programs.* New Haven, CT: Yale University Press.

Weiss, H. B. (1989). State family support and education programs: Lessons from the pioneers. *American Journal of Orthopsychiatry, 59,* 32–48.

Weiss, H. B., & Jacobs, F. H. (Eds.). (1988). *Evaluating family programs.* New York: Aldine de Gruyter.

Weissbourd, B. (1993). Family support programs. In C. H. Zeanah (Ed.), *Handbook of infant mental health* (pp. 402–413). New York: Guilford Press.

See also: Education, parenting; Home visitation; MELD; Social support, informal.

JENNIFER CLARK

Family systems. Taking a *systems* approach helps the observer to look beyond the behavior of an individual child or parent and to understand that individual within the context of the larger emotional system. The relevant emotional system might include the nuclear or intergenerational family, the school, the neighborhood, or social service agencies in contact with the family. When anxiety is high in the emotional system, one or more members of that system may start to show symptoms. Often the adults in a system respond to this heightened intensity by focusing their concerns on a child, who becomes the "identified patient."

Anxiety typically rises in a family system in response to the following stressors:

- the addition of new family members
- the loss of a family member through illness, death, divorce, or imprisonment
- illness or hospitalization
- migration or a geographic move
- change in employment
- change in the leadership of relevant systems (family, school, church, social service agency)
- anniversaries of significant emotional events (such as the loss of a family member)
- prejudice and discrimination from a more dominant group

When anxiety about any of these triggers gets overfocused on one member of the emotional system, that member may display provocative behavior that invites further attention and concern from family members and professionals. To the extent that adults in the system can "expand their lens" and view the "identified patient" as just one part of an anxious system, the adult may find new and helpful ways of responding. With a systemic lens, helpers will be less likely to take sides and can help those adults most concerned about the "identified patient" to stay calm, stay in contact, define a clear position, and think systemically (see Gilbert, 1992; Lerner, 1985).

Teachers, judges, probation officers, church leaders, and others who come into contact with highly stressed family systems may enhance their effectiveness by helping the adults in the family get curious about the larger context of their family's problems and the part they play in that emotional reactivity.

Identification of the following patterns is helpful in teaching parents to observe process, to define a position for self, and to stay calmly in contact with their children during stressful periods in their family's life:

- conflict
- distance or cutoff
- triangulation
- overfunctioning and underfunctioning

Emergence of any or all of these four patterns is likely as anxiety in a system rises. Some parents may fight about how to deal with the child's problem (conflict). Others distance from the family's problems by staying long hours at work, physically deserting the family, or just being emotionally "absent" and overfocused on alcohol, drugs, or work. Parents who have not worked out anxiety within their own intimate system may *triangulate* a child into their relationship by overfocusing on that child rather than addressing the problems in their marriage or asking the child to "take sides" and support one parent over the other. Finally, in many relationships a pattern gets established whereby one member of the family "overdoes," enabling another family member to take a less responsible position. This results in the overfunctioner "burning out" and the underfunctioner feeling angry, controlled, badgered, and depressed.

The goal is to help the adults in the system to observe patterns, to define a position for self, and to move from an anxious overfocus on a child to a confident interest in the child's response to age-appropriate challenges (Gilbert, 1992). Childhood conduct disorders and delinquency are typical of the problems addressed from a family systems perspective. In a recent meta-analysis of outcome studies, Shadish et al. (1993) identified family interventions as the most promising method of treatment for child conduct disorders. The focus of treatment includes reducing coercive patterns between parent and child, behavioral contracting, and support for parental supervision and discipline.

However, systems treatment may not end at the boundaries of the family. In recognition that adolescent delinquent behavior occurs within the context of larger systems, *Multitarget Ecological Treatment* (MET) is designed to increase contact and affiliation with prosocial peers at the same time that parents are taught to use nonviolent discipline, increase expressions of affection, and effectively monitor their children. Chamberlain and Rosicky (1995) report on the effectiveness of such multisystem intervention as well as other systemic treatments for adolescents and their parents.

References

Chamberlain, P., & Rosicky, J. G. (1995). The effectiveness of family therapy in the treatment of adolescents with conduct disorders and delinquency. *Journal of Marital and Family Therapy, 21* (4), 441–459.

Gilbert, R. M. (1992). *Extraordinary relationships: A new way of thinking about human interactions.* Minneapolis, MN: CHRONIMED Publishing.

Lerner, H. G. (1985). *Dance of anger.* New York: Harper & Row.

Shadish, W. R., Montgomery, L. M., Wilson, P., Wilson, M. R., Right, I., & Okwumabua, T. (1993). Effects of family and marital psychotherapies: A meta-analysis. *Journal of Consulting and Clinical Psychology, 61,* 992–1002.

See also: Community; Conflict resolution; Stress.

CANDYCE S. RUSSELL

Family therapy. Family therapy was preceded by the child guidance movement and a variety of individual treatment approaches for childhood disorders (Estrada & Pinsof, 1995; Roy & Frankel, 1995). Family therapy has been broadly defined as "any psychotherapeutic endeavor that explicitly focuses on altering the interactions between or among family members and seeks to improve the functioning of the family as a unit, or its subsystems, and/or the functioning of the individual members of the family" (Gurman, Kniskern, & Pinsof, 1986, p. 565). Family therapy is a common treatment method for childhood and adolescent disorders and dysfunctional parent-child relationships that focuses on the interactions among family members.

Family therapists typically request that all members of the household attend the therapy session, even if only one family member is identified as having the problem. However, during the course of therapy the therapist may also meet separately with the parents and the child/adolescent, in order to garner information that might not or should not be shared in front of the entire family. Historically, family therapists often assumed that an acting-out child was a result of dysfunctional parenting or family interaction. Currently, family therapists tend to adopt a more balanced stance, integrating into the assessment and treatment process child/adolescent biological or psychological issues as well.

There is a growing body of outcome research evaluating the efficacy of family therapy for several disorders of childhood and adolescence (cf. Chamberlain & Rosicky, 1995; Estrada & Pinsof, 1995; Liddle & Dakof, 1995; Roy & Frankel, 1995). This body of literature contains research examining the effectiveness of several different family therapy models, including structural family therapy, strategic family therapy, and behavioral family therapy, although the most convincing research has come from the behavioral tradition. In their review of this research, Estrada and Pinsof (1995) noted that many of the approaches are based on Gerald Patterson's conceptual model and treatment approach to antisocial behavior (Patterson, 1986, cited in Estrada & Pinsof, 1995). Patterson's work is based on social learning theory and proposes that the origin and maintenance of behavioral problems are inadvertent and the result of dysfunctional parent-child interaction. As a result, the goals of intervention include changing problematic interactions, examining factors within the family constellation that contribute to the maintenance of the behavior, a focus on prosocial behavior, and decreasing deviant behavior (Estrada & Pinsof, 1995).

Several disorders have been treated with family therapy approaches based on parent management training, including conduct problems or disorder, Attention-Deficit/Hyperactivity Disorder (ADHD), fear and anxiety disorders, and autistic disorder (Estrada & Pinsof, 1995). Of these disorders, the functioning of children and parents improved the most in families whose children evidenced conduct disorders or autistic disorder, while the long-term gains for ADHD and fears and anxieties were minimal (Estrada & Pinsof, 1995).

Adolescent juvenile delinquency or conduct problems have also been successfully addressed with family therapy approaches based on social learning or structural family therapy, although data demonstrating the superiority of family therapy over other approaches (such as individual therapy for the child or adolescent) are limited. This research has also documented one of the challenges to the efficacy of family therapy, resistance to family participation in treatment (Chamberlain & Rosicky, 1995). Because family therapists conceptualize children with problems as affecting other family members and in turn being affected by them, the goal is to get the entire family in treatment, so that problematic interactions can be understood and altered. This approach may clash with the stated goal of the parent, which is often to "fix this child." Consequently, family therapists must frequently spend time during the telephone intake or the initial session providing a rationale for treating the whole family.

The effectiveness of family therapy with a variety of other problems of childhood or adolescence has also been examined, although much more research is needed before the field can document these claims with certainty. For example, there is very limited, tentative data supporting the efficacy of family therapy in cases of chronic childhood illnesses, such as brittle diabetes and asthma (Roy & Frankel, 1995). There is also some data demonstrating that family therapy is a valuable part of the treatment approach for the eating disorders (anorexia nervosa and bulimia) (Roy & Frankel, 1995).

Surprisingly, there is a lack of research on family therapy as a possible intervention for a variety of other disorders, including schizophrenia, depression, suicide, and learning disabilities in childhood/adolescence (Estrada & Pinsof, 1995). The research on family therapy approaches for adolescent substance use is promising but not yet conclusive (Liddle & Dakof, 1995).

References

Chamberlain, P., & Rosicky, J. G. (1995). The effectiveness of family therapy in the treatment of adolescents with conduct disorders and delinquency. *Journal of Marital and Family Therapy*, *21*, 441–459.

Estrada, A. U., & Pinsof, W. M. (1995). The effectiveness of family therapies for selected behavioral disorders of childhood. *Journal of Marital and Family Therapy*, *21*, 403–440.

Gurman, A. S., Kniskern, D. P., & Pinsof, W. M. (1986). Research on the process and outcome of marital and family therapy. In S. L. Garfield & A. E. Bergin (Eds.), *Handbook of psychotherapy and behavior change* (3rd ed., pp. 565–624). New York: Wiley.

Liddle, H. A., & Dakof, G. A. (1995). Efficacy of family therapy for drug abuse: Promising but not definitive. *Journal of Marital and Family Therapy*, *21*, 511–543.

Roy, R., & Frankel, H. (1995). *How good is family therapy? A reassessment*. Toronto: University of Toronto Press.

See also: Conflict resolution; Family support; Family systems.

MARK B. WHITE

Fathering. No longer are fathers viewed as the forgotten contributors to child development. Decades of research have documented that fathers influence their children's sex-role identification, cognitive and moral development, social competence, and psychological adjustment. But until the mid-1970s, fathers and their roles in child development were virtually ignored in the socialization literature, thereby lending credence to Margaret Mead's statement that "fathers are a biological necessity but a social accident."

Over time, the father's role has undergone transformation—from the colonial period when fathers were primarily responsible for moral teaching, through the mid-1930s when fathers were valued as gender-role models, to the current interest in fathers as active and nurturant caregivers. Although today's fathers are expected to be more actively involved in child care than in the past, to assume that this increased involvement is necessarily beneficial in all family circumstances may be a mistake. Rather, individual circumstances must be considered to understand how children are affected by variations in father involvement (Lamb, Pleck, & Levine, 1985).

Fathers with unemployed wives typically spend about one fourth as much time directly interacting with young children and are accessible to their young children about a third as often as mothers (Lamb, 1986). In two-earner families, the levels of paternal as compared to maternal engagement and accessibility are substantially higher than in one-earner families. Yet regardless of maternal employment status, fathers assume little or no responsibility for children's day-to-day care. In light of controversies about maternal versus paternal involvement, it is worth noting that when employed mothers tend to spend less time in child care, this tends to inflate the paternal involvement estimates. In reality, fathers are proportionally more involved when mothers are employed, although the extent of their involvement does not change in any meaningful way.

During the infancy period, fathers are less accessible, hold less responsibility for child care, and engage in less one-on-one interaction with their children than mothers. Mothers' interactions usually involve caregiving, but fathers' interactions usually involve play. When fathers have been observed feeding their infants, for example, they respond as sensitively as do mothers to the babies' feeding rhythms and engage their babies in social episodes as often (Parke & Tinsley, 1981).

Fathers tend to play in a more physical, idiosyncratic, and emotionally arousing way, whereas mothers tend to play in ways that are less arousing, more verbal, and more often involve toys and conventional games such as peek-a-boo (Bridges, Connell, & Belsky, 1988). When compared to nonemployed mothers, mothers who work outside the home tend to engage in more playful stimulation of their babies, and their husbands are somewhat more involved in caregiving. When fathers are the primary caregivers, they usually retain their arousing play style of interaction in addition to meeting basic caregiving responsibilities. These highly involved fathers hold less gender-stereotyped beliefs, have sympathetic and friendly personalities, and see parenthood as an enriching experience (Lamb, 1987).

In general, research has shown that fathers tend to be more interested in and involved with their sons than their daughters, regardless of the child's age. Fathers are more concerned about sex typing than are mothers and tend to hold more traditional attitudes. Nurturant fathers and those who are more highly involved in caregiving foster altruism and generosity in their children. Fathers generally interact with daughters in more expressive ways and with sons in a more instrumental fashion. Research also shows that the warmth of father/son relations is associated with social competence, self-esteem, and personality adjustment in boys and with personality adjustment and happiness in later heterosexual relations in girls.

Both the quality and the quantity of fathering have been studied. The salience of a number of ecological variables, in the psychological, marital, sociocultural, and parental domains, has been demonstrated. Research indicates that paternal competence and child adaptation are influenced by a man's psychological health, his relationship with his own father, his autonomy and affiliation, and sex-role identification. The quality of the marital relationship, support available for meeting family and work responsibilities, personal resources, such as time and money, and employment also affect father involvement (Grossman, Pollack, & Golding, 1988).

Unfortunately, in 1990, more than one third of all children in the United States were living apart from their fathers—more than double the rate of 1960. Scholars anticipate that before reaching 18 years of age, more than half of all American children will live apart from their fathers, either in single-parent or stepparent families for a significant portion of their childhood. The disintegration of the two-parent family and an accompanying weakening of commitment of fathers to their children are central causes of many individual and social problems (Popenoe, 1996). Juvenile delinquency, drug abuse, teen pregnancy, welfare dependency, and poverty are directly correlated with fathers' lack of involvement in their children's lives.

References

Bridges, L., Connell, J., & Belsky, J. (1988). Similarities and differences in infant-mother and infant-father interaction in the strange situation: A component process analysis. *Developmental Psychology, 24* (1), 92–100.

Grossman, F. K., Pollack, W. S., & Golding, E. (1988). Fathers and children: Predicting the quality and quantity of fathering. *Developmental Psychology, 24*, 82–91.

Lamb, M. E. (1986). *The father's role: Applied perspectives*. New York: Wiley & Sons.

Lamb, M. E. (1987). *The father's role: Cross-cultural perspectives*. Hillsdale, NJ: Erlbaum.

Lamb, M. E., Pleck, J. H., & Levine, J. A. (1985). The role of the father in child development: The effects of increased paternal involvement. In B. S. Lahey, & A. E. Kazdin (Eds.), *Advances in clinical child psychology* (Vol. 8, pp. 247-268). New York: Plenum.

Parke, R. D., & Tinsley, B. R. (1981). The father's role in infancy: Determinants of involvement in caregiving and play (pp. 429-458). In M. E. Lamb (Ed.), *The role of the father in child development*. New York: Wiley.

Popenoe, D. (1996). *Life without father*. New York: Free Press.

See also: Dual-earner families; Mothering; Styles, parenting.

MARY DELUCCIE

Fear. Fear involves the perception of real or imagined danger. The experience of fear involves a combination of *psychological discomfort*, such as wariness, worry, apprehension, or horror, and *physical arousal*, such as increased heart rate or perspiration. Fear is a potentially adaptive and protective response important to survival (Sarafino, 1986). Its purpose within the self-system is to identify a threat and engage in flight or attack. Within the interpersonal system, fear elicits protection from another or signals submission to ward off attack (Malatesta, 1990). The anticipation of danger and the experience of fear may motivate children to be cautious and prudent.

Phobias are intense and irrational fears that are directly associated with specific situations. *Anxiety* is a vague, less-focused state of distress or discomfort. Fears, phobias, and anxiety are related because they involve a response to a perceived threat (Sarafino, 1986).

Young children reveal their fear and anxiety mainly by crying, screaming, clinging, and avoidance reactions. There is an increase in heart rate and blood supply and disturbances of sleep rhythms or appetite. Anxious toddlers may be less adventurous than usual. They may experience nightmares or seek comfort in a familiar object, such as a soft blanket, a teddy bear, or their own thumb. Older children may engage in nail biting, "nervous" coughs or headaches, pulling and picking, blinking or screwing-up of eyes, or vomiting in response to stress.

Fears appear in the second half of a child's first year of life, reach their peak during the second year, and then stabilize or decline thereafter. Girls tend to show fear more than boys do, probably because of sex-typed socialization. First fears are associated with separation from a familiar caretaker and unexpected and strong sensory experiences like sudden loud noises, bright lights, or the loss of physical support. Some of the most common sources of fear in preschoolers are animals, the dark, death, doctors and dentists, heights, monsters and other imaginary creatures, nightmares, school, storms, and deep water. During middle childhood, fears related to peer relationships and competence appear (Sarafino, 1986). Young children are the most fearful because of their limited capacity to comprehend the danger and take effective action.

Fears are acquired in three ways (Rachman, 1990). *Conditioning* includes exposure to traumatic or aversive stimulation or repeated exposures to aversive sensitizing conditions. This involves fear through association. The strength of the fear is linked to the number of repetitions and the intensity of the fear or pain they experience. Fear of doctors would be an example of conditioned fear. *Vicarious acquisition* involves the direct or indirect observations of people displaying fear. A child might become frightened of spiders after watching a parent show panic and repulsion when seeing a spider crawling across a wall in the kitchen. The third pathway involves the *informational acquisition of fear*. In this case, a child acquires information that is open to being interpreted (or misinterpreted) as threatening. A parent might tell a child, for example, "If you keep sucking that thumb, you will blow up and burst!" Because they take such comments literally, young children can easily become frightened by information that is misinterpreted.

Parents can reduce conditioned fears through *desensitization*. This involves exposing children to what is feared a little at a time, accompanied by pleasant or calming experiences. If a young child was conditioned to fear dogs, for example, a parent might start with a small stuffed toy animals, then graduate to a larger stuffed animal while providing lots of reassurance. Once the child was comfortable with this play, small, quiet dogs could be introduced, followed by others of gradually increasing size. Fears that were acquired vicariously could be reduced by *observing parents* mastering a fear of potentially fearful circumstances. *Accurate information* about what is feared could prove to be effective with any type of fear that is based on misunderstanding. A child who was afraid to use the toilet after hearing his mother talk about having "butterflies in my stomach" might be reassured by accurate information and pictures about how the body operates.

The *primary-secondary control model* provides three levels of coping with fear that cannot be eliminated at its source (Band & Weisz, 1988). *Problem-coping* efforts involve changing the environment to achieve control. *Emotion-focused* control consists of adaptive secondary efforts to improve one's emotional state within the existing conditions. Learning to calm oneself physically or use affirmative self-talk are examples of this form of coping. With *relinquished* control fear is endured without any attempt to exert control. There is no attempt to cope with the fear.

Stories can prove useful in the management of children's fear. Tremewan and Strongman (1991) examined children's books for the types of coping strategies they suggest. They found 10 themes related to the three levels of the primary-secondary control model. Themes emphasizing secondary control (adaptive efforts) (e.g., social support, emotion-focused crying, emotion-focused aggression, cognitive avoidance, and pure cognition) were especially important to young children in coping with fear in their own lives.

References

Band, E., & Weisz, J. (1988). How to feel better when it feels bad: Children's perspectives on coping with everyday stress. *Developmental Psychology*, *24*, 247–253.

Malatesta, C. Z. (1990). The role of emotions in the development and organization of personality. In R. Dienstbier & R. A. Thompson (Eds.), *Nebraska Symposium on Motivation 1988* (pp. 1–56). Lincoln: University of Nebraska Press.

Rachman, S. (1990). The determinants and treatment of simple phobias. *Advances in Behaviour Research and Therapy*, *12*, 1–30.

Sarafino, E. P. (1986). *The fears of childhood*. New York: Human Sciences Press.

Tremewan, T., & Strongman, K. T. (1991). Coping with fear in early childhood: Comparing fiction with reality. *Early Child Development and Care*, *71*, 13–34.

See also: Imagination; Nightmares; Television violence; Violence, community.

CHARLES A. SMITH

Feminism. Feminism is a sociopolitical philosophy that increases gender awareness and gender sensitivity. Feminists identify and try to alter patriarchal assumptions and actions. Patriarchal ideas value male-oriented concepts and activities while devaluing beliefs and behaviors associated with women. Feminists confront patriarchal expectations, actions, and laws pertaining to women in personal, economic, and political domains.

Feminists also believe women's choices will be restricted as long as women continue to have the lion's share of responsibility for child rearing and as long as work in the home is devalued (Doucet, 1995). People assume women should take care of children because they believe women possess a natural maternal instinct (Balbus, 1992). However, feminists conclude, "women are not, by definition, suited only for child care, and men are not, by definition, unable to nurture children" (Meyer & Rosenblatt, 1987, p. 250). Both men and women should be responsible for children. Therefore, changes in expectations and laws pertaining to work and child care should be seen as helping both women and men (Meyer & Rosenblatt, 1987).

Some believe coparenting (equal sharing of child-raising responsibilities) is the only way to achieve gender equality and is essential to the success of feminism (Balbus, 1992). Traditionally structured families place responsibility for child rearing at the feet of mothers and keep fathers distant. Because society expects them to be perfect, ideal mothers, women become the object of much love and much hate (Balbus, 1992). In contrast, fathers are perceived as distant and blameless (Balbus, 1992). Coparenting permits the desires and frustrations of children to be equally distributed among both parents, allowing for a balanced model of relationships. Coparenting provides children with a more balanced view of women and men. The significant involvement of both women and men in child rearing grants flexibility to women, men, and children.

However, both women and men may be hesitant to move toward coparenting. For instance, women may be hesitant to share the responsibility of parenting until they share economic and political power with men. Parenting is one of the few areas where women have power and are usually considered more competent than men. In addition, men may be torn between their socialization to be autonomous and their fear of taking care of a dependent child (Balbus, 1992). Both women and men will have to give up power in some areas in order to gain power in other areas.

Coparenting is one way in which feminists challenge the assumption that the traditional, nuclear family is the healthiest family form. Feminists believe that no one family structure is intrinsically superior to another family form (Meyer & Rosenblatt, 1987). They value the two-parent family as well as single-parent families, divorced families, and families led by lesbian and gay parents. Diverse family forms should be valued rather than pathologized by society.

Rigidly adhering to traditional family structures and gender roles restricts the choices of women and tends to isolate them. Expecting mothers to fulfill a very stressful role with little support may lead to ambivalence around mothering. Mothering may involve feelings of great joy and happiness along with despair, resentment, and frustration (Davies & Welch, 1986). Society pressures women to take responsibility for others and sacrifice self. Those who do not abide by the ethic of self-sacrifice are labeled deviant and may be considered inferior mothers (Davies & Welch, 1986).

Feminists do not consider mothering in and of itself as bad for women. They consider parenting under conditions of isolation along with societal pressures to be the ideal mother as unhealthy. Davies and Welch (1986) found that women who stayed at home with their children often considered themselves unhappy. The women interpreted these feelings as normal or attributed them to not putting enough energy into being a housewife and mother and tended to buy into societal expectations that women are supposed to put the needs of men and children first and foremost. The unhappiest mothers held onto an ideal model of mothering and believed they should behave and feel in ways commensurate with societal expectations of self-negation for women. On the other hand, the happiest women felt they had the right to fulfill their own needs and believed they had the power to do so.

Feminism aspires to create a context that values flexibility and variety for both genders. Modern feminism embraces pluralism. This concept respects diversity. Instead of focusing on the similarities and differences between the genders, pluralism highlights the inherent problems in one group dominating another group (Doucet, 1995). Basically, feminists believe that wherever domination exists, so does oppression, prejudice, and inequality.

References
Balbus, I. D. (1992). De-Kleining feminist mothering theory? *Theory and Society*, *21*, 817–835.
Davies, B., & Welch, D. (1986). Motherhood and feminism: Are they compatible? The ambivalence of mothering. *Australian and New Zealand Journal of Sociology*, *22* (3), 411–426.
Doucet, A. (1995). Gender equality and gender differences in household work and parenting. *Women's Studies International Forum*, *18* (3), 271–284.
Meyer, C. J., & Rosenblatt, P. C. (1987). Feminist analysis of family textbooks. *Journal of Family Issues*, *8* (2), 247–252.

See also: Employment, early maternal; Fathering; Mothering; Sex roles.

SHANNON DERMER AND CRYSTAL WILHITE HEMESATH

Fertilization, in vitro. For female infertility, in vitro fertilization (IVF) may be used to obtain conception. This is a process whereby several oocytes are removed from the ovaries before ovulation and placed in a laboratory dish or tube with about 50,000 spermatazoa from the woman's husband/partner. Fertilization takes place in this environment and the embryos (up to three in New Zealand) are replaced in the uterus after cell division (three- to four-cell stage) has occurred. At the three- to four-cell stage of the process, selection occurs to ensure that only the most viable embryos are used. In vitro fertilization can occur with frozen embryos and with donor egg, embryo, or sperm. A number of related processes can be used such as gamete intrafallopian transfer (GIFT) where both oocytes and sperm are transferred directly into the fallopian tubes, and zygote intrafallopian transfer (ZIFT), where zygotes (fertilized ova that have not yet developed into embryos) are transferred into the fallopian tube. In general, in vitro fertilization is indicated when the woman has tubal damage or endometriosis or when the man has less than the normal amount of sperm in the semen.

The procedure of in vitro fertilization became successful in 1968 with the first child being born in 1978, in the United Kingdom. Since then the process has been successfully used in technologically advanced countries. Since that first successful birth, the debate on assisted conception from moral and ethical perspectives has increased, as the creation of living human tissue by scientific means in a laboratory as distinct from conventional sexual intercourse became possible. The issues for couples successfully conceiving by this method revolved around the subsequent development of the children and in particular whether the circumstances of conception would affect parenting experiences.

Couples who experience female factor infertility appear to have particular needs in pregnancy (Garner, 1985). The study by Adair (1994) reported that women in the IVF group invested less in the pregnancy because of a history of obstetric failure and expected to have more difficulties adjusting to parenthood because of age.

Mushin, Barreda-Hanson, and Spensley (1986) in the first study to report on children conceived by in vitro fertilization hypothesized that these children may be seen as special and therefore have unrealistic concerns or expectations placed on them by their parents. This may result in overprotection or place undue emphasis on the nature of the conception as an explanation for problems that may arise. Subsequent studies have not shown these effects.

All of the studies that have focused on the parenting of couples who conceived by IVF or on the development of the children have shown very positive outcomes. For example, parental variables such as quality of parenting, mother-child and father-child interactions, parents' marital and psychiatric state and parenting stress were shown by Golombok et al. (1995) to be superior to those for couples who conceived naturally. Adair (1994) reported that although marital stress for all groups was lower than the population mean, the IVF group reported higher levels than either the donor insemination or the natural conception group. All other parental variables showed no differences. In both of these studies children were functioning above the mean for cognitive and psychomotor development as measured by the Bayley Scales of infant development. These results may be explained at least in part by studies that included the psychological characteristics of people seeking treatment by ART that showed couples as good copers, highly motivated, on average older (30 to 35 years), and highly educated (Abbey, Halman, & Andrews, 1992).

The issues of what information to give children when donor gametes are used will be similar to those for children conceived using donor insemination.

References

Abbey, A., Halman, L. J., & Andrews, F. M. (1992). Psychosocial, treatment and demographic predictors of the stress associated with infertility. *Fertility and Sterility, 57* (1), 122–128.

Adair, V. A. (1994). *Parenting after assisted conception by in vitro fertilisation, GIFT or donor insemination.* Unpublished dissertation, University of Auckland, New Zealand.

Garner, C. H. (1985). Pregnancy after infertility. *Journal of Gynecologic and Neonatal Nursing, 11,* 58–62.

Golombok, S., Cook, R., Bish, A., & Murray, C. (1995). Families created by the new reproductive technologies: Quality of parenting and social and emotional development of the children. *Child Development, 66,* 285–298.

Mushin, D., Barreda-Hanson, M. C., & Spensley, J. C. (1986). IVF children: Early psychosocial development. *Journal of In Vitro Fertilisation and Embryo Technology, 3,* 247–252.

See also: Donor insemination; Infertility; Surrogate motherhood.

VIVIENNE ADAIR

Fetal Alcohol Syndrome. A *teratogen* is a substance that can produce lasting birth defects by affecting the growth and proper formation of the brain and body of the fetus. *Fetal Alcohol Syndrome* (FAS) is a pattern of growth retardation, facial dysmorphology, and neurobehavioral deficits shown by individuals exposed to alcohol prenatally. *Fetal Alcohol Effects* (FAE) consist of physical anomalies and developmental disabilities shown by individuals exposed to alcohol prenatally but who do not have the full FAS.

Throughout recorded history there has been recognition that the mother's use of alcohol during pregnancy may have a negative impact on the fetus and developing child. It was not until 1973, however, that Jones and Smith described a "characteristic pattern of malformation" in the children of a small group of alcoholic women (Jones & Smith, 1973). They coined the term *Fetal Alcohol Syndrome* to describe three features of these children including prenatal onset growth deficiency, specific facial dysmorphology, and central nervous system (CNS) problems. Some children who have been exposed to alcohol in utero may manifest some, but not all, signs of FAS. These children are described as having FAE. In all cases, diagnosis of FAS or FAE can only be made if there is a history of maternal alcohol use during pregnancy.

Not all alcoholic women deliver children with FAS; estimates range from 4.3% to 33%. Risk factors include advanced maternal age and possible genetic predisposition. Few effects have been found to relate to paternal alcohol abuse, although a recent animal study suggested soft tissue anomalies (i.e., hydrocephalus) and growth retardation (Bielawski & Abel, 1996).

Growth retardation. The majority of children with FAS has growth deficiency of prenatal onset and height and weight that average around the 10th percentile in infancy and early childhood. Growth deficiency may possibly be avoided if alcohol use is discontinued during the third trimester. Young infants with FAS often have a poor sucking reflex and may exhibit failure to thrive. These children often appear quite thin in spite of adequate nutrition. Although as they reach adolescence FAS individuals may show a more rapid acceleration in weight gain, most remain small in stature. Girls tend to acquire more average body weight than boys.

Dysmorphic facial features and other physical anomalies. The diagnosis of FAS is most easily made for children between 8 months and 8 years of age because of a set of characteristics that are easily recognized at these ages. The most common features are short palpebral fissures (short eye openings), a flat midface, short upturned nose, indistinct philtrum (groove in the midline of the upper lip), and a thin upper lip. Many children also have epicanthal folds (a vertical fold of skin on either side of the nose) and micrognathia (small chin). Strabismus (crossed eyes) and ptosis (droopy eyelids) are also common. The facial features of FAS are less distinctive after puberty, and changes include an elevation of the nasal bridge and lengthening of the nose, disappearance of midface hypoplasia, clearer delineation of the philtrum and upper lip, and elongation of the chin (Streissguth, 1994). Because alcohol is nonspecific in its effects, all organs of the body can be affected. Other organ abnormalities include atrial septal heart defects, skin hemangiomas, cervical abnormalities, hernias, and malformation of the genitals.

CNS deficits. Neurobehavioral sequelae of alcohol exposure can be seen in children with FAS and even in the less severe cases of FAE. Three quarters of FAS infants are irritable at birth, showing signs of tremulousness and poor state regulation. Mild to moderate mental retardation is common in the majority of children, although some children have been shown to function in the severe to superior ranges of intelligence. Other signs of CNS dysfunction include hyperactivity, problems in attention and memory, poor social judgment, and learning deficits (Streissguth, 1994).

Emotional development also appears to be affected in that even children exposed to moderate levels of alcohol exhibit increased negative affect resulting in less optimal mother-child interactions and poorer attachment relationships in infancy (O'Connor, 1996). Older children show more depressive features, more difficulty functioning in social situations, and poor social judgment. These social skill deficits are not attributable simply to deficits in intelligence. Problems continue into adulthood. Nonretarded alcohol-exposed young adults were found to have significant problems with alcohol and drug dependence, depression, and psychotic disorders (Streissguth et al., 1997).

Much research now exists that demonstrates that alcohol is teratogenic across a variety of species. The incidence of full FAS is estimated to be 1 to 3 per 1000 live births, with the prevalence of FAE about three times higher (National Institute on Alcohol Abuse and Alcoholism, 1990). Thus, the use of alcohol during pregnancy is the most common cause of developmental disabilities of known etiology. Clearly, exposure to alcohol represents a significant mental health problem and presents challenges to future research.

References

Bielawski, D. M., & Abel, E. L. (1996). *Increased malformations in progeny of males treated with alcohol.* Poster session presented at the joint scientific meeting of the Research Society on Alcoholism and the International Society for Biomedical Research on Alcoholism, Washington, DC.

Jones, K. L., & Smith, D. W. (1973). Recognition of the Fetal Alcohol Syndrome in early infancy. *Lancet, 2* (7836), 999–1001.

National Institute on Alcohol Abuse and Alcoholism. (1990). *Seventh special report to the U.S. Congress on alcohol and health* (DHHS Publication No. ADM 90–1656). Washington, DC: U.S. Government Printing Office.

O'Connor, M. J. (1996). Implications of attachment theory for the socioemotional development of children exposed to alcohol prenatally. In H. C. Steinhausen & H. L. Spohr (Eds.), *Alcohol, pregnancy, and the developing child* (pp. 183–206). Cambridge: Cambridge University Press.

Streissguth, A. P. (1994). A long-term perspective of FAS. *Alcohol Health & Research World, 18* (1), 74–81.

Streissguth, A. P., Barr, H. M., Kogan, F., & Bookstein, F. G. (1997). *Secondary disabilities in fetal alcohol syndrome (FAS) and fetal alcohol effects (FAE) in a large sample.* Poster presented at the annual meeting of the Research Society on Alcoholism, San Francisco, CA.

See also: Disability, learning; Disability, physical; Mental retardation.

MARY J. O'CONNOR

Floortime. Floortime is a practice advocated by Stanley Greenspan for making emotional connections with infant, toddlers, and young children. Greenspan devised the practice originally for use in therapy with disturbed children (Greenspan, 1987) but now advocates the regular use of floortime by all parents and child care providers (Greenspan, 1990).

Floortime entails getting down on the child's level to play on a daily basis. The goal of floortime is not to teach a child specific skills, like how to count or identify shapes, letters, or colors. It is rather a philosophy and a technique of tuning into a child's experiences and helping to infuse these experiences with emotional meaning.

Greenspan describes the technique as comprising five simple steps (Greenspan, 1990):

Step 1. *Observation*. Parents watch and listen in order to gauge the child's mood and style of relating before opening a circle of communication.

Step 2. *Approach*. Based on observation of the child's mood and ongoing activity, parents open a circle of communication with gestures and with words.

Step 3. *Follow the child's lead*. Parents are supportive play partners who follow the child's lead and allow the child to direct the course of play.

Step 4. *Extend and expand play*. Without being intrusive, parents help the child elaborate his or her play by taking it one step further. Parents ask questions or make suggestions to stimulate creativity in play.

Step 5. *Child closes the circle of communication*. Parents let the child close a circle of communication by making comments and gestures of their own.

By using this approach, Greenspan claims that children will become more assertive and self-confident, feel understood, appreciate the value of two-way communication, and engage in more creative emotional dramas in their play.

Greenspan has described four stages in the development of relating and communicating (Greenspan, 1985). Although the principles of floortime are the same, the content of play will vary depending on the age and stage of emotional development of the child (Greenspan, 1990):

Stage 1. *Engagement* (0–8 months). During floortime, parents acknowledge and imitate the baby's behavior such as coos and facial expressions.

Stage 2. *Two-way communication* (6–18 months). During floortime, parents tune into the child's interests and build an appreciation for cause-effect relationships.

Stage 3. *Shared meanings* (18–36 months). During floortime, parents become a partner in pretend play and try to verbalize what the child is trying to act out in play.

Stage 4. *Emotional thinking* (3–5 years). During floortime, parents encourage the child to talk about and act out strong feelings through play.

Greenspan advocates that parents engage in floortime for at least 30 minutes each day (Greenspan, 1990). This does not have to be done literally on the floor but can occur while dressing or bathing the child, during a meal, in the car, while reading a book, or at bedtime. The essential principles of tuning into the child and letting the child make choices can be practiced in many settings throughout the day.

Greenspan (1990) also urges child care providers to use floortime principles in one-to-one communication with children in their care as often as possible. This can be during arrival, free choice/play time, group time, lunchtime, naptime, outdoor play, and at departure. Teachers can respectfully join children in play as supportive play partners without being intrusive. They can also provide support and comfort during difficult times like separating from parents or falling asleep at naptime.

References

Greenspan, S. I. (1985). *First feelings*. New York: Viking.
Greenspan, S. I. (1987). *The essential partnership*. New York: Viking.
Greenspan, S. I. (Producer). (1990). *Floortime: Tuning into each child* [Video]. New York: Scholastic, Inc.
Greenspan, S. I. (1992). *Infancy and early childhood: The practice of clinical assessment and intervention with emotional and developmental challenges*. Madison, CT: International Universities Press.

See also: Communication; Empathy; Mutuality.

ANN D. MURRAY

Foster parenting. Foster family care is recognized as an essential option for child welfare agencies. Foster care responds to the distinct needs of children and families through the strength of family living and community-based supports (Pasztor & Wynne, 1995). Federal and state statutes stress the importance of least restrictive, familylike settings for children who must be separated from their families because of physical abuse, neglect, sexual abuse, or special circumstances (Myers, 1992).

The role of the foster parent is continually evolving as the needs of youth and their families become more complex. Today, foster parents are providing safe, nurturing environments for children who are abused or neglected, who exhibit emotional and behavioral problems, and who have special medical needs. Recently, the role of fostering is being professionalized to meet the changing needs of society (Hawkins, 1989). States require families to meet specific licensing criteria regarding the structure and safety of their home and their functioning as a family. Ongoing training is required each year in areas related to the difficulties experienced by children entering care. Foster parents are, at times, included in the treatment planning for children in their care, are members of the community treatment teams, and are asked to work closely with parents to develop parenting abilities and parent-child relationships.

Foster care services provide one aspect of a continuum of services for children and youth who are at risk of placement outside their natural environment. Treatment options can be viewed along a continuum of increasing restrictiveness. Outpatient and home-based services for children at home would be at the least restrictive point. Detention or residential services in an institution would be at the most restrictive point. Foster care falls near the middle of the continuum. Services become more restrictive as the intensity of treatment increases, moves further from the natural environment, and limits the normal freedoms of the child (Hawkins, 1989).

For many professionals, foster parents, and parents of children placed out of the home, roles and responsibilities in relation to the child in care can become confused. In most cases, parents retain ultimate rights to their child, whereas foster parents have temporary rights as care providers. Blumenthal (1984) examined differences between parents and foster parents. He concluded that parents are responsible for decisions regarding their child, including education, discipline, religion, health care, and lifestyle. Foster parents will share or consult in decision making regarding these issues. Physical discipline is not an option in foster care placement, regardless of parental desire.

Blumenthal (1984) emphasized that natural parents are the primary attachment figures for their child and have a right to a relationship with their child. While they may offer a special relationship to the child, foster parents are temporary treatment providers who are more like a mentor or advocate rather than a parent. Foster parents are "supporters" of both the child and the family. Their charge is to listen and encourage in a respectful manner. In listening, foster parents and professionals learn that the natural parents are experts on their child, having knowledge of their child's development, growth, and history, including school, friends, family, major influences, comforts, and daily activities. Foster parents, on the other hand, will be "teachers," sharing their knowledge of children and child development. Blumenthal explicitly states that foster parents, as with all treatment providers, do not assume the responsibility for the child but, rather, share it.

Responsibilities generally assumed by foster parents include providing guidance, support, and direction to the child placed in their care; providing adequate food, clothing, and shelter; abiding by the discipline policy and procedure set forth in the care agreement, pursuant to state statutes; and working collaboratively with service providers and ensuring that the child attend medical, psychological, parental visitation, and other needed routine appointments and services. Foster parents share with the caseworker all pertinent information about the needs of the child and significant incidents related to the child. Support, guidance, or assistance should be requested and received by the foster care providers when needed in working with the individual needs of a child in their home. In addition, foster parents often assume the role of an advocate for the best interest of the child placed in their care.

Although the anticipated outcome of foster placement is reunification between parent and child, there will be times when return home is not an option. Foster-adopt programs specifically recruit foster parents who are seeking to permanently commit to a child who is placed in their home. In many other situations, foster parents develop an attachment and commitment to the foster child and wish to adopt. Goals regarding permanency for children placed in foster care should be clear from the beginning in order to avoid role confusion and conflict of interest.

References

Blumenthal, K. (1984). Involving parents: A rationale. In K. Blumenthal & A. Weinberg (Eds.), *Establishing parent involvement in foster care agencies* (pp. 1–16). New York: Child Welfare League of America.

Hawkins, R. P. (1989). The nature and potential of therapeutic foster family care programs. In R. P. Hawkins & J. Breiling (Eds.), *Therapeutic foster care: Critical issues* (pp. 5–36). Washington DC: Child Welfare League of America.

Myers, J. E. B. (1992). *Legal issues in child abuse and neglect*. Newbury Park, CA: Sage
    Publications.
Pasztor, E. M., & Wynne, S. F. (1995). *Foster parent retention and recruitment: The
    state of the art in practice and policy*. Washington, DC: Child Welfare League of
    America.

See also: Abuse, child; Family preservation; Runaway children; Throwaway children.

VICKY PRIMER AND WILLIAM F. NORTHEY JR.

Freud, Anna (1895–1982). Anna Freud, Sigmund Freud's youngest child,
devoted her life to the study of the inner world of the child, integrating psychoanalytic thinking into every aspect of her daily living and her work. She established her first school for the four children of her close friend Dorothy Burling-
ham and a small group of other children who were in analysis. She believed that
the work that children undertook in analysis could be integrated into their everyday lives at school and that parents should understand their child's analysis.
Anna Freud supported her father's view of the *Oedipus complex* which, from the
psychoanalytic perspective, emerges and is resolved between the ages of 3 and
7, so she saw no point in carrying out formal psychoanalytic work with children
until they were 7. Instead, she proposed that the analyst should form a warm,
supportive relationship with the child in order to prepare him or her for later
analysis. This approach brought her into conflict with Melanie Klein, who believed that psychic distress arises from the very condition of being human rather
than being environmentally caused. In contrast to Anna Freud, Klein advocated
working psychoanalytically with young children as early as possible.

Anna Freud argued that the child's superego is dependent on the external influence of the parents and, as an essential part of her therapeutic work, kept in
close touch with the external "reality" of the child's ongoing relationship with
the parents. She also added an educational dimension to therapy and believed
passionately in involving the parents so that the child's work in analysis could
be integrated with home and school life.

Her original research into the normal development of the parent-child relationship was based on documentation of the play, behavior, and social relationships of children. She believed that the child had the capacity to learn from experience and that each stage of life offered new opportunities for growth; for example, in adolescence the young person had the chance to resolve earlier conflicts (Freud, 1966, 1976).

Anna Freud devised a system for charting the everyday interactions of disturbed children and documenting the development of resilience in the face of
adversity. Freud and Dann (1951) made detailed observations of six orphans
who had been liberated from concentration camps and placed in Anna Freud's
therapeutic nursery. The children had been separated from their parents as babies and had been severely deprived of any continuous care from adults since
most of their caregivers themselves perished in the gas chambers. Understandably, they were extremely disturbed, destructive in their behavior, and mostly
very hostile to adult caregivers. However, the continuity of relationship had

been within the peer group, and, despite their extreme hardships they had formed strong, mutual bonds with one another. Gradually, in the supportive environment of the therapeutic nursery, they came to trust their caregivers. In adult life, they overcame the early deprivation and were able to form close relationships. The peer group probably provided the care and support that would normally be given by parents. Studies like this have been influential in helping us to understand why children act out or become withdrawn when they are experiencing emotional difficulties. She also pioneered work on the value of the "holding relationship" as a way of supporting disturbed children through their distress.

Anna Freud has been criticized for her failure to place any emphasis in her writing on the problem of child abuse, though in the year before she died she wrote of the dangers of underestimating either the frequency or importance of incest for damaging the child's normal development (Masson, 1992). Unfortunately, neither she nor her father addressed this problem in any of their publications on children.

Unlike other child analysts of this period, Anna Freud emphasized talking to children, observing how they played, and being sensitive to the images they used in order to gain insight into children's experience. This emphasis has to be seen in historical context, however, since like all psychoanalysts she was more concerned with the child's inner space than with the actual external reality of the child's life and environment.

References
Freud, A. (1966). *Normality and pathology in childhood*. London: Hogarth Press.
Freud, A. (1976). Psychopathology seen against the background of normal development. *British Journal of Psychiatry, 129*, 401–406.
Freud, A., & Dann, S. (1951). An experiment in group upbringing. *Psychoanalytic Study of the Child, 6*, 127–168.
Gomez, L. (1997). *An introduction to object relations*. London: Free Association Books.
Masson, J. (1992). The tyranny of psychotherapy. In W. Dryden & C. Feltham (Eds.), *Psychotherapy and its discontents* (pp. 7-29). Milton Keynes, England: Open University Press.

See also: Family therapy.

HELEN COWIE

G

Gay fathers. Gay fathers are newly emergent figures in homosexual culture. However, there is a limited amount of information about these individuals. It is impossible to estimate the exact percentage of gay fathers in the population. Researchers estimate that about 20% to 25% of self-identified male homosexuals are also fathers (Bozett & Sussman, 1989). Because their numbers are small, gay fathers clearly constitute a minority within a minority.

A homosexual man who also is a father is a social enigma; even the term *gay father* is a contradictory term. *Gay* connotes homosexuality and an antifamily stereotype; *father* connotes heterosexuality and a strong interest in sexual reproduction. Gay fathers must resolve a dilemma of having a conflicting personal identity because of their divided ties to both heterosexual and homosexual worlds. They do not fit easily into either homosexual or heterosexual culture. The conflict is resolved when they are able to establish their personal identity as a gay father. This is accomplished by a process known as *integrative sanctioning* (Bozett, 1981). This occurs when these men are successful in disclosing their homosexual orientation to heterosexual allies and their father identity to gays. Liaisons are formed with those who are accepting and supporting of both identities and by distancing themselves from those who cannot support the gay father's identity.

The reasons why a homosexual man becomes a father are not well understood, but researchers have explored several explanations (Barett & Robinson, 1990; Bigner & Bozett, 1989). First, some men know that they are gay but have extreme difficulty accepting themselves, perhaps because of the social stigma.

They enter a heterosexual marriage and become fathers. Maintaining this cha-
rade becomes more difficult over time. A divorce occurs, which allows the man
to come to terms with his homosexuality while reconciling the demands of being
a father. Second, some gay men willfully choose to pursue parenthood and establish a liaison with a lesbian woman or couple who also desire parenthood.
Conception usually occurs by artificial insemination, and arrangements are made
for joint custody. Third, some gay men enter into a heterosexual relationship
where both partners are fully aware in advance of the man's sexual orientation.
In some cases, the men are bisexual, and their marriages are maintained for
multiple reasons. Fourth, other reasons may motivate gay men into parenthood
such as a genuine desire to nurture children just as heterosexuals.

Society holds prejudicial opinions about gay fathers as parents and their effects on children. For example, homosexuals are thought to molest children and
to recruit them into their lifestyle, to be poor sex-role models for children, and to
be detrimental to children's welfare simply because they are gay. What does research report about such matters? There is no evidence or data that proves that
the homosexual orientation of a father or other caregiver is detrimental to children's welfare (Patterson, 1992). On the contrary, every reputable scientific investigation examining the parenting abilities and effectiveness of gay fathers has
failed to show that children's development or well-being is harmed in any way
by being raised by a gay father. Credible studies have repeatedly shown that gay
fathers are as effective as heterosexual fathers as parents and provide quality
care for their children.

Regarding the belief about sexual molestation, research repeatedly finds that
the majority (about 99.5% estimated) of perpetrators are heterosexual relatives
of victimized children of both sexes. Investigators also have found that the origins of sexual orientation are unclear but are likely to have biological determined origins rather than strong environmental causes, as was once suspected.
People are not recruited to become homosexual no more so than they are recruited to become heterosexual, and sexual orientation is not a matter of personal choice. Finally, researchers note that the percentage of children who become homosexual is the same for both gay and heterosexual parents.

Only a small number of gay fathers remain in heterosexual marriages for any
length of time following disclosure of their sexual orientation to their wives.
Adjustment of both individuals following disclosure is not well documented but
is particularly difficult for some wives. Many gay fathers find their adjustment
following divorce problematic. Many wish for and are successful in establishing
a committed relationship with another gay man, although little is known about
the family systems that are formed from these liaisons. Some gay fathers have
custody of children, and many have visitation rights. Many consider that they
have formed a gay stepfamily, and research finds that these families experience
many of the challenges and accomplishments of heterosexual stepfamilies.

References
Barett, R. L., & Robinson, B. E. (1990). *Gay fathers*. Lexington, MA: D. C. Heath.
Bigner, J. J., & Bozett, F. W. (1989). Parenting by gay fathers. *Marriage and Family Re-
     view, 14*, 155–176.

Bozett, F. W. (1981). Gay fathers: Identity conflict resolution through integrative sanctioning. *Alternative Lifestyles, 4,* 90–107.

Bozett, F. W., & Sussman, M. B. (1989). Homosexuality and family relations: Views and research issues. In F. W. Bozett & M. B. Sussman (Eds.), *Homosexuality and family relations* (pp. 1–7). New York: Harrington Park Press.

Patterson, C. J. (1992). Children of lesbian and gay parents. *Child Development, 63,* 1025–1042.

See also: Gender socialization; Lesbian mothers; Sex roles.

JERRY J. BIGNER

Gender socialization. *Sex* and *gender* often are used interchangeably in both professional and popular literature. They are not the same, however. *Sex* refers to the biological aspects of being a female or male. This includes a person's anatomical, hormonal, and chromosomal structure. *Gender,* on the other hand, refers to the social and cultural components of one's biological sex. As such, gender is a product of socialization. People learn to identify themselves as either a male or a female and what behaviors they should exhibit and what attitudes they should hold according to their label of male or female. Therefore, gender socialization encompasses two processes—the development of a gender identity and the acquisition of a gender role.

Gender identity refers to a person's self-conception of being either a female or a male. Gender identity involves a decision, not anatomical recognition. Children are certain of the existence of two sexes and of their own identification with one of them long before they are aware of the biological basis for these distinctions. Nearly all children know the labels *girl, boy, woman,* and *man* by 3 years of age and are able to apply them correctly to both themselves and others. Children of this age may not yet realize that these categories are constant. They may think that changing clothing or hairstyles can actually change sex as well.

In contrast to gender identity, *gender roles* refer to sets of expectations that prescribe the different ways men and women are supposed to act and the different tasks they are expected to undertake. Basic expectations for the sexes are learned in the family environment very early in life and are reinforced in children's literature, in the schools, in peer groups, in the mass media, in religious organizations, and in many other social settings and institutions. While gender roles in the United States are far less rigid than in other countries, males are still stereotypically thought to possess instrumental traits that enable them to accomplish difficult tasks or goals. Females, on the other hand, are still thought to possess such expressive traits as warmth, sensitivity, and the ability to express tender feelings.

Different parenting styles play an important part in promoting children's gender-role development (Fagot, 1995). While most parents in the United States report treating their daughters and sons similarly, subtle differences start as soon as the infant's sex is known. Some mothers apply gender stereotypes to movement patterns in utero when the sex of the fetus is known (Beal, 1993). Following birth, nurseries and furniture are color coded, gifts are selected by sex, and infants are dressed in sex-typed clothing. Parents handle infant sons more roughly and respond quicker to a crying baby girl. Boys are given toys that develop spatial ability and creative construction while girls are given toys that encourage social skills. From approximately 5 years of age on, parents allocate household chores according to sex, with girls being assigned more and different chores than boys. In addition, parents model different behavior, with mothers providing a significantly greater portion of the care of children than fathers.

While this differential treatment begins early, research focusing on children of several ages indicates that gender expectations are increasingly powerful from early toddlerhood through early adolescence. There is no clear-cut answer to just how much influence parenting styles and culture, as opposed to biology, have on the developmental paths and behavior of boys and girls. The fact that they affect both females and males is undeniable, however. Among the many consequences are lowered self-esteem and confidence and lessened needs for achievement among females. For years, the polar opposites of traditional gender expectations were seen as evidence of psychological health. This view has been challenged over the last quarter of a century by the belief that a standard of psychological health is needed that allows individuals to express the full range of human emotions and behavior. Called *androgyny*, this standard expands the range of behavior open to everyone and permits them to cope more effectively with diverse situations (Bem, 1975).

In general, contemporary parents are making efforts to socialize their children in less rigid ways than previous generations. Similar treatment of boys and girls does not necessarily lead to similar outcomes, however. Regardless of how persistent they might be to raise their children free of traditional gender expectations, parents are likely to face cultural opposition. Peer groups, the media, schools, and social structure reinforce gender stereotyping. Children do, however, tend to adopt the attitudes and values of their own parents in the long run (Fagot, 1995).

References

Beal, C. R. (1993). *Boys and girls: The development of gender roles*. New York: McGraw-Hill.

Bem, S. (1975). Androgyny vs. the tight little lives of fluffy women and chesty men. *Psychology Today, 9*, 58–62.

Fagot, B. I. (1995). Parenting boys and girls. In M. H. Bornstein (Ed.), *Handbook of parenting: Volume 1. Children and parenting* (pp. 163-183). Mahwah, NJ: Lawrence Erlbaum Associates.

See also: Identity development; Sex roles; Toys.

GARY L. HANSEN

Genetic disorders. The development of an individual depends on two interacting influences: heredity and environment. The genetic composition of an individual is determined at conception. A complex interaction of genetic and environmental factors will then shape the person's future development. There has been a growing appreciation of the importance of genetic factors in human disease, and revolutionary developments have occurred in the basic science of genetics. Genetic abnormalities are a common cause of disease, handicap, and death among children.

Genes, the basic molecules of heredity, are composed of DNA (deoxyribonucleic acid). The capacity of DNA to replicate itself constitutes the basis of heredity transmission. Genes are carried by chromosomes located in the nuclei of cells. Each gene has its own specific locus on the chromosome. In humans, each body cell normally has 46 chromosomes, arranged in 23 pairs. Each person possesses two alternative forms of a gene, inheriting one from each parent. A person with a pair of similar genes is a homozygote; one with a dissimilar pair is a heterozygote. If a mutant or defective gene has an effect in a heterozygous state, it is called a dominant gene. If two mutant genes are needed to manifest their clinical effect, they are called recessive.

There are three types of genetically determined disorders: (1) Mendelian or single-gene mutations that are inherited in recognizable patterns; (2) polygenic or multifactorial conditions in which genetic mutations are not always clear; and (3) chromosomal aberrations that include both structural defects and deviations from the normal number (Collins & Gelehrter, 1990). Genetic disorders determined by a single gene are the easiest to analyze and therefore have been the most fully studied. Single-gene defects may be dominant, recessive, or X-linked. In a *dominant* inherited genetic disorder, every affected person has at least one affected parent. An affected person who marries a nonaffected individual has a 50% risk that an offspring will inherit the disorder. Nonaffected children of an affected parent have nonaffected children and grandchildren. Huntington's disease, a painful, fatal disorder that afflicts young adults, is an example of a dominant inherited disorder.

In a *recessive* inherited disorder, the child of two nonaffected parents has a 25% chance of inheriting the disorder. The children of an affected homozygous person are all heterozygotes and though not affected are carriers of the trait. If two affected people marry, all of their children will be affected. Examples of recessive inherited disorders are phenylketonuria (PKU), Tay Sachs disease, cystic fibrosis, and sickle-cell anemia. In *X-linked* recessive inheritance, nearly all affected persons are males, and the trait is always transmitted through the mother, who is not affected. An affected male never transmits the trait to his sons. The carrier female transmits the trait to 50% of her sons. None of the daughters will show the trait, but 50% will be carriers. Examples of X-linked disorders are hemophilia and Duchenne muscular dystrophy.

Several genetic disorders do not fit the expectations for Mendelian inheritance. More likely these conditions result from multifactorial inheritance. Neural tube defects, often referred to collectively as spina bifida, is a common example. Characteristics such as intelligence, creativity, and sociability have not been demonstrated to be caused by a single gene, and it is likely that personality attributes are the result of the interaction of multiple genes and environmental factors (Plomin, 1990). In chromosomal abnormalities there can be chromosomal damage, the presence of an extra chromosome, or the deletion of a chromosome. There is a laboratory test that provides visible evidence of the type of chromosomal abnormality. In about 95% of the cases of Down Syndrome, a dis-

, characterized by physical and mental retardation, there is an extra chromo-
ome at the 21st pair.

The most striking advantage of the diagnosis of genetic disease is that a gene
can be identified through examination of the DNA from almost any cell of an
individual. The cell can be obtained any time in the life of the person. The genes
can then be examined for mutations associated with a disease. One or both parents can be tested for some genetic disorders before or during pregnancy. *Amniocentesis* and *chorionic villus sampling* (CVS) are the most common prenatal
tests used for the detection of genetic disorders. The amniotic fluid surrounding
the fetus provides a wide range of information such as genetic composition, fetal
maturity, and current status of development. Amniocentesis involves the aspira-
tion of amniotic fluid and is usually performed between the 16th and 18th week
of pregnancy. In CVS, a sample of the villi are extracted from the chorion, usually between the 9th and 12th week of pregnancy, and the genetic makeup of the
fetus is then examined. Diagnostic study can begin within a week of CVS rather
than after weeks of growing the cells in the laboratory, as is usually the case
with amniocentesis. This allows for a first trimester termination, if desired, with
CVS versus a second trimester termination with amniocentesis. Prenatal testing
is not routinely performed and is typically recommended if the woman is over
the age of 35, if there is a family history of genetic disease or exposure to substances that might be harmful to the fetus, or if there is a history of unsuccessful
pregnancies (Behrman, Kliegman, & Vaughan, 1992).

Diagnosis of a genetic disorder can also be done indirectly by following a
gene across generations. This is known as *genetic mapping* and is usually performed by a genetic counselor (McKusick, 1989). Advances in genetics have
opened new opportunities for influencing the course of human development.
Scientists hope not only to identify and locate the genes responsible for inherited
diseases but also to eventually use gene therapy to prevent or cure such disorders. By inserting good genes into human cells, scientists hope to counter the effects of deleterious genes.

References
Behrman, R. E., Kliegman, R.M., & Vaughan, V. C. (1992). *Nelson textbook of pediat-
rics* (14th ed.). Philadelphia: W. B. Saunders.
Collins, F. S., & Gelehrter, T. D. (1990). *The principles of medical genetics.* Baltimore,
MD: Williams & Wilkins.
McKusick, V. A. (1989). Mapping and sequencing the human genome. *New England
Journal of Medicine, 320,* 910.
Plomin, R. (1990). *Nature and nurture: An introduction to human behavioral genetics.*
Pacific Grove, CA: Brooks-Cole.

See also: Disability, physical; Illness, chronic, in children.

STEVEN M. ALESSANDRI

Gifted children. According to Public Law 95-561, gifted and talented children are those youth demonstrating a high level of performance in intellectual
ability, creativity, leadership skills, the performing or visual arts, or an identified

academic area. Furthermore, the definition states that these children require special school services because of their gifts. While not formally included in this definition, some professionals also believe that talents in psychomotor skills, such as drafting and athletics, should be considered (Tuttle, Becker, & Sousa, 1988).

According to Tuttle and colleagues (1988), children can be identified as gifted and talented students in several different ways. The most common methods are standardized group tests, culture-fair tests, creativity tests, individual IQ tests, behavior rating scales, teacher nomination, transcripts, biographical inventories, parent recommendation, and peer recommendation. Many professionals believe that a combination of procedures is most effective in identifying the broadest range of gifted students.

Gifted children are often curious and extremely perceptive and easily make numerous connections between disparate ideas (Tuttle, Becker, & Sousa, 1988). They may be class leaders with excessively high expectations of themselves and others and display some degree of perfectionism in their work. Their awareness of social injustices may be so acutely developed that they become personally distressed at the plight of others. Parents of gifted children may become overwhelmed by the persistence these children display in their rejection of simplistic responses to questions and quest for deeper understanding of complex issues.

Several researchers have examined parenting styles with gifted children, as well as the expectations and attitudes parents have about their talented offspring. Weissler and Landau (1993) studied families with and without gifted children to determine which parenting characteristics contributed to the development of gifted children. They found that in families with gifted children mothers and fathers modeled problem solving as a group activity and encouraged children to seek out further information from other sources. Parents with gifted children also felt strongly about exposing children to new experiences, developing intelligence, and encouraging social accomplishments. Furthermore, parents of gifted children had numerous books, toys, and pieces of art in the home to encourage development. Additionally, several family trips were taken during the year to expose the child to novel experiences. Many of these traits were more typical of mothers and more firmly established in families with more than one gifted child. Fathers, on the other hand, were quite authoritarian in families with more than one gifted child and less authoritarian in families with one gifted child. In both cases, fathers were more authoritarian than mothers.

In another study examining parenting styles, Moss and Strayer (1990) compared mothers of gifted and nongifted children to examine how mothers approach problem solving with their children. They found that mothers of gifted children encouraged their children to predict consequences, relate pieces of tasks to each other, and monitor their own progress during problem solving. These mothers were also more likely to allow their child to think through the problem on their own, before intervening with leading questions or comments. Mothers of nongifted children, on the other hand, more often showed the child a task's solution without encouraging cognitive problem solving.

Strom et al. (1992) looked at the differences between Anglo and Hispanic parents to determine the activities they value for their gifted children. Compared to Anglo parents, Hispanic parents felt more comfortable and played more often with their children. Furthermore, Hispanic parents felt that play was a more important influence on development than Anglo parents. Conversely, Anglo parents allowed more time for play and encouraged children to play alone more often than Hispanic parents. Additionally, they encouraged imaginative play and verbal creativity more than parents of Hispanic children. All parents in this study valued the child's imagination, were patient with chaotic play, and believed that children need to play with both parents and peers.

Finally, Keirouz (1990) conducted a literature review to determine common parent-child issues in families with gifted children. She concluded that parents are often ambivalent about the "gifted" label. Some parents are proud, while others resent the child. At times, parents expect more from these children and forget that social and emotional development may be less developed than cognitive skills. Parents also may feel guilty or threatened by their perceived inability to provide sufficient cognitive stimulation for the child.

References
Keirouz, K. S. (1990). Concerns of parents of gifted children: A research review. *Gifted Child Quarterly, 34* (2), 56–63.

Moss, E., & Strayer, F. F. (1990). Interactive problem solving of gifted and non-gifted preschoolers with their mothers. *International Journal of Behavioral Development, 13* (2), 177–197.

Strom, R., Johnson, A., Strom, S., & Strom, P. (1992). Parental differences in expectations of gifted children. *Journal of Comparative Family Studies, 23* (1), 69–77.

Tuttle, F. B., Becker, L. A., & Sousa, J. A. (1988). *Characteristics and identification of gifted and talented students* (3rd ed.). Washington DC: National Education Association.

Weissler, K., & Landau, E. (1993). Characteristics of families with no, one, or more than one gifted child. *Journal of Psychology, 127* (2), 143–153.

See also: Academic achievement; Family-school partnerships; Imagination.

SHEILA A. BALOG

Ginott, Haim (1922–1973). Haim Ginott lived in Israel where he was trained and worked as an elementary school teacher before immigrating to the United States (June, 1947). He was admitted into graduate training at Columbia University in clinical psychology and received his Ph.D. in 1952. He studied children's play therapy with Virginia Axline before joining the Jacksonville (Florida) Child Guidance and Speech Correction Clinic as chief psychologist (1952–1960).

After leaving Jacksonville, Ginott taught at New York University and Adelphi University. His professional activity moved increasingly toward parent education. The last years of his life were largely spent in such parent education efforts as general-audience book writing, radio and television programs, lecturing and leading parent education groups based in New York City.

Ginott's approach to parent education was distinctive in important ways. In contrast to the common orientation that parents must have a substantial psychological overhaul before their children's problems could be fully addressed, Ginott believed that many children's problems were simply the result of uninformed and, as a result, unhelpful parenting. By dealing with parents' ignorance and lack of skill, many problems could be remedied. Ginott distinguished between the different levels of psychological response in therapy, counseling, guidance, and education.

In his books about parenting, Ginott teaches a process of responding to children's distress and misbehavior with statements of acceptance and understanding. Rather than contradicting or denying children's feelings, this process allows children to explore, experience, and understand their feelings. When children feel understood, they feel loved. Ginott, while accepting children's feelings, did not teach that all behaviors should be accepted. He believed that simple statements of limits for behavior together with acceptance of feelings helped children to grow up to be decent human beings, people with compassion, commitment, and caring. The "language of understanding" that he recommended for responding to children has been called *childrenese*.

Ginott's approach to parent education involved large doses of understanding for the parents as well as the children. His anecdote-filled books show the compassion he felt for the challenged parent even as he showed compassion for the children's distress.

Orgel (1980) has described four phases in Ginott's process of parent guidance or education. In the first phase, the parent educator responds to parent complaints with *attention*, *understanding*, and *acceptance*. The educator provides parent participants with the healing empathy that they will be encouraged to provide for their children. In the second phase, *sensitization*, the parents' attention is directed toward the challenges and distress that the children may be feeling. Such parental perspective-taking prepares them to respond compassionately to their children. In the third phase, *learning of concepts*, the parent educator guides parents to conclusions about effective child guidance. In the final phase, *the teaching and practice of better coping skills*, the leader helps parents try out and become comfortable with their new skills. More detail about this process can be found in the *Handbook on Parent Education*.

Ginott's books—*Between Parent and Child*, and *Between Parent and Teenager*—were best sellers when they were published and are still popular today, decades after their first publication. In fact, in an evaluation of self-help books (Santrock, Minnett, & Campbell, 1994), both books received the highest rating ("Strongly recommended") and appeared on the short list of best self-help books. Ginott's book *Teacher and Child* is also popular in the training of teachers and parents. Two of Ginott's parent-students, Adele Faber and Elaine Mazlish, have written books about parenting that are also popular (e.g., Faber & Mazlish, 1980).

Ginott's books remain popular for several reasons. They show compassion and patience with the struggling parent. They pick a course between permissive and authoritarian parenting by recommending practices that set limits while understanding the frustration that motivates much child misbehavior. Ginott's books are especially useful and practical because of the wealth of anecdotes they contain.

References

Faber, A., & Mazlish, E. (1980). *How to talk so kids will listen & listen so kids will talk.* New York: Avon Books.

Ginott, H. G. (1965). *Between parent and child.* New York: Macmillan.

Ginott, H. G. (1969). *Between parent and teenager.* New York: Macmillan.

Ginott, H. G. (1972). *Teacher and child.* New York: Macmillan.

Orgel, A. R. (1980). Haim Ginott's approach to parent education. In M. J. Fine (Ed.), *Handbook on parent education* (pp. 75–100). Orlando, FL: Academic Press.

Santrock, J. W., Minnett, A. M., & Campbell, B. D. (1994). *The authoritative guide to self-help books.* New York: Guilford Press.

See also: Acceptance, parental; Education, parenting.

H. WALLACE GODDARD

Goodness of fit model. The goodness of fit model (Chess & Thomas, 1983; Lerner, 1982; Thomas & Chess, 1977) posits that a match between a child's characteristics (e.g., temperament, behavioral style) and the requirements of a particular setting or environment result in "adaptive" (productive) outcomes that accumulate in the setting. This notion is an example of a bidirectional view of child socialization. The child is not seen as a passive recipient of environmental influence. Rather, the child enters the world with characteristics that elicit varying responses, depending on the environment (including people) from which responses are elicited. These various responses in turn result in a variety of developmental outcomes. Lerner and others have captured this concept in the descriptive phrase "individuals as producers of their own development" (Lerner & Busch-Rossnagel, 1981).

The requirements or demands of the environment can take several forms (Lerner, 1982). First, demands may be in the form of attitudes, values, or stereotypes held by others in the context about the child's characteristics. Second, these demands may be attributes or characteristics of others with whom the child must coordinate or fit his or her attributes. Finally, demands may be in the form of the physical characteristics of the environment that make certain requirements of the individual before successful (adaptive) interaction can occur. The unique characteristics of a child will elicit differing types of feedback from differing environments.

The goodness of fit model is illustrated in the following examples. A child with a physical disability requiring a wheel chair for mobility will not exhibit adaptive outcomes in an environment that is physically not accessible to the wheel chair. Here a lack of fit is apparent. Similarly, a child with a high physical activity level will not match well with an environment that does not offer opportunity for physical activity and requires a high degree of concentration and sitting quietly while completing tasks. A parent-to-be expecting a child with a high need for physical contact (cuddling) may be presented with an infant that is not soothed by close contact. Here too, is an example of a less than optimal fit or match between child and environment.

The goodness of fit model has been applied to various areas of research. Lerner has utilized this concept to discuss the response of adults to children's physical characteristics (see Lerner, 1982 for a review), which suggests that children's individual physical appearance influences the feedback received by children and this differential feedback has implications for the psychological and social development of children. Alexander Thomas and Stella Chess (Chess & Thomas, 1983; Thomas & Chess, 1977) provide perhaps the best example of a parent-child application of the goodness of fit model. Their research on temperament as part of the New York Longitudinal Study suggested that an individual's temperament is less important than the match between parental expectations for the child and the child's actual makeup. In other words, there is no one best temperament; what is significant is the degree of fit between parent and child.

The importance of this conception for parents is twofold. First, if parents can be assured that difficulties are not completely due to parents' inability to parent, but instead may be due to characteristics inherent in the child, some degree of pressure and/or guilt can be removed from parents. The removal of this sort of pressure will hopefully lead to the second way in which this notion can be important. If a child is not fitting within a setting, context, or environment, adults have a responsibility to adapt their expectations and stereotypes or the physical environment in a way that better matches the attributes of the child. This sort of adaptation may often be critical in optimizing the development of the child.

References
Chess, S., & Thomas, A. (1983). Dynamics of individual behavioral development. In M. D. Levine, W. B. Carey, & A. C. Crocker (Eds.), *Developmental-behavioral pediatrics* (pp. 158– 175). Philadelphia: W. B. Saunders.

Lerner, R. M. (1982). Children and adolescents as producers of their own development. *Developmental Review, 2*, 342–370.

Lerner, R. M., & Busch-Rossnagel, N. A. (Eds.). (1981). *Individuals as producers of their own development: A life-span perspective.* New York: Academic Press.

Thomas, A., & Chess, S. (1977). *Temperament and development.* New York: Brunner/Mazel.

See also: Temperament.

BRENDA J. BOYD

Grandparenting. About 70% of middle-aged and older people become grandparents. The average age of becoming a grandparent, in Western societies, is about 50 years for women, a couple of years older for men; so it is an important part of the life cycle for most people, some 25 years or more. Typically, grandparents keep in contact with their adult children and grandchildren, often visiting weekly.

The four standard types of grandparent are maternal grandmother, maternal grandfather, paternal grandmother, and paternal grandfather. Many studies find that the maternal grandmother is the most involved and has the most frequent contact with grandchildren, with the others in generally decreasing order. With increased rates of divorce and remarriage, many families now also have step-grandparents.

The grandparent role is important as a personal experience and for its impact on parents and children (Denham & Smith, 1989; Smith, 1994). A generation or two ago, in the 1930s to 1950s, grandparenthood was often seen in a rather negative light. Grandparents were seen as older people who were likely to be frail and cantankerous and to interfere in the raising of grandchildren, being inflexible and either too lenient and indulgent or too strict and old-fashioned in their views. By contrast, recent research reports grandparenthood in a predominantly positive light. This shift could be due both to changes in stereotypes and to changes in actual grandparental roles and relationships. Gaps between the views of grandparents and parents might have been especially large in the 1950s, because of rapidly changing child-rearing opinions over previous decades; such differences in views may have lessened. Today's grandparents will have had a much fuller education; also probably fewer live directly with the grandchild. A more positive attitude toward grandparents may have resulted also as today's grandparents recognize their role as being supportive rather than didactic.

Grandparents can influence their grandchildren's behavior both directly and indirectly. Some other person or agency mediates indirect influence. For example, the parent-child interaction will be influenced by the way the parent has been brought up and the experiences of child rearing that the parent has had modeled by his or her parent, that is, the grandparent. Thus, grandparents' disciplinary practices with their children who later become parents have been found to predict the aggression of their grandchildren over two decades later. Grandparents can also continue to provide emotional and financial support for parents. Grandparents can have a powerful indirect influence on quality of parent-child interaction through the social and economic support of parents.

The most obvious forms of grandparent influence are nevertheless direct ones. Grandparents can be surrogate parents when children are young and in a single-parent family or provide care when both parents work. There is clear evidence that grandfathers play an important role in the lives of the young grandchildren of teenage mothers. Grandparents can also be special companions who can relate supportively to young children.

Grandparents have a particularly important role to play when parents are in conflict or divorce. At a time of considerable uncertainty and distress for their grandchildren, a grandparent can be a source of continuity and emotional support for both child and parent (Johnson, 1985). Sometimes, the paternal grandmother, for example, can maintain contacts with grandchildren when the father finds it difficult to do so. A recent issue has been that of custody and the rights of grandparents of a noncustodial parent to have access to their grandchildren. In recent years, statutes granting grandparents legal standing to petition for legally enforceable visitation with their grandchildren, even over parental objections, have been passed in all 50 states of the United States (Thompson et al., 1989).

In the United States, there are now courses for grandparents. Strom and Strom (1989) report an educational program for grandparents to help strengthen families including components on: sharing feelings and ideas with peers; listening to the views of younger people; learning about life span development; improving family communication skills; and focusing self-evaluation. There are also *foster grandparent* programs. These can give elders with low income the opportunity to provide companionship and caring for a variety of high-risk children and youths in return for a tax-exempt stipend. These take place in hospitals, residential institutions, day care programs, and family shelters. The evaluation of these programs appears to be positive.

References
Denham, T. E. and Smith, C. W. (1989). The influence of grandparents on grandchildren: A review of the literature and resources. *Family Relations, 38*, 345–350.
Johnson, C. L. (1985). Grandparenting options in divorcing families: an anthropological perspective. In V. L. Bengtson & J. F. Robertson (Eds.), *Grandparenthood* (pp. 81–96). Beverly Hills, CA: Sage Publications.
Smith, P. K. (1994). Grandparenthood. In M. Bornstein (Ed.), *Handbook of parenting: Status and social conditions of parenting* (Vol. 3, pp. 89–122). Mahwah, NJ: Lawrence Erlbaum Associates.
Strom, R., & Strom, S. (1989). Grandparents and learning. *International Journal of Aging and Human Development, 29*, 163–169.
Thompson, R. A., Tinsley, B. R., Scalora, M. J., & Parke, R. D. (1989). Grandparent's visitation rights: Legalizing the ties that bind. *American Psychologist, 44*, 1217–1222.

See also: Foster parenting; Intergenerational parenting.

PETER K. SMITH

Guilt. Guilt is a self-conscious affective state associated with the decision that one's specific behavior is inconsistent with one's internalized moral standards. According to Hoffman (1982), interpersonal guilt is due to the conjunction of an empathic response to someone's interpersonal distress and awareness of being the cause of that distress. Guilt has three components: *affective* (the painful feeling of dissatisfaction with the self because of the harmful consequences of one's actions), *motivation* (urge to undo the harm or make reparation and restitution), and *cognitive* (awareness that others have independent inner states and that one has caused harm).

Unlike shame, guilt has a clearer focus on the dynamics of a specific situation (Lewis, 1993). The individual evaluates his or her behavior as a failure but focuses on the specific features or actions of the self that led to the failure. In *shame* we see the body hunched over itself in an attempt to hide and disappear. In *guilt* we see the body moving in space as if trying to repair an action. Guilt is less negatively intense than shame. The emphasis is on the self's actions and behavior that are likely to repair the failure. Since the relationship between cause and effect is more clearly established with guilt, there is a greater potential for making reparation and restoring harmony. Excessive guilt is associated with a preoccupation with imagined wrongs to be undone.

Guilt has critical functions for the development of conscience (Barrett, 1995). Guilt provides the initiative to repair a damage brought about by wrongdoing and communicate awareness of proper behavior, contrition, and good intentions. Guilt highlights standards and their importance and helps teach individuals about themselves as active agents, not as passive objects.

Undifferentiated feelings of discomfort at another's distress during the first year of life grow into feelings of genuine concern (Damon, 1988). By the end of the first year, most children provide physical comfort to another in distress. Children learn that others are independent beings in their own right with emotions of their own. At this point, infants may sense that another person's unhappiness may need attention and relief.

By the end of their second year, children can understand that others have needs and feelings distinct from their own, that they can cause harm to others, and that they can repair the harm. Preschoolers cannot, however, readily grasp the relationship between intention and blame. Toddlers have been observed apologizing to upset mothers and siblings in situations where the toddlers had done nothing wrong. At about 3 years of age, children can begin to grasp the idea of hurting other people's feelings. Children 6 years and older begin to grasp a more accurate view of their role in another person's distress, attributing feelings of guilt to an actor when he or she actually caused a transgression. During the middle childhood and adolescence, children can grasp that they can have an impact on a person's identity over time and feel guilt over the effects that one's actions may have beyond the immediate situation. They begin to apply moral evaluative standards independent of outcomes (Damon, 1988). In many cases, this moral framework is given a spiritual dimension as part of a shared religious community.

The relationship between parenting and guilt has been clearly established (Zahn-Waxler & Kochanska, 1990). *Love withdrawal* is related to children's guilt experience. This involves separation imposed by the parent followed by a separation affirmation similar to "I don't want to be near you when you do that." *Induction* plays an important role in helping children to convert shame to guilt. Induction involves an explanation to children of the consequences of their actions for others and their causal role in situations of misfortune coupled with distress vocalizations and facial or bodily expressions of pain and sorrow by the parent. This synthesizes understanding with emotion. Parental *modeling* of regret and reparation can be important as well. Older children can be encouraged to recognize and discuss their own moral feelings.

Excessive love withdrawal, however, can lead to exaggerated feelings of personal responsibility for another's distress. A parent with chronic depression or frequent exposure to parental conflict can overwhelm a child with guilt. Expecting a child to achieve beyond their capacity can also create guilt and shame (Barrett, 1995). Setting reasonable expectations and responding with pride to the child's efforts offset the potential excesses of guilt.

References

Barrett, K. C. (1995). A functionalist approach to shame and guilt. In J. Tangney & K. Fischer (Eds.), *Self-conscious emotions: The psychology of shame, guilt, embarrassment, and pride* (pp. 25–63). New York: Guilford Press.

Damon, W. (1988). *The moral child: Nurturing children's natural moral growth*. New York: Free Press.

Hoffman, M. (1982). Development of prosocial motivation: Empathy and guilt. In N. Eisenberg (Ed.), *Development of prosocial behavior* (pp. 281–313). New York: Academic Press.

Lewis, M. (1993). Self-conscious emotions: Embarrassment, pride, shame and guilt. In M. Lewis & J. Haviland (Eds.), *Handbook of emotions* (pp. 563–573). New York: Guilford Press.

Zahn-Waxler, C., & Kochanska, G. (1990). The origins of guilt. In R. Thompson (Ed.), *36th Annual Nebraska Symposium on Motivation: Socioemotional development* (pp. 183–258). Lincoln: University of Nebraska Press.

See also: Conscience; Empathy; Moral development; Shame.

CHARLES A. SMITH

H

Head Start. Head Start is a federally funded preschool program for children of low-income families. It is designed to give children from resource-limited families a head start in school. Often children from these families begin school with health problems and a lack of self-confidence (Head Start Bureau, 1993). Without encouragement to press onward, these children frequently fall behind in school, creating problems that compound in later school years.

Known as a model program for comprehensive child development, Head Start is based on the philosophy that (1) a child can benefit from a comprehensive, interdisciplinary program to foster development and remedy problems as expressed in a broad range of services and (2) a child's family and community must be involved. The program should maximize on the strengths and uniqueness of each child (Office of Child Development, 1975).

With this philosophy in mind, this federal program set as its overall goal to bring about a higher degree of social competence in children of low-income families (Office of Child Development, 1975). In this context, social competence is defined as a child's everyday effectiveness in dealing with the present environment and later responsibilities in school and life. The definition takes into account the interrelatedness of cognitive and intellectual development, physical and mental health, nutritional needs, and other factors that enable a developmental approach to social competence.

The four major components of Head Start include education, health, parent involvement, and social services. The parent involvement component of Head Start was originally not clearly defined. The program proposal submitted by

Head Start proponents did not specify whether parents were to run the program or merely be participants in its parent education services. The planning committee believed that children would benefit from their parents' direct involvement in the program. They thought that the best way for parents to learn about child development was through actual participation with their children in the daily activities of the program (Zigler & Muenchow, 1992).

The initial view of committee members concerning parent involvement focused on improving the relationship between parents and their children, not organizing them for social action. The first parent-programs specialist hired by Head Start to define the role of parent involvement emphasized the phrase "maximum feasible participation of the poor" found in the Economic Opportunity Act, the legislation responsible for the Head Start program. This approach established the basis for parents becoming equal partners with professional staff and for hiring parent involvement experts as part of the program (Zigler & Muenchow, 1992).

Objectives for the Head Start parent education component of Head Start can be found in the *Head Start Program Performance Standards* (Office of Child Development, 1975). The standards emphasize a planned program of experiences and activities to support and enhance parental roles as the principal influences in the education and development of children. Parents are recognized as responsible guardians of their children's well-being, primary educators of their children, and contributors to the Head Start program and their communities. Head Start would provide the following kinds of opportunities for parent participation:

- direct involvement in decision making in program planning and operations
- paid employees, volunteers, or observers in the classroom and other program activities
- involvement in the development of activities for parents
- cooperation with Head Start staff in nurturing, guiding, and teaching their own children

Many parents now serve as members of policy councils and committees and have voices in administrative and managerial decisions that concern Head Start. The involvement of parents in parent education, program planning, and operating activities are essential parts of every Head Start program.

By participating in Head Start, parents acquire knowledge concerning the needs of their children and about educational activities that can be utilized at home. In addition, many parents serve as volunteers, aides to teachers, social service personnel, and other staff members.

References

Head Start Bureau. (1993). *Head Start: A child development program* [Brochure]. Washington, DC: Author.

Office of Child Development. (1975). *Head Start program performance standards: Head Start policy manual* (DHEW Report No. OCD-N-30-364-4). Washington, DC: United States Government Printing Office.

Zigler, E., & Muenchow, S. (1992). *Head Start, the inside story of America's most successful educational experiment*. New York: Basic Books.

See also: Child care; Family-centered services; Family support.

GWEN LAYFIELD

Hispanic/Latino parents. Hispanic/Latino people, migrating to the United States from Central and South American countries and various Caribbean Islands, often come seeking a more favorable economy for their families. Two groups well represented in the literature on Hispanic/Latino parents are Mexicans and Puerto Ricans. Although vast differences exist between individuals from different Latin American countries, these two parent groups and other Latinos share four sets of values: *hierarchical regard, familism, collective identity,* and *simpatía.*

Hierarchical regard. This set of values involves the respect that Latino people accord those with power and positions of authority within the home, state, and church (DeBord & Reguero de Atiles, 1998; Reguero, 1991; Saracho & Hancock, 1986). One's age, gender, and social class determine the level of respect paid and the kinds of interpersonal relationships formed. Elders hold higher status, and thus respect, within the Mexican American community and the family.

Familism. This set of values recognizes one's significant membership within an extended family (Fitzpatrick, 1971; Mizio, 1974; Reguero, 1991; Saracho & Hancock, 1986). Family members (those related by blood or marriage) as well as *compadrazgo* and *hijos de crianza* are a part of one's extended family. *Compadrazgo* is a coparenting relationship established between the parents of a child and the persons selected by them to act as godparents of their child when he or she is baptized. *Hijos de crianza* or "children of upbringing" are informally adopted. These children, who may or may not be related to the couple's bloodline, are accepted and reared as their own. Traditionally, these extended family members occupy the same home or live within close proximity to one another. Because family members are bound by important mutual responsibilities to each other, they frequently and intensely interact.

Traditionally, both parents share child rearing; however, the father is respected as the authority. In this patriarchal unit, the father provides financially for the family and protects the honor of his wife and daughters. As the head of the household, the man has the freedom to make decisions without consulting his wife. As his subordinate, the wife is expected to be passive, submissive, loyal, and unquestioning.

Within traditional families, male and female children are raised with different standards. Females are carefully protected and sheltered by their parents and brothers with the goal that they enter marriage as virgins (Fitzpatrick, 1971; Reguero, 1991; Saracho & Hancock, 1986). Male children, not bound by the same moral standards, are expected to engage in sexual relations prior to marriage (Fitzpatrick, 1971; Reguero, 1991; Saracho & Hancock, 1986). *Machismo* (involving pre- and extramarital sexual relations, power over women, vigorous romanticism, and jealousy) is considered a virtue when practiced by Latino fathers and sons.

Collective identity. Open communication and a feeling of unity and support exist for Latino people as a result of the respect shown to members of the community and to the extended family (DeBord & Reguero de Atiles, 1997; Reguero, 1991). Collective unity values cooperation and a sense of loyalty to members of one's family and community. Social gatherings provide families with emotional support and close contact with others.

Simpatía. This sense of collective identity, cooperation, and loyalty, is enhanced by *simpatía* (Triandis et al., 1984). With no equivalent English word, *simpatía* refers to "a permanent personal quality where an individual is perceived as likable, attractive, fun to be with, and easygoing . . . shows certain levels of conformity and an ability to share in other's feelings, behaves with dignity and respect toward others, and seems to strive for harmony in interpersonal relations" (Triandis et al., 1984, p. 1363). Rather than argue or disagree, Latino people would prefer to remain polite, respectful, and nonconfrontational. Being well liked, respected, friendly, and agreeable are desirable virtues.

The cultural values of the Anglo community are not easily reconciled with this value framework. Latino children, especially females, may experience conflict between the values and expectations of the family and those of the peer group and community. They may rebel against their parents' strict control of their social lives (Fitzpatrick, 1971; Reguero, 1991; Saracho & Hancock, 1986). Parents become anxious with this loss of influence over their children. Compounding these conflicts is the diminishing influence of extended kinship due to geographical dislocation. As second and subsequent generations of Latino parents become involved in child rearing in the United States, their cultural values assimilate more with those of Anglo Americans. Despite the cultural conflict, Latino parents continue to teach their children to be bilingual, to respect authority, and to maintain family honor.

Consequently, when working with these children, teachers must recognize that Latino children strive to achieve in order to honor their families. Cooperative learning experiences with friends whom they trust may be a more successful instructional technique for Latino children and parents (DeBord & Reguero de Atiles, 1997). The strength with which these cultural values are embraced will be strongly determined by level of education, socioeconomic status, and length of time the family has been living in the United States.

References

DeBord, K. B., & Reguero de Atiles, J. T. (1998). *Latino parents: Preferences for receiving parenting information.* Manuscript submitted for publication.

Fitzpatrick, J. P. (1971). *Puerto Rican Americans: The meaning of migration to the mainland. Ethnic groups in American life series.* Englewood Cliffs, NJ: Prentice-Hall.

Mizio, E. (1974). Impact of external systems on the Puerto Rican family. *Social Casework, 55,* 76–83.

Reguero, J. T. (1991). Relationship between familism and ego identity development of Puerto Rican and immigrant Puerto Rican adolescents. *Dissertation Abstracts International, 52* (3-B), 1750–1751.

Saracho, O. N., & Hancock, F. M. (1986). Mexican-American culture. In O. N. Saracho & B. Spodek (Eds.), *Understanding the multicultural experience in early childhood education* (3rd ed., pp. 3–15). Washington, DC: NAEYC.

Triandis, H. C., Marin, G., Lisansky, J., & Betancourt, H. (1984). Simpatía as a cultural
   script of Hispanics. *Journal of Personality and Social Psychology, 47*, 1363–1375.

See also: Cultural competence; Racial identity.

                          JULIA REGUERO DE ATILES AND SANDRA GLASNER

HOME Inventory. The HOME Inventory, or *Home Observation for Measurement of the Environment,* is a widely used measure of the quality of a child's
home environment (Bradley, 1993). The instrument was developed in order to
understand why low-income families tend to have children who lag in intellectual and academic skills. Through a combination of direct observation and parent interview, researchers can assess the types of physical and social resources
that foster children's cognitive development. Thus, the HOME Inventory measures child-rearing processes that are only imperfect reflections of social address
variables such as poverty and parent education.

   The HOME Inventory has versions for infants and toddlers, early childhood
(3–6 years), and elementary age (6–10 years), each with 45 to 59 items on multiple scales. The instrument taps various aspects of the physical environment, including play and reading materials, the temporal and spatial organization of the
home (e.g., routines, crowding, access to the environment), and the variety of
stimulation available to the child such as visits to museums, the store, and relatives. Also measured are social aspects of the home, such as parental warmth
and acceptance, disciplinary practices, language stimulation, and encouragement
of social maturity. Trained observers can complete the instrument in approximately an hour.

   The HOME Inventory is a reliable measure with excellent validity. Some research has focused on what causes variations on the HOME Inventory. Most
correlations with social class (socioeconomic status [SES]) variables are between .25 and .55. Although statistically significant, these relations do indicate
only modest overlap with SES (Bee et al., 1982). However, some wonder
whether the instrument is useful in making distinctions among low-income
families because HOME scores and income share so much variance. The best
response to this concern is that even when status variables are controlled, the
HOME Inventory still explains variations in children's development (Gottfried,
1984).

   Other social address variables are related to HOME scores, including divorce, age, and parent education. Even after accounting for income, divorced
parents provide less cognitive stimulation, possibly because of multiple demands
on their time and attention. In addition, older mothers have higher scores on the
HOME, compared to adolescent mothers, even after taking stress and income
into account. Language stimulation is a key component of the HOME Inventory,
so parents who have more education may also place more emphasis on verbal
skills. As well, parents who know more about child development are more adept
at tailoring cognitive stimulation to child readiness.

   The effect of the home environment on children's intellectual development is
evident regardless of family income, parent IQ, or perinatal insults. Research

finds that the HOME Inventory accounts for much of the effect of income on later child IQ—or stated differently, HOME scores correlate with children's intellectual performance even after controlling for SES. More intelligent parents may provide both a genetic endowment and a home environment that promote cognitive ability, yet various studies have found the HOME to predict child IQ independent of the mother's IQ. Finally, the quality of the home environment is a better predictor of later child IQ than medical risks such as low birth weight or poor Apgar scores. As a whole, these findings led Bee et al. (1982) to conclude that the HOME Inventory was the single best risk indicator for a 2-year-old.

When programs have a significant parent education component, and target low-income families, effects on the HOME are consistently observed. For instance, the Infant Health and Development Project (IHDP) combines pediatric follow-up services with home visits and early, enriched day care. At two sites, the IHDP had an impact on the HOME, especially "learning" stimulation but not the physical environment. The Elmira Nurse Home Visitation Program and the Houston Parent-Child Development Center similarly had beneficial effects on HOME scores.

Potent predictors of development are excellent sources for screening children. For instance, families who are at risk for psychosocial reasons might be selected for prevention services with a short self-report version of the HOME Inventory. In fact, Molfese and DiLalla (1995) found that a combination of four HOME subscales, biomedical risk, and maternal education effectively identified later cognitive delays. Similar procedures have been used to identify resilient children who fared well despite being low birth weight and growing up in poverty. The HOME Inventory is used often in basic research on dimensions of the home environment that affect child development. It also has the potential for use as a tool to select high-risk families for services and to determine whether they benefit from those services.

References

Bee, H. L., Barnard, K. E., Eyres, S. J., Gray, C. A., Hammond, M. A., Spietz, A. L., Snyder, C., & Clark, B. (1982). Prediction of IQ and language skill from perinatal status, child performance, family characteristics, and mother-infant interaction. *Child Development, 53*, 1134–1156.

Bradley, R. H. (1993). Children's home environments, health, behavior, and intervention efforts: A review using the HOME Inventory as a marker measure. *Genetic, Social, and General Psychology Monographs, 119*, 437–490.

Gottfried, A. W. (Ed.). (1984). *Home environment and early cognitive development: Longitudinal research.* Orlando FL: Academic Press.

Molfese, V. J., & DiLalla, L. F. (1995). Cost effective approaches to identifying developmental delay in 4- to 7-year-old children. *Early Education and Development, 6*, 265-277.

See also: Family systems; Nature versus nurture; Social context.

DAVID MACPHEE

Home schooling. Parents have always served as their children's first, and most influential, teacher. Yet due to political, economic, social, and ideological factors, parents abdicated their role as teacher to formal educational institutions (Van Galen & Pitman, 1991). Over the past three decades, however, a resurgence of interest in educating school-aged children at home has occurred. Home schooling is defined as "instruction or learning, at least some of which is through planned activity, taking place primarily at home in a family setting with a parent acting as teacher or supervisor of the activity, and with one or more pupils who are members of the same family and who are doing grade K–12 work" (Lines, 1991, p. 10).

No one questions the salience of parent involvement in the educational interests of their children. However, heated debate has occurred concerning who should have primary responsibility for directing childhood education: parents, who may or may not be formally trained in education, or schools composed of professional educators. These debates are often focused on issues much deeper than simply the academic preparation of the teacher; concerns about what is taught, how it is taught, and the environment in which it is taught are usually as important as who is teaching.

Estimates regarding the number of children being home schooled vary, but all agree that this approach to education is increasing (Lines, 1991). Descriptive characteristics are an important step in understanding home education families (Ray, 1988). Although the decision to home school involves the commitment of both parents, mothers act as the teacher most of the time. Approximately equal numbers of girls and boys are educated at home. Most parents are college-educated and middle class and regularly attend religious services. There are typically three children in the family. These children are taught a wide range of conventional subjects (e.g., reading, writing, and arithmetic) in both highly structured and unstructured formats. It is important to reiterate the diversity evident in the home schooling movement, but in spite of this pluralism, most home schoolers adhere to one central tenet: The education of children is primarily the responsibility and the right of parents. In addition, Ray (1988) has noted that another belief often implied in the literature is "parents who educate their children at home are extremely interested in and concerned about the total education of their children" (p. 19).

Parents who home school have offered varied reasons for doing so. These reasons are multifaceted and complex and go beyond religious opposition to public education or self-imposed exile from it (Mayberry et al., 1995). Parents' rationales for home schooling are often understood best from the context of their life experience.

Knowles (1991) described two clusters of parental motivation for home schooling: unpleasant experiences as children and a moral imperative. Parents who home schooled experienced early family environments in their families of origin that were not supportive or nurturing. The parents' memories as children and students not only provided the impetus to educate at home but the motivation to maintain the operation of their home schools. Similarly, many parents reported innumerable or unpleasant experiences in schools as children. These negative school experiences were often due to personal learning difficulties exacerbated by apathetic or restrictive teachers, or routine, irrelevant school activities that lacked meaning to them. These experiences and perceptions were influential in their decision to provide a contrasting environment for their children.

Responding to an unpleasant history is not the only reason that parents decide to home school. When parents' perceived their family values to be in conflict with the practices, beliefs, and environments evident in public schools, they considered home schooling a viable resolution to this conflict. Also, parents decided to home school because they believed the familiar environment of the home was better suited to nurture their children's development, and they could address the particular abilities of their children at home in a manner unobtainable in a public school setting.

A number of researchers have considered the learner outcomes of children involved in home education from various areas across the United States (Mayberry et al., 1995). A synopsis of these studies supported the contention that home schooling does not impede cognitive development as measured by performance on standardized achievement tests. Furthermore, the social and emotional development of children educated at home does not appear to be adversely affected, and may actually be enhanced (Van Galen & Pitman, 1991).

References

Knowles, J. (1991). Parents' rationales for operating home schools. *Journal of Contemporary Ethnography*, *20*, 203–230.

Knowles, J., Marlow, S., & Muchmore, J. (1992). From pedagogy to ideology: Origins and phases of home education in the United States, 1970–1990. *American Journal of Education*, *100*, 195–235.

Lines, P. (1991). Home instruction: The size and growth of the movement. In J. Van Galen & M. Pitman (Eds.), *Home schooling: Political, historical, and pedagogical perspectives* (pp. 9–41). Norwood, NJ: Ablex Publishing.

Mayberry, M., Knowles, J., Ray, B., & Marlow, S. (1995). *Home schooling: Parents as educators*. Thousand Oaks, CA: Corwin Press.

Ray, B. (1988). Home schools: A synthesis of research on characteristics and learner outcomes. *Education and Urban Society*, *21*, 16–31.

Van Galen, J., & Pitman, M. (Eds.). (1991). *Home schooling: Political, historical, and pedagogical perspectives*. Norwood, NJ: Ablex Publishing.

See also: Academic achievement; Family-school partnerships; School.

JAMES J. PONZETTI, JR.

Home visitation. Home visiting has existed in England since Elizabethan times and has been offered in the United States at least since the 1890s. There is a wide variety among interventions that occur in the client's home, however. Home visiting programs are designed to increase positive pregnancy outcomes, promote child development, increase use of preventive health services, and/or prevent child abuse. These programs are offered to many different groups, from low-income and at-risk families to the general population.

Powell (1993) has identified some of the characteristics that vary among home visiting programs. Programs may focus on child outcomes or on both parents and children. They may assume that all families need support or that some need more than others. They may assume that the environment is the primary determinant of outcomes or that the parent is. Some programs focus on the parent/visitor relationship, while others focus on the dissemination of information. Programs can have tight or loose ties to the sponsoring agency. Programs may have a single focus or a broad one. The visits may last from 30 to 90 minutes and be weekly, monthly, or quarterly. Most programs last for nine months or longer. Some programs occur in isolation, while others are combined with other agency services. Programs may use formal needs assessment tools or other ways to get parent input. Home visitors may be professionals or paraprofessionals.

Wasik and Roberts (1994) surveyed home visiting programs to identify their characteristics. After surveying 1,904 programs, they found that 224 listed their primary goal as the provision of services to abused and neglected children. The social and emotional development of the child was the most common desired outcome. Programs attempted to do this by teaching parenting skills and coping.

Many home visitors are nurses, midwives, or nurse practitioners. Others have used trained paraprofessionals or volunteers, and some have used social workers, psychology students, or pediatricians. At least one program has used a team of a peer home visitor, a social worker, and a nurse.

There is a growing literature evaluating the outcomes of home visiting programs. Many of those programs have been evaluated using random assignment of families to either the home visiting program or to a control group. Programs that have used random assignment are usually designed and conducted by researchers rather than by practitioners; there may be a need for more evaluations of programs as they are normally conducted in the field. Positive outcomes that have been found include reduced frequency of child maltreatment and improved parent-child interaction, reduced use of punishment, provision of more appropriate toys, reduced subsequent pregnancies, improved health outcomes, improved social support, and decreased psychological distress.

A review of seven studies evaluating the impact of home visiting on preterm delivery and low birth weight found very limited impact (Olds & Kitzman, 1993). Some other outcomes less likely to improve as a result of home visiting intervention are infant attachment, length of labor or days in the hospital, maternal self-esteem, and child development. Some studies have found an increase rather than a decrease in child maltreatment reports, but several authors feel that the finding is due to the increased contact with the home visitors who report the abuse rather than a true increase in abusive behavior. Several studies have found that parents who are poor, unmarried, and in their teen years are most likely to respond positively to home visiting.

Program characteristics are important as well. Gomby et al. (1993) suggest that programs that attempt to meet a wide spectrum of needs and offer a variety of services are more effective than single-focus programs. There are indications that weekly visits are more effective than monthly and that at least four visits must take place before change will occur, but empirical literature to support this recommendation is limited. Some authors have suggested that professionals are more effective than paraprofessionals, but comparisons are complicated by large differences in program structure and goals.

Gomby et al. (1993) have offered several suggestions to guide the development and operation of home visiting programs.

- Programs should be offered on a voluntary basis to all families with a newborn. Families needing more intensive services can then be continued in the program.
- Programs that use home visiting should have multiple goals.
- The intensity and duration of the programs should be flexible and rely on feedback from families until more definitive research findings are available.
- Programs should attempt to recognize and be responsive to the specific needs and situations of client families.
- Only well-trained and dedicated staff should be utilized in programs.
- Evaluations should continue and be focused on questions of clientele characteristics, optimal program length and organization, recruitment and retention issues, and training and qualifications of staff.
- Programs should develop goals and objectives and ensure that they are realistic.

References

Gomby, D. S., Larson, J. D., Lewit, E. M., & Behrman, R. E. (1993). Home visiting: Analysis and recommendations. In R. E. Behrman (Ed.), *The future of children: Home visiting*. Los Altos, CA: David and Lucile Packard Foundation.

Olds, D. L., & Kitzman, H. (1993). Review of research on home visiting for pregnant women and parents of young children. In R. E. Behrman (Ed.), *The future of children: Home visiting*. Los Altos, CA: David and Lucile Packard Foundation.

Powell, D. R. (1993). Inside home visiting programs. In R. E. Behrman (Ed.), *The future of children: Home visiting*. Los Altos, CA: David and Lucile Packard Foundation.

Wasik, B. H., & Roberts, R. N. (1994). Survey of home visiting programs for abused and neglected children and their families. *Child Abuse and Neglect, 18* (3), 271–283.

See also: Family-centered services; Family support; Social support, informal.

JUDITH A. MYERS-WALLS

Hospitalization. The term *hospitalization* refers to a specific situation commonly occurring in childhood in which several potentially stressful events coincide: separation from the family, unpredictability of a new environment, medical procedures, a nonoptimal physical condition, and sensorimotor restrictions. Hospitalization may therefore be characterized as a compound factor in which the relative importance and exact nature of contributing stressors are quite variable in each individual.

From the earliest years of research in this field, numerous adverse effects of early hospitalization have been reported, including immediate upset during the admission, negative behavioral changes shortly after hospitalization, and the development of behavioral disturbances after several years. In spite of major changes in hospital practice and improvement of care, recent research still shows a disturbing impact of early hospitalization in both the short and the long term (Haslum, 1988). This does not imply that every admission for every single child inevitably leads to adverse behavioral consequences. In some cases hospitalization instead brings about positive behavioral changes, for instance, by improving the child's physical condition.

Research consistently discloses a number of child- and environment-related factors that place a child at risk for responding poorly to hospitalization and medical procedures. These comprise admission age between 6 months and 4 years; prolonged and/or multiple admissions; more severe birth defects, trauma, or illnesses; child coping styles; lack of parental contact; parental anxiety; and inadequate preparation and care of child/and or parent by hospital staff.

The curvilinear relationship between age and psychological upset reflects notable changes in cognitive and emotional development. In younger infants separation from attachment figures generally causes strong anxiety, whereas from 4 years onward growing independence from the parents and increasing comprehension of events usually lead to better adjustment. For this reason parental factors influencing the child's response to hospitalization have been addressed primarily in research with younger infants. The reverse impact of hospitalization on the parent-child relationship for younger children is also an item of focus.

The parent-child relationship. In terms of attachment theory, hospitalization can be characterized as a decreased availability of the primary attachment figure at a time when the infant needs her most. From the child's point of view, the repeated neglect in stressful moments might affect the parent's trustworthiness. As witness the consistently reported posthospital responses of stranger anxiety, clinging to mother, and separation protest, feelings of insecurity are often expressed in intensified attachment behavior. Recent studies (e.g., Koomen & Hoeksma, 1993), however, indicate that the damaged confidence may also manifest itself in an avoidant response to the primary attachment figure shortly after hospitalization. It remains unclear whether this points to a temporary coping strategy or a more permanently affected parent-child relationship. Furthermore, additional research is necessary to determine whether an avoidant response to hospitalization is merely typical for particular subcategories of hospitalized children, such as the chronically ill.

It is commonly assumed that an initially healthy parent-child relationship is a protective factor during hospitalization. Findings of Fahrenfort (1993), however, show that securely attached infants have at least as much need of their parents during hospitalization as the insecurely attached and will show posthospital maladjustment if insufficiently supported.

Lack of parental support during hospitalization. Lack of parental contact during the admission appears to enlarge the risk of negative posthospital reactions in the child. Unless the parent is overly anxious, parental presence may help to minimize psychological upset. Possible domains of parental participation are participation in regular daytime care, presence and support at stressful moments, rooming-in at night, and presence at induction of anesthesia. Especially for young infants within the age range of 1 to 3 years, the beneficial effect of extensive parental support, during both the day and night, has consistently been shown (e.g., Saile, 1987). Even children who show substantial upset during the presence of their parents in the hospital seem to benefit from it as judged by their posthospital response. From a theoretical viewpoint, the quality or sensitivity of parental care during hospitalization should add to the effect of mere presence, although this has not been substantiated by empirical data.

Parental anxiety due to hospitalization. Besides the child's upset, hospitalization generally arouses substantial anxiety in the parents. When parents themselves have difficulty adapting to the hospital setting, they may be less able to focus on meeting the needs of their children and providing adequate support. Consequently, high parental anxiety and ineffective coping with stress appear to have a significant impact on how well the child copes. Apart from self-evident worries about medical interventions and the child's physical recovery, parents may also experience anxiety with respect to their relationship with the child in the hospital. Melnyk (1994) refers to two major sources of parental stress during hospitalization: the perception of behavioral changes in their children and uncertainty about their parental role in the hospital. Intervention programs aimed at psychologically preparing parents prove to have several favorable outcomes: lower state anxiety levels and improvement of support and participation in hospital on the side of the parents and less negative behavior following hospitalization on the part of the children (Melnyk, 1994).

A discussion of parental factors in relation to effects of hospitalization requires consideration of the context of parent-child relations as well. Contextual sources of stress and social support are known to influence parenting. They may also affect parental participation and support of the child in the hospital. In this regard it should be noted that infants of high-stress and low-support families (e.g., adolescent mothers or single-mother households) are overrepresented in hospitals in the United States. In these cases the preparation and support supplied by the medical staff and the relations maintained with the parents are of particular importance.

References

Fahrenfort, J. (1993). *Attachment and early hospitalization: An experiment in the prevention of posthospital disturbance in infants*. Amsterdam, Netherlands: Thesis Publishers.

Haslum, M. N. (1988). Length of preschool hospitalization, multiple admissions and later educational attainment and behaviour. *Child: Care, Health and Development, 14*, 275–291.

Koomen, H. M. Y., & Hoeksma, J. B. (1993). Early hospitalization and disturbances of infant behavior and the mother-infant relationship. *Journal of Child Psychology and Psychiatry, 34*, 917–934.

Melnyk, B. M. (1994). Coping with unplanned childhood hospitalization: Effects of informational interventions on mothers and children. *Nursing Research, 43*, 50–55.

Saile, H. (1987). *Psychische Belastung von Kindern Durch einen Krankenhausaufenthalt: Eine Untersuchung Zum Einfluss von Rooming-in und Temperament* [Mental strain of children caused by hospitalization: An investigation concerning effects of rooming-in and temperament]. Frankfurt am Main: Peter Lang.

See also: Illness, chronic, in children; Stress.

HELMA M. Y. KOOMEN

I

Identity development. A stable ego identity is an aspect of optimal psychological functioning that involves learning to be both separate from and yet connected to others. For each human being, identity achievement is a life long process of growth and development. Across the life span (e.g., adolescence, marriage, parenthood, or midlife) an individual must integrate new intrapersonal and interpersonal experiences that challenge his or her current sense of self.

Intrapersonally, identity functions in several ways. It provides a structure for understanding who one is, provides meaning and direction through commitments, values, and goals, and provides a sense of personal control and free will. Additionally, identity provides consistency, coherence, and harmony between values, beliefs, and commitments and enables individuals to recognize possibilities and alternatives (Adams, Gullotta, & Montemayor, 1992). Interpersonally, identity is the means by which an individual is recognized by others.

Erik Erikson (1968) believed that identity development was the central task of adolescence. He viewed identity formation as a combination of conscious and unconscious processes in which one's biological capabilities are integrated with one's personal inclinations and then expressed within a particular cultural environment. The struggle to resolve the normal and inevitable identity crisis is accompanied by *identity confusion*. Confusion that overwhelms identify formation is associated with depression, substance abuse, and poor interpersonal relationships.

In our society, some aspects of identity are selected and others are assigned (see Bosma et al., 1994). That is, an individual can choose a set of psychological and interpersonal goals based on his or her personal values; however, many features of the environment such as social class, race or ethnic membership, politics, and population demographics cannot be readily chosen. Both selected and assigned aspects influence identity development (Adams, Gullotta, & Montemayor, 1992). A child interprets and assigns meaning or value to these influences through cognitive operations that construct and organize knowledge of the self. These on-going processes continue over the life span as individuals actively select, filter, process, and manage information from their environments.

Parenting styles influence children's identity development. For instance, authoritarian parenting that is overcontrolling and extremely rigid and that discourages exploration, independent thinking, and decision making may lead to a *foreclosed* identity. Foreclosed adolescents reared by very authoritarian parents struggle with the necessary exploration phase of identity formation because they have not been encouraged to question, examine, or experiment. They are likely to prematurely commit to the values and goals of their parents.

On the other hand, an overly permissive style of parenting that provides too little structure or too few limits may lead to a *diffused* identity or perhaps an excessively long moratorium. It appears that a democratic style of parenting that is warm, positive, and minimally restrictive is associated with mature identity achievement. Therefore, parents can facilitate identity achievement in at least three ways.

- Affirm the child's unique interests, values, and feelings. Adolescents are more likely to have a positive sense of identity when both parents and children are able to share their own perspectives in mutually supportive ways (Powers et al., 1983).
- Allow the child to exercise age-appropriate levels of autonomy. Let him or her make decisions and set goals.
- Encourage initiative; allow for experimentation with roles and behaviors within a mutually supportive and accepting environment that has appropriate boundaries and limits.

In conclusion, the term *identity development* itself is a paradox. *Identity* refers to sameness or continuity, whereas *development* refers to growth and change. Identity has to do with the dynamic tension between that which is the "core" of an individual and the context (historical, cultural, relational) that recognizes the individual. Identity development is facilitated through creating an optimal balance of separation and connection, autonomy and relatedness.

References
Adams, G. R., Gullotta, T. P. & Montemayor, R. (Eds.). (1992). *Adolescent identity formation*. Newbury Park, CA: Sage Publications.
Bosma, H. A., Graafsma, T. L. G., Grotevant, H. D., & de Levita, D. J. (Eds.). (1994). *Identity and development: An interdisciplinary approach*. Thousand Oaks, CA: Sage Publications.
Erikson, E. H. (1968). *Identity: Youth and crisis*. New York: W.W. Norton & Co.
Powers, S. I., Hauser, S. T., Schwartz, J. M., Noam, G. G., & Jacobson, A. M. (1983). Adolescent ego development and family interaction: A structural-developmental perspective. In H. D. Grotevant, & C. R. Cooper (Eds.), *Adolescent development in the family: New directions for child development* (pp. 5–25). San Francisco: Jossey-Bass.

See also: Self-esteem; Styles, parenting.

SHARON S. ROSTOSKY, MYRA C. KAWAGUCHI,
AND DEBORAH P. WELSH

Illness, chronic, in children. Chronic illness among children is a challenge that faces many families. Over 7 million children have a chronic illness, including about 1 million who have a severe disorder (McDaniel, Hepworth, & Doherty, 1992). Unlike adult chronic illnesses, there is a large diversity of chronic disorders among children. Consequently, each of the childhood chronic illnesses is relatively rare. The most common is asthma, which affects about 1% of all children. Congenital heart disease, seizure disorders, cerebral palsy, arthritis, paralysis, and diabetes are among the other common children's chronic illnesses.

Rolland (1994) differentiates chronic illnesses according to four criteria. First, the illness can either have a gradual or sudden *onset*. Second, the *course* of the illness can be progressive, constant, or episodic. Third, the *outcome* may or may not lead to a shortened life span and eventual death. Fourth, the level of *incapacitation* can vary from mild to severe.

The experience of the chronic illness in the life of a child begins with the *crisis* phase, when the family copes with the initial adjustment after the diagnosis has been made (Rolland, 1994). During this phase, the family must learn to deal with the symptoms of the illness and establish collaborative relationships with health care professionals. The family must also grieve the loss of the family's identity before the illness and work toward accepting the permanent changes that have occurred in the family.

The *chronic* phase is the time between the family's adjustment to the chronic disorder and the time when some families must deal with the issues of death. This phase may last from a few months to several decades. Depending upon the course of the illness, this phase will be characterized by a steady decline of functioning, relative stability, or episodic changes. The chronic nature of the illness forces the family to deal with the disorder on a day-to-day basis for an extended period of time. During this phase, the family strives to live the semblance of a normal lifestyle in the face of uncommon circumstances.

In cases where the outcome of the chronic illness is death, families at some point encounter the *terminal* phase. This includes the preterminal period when the approaching death of the child dominates the family, as well as the stage of mourning following the child's death.

Families who have a child, rather than an adult, with a chronic medical disorder face unique challenges. Depending on the degree of their physical impairment, the length of their illness, and the overall functioning of the family, children who have chronic physical conditions such as cancer, spina bifida, cystic fibrosis, juvenile rheumatoid arthritis, insulin-dependent diabetes mellitus, and asthma are at an increased risk for problems in both psychological and social adjustment when compared to healthy children (Lavigne & Faier-Routman, 1992).

Parents (mothers in particular) also face problems in light of the emotional strain, physical requirements, and financial burden placed upon them as a result of their child's illness. Parents may feel guilty for having contributed to or caused their child's illness, grief at what appears to be the loss of a normal childhood, and concern for the future of their child. A chronic illness may also have an impact upon the siblings of the ill child, depending upon the nature of both the family and the illness.

Developmental level of the child is also an important consideration in adaptation to an illness. Varying degrees of responsibility for the child's illness are shared between the parent and the child depending upon the level of the child's physical and cognitive development. While children should be encouraged to take on as much responsibility for their health care as developmentally appropriate, they should not be unduly overwhelmed by the aspects of adherence to the treatment regimen. Parents should be aware of the stressors their child faces regarding their disease management and be available to provide the appropriate level of supervision as well as a supportive role in treatment.

Patterson has developed a model to explain why families differ in their ability to adjust to a child's chronic illness (Patterson & Garwick, 1994). As part of her model, she has proposed that families' adjustment is based on their ability to balance the demands placed upon the family by the chronic illness and the capabilities of the family to adapt to the illness. The coping process involves reducing the number or intensity of demands and increasing the family's capabilities and resources.

A chronic illness creates "a chronic set of demands on the family" (Patterson & Garwick, 1994, p. 134). One demand is additional financial burdens, such as costs for home modification, reduced income from decreased time in the labor force, and costs from nonreimbursed medical expenses. Another demand is the loss of family privacy, as medical care and social support workers become closely involved with the family. A third demand is the stress that comes from strained interactions with service providers and insurance companies. Finally, there are extra caregiving responsibilities, as family members meet the day-to-day needs of the chronically ill child.

Families also bring capabilities to face these additional demands. The ability to communicate effectively, to have the flexibility to develop new routines and family rules, and to have good problem-solving skills are all important family capabilities. In addition, the personal qualities of good self-esteem and self-efficacy, as well as community resources, such as social support, the availability of adequate medical care and educational support, and positive relationships with service providers, are important resources to families. The presence of these assets enhances the ability of families to maintain healthy family relationships and improve the outcome of children's chronic illnesses (Patterson, 1991).

References
Lavigne, J. V., & Faier-Routman, J. (1992). Psychological adjustment to pediatric physical disorders: A meta-analytic review. *Journal of Pediatrics*, *17*, 133–158.
McDaniel, S. H., Hepworth, J., & Doherty, W. J. (1992). *Medical family therapy*. New York: Basic Books.

Patterson, J. M. (1991). Family resilience to the challenge of a child's disability. *Pediatric Annals, 20,* 491–499.

Patterson, J. M., & Garwick, A. W. (1994). The impact of chronic illness on families: A family systems perspective. *Annual Behavioral Medicine, 16* (2), 131–142.

Rolland, J. S. (1994). *Families, illness, and disability.* New York: Basic Books.

See also: Death of a child; Hospitalization; Social support, informal; Stress.

RICHARD B. MILLER, STACY L. KOSER CARMICHAEL,
GARY R. GEFFKEN, AND JAMES R. RODRIGUE

Imagination. Imagination is the capacity to create and manipulate an experience mentally. It could involve reconstructing a past event or envisioning a future circumstance, lucidly daydreaming, or engaging in play. Imagination is the energy that drives creative efforts, reshaping in one's mind what is not present. Because an act of imagination is an act of freedom as well as creation, it may frighten those who are more comfortable with stability and predictability. Some parents, for example, are suspicious of fairy tales for their portrayal of a fanciful, imaginative world. If so, parents may be overlooking how imaginative talent complements life as a whole.

Imagination tends to be associated with exuberance, ambiguity, and childish fun. When these experiences are linked with control, precision, and professionalism as a child grows into an adult, imagination becomes a powerful scientific and artistic tool, capable of renewing life and redeeming the world. Like a kite that needs to be strung to the ground to fly, the power of imagination resides in its ties to the real world, its friction with a sense of reality. But this relationship needs to be dynamic rather than subordinate, greeting phenomena with a set of shifting perspectives rather than seeing everything through the same rigid interpretive grid (Grudin, 1990).

From the psychoanalytic point of view, imagination involves the creation of an inner world of subjectivity against which we make a conscious or unconscious judgment of the real world and in which we have the freedom to perceive and remodel others as we wish or need them to be. Imagination enables children to develop views of themselves in relation to others and to try on and act out the consequences they anticipate in the imaginary relationships that they create (Mayes & Cohen, 1992).

Between the third and sixth years of life children develop such neurocognitive functions as distinguishing thought from action and understanding that others as well as oneself are motivated to act because of mental states such as feelings, beliefs, and fantasies (Mayes and Cohen, 1992). In her summary of the research on young children's understanding of imagination, pretense, and dreams, Woolley (1995) concluded that by the age of 3 or 4 children understand that imaginary entities are distinctly mental and not real. When asked to explain their reasoning, children will often refer to mental realm, explaining that you cannot touch a thought about a bicycle because *it's imaginary* or because *it's in the imagination.* Children with imaginary companions do not appear to differ from others in their understanding of the mental nature of imagination. In addition to separating what is real from what is imaginary, children at this age show significant improvements in the ability to distinguish performed or pretended actions from imagined actions. This demonstrates that they can represent both pretense and imagination in memory according to cognitive operation features associated with generating a fictional mental state (Welch-Ross, 1994).

Children who are good at producing fantasies have better concentration, are less aggressive, and take more pleasure in what they do than children who fantasize less. They can integrate their experiences better, learn to differentiate between inner and outer experiences, learn to organize information, and become more reflective. Through imagination, they would be more sensitive to others (Tower & Singer, 1980).

Grudin (1990) suggests inventing stories with unique cultural context that are long enough to stretch over several daily story periods. Expressing one's imagination through "what if" conversations and congratulating the imaginative efforts of one's children are the most effective responses. If the parent is too intrusive, however, children will play less imaginatively. Shaeffer, Gold, and Henderson (1986) found in their research with 40 preschool children that parents who provided a role model, were supportive of their children's fantasies, exerted less control over their children's time and activities, and used learning approaches to discipline had children who were more frequent and fanciful fantasizers. Parents who provide resources like art materials are also likely to encourage imagination in children.

References

Grudin, R. (1990). *The grace of great things: Creativity and innovation*. New York: Ticknor & Fields.

Mayes, L. C., & Cohen, D. J. (1992). The development of a capacity for imagination in early childhood. In A. J. Solnit, P. B. Neubauer, S. Abrams, & A. S. Dowling (Eds.), *The psychoanalytic study of the child* (pp. 23–47). New Haven, CT: Yale University Press.

Shaeffer, G. I., Gold, S. R., & Henderson, B. B. (1986). Environmental influences on children's fantasy. *Imagination, Cognition and Personality, 6* (2), 151–157.

Tower, R. B., & Singer, J. L. (1980). Imagination, interest, and joy in early childhood. In P. E. McGhee & A. J. Chapman (Eds.), *Children's humor*. Chichester, England: Wiley.

Welch-Ross, M. K. (1994). Developmental changes in preschooler's ability to distinguish memories of performed, pretended, and imagined actions. *Cognitive Development, 10*, 421–441.

Woolley, J. D. (1995). The fictional mind: Young children's understanding of imagination, pretense, and dreams. *Developmental Review, 15*, 172–211.

See also: Academic achievement; Intuitive parenting; Narratives, personal.

CHARLES A. SMITH

Immunization. Immunity is the defense mechanism that protects a person from infectious disease through either active or passive protection. *Active immunity* is protection that is produced when antibodies are developed by a person's own immune system. This type of immunity is generally long lasting. *Passive* *immunity* is protection by antibodies and other products produced by an animal or human immune system and transferred to a person through injection. Passive immunity often provides effective protection, but this protection wanes over time, usually a few weeks or months (Atkinson et al., 1996).

Experience in the United States in recent years has illustrated the effectiveness of immunization. Use of vaccines has reduced peak incidence of disease by at least 95%. Before the measles vaccine was approved in 1963, an average of over 500,000 cases of measles were reported each year, killing 400 to 500 people annually. By 1983, in the United States the number of cases of measles reported had dropped to a record low of 1,497 (Berger & Thompson, 1995). Before the introduction of the polio vaccine in the late 1950s, 13,000 to 20,000 paralytic cases of polio were reported annually. Sixty-one cases were reported in 1965. Public health officials feel that polio, with continued immunization practices, will be eliminated by the year 2000.

Some parents have reservations about getting vaccinations for their children. Others have declined to have their children vaccinated at all. Parents may have religious or philosophic objections to having their child immunized. Others may view vaccination as interference by the government into what they believe should be a personal choice. They may be concerned about the safety and/or effectiveness of vaccines or may believe that vaccine-preventable diseases do not pose a serious health risk. Listed below are five common reasons children are not immunized (Atkinson, 1996).

Fear that shots are not safe. Although some adverse effects have been reported, current vaccines are safe and effective. Adverse reactions, like a sore arm or a slight fever, are usually mild. A doctor or nurse can discuss these possibilities with parents before giving the shots. More serious adverse side effects occur rarely (on the order of 1 per 1,000 to 1 per million of doses). So few deaths could possibly be attributed to vaccines that it is hard to assess the risk statistically. Of all deaths reported between 1990 and 1992, only one is believed to even possibly be associated with a vaccine. There is constant improvement in vaccines to reduce adverse reactions. Vaccines are saving thousands of lives and reducing the crippling effects each year of childhood diseases.

Lack of parental knowledge. Many parents have not been exposed to information that emphasizes the importance of immunization. Most parents of infants and preschoolers have no memory of summers when children were kept out of swimming pools for fear of catching polio—nor do they know firsthand the terrors of breath-robbing whooping cough, the often fatal paralysis of tetanus, or the sometimes fatal throat infection caused by diphtheria.

Lack of an adequate tracking system. The task of immunizing preschool children is made difficult because there often is no reminder system to help parents assure their children are vaccinated and to help providers identify children in need of immunization.

Difficulty in getting vaccines to the children who need them. Parents need a more "user-friendly" and integrated immunization system, where vaccinations are obtained easily. Such a system would provide immunization opportunities through other services and avoid many of the barriers to immunization (long clinic waits, long waits for appointments, inaccessible or difficult-to-reach loca-tions).

Insufficient funds to have their children immunized. Cost continues to rise. In 1993 the federal contract price made available through public health facilities cost $93.75 to immunize a child by his or her second birthday. The cost through the private sector for the series costs $194.12. This represents nearly a tenfold increase from 1982 in both sectors. Only about half of employer-based health insurance plans cover the cost of immunization.

In addition to these challenges, many parents have two misconceptions that can undermine immunization of their children (Atkinson et al., 1996).

Misconception 1: Diseases had already begun to disappear before vaccines were introduced, because of better hygiene, nutrition, and sanitation. Better hy-giene, nutrition, and sanitation have done much to increase the life expectancy of children. The examples of how immunization has saved lives and reduced crippling of children are indisputable. Measles cases before the 1963 approval of the vaccine averaged over 500,000 cases a year, killing 400 to 500 people annu-ally. By 1983, in the United States the number of cases of measles reported had dropped to a record low of 1,497. The 13,000 to 20,000 paralytic cases of polio disappeared over night with the mass immunization programs in the late 1950s.

Misconception 2: Vaccine-preventable diseases have been virtually elimi-nated from the United States, so there is no need for my child to be vaccinated. Some of the vaccine-preventable diseases have been eliminated. However, oth-ers are still quite prevalent—even epidemic—in other parts of the world. A visit by someone to the United States who has the vaccine-preventable disease can introduce the disease to those who are not immunized, causing an outbreak. Worldwide immunization eradicated smallpox by the year 1977, and if current immunization rates continue, polio will be eradicated by the year 2000.

Innovations in vaccines and vaccine use are the reason for changes in immu-nization recommendations and the childhood immunization schedule. Recent examples of changes include the approval of vaccine for chicken pox and the introduction of an inactivated polio vaccine.

Parents should be advised to contact a physician or public health official for recent updates or changes in the immunization schedule.

References

Atkinson, W., Furphy, L., Gantt, J., Mayfield, M., & Rhyne, G. (Eds.). (1996). *Epide-miology and prevention of vaccine-preventable diseases.* Washington, DC: Depart-ment of Health and Human Services.

Berger, K. S., & Thompson, R. A. (1995). *The developing person through childhood and adolescence* (pp. 178–181). New York: Worth.

Robinson, C. A., Sepe, S. J., & Lin, K. F. Y. (1993). The president's child immunization initiative: A summary of the problem and the responses. *Public Health Reports, 108* (4), 419–425.

See also: Illness, chronic, in children.

MICHAEL BRADSHAW

Indigenous Peoples parent roles. Indigenous Peoples are diverse populations. They occupy ancestral lands, have a shared lineage with the original inhabitants of these lands, have distinct cultures and language, and consider themselves dissimilar from those who control their lands (Stamatopoulou, 1994). In the United States, Indigenous Peoples are incorrectly called Indians, American Indians, or Native Americans. They are not Indians or American Indians since they are not from India. They are the descendants of the First Nations of these lands. Calling them Native Americans is problematic since the term also refers to most native-born Americans whose ancestors are not indigenous to North America.

Many Indigenous Peoples identify themselves by their enrollment in a tribe and refer to themselves according to their nation, tribe, or band membership. In the United States, there are more than 500 federally recognized tribal groups. In 1990, 1.95 million persons identified their race as Indigenous. About 37% of these populations live on reservations, in Alaskan villages, and historic areas in Oklahoma (Snipp, 1996).

Before contact with Europeans, the roles of most Indigenous parents and parent-child relationships evolved according to tribal custom and fluctuations in social organization. Interactions with other Indigenous groups, natural disasters, intertribal warfare, mortality, and birthrates were also influential. Parents were responsible for transmitting cultural values, customs, and beliefs to children. Rites of passage were used to advance children through various life stages and to help them become part of special clans within tribal society. Protecting, nurturing, and teaching children were shared between parents and the clan membership.

A unique aspect of Indigenous parenting was the group-raising of children through multiple parenting systems. Among the Sahnish (Arikara), children have several sets of fathers, mothers, and grandparents. The biological brothers and sisters of a child's father and mother are also the child's fathers and mothers. The sisters and brothers of the child's biological grandparents are the child's grandparents. Multiple parenting systems reduced the strain of parenting and strengthened parent-child relationships. A child received more teaching, attention, and love than was possible in a two-parent system. The participation of several parents made harsh corporal punishment a rare event.

The first contacts with European cultures were disastrous. European diseases, warfare, slavery, and alcohol wiped out tens of millions of Indigenous Peoples. Some groups were completely exterminated, while other groups' numbers dropped so low that they dipped below a genetic survival rate. At the time of first contact with Europeans, the population of Indigenous Peoples was estimated to be more than 5 million (Thornton, 1987). By the end of the nineteenth century, their numbers had declined to approximately 250,000 (Driver, 1969). Disease caused many children to become orphans. The loss of elderly left parents without the knowledge needed to raise children according to custom. The mass destruction of Indigenous Peoples is referred to as an American holocaust (Stannard, 1992).

Federal polices disrupted Indigenous Peoples occupancy of their lands. The General Allotment Act passed by Congress in 1887 divided shared tribal lands

between individuals and broke up the communal relations of the villages. Extended family members, who once had indispensable parenting roles, were physically separated onto individual parcels of land away from their children. Later, the Bureau of Indian Affairs relocation program, operating from 1952 to 1972, moved over 100,000 persons from reservations to urban areas. This relocation created a mass migration of young parents and their children to the city, which fractionated the role of multiple parent systems.

European religions disrupted sacred teaching between children and parents. By 1872, government agents had assigned 238,899 individuals from 73 different Indigenous agencies to 13 different Euro American Christian religious groups (Prucha, 1975). Agents and missionaries felt the religious beliefs and practices of Indigenous Peoples prevented them from moral and religious development. Members of parenting systems who converted to Christianity often had conflicts with relatives who held traditional beliefs. The religious tradition children would follow was often at the center of these conflicts.

The government boarding schools disrupted the intellectual and cultural foundations of children. The aim of education was cultural extinction (Adams, 1995). Indigenous students were subjected to harsh and cruel physical discipline when caught speaking their languages. Children were taught to doubt and devalue the beliefs, identity, and cultures of their communities and parents.

Many parents struggle to transmit their traditional beliefs, languages, and values to their children. Values such as harmony with nature, the tribal community before the individual, and sharing instead of private accumulation often conflict with the core values of American society. Today's high rates of substance abuse, suicide, and delinquency among Indigenous youth reflect the disruption of cultural parenting more than they reflect poor parenting skills.

To prevent further loss of their Indigenous cultures, many parents are renewing their communities by preserving their languages and traditions (Watahomigie, 1995). The following 10 principles, identified by the Navajo, may help Indigenous parents promote positive parent-child relationships that do not interfere with cultural beliefs:

- giving children the opportunities to contribute
- being patient and understanding them
- encouraging them
- avoiding conditional love
- believing in them
- encouraging them to have friends
- having physical contact with them
- promoting their physical safety
- helping them to feel safe
- helping them with their self-actualizing needs (Nystul, 1982)

References

Adams, D. W. (1995). *Education for extinction: American Indians and the boarding school experience, 1875–1928*. Lawrence: University of Kansas Press.

Driver, H. E. (1969). *The Indians of North America*. Chicago: University of Chicago Press.

Nystul, M. (1982). Ten Adlerian parent-child principles applied to Navajos. *Individual Psychology: Journal of Adlerian Theory, Research, and Practice, 38* (2), 183–189.

Prucha, F. P. (1975) *Documents of United States Indian policy*. Lincoln: University of Nebraska Press.

Snipp, C. M. (1996). The size and distribution of the American Indian population: Fertility, mortality, and residence. In G. D. Sandefur, R. R. Rindfuss, & B. Cohen, (Eds.), *Changing numbers, changing needs: American Indian demography and public health* (pp. 17–52). Washington, DC: National Academy Press.

Stamatopoulou, E. (1994). Indigenous Peoples and the United Nations: Human rights as a developing dynamic. *Human Rights Quarterly, 16*, 58–81.

Stannard, D. E. (1992). *American holocaust: Columbus and the conquest of the New World*. New York: Oxford University Press.

Thornton, R. (1987). *American Indian holocaust and survival: A population history since 1492*. Norman: University of Oklahoma Press.

Watahomigie, L. J. (1995). The power of American Indian parents and communities. (Synthesis and discussion—the role of Indigenous communities in language and culture renewal). *Bilingual Research Journal, 19* (1), 189–194.

See also: Cultural context; Racial identity.

MICHAEL YELLOW BIRD

Infertility. Infertility is present when a heterosexual couple has had unprotected intercourse for 12 months without conception. Estimates of the incidence of infertility are 14% for industrially developed nations, with an increase predicted due to the postponement of childbearing and the increase of sexually transmitted diseases (Brander, 1992). The cause of the infertility may be due to female factors (approximately 40%) or male factors (approximately 40%), with the remaining 20% being caused by both male and female factors.

Placing aside the choice to live without children, the options for resolving childlessness depend on the source of the infertility. For female factor infertility, the options are adoption, ovulation induction, in vitro fertilization (and other related techniques), and in vitro fertilization with donated sperm, egg, or embryo. Surrogacy, while technically an option, is not legally available in a number of countries. In male factor infertility, the options are adoption, artificial insemination with donor sperm (DI), intracytoplasmic sperm injection (ICSI), and in some cases of subfertility, in vitro fertilization. The success rates for a live birth are about 20% for women under the age of 37.

The effects of a diagnosis and treatment for infertility on couples, regardless of the site of the infertility, are stressful. Emotional responses may lead to physiological reactions and psychological symptoms broadly categorized in terms of depression, guilt, grief, and isolation (Schover, Collins, & Richards, 1992). The isolation may be a deliberate coping strategy to limit exposure to fertile women or to keep male infertility secret. This has implications for the support networks available to infertile couples who consequently parent.

References

Brander, P. (1992). *Infertility: A review of the literature on prevalence, causes, treatment and prevention* (Discussion Paper 17). New Zealand: Department of Health.

National Perinatal Statistics Unit (1992-1993). *IVF and GIFT pregnancies, Australia and New Zealand*. Sydney, Australia: Author.

Schover, L. R., Collins, R. L., & Richards, S. (1992). Psychological aspects of donor insemination: Evaluation and follow-up of recipient couples. *Fertility and Sterility, 57* (3), 583–590.

See also: Donor insemination; Fertilization, in vitro; Surrogate motherhood.

VIVIENNE ADAIR

Instrumental versus expressive functions. "It's a girl!" or "It's a boy!" These declarations are usually the first words new parents hear from their doctor immediately after a baby is born. Our society emphasizes sex differences. If the child is a girl, she is reinforced for nurturing, supportive, and understanding behavior. A boy, on the other hand, is expected to be competitive, confident, and rational. These sex-typed functions are referred to as expressive and instrumental, respectively.

A structural functional approach to parent-child relations suggests that families are a social system that features specialized roles organized around shared values and norms (Kingsbury & Scanzoni, 1993). Two specialized roles or functions contribute to boundary maintenance and homeostasis of the family system. *Instrumental* functions are task-oriented duties in which someone represents the family to the outside world, usually through employment. These functions have become increasingly important in a postindustrial society in which achievement is emphasized (Losh-Hesselbart, 1988). Men have traditionally occupied these roles that are external to the family. *Expressive* functions are also referred to as socioemotional roles, which include emotional labor such as nurturance and support. Women have traditionally fulfilled these roles (Losh-Hesselbart, 1988). The functional perspective suggests that these distinct roles for women and men are inherent and complementary (Osmond & Thorne, 1993). Men, according to functionalists, are expected to provide economic support, while women are expected to provide emotional support. Women, therefore, are expected to be active and involved in the rearing of children, while men are excused from these responsibilities.

Historical considerations. These distinct roles, according to sociologist Susan Losh-Hesselbart (1988), are artifacts of sociohistorical forces. For example, research using cross-cultural records suggests that women have contributed equally to subsistence production in pre-industrial societies; however, reproductive constraints have negatively influenced women's ability to contribute instrumentally in an industrial society.

In preindustrial societies, instrumental tasks were fulfilled near the home so pregnancy did not impede the contributions of women (Losh-Hesselbart, 1988). Instrumental tasks were separated from the home in industrial societies, so women's participation was limited (Losh-Hesselbart, 1988), but more women fulfill instrumental tasks in postindustrial societies for two reasons. First, advances in medicine have reduced fertility demands—high infant mortality is associated with high fertility (Losh-Hesselbart, 1988, p. 536)—so women are having fewer babies and living longer. Second, skilled labor in postindustrial society does not require that work must be accomplished in a special setting, so women, as they have throughout history, are able to complete instrumental tasks closer to home.

Gender issues. The structural functional emphasis on distinct roles for women and men fails to examine power, inequality, or conflict in gender relations (Osmond & Thorne, 1993). Instrumental and expressive tasks (rather than roles) must be met in family systems (Boss & Thorne, 1989). Food must be acquired, the residence must be cleaned, faulty equipment must be repaired or replaced, family members will need money to function in the community, and children must be educated. These tasks affect parenting because children must be encouraged, nurtured, and supported emotionally. These tasks are best met if both parents contribute in both spheres. Flexibility is an asset to parents and children: Family functioning is likely to be smoother if multiple family members have the skills to attend to multiple tasks (Boss & Thorne, 1989).

Children who are able to complete both instrumental and expressive tasks have more sophisticated social skills and experience enhanced self-esteem. Children learn through direct instruction and observation of behavior. Consequently, parents are role models for their children. It is, therefore, to the child's benefit to observe fathers and mothers engaging in both expressive and instrumental tasks. Additionally, parents can encourage daughters to participate in organized sports in order to enhance her competitiveness, which is positively associated with self-confidence. Both attributes are associated with academic and career success. Likewise, boys who are taught nurturing skills will be better prepared to interact with peers at school and work.

References

Boss, P., & Thorne, B. (1989). Family sociology and family therapy: A feminist linkage. In N. Goldrick, C. M. Anderson, & F. Walsh (Eds.), *Women in families*. New York: Norton.

Kingsbury, N., & Scanzoni, J. (1993). Structural-functionalism. In P. G. Boss, W. J. Doherty, R. LaRossa, W. R. Schumm, & S. K. Steinmetz (Eds.), *Sourcebook of family theories and methods: A contextual approach* (pp. 195–217). New York: Plenum.

Losh-Hesselbart, S. (1988). Development of gender roles. In M. B. Sussman & S. K. Steinmetz (Eds.), *Handbook of marriage and the family* (pp. 535–563). New York: Plenum.

Osmond, M. W., & Thorne, B. (1993). The social construction of gender in families and society. In P. G. Boss, W. J. Doherty, R. LaRossa, W. R. Schumm, & S. K. Steinmetz (Eds.), *Sourcebook of family theories and methods: A contextual approach* (pp. 591–625). New York: Plenum.

Ritzer, G. (1988). Structural functionalism, neofunctionalism, and the conflict theory alternative. In G. Ritzer, *Sociological theory* (2nd ed., pp. 200–241). New York: Knopf.

See also: Family systems; Sex roles.

RONALD JAY WERNER-WILSON AND MEGAN J. MURPHY

Intergenerational parenting. Rules governing intergenerational relationships vary across cultures. Hines et al. (1992) provide a cross-cultural synopsis of the differing roles and interpretations of the involvement of different generations in the parenting of young children, stressing the importance of awareness of differing values when working with families. The following examples, while by no means inclusive of all cultural representation found in this country, offer an illustration of the varying roles of the generations in parenting across cultures.

Family relationships are viewed as wealth in the African American culture (Hines et al., 1992). It is quite common for three to four generations to live in close proximity to each other. Value is placed on family loyalty and responsibility to others. The main source of intergenerational conflict results from a child behaving "disrespectfully" to an elder, as elders are considered wise and revered. Caretaking of children is shared across the generations, and family support in child rearing is highly regarded.

Latino cultures are also governed by responsibility and mutual obligation to the family (Hines et al., 1992). Grandparents do not contribute financially but do contribute indirectly to the family through the caring for the children. This enables the parents to engage in activity outside the home. The elderly, in return, expect to be cared for by their adult children when it becomes necessary.

According to Hines and colleagues (1992), the Irish maintain very strong intergenerational boundaries, with the mother as the central care provider and the father as peripheral. There is little overlap in roles within or across generations. The dominant American culture, with the emphasis on "nuclear" family and independence, resembles this division of generations.

A final culture described to illustrate the differing values placed on intergenerational parenting is the Asian-Indian culture. In this culture, relationships are other-directed rather than self-directed. The role of the mother-in-law holds the greatest status. There is a *covert power* to be gained through the caretaking of grandchildren, emphasizing the importance placed on child rearing.

Regulation and negotiation of successful intergenerational involvement in parenting depend on a number of variables. Of primary importance are the shifts that occur between generations when a new generation is created. Hanson and Jacob (1992) determined multiple factors influenced the nature and perception of support between the generations when such a transition occurred. These included life stage issues, individual characteristics, the nature of the maternal and paternal relationships, contrasts between expectations and experiences of support, perceived and available quality of relationships, and the simultaneous transitions of the family members. Further, the creation of a new generation offered opportunities for positive realignment of parent/adult child relationships or dangers of increasing conflict and estrangement. Recognition of maturity was identified as the key factor in assisting a successful transition.

Although it is reasonable to assume that parenting patterns are transmitted across generations, there is evidence that parenting is evolving with our society. Hanson and Jacob (1992) suggest that each new generation created brings with it discontinuities of culture and traditions. The blending of divergent ethnic, religious, or socioeconomic backgrounds places the parenting approaches of the previous generation in a tenuous position. Modern roles and practices influence the continuation of beliefs and conventions related to parenting. Further, acculturation of first-generation children of immigrants impacts that continuation of cultural practices in their "pure" form. A primary cause of intergenerational conflict results from the pressure on young adults to integrate beliefs and practices different from those of their parents.

The belief that abusive and dysfunctional patterns of parenting are transmitted across generations is widely acclaimed in our society. Kaufman and Zigler (1989) offer evidence that being maltreated as a child puts one at risk for becoming abusive. They also suggest, however, that the path between those two points is far from direct or inevitable. Instead, patterns of dysfunctional parenting are generated by a complex combination of ecological variables, as is the interruption of such transmission. Table 1 provides a summary of the compensatory and risk factors that influence the transfer of parenting patterns into the next generation.

Table 1
Determinants of Abuse: Compensatory and Risk Factors

	Compensatory	Risk
Ontogenetic	High IQ Awareness of past abuse History of positive relationship with one parent Special talents Physical attractiveness Good interpersonal skills	History of abuse Low self-esteem Low IQ
Microsystem	Healthy children Supportive spouse Economic security	Marital discord Children with behavior problems

Exosystem	Good social supports
	Few stressful events
	Strong, supportive religious af-
	    filiation
	Positive school experience and
	    peer relationships as a child
	Therapeutic interventions
		Unemployment
		Isolation; poor social
		    supports

Macrosystem	Culture that promotes a sense of
	    shared responsibility in caring
	    for community's children
	Culture opposed to violence
	Economic prosperity
		Cultural acceptance of
		    corporal punishment
		View of children as
		    possessions

References

Hansen, L. B., & Jacob, E. (1992). Intergenerational support during the transition to parenthood: Issues for new parents and grandparents. *Families in Society, 73,* 471–479.

Hines, P. M., Garcia-Preto, N., McGoldrick, M., Almeida, R., & Wiltman, S. (1992). Intergenerational relationships across cultures. *Families in Society, 73,* 323–338.

Kaufman, J., & Zigler, E. (1989). The intergenerational transmission of child abuse. In D. Cicchetti & V. Carlson (Eds.), *Child maltreatment: Theory and research on the causes and consequences of child abuse and neglect* (pp. 129–150). Cambridge: Cambridge University Press.

See also: Family systems; Grandparenting.

                                                                    VICKY PRIMER

Intuitive parenting. Intuitive parenting refers to the many nonconscious
but highly appropriate behaviors that serve the best interests of an infant by being well matched to the young organism's limited capabilities. Developed in
Germany by Drs. Hanuš and Mechthild Papoušek, this concept provides empirical evidence and theoretical explanations of the early social interactions between
caregivers and their infants (Papoušek & Papoušek, 1987).

Human infants are able to recognize and respond very early to social stimuli
such as voices and faces. These important behaviors help the newborn become a
reciprocating social partner, and thus increase the chances for survival of a
dependent and "helpless" being. Intuitive parenting is a helpful concept for understanding characteristics of caregiving that support these emerging infant
competencies.

The new parent must find ways of establishing effective communication with
an inexperienced infant partner; yet most accomplish this with relative ease and
no particular training. Research shows that parents respond to the infant's limited repertoire by simplifying their communication and modifying their usual
methods of eliciting and maintaining attention (Koester, Papoušek, & Papoušek,
1989). Such behaviors occur with great regularity and serve to share knowledge,
convey information, or enhance the infant's learning opportunities. However,
parents are not consciously aware of these behaviors, typically cannot recall or
describe them, and are often not aware of their own infant's specific levels of
competence. The *intuitive* side of parenting implies that parents do not rely on
rational decision-making processes that would be too slow to permit instantane-
ous responses to an infant's ongoing stream of vocal and nonvocal behaviors.

Babytalk. Parents engage in intense communicative interactions long before
an infant begins to use language, thus setting the stage for subsequent linguistic
development. During these early interactions, parents feel a compelling desire
for "dialogue" although they clearly do not expect a coherent response from the
infant. The adjustments adults make when vocalizing to infants provide excellent examples of how parental behaviors are precisely tuned to the needs and
abilities of their young (Papoušek, 1989).

Parents exaggerate their vocal input to a young child by asking many questions and using frequent repetition and "theme and variation" patterns. Specific
melodic contours are also related to the parents' efforts to soothe, console,
arouse, or praise the infant. "In other words, the melody of babytalk carries messages while its words are still meaningless to the infant" (Papoušek & Papoušek,
1990).

Testing infant alertness. At times, the caregiver may be uncertain of the infant's level of arousal, attention, or readiness for interaction. Parents frequently
engage in behaviors such as subtle testing of the infant's muscle tone, which
help to evaluate the baby's state and determine the need for additional or re-

duced stimulation. These appear to inform the parent of the infant's readiness for more interaction, sleep, or feeding.

Another cue to which parents respond is the position or activity of the infant's hands. These cues facilitate appropriate parental responses, such as altering the baby's position to increase visual alertness or to permit sleep, and therefore serve to protect the infant from too little or too much stimulation.

Visual distance. Another example of intuitive parenting relates to visual perception. Although even newborns can see and focus quite well, their range of visual acuity is nonetheless limited. Adults typically use two specific eye-to-eye distances with infants; an *observational distance* (about 16 to 20 inches) is normally used when watching an infant who is not attending to the adult. The closer *dialogue distance* (8 to 10 inches) corresponds to the infant's range of visual acuity and is used as soon as the infant shows interest in communicative interaction (Papoušek & Papoušek, 1987).

When the infant turns toward the partner, caregivers frequently reward this behavior with a contingent *greeting response*: head tilted back, raised eyebrows, widely opened eyes, open mouth, and finally a smile or verbal greeting to the infant. These visually related behaviors ensure that the caregiver is a salient feature of the infant's perceptual world—by reducing the distance to match the infant's optimal range, incorporating movement and exaggerated facial expressions to capture the infant's attention, and reinforcing the infant's social responsiveness.

Thus, within the framework of intuitive parenting, nonvocal as well as vocal behaviors offer important insights about the subtle but skillful methods used by parents—strategies that appear to facilitate the early integrative processes of the human infant. The parent's intuitive behavioral patterns match the infant's communicative and learning abilities at each stage of development (Papoušek & Papoušek, 1990). Many of these human caregiving behaviors seem to be well adapted to support and enhance precisely those capabilities that distinguish human infants from the young of other species.

Given this human tendency to modify behaviors appropriately in support of an infant's optimal development, health care and family service professionals should be alert to situations in which parents are not responsive to their infant's limited capacities. In some cases, the parental repertoire may appear restricted or inhibited due to factors such as maternal depression, domestic violence, or fears related to infant illness. Providing models of appropriate interactions, either by intervention workers or by other parents, can be an effective method to help elicit these intuitive behaviors and lead to more reciprocal and rewarding parent-infant exchanges.

References

Koester, L. S., Papoušek, H., & Papoušek, M. (1989). Patterns of rhythmic stimulation by mothers with three-month-olds: A cross-modal comparison. *International Journal of Behavioral Development, 12* (2), 143–154.

Papoušek, H., & Papoušek, M. (1990). The art of motherhood. In N. Calder (Ed.), *Scientific Europe: Research and technology in 20 countries* (pp. 382–387). Matricht, Holland: Scientific Publishers Limited.

Papoušek, H., & Papoušek, M. (1987). Intuitive parenting: A dialectic counterpart to the infant's precocity in integrative capacities. In J. D. Osofsky (Ed.), *Handbook of infant development* (2nd ed., pp. 669–720). New York: Wiley.

Papoušek, M. (1989). Determinants of responsiveness to infant vocal expression of emotional state. *Infant Behavior and Development, 12,* 507–524.

See also: Communication; Imagination.

LYNNE SANFORD KOESTER

J

Jealousy. While the words *jealousy* and *envy* often are used interchangeably, they are not the same. Jealousy is the negative reaction that arises when an agent poses a real or imagined threat to a person's relationship with someone (Hansen, 1991). Envy is the negative reaction that is precipitated when someone else has a relationship with a person or object.

Jealousy is best viewed as a compound emotion (Hupka, 1984). It results from the situational labeling of one or more of the primary emotions such as anger or fear. The primary emotion words of *anger* and *fear* describe the emotional state, while the compound emotion word of *jealousy* explains that emotional state.

This conceptualization of jealousy assumes that it is a social phenomenon that is at least partially learned and is manifested in response to symbolic stimuli that have meaning to the individual. For example, a couple has just had a baby. One of the partners devotes nearly all of his or her free time to playing with and taking care of the child, which has drastically reduced the amount of time the couple has for being together. Depending upon a variety of cultural, personal, and relationship factors, the other partner may define such devotion and expenditure of time as inappropriate and view it as a threat to their relationship. Therefore, he or she may experience such primary emotions as anger or sadness over the loss of time together. In other words, he or she may become jealous.

This view of jealousy focuses on the social psychological and sociological aspects of the emotion. *Psychoanalytic* speculation holds that early sibling conflicts may increase the intensity of jealousy in adult romantic relationships, while *attachment* theory postulates that ill-formed or disrupted attachment with early caretakers often results in *anxious attachment*. Anxiously attached people remain excessively sensitive to the possibility of separation or loss of love and are particularly susceptible to adult jealousy. Clanton and Kosins (1991) designed a study to test these two perspectives and found little support for them. They concluded that a sociological view emphasizing jealousy's role as a protector of valued relationships is a theoretical framework with greater utility.

Various efforts have been made to identify different types of jealousy. Many differentiate between "normal" jealousy, which is based upon a real threat to a person's relationship with another, and other types of jealousy. For example, White and Mullen (1989) identify three major classes of jealousy. *Symptomatic* jealousy is a consequence of a major mental illness such as paranoid disorder, schizophrenia, substance abuse, or organic brain disorders. Some people experience *pathological* jealousy because of a personality disorder or strong sensitizing experiences. *Normal* jealousy, in contrast, occurs in people who are neither sensitized nor suffering from a major mental illness. These three classes of jealousy differ according to the relative influences of biology, personality, and relationship on the development of jealousy; in the person's capacity for reality testing; and in suggested treatment approaches.

Jealousy is most likely to become a parenting issue in two instances. As in the previous example, one parent may view the other parent's relationship with a child or the children as a threat to the relationship between the two of them. Jealousy may emerge as well in sibling relationships. The difficulty children have in sharing their parents is a major factor in sibling rivalries. The degree of conflict between them may have considerable influence on parental stress and family contentment (Newman, 1994). Competition between siblings is inevitable since they must compete for numerous resources such as preferred space, television programming, and toys. Parental attention, approval, and affection are highly sought. Since children perceive this to be a finite resource, competition for these resources is particularly intense. The jealousy that results is difficult for children to manage, producing frequent conflict and aggression. As children move from the preschool to the school years, that aggression becomes more verbal and less physical.

References

Clanton, G., & Kosins, D. J. (1991). Developmental correlates of jealousy. In P. Salovey (Ed.), *The psychology of jealousy and envy*. New York: Guilford Press.

Hansen, G. L. (1991). Jealousy: Its conceptualization, measurement, and integration with family stress theory. In P. Salovey (Ed.), *The psychology of jealousy and envy*. New York: Guilford Press.

Hupka, R. B. (1984). Jealousy: Compound emotion or label for a particular situation. *Motivation and Emotion, 8*, 141–155.

Newman, J. (1994). Conflict and friendship in sibling relationships: A review. *Child Study Journal, 24*, 119–152.

White, G. L., & Mullen, P. E. (1989). *Jealousy: Theory, research, and clinical strategies*. New York: Guilford Press.

See also: Conflict resolution; Moral development.

GARY L. HANSEN

K

Kinship care. More than 1 million children live apart from their parents and in the care of kin. Although many cultural groups have long-standing traditions of informally arranged kinship care, *formal* agency-sanctioned kinship care is a fairly new phenomenon. Such care has grown dramatically in recent years, in part because child welfare agencies have come to favor family members as foster care providers (Wilson & Chipungu, 1996). Does this mean that kinship care is the "best" form of out-of-home care? Studies have indeed shown that children in formal kinship foster care have a slight edge in well-being over children in traditional foster homes (Berrick & Barth, 1994). An important caveat, however, is that it is unknown whether there were significant differences between the two groups of children in reasons for entering foster care or in socioemotional functioning at the time of placement.

Further, whether kinship care is advisable will vary from family to family, so that a careful assessment ought to be made of any potential kinship care placement. Problematic patterns of family functioning are not inevitably handed down from one generation to the next, but they can be. Consequently, family dysfunction may characterize a child's extended family as well as his or her immediate one. Kinship care also may lead to deleterious contact with a parent that otherwise would be prevented, or it may expose children to conflict between their parents and the caregiving relative (Clark, 1995).

Nevertheless, many kinship caregivers are adequate or better as foster parents, even if they may have fallen short as parents at an earlier, less-mature time of life. There is also evidence that some fostering relatives help a child to negotiate a relationship with an inadequate parent and to accept the nature of the situation without self-blame. A child in kinship care may derive feelings of connectedness, belonging, and security from familiar family habits and customs and from a sense of the long-term nature of family ties. He or she also may have a pre-existing attachment to a kin caregiver. In addition, if keeping a child within the extended family preserves cultural group ties along with family ties, the child's identity development is likely to benefit (Clark, 1995; Wilson & Chipungu, 1996).

Despite the advantages of kinship care, it can entail numerous stresses for kinship caregivers, who are disproportionately members of ethnic minority groups. One source of stress is the frequent difference between the family-related norms of such groups and the norms of the dominant culture, which have helped shape traditional foster care policies. For example, the child welfare system may overlook *fictive kin*, who lack a genetic tie but who are nonetheless important family members in some cultural groups. If preplacement screening is done, inflexible application of any of several criteria can eliminate a potentially excellent home. Then, once a foster care placement is made, it is usually considered undesirable to return the child to his or her home of origin unless the move promises to be permanent. In some cultural groups, though, in which family life is characteristically fluid, a child's "shuttling" between two homes may be both normative and adaptive. Finally, routine monitoring of a kinship placement may seem, to the family, a stressful and unnecessary intrusion into their life (Wilson & Chipungu, 1996).

In other areas, problems can ensue when kinship caregivers are not accorded the same treatment as traditional foster parents. Kinship foster parents are often elderly, in poor health, and caring for children with a formidable array of problems. Yet they are less likely than traditional foster parents to receive supportive services such as specialized training (e.g., caring for drug-exposed infants), respite care, or support groups (Child Welfare League, 1994). For some, financial support is unavailable, inadequate, or not in the form that would be most helpful (Takas, 1993). In short, those who are part of the child welfare system may be disadvantaged in comparison to traditional foster parents. Not uncommonly, kinship caregivers, both within and outside the system, are disadvantaged to the point of genuine hardship (Clark, 1995).

Child abuse and neglect, along with such correlates as poverty and substance abuse, spurred the growth in kinship foster care and are likely to sustain a need for it. The need may be increased still more by two societal conditions of fairly recent genesis: (1) the limits on public assistance mandated by the welfare reform bill of 1996 and (2) the AIDS (Acquired Immunodeficiency Syndrome) epidemic, which is expected to create sizable numbers of orphans. Fortunately, there is increasing recognition of the difficulties inherent in fitting relatives into policy molds constructed for traditional foster parents. In more than one locale, reform efforts are under way (Takas, 1993; Wilson & Chipungu, 1996).

References

Berrick, J. D., & Barth, R. P. (Eds.). (1994). Kinship foster care [special issue]. *Children and Youth Services Review, 16* (1/2).

Child Welfare League of America. (1994). *Kinship care: A natural bridge.* Washington, DC: Author.

Clark, J. (1995). *Kinship foster care: An overview of research findings and policy-related issues.* University Park: Pennsylvania State University, Department of Human Development and Family Studies. (ERIC Document Reproduction Service No. ED 400 061)

Takas, M. (1993). *Kinship care and family preservation: Options for states in legal and policy development.* Washington, DC: American Bar Association, Center on Children and the Law.

Wilson, D. B., & Chipungu, S. S. (Eds.). (1996). Kinship care [special issue]. *Child Welfare, 75* (5).

See also: Child care; Intergenerational parenting; Social support, informal.

JENNIFER CLARK

L

Language development. Language acquisition requires a child to understand or comprehend the language being spoken (referred to as *receptive* language), as well as being able to produce the language (referred to as *productive* or *expressive* language). While there is great variability in the ages at which children acquire language, the average child begins word comprehension at about 8 to 9 months. Production of first words occurs around 12 to 13 months of age and is characterized as single words that typically refer to familiar people, objects, or actions. A child's productive vocabulary slowly grows over the next few months until around 16 to 18 months of age when a spurt in the number of words that a child produces is reported. It has been suggested that comprehension abilities display a similar rapid spurt in the time period just prior to the productive spurt (Reznick & Goldfield, 1992). By 18 to 20 months, an average child begins to produce two-word combinations that are often referred to as *telegraphic speech* because they focus on high-content words and eliminate smaller, less important words (e.g., "Mommy sock" or "More milk"). Between 2 and 3 years of age, a child begins to demonstrate a basic understanding of word order. Throughout the preschool years, a child continues to master grammar and progressively learns the rules of conversation.

Various theoretical orientations attribute the development of language to different causes (McCormick & Schiefelbusch, 1990). For example, the psycholinguistic perspective proposed by Noam Chomsky assumes that an innate and detailed program for language acquisition, the language acquisition device (LAD), is present in all humans, and only a minimal amount of linguistic input in necessary to activate the program (McCormick & Schiefelbusch, 1990). Hence from a psycholinguistic perspective, parental input is not considered an essential contribution to language learning. An extreme opposite viewpoint is that of a behavioral model of language development. In this theoretical orientation, language acquisition is believed to result from adult input, and thus language learning occurs through adult modeling, child imitation and practice, and selective reinforcement of correct language output. A more moderate theoretical perspective is that of interactionist theory, which is a compromise between psycholinguistic and behaviorist viewpoints. Interactionists believe that many factors, such as cognitive abilities, motor skills, maturation, biology, and social interaction, are important for optimal language development.

Many interactionists such as Jerome Bruner, Michael Tomesello, and Lev Vygotsky have asserted that the social context in which language occurs is essential to language development. Jerome Bruner suggests that infants are born with a readiness to acquire the linguistic forms from the culture and the language environment. Caregivers are said to contribute to this process through the adult *Language Acquisition Support System* (LASS). The LASS assists the infant in the transition from prelinguistic to linguistic communication by the use of routines (e.g., dressing, eating). In such interactions, the adult can highlight those features of the environment that are already meaningful to the child and provide a simplified model of language (Bruner, 1983).

Interactionists have suggested that various types of parental behaviors can facilitate optimal language learning. Ideally, these parental behaviors evolve according to the child's developmental level. For example, parental speech that is directed to young children, referred to as *child-directed speech* (CDS) or *motherese*, is different from speech to other adults, and this CDS has been said to be "fine-tuned" to the child's language learning level (Snow, 1995). Thus, in early infancy CDS is characterized by higher pitch, more varied and exaggerated intonation, and frequent repetition. Infant CDS is believed to be an adult's response to infants' attentional patterns and to provide the infant exposure to its own language's phonetic structure. Later in infancy, the CDS is tailored by adults in that the length of utterances are reduced and utterances are directed more to objects and actions in the here and now. These parental modifications occur around the time that the child is beginning to understand and produce single words.

Another example of a supportive parental behavior is that of *joint attentional focus*. When both the child and parent are jointly focused on objects or actions, the parent can provide verbal labels for the language learning child. An example of joint attention is joint book reading, which is a highly effective language learning task involving consistency and frequent repetition.

There is a substantial body of research that suggests an enriched home environment, typically measured by the *Home Observation for Measurement of the Environment* (HOME), is associated with greater language abilities in young children. In a detailed, longitudinal study, Hart and Risley (1995) have documented large differences between socioeconomic groups on a number of parental linguistic input variables. Young children from middle-class families received significantly more parental linguistic input than did children from working-class and welfare families. The middle-class parental linguistic input was characteristically different from other families in that there were more questions directed to the child, fewer prohibitions toward the child, and more complexity and responsiveness in the parental speech.

While language delays in young children do occur, they are seldom solely explained by parental behaviors. Other causes may be related to biological factors, such as hearing deficits (either conductive or sensorineural) or neurological problems. Parents should seek a language screening or assessment if they are concerned about their child's language abilities.

References

Bruner, J. (1983). *Child's talk: Learning to use language.* Oxford: Oxford University Press.

Hart, B., & Risley, T. R. (1995). *Meaningful differences in the everyday experiences of young American children.* Baltimore, MD: Paul H. Brooks.

McCormick, L., & Schiefelbusch, R. L. (1990). *Early language intervention: An introduction* (2nd ed.). Columbus, OH: C. E. Merrill.

Reznick, J. S., & Goldfield, B. A. (1992). Rapid change in lexical development in comprehension and production. *Developmental Psychology, 28*, 406–413.

Snow, C. E. (1995). Issues in the study of input: Finetuning, universality, individual and developmental differences, and necessary causes. In P. Fletcher & B. MacWhinney (Eds.), *The handbook of child language* (pp. 180-193). Cambridge, MA: Blackwell.

See also: Communication; Deaf children, parenting; Deaf parent; HOME Inventory; Narratives, personal; Vygotsky, Lev Semenovich.

CARMEL PARKER WHITE

Lesbian mothers. The percentage of women who are lesbian mothers is not known. Like gay fathers, lesbian mothers constitute a minority within a minority. However, it is likely that a greater percentage of lesbians are mothers than gay men are fathers. This is because lesbian women differ from gay men in the ways they become involved in parenthood. For example, while there are a substantial number of lesbian women who have children as a product of a past heterosexual marriage, many others have used artificial insemination as a means for achieving parenthood. In addition, lesbian women may adopt more commonly than gay men (Pies, 1989).

Like the term *gay father*, *lesbian mother* is a contradictory term. It is difficult for the public to understand how a woman who has a same-sex orientation would want to be a parent. However, since people generally are more accepting of lesbianism as opposed to male homosexuality, lesbian mothers may not experience identity resolution problems similar to gay fathers, upon discovering and accepting their sexual orientation.

Another observed difference between male and female homosexuals is the greater tendency among lesbians to participate in long-term committed relationships. This leads to the formation of a lesbian stepfamily system when at least one of the women already has children or one partner of a lesbian couple becomes artificially inseminated. These stepfamilies resemble heterosexual stepfamilies (Baptise, 1987). Differences can be observed that distinguish lesbian stepfamilies from other family forms. These can be traced to the problems these families experience due to homophobic and heterosexist attitudes found in their communities that force them to cope with prejudice and discrimination.

Four characteristics distinguish these families from others. First, they *lack legitimacy* afforded to heterosexual families because our society does not recognize homosexual relationships vis-à-vis marriage. This lack of legitimacy presents unique problems such as how to relate to schools in which children are enrolled. Lesbian mothers must carefully consider whether to disclose their home situation and sexual orientation to children's teachers, whether their partner may feel ignored and unable to participate in parent-teacher conferences, and so on.

Second, because women typically have custody of their children, lesbian mothers may *experience more confrontations* with the negative stigmas and heterosexist attitudes in their community than gay fathers who typically do not have custody but do have visitation rights. Researchers note that sexual orientation of the two adult women in lesbian stepfamilies is likely to be a family secret shared by children. Any secret to which shame is attached is unhealthy in any family system but may be intensified in lesbian stepfamilies because it is dealt with daily. Children may not feel free to invite other children to their home to play, for example.

Third, lesbian stepfamilies typically *isolate themselves* from other family forms in their communities for a variety of reasons. Topping the list, however, may be a fear of losing custody of children if sexual orientation of the adults becomes public knowledge. When any family fails to develop social support networks as fully as possible, there is the likelihood that coping and recovery from crises will be more difficult to accomplish in healthy ways.

Finally, lesbian couples can *face legal problems* not usually encountered by other family forms. This is especially related to the use of artificial insemination in achieving parenthood. Laws regarding custody of children in most states are not clear on this procedure and particularly when a couple performs the procedure themselves rather than using a physician. In most instances, the law recognizes the biological mother as entitled to custody, and the mother's partner may have to pursue special legal proceedings in order to become legally recognized as a parent.

Lesbian families usually find ways to solve such problems creatively and in healthy ways. Like children of gay fathers, those of lesbian mothers are found by researchers to be well adjusted (Patterson, 1992). Children growing up in lesbian stepfamilies typically experience several challenges, however. First, children must cope not only with issues related to their mother's sexual orientation but to adjusting to the effects of parental divorce. This is different from children of gay fathers since those of lesbian mothers typically live with their mother during this process. Adjusting to divorce is different for men and women, and children of lesbian mothers experience more of their mother's problems in becoming a single parent. Second, researchers report that boys are more accepting of their mother's disclosure of homosexuality than girls are. This may relate to the sex-role identification issues of the girl, who may fear that she can become homosexual as well. This fear is largely unfounded. Third, lesbian women who are coparenting appear to become more flexible in how they define parenting roles. This affords children a different learning experience than in homes where parenting roles are more rigidly defined. Finally, many lesbian mothers look to their children for approval of their sexual orientation because this is generally lacking from others. This can place a special strain on their relationship.

References

Baptise, D. A., Jr. (1987). The gay and lesbian stepparent family. In F. W. Bozett (Ed.), *Gay and lesbian parents*. New York: Praeger.

Patterson, C. J. (1992). Children of lesbian and gay parents. *Child Development, 63,* 1025–1042.

Pies, C. A. (1989). Lesbians and the choice to parent. *Marriage and Family Review, 14,* 137–154.

See also: Gay fathers; Gender socialization; Sex roles.

JERRY J. BIGNER

Limit setting. Limit setting is a relational process wherein one person motivates another person to internalize rules and values, control impulses, delay satisfaction, and work within societal and parental parameters (Millstein, 1993). Limits are guidelines that caretakers construct for children or adolescents and may be imposed on a variety of levels (i.e., society, community, family) in order to let people know the "do's" and "don'ts" of behavior. They teach children what is right or wrong and what is acceptable or not acceptable. These guidelines constitute a crucial element in shaping children's judgment, developing conscience, and learning reality testing (Millstein, 1993). Limits should facilitate a child's psychological growth while protecting his or her safety. Generating and enforcing limits is an active process because limits should be matched to the person's developmental level, temperament and environment and should be adjusted over time.

Limits may pertain to moral issues (acts considered right or wrong, depending on their influence on the welfare of others), conventional issues (rules about social interaction in various situations), personal issues (actions that have consequences only to the child or adolescent), and prudential issues (pertaining to safety, self-harm, comfort, and health) (Smetana, 1995). As children get older, limit setting tends to focus less on physical safety and more on self-care, social interactions, and moral issues (Kuczynski & Kochanska, 1995). Throughout development, especially in adolescence, parents and children will differ on their ideas of how much control parents should have over these areas. The ability of parents and adolescents to negotiate and openly discuss the boundaries of parental control and adolescent self-regulation may have a positive influence on parent/adolescent relationships (Smetana, 1995).

The type of limits parents set and how they choose to enforce limits are partially dictated by parenting style. An authoritative parenting style (demanding but also responsive to a child's needs) is associated with positive outcomes. Authoritative parents impel their children to live up to or beyond their social, intellectual, and emotional abilities (Kuczynski & Kochanska, 1995). These expectations are reflected by parental guidelines about what children should and should not do. Authoritative parents focus on increasing competent behavior rather than using reactive or restrictive strategies (Kuczynski & Kochanska, 1995).

Although limit setting is associated with restrictions and prohibitions, too much emphasis on "don'ts" may have negative consequences. Excessive limits may inhibit the exploratory behavior needed to gain knowledge about oneself and one's environment, therefore jeopardizing the development of a sense of competence (Millstein, 1993). Alternately, focusing on do's early in a child's life may have positive effects on compliance with parental demands later in life. For example, one study demonstrated that parental demands for children to perform competent behaviors (play, chores, helping others) were associated with heightened compliance and less behavior problems several years later (Kuczynski & Kochanska, 1995). Requesting children to do age-appropriate behavior, instead of focusing on restrictions, is an advantageous form of limit setting.

Authority figures may be tempted to increase restrictions during times of limit testing, such as during toddler and adolescent years. However, phases of limit testing are important times because of their association with exploration, experimentation, and confidence building. Authority figures have the difficult task of allowing room for experimentation and exploration while still maintaining clear and consistent boundaries. There is a tension between the child's or adolescent's need to begin establishing independence and the need to feel protected by parents. Children and adolescents should be allowed to try new experiences and experiment as long as this process is kept mostly within the guidelines of what parents find acceptable. Adolescents should be given freedom of choice, but they should know that there are also limits to those choices (Gaoni, Kronenberg, & Kaysar, 1994).

The specific content of limits needs to be renegotiated throughout the child's development while maintaining the basic principles behind parental expectations. Children will test the guidelines that authority figures generate. However, this testing should be viewed as a developmental process rather than a personal affront to authority. Nevertheless, certain parenting strategies (i.e., authoritative) will enhance the child's development and increase the likelihood of compliance with parental expectations.

References

Gaoni, B., Kronenberg, J., & Kaysar, N. (1994). Boundaries during adolescence. *Israel Journal of Psychiatry and Related Sciences, 31*, 19–27.

Kochanska, G. (1995). Children's temperament, mothers' discipline, and security of attachment: Multiple pathways to emerging internalization. *Child Development, 66*, 597–615.

Kuczynski, L., & Kochanska, G. (1995). Function and content of maternal demands: Developmental significance of early demands for competent action. *Child Development, 66*, 616–628.

Millstein, K. H. (1993). Limitsetting, coping and adaptation: A theoretical context for clinicians and caregivers. *Child and Adolescent Social Work Journal, 10*, 289–300.

Smetana, J. G. (1995). Parenting styles and conceptions of parental authority during adolescence. *Child Development, 66*, 299–313.

See also: Discipline; Misbehavior; Physical punishment.

SHANNON DERMER AND KRISTIN PRUETT

Listening. Listening is the process where parents try to hear and understand what children are attempting to communicate. To be an effective listener, parents do not have to agree or to disagree; rather, the expectation is that parents will simply listen to understand rather than listening to evaluate or to judge. Ginott (1965) found that when parents listen sympathetically, they listen for hidden messages often conveyed in their children's verbal and nonverbal behaviors.

Nonverbal interaction often leaves room for interpretation. After extensive research in nonverbal communication, Harper, Wiens, and Matarazzo (1978) concluded that nonverbal communication can modify the meaning of, and places greater emphasis on, the verbal content. Additionally, they found that each culture and each individual have significantly different meaning in nonverbal communication. That is, the meaning of one thing to one person may have a totally different understanding to someone else. This same application to parent-child relationships would be appropriate.

There are at least two basic skills that facilitate a parent's listening: (1) *nonreactive listening* and (2) *active listening*. Nonreactive listening by the parent usually involves silence, the manifestation of genuine interest (showing undivided attention), some form of acknowledgment (such as the nod of the head), and/or the invitation or encouragement for the child to continue talking. During active listening, parents attempt to briefly summarize what children have said, reflect back what they think children have said or are feeling, or help the child with the question or emotion.

Parental barriers to effective listening may include giving advice when advice is not sought, asking interrogating questions, ordering, attacking/criticizing, and/or evading or sidestepping the problem or question being presented by the child.

When children are upset, parents are especially helpful when they listen to understand and incorporate the language of encouragement into the process. Parents can express their encouragement by using such phrases as "I" statements. That is, "I feel_____ when_____ and because_____," directing the words specifically to the actions (behavior) of the child rather than to the person. For example, the parent might respond to the child's loss of a bicycle by stating, "I feel so sorry that your bicycle was stolen because I understand how much you enjoy riding it." This permits children to know that they have been heard and that the parent understands the magnitude of the loss to them. Also, conflict is avoided, and unity between child and parent is increased.

When parents listen effectively, they can support their children's emotional expressiveness through encouraging both verbal and nonverbal communication. In one study completed by Dunn, Bretherton, and Munn (1987), mothers were found to encourage their young daughters, more than their sons, to express their feelings. They felt their findings perhaps set the stage for why females, later on in life, tend to be more emotionally expressive than are males. Additionally, Roberts and Strayer (1987) found that listening to and being responsive to their children's distresses and encouraging their children's emotional expressiveness did predict their children's competence in preschool.

References

Dunn, J., Bretherton, I., & Munn, P. (1987). Conversations about feeling states between mothers and their young children. *Developmental Psychology, 23* (1), 132–139.

Ginott, H. G. (1965). *Between parent and child*. New York: Macmillan.

Harper, R., Wiens, A., & Matarazzo, J. (1978). *Nonverbal communication: The state of the art*. New York: Wiley.

Roberts, B. E., & Strayer, J. (1987). Parents' responses to the emotional distress of their children. *Developmental Psychology, 23* (3), 415–422.

See also: Communication; Empathy; Language development.

JOSEPH G. TURNER

Literacy. Children acquire knowledge, skills, and attitudes crucial to literacy during the preschool years. Families significantly influence this development by providing access to print and graphic materials, by talking and reading with children, by modeling the uses of literacy, and by exhibiting a positive attitude toward literacy activities.

Literacy skills are central to school achievement, employment, and later success in life. Nevertheless, many adults and children in the United States appear to have problems in this area. For example, the 1993 *National Adult Literacy Survey* found that nearly half of the adult population performed at the two lowest levels on their literacy scales. Similarly, the *National Assessment of Educational Progress* found that at least 30% of all children tested at the fourth, eighth, and twelfth grades failed to reach even the basic (partial mastery) level of achievement in reading, and nearly half of the students wrote material on some writing tasks that was rated unsatisfactory or minimal (National Center for Education Statistics, 1994).

Estimates of functional illiteracy in the United States have often conflicted due to lack of agreement about the meaning and assessment of literacy. A more comprehensive definition of literacy should include not only basic skills such as knowledge of letter sounds, spelling patterns, and vocabulary in the primary language but also "higher-order" understandings such as the nature of different types of texts, ways to identify themes and points of view, and how to use background knowledge to interpret text. The meaning of literacy is not static; it evolves with changes in culture and society (Benjamin & Lord, 1996). For example, widespread use of computers is currently expanding our definition of literacy.

The preschool years of a child's life are crucial for successful literacy development. A wealth of recent research describes the literacy knowledge, skills, and attitudes that young children often acquire before coming to school, the ways that literacy development draws upon oral language abilities, and the effects that early experiences at home have on literacy development (Benjamin & Lord, 1996; Morrow, 1995).

During the first two years, children learn both the forms and functions of communication and patterns found in their language. Conversational, storytelling, and book-reading routines introduce very young children to ways of interacting through language, help them learn to label pictures and objects, and familiarize them with the purposes of books and other print materials. As children near school age, their knowledge of word meanings and word arrangement expands significantly. In addition, they usually become more aware of the features of written language and relationships between symbols, sounds, and meaning. When reading and writing is done frequently around them, and when adults respond to their questions about print and to their requests for help in reading and writing, young children often begin experimenting on their own with reading and writing processes. Children talking about storybook characters or about words on street signs, scribbling and drawing, and pretending to write a list or read a book all show a beginning awareness of print use (lists, labels, instructions, stories), of our writing system (letters and words), and of writing conventions (such as the fact that print is read from left to right).

Leicter (1984) summarizes early influences on early literacy development by describing three types of climates in the home—physical, interpersonal, and emotional. The *physical* climate for literacy development consists of the presence of print materials and written language in the home and/or access to books, magazines, or other print and graphic materials through visits to libraries, museums, or other community resources. The *interpersonal* climate for literacy involves the family interactions and activities surrounding literacy events. Included in this category are both the quality and quantity of verbal interaction, parent/child book reading, modeling of reading and writing in the home, and opportunities for literacy experiences within routine family interactions. The *emotional* climate describes the attitudes and expectations about literacy and school-like literacy tasks in the home and community. Despite correlational research showing that specific kinds of early experience are predictive of later literacy abilities, more evidence is needed to establish a causal relationship. It is important to note that there is considerable variation in literacy outcomes even within families exhibiting the most favorable or unfavorable contexts. This suggests that the relationship between the home environment and literacy is bi-directional and dynamic. The impact of literacy experiences is influenced to some extent by children's own dispositions and verbal abilities, and parents' literacy-related responses are affected by their perception of their children's interests, capabilities, and motivation.

Research highlighting the nature of early language and literacy development and the relationship between literacy support in the early years and later reading and writing competence has led to the development of programs designed to encourage teachers and parents to provide children with additional language and text-related experiences. Recent evaluations of family literacy programs such as Evenstart have suggested that changes in literacy and parenting behavior occur only when programs are of considerable duration and intensity and are targeted at adults and children in the family both individually and together (Benjamin & Lord, 1996).

References

Benjamin, L. A., & Lord, J. (1996). *Family literacy: Directions in research and implications for practice* [Summary and papers of a national symposium]. Washington, DC: United States Department of Education.

Leicter, H. J. (1984). Families as environment for literacy. In H. Goelman, A. Oberg, & F. Smith (Eds.), *Awakening to literacy* (pp. 38–50). Portsmouth, NH: Heinemann.

Morrow, L. (1995). *Family literacy: Connections in schools and communities*. Newark, DE: International Reading Association.

National Center for Education Statistics. (1994). *NAEP 1992 writing report card*. Washington, DC: National Center for Education Statistics.

See also: Language development; Narratives, personal.

MARY SUE AMMON

Locke, John (1632–1704). John Locke was a man of medicine, politics, and philosophy who challenged the philosopher Descartes who believed that children are born with certain innate understandings of the world (Caruth, 1991). Additionally, religious doctrine at the time said that man was a sinner and inherently wicked. Locke reacted against these views. In seeking to answer the question of the origin of ideas, he decided to simply sit and observe infants in their environment. He concluded that there was no evidence of any settled or inborn idea in infancy (Biehler, 1976). Rather, he affirmed the earlier ideas of Aristotle that the mind of a newborn was like a tabula rasa, or blank slate. Locke believed this slate would fill over time as newborns grew and interacted with their world. It was this experience with their environment that he thought would eventually lead children to higher learning and abstract thought.

Locke believed children had a natural curiosity about the world, and he encouraged parents to promote this curiosity in their children (Biehler, 1976). He thought one of the ways to do this was for parents and children to play together. He noted that children's curiosity is often reflected in a seemingly endless number of questions. Since this is how children learn, Locke recommended that parents be patient in answering their questions. He also encouraged parents to make educational toys for their children and to appreciate the individual differences in personality and temperament among them. Locke reacted against the adage of "Spare the rod and spoil the child," saying the use of this principle equated oppressive discipline where the more likely outcome would be a child of "low spirit" or one who would conform only while the fear of the rod was present (Biehler, 1976). Instead, Locke promoted the use of praise and reward as effective strategies for children because of the great pleasure they find in being held in high esteem and valued by other people, especially their parents (Biehler, 1976). However, for this principle to work at its best, both parents should consistently practice it.

Locke's influence can be seen today in education, psychology, and child development theory. His ideas on positive reinforcement and human nature are the hallmarks of early behaviorism and humanistic psychology. His influence on early child development can be seen in almost every infant nursery where there are typically mobiles and all kinds of toys that provide stimulation and avenues for play. In education, Locke challenged teachers to observe and appreciate the individual differences between children and base their instruction accordingly. Many of his early writings in education and child development are still widely read and can be found at most local libraries.

References
Biehler, R. F. (1976). *Child development: An introduction*. Boston: Houghton Mifflin.
Caruth, C. (1991). *Empirical truths and critical fictions: Locke, Wordsworth, Kant, and Freud*. Baltimore, MD: Johns Hopkins University Press.

See also: Nature versus nurture; Social context.

SCOTT PHILLIPS AND KIER MAXWELL

M

Marital boundaries. According to marriage and family therapists Minuchin and Fishman (1981), families are living systems that develop and change; family development occurs in stages that become more complex over time. Carlfred Broderick (1993), a sociologist as well as a marriage and family therapist, suggests that family systems are regulated by rules. One set of family rules manages barriers between the family and outsiders (e.g., children are instructed to avoid strangers; family members censor what they say to people outside of their family). These barriers are called *boundaries*.

In addition to boundaries between the family and the outside world, boundaries exist between parts of the family. These parts are called *subsystems*, which can be either individual or relational (Minuchin & Fishman, 1981). These internal family boundaries, according to family therapists Simon, Stierlin, and Wynne (1985), often feature different rules for each subsystem. For example, parents are responsible for managing the behavior of their children; older children may enjoy more privileges than younger siblings.

Most family relationships are influenced by the couple relationship. For example, a child's exposure to intense conflict between parents negatively influences the child's development. Unresolved marital conflict may also be projected toward a particular child who becomes the family scapegoat (Pillari, 1991). A healthy marital boundary surrounds the couple and helps them meet their unique needs; it includes and excludes others as necessary. Spouses who have developed appropriate boundaries are able to separate themselves from their larger family unit while simultaneously integrating themselves into the family system.

Enmeshment. Excessively weak boundaries are associated with chaotic relationships that are described as enmeshed or fused (Simon, Stierlin, & Wynne, 1985). An enmeshed relationship between one marital partner and her or his biological parent may interfere with parenting if her or his parent and partner disagree about parenting. Torn between conflicting ideas, the enmeshed parent may inconsistently enforce family rules, which may confuse children. An enmeshed relationship can also occur within the family. One parent may have an overly close relationship with one child that may produce sibling jealously as well as perpetuate family triangles.

Disengagement. In contrast to enmeshment, *disengagement* describes boundaries that are too strong; this may lead to isolation (Simon, Stierlin, & Wynne, 1985). Rigid boundaries may interfere with children's ability to receive nurturance within the family and from people outside of the immediate family such as grandparents. Rigid boundaries may also limit parenting information because marital partners may avoid consultation with their parents or other parents. Within the family, a marital boundary that is too rigid interferes with negotiation of rules between parents and children; this is a significant problem during adolescence because of their need to separate from family.

Healthy marital boundaries. Marital boundaries, according to Minuchin and Fishman (1981), are important at all stages of family development. When two individuals become a couple, they must establish boundaries between their newly formed unit and their friends, work, and extended families (Minuchin & Fishman, 1981). The new couple must also, according to Minuchin and Fishman (1981),

- learn to accommodate their different styles of being in the world
- develop interactional rules
- reach some agreement about methods to handle differences
- learn to deal with conflict

Parents expend a great deal of energy on parenting responsibilities, but they must remain engaged with each other (e.g., they should establish some time to spend together as a couple) in order to avoid cross-generational coalitions. Research suggests that marital satisfaction declines after children are born and remains low as long as children remain at home. This finding is clinically relevant because couples with children often report that they experience limited intimacy. As a result, marriage and family therapists routinely encourage couples to spend time alone as a couple.

There are direct and indirect benefits to children whose parents maintain healthy boundaries. Children will, for example, directly observe and integrate their parent's relational style. At earlier ages, the parents may avoid discussing conflict with the child in order to avoid triangulation, but the parents may discuss their methods of conflict resolution with an older child. These interactions will help children deal with their peers and also prepare them for adult intimate relationships. Additionally, children who observe healthy marital boundaries may find it easier to set personal boundaries.

References

Broderick, C. B. (1993). *Understanding family process: Basics of family systems theory.* Newbury Park, CA: Sage Publications.

Cobb, C. L. H. (1996). Adolescent-parent attachments and family problem-solving styles. *Family Process, 35*, 57–82.

Minuchin, S., & Fishman, H. C. (1981). *Family therapy techniques.* Cambridge, MA: Harvard University Press.

Pillari, V. (1991). *Scapegoating in families: Intergenerational patterns of physical and emotional abuse.* New York: Brunner/Mazel.

Simon, F. B., Stierlin, H., & Wynne, L. C. (1985). *The language of family therapy: A systemic vocabulary and sourcebook.* New York: Family Process Press.

See also: Alliance, parenting; Conflict, interparental; Styles, parenting; Triangulation.

RONALD JAY WERNER-WILSON AND MEGAN J. MURPHY

Marital interaction. Marital interaction includes exchanges of information, relationship attitudes, and verbal and nonverbal comment on rules that underlie partner communication. Marital communication involves complex decision making, problem-solving, and conflict resolution processes. A couple's unique blend of *verbal* (word) and *nonverbal expressions* ("I statements," inattentive listening) is influenced by personality, energy level, values, history, culture, and other factors. Researchers are just beginning to understand these processes and unravel their influences on children.

Parent-to-parent communication creates both a context and a model for a child's attachment and development. Observations of parent communication may directly affect a child's moods, attitudes, and behaviors, although these influences tend to be cumulative unless an event is traumatic. In one such case, a 3-year-old was brought to a therapist with psychosomatic symptoms of cracked fingernails and nervous behaviors. Although his parents both valued and nurtured him, their daily hostile shouting and wielding of kitchen utensils toward each other resulted in a stress trauma response. Such examples illustrate why marital conflict affects children even more than divorce.

More often, children are affected indirectly, as parents' conflict and cooperation behind the scenes shape a family climate of affection or anxiety. Studies with young children suggest that security and sociability behaviors are related to a mother's premarital and prebirth relationship satisfaction. Child dependency correlates with a father's satisfaction. Marital conflict tends to increase the quality of mothers' and quantity of fathers' caring for young children. Dads in conflict tend to withdraw from children; moms have less emotional energy to share with children. While father involvement with children is critical, husband support of a mother often has stronger indirect impact, especially for infants or toddlers. Family environment plays a major role in school achievement, peer relations, juvenile delinquency, and other mental health indicators (Belsky & Pensky, 1988; Black & Pedro-Carroll, 1993; Gottfried, Bathurst, & Gottfried, 1994).

Negative affect or emotional tone, and conflict, especially when expressed as contempt and belligerence toward a partner, is correlated to depression and externalizing (aggression), especially in boys, and internalizing (self-rejection) typically in girls. Symptoms vary with intensity and duration of conflict, the child's age, personality, and other sources of support. Not surprisingly, adults experience similar symptoms. Unfortunately, breakdown in support and escalating conflict often breed a toxic cycle of hostility and violence from which families are unable to extricate themselves. Recent research suggests that some children display a physiological capacity known as *vagal tone*, a physiological measure of parasympathetic nervous system activity that indicates the body's response to arousal as well as the capacity to self-soothe or regain composure after upset. This capacity enables children to overcome the negative effects of parental conflict (Black & Pedro-Carroll, 1993; Katz & Gottman, 1993, 1995).

Parent interaction is a powerful model to children. Verbal and physical aggression between partners reinforce sexist and abusive attitudes among boys, lower self-esteem in girls. Egalitarian relationships tend to have the opposite effects on children's attitudes toward themselves and their peers. Moreover, equal partnerships promote stronger feelings of support and greater involvement with children (Olson et al., 1983).

Parents seeking education or therapy with a "problem child" may benefit from exploring ways of enjoying and enriching their marital interaction for the sake of that child (since most do not want to focus attention on their own inadequacies). Parents who respect, understand, and enjoy each other gain more energy for parenting, model positive interaction skills, and avoid attempts to play each against the other.

Marriage enrichment and support are particularly critical for couples in life-cycle transitions (new baby, school entry, teenage, launching) and unexpected stressors (health or financial crisis). Research suggests that conflict or divorce is most likely at such times but that couples who mobilize their coping resources are able to recover marital and parenting effectiveness in 6 to 12 months' time. Educators, employers, and friends who continue to support and believe in parents and children sustain them through these tough times (Howes & Markman, 1989).

More research is needed on the positive effects of marital interaction on parents and on children, especially regarding teachable skills and insights that facilitate nurturant relationships. Investigations of transition to parenting and preschool years tell us much about these patterns and should be supplemented with greater attention to parenting middle school and teenage children.

References

Belsky, J., & Pensky, E. (1988). Marital change across the transition to parenthood. *Marriage and Family Review, 12*, 133–156.

Black, A. E., & Pedro-Carroll, J. (1993). The role of parent-child relationships in mediating the effects of marital disruption. *Journal of the American Academy of Child and Adolescent Psychiatry, 32*, 1019–1027.

Gottfried, A. E., Bathurst, K., & Gottfried, A. W. (1994). Role of material and dual earner employment in children's development: A longitudinal study. In A. E. Gottfried & A. W. Gottfried (Eds.), *Redefining families: Implications for children's development* (pp. 57–62). New York: Plenum.

Howes, P., & Markman, H. J. (1989). Marital quality and child functioning: A longitudinal investigation. *Child Development, 60*, 1044–1051.

Katz, L. F., & Gottman, J. M. (1993). Patterns of marital conflict predict children's internalizing and externalizing behaviors. *Developmental Psychology, 29*, 940–950.

Katz, L. F., & Gottman, J. M. (1995). Vagal tone protects children from marital conflict. *Development and Psychopathology, 7* (1), 83–90.

Olson, D. H., McCubbin, H. I., Barnes, H., Larsen, A. Muxen, M., & Wison, M. (1983). *Families: What makes them work.* Beverly Hills, CA: Sage Publications.

See also: Conflict, interparental; Marital boundaries; Paradigms, parenting; Triangulation.

BENJAMIN SILLIMAN

Mathematics. Mathematical concepts and skills begin developing in infancy well before children enter formal schooling. Parents play a role in the development of children's mathematical skills and concepts both before children enter elementary school and after. Most of the research on the influence of parents on children's mathematical development has examined the relationship between the beliefs and behaviors of parents and children's performance in mathematics.

The research with parents and preschool children indicates that parents are involved with their children on math activities. Saxe, Guberman, and Gearhart (1987) have found that many children and their mothers in the middle and working class engage in some form of number activity on a daily basis. Middle-class 4-year-olds perform better on complex number tasks than working-class children, and correspondingly, middle-class mothers engage in more complex number activities with their children. Both middle- and working-class mothers adjust their instruction to the child's level. Cross-cultural work has revealed that by kindergarten Japanese children outperform American children, even though American mothers report more involvement with their children in math activities (Bacon & Ichikawa, 1988). Work with preschool children in the United States has found that how accurate parents are about what their child can and cannot do in mathematics is also related to children's performance. One explanation for this is that the more accurate parents provide math activities that are better suited to the level of the child. Prior to first grade, it looks as if parental involvement with children on mathematics is not enough; parents also need to provide developmentally appropriate activities.

One major step in a child's education is entry into first grade. Once children enter first grade, researchers find both parents' and children's expectations for the child's performance are too high when math grades are used as the yardstick. Over time, parents' expectations change and become more linked to children's performance. The expectations of African American parents, however, are not as influenced by the performance of their child as are those of white parents (Alexander & Entwisle, 1988). Cross-cultural work also finds that parents in the United States are too generous in evaluating their children's mathematical performance. American parents are more likely to believe their child will succeed in math than Japanese and Chinese parents, even though Japanese and Chinese children outperform American children on word and calculation problems (Stevenson et al., 1990). America mothers report being more satisfied than parents from other countries with their child's performance in math except in cases where it falls below average. These results apply not only to parents of first graders but also to parents of fifth graders. During the elementary school years, parents tend to see their children's math performance in an optimistic, but not entirely realistic, way.

Parents of elementary school children have been asked to explain their children's level of performance in mathematics. When children are successful, parents give credit to ability, and when children fail, to lack of effort. By second grade parents' explanations for and beliefs about children's performance differ according to the child's gender (Alexander & Entwisle, 1988). Mothers of girls say that effort is responsible for their daughters' success, while mothers of boys attribute success to ability. The data about whether boys or girls are performing better is contradictory, but mothers consistently predict that boys perform better. Parents' beliefs about their children's math performance matter. By fifth grade, children's beliefs about their own abilities are influenced more by their parents beliefs than by their own performance (Eccles-Parsons, Adler, & Kaczala, 1982).

A consistent finding is that parents are involved with their children on mathematics and that their beliefs and behaviors influence their children's beliefs and behaviors. This fits with the position that parents are a major source of influence on children's lives. What parents are doing with their children may be more important than the fact that they are involved.

When parents provide developmentally appropriate activities and communicate messages about the importance of hard work and meeting high standards, children perform better. Unfortunately, many American parents communicate the opposite messages: that success in mathematics is due to innate ability, especially for girls, and that relatively low standards for performance are acceptable. These messages may not motivate children to perform well in mathematics.

References

Alexander, K., & Entwisle, D. (1988). Achievement in the first 2 years of school: Patterns and processes. *Monographs of the Society for Research in Child Development*, *53* (2, Serial No. 218).

Bacon, W., & Ichikawa, V. (1988). Maternal expectations, classroom experiences, and achievement among kindergartens in the United States and Japan. *Human Development*, *31*, 378–383.

Eccles-Parsons, J., Adler, T., & Kaczala, C. (1982). Socialization of achievement attitudes and beliefs: Parental influences. *Child Development*, *53*, 310–321.

Saxe, G., Guberman, S., & Gearhart, M. (1987). Social processes in early number development. *Monographs of the Society for Research in Child Development*, *52* (2, Serial No. 216).

Stevenson, H., Lee, S., Chen, C., Stigler, J., Chen-chin, H., & Kitamura, S. (1990). Contexts of achievement. *Monographs of the Society for Research in Child Development*, *55* (1–2, Serial No. 221).

See also: Academic achievement; Family-school partnerships; Money and children; School.

BELINDA BLEVINS-KNABE

Media, mass. The twentieth century has seen a surge of professional and popular interest in parenting education and also a surge in technological and economic growth in the mass media within the United States. Not surprisingly, these two trends have converged to generate an explosion of information about parenting in the mass media.

The term *mass media* refers to books, magazines and newsletters, newspapers, radio, television, film, videotapes, software, and the Internet. While technically some are media (such as radio and newspapers) and some are materials typically distributed by media (such as videos) (see Manoff, 1985), they are considered together and defined as mass media here, according to common practice.

In assessing the current state of media attention to parenting, a recent study by the Center for Health Communication, Harvard School of Public Health (Simpson, 1997), supported by the John D. and Catherine T. MacArthur Foundation, found four major trends:

Parenting has become a staple among topics in many print media. Parenting books, magazines, and regional controlled-circulation papers, as well as child and family beat reporters at major newspapers, have increased dramatically. Almost every parent is exposed to printed information about parenting, many repeatedly.

Parenting initiatives within the electronic media are expanding. In particular, rapid growth is occurring in public television, cable television, local news, and the Internet, and new developments are occurring on the commercial networks as well.

The demand for media information among parents is substantial and increasing. By a number of measures, many parents have a high level of interest in information about child rearing, including information from the mass media, on a broad range of topics. The extent to which particular parents are reached, however, varies according to a number of important factors, including age, gender, communication skills and style, cultural and language preferences, and economic resources (see, e.g., Young, Davis, & Schoen, 1996).

The preponderance of professional opinion, supported by theory and research, is that the media, as part of a complex set of factors, can and do have a significant impact on parents and parenting. Although little direct research has been done on the effects of the media on parents, inferences can be drawn from theory, related research, and professional experience. Together, they make a strong case that the media have important influences, in conjunction with other forces and strategies, on parents' attitudes and behaviors and hence on child outcomes. Resources are also available to assist parenting and media professionals in designing media efforts in ways that are effective in reaching their goals (see, e.g., Dombro et al., 1996).

On the other hand, a number of drawbacks undermine the ability of the media to contribute effectively to the well-being of parents and families. Of these drawbacks, four were identified in the Harvard Center for Health Communication study as especially important:

Easily accessible sources of information on parenting topics for use by the media are scarce and scattered. Contributing in particular to the inaccessibility of information is the fact that researchers and resources related to parenting are embedded in hundreds of organizations and dozens of disciplineš, with no centralized access to information.

Parenting advice conveyed by the media is often confusing and conflicting. Caught in the interaction of economic, intellectual, cultural, and social forces, the only constant in child-rearing advice has been change. Amid this fluctuation and controversy, researchers, practitioners, the media, policy makers, advocates, and parents have all been frustrated in their efforts to seek reliable information from each other.

Parents of adolescents receive less information and support from the media than parents of younger children. Although parents play a critical role in influencing outcomes for teenagers, the media provide them with relatively little information and support. Exacerbating the problem are negative images of teenagers in the news and entertainment media (see, e.g., Kunkel, 1996).

Entertainment television has been largely overlooked as a source of influence on parenting and as a vehicle for supporting and informing parents. What little is known about parenting messages in entertainment programming is mixed, suggesting that parents receive both positive and negative messages about raising children from the many situation comedies, dramas, talk shows, films, and other entertainment formats that portray family life (see, e.g., Lichter, Lichter, & Rothman, 1994).

The potential of the media to reach parents can be expected to continue to grow, providing opportunities for professionals and parents to shape their influence in meeting the critical needs of families.

References

Dombro, A. L., O'Donnell, N. S., Galinsky, E., Melcher, S. G., & Farber, A. (1996). *Community mobilization: Strategies to support young children and their families* (chap. 9). New York: Families and Work Institute.

Kunkel, D. (1996). How the news media "see" kids. In E. E. Dennis & E. C. Pease (Eds.), *Children and the media* (pp. 57–62). New Brunswick, NJ: Transaction.

Lichter, S. R., Lichter, L. S., & Rothman, S. (1994). *Prime time: How TV portrays American culture.* Washington, DC: Regency Publishing.

Manoff, R. K. (1985). *Social marketing: New imperative for public health.* New York: Praeger.

Simpson, A. R. (1997). *The role of the mass media in parenting education.* Boston, MA: Center for Health Communication, Harvard School of Public Health.

Young, K. T., Davis, K., & Schoen, C. (1996). *The Commonwealth Fund survey of parents with young children.* New York: Commonwealth Fund.

See also: Television viewing; Television violence.

A. RAE SIMPSON

Mediation, parent-child. Parent-child mediation is one form of a broader set of interventions referred to as family mediation, defined as the application of dispute resolution techniques, conventionally used in labor-management disputes and international relations, to conflicts within the nexus of the family and its component members. The use of mediation for parent-child conflicts originated in a variety of environments (e.g., criminal justice system, therapeutic settings) but is currently most often provided by community-based agencies referred to as *dispute resolution centers*. These centers receive referrals from a variety of agencies; however, they usually have a relationship with the juvenile justice system and receive the majority of their referrals from this source. Consequently, the parent-child conflicts that come to mediation are typically identified as arising from the child's (usually an adolescent) problematic behavior (e.g., truancy, running away). However, this characterization has been challenged as inappropriately focused on the child's behavior while ignoring the role of family dynamics.

Parent-child mediation focuses on resolving the specific conflict between the parents and the juvenile in an effort to maintain the family unit. Thus, it differs from most other applications of family mediation because it involves an adult and a minor as disputants rather than two adults and involves families that wish to remain intact (Van Slyck, Stern, & Newland, 1992).

A number of goals have been articulated for parent-child mediation. The fundamental goal is to assist family members in defining the underlying issues in the conflict and facilitate their movement toward some common agreement focusing on future behavior as a basis for resolving it, usually codifying the resolution in the form of a written contract (e.g., Huber, Mascari, & Sanders-Mascari, 1988). An additional goal is to educate family members in positive conflict resolution techniques to enhance the family's ability to resolve future conflicts. If these goals are achieved, it is often hoped that mediation can thereby effect a positive change in the dynamics of the interactions of family members on a long-term basis (Van Slyck, Stern, & Zak-Place, 1996).

Only a limited amount of research has examined the use of mediation for parent-child conflicts to determine its success in achieving its goals. Initial research was narrowly evaluative in its approach, focusing on such issues as participation in, completion of, and compliance with the process. More substantive research efforts have attempted to go beyond these traditional evaluation criteria to assess the impact of the mediation process on the lasting quality of the resolution of the specific conflict and on long-term family relationships. The findings from this body of research are reasonably consistent and support the conclusion that mediation can be an effective intervention for helping distressed families in conflict. In terms of traditional program evaluation criteria, the studies report similar rates of successful resolution of referred cases. In addition, client families generally express a high level of satisfaction with the process and indicate that mediation is a useful intervention. On a more fundamental level, these studies consistently report improvement on one or more index of family interaction or functioning. Specifically, such factors as manageability of the child, occurrence of family conflict, communication, expressiveness, independence, and achievement have been found to improve (Van Slyck, Newland, & Stern, 1992).

Research has clearly demonstrated that the families involved in these cases can be characterized as *dysfunctional*, supporting the contention that the problem is not fairly attributed solely to the adolescent's behavior. One potentially important finding is a positive relationship between the degree to which the parent involved viewed the situation as serious and the likelihood of the conflict being resolved through mediation. This relationship did not hold for the adolescents involved (Stern & Van Slyck, 1992). This finding indicates the importance of parental attitude in the successful resolution of these types of conflicts. In addition, the fact that cases that are characterized as serious (at least by parents) are amenable to mediation supports the use of this intervention for such cases, which are often viewed as necessitating "firmer" intervention modalities (e.g., probation services).

Mediation may be more effective than court processing in resolving parent-child disputes (Merry & Rocheleau, 1985). Mediation is viewed more favorably than a counseling intervention but not more favorably than a probation intervention (Stern & Van Slyck, 1992). Overall, these results suggest that mediation can both resolve specific disputes as well as produce a positive impact on the general quality of (often dysfunctional) family interactions and may do so more effectively than standard interventions such as criminal justice approaches and counseling.

This literature suggests that mediation is successful in improving family interactions because its approach is consistent with both the developmental needs of the adolescents involved as well as with the dynamics of the family system. The effectiveness and positive impact of mediation result from the problem-solving orientation to resolving conflict that it takes, which has been labeled as *developmentally appropriate* (Van Slyck, Stern, and Zak-Place, 1996). This designation is based on the goals of conflict resolution, which among other things encourage the development and use of problem-solving skills in the formalized setting of negotiation and mediation. The development of such coping skills by adolescents is related to more positive developmental outcomes and improved family functioning and would thus in part explain the positive impact associated with parent-child mediation.

References
Huber, C., Mascari, J., & Sanders-Mascari, A. (1988). Family mediation: An idea whose time has come. In J. Carlson & J. Lewis (Eds.), *Counseling the adolescent* (pp. 135–158). Denver, CO: Love Publishing Co.
Merry, S., & Rocheleau, A. (1985). *Mediation in families: A study of the children's hearing project*. Cambridge, MA: Cambridge Family and Children's Services.
Stern, M., & Van Slyck, M. (1992). *PINS diversion research project: Final report*. Washington, DC: Fund for Research on Dispute Resolution.
Van Slyck, M., Newland, L., & Stern, M. (1992). Parent-adolescent mediation: Integrating theory, research and practice. *Mediation Quarterly*, *10*, 193–208.
Van Slyck, M., Stern, M., & Newland, L. (1992). Parent-child mediation: An empirical assessment. *Mediation Quarterly*, *10*, 75–88.
Van Slyck, M., Stern, M., & Zak-Place, J. (1996). Promoting optimal adolescent development through conflict resolution education, training, and practice: An innovative approach for counseling psychologists. *Counseling Psychologist*, *24*, 433–461.

See also: Conflict resolution; Delinquency, juvenile; Problem solving.

MICHAEL R. VAN SLYCK AND MARILYN STERN

MELD. Since 1973, MELD (formerly *Minnesota Early Learning Design*) and its affiliated agencies have provided group-based parenting education to thousands of parents in 25 states. A national program with headquarters in Minneapolis, Minnesota, MELD's ongoing mission is to strengthen families in critical periods of transition. MELD is a private, not-for-profit family support agency that is funded by a variety of grants and fee-for-service contracts.

The MELD approach brings together groups of parents who have similar needs, provides them with pertinent information, and helps them to develop into supportive peer groups. MELD programs have been replicated by almost 200 agencies, including hospitals and health clinics, schools, family centers, child care centers, job training centers, and community-based not-for-profit groups.

Primary development of the MELD model began in 1973 when founder Ann Ellwood reviewed literature, surveyed needs, and assessed resources related to young children, parenting, and early learning. The program design was piloted from 1975 to 1978 with five parent groups that included 19 Parent Group Facilitators and 89 parents.

MELD's impact lies in mediating factors related to the potential for child abuse and neglect. Family isolation is reduced through the support of other parents and through improved connections with community resources. Parents increase their knowledge of child growth and development and age-appropriate behavior. Parents become skilled at solving problems and making decisions that support their own health and well-being, as well as those of their children.

In every MELD community and target population, the program is recognizable through the replication of these essential program components:

- group facilitation by parents who have experienced life situations similar to those of group members
- long-term availability of programming, generally two years
- integrating information into a supportive group environment
- program content that addresses the concerns of the group, the parent, and the child
- a persistent focus on parent strengths
- an emphasis on how to solve problems and make decisions, rather than on the "quick fix"
- support for volunteers and professionals through ongoing training and technical assistance

MELD programs have been designed for teenage mothers, young fathers of preschool children, parents of children with special needs, and a variety of additional audiences where parents seek mutual support and information.

Paraprofessional leaders are emphasized for their investment in the community, for the trust they inspire due to their knowledge of community networks, and for their lower cost that allows programs in settings that otherwise might not be able to hire an equivalent number of family workers (Family Impact Seminar, 1996).

When integrated with a home visiting program, MELD was one of two Philadelphia programs that had significant improvements in factors that predict child abuse and neglect (Daro, Jones, & McCurdy, 1995). A 1985 study demonstrated that the amount of support MELD participants get from the program is high and that much of their support comes directly from the parent group. The only source of support ranked more highly was "spouse." Furthermore, the MELD program group was the only group among those studied with a statistically significant increase in knowledge of child development (Powell, 1993).

For more information about MELD's parent education and support groups, contact MELD, Suite 507, 123 North Third Street, Minneapolis, MN 55401.

References

Daro, D., Jones, E., & McCurdy, K. (1995). *Final evaluation of nine child abuse prevention programs*. Chicago, IL: National Committee to Prevent Child Abuse.

Family Impact Seminar. (1996, March). *Devolution's missing link: Investing in family-centered, front-line training*. Washington, DC: Family Impact Seminar.

Powell, D. R. (1993, December). *Effects of information and social support during the early years of parenthood: A longitudinal study of MELD*. West Lafayette, IN: Purdue University.

See also: Adolescent parenthood; Empowerment; Family support; Social support, informal.

ELIZABETH J. SANDELL

Mental illness, children. Professionals typically use the term *mental illness* to refer to the more severe disorders that have a strong biological or genetic base: schizophrenia, major depression, and bipolar disorder (formerly known as manic depression) (Engler & Goleman, 1992). Most emotional and behavioral problems are not considered mental illnesses.

A mental illness has the potential to incapacitate a child if left untreated. The *Diagnostic and Statistical Manual of Mental Disorders* (American Psychiatric Association, 1994), or *DSM*, defines specific criteria that must be present for the diagnosis of a mental illness. These criteria include symptoms that can develop slowly or have a sudden onset, although sudden onset is more common with adolescents (Klein & Wender, 1993). Hallucinations (e.g., seeing or hearing things that are not there), suicidal thoughts, social withdrawal, and insomnia are some of the symptoms listed by the *DSM* that may indicate mental illness. Other symptoms that should be addressed if they occur for more than a two-week period include irritable or depressed moods, mood swings, and changes in appetite, weight, or sleep patterns.

Explanations for why mental health problems develop typically focus on biological factors, environmental factors, or some combination of the two.

Biological explanations. Just as with physical illness, it appears that mental illness is linked to genetics based on findings that suggest it runs in some families (Reiss, 1995). Many of the mental illnesses respond to medication, which is seen as further support for a biological base. Extremely high fevers or a head injury can also lead to later behavioral or emotional problems.

Environmental influences. Ideally, families provide love, support, stability, and safety for their children, while peer groups provide social experiences and opportunities for children to form identities outside of their families. For some children there appears to be a strong association between a lack of these experiences and mental health problems.

Understandably, parents of mentally ill children often want to know if they caused their child's illness. Given what we know about mental illness, the development of the more severe disorders is governed mainly by laws of nature. Abusive or conflictual family relations do not appear to cause conditions such as schizophrenia or bipolar disorder, although these experiences may lead to low self-esteem, depressive episodes, other behavioral or emotional problems or the worsening of an already present illness.

The interaction of biology and environment. Theoretically, either "bad" genes or a negative environment can contribute to mental illness, just as "good" genes or a positive environment can foster mental health. Most professionals see mental illness as resulting from some interaction of biology and environment.

Families of mentally ill children face difficult challenges that can create and maintain high levels of stress. Often they respond to the chronic stress in one of the following three ways.

Underresponse. All parents will at times excuse misbehavior. Sometimes this becomes a habitual pattern for parents of mentally ill children due to fear over making things worse, a lack of information about a child's illness, or parental guilt. A mentally ill child, however, needs structure and behavioral limits, just as with any other child.

Overresponse. Parents of mentally ill children can become too sensitive to their child's emotional state. It is important to avoid reinforcement of angry outbursts (if they occur) by giving in to the child. Likewise, it is also important to resist the pattern of avoidance some children develop where they seem to become sickly when given directions or asked to assume more responsibility. It is true that a mentally ill child can have frightening symptoms, but it is important that these symptoms not handcuff parents from asking the child to meet reasonable expectations.

Problem solving at the wrong level. Everyone has "do it yourself" projects around the house. Coping with mental illness should not be one of them. Mental illness requires outside intervention and support. In fact, some conditions can become a terminal illness (through suicide) if left untreated. If parents suspect emotional or behavioral problems in their child, they seek out a competent mental health professional for an assessment. Engler and Goleman (1992) wrote an excellent resource guide for people who want to make an informed decision about mental health services. Their book provides detailed information on every psychological problem listed in the *DSM* along with the training and qualifications of the professionals who work with these conditions.

Parents should note that even an accurate diagnosis of a mental illness could be a double-edged sword. Diagnostic labels can be stigmatizing, but they may be required to access necessary social or special education services (if needed). In many cases therapy can help families to organize in a way that supports development of the child and family. Some combination of medication and psychotherapy is a common recommendation. Medication may be more useful in the short term for serious, acute problems; however, both approaches can produce noticeable changes.

The good news is that many childhood disorders are treatable. Parents should expect to be included in any treatment their child receives, and they have the right to request inclusion if this is not already happening. For chronic or severe disorders, therapy can be a supportive effort between the therapist and family members to prevent or minimize more severe symptoms.

References

American Psychiatric Association. (1994). *Diagnostic and Statistical Manual of Mental Disorders* (4th ed.). Washington, DC: Author.

Engler, J., & Goleman, D. (1992). *The consumer's guide to psychotherapy.* New York: Simon & Schuster.

Klein, D., & Wender, P. H. (1993). *Understanding depression.* New York: Oxford University Press.

Reiss, D. (1995). Genetic influence on family systems: Implications for development. *Journal of Marriage and the Family, 57,* 543–560.

See also: Depression in children; Family therapy.

SCOTT PHILLIPS AND JAMES M. SEIBOLD

Mental retardation. The American Association on Mental Retardation (AAMR) defines *mental retardation* as "substantial limitations in present functioning. It is characterized by significant subaverage intellectual functioning, existing concurrently with related limitations in two or more of the following applicable adaptive skill areas: communication, self-care, home living, social skills, community use, self-direction, health and safety, functional academics, leisure, and work. Mental retardation manifests before age 18" (AAMR, 1992, p. 1). The AAMR manual provides guidance on classification and suggests using the intensity of support needed by the person with mental retardation (intermittent, limited, extensive, and pervasive). This replaces the earlier IQ-based levels of mental retardation (i.e., mild, moderate, severe, and profound) established in 1983. Although some groups, including the American Psychological Association, would prefer the earlier definition, the basic concept of mental retardation including subaverage intellectual functioning and deficits in adaptive behavior is commonly accepted.

Aging caregivers of adults with mental retardation face numerous unique experiences. Seltzer and Krauss (1989) identified three specific phenomena that occur as the caregivers age: arrest in the normal family life cycle, overall length of time care is needed, and out-of-home placements. Older caregivers become out of synch with peers whose children do not have a disability. Direct caregiving by a parent for a child is not normative when the parent is reaching old age and the child becomes an adult. Being off cycle may effect the personal and social well-being of the caregiver. The caregiver may care for the child for a significantly lengthy period as compared with those adults who care for elderly family members. Finally, out-of-home placements of the adult child with a disability increase as the caregivers reach old age.

Seltzer and Krauss (1989) measured maternal well-being across several domains and found that aging maternal caregivers of adults with mental retardation demonstrated resiliency and optimism and functioned well in multiple roles. Mothers in the study reported to be in good health and compared well to age peers. Higher socioeconomic status (SES) factors improved the mother's well-being, and fewer disabling conditions of the adult child reportedly resulted in decreased stress. Older caregiving mothers had smaller social networks than same-age peers did. Finally, a salient family social climate (relationships of family members, values, and organization of the family) and family risk factors shape the well-being of aging parents caring for adult children with disabilities.

Parents and caregivers of children with disabilities report more stress than their peers without disabled children (Baxter & Kahn, 1996; Beckman, 1991; Orr et al., 1993). The mentally retarded child's lack of adaptation to new activities and changes in routine and increased and unique demands placed on caregivers, as well as failing to meet parent expectations, present special difficulties. Parents need opportunities to discuss these issues, as they do not seem to resolve over time (Orr et al., 1993). Informal supports most effectively help mediate the maternal stress (Baxter & Kahn, 1996; Orr et al., 1993) while formal supports help to minimize paternal stress (Beckman, 1991).

Children with disabilities (ages 2 to 18) were strong sources of stress for mothers, yet these women are fairly typical in terms of stress characteristics, when compared to their peers, and adapt quite well over time (Orr et al., 1993). Mothers of young children with disabilities reported significantly increased problems with depression, restrictiveness of her parental role, decreased sense of competence, decreased general health, and increased trouble in marital relationships. Stress related to a child increases sharply from early to late preschool (Orr et al., 1993). Fathers of young children with disabilities reported significantly more problems with attachment (Beckman, 1991). Both parents reported increased caregiving needs of a child with a disability (Baxter & Kahn, 1996; Beckman, 1991; Orr et al., 1993; Seltzer and Krauss, 1989).

Middle childhood (6 to 12 years old) seems to be an extremely stressful and difficult time to parent a child with mental retardation (Orr et al., 1993). Perhaps this is because early childhood programs closely involve caregivers, but traditional school programs do not necessarily have close family involvement. Furthermore, during middle childhood, there is a greater frequency of behavioral problems than found during adolescence. This may be due to an increase in mortality rates or out-of-home placements for adolescents with disabilities.

References

American Association on Mental Retardation. (1992). *Mental retardation: Definition, classification, and systems of supports* (9th ed.). Washington, DC: Author.

Baxter, A., & Kahn, J. V. (1996) *Effective early intervention for inner-city infants and toddlers: Assessing social supports, needs, and stress*. Paper presented at the annual conference of the Council of Exceptional Children, Orlando, FL.

Beckman, P. J. (1991). Comparison of mothers' and fathers' perceptions of the effect of young children with and without disabilities. *American Journal on Mental Retardation, 95* (5), 585–595.

Orr, R. R., Cameron, S. J., Dobson, L. A., & Day, D. M. (1993). Age-related changes in stress experienced by families with a child who has a developmental delay. *Mental Retardation, 31* (3), 171–176.

Seltzer, M. M., & Krauss, M. W. (1989). Aging parents with adult mentally retarded children: family risk factors and sources of support. *American Journal on Mental Retardation, 94* (3), 303–312.

See also: Disability, learning; Disability, physcial

ABIGAIL BAXTER, JAMES V. KAHN, AND ROBERTA O'SHEA

Military families. Military families are families in which one or both parents are employed by the United States armed services. As of September 1995, 1,358,021 children under 18 years of age resided in military families (Department of Defense, 1996).

For military families, threats to the family unit are confounded by the uniqueness of military life—frequent moves, hectic and varying schedules, extended separations, and concern for the military member's safety. These challenges provide unique dilemmas for parents and the parent-child relationship.

Geographic mobility. On average, military families move every three years (with an average of five to eight moves during a typical 20-year military career). This rate is approximately four times the rate of nonmilitary families. Although relocation does not appear to affect children's academic achievement, the frequency and distance of the moves may affect social contacts for both parents and children, as well as parent-child relationships. Families moving greater distances may experience more disruptions in social activities than those moving short distances. Poor parent-adolescent relationships and the adolescent's unwillingness to use family members as sources of social support predicted poorer adjustment after relocation (Pittman & Bowen, 1994). Difficulty making new friends and dissatisfaction with treatment by civilians in the new location also contributed to poorer adjustment in adolescents. On average, adolescents preferred to minimize moves and may actually blame parents for moves.

Parents should attempt to maintain strong parent-child relationships and supportive family environments during and after moves. Moreover, for older adolescents, support from friends my enhance adjustment. Some researchers contend, however, that structure, consistency, and the highly mobile nature of military life may reduce the disruptiveness of relocation.

Extended separation. A recurrent challenge faced by military families is extended separations. Studies of traditional father-deployed military families experiencing extended separation (known as deployments) have suggested a cyclic pattern of depressive behavior in both mothers and children, with higher levels of depressive mood and behavior reported prior to and during the deployment than during the reunion period (e.g., Jensen, Lewis, & Xenakis, 1986). Parents and parent-child relationships may be affected as some women whose husbands are deployed report increased anxiety, emotional withdrawal, and disruptions in parenting rules and expectations (e.g., Amen et. al., 1988). For the absence parent, reintegration back into the family also presents a challenge. Separated fathers report disrupted communication patterns, feeling "out of sync," missing developmental milestones, and the challenge of maintaining strong parent-child attachment given occasional absences. Although less is known about alternative military families, navy women anticipating separation reported more parenting stress and more sensitivity toward children than those who had recently returned. Single mothers reported more separation anxiety, less family cohesiveness, and less family organization than did married military mothers (e.g., Kelley, Herzog-Simmer, & Harris, 1994).

Because younger children require more care and supervision, the temporary loss of a parent may be more difficult for families with young children. Similar to the divorce research, boys may have more difficulty adjusting to separation than girls. Officers' families and higher-ranking enlisted military personnel, because they have less finance-related stress, generally experience less difficulty in relation to separation. However, in the case of reservists, because the military may not be able to compensate higher-ranked soldiers, the opposite may be true.

Fortunately, parents can ease the stress associated with extended separations. Most important, both parents should remain actively involved in parenting during separations. If this is not feasible, extended family members and friends need to become involved so that the impact of the parent's leaving is diminished. Additionally, positive identification with the military, increasing social contacts for both parents and children, preserving normal rules and expectations during the separation, and avoiding "parentification of a child," or giving a child adult responsibilities as a result of a missing parent, are all important aims. The quality of the preexisting relationship between the child and the service-member parent also affects children's ability to cope with deployment. Specifically, children with better relationships with fathers (or mothers) may exhibit less difficulty during separation.

Even during routine peacekeeping missions or training exercises, spouses and children fear for the service-member's safety. These fears are exacerbated when service-members are in a high-combat area. For instance, during the Persian Gulf War, families experienced the mounting anticipation of war, fear of mission attacks (including "friendly" fire), other enemy attacks, and the potential loss of the service member's life.

Parents can help children cope with these concerns, as well as maintain healthy parent-child relationships, in a number of ways. These include continuing contact with the absent parent to eliminate misinformation, encouraging children to pursue peer contacts, informing the child's teachers about any concerns, channeling energy into positive activities, providing a supportive, democratic family environment, and maintaining regular routines.

References

Amen, D. J., Jellen, L., Merves, E., & Lee, R. E. (1988). Minimizing the impact of deployment on military children: Stages, current preventive efforts, and system recommendations. *Military Medicine, 153,* 441–446.

Department of Defense (1996). *Worldwide manpower distribution by geographical area* [available from Directorate for Information, Operations and Reports]. Washington, DC: U.S. Pentagon

Jensen, P. S., Lewis, R. L., & Xenakis, S. N. (1986). The military family in review: Context, risk, and prevention. *Journal of the American Academy of Child Psychology, 25,* 225–234.

Kelley, M. L., Herzog-Simmer, P. A., & Harris, M. A. (1994). Effects of military-induced separation on the parenting stress and family functioning of deploying mothers. *Military Psychology, 6,* 125–138.

Pittman, J. F., & Bowen, G. L. (1994). Adolescents on the move: Adjustment to family relocation. *Youth and Society, 25,* 69–91.

See also: Separation anxiety.

MICHELLE L. KELLEY

Misbehavior. Misbehavior generally refers to an act or set of actions by children that are not acceptable to parents or caregivers. According to Dreikurs and Soltz (1990), all behaviors on the part of children are purposeful. However, children often are only dimly aware of the purpose or goal of their misbehavior. Children often misbehave because they feel discouraged and want to be recognized, to belong. Children are not readily aware of such goals, especially at a young age.

Additionally, Dreikurs and Soltz (1990) conclude that in the process of finding where one belongs the child may be discouraged and turn to mistaken behaviors. These behaviors include seeking *attention*, seeking *power*, seeking *revenge* and/or displaying *inadequacy*. To help parents remember these four misbehaviors, Allred (1976) created the A,B,C,D Model of misbehavior. He suggested these four misbehaviors be relabeled as (A) *attention* seeking, (B) desiring to *boss*, (C) wanting to *counter-hurt* and (D) appearing to be *disabled*.

When children misbehave, parents should first try to intuitively determine the child's purpose. For example, parents who feel annoyed by a child (*attention* seeking) could ignore the child's behavior in order to "extinguish" unacceptable behavior. When the child tries to control (*boss*), parents may feel angry. In this situation parents could withdraw from a possible power struggle. When a child feels hurt and, therefore, attempts to hurt someone else (*counter-hurt*), parents may feel distress themselves. Rather than retaliate, parents could respond supportively to the child's pain. When the child does not want to participate in an activity (appears *disabled*), parents could emphasize and encourage the child's involvement.

Children will often misbehave knowing there will be negative consequences to their actions. In these cases their need for attention or wanting to belong becomes greater than the negative response that this behavior elicits from their parents.

As children progress from attention seeking (A) to one of the other misbehaviors (B, C, D), the problem of misbehavior becomes more serious. The misbehavior on the part of the child who displays inadequacy (D) is more serious than A, B, or C and is more difficult to change. In this case, parents are encouraged to avoid criticism and encourage positive attempts by the child to behave more acceptably. Parents should avoid contributing to the inadequacy by responding punitively or giving-up on the child.

When the child acts more appropriately, parents are encouraged to reinforce the child's positive behavior. Pettit and Bates (1989) observed 29 4-year-olds and their mothers. They determined that positive behaviors on the part of the mothers were related to fewer behavior problems with their children.

References

Allred, G. H. (1976). *How to strengthen your marriage and family.* Provo, UT: Brigham Young University Press.

Dreikurs, R., & Soltz, V. (1990). *Children: The challenge*. New York: Plume.

Pettit, G. S., & Bates, J. E. (1989). Family interaction patterns and children's behavior problems from infancy to 4 years. *Developmental Psychology, 25* (3), 413–420.

See also: Consequences, natural and logical; Control strategies; Discipline; Physical punishment.

JOSEPH G. TURNER

Money and children. Children acquire most of their money knowledge and become socialized as consumers through family interaction. Ward, Wackman, and Wartella (1977) identified several methods mothers use to teach their children monetary skills. These include limiting certain behaviors, giving lectures, serving as examples, and allowing the child to learn from various hands-on experiences. Parents use few direct teaching methods, and there is great variation among families. Positive associations between children's saving patterns and parents' savings and money management habits have been noted. In the United States, children influence more than $150 billion spent by their families and are directly responsible for some $20 billion in purchases. The mass media has a great impact on children's spending patterns.

Some researchers have suggested that children need to understand numbers before money concepts are mastered. Children must be able to grasp Piagetian-based concepts of conservation, reversibility, classification, seriation, and numeration to achieve the concept of numbers. Piagetian-based numerical knowledge is a prerequisite of monetary knowledge (Berti & Bombi, 1988). Furth (1980) has argued that understanding money and how it functions in society is a critical component of social development that develops in four stages.

At the earliest ages, children think that money is available on demand and do not recognize basic money functions. For example, a child may think that any coin will buy any object or that more coins always equal more money than fewer coins, regardless of their value. Around 7 or 8 years of age, children understand fundamental functions of money—for example, that money is needed to obtain goods—but the concept of payment is not clearly understood, nor is the role of change following payment. Between 9 and 10 years, children still do not understand the multiple conditions surrounding a buy or sell exchange. For example, they may not understand that the shopkeeper has to pay for the goods in the store. In the fourth stage, by ages 11 and 12, children are able to handle basic financial transactions and recognize that money has both personal and societal functions.

Financial experts and parenting authorities generally recommend that parents begin teaching their children about money between 3 and 4 years of age. By this age, most children have observed their families shopping and may have even participated in buying by making requests for specified items or handing shopkeepers change for small treats. By age 5, most children begin to acquire monetary knowledge by associating money with buying and recognize that money can be exchanged for goods, although they generally fail to discriminate among kinds of money.

Most parents who give their children allowances begin between ages 6 and 11 years. Before this time, counting money and understanding money concepts are likely beyond the child's cognitive capacity. In addition to determining a suitable amount (which some suggest should approximate a dollar per year of age), parents and children need to agree on what an allowance is expected to cover. While definitions of allowance vary, an allowance must permit some discretionary spending even if it is also expected to cover certain fixed expenses such as lunch and bus fare. Experts also suggest that parents help children open their own bank account around this time.

Between 12 and 16 years, teens should be given increasing responsibility to pay for certain items. Parents may wish to introduce their children to checking accounts and investing. By now, many teens are also earning extra money through part-time work, and some suggest that earned money should begin to exceed that provided by the allowance.

Between 16 and 18 years of age, many teens are ready to learn about responsible use of credit and should be beginning to assume the primary responsibility for their financial matters.

According to Marshall (1964) and Hollister, Rapp, and Goldsmith (1986), there is no difference in financial knowledge and responsibility among children who do and do not receive an allowance. Others have argued that regular allowances help children learn good money management techniques such as making wise decisions about how to spend and/or save money, how to plan ahead for future purchases, and how to budget (Mortimer et al., 1994). However, many children who do not receive allowances actually have as much spending money as do children who receive allowances. There is also little agreement on whether children should be expected to perform household chores in order to receive an allowance. While many parents do require their children to help around the home, some believe that receipt of an allowance should be contingent on successful completion of the chores, and others believe that allowances should be paid independently of chores, which should be done for the common good of the family. Similarly, there is little consensus on withholding allowances as a disciplinary technique.

References

Berti, A., & Bombi, A. (1988). *The child's construction of economics.* Cambridge: Cambridge University Press.

Furth, H. (1980). *The world of grown-ups: Children's conceptions of society.* New York: Elsevier.

Hollister, J., Rapp, D., & Goldsmith, E. (1986). Monetary practices of sixth-grade students. *Child Study Journal, 16* (3), 183–190.

Marshall, H. (1964). The relation of giving children an allowance to children's money knowledge and responsibility and to other practices of parents. *Journal of Genetic Psychology, 104,* 35–51.

Mortimer, J., Dennehy, K., Lee, C., & Finch, M. (1994). Economic socialization in the American family: The prevalence, distribution, and consequences of allowance arrangements. *Journal of Applied Family and Child Studies, 43,* 23–29.

Ward, S., Wackman, D., & Wartella, E. (1977). *How children learn to buy.* Beverly Hills, CA: Sage Publications.

See also: Chores; Mathematics.

ELIZABETH A. LEVIN

Moral development. There are many behaviors that society may label as more or less moral—for example, sharing, helping, honesty, stealing, and lying. Even very young children can show basic understanding and sympathy for other people. As children grow, they may develop more mature moral reasoning and behavior.

One of the most influential theories of moral development was developed by Lawrence Kohlberg. According to Kohlberg, children can progress through a series of predictable stages in their moral reasoning. Younger children make decisions based on considerations of rules and rewards. As they learn to think in more sophisticated ways, they may come to understand other people's point of view. This more mature thinking allows them to make moral decisions based on consideration, relationships, and conscience. Ultimately, people may mature to a level of morality based on concern for the greater good and universal ethical principles.

Kohlberg's theory has been useful for understanding progressive moral development. It has also been criticized for being largely cognitive. The ability to know what is best does not guarantee that people will do it.

There are other influential views of moral development. Freud's psychoanalytic view suggested that parents could get their children to internalize their values in order to control their destructive drives. Behaviorism teaches that parents can use rewards and punishments to train a child to behave in moral ways. Hoffman's theory of moral internalization suggests that parents who use the reasoning and perspective-taking that are characteristic of inductive discipline will develop an internal moral force that he called moral internalization.

In the process of moral development, parent behaviors can make an important difference. For example, parents who ask their children's opinions, ask clarifying questions, and check for understanding have children who demonstrate more mature moral reasoning. Parents who use power to control their children are less likely to have children who use more mature moral reasoning. Parents who use induction are more likely to have children who demonstrate more mature moral reasoning. Parents who use moral reasoning that is only slightly more mature than the level of reasoning used by the child are most effective in helping children progress in their moral reasoning. Further, parents who model helpful, caring behaviors are more likely to have moral children.

Of particular interest in any discussion of moral development is prosocial behavior, which is defined as voluntary behavior intended to benefit another person. Children are more likely to demonstrate prosocial behavior if their parents use constructive discipline, involve their children in decision making, model prosocial behavior, and involve the children in helping.

There are also parent behaviors that make antisocial behavior more likely in children. Examples of such behavior include rejection, ineffective parenting, blaming, and modeling of antisocial behavior.

Eisenberg (1992, p. 144) has summarized important knowledge about moral development: "In general, cultures and families are likely to produce prosocial children when cooperation, helpfulness, generosity, and harmony are valued and modeled, children are loved and treated with respect, and the similarity of diverse groups of people is emphasized."

References
Eisenberg, N. (1992). *The caring child*. Cambridge, MA: Harvard University Press.
Eisenberg, N., & Murphy, B. (1995). Parenting and children's moral development. In M. H. Bornstein (Ed.), *Handbook of parenting: Vol. 4. Applied and practical parenting* (pp. 227–257). Mahwah, NJ: Lawrence Erlbaum Associates.

See also: Conscience; Empathy; Prosocial behavior; Victim-centered discipline.

H. WALLACE GODDARD

Mothering. *Mothering* refers to a mother's style of interaction with her child. A mother's early interaction style has been related to a variety of outcomes, including the development of the mother-infant relationship, children's prosocial behavior, and later behavioral problems. Specifically, mothers who were highly *responsive* and *available* to their children were more likely to have infants who developed more harmonious relationships with their mothers. Further, when mothers were more sensitive, their children were more empathic, more compliant with adults, and less likely to develop behavior problems (Sroufe & Fleeson, 1988).

Many researchers agree that infants' early interactions with their primary caregivers are foremost in determining the quality of the mother-infant relationship, or attachment bond. Sensitive mothering in the first year of life is thought to predict the quality of the mother-infant attachment. Mothers who are more sensitive and responsive in their interactions (i.e., mothers who notice infant signals and respond to them appropriately) will have infants who will eventually develop a more adaptive (secure) attachment relationship. On the other hand, mothers who are more insensitive, rejecting, underinvolved, or intrusive are more likely to have infants who develop an insecure bond. The mother-infant attachment relationship is thought to set the tone for all future relationships. Research has shown also that infants who develop a harmonious relationship with their mothers tend to be less dependent on their teachers, more competent with their peers, and more cooperative with adults as children (Sroufe & Fleeson, 1988).

Mothering also has been linked with children's prosocial and antisocial behavior. Specifically, the way mothers attempt to control their children has been associated with children's compliance, impulse control (i.e., not touching a forbidden object), and self-assertion. Mothers' use of suggestions and reasoning has been linked to higher compliance, whereas mothers' use of physical force, power-assertive behavior, or negative actions has been related to children's noncompliance and defiance (Crockenberg & Litman, 1990).

Although sensitive mothering is thought to predict the quality of the mother-infant relationship and children's later behavior, there are several important factors that contribute to the way mothers interact with their children. For example, maternal characteristics such as depression are related to less sensitive caregiving. Research indicates that depressed mothers showed less positive affect with their babies and were less responsive to their infants' cues (Downey & Coyne, 1990). Additionally, mothers' positive personality characteristics (e.g., extroversion, self-esteem) have been linked to more positive mothering (Fish, Stifter, & Belsky, 1993).

In addition, researchers have found a link between the way infants behave and mothering. Clearly, a mother's ability to respond to her infant is related to infant characteristics, as it is easier to respond sensitively to a baby who is easier to manage. There is evidence to suggest, for example, that mothers who rated their infants as more adaptable, approaching, and positive at 6 months provided more sensory and social stimulation to their infants at 6 and 12 months of age (Klein, 1984). On the other hand, maternal sensitivity is thought to impact infant behavior, specifically the infant's reactivity level. Sensitive mothers, for example, have infants whose crying is significantly reduced over time.

Further, sensitive mothering may be determined by family context, such as the marital relationship, the mother's social support network, or maternal employment. For example, mothers who were in more satisfied marriages and believed they had more supportive social networks were more responsive to their children (Fish, Stifter, & Belsky, 1993). Although there is considerable controversy regarding the impact of maternal employment on the mother-infant bond, there are few consistent findings regarding the link between maternal employment status and mothering style. Researchers have proposed that maternal attitudes (i.e., role satisfaction, separation anxiety) may contribute more to mothering than does employment status (Stifter, Coulehan, & Fish, 1993).

Recent research stresses the importance of considering the interactions among these variables to influence mothering. For instance, there is evidence that maternal employment interacts with mother characteristics to explain mothering. Consider an investigation by Stifter, Coulehan, and Fish (1993) that explored the interaction between maternal employment and separation anxiety in explaining maternal interaction style. The results of this work revealed no main effects for maternal employment status or separation anxiety. However, the researchers found that mothers who were highly anxious about separation from their children and employed outside of the home were more intrusive with their infants, and in turn, these children were more likely to be rated as having an insecure relationship with their mothers.

References

Crockenberg, S., & Litman, C. (1990). Autonomy as competence in 2-year-olds: Maternal correlates of child defiance, compliance and self-assertion. *Developmental Psychology, 26*, 961–971.

Downey, G., & Coyne, J. C. (1990). Children of depressed parents: An integrative review. *Psychological Bulletin, 108*, 50–76.

Fish, M., Stifter, C. A., & Belsky, J. (1993). Early patterns of mother-infant dyadic interaction: Infant, mother, and family demographic antecedents. *Infant Behavior and Development, 16*, 1–18.

Klein, P. S. (1984). Behavior of Israeli mothers toward infants in relation to infants' perceived temperament. *Child Development, 55*, 1212–1218.

Sroufe, L. A., & Fleeson, J. (1988). Relationships within families: Mutual influences. In R. A. Hinde & J. Stevenson-Hinde (Eds.), *The coherence of family relationships* (pp. 27–47). Oxford: Oxford University Press.

Stifter, C. A., Coulehan, C. M., & Fish, M. (1993). Linking employment to attachment: The mediating effects of maternal separation anxiety and interactive behavior. *Child Development, 64*, 1451–1460.

See also: Employment, early maternal; Fathering; Feminism; Instrumental versus expressive functions.

TRACY SPINRAD AND CYNTHIA STIFTER

Motor development. Motor development is as important an aspect of child and adolescent development as is cognitive, psychological, and social development. It involves the progressive development of movement skills and abilities with age. Motor development is an academic area of study and research within university faculties of physical education and kinesiology. Research in this area has made significant contributions to knowledge about changes in motor behavior and the reasons for those changes (see Roberton, 1995).

There are two main categories of motor skills: *gross motor* and *fine motor*. Gross motor skills involve the large muscle groups and include such activities as running, jumping, throwing, and catching. Fine motor skills involve the small muscles of the hands and fingers and include such activities as writing, cutting, and manipulating small objects (manual dexterity). Fine motor skills are important in academic and many job settings. This entry will focus only on gross motor development.

Gross motor skills are important for participation in a variety of physical activities and sports and can be divided into three categories: (1) *locomotor*, for example, running, jumping, hopping, skipping; (2) *object control* (manipulation), for example, throwing, catching, kicking, striking; and (3) *balance/stability*, both static and dynamic. Research has been conducted on each of these skills, and it has been found that children go through identifiable stages in their skill development. Texts such as *Human Motor Development* by Payne and Isaacs (1995) outline the initial, formative (intermediate), and mature stages of the major fundamental movement patterns. For example, for throwing, children typically begin throwing with their legs stationary, using only limited arm action. At the formative stage, children step with the leg on the same side as the throwing arm (homolateral step), while at the mature stage, children step with the leg opposite the throwing arm (contralateral step). Parents, teachers, and anyone working with young children should be aware of the characteristics of each stage and should be able to identify at which stage a child is performing a skill. Children will develop motor skills in similar sequences but at different rates, depending on a number of factors to be discussed later.

There are two main factors affecting a child's rate of motor development: *biological* and *environmental*. The biological factors are largely controlled by genetics and include type of physique (larger, more muscular physiques have an advantage), rate of maturity (early maturing children will have an advantage until puberty), neuromuscular control, and perceptual ability. The most important environmental factors are opportunities for practice, which are determined by availability of facilities, equipment, fees for programs, transportation to programs, and support from significant others, especially parents.

Parents can facilitate their child's motor development by providing opportunities in a wide variety of structured activities (lessons, sport teams) and unstructured activities (neighborhood games and play, playground play). This will ensure that a child finds several activities that they enjoy and thus will be more apt to participate. Practice is very important for developing proficiency in the basic motor skills. It requires many repetitions of a motor skill to become proficient at it.

A good school physical education program should provide instruction and some practice in these basic skills, but much practice outside of school hours is necessary. Parents should encourage their child to practice their skills and should spend time participating with them. Numerous resources are available to assist parents (see Gallahue, 1996). With a good foundation of basic movement skills, children will feel competent and eager to participate in a wide variety of physical activities and sports as adolescents and adults, thus contributing to their lifelong health and wellness.

Finally, several tests are available to measure a child's level of motor development, for example, *Bruininks-Oseretsky Test of Motor Proficiency* and *Ulrich Test of Gross Motor Development* (Payne & Isaacs, 1995). Many schools use simpler screening tests to determine if elementary-aged children are delayed in motor development and require a remedial program to improve their motor skills. Parents of children with delayed motor development should consult their school to determine if such a program exists.

Some children (about 5%) with no known neuromuscular problems will experience severe delays in motor development and are termed "physically awkward" children (Wall, Reid, & Paton, 1990). These children will require specialized programs with numerous repetitions of skills to be able to function satisfactorily in the motor domain.

References

Gallahue, D. L. (1996). *Developmental physical education for today's children* (3rd ed.). Dubuque, IA: Brown & Benchmark.

Payne, V. G., & Isaacs, L. D. (1995). *Human motor development: A lifespan approach* (3rd ed.). Mountain View, CA: Mayfield Publishing.

Roberton, M. (Ed.). (1995). *Advances in motor development research* (Vol. 4). New York: AMS Press.

Wall, A. E., Reid, G., & Paton, J. (1990). The syndrome of physical awkwardness. In G. Reid (Ed.), *Problems of motor control* (pp. 283–316). Amsterdam: Elsevier Publishers.

See also: Physical activity; Physical fitness; Playground skills; Sports.

JANICE BUTCHER

Multiples. There has been a remarkable rise in the number of twins, triplets, and other higher-order multiple births over the past two decades. This rising number represents the increase in births to women in their thirties, who are more likely to have multiple births and to have used fertility-enhancing drugs and techniques (National Center for Health Statistics, 1997). Multiple births have a higher incidence of infant mortality, low birth weight, and shorter periods of gestation (National Center for Health Statistics, 1997). In addition, the demands of a multiple birth pregnancy and raising twins, triplets, quadruplets, quintuplets, or more put families at high risk for birth defects, child abuse, financial stress, and marital problems.

Parents of multiples face many unique challenges. Some of the most common challenges and suggestions for parents to successfully negotiate these challenges are summarized below.

Pregnancy. Multiple birth pregnancies are at a higher risk of experiencing complications such as toxemia, placenta previa, and fetal growth restriction. Mothers expecting a multiple birth should attend all prenatal visits to ensure their health and that of their unborn children. Mothers expecting twins should pay careful attention to nutrition and should get adequate sleep.

Health. Many multiples, even full-term multiples, require neonatal hospitalization. Some twins go home within a few days; others (especially triplets, quadruplets, and more) may remain in neonatal care for weeks or months until they are healthy enough to leave the constant care of nurses. This special care required necessitates time away from parents. This parental absence may reduce early bonding and increase stress related to feelings of parental competency. Frequent hospital visits to care for the infants may reduce separation anxiety, increase parenting skills, and aid in parent-child bonding.

Demands on parents. The overload of baby care for parents of multiples allows little time for early individual exchanges with the infants. Many parents feel there is barely enough time to meet the basic physical needs of each child, much less the individual emotional needs. Mothers of multiples often report a lack of sleep, increased emotional disturbance, increased marital conflict, financial strain, and a lack of time to care for the needs of their other children. The most difficult period appears to be the first year. Support from fathers is important but must include child-rearing tasks in addition to emotional support. Over half of mothers rearing multiples report receiving little, if any, assistance from others (Chang, 1990).

Avenues of support. Multiple birth families must struggle to cope with extraordinary issues with little or no information or support. For this reason, pediatric care of a family with multiple births should begin prenatally and should prepare parents for the unexpected emotional, physical, and financial stresses that accompany multiple births. Parents should also seek and accept assistance from others such as family, friends, neighbors, churches, twin support groups, and child care providers.

Dependency. Twins commonly become overly dependent on each other. Identical twins tend to be more dependent on each other and to spend more time together than fraternal twins, especially identical twin girls (Fischbein, Hallencreutz, & Wiklund, 1990). Their preference for each other over others can often cause the parent to feel left out. This comradery also encourages parents to leave the twins to play together alone, thus spending more time with each other and

less around adults or other children. This isolation can exacerbate already existing overdependency on the other twin as well as contribute to partner-dependent
interactive styles. Parents should attempt to spend individual time with each
child on a regular basis and talk often to each child and avoid treating the pair as
a single individual.

Encouraging friendships. Multiples are more likely to play with one another
than with a peer. Development of social characteristics, language, and intelligence is affected by "twoness" (Lytton, Singh, & Gallagher, 1995). Therefore, it
is important to make friends outside the twinship. Parents need to recognize that
friendships are an important avenue for children to become independent; this
may be especially true for twins. Having friends outside of sibling relationships
aids in the development of their separate identities and offers the twins time
within a "nonshared" environment. It is the time spent within these nonshared
environments that is the most influential factor for individual personality development (Lytton, Singh, & Gallagher, 1995).

Goals for parents of multiples. Parents of multiples must successfully resolve issues related to parent-child bonding, parental preference, temperament
and personality, the separation-individuation process, cognitive development,
and child abuse. According to Showers and McCleery (1984), optimal parenting
involves recognizing the difficulties associated with being a twin or triplet, particularly each child's desire to establish a strong sense of self. Both parents must
establish positive feelings for each infant and their individual personalities and
needs.

References

Chang, C. (1990). Raising twin babies and problems in the family. Sixth International
    Congress on Twin Studies. *Acta Geneticae Medicae et Gemellogiae, 39* (4), 501–505.
Fischbein, S., Hallencreutz, I., & Wiklund, I. (1990). What is it like to be a parent of
    twins? Sixth International Congress on Twin Studies. *Acta Geneticae Medicae et
    Gemellogiae 39* (2), 271–276.
Lytton, H., Singh, J. K., & Gallagher, L. (1995). Parenting twins. In M. H. Bornstein
    (Ed.) *Handbook of parenting: Vol. 1: Children and parenting* (pp. 185–208).
    Mahwah, NJ: Lawrence Erlbaum Associates, Publishers.
National Center for Health Statistics. (1997). *Triplet births: Trends and outcomes, 1971–
    94* [On-line]. Available: http://www.cdc.gov/nchswww/releases/97facts/97sheets/trip-
    lets.htm.
Showers, J., & McCleery, J. T. (1984). Research on twins: Implications for parenting.
    Child: Care, Health, & Development, 10 (6), 391–404.

See also: Siblings; Social support, informal.

JACQUELINE J. KIRBY

Munchausen Syndrome by Proxy. Munchausen Syndrome by Proxy is
a form of child abuse in which primary caregivers induce physical illness or
contrive symptoms in their children in an effort to obtain attention from medical
professionals. Coury (1994) has identified core symptoms associated with the
disorder that include the following: (1) physical illness in a child that is either
simulated or induced by a primary caregiver or parent; (2) ongoing medical

treatment that often requires excessive and sometimes intrusive medical procedures; (3) denial by the perpetrator as to the etiology of the child's presenting symptoms; and (4) diminution of symptoms upon separation of the child from the perpetrator.

Munchausen Syndrome by Proxy is rarely identified. In part, this is due to a lack of objectively quantifiable diagnostic criteria for the disorder. Additionally, the condition involves not only the child but the caretaker, who may be reluctant to acknowledge abusive behavior. This caretaker is almost always the mother. Furthermore, children are not apt to acknowledge the abuses due to developmental considerations and limitations regarding self-report that preclude an understanding of such events. Moreover, the children have become accustomed to and accepting of their parents' maladaptive behavior. For these reasons, accurate prevalence data are understandably difficult to ascertain. In an extensive review of the literature, Coury (1994) has documented only 150 cases of the disorder that are reported. Based on the difficulties associated with diagnosis, experts contend that this is likely an underestimation of actual prevalence (Kaufman, 1994). Prevalence among male and female children is similar.

Due to a paucity of research pertaining to Munchausen Syndrome by Proxy, the etiology of the disorder is not entirely understood. Kaufman (1994) has posited specific familial factors that characterize the perpetrators' families of origin. These factors include a family environment lacking nurturance, support, and warmth. Individuals reared under such conditions seek this emotional support from health care providers through their children's alleged illness. In a recent investigation of psychopathology among mothers of children identified as having Munchausen's Syndrome by Proxy, Bools, Neale, and Meadow (1994) found that over 80% of the mothers interviewed were characterized by some type of psychiatric disturbance including personality and somatoform disorders. Moreover, many of the mothers reported some type of abuse during childhood.

The more common presentations of the syndrome include seizures, apnea, vomiting, diarrhea, and bleeding (Coury, 1994). Typically, these symptoms are induced by means of suffocation or the administration of some type of noxious substance or medication (i.e., poisonous substances, laxatives, and stimulants) on the part of the perpetrator. Less common manifestations of the disorder include infections and developmental disorders. In contrast to symptom induction, primary caretakers may also fabricate nonexistent symptoms. These fictitious symptoms often lead to extensive medical evaluations and sometimes-inaccurate diagnoses, which may have iatrogenic effects that may result in additional physical symptoms and complaints. As Schreier and Libow (1993; 1994) conclude, Munchausen Syndrome by Proxy places children at significant risk for physical and psychological morbidity as well as mortality.

The diagnosis of *Munchausen Syndrome by Proxy* requires either direct observation of the perpetrator inducing physical symptoms or objective verification of reports of factitious illnesses. Once the disorder is identified, a multidisciplinary team including psychologists, social workers, and physicians should be involved in order to provide optimal management of symptoms. First, the child must be protected from any possible harm that may occur as the result of the caretaker's administering unnecessary medications and requesting unwarranted procedures. This is often accomplished through the removal of the child from any unsupervised contact with the perpetrator. Subsequently, the perpetrator must be carefully evaluated to rule out the possibility of any thought disturbances. The perpetrator should be involved in individual psychotherapy in order to understand underlying motives that may provide an explanation of the behavior. In addition, family psychotherapy should be made available to family members including the child to assist in the adjustment of the separation from the perpetrator. Finally, supportive psychotherapy is necessary for the victimized child to assist in any posttraumatic stress symptoms as well as repetitions of abuse that may ensue following separation from the perpetrator. For the caregiver, a therapeutic goal would be to model appropriate behaviors that are incompatible with illness, while at the same time discouraging manipulative means of seeking attention.

There is a limited extant literature pertaining to the management and treatment of children who have been identified with Munchausen Syndrome by Proxy. In the absence of such research, the practitioner must rely on current theoretical notions of the etiology and manifestations of the disorder. The complexity of the disorder, coupled with the primary caretaker's psychopathology, leads to a guarded prognosis for the perpetrator. However, if the syndrome is identified early, and if appropriate interventions are made, the prognosis for the victimized child may be more optimistic.

References

Bools, C., Neale, B., & Meadow, R. (1994). Munchausen Syndrome by Proxy: A study of psychopathology. *Child Abuse and Neglect, 18* (9), 773–788.

Coury, D. L. (1994). Munchausen Syndrome by Proxy: Medical issues. In R. A. Olsen, L. L. Mullins, J. B. Gillman, & J. M. Chaney (Eds.), *The sourcebook of pediatric psychology* (pp. 335–360). Boston, MA: Allyn & Bacon.

Kaufman, K. L. (1994). Munchausen Syndrome by Proxy: Psychological issues. In R. A. Olson, L. L. Mullins, J. B. Gillman & J.M. Chaney (Eds.), *The sourcebook of pediatric psychology* (pp. 361–374). Boston, MA: Allyn & Bacon.

Schreier, H. A., & Libow, J. A. (1993). Munchausen Syndrome by Proxy: Diagnosis and prevalence. *American Journal of Orthopsychiatry, 63* (2), 318–321.

Schreier, H. A., & Libow, J. A. (1994). Munchausen by Proxy Syndrome: A clinical fable for our times. *Journal of the American Academy of Child and Adolescent Psychiatry, 33* (6), 904–905.

See also: Abuse, child; Stress.

KELLY C. BYARS, WENDY RODENBERGER KUPPENHEIMER, AND RONALD T. BROWN

Mutuality. Mutuality is a term that is used to refer to the mutual regulation of social interaction by mothers and their infants. Researchers from a variety of fields (developmental psychology, infant psychiatry, language development, neuroscience) have addressed this phenomenon, often using different labels for a similar concept (e.g., reciprocity, synchrony, intersubjectivity, affective attunement, affective matching).

At the core of the concept of mutuality is the notion that responsive parents attend closely to the behavioral signals of their infants and match their behaviors to their infants' levels of arousal and interest. In this way, parents assist their infants in regulating their emotions and states of arousal. A history of repeated success in modulating affect in the context of the relationship with the primary caregiver is eventually internalized to become part of the child's own capacity for self-regulation. Affective matching by parents also confers meaning to the infant's (initially random) actions and builds infants' expectations that their actions are effective in bringing responses from the environment.

According to Trevarthen (1980), there is an early period of mutual regulation (3 to 9 months) that reflects primary intersubjectivity, or the infant's capacity for shared emotional experiences. However, a qualitative change occurs at 9 to 12 months when the infant becomes capable of secondary intersubjectivity, or the capacity to share meanings and understandings with others about objects and events in their world. During this period, infants deliberately seek to share a focus of attention and states with others.

Developmental psychologists have studied mutuality primarily within the context of mother-infant face-to-face play. For example, Tronick and his colleagues (Tronick & Cohn, 1989) have observed an increase in the matching of states in social play from 3 to 9 months of age. Mutual regulation is clearly demonstrated in Tronick's *still-face* paradigm in which mothers are instructed to be unresponsive to their infants' bids for attention. Infants quickly look away, protest, become disorganized and distressed, and attempt to soothe themselves. Tronick's research focused attention on the plight of infants whose mothers are depressed and tend to be either unresponsive or intrusive in their social interactions. Such early experiences could lead to later interactional disturbances in this population of infants.

Stern (1985), an infant psychiatrist, goes beyond the concept of affect matching to speak of *affect attunement*. He argues that parents do not simply imitate or match their infants' behaviors, but they often reflect or mirror the emotional tone of the infants' behaviors in another modality. For example, as the infant is pounding rhythmically and with increasing intensity on a table, the mother says, "Bang! Bang!! Bang!!!" with increasing vocal intensity in coordination with the baby's motor actions. Stern argues that such experiences of emotional resonance are influential in the infant's formation of a core sense of self.

Researchers of language development (Bruner, 1983) have described mutuality in the development of reciprocal vocal turn taking from 3 to 9 months of age. This reciprocal interaction lays the groundwork for a later ability to engage in conversational dialogues. Concomitant with the shift to secondary intersubjectivity, a qualitative shift in communicative development occurs at about 9 to 12 months of age when infants begin to use gestures and vocalizations to communicate intentionally. A mother who scaffolds her infant's communicative efforts by establishing a joint focus of attention and following her infant's lead in play provides a *language acquisition support system* that facilitates the infant's language development (Bruner, 1983).

Neuroscientists have described psychobiological mechanisms by which early experiences of attunement or misattunement can have lasting effects on the developing child (Schore, 1994). Much of the maturation of the brain and the development of its cortical pathways are dependent upon the experiences of the child during the first two years of life. Synchronous interactions that result in a predominance of shared positive states promote the development of brain circuits responsible for emotion regulation. Repeated experiences in which caregivers are unresponsive and fail to help infants modulate their distress lead to impairment in brain mechanisms that underlie emotion regulation. What is needed is a sensitive and responsive parenting style with infants in which caregivers contingently respond to the infant's distress signals, tune into the infant's ongoing interests, and follow the infant's lead in play. Unresponsive, inconsistently responsive, or intrusive caregiving in infancy can have lasting negative consequences for cognitive, language, and emotional development.

References
Bruner, J. (1983). *Child's talk: Learning to use language*. New York: Norton.
Schore, A. (1994). *Affect regulation and the origin of self: The neurobiology of emotional development*. Hillsdale, NJ: Erlbaum.
Stern, D. (1985). *The interpersonal world of the infant*. New York: Basic Books.
Trevarthen, C. (1980). The foundations of intersubjectivity: Development of interpersonal and cooperative understanding in infants. In D. R. Olson (Ed.), *The social foundations of language and thought* (pp. 1–39). New York: Norton.
Tronick, E., & Cohn, J. (1989). Infant-mother face-to-face interaction: Age and gender differences in coordination and the occurrence of miscoordination. *Child Development, 60*, 85–92.

See also: Attachment, secure; Developmentally Appropriate Practice; Floortime; Instrumental versus expressive functions; Scaffolding.

ANN D. MURRAY

N

Narratives, personal. The ability to comprehend and create narratives is a critical accomplishment that has implications for both personal and social development. Personal narratives are fundamental forms of thought and expression that allow us to structure and communicate a social experience in which the self is presented to listeners and integrated into the surrounding culture (Engel, 1995). Over time, we create ourselves by shaping and sharing the stories we tell about our lives.

A *narrative* is a logical sequence of meaningfully related events, imaginary or real, placed within a dramatic context. The challenges of narrative involve reconstructing experience and *decontextualizing* language (McCabe & Peterson, 1991). "Decontextualizing" means that language is used to shape an image of a past or future that can be recreated in the minds of listeners, not to describe immediate here-and-now experience. Narratives that are told intentionally are *stories*. Children are exposed to models of narrative in imaginary stories that are read to them (McCabe & Peterson, 1991).

Children construct narratives in the context of play or playful conversation (Engel, 1995). When parents engage their young children in collaborative storytelling involving personal narratives, they socialize their children into certain linguistic, social, and cognitive structures and practices that constitute "scientific" discourse and thought, potentially long before they enter kindergarten. This narrative activity is scientific because children construct and evaluate explanations of events and thus engage in basic processes of scientific thought (Ochs et al., 1992).

Becoming skilled in narrative begins with infant-parent collaborative conversation about the past with the parent as the central and predominant constructor of the narrative. By 24 months, their respective roles become more differentiated between teller and listener, though the parent supports the conversation through framing questions and supportive interpretations (Engel, 1995). This practice is called *scaffolding*. At 30 months, children need less prodding, framing, and direct questioning by the parent. Toddlers learn that they have a past that can be described. As their language skills improve, they learn that narrative is a means for them to learn about themselves and convey that knowledge to others.

By age 3, children can shift from elaborating events inferring a story character's motives in hypothetical situations. They can provide plausible reasons why a story character might feel sad, happy, or angry. They can respond to parents' encouragement to "remember that?" At this point, children gradually increase their ability to employ more accurate sequences in their narratives, to diverge from the plot to add detail. Stories that involve other family members can reinforce the child's sense of family and belonging. Unfortunately, narratives can place children in a negative context that is discouraging and demeaning. During later years, the child's peers and other family members become an important audience for narrative as well as a source of stories for the family (Bretherton, Prentiss, & Ridgeway, 1990).

McCabe and Peterson (1991) found several styles of parental response to a toddler's narrative. *Topic switching* involved changing the topic. *Repetitive* is a passive response that simply repeats something the child said. A *topic-extensive* style responds to a child's remarks with open-ended questions linked to where the child left off. The parent may move from general open-ended questions to progressively more specific questions in the face of nonresponsiveness. This scaffolding strategy makes few, if any, directives or overt corrections of the child's behavior. Parents with a *confrontational topic-extensive* style kept correcting the child's grammar mistakes or disputed the facts of the child's narrative. A *supportive topic extensive* style proved predictive of longer child narratives over time, whereas topic switching was associated with subsequent relatively shorter narratives.

Engel (1995) suggests six strategies for promoting narrative skill in children:

- Listen attentively.
- Respond substantively by asking questions that reflect genuine, specific attention and interest.
- Collaborate by engaging oneself in the story.
- Provide a multiplicity of voices and genres for children to experience.
- Encourage the use of a wide range of story forms.
- Permit stories about things that matter.

References

Bretherton, I., Prentiss, C., & Ridgeway, D. (1990). Family relationships as represented in a story-completion task at thirty-seven and fifty-four months of age. *New Directions for Child Development, 48*, 85–105.

Engel, S. (1995). *The stories children tell: Making sense of the narratives of childhood*. New York: W. H. Freeman.

McCabe, A., & Peterson, C. (1991). Getting the story: A longitudinal study of parental styles in eliciting narratives and development of narrative skill. In A. McCabe & C. Peterson (Eds.), *Developing narrative structure* (pp. 217–253). Hillsdale, NJ: Lawrence Erlbaum Associates.

Ochs, E., Taylor, C., Rudolph, D., & Smith, R. (1992). Storytelling as a theory-building activity. *Discourse Processes, 15,* 37–72.

See also: Communication; Language development; Literacy.

CHARLES A. SMITH

National Extension Parent Education Model (NEPEM). The National Extension Parent Education Model (NEPEM) is a parent education framework that serves as common ground for parent education conducted through county extension offices throughout the United States (Smith et al., 1994).

NEPEM was created to establish a core unifying conceptual framework that would serve to guide local programs, increase collaboration across state lines, and provide a basis for synthesizing evaluations of common efforts. By creating a unifying vision of parent education, the team that created the model hoped to provide a powerful tool for teaching decision makers, state and federal organizations and agencies, and the public about the Cooperative Extension System's concern about children and their parents (Goddard et al., 1994).

The model consists of 29 parent practices divided into six categories:

- *Care for self* emphasizes the parent's personal skills (e.g., managing personal stress).
- *Understand* emphasizes parent knowledge about children (e.g., observing and understanding one's children and their development).
- *Guide* involves the use of influence and authority (e.g., establishing and maintaining reasonable limits).
- *Nurture* emphasizes emotional support for children (e.g., expressing affection and compassion).
- *Motivate* focuses on more intellectual pursuits (e.g., teaching children about themselves, others, and the world around them).
- *Advocate* emphasizes reaching out beyond one's immediate family (e.g., finding, using, and creating resources when needed to benefit one's children and the community of children).

The 29 practices and six categories were shaped around the suggestions provided by extension human development specialists at the land-grant universities for each state. At each step of the revision process emphasis was placed on achieving consensus. There were regional and state differences in priorities. Skills that could not be enthusiastically supported as key priorities by all states, however, were not included in the final model. The model would serve to bring professionals together rather than serving as a point of conflict.

The resulting model focuses exclusively on what parents do to enhance the well-being of their children. It emphasizes priority parent practices across the full range of childhood and adolescence. The emphasis is on core priorities related to parent strengths with no claim on identifying all of the important parent skills. The categories are viewed as having fluid, not rigid boundaries. The practices were also identified at a level of abstraction that would make them applicable across the cultural spectrum. "Expressing affection," for example, was considered important for all children. The manner in which this practice is expressed could vary a great deal from one culture to another. This latter goal of cultural commonality was intended to have a unifying effect on programs that serve parents across in the United States.

The final report was distributed to every county extension office in the United States and key agencies at the state level. Current efforts are now underway to develop common evaluation tools to measure the effectiveness of parent education programs.

References
Smith, C. A., Cudaback, D., Goddard, H. W., & Myers-Walls, J. (1994). *National Extension Parent Education Model of Critical Parenting Practices.* Manhattan, Kansas: Kansas State Research and Extension.

Goddard, H. W., Smith, C. A., Cudaback, D., & Myers-Walls, J. A. (1994). A national model for parent education: Practices and empirical bases. *Family Science Review*, 7 (3–4), 79–92.

See also: Cooperative Extension Service; Education, parenting.

CHARLES A. SMITH

Nature versus nurture. Few issues have been more divisive in the field of human development than assigning cause to human outcomes. To what extent is human development the result of socialization, training, or the environment of development? To what extent is development the result of inborn, genetic, or biological factors? How do we account for successful children of maladaptive parents? How do we account for troubled children in good families?

The field has not lacked for disciples of extreme views. Different opinion leaders have suggested that human nature is despicable, benign, or angelic. What these varying views have in common is the belief that human behavior is largely the result of inborn factors. Such theories are therefore labeled as biological, genetic, or nurture theories.

Such a biological orientation has made for strange bedfellows. John Calvin with his emphasis on innate depravity and Sigmund Freud with his view that humans are a bundle of destructive drives fall in the same camp with Maria Montessori, Carl Rogers, and Abraham Maslow who believed in the inherent goodness of human nature. Within these biology-emphasizing theories, the responsibility of caregivers ranges from taming the instincts to staying out of the way of flowering development. In this biological view, outcomes are largely explained in terms of basic nature rather than effective socialization.

At the opposite end of the nature/nurture spectrum are behaviorists who take as a basic premise the view that human behavior can best be understood as a reaction to past and prospective rewards and punishments. Such a view sees humans as malleable clay to be formed or blank slates to be marked by people and circumstances. As a result they are labeled as environmental or nurture theories. With such a view, the responsibilities of "trainers" are immense.

John Watson represents the extreme environmental view with his inflammatory pronouncement offered over 70 years ago: Give me a dozen healthy infants, well-formed, and my own specified world to bring them up in, and I'll guarantee to take any one at random and train him to become any type of specialist I might select—doctor, lawyer, artist, merchant-chief and, yes, even beggar-man and thief, regardless of his talents, penchants, tendencies, abilities, vocations, and race of his ancestors (Watson, 1924/1930, p. 104).

Behaviorism has been a dominant or influential paradigm in American psychology for much of this century. For several decades it seemed as if the nature/nurture debate was settled in favor of nurture. But a new wave of biological thinking is assaulting the behaviorists. The relative calm was shattered in the scientific community by a controversial article by Sandra Scarr (1992) and in the public arena by the publication of *The Bell Curve* by Herrnstein and Murray (1994). Additional scholars have weighed in for the battle (Rowe, 1994). The new biological thinking suggests that our genetic codes determine much of our development and that the influence of family and society is less than we have traditionally assumed.

"Fortunately, evolution has not left development of the human species, nor any other, at the easy mercy of variations in their environments. Developmental research of the past 25 years supports the idea that normal genes and normal environments promote species-typical development and that, given a wide range of opportunities, individuals make their own environments, based on their own heritable characteristics" (Scarr, 1992, pp. 15, 17). Scarr concludes that "good-enough parenting" has the same effects as super parenting. Her counsel: Just provide a safe and stimulating environment, and children will do fine.

But the new biological thinking has not gone unchallenged. Baumrind (1993, p. 1308) has asserted that "the average expectable environment is not good enough." Reviewing extensive research, she concludes that there is consensus today that adolescents, as well as younger children, require a family environment that fosters security of attachment and provides close supervision. According to Baumrind, differences in parenting behavior make very big differences in child outcomes.

Scholars have tried to replace competing nature/nurture extremes with a view of complex interactions between genes and environments (Horowitz, 1993). Some (Wachs, 1993) have even suggested that the nature versus nurture dichotomy is meaningless. But even with attempts at synthesis, the debate continues to be ardent and polarized.

The most sensible modern view is probably that genes not only can form a path for individual development but also can determine what effect various experiences will have on a person. At the same time, life experiences will determine which genetic messages are activated and which will lie dormant. Both nature and nurture have important impact on development.

References

Baumrind, D. (1993). The average expectable environment is not good enough: A response to Scarr. *Child Development, 64,* 1299–1317.

Herrnstein, R. J., & Murray, C. (1994). *The bell curve: Intelligence and class structure in American life*. New York: Free Press.

Horowitz, F. D. (1993). The need for a comprehensive new environmentalism. In R. Plomin, & G. E. McClearn (Eds.), *Nature, nurture, & psychology* (pp. 341–353). Washington, DC: American Psychological Association.

Rollins, B. C., & Thomas, D. L. (1979). Parental support, power, and control techniques in the socialization of children. In W. R. Burr, R. Hill, F. I. Nye, & I. L. Reiss (Eds.), *Contemporary theories about the family* (Vol. 1, pp. 317–364). New York: Free Press.

Rowe, D. C. (1994). *Limits of family influence: Genes, experience, and behavior*. New York: Guilford Press.

Scarr, S. (1992). Developmental theories for the 1990s: Development and individual differences. *Child Development, 63*, 1–19.

Wachs, T. D. (1993). The nature-nurture gap: What we have here is a failure to collaborate. In R. Plomin, & G. E. McClearn (Eds.), *Nature, nurture, & psychology* (pp. 375–391). Washington, DC: American Psychological Association.

Watson, J. B. (1930). *Behaviorism* (Original work published in 1924) (rev.ed.). New York: W. W. Norton & Company.

See also: Locke, John; Paradigms, parenting; Rousseau, Jean Jacques.

H. WALLACE GODDARD

Nightmares. Nightmares are unpleasant or frightening dreams that occur during REM (rapid eye movement) sleep, typically late in the sleep cycle, in the early morning hours. Nightmares are vivid and disturbing, and children remember the content and the emotional experience after waking. Children typically wake abruptly from a nightmare. Nightmares and *night terrors* are very different sleep disturbances; night terrors happen during slow-wave sleep earlier during the night. Both are classified as *parasomnias*, a group of sleep disorders involving an abnormal event that disrupts sleep. It is important for parents to identify whether a child has experienced a nightmare or sleep terror because parenting response differs depending on the type of disturbance. Although the terms *nightmares* and *bad dreams* are often used interchangeably, technically bad dreams are not as frightening and are not accompanied by the physiological changes that accompany nightmares (Golbin & Sheldon, 1992).

Everyone experiences occasional nightmares. Somewhere between 10% and 50% of children between the ages of 3 and 6 have nightmares often enough to concern parents (Mindell, 1993). After age 5 or 6, children in middle childhood and adolescence appear to experience fewer nightmares. The particular theme or "story" in the nightmare depends on the child's stage of development, general emotional conflicts being experienced at the time, and specific events from the day. Often the content involves immediate threats to the child's safety or emotional well-being, such as being attacked or killed or falling. A variety of experiences that increase children's general nighttime fears also increase the likelihood of nightmares. For example, young children may hear confusing messages about the death of a loved one or pet that indicate that death is like sleeping; such comparisons may increase children's fears of dying during sleep. Preverbal toddlers cannot use language to describe the frightening nightmare or label their emotional reactions. After children acquire verbal skills, they often do not tell adults about their frightening dreams. Children may believe that if they talk about a dream, the dream will come true.

Most parents can be reassured that nightmares are part of normal child development and not an indication of psychological disturbance. To reduce the likelihood of nightmares, parents may need to review the child's daily experiences to see if any changes could be made to facilitate the child's sense of security and promote a positive view of sleep. There are many excellent children's books dealing with nightmares and scary dreams that can be read with children during the day (Ferber, 1985). Parents can monitor children's exposure to violence and suspenseful television programs. Children may not appear frightened when watching such shows and may even seem to enjoy the excitement but, nevertheless, experience enough anxiety to cause nightmares during sleep. Parents should consider seeking professional help for children with frequent nightmares that continue for more than a month. A child psychologist or psychiatrist usually conducts treatment, with strategies often consisting of behavioral anxiety management interventions such as deep relaxation and systematic desensitization.

Although nightmares do not indicate that a child has a psychological disorder, many children experiencing temporary or chronic emotional maladjustment may have disturbing nightmares. For example, a nightmare in which an individual vividly relives a trauma is one of the hallmarks of posttraumatic stress disorders (Terr, 1987). Nightmares may also occur when children are experiencing significant emotional distress. For example, children with major difficulties with depression or anxiety often have some type of disturbed sleep, such as difficulty falling asleep or waking up several times during the night, bad dreams, and possibly nightmares.

Although nightmares are by definition frightening and overwhelming, the approach parents take to explaining or interpreting the significance of the nightmare plays a large role in how children understand the meaning of having a nightmare. Parents who communicate messages to children that dreams are omens or have the power to forecast the future may increase children's fearfulness following a nightmare. Those with a psychoanalytic perspective may view nightmares as symbols of unconscious wishes, projections, and displacements, which may sensitize children to a sense that their nightmares are very important messages. Most children respond well to parents' comfort and reassurances after a nightmare, although many children remain frightened for some time and do not return to sleep easily. Children benefit from calm reassurance that they are safe, and the parent is there to care for and protect them.

References

Ferber, R. (1985). *Solve your child's sleep problems*. New York: Simon & Schuster.

Golbin, A. Z., & Sheldon, S. H. (1992). Parasomnias. In S. H. Sheldon, J. P. Spire, & H. B. Levy. *Pediatric sleep medicine*. Philadelphia, PA: W. B. Saunders.

Mindell, J. A. (1993). Sleep disorders in children. *Health Psychology*, *12*, 151–162.

Terr, L. C. (1987). Nightmares in children. In C. Guilleminault (Ed.), *Sleep and its disorders in children* (pp. 231–242). New York: Raven Press.

See also: Fear; Night terrors; Night wakings; Nighttime fears.

SUZANNE M. THOMPSON

Night terrors. Night terrors, also called *sleep terrors*, are a very different form of sleep disturbance than nightmares, although the two terms are often confused. Sleep terrors are officially classified as *parasomnias,* which are sleep dysfunctions associated with sleep, sleep stages, or partial arousals from sleep and include sleepwalking, head banging, and bruxism (grinding teeth during sleep). Night terrors involve difficulties in the transition between sleep stages, as children partially awaken from deep, nondreaming sleep. Partial arousals from sleep occur because all children and adults pass through distinct stages of sleep several times every night. Some of these sleep stages are called REM (rapid eye movement) sleep and are typically associated with dreaming, and other stages involve non-REM, or nondreaming, sleep. At the end of one cycle, we all typically experience what is known as a partial waking. Children move about in bed and may briefly open and close their eyes and look around the room to assure they are in familiar surroundings. The vast majority of the time, children, like adults, quickly begin the next sleep cycle and go into deeper sleep. The arousal is only partial, as we do not fully awaken. Thus, sleep terrors are arousal disorders, as they are due to impaired or partial arousal from slow-wave sleep (Sheldon, Spire, & Levy, 1992).

Children who experience these partial arousal disturbances may simply sit up in bed calmly and look around with a blank expression, may talk in their sleep, or may sleepwalk or urinate in an inappropriate place. Sleep terrors involve more agitated and intense behaviors such as thrashing, yelling, kicking, screaming, and chaotic movement. The beginning of a sleep terror episode is sudden, dramatic, and frightening. Children experience a variety of changes in autonomic nervous system functions. The child may bolt upright in bed and scream loudly and may get out of bed and exhibit wild, chaotic behavior, possibly injuring himself or herself or someone else. Children are typically not aware of or responsive to parents' attempts to soothe or support them. Usually episodes of sleep terrors last only a few minutes, and the child abruptly returns to sleep. If the child is awakened, he or she is likely to be confused and disoriented and will probably not remember the episode (Guilleminault, 1987).

Like all parasomnias, night terrors are related to general central nervous system functioning. The exact prevalence of sleep terrors is unknown but appears to occur in approximately 3% of children and less than 1% of adults. Boys experience night terrors more frequently than girls, and there is some thought that the disturbance may have a genetic component (Mindell, 1993). Night terror difficulties usually begin in childhood, often between the ages of 2 and 4. They are most common up until approximately age 5 or 6 and typically resolve spontaneously, although they sometimes persist into adolescence and adulthood. Arousal disorders such as night terrors can occur more often in children who are experiencing fever, sleep deprivation, or stress. Emotional stress increases the frequency of brief partial arousals in normal people, and significant ongoing emotional stress appears to increase the frequency of night terrors in children predisposed to this disturbance. Although environmental stress can increase the frequency of sleep terror episodes, children who experience night terrors do not show higher rates of psychological disorders than the general population. However, frequent sleep terrors are very rare for older children and teenagers, and psychological factors may be important in maintaining the disturbance, in contrast to the situation with younger children (Rosen, Mahowald, & Ferber, 1995).

Parents who are concerned that their child may be experiencing sleep terrors should contact their pediatrician for accurate assessment and diagnosis. Parents are usually encouraged to keep distance during a child's night terror, since there is little that can be done to shorten an episode. In fact, children may become even more out of control if attempts are made to restrain them or wake them up. All episodes will eventually end fairly suddenly on their own. Parents are usually encouraged to let the episode run its course, intervene only to the extent necessary to prevent injury, and help the child back to bed. Children will not remember the event and are usually fairly calm and relaxed. Parents who mistake sleep terrors for nightmares may repeatedly question children about the nature of the "dream," and children may feel embarrassed or confused about losing control and not being able to remember what they did. Parents should simply return the child to bed, ensure his or her comfort, and not question the child at that point or in the morning about the experience.

Parents are also instructed to maintain regular bedtimes and awakening times and to try to prevent the child from chaotic sleep schedules or sleep deprivation. Often parents are encouraged to provide calm, relaxing activities during the child's bedtime routine. In moderate or severe cases of night terrors, pediatricians may prescribe medications and may consult a mental health professional to work with the parents on using approaches such as behavior training, sleep hygiene, psychotherapy, or hypnosis. Young children generally respond well to medical and behavioral interventions, unlike adolescents and adults, who in general show a less positive response (Ferber, 1985).

References

Ferber, R. (1985). *Solve your child's sleep problems*. New York: Simon & Schuster.

Guilleminault, C. (1987). Disorders of arousal in children: Somnambulism and night terrors. In C. Guilleminault (Ed.), *Sleep and its disorders in children* (pp. 243–252). New York: Raven Press.

Mindell, J. A. (1993). Sleep disorders in children. *Health Psychology, 12*, 151–162.

Rosen, G., Mahowald, M. W., & Ferber, R. (1995). Sleepwalking, confusional arousals, and sleep terrors in the child. In R. Ferber & M. Kryger (Eds.), *Principles and practice of sleep medicine in the child* (pp. 99–106). Philadelphia, PA: W. B. Saunders.

Sheldon, S. H., Spire, J. P., & Levy, H. B. (1992). *Pediatric sleep medicine*. Philadelphia, PA: W. B. Saunders.

See also: Nightmares; Nighttime fears.

SUZANNE M. THOMPSON

Nighttime fears. Most children experience bedtime fears from time to time. Some children are generally more anxious than others, but most children experience periodic fears at nighttime such as fear of "monsters," the dark, or separation from a parent. Some surveys indicate that parents are often unaware of the extent that children experience fear and worry at night (Mindell, 1997). These fears are understandable given the nature of transitioning from being awake to being asleep. When preparing for sleep, children must give up the little control they have over the world and cannot continually check in on the environment.

Many experiences can increase children's nighttime fears, just as children's daytime anxieties are often related to environmental stresses. These stressors include family conflict, illness, financial difficulties, parental depression or other psychological disorders, excessive or insufficient limit setting by parents, and exposure to frightening events. For example, sometimes children experience frightening events such as observing a conflict between parents or violence on TV and may not appear upset to the parent at the moment but experience considerable anxiety at night. Children may be busy during the day but during the quietness of night have time to think and worry. Their thoughts may seem to be out of control, and so they may try to be active (rolling around in bed, getting up) to avoid uncomfortable thoughts (Ferber, 1995).

Fears are related to the child's developmental stage. All children experience fear, guilt, and worry, but the specific form of these emotions varies with age. Preschoolers may experience strong fears of separation, fears of soiling or wetting during toilet training, fears of specific objects such as dogs, and fears of imaginary dangers such as ghosts and monsters. Children may use fantasy to transform intangible fears into concrete fears such as monsters hiding under the bed. Older children fear things of the "real world" such as physical danger or problems with family, peers, or school (Sheldon, Spire, & Levy, 1992).

Parenting relates to children's nighttime fears in a similar manner as it relates to children's daytime fears. Children need explicit and implicit messages to convince them that they are safe and secure and that parents are able and willing to protect them. Ideally, the parenting approach involves a balance between nurturance and encouragement and firm enforcement of bedtime rituals and routines. Children benefit from parents expressing calm support, reassurances, and avoidance of actions that teach the child that escalating anxiety will result in the parent remaining in the room or delaying bedtime. Parents are encouraged to stick to a schedule as much as possible, as deviating from the routine can be anxiety provoking for a child. Positive reinforcements such as praise or small rewards for staying in bed provide motivation for children to deal with anxiety and realize a sense of mastery for accomplishing a difficult goal.

Additionally, parents can facilitate children's learning how to manage fears and comfort themselves. Children whose parents tend to avoid discussing serious issues faced by children, or who discuss these issues with their children in an inappropriate or inaccurate manner, are most likely to experience repeated fears (this parenting style also contributes to children's nightmares). For example, young children often have questions and concerns about death after hearing adults refer to someone who "died in her sleep." Minimizing the child's fears or scolding the child is not helpful. Parents should try to understand why the child is feeling insecure and during the day discuss with the child how to make bed-time go better. Children benefit from parenting that helps them understand and label feelings and fears and use fantasy to resolve fears. For example, although monsters are not real, the child's fears and fantasies are real. Imagination sup-plies an explanation and concrete cause for the fears. Telling a child such fears are "only in your imagination" is not helpful to the child; imagination can be a powerful tool in children's ability to comfort themselves as well as scare them-selves. Adults can use children's fantasies to increase their sense of mastery and efficacy, perhaps by creating a story together in which the child fantasizes using powerful strategies with success (e.g., a magic word or invisible fence around the bed to banish the monster). Parents can also encourage children to label their feelings honestly and validate the naturalness of the emotional reactions before then going on to help the child reduce the fears (Ferber, 1985).

Usually nurturant and firm parenting approaches will assist children in re-solving their fears. Brief fears and sleep disturbances are common and respond well to parental support. If fears persist, become accompanied by panic or irra-tional out-of-control terror, parents should consult a pediatrician or child psy-chologist for evaluation. Such fears can reflect larger issues, such as an emo-tional disorder or family problem that needs treatment.

References
Ferber, R. (1985). *Solve your child's sleep problems*. New York: Simon & Schuster.
Ferber, R. (1995). Sleeplessness in children. In R. Ferber & M. Kryger (Eds.), *Principles and practice of sleep medicine in the child* (pp. 79-89). Philadelphia, PA: W. B. Saunders.
Mindell, J. A. (1997). Children and sleep. In M. R. Pressman & W. C. Orr (Eds.), *Under-standing sleep: The evaluation and treatment of sleep disorders* (pp. 427–439). Washington, DC: American Psychological Association.
Sheldon, S. H., Spire, J. P., & Levy, H. B. (1992). Disorders of initiating and maintaining sleep. In S. H. Sheldon, J. P. Spire, & H. P. Levy (Eds.). *Pediatric sleep medicine* (pp. 69-90). Philadelphia, PA: W. B. Saunders.

See also: Fear; Nightmares; Night terrors.

SUZANNE M. THOMPSON

Night wakings. Sleeplessness in children takes several forms, classified as *dyssomnias*, which are disorders that result in difficulty either initiating or maintaining sleep or involve excessive sleepiness. The predominant disturbance is in the amount, quality, or timing of sleep. Some dyssomnias are physiologi-cally based, such as *narcolepsy* and *obstructive sleep apnea*. Other dyssomnias are related to the environment, such as adjustment sleep disorder, due to emo-tional arousal caused by stress, conflict, or environmental change. For example, when children move or begin school, they may wake at night. These problems usually resolve naturally over time, although when ongoing stressors are present, sleep disturbance may continue. The solution to the sleep disturbance usually lies in resolving the precipitating stressor.

Another environmentally based dyssomnia is *limit-setting sleep disorder*, which involves difficulty in initiating sleep related to stalling or refusing to go to bed. Occasionally, this may be because children are truly not sleepy, and parents are attempting to enforce a sleep schedule that contains more hours of sleep than necessary. Children can experience legitimate nighttime fears. Some parents, however, are unable or unwilling to enforce nighttime rules with enough consistency to keep the child in bed and quiet so that sleep may occur. Difficulties setting and enforcing rules with supportive firmness may actually increase anxiety in children instead of providing reassurance.

Common throughout childhood, night wakings are very difficult for parents as well as children. For example, parents with children who have such difficulties often experience less accepting attitudes toward their children, increased depressed symptoms, increased marital problems, and increased anxiety. Resolution of this sleep disorder requires changes in parenting, including setting clear and firmly enforced limits and bedtime routines (Mindell, 1993).

Another environmentally based dyssomnia is *sleep-onset association disorder*, which occurs when children cannot fall asleep because certain objects or circumstances are not present. When the objects or circumstances (such as a bottle, a pacifier, a parent rocking the child) are present, sleep is normal; when absent, sleep involves delays in getting to sleep and frequent night wakings. This disturbance is very common in children ages 6 months to 3 years and can continue in older children. A related problem is *nocturnal eating (drinking) syndrome*, in which children repeatedly wake up and are unable to return to sleep without eating or drinking. This problem is common in infancy and early childhood, when children are nursed or given a bottle to fall asleep. The child awakens during the night as normal but becomes distressed when the bottle or breast is no longer present and wakes up instead of returning easily back to sleep. Resolution of these disturbances requires the parent to make changes in the child's learned sleeping patterns and to teach the child to fall sleep on his or her own without parent contact. A gradual retraining and extinction period is usually recommended to avoid having a child experience undue stress (Richman, 1987).

For adolescents, problems with night wakings begin to resemble adult insomnia. Common contributors to sleeplessness in adolescents are inconsistent and inappropriate sleep schedules (e.g., taking naps in the afternoon or evening) and poor sleep hygiene (e.g., engaging in stimulating activities such as watching television or listening to loud music just prior to bedtime). Just as with adults, adolescents experiencing stressful events such as family conflict and feelings of anxiety or sadness often have trouble sleeping. Treatment of insomnia in adolescents typically consists of similar techniques as have been proved useful for adults. Examples include improved sleep hygiene and sleep schedules, relaxation training, biofeedback, and psychotherapy.

Certain parenting styles involving discipline, nurturance, overresponsiveness to child distress, parental anxiety, parental ambivalence, feeding style, and cosleeping have been linked to night wakings, although such practices vary widely among parents with varied cultural backgrounds (Lozoff, Wolf, & Davis, 1985). Naturally, it is difficult to infer causal relations from these correlations as parental behavior is strongly influenced by the behavior of the child. However, all of the environmentally related causes of night wakings require major changes in parenting behavior to resolve the problem (Ferber, 1995). Poor limit setting around bedtime may simply reflect a lack of parental knowledge of the connection between this parenting style and children's sleep, and these parents are able to utilize education to make changes. For a variety of reasons, some parents experience difficulty making changes on their own and may benefit from consultation with a child psychologist or psychiatrist. This is particularly true when the parenting behaviors related to the child's sleep disturbance are also contributing to other child problems during the day.

References
Ferber, R. (1995). Sleeplessness in children. In R. Ferber & M. Kryger (Eds.), *Principles and practice of sleep medicine in the child* (pp. 79–89). Philadelphia, PA: W. B. Saunders.
Horn, J. L., & Dollinger, S. J. (1995). Sleep disturbances of children. In M. C. Roberts (Ed.), *Handbook of pediatric psychology* (pp. 575–588). New York: Guilford.
Lozoff, B., Wolf, A. W., & Davis, N. D. (1985). Sleep problems seen in pediatric practice. *Pediatrics, 75*, 477–483.
Mindell, J. A. (1993). Sleep disorders in children. *Health Psychology, 12*, 151–162.
Richman, N. (1987). Surveys of sleep disorders in children in a general population. In C. Guilleminault (Ed.), *Sleep and its disorders in children* (pp. 115–127). New York: Raven Press.

See also: Nightmares; Night terrors; Nighttime fears; Toilet learning.

SUZANNE M. THOMPSON

Nurturance. Parental *nurturance* is defined as behavior that helps the child feel safe, valuable, and accepted. Related terms are *support, affection, love, warmth,* and *caring.* When people think of parenting, they may think first of control and discipline. Yet nurturance is central to effective parenting.

Nurturing may be the most important parenting behavior for predicting healthy development of children. For several decades, nurturance has been identified as vital for children. Research has generally shown that the combination of warm, nurturant parenting together with clear standards and reasonable control results in children who are competent, responsible, independent, confident and achievement-oriented and able to control aggression (Maccoby & Martin, 1983).

Nurturing behaviors include physical caregiving such as providing shelter, clothing, food, and protection. Nurturing behaviors also include providing for emotional and developmental needs by talking with, listening to, expressing love, and spending time with the child. Parent education can prepare parents to nurture by helping them learn to use acceptance, empathy, support, and appreciation in relationships with their children. Effective parent education can teach parents specific skills of noticing good behavior, expressing appreciation, sending messages of love, and taking time with each child.

Research suggests that nurturing has both direct and indirect impacts on children. Nurturance all by itself is important to helping children develop. In addition, nurturance has been shown to affect the way other parenting behaviors influence children. For example, a child will respond more positively to the disciplinary actions of a nurturing parent than to the disciplinary efforts of a less nurturing parent.

In addition to being nurturing in their relationships with their children, parents can also establish an environment that is nurturing. For example, a parent may provide opportunities for a child to develop talents and participate in valued activities.

For a variety of reasons, nurturing can be challenging not only because a family's emotional resources are often overextended but also because each child has different needs and different preferences for nurturing behavior. Since the objective of nurturing is to help the child feel valued and supported, the parent must be sensitive to the unique way that each child feels supported. For example, while some children may enjoy snuggling or words of love, others may feel supported primarily by actions such as participating with them in projects.

Customizing messages of love for children is consistent with research that finds synchrony as vital to effective parenting (Rothbaum & Weisz, 1994). *Synchrony* is defined as behavior that responds sensitively to the cues and initiatives of the child. It may be called *attunement*, *involvement*, or *responsiveness* and is apparently a vital part of nurturance.

Research in parent-child attachment (Ainsworth, 1978) stresses the importance of prompt and sensitive responding by parents to children's needs. The pattern of responding becomes the basis for the continuing relationship and for the child's construction of a worldview. Sensitive, nurturing caregiving will help a child develop trust and initiative in part because he or she sees the world as a safe place. Parents can become effective nurturers by learning to attend to their children's needs, by building a positive relationship, and by consistently sending loving, supportive messages.

References

Ainsworth, M. D. S. (1978). *Patterns of attachment*. Hillsdale, NJ: Erlbaum.
Maccoby, E. E., & Martin, J. A. (1983). Socialization in the context of the family: Parent-child interaction. In P. H. Mussen (Ed.), *Handbook of child psychology* (Vol. 4, pp. 1–101). New York: John Wiley.
Rothbaum, F., & Weisz, J. R. (1994). Parental caregiving and child externalizing behavior in nonclinical samples: A meta-analysis. *Psychological Bulletin, 116,* 55–74.

See also: Attachment, secure; Nature versus nurture; Synchrony.

H. WALLACE GODDARD

O

Obesity. Obesity is an excess of body fat. Professionals use varying definitions of the levels at which body fat and body weight cross a threshold and become defined as obesity or overweight, and tables of "ideal" weights differ. Obesity is commonly defined as 20% over the ideal weight, although the precise point at which increasing weight threatens health has been estimated at 5% to 30% above ideal weight. Prevalence estimates vary depending on how obesity is defined and assessed, but between 20% and 25% of children and adolescents appear to meet the criteria for obesity.

Obesity is associated with extremely adverse medical and psychosocial effects. For example, in our culture, obese children may experience social and academic/vocational discrimination. Children who become obese at younger ages, those who remain obese for longer periods of time, and those who are more severely obese are most likely to experience obesity persisting into adulthood. Most obese children do not exhibit clinically significant levels of global psychological problems. Social conflict, anxiety, and depression are the most common problems when they do occur.

Genetic, biological, behavioral, familial, cultural, and economic factors interact in complex ways to affect the development and maintenance of obesity. Some of the factors that increase children's risk for obesity include parents (biological or adoptive) being overweight, high-density eating patterns (more gulping and less chewing), low activity levels, higher amount of time spent viewing TV, and child-rearing practices.

Parenting behaviors can affect a child's risk for obesity in several ways. First, parents who are unskilled or uncomfortable setting limits with children *may not set limits around eating behaviors*, allowing children to develop unhealthy habits. Second, parents *may use food as a way of nurturing or reinforcing children*, which teaches children to rely on food for self-gratification and self-reinforcement. Third, parents *model their own eating habits and attitudes*, and over time children learn to adopt parental eating behaviors. Fourth, some parents with disordered eating are not obese but *may be preoccupied with body shape, weight, and food*; such parents may invest so much energy in behaviors to limit food intake that disruptions occur in daily living and responsiveness to children's needs. Finally, parents with disturbed attitudes regarding eating, body shape, and weight *may criticize their children's eating habits and appearance*. Meals may involve much conflict among family members, and food may come to symbolize dysfunctional parent-child issues.

The multiple causes of this problem make treatment very difficult. Different treatments may work for different individuals, and treatment must be adapted to the specific developmental stages and capabilities of the child. Diets are not effective and may be harmful; successful treatment programs focus on helping children form new habits that will persist into adulthood. Parents play an important role in facilitating children's changes in caloric intake and energy expenditure, and their involvement should be tailored to fit the age of the child or adolescent. Parent coordination is often crucial for making such pervasive changes in lifestyle, including changing normal daily activities to develop new exercise habits and limiting access to sedentary behaviors. Some studies have shown that parental modeling of new behaviors, such as parents changing their own eating and exercise habits, significantly helps children lose weight and maintain a healthier weight over time. During difficult times or "lapses," parents should recognize the unfriendly combination of environment and biology that makes it very difficult to maintain weight loss and should encourage their children not to attribute their lack of success to personal failings. Both children and parents need to be empowered to persevere with making lifestyle changes.

Parent involvement in a child's weight loss program is crucial. First, parents should know the relative weight and height of the child and *whether or not the child's weight is outside the normal range*. Many parents and adolescents are overpreoccupied with weight and body appearance, and distort body size. On the other hand, many families may not acknowledge that the child has a weight problem or the unhealthy eating habits of the family. Consultation with the child's pediatrician is an important first step in identifying whether or not a weight problem exists. Second, parents should *discuss the situation with the child*. Parents can provide honest and direct information about the child's weight status and the consequences of maintaining an obese weight. Children often need assistance from parents in generating motivation to make changes in eating patterns and activity levels. Naturally parents will want to affirm the self-confidence of the child, which can be done by reviewing positive aspects of the child's health and functioning, talking about weight problems as caused by both genetics and habits, and providing an optimistic message regarding the child's ability to make changes. Third, parents will want to *pursue education on how weight change occurs and is maintained*. For example, short-term approaches such as dieting are not useful and may result in long-term weight gain. The focus needs to be on making long-term changes in daily behaviors, including changes in eating and exercise habits. Many people find it helpful to participate in a multidisciplinary weight management program.

References
Dietz, W. H. (1995). Childhood obesity: Prevalence and effects. In K. D. Brownell & C. G. Fairburn (Eds.), *Eating disorders and obesity: A comprehensive handbook* (pp. 438–440). New York: Guilford.
Epstein, L. H. (1995). Management of obesity in children. In K.D. Brownell & C. G. Fairburn (Eds.), *Eating disorders and obesity: A comprehensive handbook* (pp. 516–519). New York: Guilford.
Epstein, L. H., Klein, K. R., & Wisniewski, L. (1994). Child and parent factors that influence psychological problems in obese children. *International Journal of Eating Disorders, 15*, 151–157.
Epstein, L. H., Valoski, A., Wing, R. R., & McCurley, J. (1990). Ten-year follow-up of behavioral, family-based treatment for obese children. *Journal of the American Medical Association, 264*, 2519–2523.
Epstein, L. H., & Wing, R. R. (1987). Behavioral treatment of childhood obesity. *Psychological Bulletin, 101*, 331–342.

See also: Eating behavior, children and; Eating disorders.

SUZANNE M. THOMPSON

P

Pain, children and adolescents with. Pain is an experience that affects all children to some degree during childhood and adolescence. However, when a child's pain persists and is resistant to medical treatments, is considered excessive to the organic cause, interferes with family functioning, and/or interferes with participation in age-appropriate activities the child may be referred to a psychologist for pain management (Coleman, Friedman, & Gates, 1994). Children experience and cope with pain in a variety of ways. When children are referred to a psychologist to learn pain management skills, parents or the child may be concerned that the health professionals believe that the pain is "in the child's head." However, children rarely fabricate pain symptoms. The difficulty in defining and quantifying pain comes from the lack of a relationship between an observable injury (i.e., swelling) and the subjective experience and expression of pain. Two children with an identical injury or condition will likely have different experiences of pain. Sensory, neurochemical, cognitive, affective, motivational, behavioral, developmental, and historical factors all impact a child's subjective experience of pain.

Pediatric pain categories include: (1) pain associated with chronic diseases (e.g., sickle cell disease, cancer); (2) pain associated with observable physical injuries or traumas (e.g., fractures, burns); (3) pain that is not associated with a identifiable disease or physical trauma (e.g., headaches, abdominal pain); and (4) pain associated with medical and dental procedures (e.g., bone marrow aspirations, injections, extractions) (Varni, 1983). Pain is also classified as *acute* (rapid onset, typically resulting from an identifiable trauma or event, predictable course) or *chronic* (persistent, less predictable course, recurrent, or continuous).

Assessment of pediatric pain typically involves obtaining information from both the parents and child via interview, self-report, and parent-report question-naires. During the initial pain interview it is important to assess the child and family's functioning in several areas (Karoly, 1985):

- current environment and health and medical history (success of and attitude toward previous medical interventions)
- pain onset (including any corresponding changes in the family or environment) and the child's perception of the pain
- advantages and disadvantages of the pain (increased parental attention, intrusive medical procedures)
- such family issues as changes in family relationship patterns (including changes in routine to accommodate child's pain), the mental and physical health of family, and parental beliefs and coping resources
- antecedents, consequences, and accompanying emotions to pain
- current medication use and compliance

How children cope with specific painful situations or aspects of their illness has received more attention in the literature than how children cope with pain in general. Successful *copers* were found to have more accurate information re-garding their hospitalization, were categorized as information seekers, described using multiple strategies for different painful experiences, used behavioral, cog-nitive and decisional control strategies and coping responses, and engaged in positive self-talk (Siegel & Smith, 1991). Factors that appear to impact the use of coping strategies include the degree of control the child has over the painful event, the predictability of the event, and the appraisal of the event (as a threat that they either do or do not have the resources to cope with).

In order to increase a child's sense of control and predictability, it may be helpful to provide the child with information and include the child as much as possible in decision making and actual treatment procedures (e.g., asking them to choose an arm for an injection). Parental factors have also been demonstrated as having an impact on children's coping. The manner in which a parent re-sponds to a child's verbal and nonverbal expression of pain affects the child's experience and/or report of the pain. Parental anxiety and distress during a pain-ful medical procedure may result in maladaptive child coping, and children may model a parent's dysfunctional somatic response to stressful situations.

Personal resources may mediate a child's experience of pain. For example, the child's level of cognitive development influences their understanding of the causes of their pain as well as the treatment options. In addition, children ascribe various meanings to their pain, which influence their experience and pain ex-pression. Meaning attributed to pain likely differs according to disease-related pain (i.e., loss issues, feeling different from peers) versus more acute trauma. Previous experience with pain can have both a positive and negative impact on coping with subsequent pain. Prior experience affects the child's expectation re-garding the controllability of the situation as well as their ability to cope with the pain. Investigating how a child coped with previous painful experiences may provide useful information for facilitating future coping; however, it may also sensitize a child and increase his or her anxiety before a painful procedure.

There are multiple approaches to treating childhood pain. When selecting a treatment approach, it is critical to consider the individual, familial, situational, and emotional issues affecting the pain, rather than matching a treatment intervention to a certain pain category (e.g., biofeedback for migraine headaches). While a detailed discussion of treatment approaches is beyond the scope of this entry, possible treatment approaches can be categorized as physical, behavioral, and cognitive and are shown in Table 1.

Table 1
Nonpharmacological Pain Interventions

Physical	Behavioral	Cognitive
Surgical techniques	Exercise	Distraction
Anesthetic blocks	Operant conditioning	Attention
Hot and cold stimulation	Relaxation	Imagery
Electrical nerve stimulation	Biofeedback	Thought stopping
Acupuncture	Modeling	Hypnosis
	Desensitization	Music therapy
	Art and play therapy	Psychotherapy

McGrath, 1990, p. 133. © 1990 Guilford Publications, Inc. *Reprinted by permission.*

References

Coleman, C. A., Friedman, A. G., & Gates, D. (1994). Behavioral assessment and treatment of chronic pain in children. In L. Vandecreek, S. Knapp, & T. L. Jackson (Eds.), *Innovations in clinical practice: A source book* (Vol. 13, pp. 55–72). Sarasota, FL: Professional Resource Press.

Karoly, P. (1985). The assessment of pain: Concepts and issues. In P. Karoly (Ed.), *Measurement strategies in health psychology* (pp. 461–515). New York: Wiley.

McGrath, P. (1990). *Pain in children: Nature, assessment and treatment*. New York: Guilford Press.

Siegel, L. J., & Smith, K. E. (1991). Coping and adaptation in children's pain. In J. Bush & S. Harkins (Eds.), *Children in pain: Clinical and research issues from a developmental perspective* (pp. 149–170). New York: Springer-Verlag.

Varni, J. W. (1983). *Clinical behavioral pediatrics: An interdisciplinary biobehavioral approach*. Elmsford, NY: Pergamon Press.

See also: Illness, chronic, in children.

KATHLEEN L. MACNAUGHTON, JAMES R. RODRIGUE,
AND GARY R. GEFFKEN

Paradigms, parenting. Parenting paradigms are sets of assumptions, beliefs, and knowledge held by parents that guide them in rearing their children. According to Grusec, Hastings, and Mammone (1994), parenting beliefs focus on naive theories about what children are like, beliefs about how they develop, notions about the relative importance of internal and external events, and ideas about parental influence and responsibility and about the practical approaches to achieving goals. Grusec and colleagues (1994) identified two important sources of parental cognitions: the *surrounding culture and the local community* and the *parents' childhood experiences* with their own caregivers. Similarly, Reiss, Oliveri, and Curd (1983) argued that family paradigms may be relatively stable and persist over time, possibly even generations; thus, parenting paradigms may become family paradigms when children come to hold the same views of children and parenting as did their own parents.

At the same time, however, Reiss and coworkers (1983) acknowledged that crises and periods of family disorganization may bring about transformations in family paradigms. In his review of the literature, Youniss (1994) showed that parents are sensitive to the broader social environment. Because they are aware of shifts that occur in the social milieu, they can act as mediators of social change by modifying their child-rearing practices in order to better prepare their children to function effectively in these changed social conditions. Hence, the concept of parenting paradigms or approaches explicitly acknowledges that parents are cognitive agents with goals (intended outcomes) for their children and with attitudes, beliefs, and abilities about how their children should be raised. These parental attributes manifest themselves in the particular parenting practices that the parents adopt in daily family life.

One example of the impact of parenting paradigms on the experiences of children in families is in the area of discipline. Historical analyses have shown that a concept of children as inherently bad was prevalent in the past; this view, which stems from the Christian notion of Original Sin, was actively promoted by Calvinist Reformers, by American Puritans, and more recently, by Sigmund Freud, albeit in a secular form. This view of children implies that they require firm parental guidance, strict and even harsh discipline, and education in order to ensure that they learn how to control their impulses and desires. The persistence of the idea that some physical punishment is normal, necessary, and even good may reflect the traditional parenting paradigms and conceptions about the nature of children.

The social constructivist view asserts that parental beliefs reflect the existing values and norms of culture or subculture in which parents live. A fair amount of evidence supporting the constructivist view exists. For example, there is evidence that low and high socioeconomic status (SES) parents differ with respect to concepts of development. Compared to low SES parents, perspectivistic views of development are endorsed more strongly, and categorical views are endorsed less strongly by high SES parents. Research has also revealed that parental SES is related to endorsement of conforming and self-direction values for children and to authoritarian beliefs (Siegel, 1985). In addition, comparison of different ethnic groups within the United States has indicated that Anglo American parents stressed cognitive aspects of intelligence and autonomy more than Asian immigrant and Mexican American parents. Evidence also exists with respect to greater emphasis placed on effort by Chinese and Japanese than American mothers in explanations of academic failure (Miller, 1995).

While parenting paradigms may be relatively stable and even persist for generations within some families, there is considerable evidence that they are likely to vary as the characteristics and circumstances of families and the larger society change. Youniss (1994) discussed evidence that parenting paradigms have changed historically, have varied by social class, and are modified when immigrants move to a new cultural setting.

Child academic outcomes are related positively to parental beliefs stressing an active role of children in cognitive development and are related negatively to beliefs endorsing maturational explanations of cognitive development. Parental endorsement of conformity is related to lower achievement on tests of cognitive development and teacher ratings of incompetence. Parental emphasis on independence is related to academic achievement. Parental endorsement of authoritarian beliefs is related to low levels of child creativity and curiosity. Research also indicates that parental attribution of failure to lack of effort is associated with academic success (Ogasaki & Sternberg, 1993). In short, children's cognitive achievement is related to complex, active, and multidimensional views of children and of cognitive development.

References

Baumrind, D. (1991). Effective parenting during the early adolescent transition. In P. A. Cowan & E. M. Hetherington (Eds.), *Advances in family research* (Vol. 2, pp. 111–163). Hillsdale, NJ: Erlbaum.

Grusec, J., Hastings, P., & Mammone, N. (1994). Parenting cognitions and relationship schemas. *New Directions for Child Development, 66*, 5–19.

Miller, S. A. (1995). Parents' attributions for their children's behavior. *Child Development, 66*, 1557-1584.

Ogasaki, L., & Sternberg, R. J. (1993). Parental beliefs and children's school performance. *Child Development, 64*, 36–56.

Reiss, D., Oliveri, M. E., & Curd, K. (1983). Family paradigm and adolescent behaviour. *New Directions for Child Development, 22*, 77–93.

Siegel, I. E. (Ed.). (1985). *Parental belief systems. The psychological consequences for children.* Hillsdale, NJ: Erlbaum.

Youniss, J. (1994). Rearing children for society. *New Directions for Child Development, 66*, 37–50.

See also: Feminism; Instrumental versus expressive functions.

CAROL KAUPPI AND NURAN HORTAÇSU

Parents Anonymous. *Parents Anonymous* (PA) was cofounded in California in 1970 by Jolly K., an abusive mother, and Leonard Lieber, a psychiatric social worker. Jolly K. felt that frustrated or abusive parents might be better able to understand one another and thus provide the most help. Peer support and understanding develop in PA meetings over time as members discover they share similar negative feelings and child-rearing practices. This community building is important because fear of rejection or punishment often prevents abusive parents from getting the help they need. Members should be aware that the group facilitator has a legal obligation to report current or past child abuse, just as with any other case.

Currently, there are more than 2,000 active PA groups in 48 states across the country. In some states, PA groups also have children's groups. Recognized in 1973 as a nonprofit organization based in Clairmont, California, Parents

Anonymous is staffed by volunteers and relies on outside funding to provide services free of charge to its members.

The philosophy behind Parents Anonymous is similar to other anonymous self-help groups. The qualities shared among self-help groups are to provide a safe environment of nurturance, education, social connection, and alternative resources. PA's daily guidelines encourage parents to claim responsibility for their actions and to recognize that change happens one day at a time. Ultimately, the primary goal of PA is to promote better relationships between parents and their children by instilling within the parents the strength and self-confidence to re-channel destructive attitudes and actions.

All of PA's programs operate on a model of shared leadership between members. The program has seven guiding principles: mutual assistance, empowerment, support, ownership, caring, nonviolence, and anonymity and confidentiality. Parents Anonymous uses these principles to handle related forms of child abuse such as physical abuse, physical neglect, emotional abuse, emotional deprivation, verbal assault, and sexual abuse.

To help parents feel safe, the identity of group members is protected by policies requiring strict anonymity and confidentiality. Group members use only their first names, and no records of the meetings or group discussions are kept. Also meeting times and locations are not publicly disclosed. Only a contact telephone number is given to the public. Sponsors are available for members to contact in a crisis, but perhaps most important, they may call upon other members for help, support, or advice at any time.

PA is believed to be one of the more effective programs for reducing the frequency and severity of child abuse and neglect. However, it is probably true that those parents who are motivated to change stay with the program, while those parents who are not tend to drop out. Some have estimated PA attendees dropout rate at around 20% to 30%, which is still well below that of some psychotherapy approaches. The problem with providing more detailed information on the program's effectiveness comes from the structure of the program itself: Members remain anonymous, no records are kept, and the method of intervention (e.g., therapy and mutual support) is difficult to measure.

Rererences
Ehresman, L. W. (1988, Fall). Parents Anonymous. *Missing/Abused*, *4*, 10–11.
Hunka, C. D., O'Toole, A. W., & O'Toole, R. (1985). Self-help therapy in parents. *Journal of Psychosocial Nursing*, *23* (7), 24–32.
Lieber, L. L. (1983). The self-help approach: Parents Anonymous. *Journal of Clinical Child Psychology*, *12* (3), 288–291.
Moore, J. B. (1983, December). The experience of sponsoring a parents anonymous group. *Social Casework: The Journal of Contemporary Social Work*, *64* (10), 585–593.

See also: Abuse, child; Social support, informal; Stress.

KIER MAXWELL AND SCOTT PHILLIPS

Parents Without Partners. *Parents Without Partners* (PWP) is an international, nonprofit organization founded in 1957 in New York by two single parents: Jim Egleson, a noncustodial parent, and Jacqueline Bernard, a custodial parent. As concerned parents, they felt isolated from society because of their marital status and decided to form a mutual support organization. Following their first newspaper advertisements directed to "Parents Without Partners," 25 single parents attended the first meeting in a Greenwich Village church basement. Later, media attention brought inquiries from all over the United States (Parents Without Partners, 1998).

Parents Without Partners provides single parents and their children with an opportunity for enhancing personal growth, self-confidence, and sensitivity toward others by offering an environment for support, friendship, and the exchange of parenting techniques. Membership consists of 63,000 individuals organized into 400 chapters in the United States and Canada. Ages of members range from 18 to 80 (most have teenage children), and 55% are female. Chapters range in size from 25 to 1,500 members and are run entirely by volunteer members. Information about local chapters and their scheduled activities can be found in local newspapers or in the white pages of the telephone book.

The informal support system of PWP helps provide single parents with an opportunity to socialize with others that are experiencing the same parenting issues and concerns. The diversity of membership can provide an invaluable source for networking and assistance.

The educational programs may vary from chapter to chapter based mainly on the specific needs of the members and the resources available from the community. The social programs provide a mechanism for parents to meet other adults and for their children to meet other children who are sharing some of the common experiences of single-parent families. Furthermore, PWP speaks on behalf of all single parents and their children at conferences, in national coalitions, and in workshops. The International Board of Directors supports legislative policies and priorities to further the interests of single-parent families (Parents Without Partners, 1998)

Parents Without Partners can be contacted at their national headquarters at 401 North Michigan Avenue, Chicago, Illinois 60611-4267.

Reference

Parents Without Partners (1998). *What is Parents Without Partners, Inc.?* [On-line]. Available: http://www.parentswithoutpartners.org/whatis.html.

See also: Divorced families; Single parents.

DEBORAH J. THOMASON

Peace education. There are a number of schools of thought that guide parent education materials and programs. One school teaches a democratic family style and is generally based on the psychology of Alfred Adler. Another school is behavioral in nature and grows from the work of B. F. Skinner and Alfred Bandura. A third group is based on communication theory and on the child's sense of self-expression and responsibility, growing out of the work of Haim

Ginott. Although it is not as widely recognized, another body of parent education literature can be identified and has been called *Parenting for Peace and
Justice* (McGinnis & McGinnis, 1991) or *Parenting for Social Responsibility*
(Myers-Walls, 1996a). This school of thought is not based on a single author or
theorist. The programs place parents and children in their larger world context
and recognize that all people are affected by the events and conditions around
them and also that parenting styles and behaviors have an impact on the surrounding environment. The parenting goals associated with these programs are
that children show empathy and respect for themselves and others, that they
show understanding of the implications of their behavioral choice for others, and
that they feel empowered to change situations they feel are unjust (Myers-Walls,
1996b).

Parents and children live in their homes and interact with their families.
They also live in communities and interact with other institutions and groups.
The skills that are learned in the family and the attitudes and values that are created there impact and are impacted by the larger political and economic context
as well. Most parent education programs address the home and family context
but have nothing to say about the larger world. That is a void filled by peace and
justice or social responsibility programs.

Myers-Walls (1996a) has defined seven key characteristics of Parenting for
Social Responsibility and related programs. First, such programs encourage *an
awareness and sharing of power*. Realizing that power operates in every relationship, the programs teach parents to be aware of their own power and to make
children aware of power relationships. Individuals are encouraged to use their
power for common goals shared by others and to use power with instead of
power over.

Nurturance and empathy comprise the second set of characteristics that allow decisions to be based on the feelings of others. By listening to others, parents and children are encouraged to try to understand perspectives beyond their
own. Unique among parent education programs, programs that teach social responsibility ask that individuals consider people in general, not only family and
friends.

Communication skills are critical and are related to several other sets of
characteristics. This means using active and effective listening as a tool for establishing nurturance and empathy. Sensitive communication also means being
aware of the power of language and whether it is inclusive or exclusive.

Responsibility and empowerment are critical concepts. Rather than blaming
others or withdrawing from difficult situations, problems are seen as related to
one's own life. Boundaries around "home" and "family" are drawn very wide,
perhaps including the earth and all people. A danger is that parents and children
can become overwhelmed with a sense of responsibility or feel guilty about their
contribution to the problems of others when they take on a sense of personal responsibility. Therefore, it is important to encourage a realistic level of
empowerment.

Problem solving and conflict resolution comprise the fifth set of characteristics. Parents and children are encouraged to seek win/win solutions and to look
at conflicts as problems to be solved and as a normal part of life. Solutions to

conflicts should meet the needs of many individuals by using cooperation and creativity.

The sixth group of characteristics stresses *connections and personal impact*. Unlike other parent education programs, these programs address lifestyle and encourage decisions that express caring—for self, others, and the earth. This is based on the concept that all actions impact others and that decisions and lifestyle are not entirely personal. Parents and children are taught to build a sense of community.

Finally, a *sense of hope and commitment to the future* are critical characteristics. Personal responsibility and a focus on the world situation can create despair and hopelessness, so programs emphasize that there is a peaceful and caring future possible. Through understanding social change, parents and children stress the importance of learning and growing and celebrate growth and possibilities.

Myers-Walls (1996a) reported that parent educators appear to support the values and solutions consistent with peace and justice parenting but that they are uncomfortable with the political tone in the Parenting for Peace and Justice label. Therefore, she proposed the Parenting for Social Responsibility reference. Initial reactions indicate increased openness to the latter phrase.

The Institute for Peace and Justice in St. Louis has been the source of much of the practice-oriented literature and programming in this area (see e.g., McGinnis & McGinnis, 1986). Although ecumenical in focus, much of the programming remains religious in nature. The Bahai' community has also produced some literature using this approach (Goding, 1989). Much of the related literature is designed for schools and addresses conflict resolution, diversity training, and communication skills (e.g., conflict negotiation). There is a need for further curriculum development for parent educators using this approach.

References

Goding, P. (1989). *Raising children as peacemakers*. Los Angeles, CA: Kalimat Press.

McGinnis, K., & McGinnis, J. (1991). *Parenting for Peace and Justice*. Maryknoll, NY: Orbis.

McGinnis, J., & McGinnis, K. (1986). *Building shalom families: Christian parenting for peace and justice*. St. Louis, MO: Institute for Peace and Justice.

Myers-Walls, J. A. (1966a, October). *Parenting for peace: Building skills for living at home and in the world*. Keynote presented at the Northwest Parenting Conference, Yakima, Washington.

Myers-Walls, J. A. (1996b). *What are your parenting recommendations?* [questionnaire for parent educators]. West Lafayette, IN: Purdue Cooperative Extension Service.

See also: Conflict resolution; Problem solving.

JUDITH A. MYERS-WALLS

Peer influence. A child's peer is another child, an age mate, who is at an equal level in many respects but not necessarily every aspect. Children's peer relations vary according to the extent of attraction, acquaintance, feelings of liking, and common interests and may take many different forms, such as friend, acquaintance, playmate, adversary, classmate, and teammate. Friends are voluntarily selected associates, whose roles change depending on age and situational variables, and friendship is a specific, bilateral construct that refers to the evolving experience of having a close, mutual, dyadic relation. As children grow older, a peer group, whether it is an informal small clique (a girls' or a boys' clique), a crowd (association of two or more cliques), a gang, a club, or a team, is of major importance. A *peer group* refers to a cluster of associates with a specific structure, and individual members have a sense of belonging and serve as a source of reference or comparison for one another. *Peer status* refers to the standing of a child in a group, based on the view of the group members toward this child. The most common methods used in recent research to assess peer relations are nomination and rating scale sociometrics.

Children's friendships have multiple functions supporting the premise that "peer interaction is a socializing context, not merely the reflection of repertoires acquired in other settings" (Hartup, 1983, p. 164). Children with poor peer relations are at risk for later maladjustment (e.g., dropping out of school, criminality, and psychiatric disturbance) (Parker & Asher, 1987).

Children's conceptions of their friends and their specific expectations undergo a series of transformations with increasing age, mainly deriving from changes in cognitive and language development as well as changes in the child's understanding of social reciprocity. There is considerable evidence that early friendship expectations stress participation in common activities and concrete reciprocities, while later friendship expectations emphasize mutual understanding, intimacy, loyalty, trust, and self-disclosure.

Peer friendships and peer groups tend to be structured around several characteristics—sex, age, and race—and are usually fostered by frequent interactions or physical proximity within the school and community. Children of all ages interact more frequently with same-sex peers and like them better, mainly attributed by many investigators to a combination of encouragement from adults (parents and teachers) and other children, and intrinsic gratification contained in same-sex play activities. With increasing age, peer groups take on their greatest importance, when children have to leave the safety of the family. Peers can play a supportive role mainly in the emotional and sexual domains of development and can further compensate for deficiencies and problems in family relations.

Parents and family relationships influence the quality of children's peer relationships and social competence in indirect and direct ways (Parke & Ladd, 1992). Indirect influences include the parents' relationships with their children (attachment, child-rearing and discipline styles, abuse) and each other (marital discord, divorce), parents' perceptions and attitudes about their children, family stressors (economic deprivation), and parental pathology. Parent-child interactions may serve as models for social behaviors (e.g., sharing, affect regulation) and as teaching context by providing, supporting, or suppressing opportunities for the child to develop and practice social skills.

Available evidence suggests that a secure parent-child attachment relationship and an authoritative parenting style that is characterized by responsiveness and age-appropriate maturity demands facilitate children's development of social competence. On the contrary, children exposed to negative (harsh, coercive) or unpredictable disciplinary styles, marital discord, or child abuse have more difficulties in their peer relationships and are more likely to develop conduct problems, such as aggression and social withdrawal.

Parents influence their children's peer relationships directly (Parke & Ladd, 1992) by "managing" various aspects of children's social lives. Parents set the stage for peer interactions by choosing a neighborhood, school, community activities, and adult friends and by arranging and facilitating peer contacts and activities. There are times when parents need to remove a child from a negative friendship or group, but usually it is important to help children understand friendship and peer breakups and separations. As children grow older, parents appear to use more subtle styles of supervision. Parents may monitor children's contacts by gathering information about peers and activities and advise or "consult" with children.

Several studies indicate that although adolescents and parents have different attitudes about issues of contemporary social concern (e.g., war, drug use, and sexuality), most of these differences rather reflect contrasts in attitude intensity rather than attitude direction. Adolescents' attitudes further depend on parental rearing practices and characteristics of parents. A combination of independence fostering and continued guidance in parents' behavior was found to be critical for close relationships of adolescents with their parents, usually choosing friends with congruent values. Furthermore, the values of a subgroup of similar peers were found to be more influential for adolescents with low performance in school.

References

Hartup, W. W. (1983). Peer relations. In E. M. Hetherington & P. H. Mussen (Eds.), *Handbook of child psychology: Socialization, personality, and social development* (Vol. 4, pp. 103–196). New York: Wiley.

Parke, R. D., & Ladd, G. W. (Eds.). (1992). *Family-peer relationships: Modes of linkage.* Hillsdale, NJ: Lawrence Erlbaum.

Parker, J. G., & Asher, S. R. (1987). Peer relations and later personal adjustment: Are low-accepted children "at risk"? *Psychological Bulletin, 102,* 357–389.

Selman, R. L. (1980). *The growth of interpersonal understanding: Developmental and clinical analyses.* New York: Academic Press.

See also: Siblings.

CHRYSE HATZICHRISTOU

Pets and children. Pets may play an integral part of many families. Over 61% of households (52.5 million) in the United States have one or more pets (Beck, 1990). Children and parents can benefit from the relationship that children can develop with family pets. The companionship of pets is believed by some to help children develop mentally and experience more success during adulthood (Swift, 1996). Parents can use pets to help children to learn responsibility and to provide them with companionship. However, parents should be careful to note any signs of exaggerated cruelty that the child may show toward the pet, which may be a symptom of an emotional problem that needs attention.

The role that pets play in treating children with special needs can be seen in work done with hyperactive children and children in residential group care living environments. This arrangement of pets as therapeutic adjuncts can provide opportunities for improvements when working with children but may have pitfalls as well (Mallon, 1994, 1989). Wishon and Huang (1989) warn that although pets provide companionship, the frequency of pet-associated injuries should be taken into account. Animal assaults often cause permanent and serious physical and emotional injury and even death in some cases. Negative experience with pets can cause children to develop lifelong fears and anxieties. The selection of an appropriate pet is a key factor in preventing pet-related injuries. The following questions may provide some guidance in selection of appropriate pets.

- *Desire.* Does the child "want" a pet? Do they have a clear and complete understanding of all that is involved in caring for a pet? Is it just a "whim"?
- *Type.* What species or breed of pet is most appropriate for the child? Will the adult or mature animal still be appropriate for the home setting?
- *Responsibility.* Can or will the child assume the responsibility for the care and maintenance of the pet? Is the child mature and responsible enough to provide adequate care?
- *Safety.* Is the animal appropriate in size (consider mature size as well), temperament and disposition for the child? Will the animal be in a safe and humane environment?
- *Family lifestyle.* Will the family be able to provide continuous care for the animal? Who will care for the pet when the family is away from home?

Parents can use pets as a valuable asset in the development of a child. Many life skills can be learned by caring for a pet properly. Lessons about grief and death can sometimes be approached when a teachable moment arises. Safety for the child and humane care for the pet must be the primary considerations when selecting a pet.

References
Beck, A. (1990). *The role of animal interaction with children and adolescents: A presentation of studies and practice.* A paper presented at the Center for Applied Ethology and Animal/Human Interaction, West Lafayette, IN.
Mallon, G. P. (1989, May). The trouble with children's best friends. *Children Today*, p. 24.
Mallon G. P. (1994, April). Some of our best therapists are dogs. *Child and Youth Care Forum*, p. 89.
Swift, W. B. (1996, May). What pets teach kids. *Animals*, p. 10.
Wishon, P. M., & Huang A. (1989, May). The trouble with children's best friends. *Children Today*, p. 24.

See also: Prosocial behavior.

DEBORAH J. THOMASON

Physical activity. Physical activity is defined as energy expenditure through body movement. There are many types of physical activity including competitive sports, individual or group recreational activities, exercising, physical activity for transportation (e.g., walking, cycling), and occupational physical activity (e.g., on the job, yard, or housework). Children and youth can derive many benefits from participation in physical activity, and thus it should be encouraged and facilitated by parents, teachers, and other adults working with this age group.

The benefits from physical activity are dependent on the amount of energy expended; there is a dose-response relationship. Moderate levels of physical activity (e.g., a brisk walk) provide numerous health benefits. More intense levels of physical activity will improve physical fitness.

The International Consensus Conference on Physical Activity for Adolescents recommended two guidelines for the amount of physical activity. First, all adolescents should be *physically active daily* or nearly every day as part of their lifestyles. Second, adolescents should engage in *three or more sessions per week* of activities that last 20 minutes or more and that require moderate to vigorous levels of exertion. Available data suggest that the vast majority of United States adolescents meet the first guideline, but only about two thirds of boys and one half of girls meet the second guideline (Sallis & Patrick, 1994, p. 302).

These guidelines ensure that youths derive both the health and the fitness benefits. Youths should also be aware of and be prepared to follow the recent surgeon general's recommendation (U.S. Department of Health and Human Services, 1996) for adults: a moderate amount of physical activity daily.

A brief summary of the physical health benefits from physical activity include reduced incidence of coronary heart disease, stroke, non-insulin-dependent diabetes, osteoporosis, and some cancers (Bar-Or, 1995; U.S. Department of Health and Human Services, 1996). Physical activity also has positive mental health benefits, particularly for depression, and psychological benefits including improved self-esteem and feelings of well-being (Landers, 1997). The 1996 surgeon general's report on physical activity and health endorses the benefits of physical activity and the risks associated with inactivity. It should have a major impact on encouraging physical activity for all ages.

In spite of these important benefits, research has shown that physical activity tends to decline during adolescence. It is important to understand the factors related to participation in physical activity so that it can be promoted. Sallis (1994) provides a summary of the research on the determinants of physical activity. The psychological factors of knowledge, beliefs, and attitudes about physical activity are weak or inconsistent correlates, while self-efficacy (confidence in one's ability to be active) and intentions are stronger correlates and predictors. Sociocultural factors, including socioeconomic status and parental influences, have been shown to be strong influences, and physical environmental variables such as seasonal variations and time spent outdoors have also been found to be related to activity. Enjoyment is another important variable influencing activity levels. One of the main influences on enjoyment is the amount of exertion required.

Sallis (1994) suggests several ways that parents can support children's physical activity. Serving as active role models and providing encouragement are important, but some research shows that parents can have the most impact by directly helping children be active. Parents who participate in activities with their children, organize activities, or transport children to places where they can be active are the most effective supporters. In addition, providing opportunities for a variety of physical activities will ensure that children and youths are able to discover activities that they enjoy. Children should be encouraged to play outdoors everyday, as this is where they are more active.

Several organizations have published documents to assist in promoting physical activity (e.g., Centers for Disease Control and Prevention, 1997; Sammann, 1998). The newly formed *National Coalition for Promoting Physical Activity* should also provide a coordinated effort to encourage all age groups, including children and adolescents, to be more physically active.

In conclusion, research suggests that the effectiveness of physical activity programs should be maximized when participants' confidence about their ability to participate in physical activity is nurtured, they enjoy the activities they have chosen, they receive encouragement and assistance from other people in their lives, and they reside in a supportive environment that provides convenient, attractive, and safe places for physical activity (Sallis, 1994).

References

Bar-Or, O. (1995). Health benefits of physical activity during childhood and adolescence. *Physical Activity and Fitness Research Digest, 2* (4), 1-6.

Centers for Disease Control and Prevention (1997). Guidelines for school and community programs to promote lifetime physical activity among young people. *MMWR 46* (No. RR-6), 1-24.

Landers, D. M. (1997). The influence of exersize on mental health. *Physical Activity and Fitness Research Digest, 2* (12), 1-8.

Sallis, J. F., & Patrick, K. (1994). Physical activity guidelines for adolescents: Consensus statement. *Pediatric Exercise Science, 8,* 302–314.

Sallis, J. F. (1994). Influences on physical activity of children, adolescents, and adults OR determinants of active living. *Physical Activity and Fitness Research Digest, 1* (7), 1–8.

Sammann, P. (1998). *Active youth: Ideas for implementing CDC physical activity promotion guidelines.* Champaign, IL: Human Kinetics.

United States Department of Health and Human Services. (1996). *Physical activity and health: A report of the surgeon general.* Atlanta, GA: United States Department of Health and Human Services.

See also: Obesity; Physical fitness; Sports.

JANICE BUTCHER

Physical fitness. Physical fitness is the body's ability to function efficiently and effectively (Corbin & Lindsey, 1996). It affects a person's ability to work effectively, to enjoy leisure time, to be healthy, and to meet emergencies. It is related to but different from physical health and contributes to total quality of life. Thus, physical fitness is important for the well-being of children and youths.

There are two types of physical fitness: health-related fitness and skill-related fitness. *Health-related fitness* is important for daily functioning at an optimal physical level and for lifelong health. *Skill-related fitness* involves components that are important for skilled athletic performance such as speed, agility, balance, power, coordination, and reaction time. Only health-related physical fitness will be discussed in this entry.

Health-related physical fitness consists of four components: *cardiovascular endurance, muscular strength and endurance, flexibility*, and *body composition*. To improve any of these fitness components, the overload principle must be used (Corbin & Lindsey, 1996). The body must be "overloaded" or worked against a load greater than normal. If exercise is less than normal for a specific component of fitness, the result will be a decrease in that particular component. A normal amount of exercise will maintain the current fitness level. Thus, there is a threshold of training for each fitness component.

Physical fitness can be improved or maintained through participation in general physical activity if it approaches the training threshold. For children, this is usually sufficient. However, adolescents should add a structured exercise program for each of the fitness components to their regular physical activity. This will improve/maintain their fitness levels and will prepare them for adulthood when regular exercise will be essential. Children do not respond to exercise in exactly the same way as adults, but information is well established about developmental exercise physiology and guidelines for training (Rowland, 1996).

Cardiovascular endurance. Cardiovascular (CV) fitness is the efficiency of the heart, lungs, and vascular system in delivering oxygen to working muscles so that prolonged physical work can be maintained (Corbin & Lindsey, 1996). Typical CV activities include running, swimming, cycling, and skiing for relatively long periods of time at moderate intensities. Field assessments done in schools or other programs typically involve running for distance or time. The FITT Principle is a useful guideline for producing the exercise threshold necessary to improve CV fitness: *frequency* (minimum of three times per week), *intensity* (60% to 90% of maximum heart rate, or moderate to high perceived exertion), *time* (the heart rate should be kept in the target zone for at least 20 minutes for a training effect to occur), and *type of activities* (repetitive activities using the large muscle groups).

Muscular strength and endurance. Muscular *strength* is defined as the maximal force exerted in one contraction, while muscular *endurance* involves submaximal force exerted over several contractions. In field tests, muscular strength and endurance are usually measured together using chin-ups, push-ups, and sit-ups. They are improved by performing exercise against a resistance provided by the body itself, free weights, or machine weights. Prepubescent children can derive benefit from weight training but should follow safety guidelines (Kraemer & Fleck, 1993). They should not engage in power lifting of maximum weights.

Flexibility. Flexibility is the range of motion possible at a joint and is quite joint specific. It can be measured with protractorlike instruments (flexometers) but most commonly with a sit-and-reach test. Flexibility declines at any age if joints are not regularly put through a full range of motion. Thus, children and youth should be encouraged to work on their flexibility by performing stretching exercises on all major joints. The best stretches are slow, controlled stretches held for 15 to 30 seconds, done after the body is warmed up. Good flexibility decreases the chances of injuries and improves motor performance.

Body composition. This component involves the relative percentage of fat, muscle, bone, and other tissues of which the body is composed (Corbin & Lindsey, 1996). Although fat serves some important functions in the body, excessive fat is detrimental to good health and performance of motor skills. Individuals should strive for an optimal level of body fat. The best method of fat control is balancing calorie intake and energy expenditure (physical activity). The goal is to eat less and exercise more. Too little fat as a result of eating disorders is also a health problem.

Parents should educate their children about the fitness components and how they can be improved. They should encourage participation in physical activity and exercise programs that will enhance their children's physical fitness and thus their health and well-being. Numerous resources are available including books by Corbin and Lindsey (1997), Foster, Hartinger, and Smith (1992) and Kalish (1996).

References

Corbin, C., & Lindsey, R. (1997). *Fitness for life* (4th ed.). Glenview, IL: Scott Foresman.

Corbin, C., & Lindsey, R. (1996). *Fitness and wellness concepts*. Dubuque, IA: Brown & Benchmark.

Foster, E. R., Hartinger, K., & Smith, K. A. (1992). *Fitness fun: 85 games and activities for children*. Champaign, IL: Human Kinetics.

Kalish, S. (1996). *Your child's fitness: Practical advice for parents*. Champaign, IL: Human Kinetics.

Kraemer, W. J., & Fleck, S. J. (1993). *Strength training for young athletes*. Champaign, IL: Human Kinetics.

Rowland, T. W. (1996). *Developmental exercise physiology*. Champaign, IL: Human Kinetics.

See also: Eating disorders; Obesity; Physical activity; Playground skills; Sports.

JANICE BUTCHER

Physical punishment. Some researchers have suggested that physical punishment is always harmful (Straus & Yodanis, 1996). Physical punishment, however, must be distinguished from child maltreatment. Hitting the face, use of an object (e.g., a belt), or hitting any area of the body repeatedly is inappropriate. An open-handed swat or two on the bottom, however, may be effective with some children in cases of deliberate disobedience. Shaking as a means of physical punishment can have permanent, sometimes fatal, consequences in young children. Excessive use of even mild physical punishment, however, may give children the wrong message about how to handle problems and may contribute to aggressive behavior (Straus & Yodanis, 1996).

Physical punishment, if used, should be an infrequently employed part of a repertoire of various discipline strategies for different situations and developmental stages (Baumrind, 1996). Spanking tends to be less effective than other disciplinary methods for long-term behavioral change. Mild spanking, however, has not been consistently shown to cause long-term damage to children and has been shown to be an effective disciplinary form for young children (Baumrind, 1996). A warm, supportive relationship between parent and child is important for discipline to be beneficial. Mild spanking should occur immediately following the infraction to be effective.

Adults who are not in control of anger, however, should avoid physical punishment. Sometimes a parent who is attempting to physically punish a child can get "carried away." When this happens, the parent may inflict more intense, severe, and repetitive punishment on the child than was originally intended (Belsky, 1993). Many instances of physical child abuse begin as efforts to physically discipline a child (Belsky, 1993), particularly in families with disciplinary repertoires limited to physical punishment. Spanking should be avoided with children who have experienced maltreatment, as it may further undermine the child's trust of adults. Even in the absence of maltreatment, the frequent use of physical punishment can contribute to a loss of respect for authority figures and damage to a child's self-image. Physical punishment may also teach children that the use of physical force is an appropriate means of getting what they want (Straus & Yodanis, 1996).

The parenting process combined with other life stressors, such as economic disadvantage and related problems, may lead to an increase in use of physical punishment. McLoyd (1990), for example, states that economically stressed parents more commonly use power assertion, including physical punishment, in discipline. Parenting children with highly active temperaments may also add to the stress experienced by some parents and contribute to an increase in the use of physical punishment (Belsky, 1993).

The use of physical punishment is widely distributed among various cultures of the world, occurring in 77% of 90 societies studied by Levinson (1989). Within these societies, there are differences in the use of physical punishment among subcultures. Some religious groups, for example, encourage the use of severe forms of corporal punishment even on very young children (Greven, 1991). Developmental stage of a child affects the suitability of corporal punishment. For example, children younger than 2 years of age are too young for spanking to be an effective means of discipline. Similarly, the use of physical punishment with adolescents may be counterproductive (Straus and Yodanis, 1996).

Larzelere (1996) reviewed 35 research articles on child outcomes and parental use of corporal punishment. Outcomes from nonabusive physical punishment were predominantly positive in 26% of studies; negative in 34%; and neutral in 40%, that is, neither positive nor negative. Physical punishment was detrimental in all of the studies that explicitly measured corporal punishment of teenagers but was less harmful with children between the ages of 2 and 6. Severity of punishment was also important. Two spanks to the buttocks, used as a backup to less aversive methods, was primarily associated with beneficial outcomes. More severe punishment was associated with more negative outcomes. African Americans had more positive results from corporal punishment, whereas European Americans had less positive results. In addition, less negative outcomes from physical punishment were found in cases of less frequent use, use in private, use in combination with reasoning, and use in an environment of positive parent-child involvement.

References

Baumrind, D. (1996) The discipline controversy revisited. *Family Relations, 45,* 405–414.

Belsky, J. (1993). Etiology of child maltreatment: A developmental-ecological analysis. *Psychological Bulletin, 114,* 413–434.

Greven, P. (1991). *Spare the child: The religious roots of punishment and the psychological impact of physical abuse.* New York: Alfred A. Knopf.

Larzelere, R. (1996). A review of the outcomes of parental use of nonabusive or customary physical punishment. *Pediatrics, 98,* 824–827.

Levinson, D. (1989). *Family violence in cross-cultural perspective.* Newbury Park, CA: Sage Publications.

McLoyd, V. C. (1990). The impact of economic hardship on Black families and children: Psychological distress, parenting, and socioemotional development [Special issue: Minority children]. *Child Development, 61,* 311–346.

Straus, M. A. & Yodanis, C. (1996). Corporal punishment in adolescence and physical assaults on spouses later in life: What accounts for the link? *Journal of Marriage and the Family, 58,* 825–841.

See also: Conflict resolution; Discipline; Limit setting; Violence, community.

MIRIAM MULSOW AND VELMA MCBRIDE MURRY

Play. Play is the most common activity of young children, integrating and balancing all aspects of human functioning (Rogers & Sawyers, 1988). Play is intrinsically motivated and relatively free of externally imposed rules and is carried out as if the activity were real. In play, the focus is on the process rather than any product. It also requires the active involvement of the players who feel in control (Rubin, Fein, & Vandenberg, 1983).

Play has significant effects on social skills and perspective-taking. *Social skills* refer to children's ability to manage the environment through cooperation, helping, sharing, and successful social problem solving (Rogers & Sawyers, 1988). Conflicts occur between peers because children are egocentric. When children resolve these conflicts, they learn how to manage their environment (Rogers & Sawyers, 1988). Children's social competence with peers is related to the amount of their physical play in the home. Children who have been rated by their teachers as popular are most likely to have parents who engage in physical play with them. Physical play teaches self-control because children learn to become intensely engaged with another person, to stay engaged, and then to disengage when the physical play ends. In addition to self-control, children also learn to decode the emotional states of other people, encode their own emotional states, and communicate their feelings with appropriate facial expressions. Play materials such as blocks, clay, and music may help socially awkward children gain entrance into their social peer groups (Hughes, 1995).

Involvement in dramatic play improves children's ability to understand human relationships. Rogers and Sawyers (1988) reviewed research that indicates that children's frequency of social pretend play predicted their social competence, popularity, and role-taking ability. Also, when children were trained in sociodramatic play, their scores have been found to increase in perspective-taking ability, group cooperation, social participation, impulse control, and social problem-solving skills.

Perspective-taking can be defined as being able to simultaneously consider one's own thoughts, feelings, and visual views of the world along with another's (Rubin & Howe, 1986). Pretend play enables children to develop and practice decentration and reversibility. Decentration involves the ability to simultaneously consider more than a single perspective of an object or event, and reversibility is understanding that a thought carried out in one direction can always be carried out in the opposite direction (Rubin & Howe, 1986). In order to have successful sociodramatic play, children must be able to infer intentions, make distinctions between literal and nonliteral behaviors, and conceptualize role expectations for themselves and their playmates. Psychologists have advocated training young children in sociodramatic play to help them develop decentration skills and perspective-taking or role-playing skills (Rubin & Howe, 1986).

Parents and teachers can ensure that preschool-aged children have the opportunity for play by providing time, space, and materials. Adults should remain available to the children and restrain from interrupting children who are really absorbed in play. In order to avoid play from becoming adult directed, adults can be part of the play, but they must remain in a playful mode and be open to what happens without setting up goals or playing for particular results. Adults also need to provide safety because without it, there is no free play (Gonzalez-Mena & Widmeyer Eyer, 1989).

Adults can also structure a free play environment in order to provide choices for the children. By watching children, parents and teachers make wise choices of play materials to put into the environment to promote *optimum incongruity* between what is already known and a new situation (Gonzalez-Mena & Widmeyer Eyer, 1989). By providing a number of choices of appropriate toys, objects, and occurrences, the parent or teacher gives children the opportunity to move to new situations and new uses of the materials.

Rogers and Sawyers (1988) suggest that adults can foster children's play by providing an environment without excessive verbal or physical restrictions, by being sensitive and responsive to children's play, by offering toys that provide sensory stimulation or feedback, and by matching toys and equipment to children's development. Also, adults should emphasize the process rather than the product, help children take advantage of opportunities to solve problems and think divergently, add more and more complex materials as children become more capable, and provide ample periods for children to select their own activities. Finally, adults should give children control of their make-believe play, build on children's experiences, let the children direct their play, and challenge children to extend their play (Rogers and Sawyers, 1988).

References
Gonzalez-Mena, J., & Widmeyer Eyer, D. (1989). *Infants, toddlers, and caregivers.* Mountain View, CA: Mayfield Publishing Co.
Hughes, F. P. (1995). *Children, play, and development.* Boston, MA: Allyn & Bacon.

Rogers, C. S., & Sawyers, J. K. (1988). *Play in the lives of children*. Washington, DC: National Association for the Education of Young Children.

Rubin, K. H., Fein, G. G., & Vandenberg, B. (1983). Play. In E. M. Hetherington (Ed.), *Handbook of child psychology* (Vol. 4, pp. 693–774). New York: Wiley.

Rubin, K. H., & Howe, N. (1986). Social play and perspective-taking. In G. Fein & M. Rivkin (Eds.), *The young child at play* (pp. 127–139). Washington, DC: National Association for the Education of Young Children.

See also: Imagination; Playground skills; Toys.

TRICIA K. NEPPL

Playground skills. Playground play can have a significant impact on the development of preschool and elementary-age children. Frost and Wortham (1988) summarize the major contributions of playground play to motor, cognitive, social, and emotional development. This entry emphasizes physical playground skills that lead to the development of motor skills and physical fitness.

Physical playground skills are movement skills performed on apparatus typically found in playgrounds such as climbing bars, ladders, swings, and platforms. The most common movement skills and equipment are the following: (1) climbing on ladders, cargo nets, climbing bars, and ropes; (2) hanging (body held stationary) and swinging (body moving) on horizontal bars and ladders, swings, ropes, and rings; (3) locomoting (moving) on beams, bridges, horizontal bars and ladders, and platforms; (4) upper body supports (supporting weight on arms) on horizontal bars and railings; (5) takeoffs and landings by jumping from heights and across spaces (crevices).

These skills are particularly useful for developing the skill-related fitness components of static and dynamic balance, agility, and coordination and perceptual motor skills such as spatial awareness, directionality, and kinesthetic awareness (Alston, 1985). They also develop the physical fitness component of muscular strength and endurance, particularly upper body strength. Playground play is one of the best ways of developing upper body strength, a common deficiency in children.

Like other motor skills, children benefit from instruction, opportunity for practice, and encouragement. Preschool and elementary schools should offer instruction in playground skills to supplement free play. Alston (1985) presents many varied and challenging ideas for promoting playground skills. Parents can also assist by frequently taking young children to playgrounds and encouraging older children to improve their skills. Although Butcher (1993) found that playground proficiency (measured by the Playground Skills Test) was not related to direct parental support, parental perceptions of children's skills and attempts at risk taking were significantly related. Thus, interested parents can facilitate playground skills.

In addition to the motor development and physical fitness benefits, playground play has two other unique features: Children can play on their own without constant direction and organization from adults, as is common in physical education classes and organized sport programs; and second, the activities are self-testing. This means that children can attempt skills that are appropriate for their skill level and can progress at their own rate. Both these features contribute to many psychological benefits for children, including a sense of achievement and competence, improved self-esteem, and a realistic appraisal of their own abilities. Playground play also facilitates risk taking. If children are encouraged to challenge themselves (sensibly) and meet these challenges, psychological development will be enhanced.

One of the primary concerns adults have regarding playground play is safety because the large equipment has potential for injury. Frost (1994) outlines the four major factors that contribute to safety on playground equipment: design of the equipment, proper installation, regular maintenance, and trained supervision. Frost, Bowers, and Wortham (1990) reported on three recent surveys of public elementary school playgrounds (1988), public park playgrounds (1989), and preschool centers (1990) completed by the American Association for Leisure and Recreation. All three found "antiquated design, hazardous conditions, and poor or absent maintenance." Individuals responsible for establishing playgrounds should consult the guidelines of the United States Consumer Product Safety Commission or the Canadian Standards Association.

Those responsible for the design and construction of children's playgrounds should consider several guidelines for building developmentally appropriate playgrounds, as outlined by Frost and Wortham (1988): plan with children; preserve and enhance natural features; establish guidelines for safety; and consider the play, developmental, and curriculum needs of children.

References

Alston, W. G. (1985). *The developmental challenge course in elementary physical education*. Ithaca, NY: Movement Publications.

Butcher, J. (1993). Socialization of children's playground skill. *Perceptual and Motor Skills, 77*, 731–738.

Frost, J. L., & Wortham, S. C. (1988). The evolution of American playgrounds. *Young Children, 43*, 19–28.

Frost, J. L. (1994). Preventing playground injuries and litigation. *Parks and Recreation, 29*, 53–60.

Frost, J. L., Bowers, L. E., & Wortham, S. C. (1990). The state of American preschool playgrounds. *Journal of Physical Education, Recreation and Dance, 61*, 18–23.

See also: Motor development; Physical activity; Physical fitness; Play.

JANICE BUTCHER

Popularity. Popularity is a group-based evaluation of children's sociometric standing within a peer group and should not be confused with *friendship*, a reciprocal relationship between two people. Research on popularity has adopted a classification system utilizing the number of both positive and negative friendship choices received by children within a peer group: *popular* (children who receive a large number of positive nominations and few negative nominations), *rejected* (children who receive a large number of negative nominations and few positive nominations), *controversial* (children who receive large numbers of both positive and negative nominations), *neglected* (children who receive few numbers of either positive or negative nominations), and *average* (children who cannot be placed within either of the four previous categories) (Asher & Coie, 1990). Later research has also shown that the rejected category has two sub-types, namely, high aggressive children, characterized by high aggression, low self-control, behavioral problems, and withdrawal, and low aggressive children, characterized only by withdrawal.

Evidence for the relationship between peer group difficulties and later mal-adjustment exists. Low acceptance in childhood is associated with dropping out of school and juvenile delinquency and crime and other forms of psychopathol-ogy at a later period of life. The risk factor seems to be greater for aggressive than for withdrawn children. There are several explanations for the relationship between peer rejection and later negative life experiences: (1) the same deficit may be responsible for both peer rejection and later maladjustment, (2) peer group acceptance may play a protective role for life stresses, and (3) lack of good relationships within the peer group is detrimental for development of skills necessary for adjustment (Parker & Asher, 1987).

Physical attractiveness, obesity, and motor skill have been associated with acceptance scores among primary school children. Studies comparing different categories of children on a number of dimensions have revealed that popular children are more cooperative, more prosocial, and less disruptive than rejected children. Popular children also engage in leadership behaviors more frequently and ask for help less frequently than rejected children. Neglected children, on the other hand, demonstrate higher levels of academic motivation, are better liked by teachers, and are described by teachers as more prosocial and compliant and as more self-regulated learners than other groups of children. One point to note is that the associations between different behavioral characteristics and peer acceptance show variations with respect to age and sex of child (Schneider, Ru-bin, & Ledingham, 1985).

Research has shown that popular and other groups of children differ with re-spect to cognitive skills. Popular and neglected children are more accurate at identifying facial emotions than rejected children, and popular children demon-strate higher accuracy at interpretation of intentions than average children, who, in turn, are more accurate than rejected children. Rejected children are especially poor at identifying prosocial intentions. Rejected children also display a hostile attribution bias. They perceive hostile intent, especially toward themselves, when the situation is ambiguous. Another cognitive difference between rejected and other categories of children is that rejected children are less likely to attrib-ute the cause of social success to themselves and the cause of social failure to external causes than are other groups of children. Rejected children, especially those classified as low aggressive and withdrawn, also report higher levels of loneliness than any other group (Asher & Coie, 1990; Schneider, Rubin, & Ledingham, 1985).

Differences between rejected and popular children with respect to communi-cation skills and entry behaviors into existing peer groups have also been re-ported. Research has shown that popular children are better at persuading their peers, comforting others, and referential communication—that is, being able to take the other's point of view while explaining something—than rejected children. They also are more likely to take turns and provide explanations than rejected children, who interrupt and respond with irrelevant comments during conversations. In addition, entry behavior of popular children includes more context-relevant comments and better timing of attempts than those of rejected children (Asher & Coie, 1990).

Parents may influence children's peer acceptance through the quality and warmth of their parent-child attachment, the way they respond to their children's aggressive behavior, modeling, coaching social skills, and indirectly monitoring their child's peer relations. Research has shown that parents of rejected children are more likely to make irrelevant comments, more likely to make requests without leaving time for answers, and more likely to leave their child's requests unattended. Mothers of popular children, on the other hand, were more sociable and less disagreeable, were more focused on feeling, were more skilled at group entry behavior, and exhibited more positive-direct and less avoidant and vague behaviors as supervisors than mothers of rejected children (Black & Logan, 1995).

References
Asher, S. R., & Coie, J. D. (1990). *Peer rejection in childhood*. Cambridge: Cambridge University Press.

Black, B., & Logan, A. (1995). Links between communication patterns in mother-child, father-child, and child-peer interactions and children's social status. *Child Development, 66,* 255–271.

Schneider, B. H., Rubin, K. H., & Ledingham, J. E. (1985). *Children's peer relations: Issues in assessment and intervention*. New York: Springer-Verlag.

Parker, J. G., & Asher, S. R. (1987). Peer relations and later personal adjustment: Are low-accepted children at risk? *Psychological Bulletin, 102,* 357–389.

See also: Peer influence.

NURAN HORTAÇSU

Poverty. The United States government defines poverty as the minimum annual income needed to support a family. Specifically, it is the estimated cost of an *economy food budget* multiplied by 3 and adjusted for family size, age of the head of the household, and number of children under age 18. In 1995, the poverty threshold for a two-parent family with two children was $15,455. Low-income families typically include those making 150% of the poverty threshold. Poverty encompasses more than just economic deprivations and so is more pervasive than related concepts such as unemployment and socioeconomic status.

Many American families were under siege in the 1970s and 1980s, due to a combination of a stagnant economy, decreased value of transfer benefits, and policies that magnified income disparities (Huston, 1990). Between 1973 and 1990, the inflation-adjusted median income of families with children, headed by a parent under 30, dropped 32%. Particularly salient is the erosion of real income among the lowest-income families, a decline attributed largely to the higher incidence of female-headed households.

Census data show that poverty is more likely to affect those who are young, unmarried, and minority. First, children constituted 48% of the chronically poor in 1993. Second, mother-only families are much more likely to be poor than married couples with children (52.9% versus 10.8% in 1994) and also are more likely to experience persistent poverty of more than six years. Also, among poor children under age 6, 47% had mothers who first gave birth before age 20; the comparable figure was 17% for nonpoor children. Third, minority families are disproportionately affected by poverty. In 1994, 49% of African American children and 44% of Hispanic children under 6 years of age lived in poverty, compared to 19% of white children. Ethnic disparities are more dramatic when persistent poverty is considered: Of families in poverty, fewer than 5% of white children but 49% of African American children experience chronic poverty.

The most consistent and powerful predictor of youths' well-being is family income. Research shows that children living in poverty are at elevated risk for behavior problems, depression, low self-confidence, and school failure (McLeod & Shanahan, 1993), effects that are independent of family structure and maternal education. Many of the social issues that concern policy makers and citizens alike—delinquency, adolescent pregnancy, school dropout—are more likely to occur among teens living in poverty (National Research Council, 1993). Poverty does have some direct effect on these outcomes by (1) increasing the odds of giving birth to preterm or low-birth-weight infants as a consequence of the mother's inadequate prenatal care; (2) limiting a family's ability to purchase essentials such as adequate housing, food, and health care, which are detrimental to children's health; and (3) restricting the social capital available to them in their neighborhoods and schools. However, poverty seems to cause the most harm to youth because of its corrosive effects on parents.

General barometers of poverty' impact on families include a link between unemployment and the divorce rate, attributable to the impact of financial hardship on family conflict, and an association between poverty and child maltreatment, whether neglect or abuse. The rate of child abuse is nearly seven times higher for those below the poverty line, yet few low-income parents (54 of 1,000) do abuse their children.

More thorough examinations of child-rearing practices show that low-income parents are more likely to be authoritarian in that they value obedience and are less likely to use reasoning, to seek their children's opinions, and to be warm and responsive to their children (McLoyd, 1990). Mothers who are poor also tend to use inconsistent, harsh punishment and are less likely to monitor their children carefully. These differences in social control in turn explain the relation between poverty and children's behavior problems as well as delinquency.

Research on parents' mental health illuminates processes by which poverty affects child rearing (Conger et al., 1994). First, low-income families face much more social adversity than more advantaged families, including neighborhood violence, low education, father absence, and limited access to basic necessities. On the Deprivation Index, for instance, 55% of families in poverty had at least one deprivation as compared to 13% of nonpoor families. These deprivations include eviction, gas or power turned off, not having enough food, crowded housing, and no access to a refrigerator, stove, or phone.

Poverty and its attendant stress create emotional distress, especially depression and irritability. Careful follow-up studies of workers who become unemployed find increased levels of dysphoria and marital conflict. Similarly, individuals in poverty are at much greater risk for a major psychiatric illness. Research with parents consistently shows that poverty produces depression, with clinical levels as high as 60% among low-income single mothers.

Parental depression and irritability affect children by two routes: through increased marital discord, which has a spillover effect, and directly by means of more hostile, coercive interchanges with children. Parents who are emotionally distressed display fewer positive behaviors and are more rejecting in terms of threats, derogatory statements, and hostility (McLoyd & Flanagan, 1990). Depression is strongly related to child neglect and inconsistent, harsh parenting, across economic strata and among families in poverty, although parents' feelings about their role may mediate these effects. Similarly, irritability, especially in relation to children's defiance, predicts child abuse and harsh punishment.

Low-income parents are not uniformly punitive or nondemocratic because studies observe much variability in parenting practices among families living in poverty. This variability is partly due to the impact of social support, which tempers parents' emotional distress and punitive child rearing. The benefits of support can be observed at the neighborhood level as well, where rates of child abuse in low-income areas are lower if there are more social exchanges among families.

Finally, poverty affects the cognitive stimulation available in the home, which in turn influences children's cognitive development and academic success. Although income is not strongly related to parents' expectations for their children's school success, there are consistent differences in family resources and parenting strategies that promote academic achievement. Even after other factors are taken into account, such as parent education and marital status, poverty still explains variations in the home learning environment. Within poverty samples, resilient children are much more likely to grow up in family environments that have adequate stimulation and that are relatively uncrowded and safe. It is for this reason that early interventionists focus on home-based parent education or enriched substitute care as means to compensate for the detrimental effects of poverty.

References

Conger, R. D., Ge, X., Elder, G. H., Lorenz, F. O., & Simons, R. L. (1994). Economic stress, coercive family process, and developmental problems of adolescents. *Child Development, 65*, 541–561.

Huston, A. C. (Ed.). (1990). *Children in poverty: Child development and public policy.* Cambridge: Cambridge University Press.

McLeod, J. D., & Shanahan, M. J. (1993). Poverty, parenting, and children's mental health. *American Sociological Review, 58*, 351–366.

McLoyd, V. C. (1990). The impact of economic hardship on black families and children: Psychological distress, parenting, and socioemotional development. *Child Development, 61*, 311–346.

McLoyd, V. C., & Flanagan, C. (Eds.). (1990). *New directions for child development (#46). Economic stress: Effects on family life and child development*. San Francisco: Jossey-Bass.

National Research Council. (1993). *Losing generations: Adolescents in high-risk settings*. Washington, DC: National Academy Press.

See also: Socioeconomic status.

DAVID MACPHEE

Premature birth. Approximately 5% to 7% of all infants born in the United States are born prematurely, have low birth weight, or both. Most premature infants are born to middle-class mothers. However, factors related to poverty such as quality of prenatal care are strongly associated with high-risk births. Proportionately, preterm births are more common in the African American population (O'Brien, Soliday, & McClusky-Fawcett, 1995).

Prematurity is defined by the American Medical Association Standards as birth occurring before 36.5 weeks gestation, or earlier than 3.5 weeks before the expected date of birth. A second commonly used criterion for prematurity is low birth weight. Infants weighing less than 2,500 grams (5.5 pounds) are classified as low birth weight, those weighing less than 1,500 grams (3.5 pounds) are classified as very low birth weight, and those weighing below 1,000 grams are considered extremely low birth weight. Approximately 1% of infants born prematurely in the United States weigh less than 1,500 grams. It is important to consider both criteria of age and weight in determining prematurity because although small, birth weights of these infants are often in proportion to their gestational age. Infants weighing below the 10th percentile who are considered "small for their gestational age" are at higher risk for later health and developmental difficulties than other prematurely born infants (Nowicki, 1994).

The survival rate of preterm and low birth weight infants has increased dramatically over the past 20 years. Today, even infants weighing under 1,000 grams are given a better than 50% chance of survival. Concomitant with increased survival rates has come a dramatic increase in the amount of time high-risk infants are hospitalized after birth. Admission to a Neonatal Intensive Care Unit (NICU) is a stressful experience for both infants and parents (Miles, 1989). For infants, the continuous presence of monitors and other technological equipment makes the NICU experience very different from the uterine environment or from a standard hospital nursery. The infant's appearance may also be a source of stress for parents. Premature infants often have ruddy complexions, long, narrow heads, poor muscle tone, and highly flexible joints. They may also startle more easily and emit a high-pitched cry. Sleep and feeding disturbances are also characteristic and may persist into the first two years of life (O'Brien, Soliday, & McClusky-Fawcett, 1995).

Additional parental stressors include those produced by an unexpected delivery and concern about the infant's health. The sterile medical environment of the NICU can exacerbate the difficulties parents experience in their attempts to bond with and feel close to their infant (Meyer et al., 1995). Additionally, they may feel a sense of helplessness in their inability to comfort and alleviate their infant's pain. Uncertainty about treatment outcome and the need to communicate with a wide array of medical personnel may also exacerbate parental stress. Parents may become hypervigilant to health care providers' nonverbal behaviors and thereby form expectations based on information that may be unrelated to their infants' health status. Staff behaviors and communications clearly can have a profound impact on parents' attitudes toward their premature infants (Miles, 1989). Overall, these very early stressful experiences of prematurely born infants and their parents can subsequently affect parental attitudes, behaviors, and the parent-child relationship.

Prematurely born infants who spend time in the NICU tend to be less responsive and less socially active when released from the hospital than their full-term counterparts. At their expected date of birth, premature infants have been observed to fuss and cry more, to be harder to soothe, and to change their state more frequently than full-term infants. While the smallest preterms tend to experience the greatest difficulties, all infants born prematurely may experience delayed development in the physical, cognitive, social-emotional, and behavioral areas. Despite these initial delays, most infants catch up to their full-term peers during the first year of life, although a higher than would be expected proportion of premature infants are classified with learning disabilities and/or require special services later in childhood (O'Brien, Soliday, & McClusky-Fawcett, 1995).

The potential impact of parental beliefs and attitudes on the developing relationship between parents and these infants has become an area of concern. Negative beliefs about prematurity are thought to influence parental expectations, thus laying the groundwork for the development of a self-fulfilling prophecy. Parents' reactions to and behaviors toward prematurely born infants become based on beliefs that the infant is vulnerable rather than the actual cues and capabilities exhibited by the infant. Nonexperimental evidence for such a process is available. Research examining mother-infant interactions has shown that mothers treat premature infants differently from full-term infants even when evidence is available that the premature infants are capable and competent and that their behavior is objectively no different from their full-term counterparts (Barnard, Bee, & Hammond, 1984). The potential for long-term consequences of this differential treatment is suggested by studies that find a persistent relationship between behaviors observed in early mother-infant interactions and later infant and child competence (Beckwith, Rodning, & Cohen, 1992).

Parental beliefs about their premature infants' level of development and subsequent attributions regarding behaviors can have a damaging impact on future parent-child interactions (Himelstein, Graham, & Weiner, 1991). One program of research has experimentally documented that parents hold a negative set of beliefs about premature infants and that these beliefs may be associated with undesirable adult behaviors and infant outcomes. This set of beliefs has been labeled a *prematurity stereotype*, and evidence is available suggesting that it is a pervasive phenomenon that subsequently affects parenting and child developmental outcomes (Stern & Karraker, 1992).

References

Barnard, K., Bee, H., & Hammond, M. (1984). Developmental changes in maternal interactions with term and preterm infants. *Infant Behavior and Development, 7*, 101–113.

Beckwith, L., Rodning, C., & Cohen, S. (1992). Preterm children at early adolescence and
continuity and discontinuity in maternal responsiveness from infancy. *Child Development, 63*, 1198–1208.

Himelstein, S., Graham, S., & Weiner, B. (1991). An attributional analysis of maternal
beliefs about the importance of child-rearing practices, *Child Development, 62*, 301–
310.

Meyer, E. C., Garcia Coll, C. T., Seifer, R., Ramos, A., Kilis, E., & Oh, W. (1995). Psychological distress in mothers of preterm infants, *Journal of Developmental and Behavioral Pediatrics, 16*, 412–17.

Miles, M. S. (1989). Parents of critically ill premature infants: Sources of stress. *Critical
Care Nursing Quarterly, 12*, 69–74.

Nowicki, P. T. (1994). Neonatal problems. In R. A. Olson, L. L. Mullens, J. B. Gillman,
& J. M. Chaney (Eds.), *The sourcebook of pediatric psychology* (pp. 11–25). Boston,
MA: Allyn & Bacon.

O'Brien, M., Soliday, E. & McClusky-Fawcett, K. (1995). Prematurity and the neonatal
intensive care unit. In M. Roberts (Ed.), *Handbook of pediatric psychology* (pp. 463–
478). New York: Guilford Press.

Stern, M., & Karraker, K. (1992). Modifying the prematurity stereotype in mothers of
premature and ill full-term infants. *Journal of Clinical Child Psychology, 21*, 76–82.

See also: Attachment, secure; Self-fulfilling prophecy; Vulnerable Child Syndrome.

MARILYN STERN AND LUCILLE LARNEY

Prevention. Ineffective parenting, in concert with family stress, contributes
to a host of dysfunctions in youth, ranging from antisocial behavior and delinquency to substance use and early childbearing. The current child welfare system reacts to such problems, especially child abuse, by treating the full-blown
symptoms rather than their causes. Remedial approaches for troubled families
are expensive and often ineffective, with over half of abusive families involved
in intensive treatment likely to mistreat their children again. An alternate strategy is to prevent the occurrence of parenting problems by either attacking
known risk factors or optimizing family resources and strengths. Put differently,
prevention is about changing the odds, not beating them.

Effective prevention requires a theory that links risk conditions, mediating
processes, and maladaptive outcomes (Coie et al., 1993). A program can then be
designed to modify one or more of these causal mediators. Certain risk factors
are common to a variety of family problems, including poverty, single or adolescent parenthood, and domestic violence in the family of origin. As well, key
mediating processes are implicated in a variety of family dysfunctions, such as
inconsistent, punitive parenting, unrealistic expectations, distorted appraisals of
the child, low self-esteem and social support, and ineffective coping skills. Thus,
well-conceived prevention efforts can both test the efficacy of programs and
provide insights into etiology, if a risk factor is minimized but the problem is not
altered.

Prevention efforts can be initiated at different stages in the emergence of a problem. *Primary or universal* prevention is a public health approach that provides services to the general population, with the intention to educate or alleviate a widespread risk. Public service announcements about child abuse and family life programs in public schools are examples. *Secondary or targeted* prevention focuses on families who are at risk and tries to prevent that high-risk status from being translated into maladaptive behavior. Thus, adolescent mothers often are recruited for secondary prevention because they are under much stress, are less knowledgeable about development, and are less likely to use nurturant child-rearing practices. Secondary prevention is particularly critical with parents at high risk for maltreatment, before coercive and avoidant patterns become ingrained. Finally, *tertiary or indicated* prevention is a remedial approach that treats a manifest problem on a case-by-case basis. One example is *Homebuilders*, an intensive family support program for parents who are facing removal of their children from the home.

Prevention efforts also can vary in scope, from categorical to comprehensive. Schorr (1989) is critical of single-purpose programs because they fragment lives, dilute effectiveness, and duplicate services. One common denominator of successful programs is that they provide comprehensive services to the family, such as health care, education, family support, and a liaison to community resources (Price et al., 1989). The emergence of ecological models of parenting has led to more emphasis being placed on family interactions, stresses, and supports in both family resource programs and abuse prevention efforts (Weissbourd & Kagan, 1989). This emphasis reflects the assumption that "the stresses and oppressive conditions in parents' own lives must be addressed before they will embrace their role as parents" (Bernstein, Hans, & Percansky, 1991, p. 32). On the other hand, comprehensive services can be costly.

Contemporary prevention programs are distinguished by their emphasis on (1) protective factors that enhance resilience, notably competent parenting, (2) attention to families' individual needs and strengths, (3) ecological factors, especially coping with stress, and (4) attention to the developmental origins of problems (Roberts et al., 1991). These elements are evident in the sample prevention strategies discussed next. The reader is cautioned that many local programs are never evaluated, and many that are evaluated are badly flawed in their design and implementation. Shortcomings include lack of comparison groups, informal self-reports of change, small samples, poorly defined or unmeasurable objectives, and short-term interventions that are not intense enough to effect change. Thus, our knowledge of what works with families is based on a limited number of prevention programs.

Instructional media. This prevention strategy emphasizes the dissemination of information through age-paced newsletters or advice booklets. Written material may, however, be an impediment for low-literacy groups, including teen mothers.

Classes and workshops. When parenting information is conveyed to groups, new opportunities arise for modeling, practice, social support, and verifying that skills are being learned.

Home visitation. In England, public health nurses visit all new mothers in order to provide parent education, support, and referrals to community resources. More intensive services are given to families who need them. The United States, in contrast, has a piecemeal approach that is focused on high-risk parents. Demonstration studies have shown that home visitation is highly effective with at-risk populations, particularly young mothers and low-income or multiproblem families.

Comprehensive services. The above approaches can be combined, typically when a community undertakes a concerted primary prevention program to reduce child abuse or when the problem has multiple causes and is intractable in its later stages.

Prevention efforts that target parents usually are more effective and less costly than treatment or social casework models. It is therefore surprising that family resource programs, as a means to address social ills, are neglected in the policy arena.

References
Bernstein, V. J., Hans, S. L., & Percansky, C. (1991). Advocating for the young child in need through strengthening the parent-child relationship. *Journal of Clinical Child Psychology, 20*, 28–41.
Coie, J. D., Watt, N. F., West, S. G., Hawkins, J. D., Asarnow, J. R., Markman, H. J., Ramey, S. L., Shure, M. B., & Long, B. (1993). The science of prevention: A conceptual framework and some directions for a national research program. *American Psychologist, 48*, 1013–1022.
Price, R. H., Cowen, E. L., Lorion, R. P., & Ramos-McKay, J. (1989). The search for effective prevention programs: What we learned along the way. *American Journal of Orthopsychiatry, 59*, 49–58.
Roberts, R. N., Wasik, B. H., Casto, G., & Ramey, C. T. (1991). Family support in the home: Programs, policy, and social change. *American Psychologist, 46*, 131–137.
Schorr, L. (1989). *Within our reach*. New York: Anchor.
Weissbourd, B., & Kagan, S. (1989). Family support programs: Catalysts for change. *American Journal of Orthopsychiatry, 59*, 20–31.

See also: Discipline; Limit setting; Misbehavior.

DAVID MACPHEE

Prison, parents in. Parents in prison are incarcerated mothers or fathers with children below the age of 18. About 1.5 million American children have a parent who is incarcerated (Adalist-Estrin, 1995). While the overall imprisonment rate has increased substantially during the last 15 years, the rise has been particularly dramatic among women. From 1984 to 1994, the number of incarcerated women tripled (Boudouris, 1996). Even so, more than 90% of prisoners are male.

Research on how children are affected by parental imprisonment is limited. Historically, incarcerated offenders have been the focus of public policy concerns, not their families. Parents in prison tend to have low educational and job skill levels. As children, they were often separated from their own parents, and their backgrounds frequently include parental addiction to alcohol or drugs, molestation, and exposure to domestic and community violence. Approximately 6% of women enter prison pregnant (Gabel & Johnston, 1995).

When a parent goes to prison, children experience a difficult separation, loss, and grief process. Common emotional reactions include shock, rage, depression, guilt, and blame as well as accompanying physical problems such as sleep disturbances and stomachaches. Although embarrassment about having an incarcerated family member appears to vary somewhat across subcultures, children and other family members struggle with powerful feelings of shame and isolation. In addition to the emotional trauma and role strain, the family usually suffers financially. In two-parent families, children instantly find themselves living in a solo parent home.

Particularly in cases of a mother's incarceration, children may need to move out of their primary residence into a home with a grandparent, another family member, or foster parents. Often the children are traumatically separated from their familiar settings, routines, and friendships. These family stressors result in challenges in areas such as self-esteem, sociability, concentration, health, and participation in school and extracurricular activities (van Nijnatten, 1997).

A primary need of incarcerated parents and their children is contact with each other. Both mothers and fathers in prison need parent-child contact, but incarcerated mothers usually require additional services because their parental rights are more likely to be terminated because of their offense (Gabel & Johnston, 1995).

Visitation programs are vital to family functioning, as are other forms of familial contact. The parent-child relationship thrives on personal visits and regular telephone and letter exchanges (Gabel & Johnston, 1995).

Children need to feel loved, understood, and encouraged regardless of their parental circumstances. When a parent is incarcerated, children receive mixed signals about the formulation of values (Hostetter & Jinnah, 1993). In a developmentally appropriate way, a child needs accurate information about the events surrounding his or her parent's incarceration. Children require plenty of opportunities to talk about their feelings, process their value questions, and work through the shame, grief, and isolation associated with having a parent jailed or imprisoned.

A growing number of parenting education and family strengthening programs serve parents in prison. Interventions include children's centers in prisons, parenting skill programs, tutorial assistance, camping experiences, self-help groups, transportation services, emergency provisions, and legal advice. The *Family and Corrections Network* provides a state-by-state listing of such programs on the Internet.

Given current societal trends, the number of children with parents in prison may continue to rise in the immediate future. Currently only a small number of states have legislation that recognizes problems in children associated with parental incarceration (Gabel & Johnston, 1995). Among pressing needs that correctional professionals, researchers, social workers, educators, and therapists must address are the following:

- The parenting role of incarcerated men and women needs more attention in the arenas of research, public policy, and service delivery. In addition to issues of personal responsibility, key systemic factors, such as poverty, that feed the cycle of incarceration should also be examined.

- In an age-appropriate way, children need to receive open and honest communication about the events leading up to and surrounding the incarceration of their parents. Secrets, deception, and misinformation only serve to worry, confuse, and undermine a child's sense of trust. In rare cases where contact with an imprisoned parent would be clearly detrimental, children require assistance in coming to terms with this devastating fact.
- Children need many opportunities to share their feelings, thoughts, and struggles about having a parent in prison. In order to heal from their multiple losses, children, parents, and key family members must journey through a difficult grief process.
- Healthy parent-child contact and bonding are critical during the prison experience. Regular visitation and sharing by mail and phone build a foundation for successful family functioning after the parent's release. Parenting education is essential.
- Imprisoned parents should be treated with dignity and compassion while being held responsible for making positive life changes. For both parent and child, acceptance, forgiveness, courage, and the willingness to start afresh are indispensable skills.

References

Adalist-Estrin, A. (1995). Strengthening inmate-family relationships: Programs that work. *Corrections Today, 57* (7), 116–117.

Boudouris, J. (1996). *Parents in prison: Addressing the needs of families.* Philadelphia, PA: Braceland.

Gabel, K., & Johnston, D. (Eds.). (1995). *Children of incarcerated parents.* New York: Lexington Books.

Hostetter, E. C. & Jinnah, D. T. (1993). *Families of adult prisoners* [On-line]. Available: http://www.ifs.univie.ac.at/uncjin/mosaic/famcorr/famcorrpt.html.

van Nijnatten, C. (1997). Children in front of the bars. *International Journal of Offender Therapy and Comparative Criminology, 41* (1), 45–51.

See also: Attachment, secure; Role strain; Separation anxiety; Single parents.

MARCIA M. BELL AND SAM QUICK

Problem solving. Children differ dramatically in the way they approach a problem. When a request for the coveted toy a 4-year-old wants from another child is predictably rejected, one child might hit the child, another might grab the toy, a third might tell his mother, and a fourth might walk away, giving up in despair. When one particular boy, Richard, wanted a wagon that Peter was pulling, a request Peter also rejected, Richard did something different. He asked Peter why he could not have it. When told, "I need it, I'm pulling the rocks," Richard then suggested, "I can help you pull the rocks. We can pull them together." Then the two boys went off playing happily together.

Richard's ability to mesh his needs with those of Peter's, instead of thinking only of "me, me," resulted in success and a feeling of pride instead of frustration and failure. A series of research studies have shown that while children who are socially competent can *think* of grabbing and hitting others for what they want, they can also think of more prosocial, nonforceful ways such as the one Richard executed (Shure, 1993).

Why is ability to think through and solve everyday conflicts so important? Research (reviewed in Spivack & Shure, 1982) has shown that youngsters who can recognize that behavior has causes and consequences, that people have feelings, and that there is more than one way to solve a problem are less likely to behave aggressively, be less impatient, and are less likely to lose control in the face of frustration than poor problem solvers. These are the very behaviors that can predict later, more serious problems such as violence, substance abuse, and teen pregnancy. Poor problem solvers can also display overly shy, withdrawn behaviors, an early high-risk sign of later depression and, in extreme cases, even suicide.

Another series of studies (Spivack & Shure, 1982) set out to test whether behavior could be guided by teaching children how to think about what they are doing, in light of how they and others feel, the impact their behavior has on others (consequences), and what else they could do to solve the problem (alternative solutions), instead of focusing directly upon the behaviors themselves. If these problem-solving skills do mediate behavior, the intervention designed to train these skills would pinpoint those problem-solving skills that play the most significant role in the behavior adjustment of youngsters 4 to 6 years of age.

A four-month intervention program (Shure, 1996b) was designed with early games consisting of word concepts that can set the stage for later problem-solving thinking. For example, the word *different* is taught to help children later think about *different* ways to solve a problem (alternative solution thinking). The words *not*, *because*, and *might* are taught to help children later think about whether an idea *is* or is *not* a good one *because* of what *might* happen next (e.g., "I might hurt him if I hit him," "He hit me because I hit him" [consequential thinking]). Subsequent games focus on recognition and awareness of children's own and others' feelings to help enrich the range and nature of solutions and consequences to problems in hypothetical children (in pictures or with puppets). Children are never told specific solutions or consequences. Rather, they are encouraged to generate their own ideas and then to think about how people might feel or what they might do. The goal is to teach children *how* to think, not what to think, so they can choose and evaluate for themselves what, and what not to do, and why.

In addition to parents teaching their children problem-solving skills, the program helps parents reach the capacity for problem solving through a progression along four levels (in Shure, 1996a, 1996b, 1996c).

1. *Power Assertion: punishment, demanding, commanding, Belittling* (e.g., Go to your room right now!)

2. *Positive Alternative: suggestions without explanation* (e.g., You should share)

3. *Induction: explanations and reasoning* (e.g., If you hit him, you might hurt him)

4. *Problem Solving: child is guided to think of feelings, solutions, consequences* (e.g., What's the matter? What's the problem?).

Level 4 dialoguing and problem-solving skills reduce high-risk behaviors at all ages (Shure, 1993; Spivack & Shure, 1982).

References

Shure, M. B. (1993). *Interpersonal problem solving and prevention* (Research and training final report, No. MH-40801). Washington, DC: National Institutes of Mental Health.

Shure, M. B. (1996a). *Raising a thinking child audio*. New York: Bantam, Doubleday, Dell Audio Pub.

Shure, M. B. (1996b). *Raising a thinking child: Help your young child to resolve everyday conflicts and get along with others*. New York: Henry Holt.

Shure, M. B. (1996c). *Raising a thinking child workbook*. New York: Henry Holt.

Spivack, G., & Shure, M. B. (1982). Interpersonal cognitive problem solving and clinical theory. In B. Lahey & A. E. Kazdin (Eds.), *Advances in child clinical psychology* (Vol. 5, pp. 323–372). New York: Plenum.

See also: Aggression, childhood; Conflict resolution; Prosocial behavior; Shyness.

MYRNA B. SHURE

Prosocial behavior. Prosocial behavior is voluntary, intentional behavior intended to benefit others, such as helping, sharing, and comforting. Many factors including self-gain, social approval, sympathy, and moral values may motivate prosocial behavior. One type of prosocial behavior is altruistic behavior, prosocial behaviors that are motivated by sympathy or moral values rather than rewards, social approval, or concern about guilt (see Cohen, 1990; Eisenberg & Fabes, 1998).

By 12 months of age, infants frequently express agitation and disturbance in reaction to viewing others in distress, and by 18 months of age, they sometimes try to help, share with, or comfort other people. At a young age, children may not fully distinguish between their own and another person's inner states and are apt to confuse the two; thus, their attempts to help others often consist of giving the other person what they themselves find most comforting or helpful. The appropriateness and quantity of children's prosocial behaviors increase with age (Eisenberg & Fabes, 1998).

Because young children are capable of performing prosocial behaviors, it is likely that their prosocial responding can be influenced even at 1 or 2 years of age. Socializers of children's prosocial responding include cultural influences, parents, siblings, and the schools.

The frequency of children's prosocial and cooperative actions differs considerably across cultures. Children reared in traditional rural subcultures and traditional, semiagricultural settlements cooperate more than do children reared in modern, urban settings (i.e., they are more likely to work well on a task that benefits both oneself and others). Children who are in the process of assimilating or are exposed to the dominant, urban culture in their school tend to be less cooperative than children from the same cultural group with less exposure to urban society. Although it is not very clear why such cross-cultural differences occur, there is some evidence that cultures characterized by warm, supportive parenting produce more cooperative, prosocial children. In addition, cultures vary in the degree to which they specifically value, teach, and reinforce positive or negative values and behaviors. In traditional cultures, the survival of the family and the group often is dependent on cooperation and helping among kin and neighbors. Consequently, the child's routine, everyday chores and activities in-

volve cooperation and prosocial actions. In fact, cultural variation in the degree to which children are assigned chores that significantly contribute to the well-being of the family has been associated with cultural differences in children's prosocial behavior. Thus, the structure of traditional, nonurban, subsistence cultures seems to promote a cooperative, prosocial orientation, at least in regard to other members of the child's own community (see Eisenberg & Mussen, 1989).

Differences among children in their prosocial behavior also appear to be related to socialization within the home and the schools. Prosocial children tend to have parents who model prosocial actions and value prosocial behaviors. In addition, children's prosocial behavior appears to be fostered by parental use of reasoning in disciplinary interactions rather than primarily punishment or threats. Socializers also can foster prosocial tendencies by providing opportunities for children to engage in prosocial actions; children who are subtly induced to assist others but do not feel forced to do so are more likely to help on subsequent occasions. Although praising children for prosocial behavior may foster such behavior, particularly if children are led to believe that they are helpful people, concrete rewards for prosocial behavior may undermine prosocial development in the long run (even though they can increase prosocial responding in a particular context). Moreover, parents' and teachers' verbalizations that encourage children's perspective-taking, empathy, and sympathy seem to be linked to prosocial action. For example, parents of Europeans who rescued Jews from the Nazis during World War II tended to model and teach their children prosocial values, emphasized caring for others and extending ethical principles to a wide spectrum of humanity, used reasoning rather than punitive discipline with their children, and had warm, respectful relationships with their children (Eisenberg & Murphy, 1995).

Parental practices that foster children's tendencies to experience others' negative emotion (empathy) and to sympathize are perhaps most clearly associated with the development of children's altruism. This is not surprising because sympathetic people are more prosocial than are other people. It appears that parents can facilitate sympathetic and altruistic responding even in young children (e.g., 1- and 2-year-olds) if they encourage their children to consider the consequences of their behaviors for others and, through their level of affect, make it clear that the parent is concerned about the child's behavior (Eisenberg & Fabes, 1998; Radke-Yarrow, Zahn-Waxler, & Chapman, 1983).

Children also may learn prosocial behaviors in their interactions with siblings. By 18 months of age, siblings are capable of sharing, comforting, and cooperating with each other. There is some evidence that the quality of the sibling relationship influences the degree to which siblings engage in prosocial actions with one another. Older children, in particular, are exposed to opportunities to learn prosocial behaviors because of their opportunities for caregiving and helping of younger siblings (see Eisenberg & Fabes, 1998).

In addition, teachers and schools influence children's prosocial development. For example, school-based programs that emphasize rational discipline (e.g., the use of reasoning), cooperation, prosocial values, and student participation in rule

setting, and that provide activities designed to enhance children's sympathy and understanding of others, appear to foster elementary school children's prosocial behavior. Moreover, quality of the teacher-child relationship has been related to children's sensitivity and empathy with unfamiliar peers. Moreover, contemporary teacher-child relations better differentiated peer outcomes for children than did contemporary maternal attachment relations or child care history. In addition, television appears to be a socializer of prosocial as well as aggressive behavior; children who view programs with prosocial content tend to be slightly more prosocial (Eisenberg & Fabes, 1998; Radke-Yarrow, Zahn-Waxler, & Chapman, 1983).

Of course, the influences of the culture, home, and school must all be considered, as must aspects of the child's personality that could affect how socializers interact with and discipline a child. However, it appears that it is possible to foster caring behavior in children.

References

Cohen, A. (1990). *The brighter side of human nature: Altruism and empathy in everyday life*. New York: Basic Books.

Eisenberg, N. (1992). *The caring child*. Cambridge: Harvard University Press.

Eisenberg, N., & Fabes, R. A. (1998). Prosocial development. In W. Damon (Series Ed.) & N. Eisenberg (Vol. Ed.), *Handbook of child psychology: Vol. 3. Social, emotional, and personality development* (5th ed., pp. 701–778). New York: Wiley.

Eisenberg, N., & Murphy, B. (1995). Children's prosocial and moral development. In M. Bornstein (Ed.), *Handbook of parenting: Vol. 4. Applied and practice parenting* (pp. 227–257). Hillsdale, NJ: Lawrence Erlbaum.

Eisenberg, N., & Mussen, P. H. (1989). *The roots of prosocial behavior in children*. Cambridge: Cambridge University Press.

Radke-Yarrow, M., Zahn-Waxler, C., & Chapman, M. (1983). Prosocial dispositions and behavior. In P. H. Mussen (Series Ed.) & E. M. Hetherington (Vol. Ed.), *Handbook of child psychology: Vol. 4. Socialization, personality, and social development* (4th ed., pp. 469–545). New York: John Wiley & Sons.

See also: Conscience; Moral development.

NANCY EISENBERG

Psychological testing. Psychological testing refers to the use of psychometrically precise tests to measure individual characteristics and achievement (Simeonsson, 1986). A psychological test is administered and scored according to procedures specified in the test manual. Psychological tests are said to be standardized because these procedures remain the same for each administration of the test.

An individual's test score obtained during the administration of a psychological test can be compared to a norm. As implied, the norm represents average performance and is determined during development of the test when it is administered to a large sample of individuals chosen to be representative of persons for whom the test is designed. Age and other demographic characteristics usually define the norm group.

The score of an individual on a standardized psychological test therefore has meaning and is interpreted relative to the performance of others of similar age and demographic characteristics. There are no criteria for passing or failing a psychological test. For example, a score on a test measuring knowledge of vocabulary words obtained by a 6-year-old is interpreted with respect to scores obtained by a large sample of 6-year-olds during development of the test. In this way one can determine whether the individual's score is equal to, above, or below that obtained by other 6-year-olds.

Parents may have experience with psychological testing for a variety of reasons. Their child may be a participant in a research study, or parents may wish to determine if their child is eligible for participation in a gifted program. Because Public Law 94–142, the *Education for All Handicapped Children Act*, mandates parental involvement in the educational planning process for children with handicapping conditions, parents' experiences with psychological testing often results when their children are referred for psychological assessment due to suspected learning disability, emotional difficulty, mental retardation, or other condition that is compromising adjustment and educational achievement.

Psychological testing is an important component of the more broadly defined assessment procedure that entails gathering information about the child's functioning from a variety of sources as well as administering appropriate psychological tests. Test scores permit evaluation of the extent that the child differs from average. Score profiles also detail strengths and weaknesses and provide diagnostic information with implications regarding intervention and service needs.

Because of the potential misinterpretation and misuse of test results, ethical standards and guidelines to safeguard the application of psychological testing have been defined. The *Standards for Educational and Psychological Testing* details procedures for the construction and professional use of tests (American Educational Research Association [AERA], American Psychological Association [APA], National Council on Measurement in Education [NCME], 1985). Parents should become familiar with their rights and the rights of their child. In the case of testing that is part of an individualized assessment of a child, a parent or legal guardian must provide consent before the child is tested, the child should receive an explanation of the reasons for testing tailored to the child's developmental level, and test results should be reported in a timely fashion and in a manner that can be understood by the intended audience (AERA, APA, NCME, 1985; Koocher & Keith-Spiegel, 1990).

Care should be exercised in communicating test results to parents, taking into account the characteristics of the person receiving the information including their education and knowledge of psychology and testing (Anastasi, 1988). Given the limited technical knowledge of testing on the part of most nonprofessionally trained individuals, as well as the potential for misinterpretation of individual test scores, results should be presented to parents in terms of descriptive performance levels rather than isolated numerical scores (Anastasi, 1988). Interpretative explanations should also accompany the presentation of results (Anastasi, 1988).

The anticipated emotional response to the information should also be considered (Anastasi, 1988). When a child has been referred for evaluation due to suspected learning disability, emotional difficulty, or retardation, the parent is facing the possible identification of their child as disabled. Parents' response to an initial diagnosis may involve a combination of shock, disbelief, guilt, anger, and loss (Batshaw & Perret, 1992).

Children referred for testing because of educational or emotional difficulties may be feeling inadequate, different, and frightened by the testing experience. Parents can help by being accepting of the child (Batshaw & Perret, 1992). Parents should also discuss with their child the reasons for testing and provide reassurance (Smith, 1986).

When a child is referred for psychological testing, professionals should anticipate a range of reactions on the part of parents and children. Professionals should provide support and maintain a cooperative, reciprocal relationship with parents. When special needs are indicated, the role of the parent becomes one of an advocate for their child, and professionals can assist parents by informing them of their rights and procedures for obtaining services.

References

American Educational Research Association, American Psychological Association, & National Council on Measurement in Education. (1985). *Standards for educational and psychological testing.* Washington, DC: American Psychological Association.

Anastasi, A. (1988). *Psychological testing* (6th ed.). New York: Macmillan.

Batshaw, M. L., & Perret, Y. M. (1992). *Children with disabilities* (3rd ed.). Baltimore, MD: Paul H. Brookes.

Koocher, G. P., & Keith-Spiegel, P. C. (1990). *Children, ethics, and the law: Professional issues and cases.* Lincoln: University of Nebraska Press.

Simeonsson, R. J. (1986). *Psychological and developmental assessment of special children.* Boston, MA: Allyn & Bacon.

Smith, S. L. (1986). *No easy answers: The learning disabled child at home and school.* New York: Bantam Books.

See also: Family therapy; HOME Inventory; School.

SUSAN RUTH WADDINGTON

Puberty. Puberty is the attainment of reproductive capacity that includes a multitude of physical changes in body size, shape, and physical capacity. It is the most fundamental biological change during the early stages of adolescence. Along with the physical developments, changes in parent-child relationships are evidenced, pointing to a distancing process between parents and children.

Initially children perceive their bodies as one with that of the mother. This symbiosis between mother and child is a cornerstone in several developmental theories. Development leads to a gradual differentiation between child and parents. According to the psychoanalytic theory, the child's libidinal attachment to the parent of the opposite sex is highlighted during the Oedipal phase (ages 3 to 5). Resolution of this complex is accompanied by repression, which ushers in the latency stage, during which the child's erotic life is dormant and relationships with parents are relatively peaceful.

Physical maturation and pubertal changes reintroduce the issues of body self and sexual identity to the developing adolescent. The ego is overwhelmed by the emergence of the sexual instincts and the need to consolidate a mature male or female body. Anna Freud (1958) claimed that this process invokes anxiety, and former established attachments to parents can reawaken former incestuous fixations. As a response, adolescents tend to withdraw their investment from their parents. Consequently, acting out against parents and experiencing of negative emotions against parents can be evidenced. According to Blos (1967), well known for his theories on adolescence, becoming physically mature leads to a *narcissistic self-inflation* reflected in the adolescent's arrogance and rebelliousness combined with underevaluation of parents and defiance of their authority.

Studies conducted during pubescence showed changes in parent child-relationships across various domains. Schulz (1991) found that shortly before the onset of menarche the nature and amount of physical contact with both parents changed dramatically. The previous close physical contact (i.e., sitting on the lap, embracing, and kissing) was drastically reduced. A substantial number of girls even refused to have any physical contact with their father unless it was unavoidable or absolutely necessary. Similar trends were found in a study of physical contact between fathers and adolescent sons (Salt, 1991). As the son grows older and approaches adolescence, both parent and child demonstrate a decrease in the acceptance of physical contact between them.

Distancing between pubescent adolescents and their parents is not restricted to the physical domain. In fact, it is especially evidenced in the relational domain. Steinberg (1987) found that following the pubertal apex an increase in conflict between adolescent and their parents—especially mothers—was evidenced. Adolescents and their mothers tended to interrupt each other with increasing frequency and explain themselves less frequently. Relationships with fathers were more characterized by a decrease in closeness. These as well as additional studies (see Steinberg, 1988) suggest that puberty leads to a distancing between adolescents and their parents.

A number of models were suggested to explain the associations between adolescents' pubertal changes and characteristics of parent-adolescent relationships (Paikoff & Brooks-Gunn, 1991). First, changes in hormone concentration or variability are thought to heighten the adolescent's arousal or emotional liability so that his or her responses to parents' initiatives are more negative or unpredictable. A more empirically founded hypothesis claims that pubertal changes signal the maturity of the adolescent. This change is emotionally laden for both adolescent and parent and hastens changes in expectations toward one another as well as their joint relationship.

An alternative approach, mainly based on primate research, suggests that parent-child distancing accelerates pubertal maturation. Among Old World monkeys, males' sexual maturation is inhibited as long as they remain in the company of dominant males. Studies on monogamous monkeys point to the inhibition of reproduction of female adolescents by the presence of the mother. The inhibition of reproduction was reflected by the suppression of ovulation or slowing of maturation process (Steinberg, 1988). In humans, the impact of distancing on adolescent pubertal maturation appeared to be sex specific. Boys' rate of maturation was unaffected by their relations with their parents. Girls' maturation appeared to be accelerated by parent-child distance, particularly in the mother-daughter dyad.

Replicative studies of puberty and parent-adolescent relationships indicate the distancing impact of puberty and the perturbations these relationships undergo. However, conflict is typically not intense and does not indicate a diminution in the affective bond between parent and child. Moreover, only a small minority of families (5% to 10%) with adolescents experienced a marked deterioration in parent-adolescent relationships (Steinberg, 1990). Puberty is then a stage when parent-child relations undergo major transformations in which former perceptions and behaviors change in order to develop more mature and egalitarian relationships.

References
Blos, P. (1967). The second individuation process of adolescence. *Psychoanalytic Study of the Child, 22,* 162–186.
Freud, A. (1958). Adolescence. *Psychoanalytic Study of The Child, 13,* 255–278.
Paikoff, R. L. & Brooks-Gunn, J. (1991). Do parent-child relationships change during puberty? *Psychological Bulletin, 110,* 47–66.
Salt, R. E. (1991). Affectionate touch between fathers and preadolescent sons. *Journal of Marriage and the Family, 53,* 545–554.
Schulz, A. (1991). *The body image of female adolescents and its behavioral impact.* Unpublished diploma thesis, University of Bonn.
Steinberg, L. (1987). Impact of puberty on family relations: Effects of pubertal status and pubertal timing. *Developmental Psychology, 23,* 451–460.
Steinberg, L. (1988). Reciprocal relation between parent-child distance and pubertal maturation. *Developmental Psychology, 24,* 122-128.
Steinberg, L. (1990). Independence in the family: Autonomy, conflict and harmony in the parent-adolescent relationships. In S. S. Feldman & G. R. Elliot (Eds.), *At the threshold: The developing adolescent* (pp. 255-276). Cambridge, MA: Harvard University Press.

See also: Adolescent separation; Sex education; Sexuality, adolescent.

SHMUEL SHULMAN AND DANIELLE KNAFO

R

Racial identity. Racial identity is part of everyone's psychosocial self. It is based on a person's perception of having a group identity with those of similar racial heritage. Racial group identification generally arises from a common ancestry and accumulated historical experiences among persons who share specific characteristics (i.e., color of skin, facial features, language). Such attributes, however, have no innate psychological, social, or behavioral significance (Helms, 1990; Holmes, 1995; Ogbu, 1994).

Race only takes on significance when it becomes socially defined—that is, persons having similar distinguishable characteristics are treated according to what is perceived as their racial group. However, racial identity development, a psychological process evolving from racial group membership, is determined more from a person's perception than from actual racial classification.

Several age-related childhood developmental models have been proposed to explain how children develop racial concepts and attitudes (Rotheram & Phinney, 1987). Becoming aware of skin color differences and other initial concepts is thought to occur in early childhood, ages 2 to 4. Children pick up on cues around them, recognizing that social comparisons are being made. This is the beginning of a cognitive understanding of race and its relationship to the conceptualization of self (Holmes, 1995; Rotheram & Phinney, 1987). As Boyd-Franklin (1989) indicates, a parent, especially among families of color, may need to help a child reframe and normalize day-to-day experiences to help in a child's positive racial identity development.

Awareness of group affiliation begins to take shape from ages 4 to 8 and by age 10, children are thought to have processed and interpreted racial stimuli to the extent that they have developed specific attitudes about the meaning of race. They initially learn from others about the racial group to which they belong, but they eventually realize the options they have in considering themselves a part of a certain group (Rotheram & Phinney, 1987).

However, children may not realize there is such a thing as race-related behavior or racial stimuli, depending on the specific situations in which they find themselves. It depends on their status as minority or majority group members or the degree to which everyone is similar or different. For example, white children are more likely to think about race when in a class with 20 African American classmates as compared to those who are in a classroom with uniformly white peers. Asian American children living in Hawaii may feel more comfortable with their racial identity than if they were living on the mainland with far fewer Asian Americans as friends (Canino & Spurlock, 1994; Rotheram & Phinney, 1987).

Racial identity consists of how one resolves personal identity issues related to race and the extent one uses a racial reference group as a basis for personal values and ideologies. The extent a person assumes an ascribed identity and commitment to racial group membership is important as well (Helms, 1990). For instance, Mexican American adolescents may speak Spanish and consider themselves part of the culture of their parents and grandparents, while others from the same background may choose to associate mainly with European Americans and drop the Mexican American racial identity.

Helms (1995) created two separate racial identity developmental models for the following groups: (1) whites and (2) people of color—Native Americans and those with an African, Asian, and Latino heritage. These models reflect the inequitable societal positions traditionally held by the two groups and the resulting impact on the psychological processes in which persons develop racial identities. Persons may do little movement from one level to the next, or they may manage racial stimuli in increasing multifarious thought processes, moving them into more complex levels of racial identity.

For people of color, Helms's model describes several possible stages in the process of forming a racial identity. First, they are *oblivious* to the sociopolitical nature and history of race and learn to devalue their own racial group. The second stage is *confusion and ambivalence* about racial identification based on society cues that they receive. The next step involves *recognition* of the historical definitions of race, leading to the denigration of whites as they develop more racial ownership and eventually become committed to their racial group. Next, persons of color *internalize positive attributes* of their own race and simultaneously respond objectively to the dominant group when making life's decisions. This is followed by a *collective identity* with their socioracial group and an *empathy* with other oppressed groups.

Helms suggests that whites move first from being *oblivious* to racism and how racial factors influence life decisions, to an *awareness*, but intolerance of others, to coming to a *realization* of being white and *redefining* what it means in their lives. The final stage is *avoiding options* in daily behavior that takes advantage of the privilege of their whiteness.

Racial identity is a psychological characteristic that is part of everyone's self-identification. It is a function not only of the level of cognitive functioning but of a person's immediate environment. Using information about racial identity development can help parents and others optimize children's positive attitudes toward their own racial group as well as the racial groups of others (Rotheram & Phinney, 1987).

References

Boyd-Franklin, N. (1989). *Black families in therapy: A multisystems approach*. New York: Guilford Press.

Canino, I. A., & Spurlock, J. (1994). *Culturally diverse children and adolescents, assessment, diagnosis, and treatment*. New York: Guilford Press.

Helms, J. (1990). Introduction: Review of racial identity terminology. In J. E. Helms (Ed.), *Black and white racial identity: Theory, research, and practice* (pp. 3–8). New York: Greenwood Press.

Helms, J. (1995). An update of Helms's white and people of color racial identity models. In J. G. Ponterotto, J. M. Casas, L. A. Suzuki, & C. M. Alexander (Eds.), *Handbook of multicultural counseling* (pp. 181-198). Thousand Oaks, CA: Sage Publications.

Holmes, R. M. (1995). *How young children perceive race*. Thousand Oaks, CA: Sage Publications.

Ogbu, J. U. (1994). From cultural differences to differences in cultural frame of reference. In P. M. Greenfield & R. R. Cocking (Eds.), *Cross-cultural roots of minority child development* (pp. 365–392). Hillsdale, NJ: Lawrence Erlbaum Associates, Publishers.

Rotheram, M. J., & Phinney, J. S. (1987). Introduction: Definitions and perspectives in the study of children's ethnic socialization. In J. Phinney & M. Rotheram (Eds.), *Children's ethnic socialization: Pluralism and development* (pp. 10–28). Newbury Park, CA: Sage Publications.

See also: Cultural competence; Identity development; Self-esteem.

CHARLOTTE SHOUP OLSEN

Recognition/encouragement. Recognition is encouragement and support for effort based on acceptance and appreciation of the strengths and uniqueness of children. The key to encouragement is to look for the positive in children's behavior. How parents frame or interpret behavior has an impact on their relationships with children. For example, anger could be viewed as assertiveness, or stubbornness as an illustration of determination. Emphasizing the positive reduces antagonism and conflict while encouraging more acceptable behavior (Dinkmeyer & Eckstein, 1993).

According to symbolic interaction theory, a parent's or caregiver's expectations for children influences the way children define themselves (Charon, 1992). Children often think and act in ways that are consistent with the label assigned by others. Consequently, parents can influence children by how they reference their children's behavior.

Research in family strengths supports the expression of appreciation among and between family members as a characteristic of strong families (Abbott,

1988). Encouragement within the family provides support for children, contributing to their self-definition, self-appreciation, and self-confidence.

Recognition and encouragement are expressed through

- positive expectations
- showing faith and belief in capabilities
- building self-respect by drawing attention to personal resources
- recognizing effort and improvement

Effective recognition has several key qualities (Dinkmeyer & Eckstein, 1993). Recognition must be *sincere*. Fake or manipulative recognition creates cynicism and resentment. Effective recognition is *specific* with clear reference to the behavior that is appreciated. It should also be *immediate*. Time delays erode the significance of appreciation. Furthermore, encouragement that is *personal*, that has clear meaning for the person making the expression, is more significant for children. Finally, the expression should be *proportional* to the amount of effort invested by the child. Exaggerated recognition is more likely to create discomfort than serve as encouragement.

References

Abbott, D. A. (1988). Characteristics of strong families: Perceptions of ethnic parents, *Home Economics Research Journal, 17* (2), 140–147.

Charon, J. M. (1992). *Symbolic interactionism: An introduction, an interpretation, an integration* (4th ed.). Englewood Cliffs, NJ: Prentice-Hall.

Dinkmeyer, D., & Eckstein, D. (1993). *Leadership by encouragement*. Dubuque, IA: Kendall/Hunt Publications.

See also: Acceptance, parental; Communication; Identity development; Self-esteem.

VIRGINIA GOBELI

Reconstituted families. Reconstituted or blended families are formed through a remarriage where at least one spouse has custody of dependent children from a previous union. Historically, most reconstituted families were created after the death of a spouse; now such families stem mainly from divorce. They usually involve the remarriage (or cohabitation) of divorced women since women typically receive custody of children. Reconstituted families have become a prevalent family form since most Americans who divorce eventually remarry, and most women who divorce have dependent children. In addition, with increases in cohabitation, many de facto blended families are not legally or formally recognized.

There are many variations based on the previous marital status of each spouse, such as a partial remarriage involving the marriage of a divorced or widowed spouse to a never-married spouse and a joint remarriage involving two previously married spouses. Reconstituted families, by definition, include stepfathers or stepmothers. Also, some of the spouses in reconstituted families have remarried more than once. According to Furstenberg (1988), about 10% of children experience the divorce, remarriage, and subsequent redivorce of their custodial parent.

Other factors adding complexity to the forms that reconstituted families take are the parental status of each spouse and the custodial and residential arrangements for their children. For example, one or both spouses may have custodial, residential children, and the couple may or may not produce more children jointly. Furthermore, one or both spouses may have shared custody of children who reside in the home only some of the time; hence, some children may be members of binuclear families (Ahrons, 1994), that is, members of the reconstituted families of both of their biological parents. Furstenberg (1988) found that 28.6% of children consider the noncustodial parent's residence to be like their own home.

The formation of reconstituted families can affect the relationships between children and their noncustodial fathers. While most nonresident mothers maintain the same level of contact after remarriage, contact between fathers and their noncustodial children typically decreases after the remarriage of either one of the ex-spouses (Seltzer, 1994). Remarriage may establish obligations to new children, produce rivalries between stepparents and biological parents, and exacerbate tensions between former spouses (Furstenberg & Cherlin, 1991).

Considerable complexity exists in the roles and relationships of the various members in reconstituted families. Children acquire additional step- and half-siblings, grandparents, and other extended family members. Parents must cope with an array of in-law relatives. Subjective definitions of membership in the family become complicated since people living in different households may be included, while some members living in the household may be excluded. Intergenerational bonds are affected when children's relationships with the nonresident parent's extended family are weakened.

The power hierarchy in reconstituted families is usually less clearly established than in nuclear families. Children may challenge the authority of stepparents by refusing to acknowledge their power to make or enforce rules. Stepfathers may also be less interested in disciplining and supervising their stepchildren than biological fathers (Seltzer, 1994). The parental role of noncustodial parents also changes with divorce and remarriage; outside parents engage primarily in recreational activities with their children and adopt a more permissive parenting style (Furstenberg, 1988). Acquiring two sets of authority figures (biological mother and stepfather; biological father and stepmother) creates new and unfamiliar power relations and family politics that can be confusing for both children and adults.

Relatively few reconstituted families are formed after the death of a spouse since most widows and widowers are senior citizens, but such families are not uncommon. The death of a parent accounts for 13% of family disruption (Furstenberg, 1988). While all reconstituted families share some common characteristics (e.g., progression through stages in developing a family identity), the dynamics differ somewhat in families that are formed after the death of a parent rather than after divorce. Children may feel less disloyalty to deceased parents in forming relationships with stepparents than are children who have living noncustodial parents. The finality of death brings some sense of closure; however, with divorce, children hope unrealistically for the reunification of their biological parents (Furstenberg & Cherlin, 1991). Moreover, postbereavement families are unaffected by lingering animosity or bitterness between ex-spouses and conflicts over child custody and support.

Research on outcomes for children in reconstituted families has not identified the most problematic circumstances. Some studies have suggested that negative effects of divorce and remarriage on the well-being of children are inevitable (Seltzer, 1994). Stepmother families experience more difficulties than stepfather families (Furstenberg, 1988). Yet Furstenberg and Cherlin (1991) concluded that while children in reconstituted families have more problems than children in intact families, the risk of experiencing long-term problems is small. Most important, one half of stepfamilies appear to function effectively, with family members reporting high satisfaction and close, harmonious relationships. Substantial variation among blended families makes generalizations about them difficult. With divorce rates stabilizing at a high level, it can be expected that up to one quarter of American children will live in reconstituted families for some part of their lives (Furstenberg & Cherlin, 1991). Changes in prevailing beliefs, practices, and legislation regarding custody and support, as well as greater awareness of the rights and responsibilities of parents and stepparents, may produce positive benefits in the future for blended families.

References
Ahrons, C. R. (1994). *The good divorce*. New York: HarperCollins.
Furstenberg, F., Jr., (1988). Child care after divorce and remarriage. In E. M. Hetherington & J. D. Arasteh (Eds.), *Impact of divorce, single parenting, and stepparenting on children* (pp. 245-261). Hillsdale, NJ: Lawrence Erlbaum Associates.
Furstenberg, F., Jr., & Cherlin, A. J. (1991). *Divided families*. Cambridge: Harvard University Press.
Seltzer, J. A. (1994). Consequences of marital dissolution for children. *Annual Review of Sociology, 20*, 235–266.

See also: Custody; Divorced families; Family systems.

CAROL KAUPPI

Religious development. Religious development refers to two aspects of age-related changes in understanding and responding to a nonmaterial meaning of life. First, *religious knowledge*, or understanding and reasoning within particular religious traditions, undergoes systematic changes related to cognitive, social, and moral development. Second, *spirituality*, or a deeply felt personal connection with an ultimate reality or deity, may fluctuate over the life span. Religious development relates to "how young we are when we start wondering about it all, the nature of the journey and of the final destination" (Coles, 1990, p. 335).

From the perspective of cultural psychology, children actively construct their religious beliefs from available cultural resources and from personal experiences. This suggests that parents may support their children's religious development through exposing them to religion, providing them with personal models of religious commitment, and encouraging their active exploration of religion including its relationship to personal experiences. Parents who fail to communicate openly about religion and/or who criticize children's emerging understanding and experience may inhibit religious development (Oser, 1991).

Religious ideas are important, in part, because they help us to place ourselves in space and time, and provide meaning and direction beyond immediate experience (Coles, 1990). For example, the importance of religion in aiding survival is a key factor in the African American notion of faith (Hale-Benson, 1987). The following fragment from a narrative told by a 73-year-old African American woman, recounting her first experiences as a 7-year-old child walking to segregated school, illustrates both religion as a protective factor and the positive impact parents may have on their children's religious development:

> *The whites would be walking one way, and we'd be walking the other. They'd yell at us, 'You dirty, black niggers! We hate you! We hate you!' I'd go to my Mama and ask her, 'Why do they hate us?' She'd always take me to the Bible. She taught me that God loves us all. God is the judge. She taught me not to take hate inside of myself* (Haight, 1998).

The narrator went on to explain that when we hate, we destroy that part of God that he left inside each of us when he created us. Thus, from the religious perspective taught to her by her mother, the narrator was not the victim of this story: her taunters were.

Available empirical evidence also suggests a relationship between religious socialization and a number of positive developmental outcomes. For example, Brown and Gary (1991) found that self-reports of church involvement were positively related to educational attainment among African American adults. In an interview study of African American urban male adolescents, Zimmerman and Maton (1992) found that youths who left high school before graduation and were not employed, but who attended church, had relatively low levels of alcohol and drug abuse.

Despite the plethora of research in related domains such as moral development, psychologists and educators have virtually ignored religious development or have adopted a negative view of religion. Thus, many important research questions concerning the socialization of religion and the role of religion in development await systematic examination. Existing qualitative and quantitative evidence suggests that considering children's emerging religion may provide parents, teachers, social workers, and others with an important tool both for gaining a fuller understanding of children. Nurturing religious conviction may help children to find meaning in, and to cope successfully with, the stressful as well as the joyful events of everyday life.

References
Brown, D. R., & Gary, L. E. (1991). Religious socialization and educational attainment among African-Americans: An empirical assessment. *Journal of Negro Education, 3*, 411–426.

Coles, R. (1990). *The spiritual life of children*. Boston, MA: Houghton Mifflin.

Haight, W. (1998). Gathering the spirit at First Baptist Church: Spirituality as a protective factor in the lives of African American children. *Social Work, 43* (3), 213-221.

Hale-Benson, J. (1987, December 8–11). *The transmission of faith to young Black children*. Paper presented at the Conference on Faith Development in Early Childhood, Henderson, NC.

Oser, F. (1991). The development of religious judgment. In G. Scarlett & F. Osler (Eds.), *Religious development in childhood and adolescence. New Directions in Child Development, 52,* 5–26.

Zimmerman, M. A., & Maton, K. I. (1992). Life-style and substance use among male African-American urban adolescents: a cluster analytic approach. *American Journal of Community Psychology, 20,* 121–138.

See also: Conscience; Moral development; Spirituality.

WENDY HAIGHT

Reproductive technology, assisted. Assisted reproductive technology (ART) encompasses a range of techniques that increase the probability of conception. These can be grouped under male or female factor infertility or factors attributed to both partners.

There are two main techniques used when male infertility is present: donor insemination (DI), where semen from a donor is inserted into the vagina, and intracytoplasmic sperm injection (ICSI), where a single sperm is deposited in the cytoplasm surrounding the nucleus of the egg. In the first process the relationship between the father and a resulting child is social only, whereas with ICSI the relationship is both genetic and social. ICSI has been regarded as a psychological as well as medical breakthrough because the issues of access to information for children about a donor are not relevant. Evidence about harm to the egg during the process or defective genes being passed to a child has not been found (Bryan & Higgins, 1995).

For female infertility, in vitro fertilization (IVF) is a process whereby several oocytes are removed from the ovaries before ovulation and placed in a laboratory dish or tube with about 50,000 spermatazoa. Fertilization takes place in this environment and the embryos (up to three in New Zealand) are replaced in the uterus after cell division (three- to four-cell stage) has occurred. At each stage of the process, selection occurs to ensure that only the most viable sperm and embryos are used. In vitro fertilization can occur with frozen embryos and with donor egg, embryo, and sperm.

Assisted reproductive technology has provided new hope for infertile couples, but the success rates are very age dependent and still relatively low. Using live births as the criterion of success, IVF success rates for women under the age of 37 years are approximately 20% per cycle (National Perinatal Statistics Unit, 1992, 1993), DI rates are 20%, and ICSI rates are 22%.

The concerns that the techniques may produce infants who have more physical problems and genetic abnormalities than expected in the normal population have not eventuated (Amuzu, Laxova, & Shapiro, 1990). There is a higher risk of multiple births and a slightly higher risk of having a low birth weight infant for women having a first birth at 35 years or older.

Parenting with children conceived by ART appears to be positive and shows no pathology. A study of parenting after IVF, DI, adoption, and normal conception (Golombok et al., 1995) showed that the quality of parenting in families assisted in conception by in vitro fertilization or donor insemination was superior to the quality of parenting in naturally conceived families.

mentally overwhelming. Parents can encourage and shape a sense of responsibility to self and others. They can foster a desire for participation in special interests/activities that fortify self-esteem and provide a sense of personal gratification. They can be an example to the child, modeling a perspective on life that reflects proactive behavior in the face of adversity and optimism relative to outcome. Parents can also encourage children to reach out of their social comfort zone in the service of others.

When stressful life events outweigh the protective factors, children's resiliency may decrease, leaving them vulnerable and at risk (Garmezy & Tellegren, 1984). Parents and other caregivers should consistently reinforce those factors that maintain resilience.

References
American Psychiatric Association. (1994). *Diagnostic and statistical manual of mental disorders* (4th ed.). Washington, DC: Author.
Garmezy, N., & Tellegren, A. (1984). Studies of stress-resistant children: Methods, variables and preliminary findings. In F. J. Morison, C. Lord, & D. P. Keating (Eds.), *Applied developmental psychology* (Vol. 1, pp. 231-287). New York: Academic Press.
Gelman, D. (1991, Summer). The miracle of resiliency. *Newsweek*, pp. 44–47.
Honig, A. (1984). Research in review: Risk factors in infants and young children. *Young Children, 39* (4), 60–73.
O'Connell-Higgins, R. (1983). *Psychological resiliency and the capacity for intimacy.* Qualifying paper, Harvard Graduate School of Education.
Werner, E. E. (1984). Resilient children. *Young Children, 40* (1), 68–72.

See also: Resiliency in parents; Social support, informal; Stress.

D. KIM OPENSHAW

Resiliency in parents. Resiliency, or long-term adaptation through life-cycle and unexpected stresses, involves limiting risks for negative outcomes (mental or physical health problems, financial crises, divorce, or abuse) and maximizing protective factors sustaining healthy development. For parents, these risk factors likely include health and safety hazards at work or leisure, social isolation, conflict with significant others, and high stress. Protective factors might include supportive family, friend, work, and community relationships; interpersonal and financial management skills; realistic expectations and optimistic attitudes; and relaxing leisure interests. Assets such as physical endurance, child development knowledge, confidence, hard work, and supportive friendships help parents manage frequent and unexpected challenges. When illness, unemployment, divorce, neighborhood crime, or care of an elder or special-needs child overwhelm parent capacities, community support systems are critical to restoration of a resilient balance. Likewise, communities that help parents build strengths and work together are more likely to minimize risks than those where parents act only to protect themselves.

Parents who utilize a variety of coping mechanisms tend to show greater stress tolerance. Effective coping mechanisms include:

- maintaining family togetherness

- developing self-reliance and esteem
- developing social support
- taking a positive outlook
- learning about the problem
- reducing tension
- balancing coping efforts

Ironically, reliance on one method such as support from friends or escaping through exercise or hobbies may make a parent less resilient (i.e., more dependent or anxious about coping abilities). For a parent facing a medical crisis with a child, both the number and special combination of strategies are keys to managing effectively. Resiliency reflects an attitude of changing what can be changed, bearing what cannot be changed, and knowing to discern what and how things can be handled (McCubbin et al., 1995).

Self-care is critical to resilient parenting (Smith et al., 1994). A parent who is chronically ill, depressed, overstressed, or fatigued has little reserve energy to deal with unexpected challenges. When parent burnout results in apathy, hostility, or abuse, the results often spell even greater stressors for the family. Time away from children to cultivate interests, gain perspective, and refresh energy is critical to parenting effectiveness. Ironically, those who most need respite such as single parents, mothers of newborns, and individuals whose children or parents have special needs experience the most difficulty in gaining substitute care.

Flexibility in dealing with children's different personalities and stage-related changes is another key to resilient parenting. Often a parent who enjoys a quiet, attentive child becomes frustrated and discouraged with his active, challenging sibling. Especially when stressed, parents may find personality clashes difficult to manage. Likewise, a mother who is fulfilled (while the father is bewildered) in caring for an infant may struggle to relate to a rough-and-tumble 6-year-old or testy teenager who fits dad's style. Parents who view changes as normal and view challenges as opportunities for growth are most likely to adjust. Those who think through basic priorities and values can more consistently apply family rules, rather than simply react to personal dislikes. One mom, besieged nightly by a 5-year-old's pleas to stay up late, was able to say no, remind her son of his tired mornings, and tune out his protests once she thought through his need for rest and admitted her urge to please him. Promoting age-appropriate autonomy, social skills, and problem solving (keys to child resiliency) in daughters and sons also helps moms and dads avoid over- or underresponsibility in their own roles.

Each individual and culture possesses strengths and vulnerabilities for resilient parenting. Parents whose ethnic heritage values the traditional, extended family may struggle with their children's assertiveness while drawing support from other family members. Practitioners who support these inherent strengths can help parents cope more effectively, access and affirm cultural resources, and reduce their children's vulnerability to personal and social stressors. Since ethnic minority parents act as significant stress buffers and role models for children, enhancing their capacity to affirm their own heritage and bridge cultures helps their children adapt (McCubbin et al., 1995; Seligman, 1991).

References

McCubbin, H. I., McCubbin, M. A., Thompson, A. I., & Thompson, E. A. (1995). *Resiliency in ethnic minority families*. Madison, WI: Center for Family Studies.

Seligman, M. E. P. (1991). *Learned optimism*. New York: Alfred A. Knopf.

Smith, C. A., Cudaback, D., Goddard, H. W., & Myers-Walls, J. A. (1994). *National Extension Parent Education Model of critical parenting practices*. Manhattan, KS: Kansas State Research and Extension.

See also: Resiliency in children; Social support, informal; Stress.

BENJAMIN SILLIMAN

Rituals. A ritual is a special act that links people in a group (e.g., families) through shared meaning. It provides a means of giving significance to the passage of time and marking its flow. Rituals move beyond routines in that repetitive behavior takes on special symbolic value and satisfies a need for assigning purpose to certain activities in people's lives. Ritual jars and desynchronizes mundane behavior so as to facilitate the concentration of attention on relevant family events, values, sentiments, and behavior.

Bossard and Boll (1950) were among the first scholars to describe the salience of ritual to family life. They noted how ritualized behavior requires family members to engage in a prescribed sequence of activities and interactions instilled with meaning. When the prescribed behavior fails to occur, family members sense that something is amiss. By following the ritual, family members feel engaged in something larger than themselves. Ritual is characterized by prescription, rigidity, and rightness within a particular family.

Family ritual that celebrates certain life events or commemorates seasonal or religious holidays serves many purposes within families (Imber-Black & Roberts, 1992). It provides form, continuity, and predictability to mundane family interactions. Family ritual reinforces family cohesion and interdependence, enhances the sense of family stability and emotional security, provides a source of comfort and reassurance, puts a special stamp on family milestones, and is a source of family unity and pride (Fiese, 1995; Wolin & Bennett, 1984). Schvaneveldt and Lee (1983) noted that family rituals create intergenerational bonds and, when used wisely, reduce tension and conflict, generate pleasurable anticipation and excitement, and provide opportunities for the growth of family members. Ritual disciplines by its observance, educates through the deposit of its lore, and holds families together simply by having its members do significant activities together.

Family ritual provides a window for viewing a family's shared beliefs about the social world and their place within it. As contemporary family life becomes increasingly harried and stressful, ritual participation may be a mechanism that serves to support and preserve much of what is meaningful and useful to family life. Family ritual, in other words, has an *integrative* function. In addition, ritual may serve a *homeostatic* function, maintaining anxiety within an optimal range for information processing and task performance. These functions of ritual are perhaps most clearly seen in the perceptions of children.

Children give substance to the abstract idea of time by marking the intervals from one ritual to another. The importance of these rituals, celebrated by children within the family, is reinforced by information from the social world. Past cultural, ethnic, and religious practices tend to regain significance and influence decisions regarding family celebrations, rituals, and interaction practices. Children remember from year to year the activities attendant upon celebration of rituals and may measure their development in terms of their changing role in the ritual. Family ritual continues to play a central role in family interaction during adolescence and later life (Troll, 1988).

Family rituals take a variety of forms. There are daily practices such as praying before a meal or reading a special story together every night before bed. There are family rituals associated with celebrating birthdays and anniversaries. There are holiday celebrations like picnics on the Fourth of July or preparing a special family meal during Thanksgiving, and life-cycle rituals, such as graduation and retirement, that mark major transitions in life.

The truly magical quality of rituals is embedded in their capacity not only to announce change but also to actually create the change. In fact, rituals exist to ease the transition inherent in life and assist in coping with change. Change is enacted through ritual and not simply talked about. Couples, for example, do not become parents by simply talking about children but rather by bringing this wish to fruition and then sharing the birth and growth of their child with others through rituals designed to redefine their roles such as christenings or baptisms (Imber-Black & Roberts, 1992).

Rituals do not necessarily have to happen every day, but the activities must occur within a framework that holds enough significance to create a memory. When rituals are consistently observed, then the rituals and their memories help to provide a linkage between the moments. Rituals are among the best memory-makers in family life. Rituals give families possibilities to be the interpreters of their lives in several ways (Bossard & Boll, 1950; Fiese, 1995; Imber-Black & Roberts, 1992). The symbolic meaning behind a ritual cannot always be easily expressed in words. *Symbolic actions* are powerful activators of sensory memory—images, textures, and sounds. Scenes and stories are recalled of previous times when similar rituals were enacted or family members were together. The symbolic significance of family ritual offers a chance to stop ordinary activity, reflect, and remember the uniqueness of family life. Because of the meaning and sensory elements inherent in ritual, it appeals to family members of all ages.

Rituals intimately affect families, giving them a common focus, bringing them together in a way everyday activities cannot. The dividing line between family rituals and other types of ritualistic behavior (e.g., routines or traditions) is not a sharp one. Family ritual is essentially prescriptive behavior that is repeated within families because it takes on special meaning and thus is particularly gratifying to family members.

References

Bossard, J., & Boll, E. (1950). *Ritual in family living*. Philadelphia: University of Pennsylvania Press.

Fiese, B. (1995). Family rituals. In D. Levinson (Ed.), *Encyclopedia of marriage and the family* (Vol. 1, pp. 275–278). New York: Macmillan.

Imber-Black, E., & Roberts, J. (1992). *Rituals for our times*. New York: HarperCollins.

Schvaneveldt, J., & Lee, T. (1983). The emergence and practice of ritual in the American family. *Family Perspective, 17*, 137–143.

Troll, L. (1988). Special issue on rituals and reunions. *American Behavioral Scientist, 31*.

Wolin, S., & Bennett, L. (1984). Family rituals. *Family Process, 23*, 401–420.

See also: Narratives, personal; Routines; Traditions.

JAMES J. PONZETTI, JR.

Rogers, Fred (1928–). Fred McFeely Rogers was born in Latrobe, Pennsylvania, in 1928. He received his undergraduate degree in music composition from Rollins College in Florida in 1951 and was ordained as a Presbyterian minister in 1962 (having studied at the Pittsburgh Theological Seminary and the Graduate School of Child Development at the University of Pittsburgh). He married Joanne Byrd, a pianist and fellow undergraduate student, in 1952, and they have two sons and two grandchildren.

"Mister Rogers" began his career in television in New York in 1951, working at NBC on *The Voice of Firestone, The Lucky Strike Hit Parade, The Kate Smith Hour*, and the *NBC Opera Theatre*. In 1953, he returned to Pittsburgh to work at the first community-supported Public TV station, WQED. He served as the producer, musician, and puppeteer with host Josie Carey on a one-hour, live, daily children's program called *The Children's Corner*. The program won the Sylvania Award for the nation's best locally produced children's program in 1955. He then moved to Toronto and created a 15-minute *Misterogers* program for the Canadian Broadcasting Corporation and then brought this program to Pittsburgh's WQED in 1966 as a half-hour program called Mister Rogers' Neighborhood.

This program is one of the longest-running children's television series. It has been nominated for over 20 Emmies and has received two Peabody Awards. Also, Fred Rogers has received honorary degrees from 32 universities and Lifetime Achievement awards from the Emmies and the TV Critics Association.

Throughout his career, Fred Rogers has focused his creative efforts on one simple tenet—respect for all. *Mister Rogers' Neighborhood* is a program that respects children and their parents, and it is a program that has been shown to have a positive influence on the lives of young viewers (see Friedrich & Stein, 1973). The values that have guided the development of the program and all of the ancillary materials such as videotapes and books or brochures for parents can be summarized by the words of Fred Rogers' favorite song:

It's you I like,
It's not the things you wear,
It's not the way you do your hair—
But it's you I like,
The way you are right now,
The way down deep inside you—
Not the things that hide you.
Mr. Rogers

Parents whose children watched Mister Rogers may have learned that a low-key and patient approach to responding to young children might be an effective parenting tool. In addition, his consistent emphasis on the emotional life of the child may have encouraged parents to treat this part of their children's lives with significance equal to more traditionally academic skills emphasized in programs like *Sesame Street*.

References/Sources
Family Communications Inc. (1997). *Fred Rogers' biography*. Available from Family Communications Inc., 4802 Fifth Avenue, Pittsburgh, PA 15213.
Friedrich, L. K. & Stein, A. H. (1973). Aggressive and prosocial television programs and the natural behavior of preschool children. *Monographs of the Society for Research in Child Development, 38* (Serial No. 151).
Sedgwick, J. (1991, February). Welcome to "Mister Rogers' Neighborhood." *Reader's Digest*, pp. 127-131.

See also: Captain Kangaroo.

JOHN P. MURRAY

Role strain. Role strain refers to the challenges and conflicts associated with the occupation of social roles such as being a parent, marital partner, or employee (Pearlin, 1983). Parental role strain involves stressors experienced while functioning as a primary caregiver for a child. Parents encounter the chronic, normative strains of everyday life that include scheduled transitions (e.g., when a child enters school) as well as sudden changes that are frequently unexpected and undesired (Pearlin & Turner, 1987).

Various types of role strain have been described by Pearlin (1983). *Role overload* refers to the perception that a role is too burdensome or stressful. For example, parents of children with a chronic illness may become overwhelmed by the numerous tasks inherent in managing the daily treatment regimen associated with the illness. *Intrarole conflict* describes the problems between individuals within a role set. An example of intrarole conflict is when parents disagree on methods of disciplining their children. Interrole conflict is the result of competing demands across various role sets (e.g., roles as a parent and as employee). Such conflict may arise for a parent who takes leave from work to care for an ill child. *Role captivity* describes occupying an undesired role (e.g., a grandparent who feels compelled to care for a grandchild due to the biological parents' inability to manage this responsibility). Finally, *role restructuring* pertains to adding or relinquishing roles (e.g., becoming a parent) as well as changing relationships among role partners (e.g., when adult children are required to take more responsibility for an elderly parent).

Measures of parental role strain have included self-reports of role overload, intrarole conflict, and/or interrole conflict (for examples see Jackson, 1992; Quittner et al., 1992). These measures of role strain consist of specific questions addressing parents' perceptions of whether their children have any health-related or behavioral problems, how caring for children impedes on personal time for parents and time with other family members, and how child care responsibilities are shared between spouses.

Research employing these self-report measures of parental role strain has revealed significant associations between greater perceived role strain and poorer psychological adjustment (i.e., decreased parental self-esteem, marital difficulties, and hopelessness) (e.g., Simon, 1992). Mothers are particularly vulnerable to parental role strains in part due to the documented gender difference that the parental identity is more salient to women than to men (Simon, 1992). In fact, mothers report greater parental role strains than do fathers, and employed mothers endorse greater interrole conflicts than do employed fathers (Quittner et al., 1992; Simon, 1992). Regardless of gender, however, parents who endorse the highest commitment to parental identity are more vulnerable to the strains of the parental role. Perceived support from a spouse has been found to be associated with lower self-reported parental role strain, and for this reason spousal support might alleviate any potential negative psychological outcomes of these strains on parents (Simon, 1992).

A behavioral measure of parental role strain has been developed for an investigation comparing mothers caring for infants and/or toddlers with cystic fibrosis (CF) and mothers of physically healthy matched controls (Quittner et al., 1992). The *Behavioral Role Strain Index* is based on a six-day evening phone diary in which mothers are tracked through activities they perform during the day employing a cued-recall procedure. With prompts from an interviewer to reconstruct the day, mothers are asked to describe the type and duration of each activity. For this investigation, role overload was conceptualized as the ratio of time spent in basic household and child care (i.e., obligatory activities) relative to time spent in recreation (i.e., discretionary activities). Mothers of children with CF, compared to those of physically healthy children, spent a significantly greater proportion of their time performing household and child care tasks in relation to recreational activities (e.g., playing with their children, going on outings, reading). This difference was found even when controlling for time spent on medical care. The findings are interpreted to indicate that by restricting opportunities for positive social and emotional parent-child interactions, role strain may lead to negative consequences for families over time.

References

Jackson, P. B. (1992). Specifying the buffering hypothesis: Support, strain, and depression. *Social Psychology Quarterly, 55*, 363–378.

Pearlin, L. I. (1983). Role strains and personal stress. In H. B. Kaplan (Ed.), *Psychosocial stress: Trends in theory and research* (pp. 3–32). New York: Academic Press.

Pearlin, L. I., & Turner, H. A. (1987). The family as a context of the stress process. In S. V. Kasl & C. L. Cooper (Eds.), *Stress and health: Issues in research methodology* (pp. 143–165). New York: John Wiley & Sons.

Quittner, A. L., Opipari, L. C., Regoli, M. J., Jacobsen, J., & Eigen, H. (1992). The impact of caregiving and role strain on family life: Comparisons between mothers of children with cystic fibrosis and matched controls. *Rehabilitation Psychology, 37*, 275–290.

Simon, R. W. (1992). Parental role strains, salience of parental identity and gender differences in psychological distress. *Journal of Health and Social Behavior, 33*, 25–35.

See also: Conflict, interparental; Instrumental versus expressive functions; Mediation, parent-child; Stress.

CAROLYN IEVERS

Rousseau, Jean Jacques (1712-1778). Theories of how children develop are not unique to our century. People have always had beliefs about how children change over time and what is important for their development. The ideas of Jean Jacques Rousseau have exerted significant influence in Europe and North America in recent centuries. In 1762, Rousseau published *Emile* (1762/1979), which established him as a visionary for twentieth century educational theorists. *Emile* was the most read child-rearing manual of its time, and it included a great deal of advice on the daily care of children (Boyd, 1963).

Emile, written in the form of a novel, was actually what its subtitle indicated: *A treatise on education*. In contrast to the prevalent eighteenth-century Puritan conception that the newborn was a sinner and possessed by motives to do evil (deMause, 1974), Rousseau proposed in *Emile* that the child is born morally good. His description of child development is focused on the search for ways of guiding children's growth so they remain true to their natural inclinations. Rousseau called his pedagogic principles a program for *negative education*. That is, no direct attempt is allowed to influence the child's beliefs, values, and morals, and the task of parenting consists in creating a social environment where the child's natural tendencies can unfold without constraints and prejudice.

According to Rousseau, there are critical periods to a child's development: physical development, mental development, and social and moral development. Nature impels children to develop different capacities at different stages. The parent and teacher must adapt the form and content of their teachings to the specific abilities of the child that characterizes the various stages that unfold in an invariant sequence according to nature's plan. *Infancy* is a critical time for establishing physical health and developing the senses based on the free play of the child's natural impulses. *Early childhood* is important for developing physical strength and agility. Throughout this period children learn best from direct experience related to their daily needs and interests. Children should be taught to make useful objects with their hands that can be used to solve everyday problems. For Rousseau, direct instruction about the world beyond immediate, daily experience should be postponed until adolescence. *Late childhood* and *adolescence* are critical for the development of reasoning, social skills, civic responsibility, and morality. This is the time when sensations are transformed into ideas. These ideas should be based on experience, not abstract theories. The conceptual basis of the child's understanding is enlarged from grasping merely the necessity of causal processes to conceiving the utility of certain courses of action. Means-end relations between complex events can now be mastered.

Four of Rousseau's ideas continue to have an impact in modern times. First, Rousseau insisted that children are not simply miniature adults but are *different in quality of mind and needs*. Nature is like a hidden tutor who prompts the child to develop different capacities at different stages of growth. His belief in the faith of nature to guide the child's growth ushered in the developmental tradition in psychology and education. Second, Rousseau *popularized maternal breastfeeding*, in contrast to the use of wet nurses, not just because of the physical properties of maternal milk but also because of the tenderness and love that a mother can thereby communicate to the infant. Following Rousseau, many books on parental advice recommended that mothers nurse their own infants and allow them the freedom to explore the environment. Third, he emphasized the *importance of firsthand experience* as the most basic foundation of learning in childhood. Parents should question and arrange their children's experiences that lead their children to infer their own conclusions about what they observe. This is how children learn to trust their own powers of judgment. What is important is not that children acquire specific information but that they learn to think for themselves. Finally, he convinced people that *childhood was worth the attention of educated adults* and encouraged an interest in the *process of development rather than just the result*. Rousseau proposed a philosophy of child rearing and education that would be identified today as *child centered*. Elements of Rousseau's beliefs are found in the writings of such educational theorists as Frederick Froebel (1782–1852), Maria Montessori (1870–1952), and Jean Piaget (1897–1980). Rousseau is often credited as being the father of modern pedagogy and as the founder of the discovery method in science.

References

Boyd, W. (1963). *The educational theory of Jean Jacques Rousseau*. New York: Russell & Russell.

deMause, L. (1974). *History of childhood*. New York: Psychohistory Press.

Rousseau, J. J. (1979). *Emile*. (Introduction, translation, and notes by Allan Bloom). New York: Basic Books. (Original work published in 1762)

See also: Lock, John; Nature versus nurture.

STEVEN M. ALESSANDRI

Routines. Intimate interaction occurs continuously among family members as they respond to one another's actions and reactions. These family interaction patterns are affected by the degree of routinization within families. Most families develop an identifiable collection of routines around which the rhythm of daily life is established. These routines appear to serve as an organizing principle integrating diverse activities and fostering regularity in the family's collective life. In the crunch and chaos of everyday life, it is easy to lose sight of the significance of family routines. Yet these routines may be a resonant and powerful stamp of a family's individuality.

Routines make life simpler. Routines are repetitive behaviors that often lack historical embeddedness; that is, they are not necessarily passed on from older to younger generations (Boyce et al., 1983). They impart a certain comfort that comes from knowing what to expect next in everyday life. Family routines can occur daily or intermittently. Specifically, family routines consist of behavior or activities engaged in by family members on a regular and predictable basis that help define expectations for roles and interaction.

Family routines may or may not have symbolic significance to the family. They can be very simple or quite elaborate. Family routines range from activities that are common to many families to those that are peculiar to a particular family (Wise, 1986). Routines can serve as a means of easing transitions that occur during the day or over time (Albert et al., 1979). In this sense, they are more than just chores. For example, a parent gives a child a bath. Although the primary objective of bathing is to maintain cleanliness, children often enjoy playing in the water. On bath night, the small things that make up the routine of cleaning oneself present a unique opportunity for interaction. Since this activity requires supervision and help from a parent, the established patterns involved in cleaning a child can be routinized into a pattern that offers reassurance and continuity through its predictability. Sharing dinner together is another example. Food consumption is essential to life, but in addition to the value of food content, sharing the same food, especially at home at certain times, weaves a social link between family members. Meal routines provide the context in which meals provide order in daily family life and establish expectations for interaction between family members.

Family routines are significant at every stage of family life and extend across the life span. In addition to the casual routines established by a couple, family routines tend to emerge fully from the family milieu as child rearing is initiated. As the toddler stage emerges and maturation to school age occurs, family routines (e.g., bedtime and mealtime) are more firmly developed. Family routines offer parents the opportunity to systematize and simplify the decisions involved in the activities of daily life. In addition to the security obtained through predictability, routines help children to clarify expectations. Children often assist in the establishment of routines by urging family members not only to adhere to the routines but to fully participate in them as well. Routines may change and evolve as children mature, responding to the changing dynamics within the family system. Some of the routines learned in childhood carry forward as children move into adulthood and provide a foundation for future family expectations.

Family routines can be elevated to the level of ritual. When a family routine has taken on, or been assigned, symbolic meaning by family members beyond the functional aspects of the activity, it becomes a family ritual.

References

Albert, S., Amgott, T., Krakow, M., & Marcus, H. (1979). Children's bedtime rituals as a prototype rite of passage. *Journal of Psychological Anthropology*, 2 (1), 85–105.

Boyce, W., Jensen, E., James, S., & Peacock, J. (1983). The family routines inventory; Theoretical origins. *Social Science Medicine*, 17 (4), 193–200.

Denham, S. (1995). Family routines: A construct for considering family health. *Holistic Nursing Practice*, 9 (4), 11–23.

Sprunger, L., Boyce, W., & Gaines, J. (1985). Family-infant congruence: Routines and rhythmicity in family adaptation to a young infant. *Child Development*, 56, 564–572.

Wise, G. (1986). Family routines, rituals, and traditions: Grist for the family mill and buffers against stress. In S. VanZandt (Ed.), *Family strengths 7: Vital connections* (pp. 243–256). Lincoln: Center for Family Strengths, University of Nebraska.

See also: Rituals; Traditions.

JAMES J. PONZETTI, JR.

Rules, implicit. Parenting exists within the context of an implicit and culturally sensitive moral code. Maccoby (1980) reminds us that virtually all societies have developed rules and norms to deal with key issues, such as safety, health, property, control of aggression and sex, self-reliance and work, maintaining trust, and respect for authority. These moral rules reflecting fairness and respect for the social order are developed during childhood, placing great emphasis on parenting and are reflected in children's expressions of social rules that are scaffolded through face-to-face encounters (Bigelow, Tesson, & Lewko, 1996).

Youniss (1980) claimed that social rules are accessible through the content of the child's descriptions of the specific interpersonal relationship in question. Bigelow and his colleagues (1996) defined social rules as linguistically represented elements of experience that describe how to behave (i.e., the "do's" and "don'ts") with a person occupying a given social relationship (e.g., parent) within which the rule is learned and give a relationship the appearance of a stable meaning.

The social rules that describe interpersonal relations and the limits governing each are often implicit (Shotter & Newson, 1982) in the social order: They are not social skills or techniques. While parenting practices (e.g., control tactics) are often explicit, a social rule is deeply embedded in the parent's and child's sense of the social order. Such rules have a powerful effect on the child's social expectations as reflected in their ratings of social rule–relational strategies in dealing with parents, close friends, teachers, and siblings (Bigelow, Tesson, & Lewko, 1996). Social rules are not externally imposed, rigid social codes (Fogel, 1993) but stem from implicitly constructed *interaction rituals* (Goffman, 1967). For example: Sister: "You can't just leave without doing the dishes!" Brother replies: "Take off, eh! You're not my mother or anything!"

Social rules are regulatory constructions that include those understandings that guide the scaffolding of the parent-child or peer relation and are learned (implicitly) through co-construction (Youniss, 1980). In peer relations, social rules reflect the checks and balances of freely expressed opinions validated through cooperation and mutual consensus, giving rise to implicitly shared relationship models (Youniss, 1980). Parent-child experiences are constructed more in terms of unilateral compliance and are similarly described by Fogel (1993) as co-constructed knowledge *frames*, which are joint actions that mutually create a set of social actions with others and with the world at large.

Parent-child social rules were identified by Bigelow, Tesson, and Lewko (1996) through in-depth interviewing of children and largely appeal to Maccoby's (1980) universally salient moral themes. Ratings of these rules-relations more directly address their implicit nature. Parent-child social rules contain the key ingredients used in dealing with close friends and with other adults, such as teachers. Such rules include:

- *Compliance* rules such as *following* (e.g., do what you are told; do obligatory work; respect property) and *deference* (e.g., be polite; accept others as they are; go along with others' initiatives)
- *Helping* rules (e.g., offer to help; help by doing things; teach them how to do things)

- *Cooperative* rules such as *reparation* (e.g., talk/make up after fighting) and *talking* (e.g., talk, tell things, discuss; reveal your personal experiences to others)
- *Loyalty* and *trust* rules (e.g., do not lie, be honest; be loyal/dependable)
- *Reciprocity* rules (e.g., share things; help each other; be fair)

Siblings were noted by their low rule ratings. Teacher-child relations are governed primarily by authority and compliance rules.

References

Bigelow, B. J., Tesson, G., & Lewko, J. H. (1996). *Learning the rules: The anatomy of children's relationships*. New York: The Guilford Press.

Fogel, A. (1993). *Developing through relationships: Origins of communication, self, and culture*. New York: Harvester.

Goffman, E. (1967). *Interaction ritual*. New York: Doubleday.

Maccoby, E. E. (1980). *Social development: Psychological growth and the parent-child relationship*. San Diego: Harcourt Brace Jovanovich.

Shotter, J., & Newson, J. (1982). An ecological approach to cognitive development: Implicate orders, joint action and intentionality. In G. Butterworth & P. Light (Eds.), *Social cognition: Studies of the development of understanding* (pp. 32–52). Brighton, England: Harvester.

Youniss, J. (1980). *Parents and peers in social development*. Chicago, IL: University of Chicago Press.

See also: Limit setting; Misbehavior; Paradigms, parenting.

                                                                          BRIAN J. BIGELOW

Runaway children. Runaway youths are those children reported by their families to be away from home without parental permission for more than 48 hours (Welsh et al., 1995). Runaway children are not a homogeneous population (Jones, 1988; Zide & Cherry, 1992). Traditionally, research has suggested that there are four types of runaways (Zide & Cherry, 1992). First, *running to* consists of children who seek adventure or leave home because they desire increased freedom. *Running from* refers to youth who leave pathological situations, including severely dysfunctional families. These youth are unhappy and alienated from their family. Even though leaving an unhealthy situation is adaptive, this behavior is associated with long-term negative consequences such as loss of social support and increased likelihood of exploitation. *Thrown out*, the third category, refers to youth who are told to leave their home. Finally, some children are *forsaken*; they leave home because their family cannot financially support them.

Intervention programs designed to assist the runaway population should be prepared to deal with each subgroup because treatment implications differ for each. For example, counseling that emphasizes reality testing may be appropriate for children seeking adventure, while support and foster placement would be more appropriate for a forsaken child.

Peggy Plass and Gerald Hotaling (1995), in their examination of intergenerational influences on running away from home, suggest that there is a basic consensus about factors that influence a child's decision to leave home, including

- personal maladjustment or problems in the child's life
- high levels of unresolved conflict between children and their parents
- emotional, physical, or sexual abuse of the child

Welsh et al. (1995, p. 22) describe the influence of physical and sexual abuse on youth from the running from category; they note that for "youths exposed to chronic mistreatment at the hands of parents or caretakers, running away from home may be viewed as a healthy and adaptive response to a negative situation." Research suggests that at least 75% of runaway youth experienced maltreatment and up to 60% experienced sexual abuse. Multiple-risk theory suggests that accumulation of risk factors (i.e., poor parental relations, poverty, limited social support) is related to negative consequences of an event such as running away (Welsh et al., 1995). Families of runaway youth feature poor conflict resolution, communication, and parental supervision. Experience of abuse before running away is positively correlated with the likelihood that the runaway will engage in delinquent behavior. These findings support multiple-risk theory.

Finkelhor, Hotaling, and Sedlak (1990) collected data from a survey of households, a survey of juvenile facilities, interviews with runaways who had returned home, police records, FBI data, and interviews with community professionals in a comprehensive study of runaways. They reported the following trends that suggest that running away is a common, benign, occurrence (Finkelhor, Hotaling, & Sedlak, 1990):

- An estimated 450,000 youth ran away from home (n = 446,700) or juvenile facilities (n = 12,800) during one year's time.
- Almost all runaways were teenagers.
- They tended to disproportionately run from stepparent type households.
- Running away was more likely to occur in the summer.
- About 66% of the runaways went to a friend's or relative's house.
- Eighty-two percent were accompanied by another youth.
- Fifty percent returned to their home within two days.
- Caretakers knew the whereabouts of their children in 39% of the cases.
- Runaway trends seem to be stable (e.g., there has been little fluctuation since 1975).

A significant number of cases were not benign. For example, 10% of the youth who left home traveled a distance of more than 100 miles, and 7% left their state. This travel increased their risk for abduction or abuse. Furthermore, running away was a regular occurrence for one third of the population which increased their chances for experiencing maltreatment while on the run (Finkelhor, Hotaling, & Sedlak, 1990).

References
Finkelhor, D., Hotaling, G., & Sedlak, A. (1990). *Missing, abducted, runaway, and thrownaway children in America. First report: Numbers and characteristics*. Washington, DC: Office of Juvenile Justice and Delinquency Prevention.
Jones, L. P. (1988). A typology of adolescent runaways. *Child and Adolescent Social Work, 5*, 16–29.

Plass, P. S., & Hotaling, G. T. (1995). The intergenerational transmission of running away: Childhood experiences of the parents of runaways. *Journal of Youth and Adolescence, 24,* 335–348.

Welsh, L. A., Archambault, F. X., Janus, M. D., & Brown, S. W. (1995). *Running for their lives: Physical and sexual abuse of runaway adolescents.* New York: Garland Publishing.

Zide, M. R., & Cherry, A. L. (1992). A typology of runaway youths: An empirically based definition. *Child and Adolescent Social Work Journal, 9,* 155–168.

See also: Family systems; Scapegoating; Self-esteem; Throwaway children.

RONALD JAY WERNER-WILSON AND MINDI R. HIGGINS-KESSLER

S

Scaffolding. Scaffolding is a supportive structure that caregivers provide to children to help them learn. The term *scaffolding* derived explicitly from Vygotsky's (1978) usage of the concept *zone of proximal development*. Bruner (1975) then incorporated this "zone" as a scaffolding process of social interaction between children and their caretakers (usually parents). Children observe and listen to their caretakers within a temporary structure, or zone, within which children are assisted to say or do things that normally lie just outside their grasp. With the caretaker's assistance they are rendered more competent. Caretakers adjust this zone to fit their children's developmental needs. In this manner, the child's verbal and intellectual skills are assisted and grow.

Scaffolding is a linguistic and cultural tool. Scaffolding has its roots in Lev Vygotsky's (1978) historic work in which he claimed that cognition is intrinsically social in origin. For Vygotsky, language is a cultural tool that shapes knowledge, and this cultural construction transpires best between the child and caretaker in mutual interaction. Vygotsky (1934/1962) described Tolstoy's failed attempt to teach peasant children literary language in the formal classroom. He found that children learn much better within the general linguistic context of interactions between parents and peers. For Vygotsky, language and dialogue shapes our thoughts and provides us with meaning and how we construct our relations with people.

Knowledge is socially and culturally cultivated. Like Vygotsky, Fogel (1993) believes that all cognition is relational. Fogel claimed that in infancy these social exchanges between child and caretaker are "co-constructed" into continually changing knowledge "frames" that are not static but are active attempts at conceptual closure. Fogel reported that infants are keenly aware of the social action within their maternal relationship. Similarly, Vygotsky (1978) believed that knowledge itself is socially cultivated by the personal interactions children have with their parents, peers, and other caretakers such as their teachers. This experience conveys the culture's accumulated knowledge.

Scaffolding continuously adapts to fit the child's increasing competence. Fischer and Bullock (1984) suggested that during the middle years of childhood cognitive competence is achieved through a *collaborative cycle*, where the child in scaffolded interaction eventually learns to complete a task, such as a puzzle, without the parent's help. Parents continuously update their scaffolding to fit their child's newly acquired knowledge and skill.

Rogoff (1990) claims that parents give their toddlers *metacognitive support* within the scaffolded zone by identifying their goal or problem through supportive questioning of their narrative. This goal is then broken down into its more manageable constituents, giving the child purpose and vision. A more experienced child assumes responsibility for managing the task. Rogoff extended Vygotsky's (1978) zone of proximal development by stressing the interrelatedness of the child's role and those of their social counterparts in *guided participation*, wherein they actively and routinely engage in ongoing cultural activities and practices. Children actively seek structure and even demand assistance to achieve it. Unlike Vygotsky (1978), Rogoff views scaffolded communication as more than language based, including verbal and nonverbal dialogue, which is especially important during infancy.

References

Bruner, J. S. (1975). The ontogenesis of speech acts. *Journal of Child Language, 2,* 1–19.

Fischer, K. W., & Bullock, D. (1984). Cognitive development in school-age children: Conclusions and new directions. In W. A. Collins (Ed.), *Development during middle childhood: The years from six to twelve* (pp. 70-146). Washington, DC: National Academy Press.

Fogel, A. (1993). *Developing through relationships: Origins of communication, self, and culture.* New York: Harvester.

Rogoff, B. (1990). *Apprenticeship in thinking: Cognitive development in social context.* Oxford: Oxford University Press.

Vygotsky, L. S. (1962). *Thought and language* (E. Hanfmann & G. Vaker, Eds.). Cambridge, MA: MIT Press. (Original work published 1934)

Vygotsky, L. S. (1978). *Mind in society: The development of higher psychological processes.* Cambridge: Harvard University Press.

See also: Communication; Developmentally Appropriate Practice; Language development.

BRIAN J. BIGELOW

Scapegoating. Scapegoating, according to Sir James George Frazer (1933), has occurred in societies throughout human history "to alleviate human sufferings by diverting them to material objects, which are then thrown away or otherwise disposed of to render them innocuous. Often, however, the transference

of evil to a material object is only a step toward foisting it upon a living person" (pp. 5–6). Family therapists Fritz Simon, Helm Stierlin, and Lyman Wynne describe scapegoating in families: "This biblical metaphor refers to a situation in which parents attempt to resolve conflict between themselves by seeking and/or exaggerating problems in another family member [who is usually a child]" (1985, p. 308).

Ezra Vogel and Norman Bell (1968) conducted one of the first investigations of scapegoating in families; they reported that parents in their study used emotionally disturbed children as distractions from marital conflict. Scapegoating, according to Vogel and Bell (1968), is both functional and dysfunctional. The main function of scapegoating is to maintain family solidarity; it also serves the following functions (Vogel and Bell, 1968):

- It stabilizes the personality of the parents.
- The projection of marital difficulties onto children minimizes and controls conflict.
- It permits parents to ignore intrapsychic difficulties so they can concentrate on work and other social obligations.

Although scapegoating enhances family stability, it also includes dysfunctional elements (Vogel & Bell, 1968):

- It produces additional family responsibilities (e.g., monitor and manage the scapegoat's behavior).
- The person who is scapegoated may respond aggressively.
- Although family stability is maintained, the scapegoat's behavior outside of the family causes external strain (e.g., behavior problems at school) that must be managed by the family.
- The person who is scapegoated experiences emotional and personality disturbances.

Clinically, psychotherapists should assess family dynamics before treating a child. Do the child's symptoms serve some function for the family? Do family members deliberately or unintentionally reinforce problematic behavior? If so, family therapy should be included in some form. Teachers and physicians should also pay attention to family dynamics because children who are scapegoated are likely to have poor social skills, exhibit poor impulse control, and engage in aggressive behavior to other children. Family processes should be evaluated as part of a comprehensive assessment of the child's mental and physical health. Families may be reluctant to change entrenched patterns, so family therapy should emphasize the dysfunctional aspects of scapegoating as leverage to motivate the family to change.

Conditions associated with scapegoating. First, differences in value orientation between parents may produce conflict (Pillari, 1991; Vogel & Bell, 1968). Religious differences, behavioral routines, and attitudes about parenting may produce conflict between partners that, in turn, becomes directed at a child. Second, regular tension between the family and the community may propel the parents to blame their difficulties on a child (Vogel & Bell, 1968). This can occur because of mobility (i.e., a family moves into a new neighborhood in which they have difficulty establishing a social network) or long-standing tension between a

particular family and members of the community. The latter may occur if a family becomes a scapegoat for the community. Third, skewed and schismatic family types are more prone to dysfunction, especially marital problems, which enhance the likelihood of scapegoating (Pillari, 1991). Skewed families feature one dominant partner and one passive partner; conflict may be channeled through one particular child who becomes the scapegoat. The marital relationship in schismatic families, on the other hand, features hostility and withdrawal. Finally, scapegoating can occur if there is triangulation (Pillari, 1991; Vogel & Bell, 1968): A third person, usually a child, is triangled into a relationship if the couple is unable to manage tension and anxiety between them.

Selection of the scapegoat. Broderick and Pulliam-Krager (1979), in a review of literature about coalitions and scapegoating, note that some scholars suggest that the weakest and most vulnerable child is chosen as a scapegoat and recruited into that role (see also Pillari, 1991). From this perspective, developmental anomalies predispose a child to being selected as a scapegoat if one of the conditions exist. Other scholars have suggested that instead of one person serving exclusively as a scapegoat the child who is the most disruptive will be chosen (Broderick & Pulliam-Krager, 1979), which results in a family having different scapegoats based on life circumstances. A family may select the most convenient target if unmanageable conflict arises (e.g., the child who is currently experiencing academic difficulty); a family may also select a new child to be the family scapegoat if the previously scapegoated child leaves home.

References

Broderick, C. B., & Pulliam-Krager, H. (1979). Family process and child outcomes. In W. R. Burr, R. Hill, F. I. Nye, and I. L. Reiss (Eds.), *Contemporary theories about the family* (Vol. 1, pp. 604–614). New York: Free Press.

Frazer, J. G. (1933). *The golden bough: Volume VI. The scapegoat* (3rd ed.). London: Macmillan.

Pillari, V. (1991). *Scapegoating in families: Intergenerational patterns of physical and emotional abuse.* New York: Brunner/Mazel.

Simon, F. B., Stierlin, H., & Wynne, L. C. (1985). *The language of family therapy: A systemic vocabulary and sourcebook.* New York: Family Process Press.

Vogel, E. F., & Bell, N. W. (1968). The emotionally disturbed child as the family scapegoat. In E. F. Bell & N. W. Vogel (Eds.), *A modern introduction to the family* (pp. 412–427). New York: Free Press.

See also: Alliance, parenting; Conflict, interparental; Distancing strategies; Family systems; Triangulation.

RONALD JAY WERNER-WILSON AND MINDI R. HIGGINS-KESSLER

School. The school is a major social institution affecting various aspects of children's intellectual, social, and emotional development. Because of compulsory primary education, elementary schools touch the lives of the majority of children in many cultures, influencing even those children who are not in the educational system because of the implications of being excluded.

The research literature documents three major functions of schools. First, schools offer literacy, math, and scientific knowledge for all children, not just

the privileged. The learning of specific knowledge and skills connected to formal educational qualifications constitutes the key factor to a child's entry into
higher education or training and employment. Second, the school transmits societal and cultural values. In the last two decades, the impact of school on children's social and personal development has been emphasized. Third, the school
is an agent of social change aiming at correcting socioeconomic and racial ine-
qualities. Schools together with families and communities are further asked to
address broader societal problems, which include discrimination, substance
abuse, violence, parental divorce, dropping out, teenage pregnancy, and the special needs of minority groups of children (learning disabled, handicapped, bilingual).

Schools and families interact as *complementary* systems. The child's experience in one context may either confirm or modify experiences in the other.
Schools can complement the child's family by reinforcing the values, traditions,
and expectations that the family members hold. Schools can also supplement the
family by teaching skills and introducing ideas that are not a part of the family's
background. When the dominant culture orientation of the school conflicts with
the values and traditions of a minority family, the two systems can be in conflict.

Family income and parents' formal education can influence student
achievement and parent involvement. Fuller and Clarke (1994) conducted a review of worldwide research on the relationship between parents and children's
school performance. They found that under some conditions school effects on
achievement are greater than family background influences within impoverished
settings and that family practices related to later school achievement vary within
social classes. They also found that family demand for schooling is shaped by
ethnicity and child's gender and age in many societies.

Regardless of parent income or education, research further suggests that students do better in their academic work and have more positive school attitudes,
higher aspirations, and other positive behaviors if they happen to have parents
who are aware, knowledgeable, encouraging, and involved and have high expectations for their children's education.

At all school levels, parents need to gather information about school organization, programs, assessment practices, grouping procedures and opportunities
to further their children's school experiences. They further need to make decisions about their children's education.

Schools determine much of the nature and form of interactions between parents and schools through the practices they use to inform, invite, and involve
families. Schools have the expertise and information that could help many parents to understand, monitor, and support children's education. Studies suggest
that teachers who do give parents specific information on their children's learning and progress in school notably influence what parents do at home to support
children's learning. Researchers have emphasized the importance of creating
two-way communication, enhancing learning at school and at home, providing
mutual support and confidence, and making joint decisions for a successful partnership between school and home.

Several school reform programs have been developed in the past one or two
decades in the United States as an outcome of the acknowledgment of the aca-

demic failure and the unmet needs of many students, especially those from low-income families. They focused on changes in the organizational structure and climate of the school, changes in the curriculum and teaching methodology, implementation of early childhood education programs and family support programs, and collaboration with community agencies and groups (Finn-Stevenson, 1992). Although these are school-based programs, they emphasize the importance of working with parents, and they include a focus on parent involvement (parent education, interactive homework, volunteer activities, family counseling).

Some of the most successful and widely publicized school improvement programs are the Comer's School Development Program, Zigler's School of the 21st Century and more recently The School of the Future. The School of the Future focuses on the implementation of a comprehensive range of services and innovative programs for children and their families with an additional emphasis on promoting self-esteem and positive human development (Finn-Stevenson, 1992).

References

Finn-Stevenson, M. (1992). Paving the way: Questions and criteria for the School of the Future. In W. H. Holtzman (Ed.), *School of the Future* (pp. 45–59). Austin: American Psychological Association and Hogg Foundation for Mental Health, University of Texas.

Fuller, B., & Clarke, P. (1994). Raising school effects while ignoring culture? Local conditions and the influence of classroom tools, rules, and pedagogy. *Review of Educational Research, 64* (1), 119–157.

See also: Academic achievement; Family-school partnerships; Teacher training.

CHRYSE HATZICHRISTOU

Self-care. Self-care generally refers to the situation in which a child spends time at home or elsewhere alone or with a sibling or peer. In a national survey of child care arrangements (Hofferth et al., 1991), just over 2% of all children ages 5 to 12 years were reported to be in self-care as the primary care arrangement during the before- or after-school hours. Self-care also appeared in the survey as a supplemental arrangement for families, with 12% of the children in self-care at least some of the time. When broken down by age group, it is clear that use of self-care increases as children get older: 2.2% for children 5 to 7 years old, 10.7% for children 8 to 10 years, and 31.5% for 11- and 12-year-olds.

Conflicting results have been reported in the research literature regarding the effects of self-care on children's adjustment. Although some studies have found that self-care children exhibit problems such as a greater number of fears and poorer cognitive development than children supervised by adults during the after-school hours, other studies have found no differences between self-care and adult-supervised children in terms of behavioral adjustment, self-esteem, anxiety, and social adjustment. A variety of demographic and contextual factors play a role in determining the consequences of self-care during out-of-school time.

Age of child. Generally, children younger than 10 years or so do not have the skills necessary to deal effectively with caring for themselves during their out-of-school time. Negative consequences of the arrangement are more common for younger children than for older children. For example, younger children in self-care are more fearful of being alone or without adults nearby than older children are (Robinson, Rowland, & Coleman, 1986). As children get older and desire greater autonomy, self-care may represent an opportunity to exhibit their ability to regulate their own behavior within the context of rules set by parents. Use of a self-care arrangement in this case acknowledges the child's readiness for responsibility and independence and his or her developmental press for autonomy.

Time spent in self-care. Children who spend 30 minutes caring for themselves before or after school experience the arrangement differently than children who spend 2 hours without adult supervision. Additionally, one afternoon per week in self-care is a different experience than five afternoons. Consideration of self-care as an arrangement during the out-of-school hours should include the time involved and the number of days per week.

Type of self-care arrangement. Some self-care children are home alone, others are home with a sibling, others are at the home of a friend without adult supervision, and still others spend their self-care time "hanging out" at places such as shopping malls and video arcades. There can be considerable variability in potential impacts and how children experience these arrangements. Some children are completely unsupervised by adults, whereas others are supervised distally, through telephone communication with their parents and rules and routines established by parents. Children who are monitored by telephone, and those who have parental rules to follow while caring for themselves, may experience no harmful effects from the arrangement. Those who are not monitored and spend their unsupervised time with peers are especially susceptible to engaging in problematic behavior (Steinberg, 1986).

Neighborhood setting. Characteristics of the neighborhood and its perceived safety play a role in determining children's adjustment to self-care. Children who live in urban areas, with attendant problems of crime and lack of safety, may experience negative consequences such as fear and social isolation when their parents require them to stay in the house after school. Research with children in suburban and rural areas has generally failed to find negative effects of self-care. These children experience fewer restrictions on outdoor play and fewer threats of physical harm (Robinson, Coleman, & Rowland, 1986).

Parent-child relationship. Another factor that plays a role in determining the outcomes of self-care is the quality of the parent-child relationship. Emotionally supportive parents who establish firm rules for their children's self-care time may protect children from negative consequences. Children who feel a strong attachment to their parents may experience fewer fears about being home alone in an urban environment, and parents who provide a great deal of emotional support protect their self-care children from exhibiting behavior problems (Vandell & Ramanan, 1991). The quality of children's experiences within their families is an important determinant of the outcomes of self-care arrangements.

Parents can teach self-care skills and safety rules to their children. This may help children to avoid injuries, emotional difficulties, and the poor selection of activities that may occur in self-care situations. Role playing, or acting out the correct response to potential problems, and occasional review sessions can help children to learn and maintain the necessary skills for caring for themselves during their out-of-school time.

References

Hofferth, S. L., Brayfield, A., Deich, S., & Holcomb, P. (1991). *National Child Care Survey, 1990*. Washington, DC: Urban Institute Press.

Robinson, B. E., Coleman, M., & Rowland, B. H. (1986, Summer). The after-school ecologies of latchkey children. *Children's Environments Quarterly*, *3*, 4–8.

Robinson, B. E., Rowland, B. H., & Coleman, M. (1986). *Latchkey kids: Unlocking doors for children and their families*. Lexington, MA: Lexington Books.

Steinberg, L. (1986). Latchkey children and susceptibility to peer pressure: An ecological analysis. *Developmental Psychology*, *22*, 433–439.

Vandell, D. L., & Ramanan, J. (1991). Children of the National Longitudinal Survey of Youth: Choices in after-school care and child development. *Developmental Psychology*, *27*, 637–643.

See also: After-school child care; Attachment, secure; Child care.

KIM M. PIERCE

Self-esteem. Self-esteem is a psychological construct that is frequently used by both research and practitioners in a variety of ways to refer to a person's sense of well-being. The lack of an established, clear definition, however, has hampered research and undermined the term's usefulness. The concept has also fallen into disfavor by some professionals who believe that its significance has been overrated.

Smith (1988) defined self-esteem as the value we place on what we believe to be true for ourselves. The emphasis in this approach is on an individual's construction and evaluation of "truth" as it applies to his or her humanity. A person's convictions of personal value are more important than superficial emotional experiences. Confidence and belief in oneself are the core of self-esteem and are not affected by transitory emotions. Individuals with self-esteem might be quite unhappy about their circumstances and might be angry toward themselves about the choices they have made. Self-esteem has little to do with putting on a "happy face." Similarly, being delighted about one's good fortune, gained at the expense of causing grief and pain to others, has nothing to do with self-esteem either. An honest self-examination would strip away the veneer of that artificial emotion. Self-esteem is the judgment we make after taking an honest look at our existence and becoming aware of the consequences of our actions. Translating this view of self-esteem into a operational form for use in research is a daunting task.

There are many research studies that show a positive relationship between supportive parental behavior and the self-esteem of children (Felson & Zielinski, 1989). Parental support in the form of praise and showing affection and respect may affect self-esteem through a process of self-appraisal. According to this view, originally proposed by Charles Cooley in 1902, self-appraisals develop through a process of role taking in which people come to see themselves through the eyes of significant others (Reiss, 1968). If children perceive their parents' supportive behaviors as reflecting positive appraisals, and if parents are highly significant others, then parental support should be a critical variable in the development of a child's self-esteem (Felson & Zielinski, 1989).

Smith (1988) identified four essential beliefs and contributing parental behaviors that establish a basis for self-esteem. The key to developing self-esteem involves fostering a child's *self-respect, hope* in the future, *courage* in making choices, and *compassion* toward others. Parents nurture self-respect in their children by coming to terms with and accepting what they cannot change in their children. They contribute to their children's hope by encouraging them to set goals and work toward a positive future. Empowering children contributes to their ability to courageously persevere, while love and affection promote the child's capacity for compassion.

Adolescents, especially girls, are especially vulnerable for the loss of self-worth. Parental affection or support is positively related to adolescent self-esteem. The relationship of the father toward his adolescent daughter appears to be particularly salient (Richards et al., 1991). A parenting style that avoids the excessive use of guilt, anxiety, and love withdrawal for use in controlling children's behavior appears to have a positive relationship to their self-esteem (Nielsen & Metha, 1994).

Roberts and Bengtson (1993) found long-term benefits of parent-child affection for a son's or daughter's psychological well-being in adulthood. Young adults who enjoyed greater parent-child affection during their late teens and early twenties reported higher self-esteem, which predicted greater psychological well-being 14 years later.

The self-esteem of parents has an impact on parent-child relationships. Low maternal self-esteem is associated with ineffective, coercive parent-child interaction. Mothers with higher self-esteem were more likely to provide their adolescent children with greater decision-making freedom and to view their children as independent. Mothers with higher self-esteem tended to have children who were more satisfied with the level of autonomy they were given to make their own decisions (Crouter & McHale, 1993).

What children and parents believe about themselves and the worth they associate with those personal truths have a significant impact on their relationships. Clear and confident conclusions, however, are difficult to make because of the variety of definitions and types of measurement used in studies on self-esteem (Nielsen & Metha, 1994).

References

Crouter, A. C., & McHale, S. M. (1993). The long arm of the job: Influences of parental work on childrearing. In T. Luster & L. Okagaki (Eds.), *Parenting: An ecological perspective* (pp. 179–202). Hillsdale, NJ: Lawrence Erlbaum Associates.

Felson, R. B., & Zielinski, M. A. (1989). Children's self-esteem and parental support. *Journal of Marriage and the Family, 51*, 727–735.

Nielsen, D. M., & Metha, A. (1994). Parental behavior and adolescent self-esteem in clinical and nonclinical samples. *Adolescence, 29* (115), 525–542.

Smith, C. A. (1988). *I'm positive: Growing up with self-esteem*. Manhattan: Kansas State Research and Extension.

Reiss, A. J. (Ed.). (1968). *Cooley and sociological analysis*. Ann Arbor: University of Michigan Press.

Richards, M. H., Gitelson, I. B., Peterson, A. C., & Hurtig, A. L. (1991). Adolescent personality in girls and boys. *Psychology of Women Quarterly*, *15*, 65–81.

Roberts, R. E. & Bengston, V. L. (1993). Relationships with parents, self-esteem, and psychological well-being in young adulthood. *Social Psychology Quarterly*, *56* (4), 263–277.

See also: Identity development; Social competence.

CHARLES A. SMITH

Self-fulfilling prophecy. Although extensive research has been conducted on the self-fulfilling prophecy, the main premise is quite simple: One's expectations of another have the potential to affect the other's behavior. The expectations that affect performance can be positive or negative. For example, a parent can either expect their children to do well in a competition or expect their children will make mistakes and perform poorly. Since the expectations of the parent have the potential to impact the outcome of their performance, children are likely to perform at the level expected of them. Explained in more detail, the self-fulfilling prophecy is a process in which the expectancies of one individual about another alter the behavior of the other in a way that observers would interpret as a confirmation of the perceiver's expectancy (Darley & Fazio, 1980). Although this concept can be applied to adult performance, the majority of research involves the effects of expectations on children.

One of the most influential applications of the self-fulfilling prophecy is when dealing with families. The parent-child relationship is especially crucial. Even a newborn baby can experience differences in parental expectations. In one study, infants who were labeled premature were both treated and perceived differently even though all the babies were actually similar. The "premature" infants were touched less, liked less, and rated as smaller and finer-featured than those babies labeled full-term. In addition, the infants labeled premature were less active than the full-term infants, presumably as a result of being treated differently due to the adult's preconceptions of premature infants. Not only did the adults treat and perceive the newborns differently; these actions appeared to produce differences in the infants' behaviors as well (Stern & Hildebrandt, 1986).

Although the education system is critical to the development of children, parents are often the key players. In the home environment, the positive involvement of parents is crucial to the competence and success of their children. If parents perceive their children as competent and relay that message to their children, the children have a better chance of perceiving themselves as capable and competent. If children perceive themselves as capable and competent, they will have an increased chance of a better self-concept and greater self-esteem. This type of positive encouragement from parents automatically provides children with a much-needed head start.

A significant relationship exists among children's self-perceptions of competence, parental beliefs about their children's competencies, and children's perceptions of these parental beliefs. Children's perceptions of academic competence and their beliefs about their parents' competence judgments are influenced more by their parents' beliefs than by their own record of achievement. Fathers of children with low perceptions of competence estimated that their children's abilities were lower than did fathers of children with average and high self-perceptions. Compared to other children, those with low perceptions of competence significantly underestimate their abilities, have more difficulty with school, prefer less challenging assignments, perceive that significant adults hold more negative perceptions of their competence, and adopt lower expectancies for success (Phillips, 1987). Again, these finding suggest that parental expectations have the potential to affect the performance of children.

Gender and culture are other important issues to consider when exploring the self-fulfilling prophecy. Both gender and cultural stereotypes have the potential to become self-fulfilling prophecies. Many examples can be used to illustrate this point. In the case of gender stereotypes, girls are often described as "nice," "good," or "cute." Boys, on the other hand, are described as "big," "strong," and "brave." In addition, many stereotypes specific to individual cultures exist. One of the first places that children learn gender and cultural stereotypes is in the home. Children not only learn that the sexes and cultures differ but that certain attributes are valued and are more relevant for one sex or culture than the other. Because of this, gender and cultural stereotypes can become self-fulfilling prophecies (Basow, 1992).

The well-supported notion of the self-fulfilling prophecy has major implications for parents, teachers, family life educators, clinicians, and researchers. Brophy (1983) offers guidelines for teachers that can be expanded for parents to minimize negative expectation effects and maximize positive expectation effects:

- Keep expectations for children current by monitoring their progress closely; stress present performance over past history.
- Set goals for children in terms of floors (minimally acceptable standards), not ceilings; let the child's progress rates, rather than limits adopted arbitrarily in advance, determine how far the child can go within the time available.
- When individualizing instruction and giving children feedback about performance, stress continuous progress relative to previous levels of mastery rather than normative comparisons or comparisons between individuals.
- When giving children feedback, stress the provision of informative information and not merely evaluation of success or failure.
- When children have not understood an explanation or demonstration, think in terms of diagnosing their difficulty in learning and following through by breaking down the task or reteaching it in a different way, rather than merely repeating the same instruction or giving up in frustration.
- Think in terms of stretching children's minds by stimulating them to achieve as much as they can and not in terms of "protecting" them from failure or embarrassment.

References

Basow, S. A. (1992). *Gender: Stereotypes and roles* (3rd ed.). Pacific Grove, CA: Brooks/Cole Publishing Co.

Brophy, J. E. (1983). Research on the self-fulfilling prophecy and teacher expectations. *Journal of Educational Psychology, 75* (5), 631–661.

Darley, J. M., & Fazio, R. H. (1980). Expectancy confirmation processes arising in the social interaction sequence. *American Psychologist, 35* (10), 867–881.

Phillips, D. A. (1987). Socialization of perceived academic competence among highly competent children. *Child Development, 58,* 1308–1320.

Stern, M., & Hildebrandt, K. (1986). Prematurity stereotyping: Effects on mother-infant interaction. *Child Development, 57* (2), 308–315.

See also: Acceptance, parental; Communication; Empowerment; Gender socialization; Nurturance; Self-esteem.

JENNIFER B. HUTCHINGS

Separation anxiety. Separation anxiety refers to the worry, trepidation, and outright distress felt by infants, toddlers, and some preschoolers when an attachment figure is absent. It is a difficult moment for children, caregivers, and parents alike. This troublesome experience is best understood by examining attachment to caregivers and the role of emotions, particularly fear.

First, attachment is the emotional tie of one person to another and refers to the special closeness that develops between the child and his or her caregivers. *Primary* attachment is the initial one-to-one relationship with a single human caretaker, usually a mother or father—the person who assumes the major responsibility for the child's care in an ongoing, consistent manner.

Secondary attachments are also formed with nonprimary caregivers such as grandparents, day care personnel, teachers, friends, and babysitters. These individuals provide supplemental support for both children and their parents. Attachments give the child internal working models for all subsequent relationships in life: "This is my person who comforts me when I am distressed and shares good times with me. I can count on this person. I just want to be near this person."

Both primary and secondary attachment relationships provide a "secure base" that allows children to explore their environment and experience a feeling of mastery over their activities and surroundings. Fear of strangers and separation anxiety are also developmentally appropriate ways in which infants and toddlers demonstrate that their attachment figures are important and unique. These manifestations of an attachment relationship are important indices of social-emotional functioning during the periods of infancy and toddlerhood. Successfully negotiating the separation anxiety milestone is particularly important for moving on to the more advanced developmental tasks of autonomy and entering the world of peers. That goal is achieved through caregiver/parent consistency, responsiveness, and emotional availability. Parents should monitor their own behavior and that of secondary caregivers to assure these qualities.

Attachment also has an emotional basis, and separation anxiety can be seen as a special case of fear. It is important to examine the intra- and interpersonal regulatory functions of emotions when discussing separation anxiety. Emotional behaviors signal a need for change in the goal-directed behavior of both self and others. The tight brows, raised and drawn together, and high-pitched voice of fear tell caregivers that the child experiencing separation anxiety needs comfort. Experiencing separation anxiety also spurs the child to perform specific behaviors, such as searching for the attachment figure. Emotions also serve adaptive functions—in the case of separation anxiety, it is adaptive to remove oneself from a dangerous situation, such as being without a caregiver.

Although fears can serve the useful purpose of acting as cues for potentially dangerous situations, in excess they create considerable discomfort and social drawbacks for the child. As a special kind of fear, then, separation anxiety can be considered on a continuum. A certain amount is common and expected, especially in infancy and toddlerhood, but the more intense and later experienced it is, the more separation anxiety gets in the way of feeling comfortable in the environment and interacting with others.

Research has shown that children can be prepared for separation before its first occurrence. The following ideas may be useful to minimize separation anxiety (see also Crosser, 1995):

- Provide children with information before leaving them. Brief preparations help children understand the departure, but extensive, lengthy preparations can actually cause more distress.
- Familiarize both primary caregiver and child with any caregiving setting in advance. The presence of primary caregiver and the introduction to the secondary caregiver help reduce stress.
- The caregiver may make a home visit before enrollment; any procedure that maximizes their familiarity to the child can be useful (Donate-Bartfield & Passman, 1995).
- Allow the child to gradually adjust to the separation and the setting, perhaps attending for just a few hours the first few days, gradually extending to full days (Field, 1991).
- Establish a routine procedure for entry and exit in the child care environment.
- Permit the child to bring a favorite toy or blanket; an attachment object can help assuage separation from the human attachment figure (Passman, 1977).
- Post photographs of the child and the family to help the child feel more at home.
- Parents and caregivers both must be sensitive to the child's signals. It is normal that some days separating from a parent is more difficult than at other times. Parents may need to linger a bit longer on these days or especially at the beginning of any new caregiving situation.

References

Adams, R. E., & Passman, R. H. (1981). The effects of preparing two-year-olds for brief separations from their mothers. *Child Development, 52*, 1068–1070.

Crosser, S. (1995). I want my Mommy now! *Early Childhood News, 7* (3), 14–18.

Donate-Bartfield, E. L., & Passman, R. H. (1995, August). *Strangers' spending time with children affects adaptation to maternal separation.* Paper presented at the annual convention of the American Psychological Association, New York, NY.

Field, T. M. (1991). Young children's adaptations to repeated separations from their mothers. *Child Development, 62*, 539–547.

Passman, R. H. (1977). Providing attachment objects to facilitate learning and reduce distress: Effects of mothers and security blankets. *Developmental Psychology, 13,* 25–28.

See also: Affectivity, positive and negative; Attachment, secure; Child care; Fear; Floortime.

SUSANNE A. DENHAM

Sex education. Sex education for children begins at birth and continues throughout their lifetime. Parents are the first and foremost sex educators of their children whether they say much or nothing about sex (Gordon & Gordon, 1989). Children are sexual beings. They are as curious about sex as they are about life in general. How questions about sex are answered, how parents and relatives act, and how the total concept of sexuality is handled are a part of a children's informal sex education within the family.

Although many parents feel it is their responsibility to teach their children about sex, most are reluctant, uncomfortable, embarrassed, or unprepared to do so. College students in human sexuality classes report that "sex was never discussed in my family," "sex was hush hush, rather akin to cursing," or "sex wasn't really talked about until it was on the TV screen, and then it was time to turn the channel" (Bergen, 1988). These same students, however, reported that parents were their first choice for receiving sex education.

Sex education began in a more formal sense in the United States in the early 1900s with references to the importance of instruction in sexual hygiene in preparation for marriage and parenthood. The 1919 White House Conference on Child Welfare suggested that sex education become a task of the school. Federal government agencies and national organizations such as the United States Public Health Service, National Education Association, American Medical Association, and American Social Health Association made statements and published documents in support of sex education (Means, 1962). The *Sex Information and Education Council of the United States* (SIECUS) and the *American Association of Sex Educators, Counselors, and Therapists* (AASECT), two groups that began in the 1960s, continue to strongly support sex education through their literature and programs.

Social forces within the twentieth century, such as two world wars, changes in family lifestyles, technological advances in communication and transportation, and the beginning of sex research influenced our thinking about human sexuality.

From instruction in sexual hygiene and parenthood preparation in the early 1990s, sex education has evolved today to embrace the totality of human sexuality, a concept involving much more than anatomy and reproduction. Sexuality is an important dimension and foundation of family life, and sexuality education is associated with knowledge, beliefs, attitudes, decisions, behaviors, emotions, responsibilities, and relationships throughout the life cycle.

Today at state and local levels, formal sexuality education is provided in schools, social agencies that serve parents and families, religious groups, health departments, and medical organizations. Programs have different goals, depending on the sponsorship and where they are held. Emphasis is placed primarily on solving existing social problems, such as unwanted teenage pregnancy, epidemic levels of sexually transmitted diseases, drug and alcohol use related to sexuality, and the high proportion of sexual assault and violence in our society.

Within the decades of the 1980s and 1990s, a majority of the states have either required or recommended that human sexuality and AIDS (Acquired Immunodeficiency Syndrome) education be taught in the schools at both elementary and secondary levels. For most parents and children, sexuality education programs within the schools have greater interest, impact, and concern for them than other agency programs. Nearly 90% of parents want their children to be informed about sex and want the schools to provide the information (Haas & Haas, 1993).

Although it is frequently viewed as important for a child to develop a healthy, happy, balanced lifestyle, sexuality education in the schools is often controversial. Parents and other vocal groups opposing sex education in the schools focus on what content is being taught, who is doing the teaching, what values are being discussed, and whether the moral fiber of the nation and the responsibility of the parent are being weakened. A major criticism of sex education is that telling children and teens about contraception and intercourse removes an inhibitory barrier and encourages sexual experimentation and an increase in sexual relations.

Does sex education work? Haas and Haas (1993) cited several research studies that have concluded that (1) sex education does provide accurate information; (2) students do gain new knowledge and understanding; (3) students feel more able to communicate their feelings and talk about their relationship with a partner; (4) sex education does *not* lead to an increase in sexual activity; (5) sex instruction reduces the peer pressure to become sexually active; and (6) sex education seems to have some success in reducing unwanted pregnancies.

Sex education is effective, but improvements can be made. Instruction by parents should begin in infancy and continue throughout adolescence and young adulthood. Parental instruction should include discussion about family values, since they are a central part of sexual behavior. School programs should involve parents and community members in planning stages, offer accurate information, be developmentally appropriate, extend from kindergarten to adulthood, encourage peer participation in teaching, be taught by teachers well trained in sexuality education, and provide for ongoing evaluation of their effectiveness.

References

Bergen, M. B. (1988). Sex education? Not from my parents? *Education n 88, 3* (2), 14–16.

Gordon, S., & Gordon, J. (1989). *Raising a child conservatively in a sexually permissive world.* New York: Simon & Schuster.

Haas, K., & Haas, A. (1993). *Understanding sexuality.* St. Louis, MO: Mosby.

Means, R. K. (1962). *A history of health education in the United States.* Philadelphia, PA: Lea & Febiger.

See also: Adolescent pregnancy; AIDS/HIV; AIDS/HIV, adolescent; Sexuality, adolescent.

M. BETSY BERGEN

Sex roles. "Is it a boy or a girl?" is generally the first question asked when an infant is born. Based on the gender distinction at birth of either male or female, children begin to learn the sex or gender role for their sex. The terms *sex roles* and *gender roles* refer to the behaviors that are expected of females and males within a particular society. These roles include dress and appearance, work and play activities, occupations and obligations within both the family and the society, and social skills and behavior (Beal, 1994).

Although some sex roles are mandated by biology—e.g., women bear children—a greater number of sex roles are socially determined by the society in which one lives. Each society has expectations for its children, and boys and girls must learn the sex roles for their gender. Often, these expectations become prescriptive "stereotypes," in that *all* boys and *all* girls must behave in the prescribed manner acceptable for their gender. Parents are expected to guide their child's development and behavior so that their child fits into the appropriate sex role. In other words, boys learn to be boys and girls learn to be girls. Fathers, more than mothers, tend to make more distinctions between their sons and daughters, especially concerning play activities. Daughters may be "tomboys," but sons can never be "sissies"!

Gender becomes a core part of a child's personal identity very early and, as such, plays an important part in one's interactions with others. Children learn what the sexes are like from about ages 1 to 3 years. Although parents are the first role models for their child, they are not totally responsible for sex-role socialization. Children have their own ideas about what boys and girls do, and in their need to be accepted, they adhere to the expectations of their peers. School and media also influence the sex-role behavior of girls and boys in specific areas, and evidence suggests that children are willing and even eager to conform (Beal, 1994).

Flexibility of sex roles in adulthood has undergone several changes in the past decades in the United States. However, most of the changes have come in expectations in what girls can do. Most women are employed outside the home, and men are encouraged to devote additional time and energy to housework and child rearing. As to the careers men and women choose, fewer restrictions and legal barriers exist. Nevertheless, both explicit and subtle pressures during the adolescent years often limit the options for choice. Beal (1994) has suggested that girls can be ambitious and sports inclined, but few adults are supportive of a gentle boy interested in fashion and ballet.

Although sex roles have become more flexible in recent decades, arbitrary and unnecessary gender distinctions that remain within our society should be confronted. Parents can emphasize nonsexist child rearing in the toys they choose, in the books they read to their children, in the television programs they permit their children to view, in the activities they support, and in the feedback they give their children. Parents can be assured that some of the early exaggerated stereotyping phases do not appear to predict a child's interests as an adult. With older children, parents can insist that gender not be the only justification for career choices and personal pursuits.

Finally, as a society, we cannot completely eliminate gender differences, but we can continue to move toward gender equity for both girls and boys. Parents, teachers, and society in general can strive to encourage both genders to be "all they can be."

Reference

Beal, C. R. (1994). *Boys and girls: The development of gender roles*. New York: McGraw-Hill.

See also: Gender socialization; Identity development.

M. BETSY BERGEN

Sexuality, adolescent. Adolescent sexuality refers to a complex set of sexual feelings and behaviors as well as adolescents' sexual identity or sense of themselves as sexual beings. In spite of this broad definition, *adolescent sexuality* is often narrowly used synonymously with *adolescent sexual intercourse*. This narrow definition can be harmful by causing parents, researchers, policy makers, teachers, therapists, and adolescents themselves to neglect discussing and understanding the importance of adolescents' feelings, sense of themselves as sexual beings, and the plethora of other sexual behaviors in which adolescents engage (Welsh, Rostosky, & Kawaguchi, in press).

Adolescence is a crucial time for the development of sexuality because it is a time when many biological, psychological, and social changes occur. For example, puberty, the biological hallmark of adolescence, represents the greatest physical change since birth. In addition to substantial growth in height, weight, and musculature, adolescents' sex hormone levels increase markedly. The increased level of sex hormones causes increased frequency and intensity of sexual arousal. Another change is adolescents' newly acquired cognitive ability, formal operational thought, which permits adolescents to think abstractly and to take others' perspectives. These new cognitive and interpersonal skills allow for more complex interpersonal relationships and facilitate the development of intimacy and identity. These changes occur within a cultural context that provides them with meaning and significance. This context includes parents, peers, schools, churches, and the mass media, each of which helps construct adolescents' sense of sexuality.

Most adolescents first experience sexual activity alone, either by having erotic fantasies and/or by masturbating. By middle adolescence, the majority of adolescents have engaged in some sexual behaviors with another person. Adolescents today engage in sexual intercourse at earlier ages than they did a generation ago. The median age at which adolescents first have intercourse is about 16 years (Scales, 1991).

The integration of sexuality into one's sense of identity and relationships is one of the primary tasks of adolescence. Harry Stack Sullivan (1953) described the integration of intimacy and sexuality into the same relationship as the primary goal of adolescence. When adolescents are not able to integrate these aspects into a single relationship, they are likely to experience relationship difficulties and lower self-esteem. Parents can facilitate their adolescent children's' healthy sexual development by modeling relationships that integrate sexuality and intimacy and by maintaining open communication with their children. Parents can inhibit the development of healthy sexual relationships in their children by forbidding their adolescents to develop romantic relationships and discouraging discussions of sexuality.

Unfortunately, adolescents and their parents generally report a lack of communication about sexuality. The most important reason given by parents for this lack of communication is their own discomfort about sex. This trend is unfortunate because it results in adolescents receiving the vast majority of their information about sexuality from peers. The information they receive is often inaccurate, as their peers are also poorly informed about the topic. In addition, the guilt and shame our culture associates with sexuality inhibit conversations about the meaning that adolescents make of their feelings and behaviors. Parental discipline is also related to adolescents' sexual behaviors. Sexual activity is lowest among adolescents who perceive their parents to be moderately strict. Families who are either very liberal or very conservative tend to have more sexually experienced adolescents (Miller et al., 1986).

Discussions of adolescent sexuality must take into account the different experiences of males and females. Adolescent girls and boys are socialized differently and, thus, imbue their sexual experiences with very different meanings. Adolescent boys are more likely to understand their sexual activities as recreational; adolescent girls tend to associate sexual activity with intimacy and commitment (Hendrick & Hendrick, 1994). These differences reflect different social attitudes toward sexuality: Society is more discouraging of females' sexual activity outside of committed relationships. Research suggests that adolescent girls' sexual behaviors are influenced by their social contexts to a much greater extent than are adolescent boys' sexual behaviors. The strongest predictor of adolescent boys' sexual behavior is their level of sex hormones. For adolescent girls, however, hormonal levels play a much less powerful role in influencing their sexual behavior. Girls' sexual behavior depends largely on their social contexts including the quality of their relations with their families and peers (Udry & Billy, 1987). Adolescent girls' family contexts also influence their rates of physiological maturation. Girls who are emotionally closer to their families experience puberty later than those from less connected families.

The facilitation of healthy adolescent sexual development requires policy makers and care providers to help create safe environments conducive for adolescents to explore and discuss their sexual feelings, behaviors, and their experience of being sexual people. These environments need to include the people who are most meaningful to adolescents such as their parents, clergy, teachers, counselors, and extended family. Adolescents benefit from the availability of appropriate role models with whom they can explore their feelings. Fear, guilt, and shame generated by current societal attitudes toward sexuality inhibit this sort of exploration by making adults afraid to talk about sexuality with adolescents. Healthy exploration must extend beyond public programs and into the lives of adolescents, involving family members and other culturally significant people, and incorporate an appreciation for diverse cultures and contexts.

References

Hendrick, S., & Hendrick, C. (1994, February). Gender, sexuality, and close relationships. In R. Turner (Chair), *Sexuality and interpersonal relationships*. Symposium conducted at the biennial meeting of the Society for Research on Adolescence, San Diego, CA.

Miller, B. C., McCoy, J. K., Olson, T. D., & Wallace, C. M. (1986). Parental discipline and control attempts in relation to adolescent sexual attitudes and behavior. *Journal of Marriage and the Family, 48*, 503–512.

Scales, P. (1991). *A portrait of young adolescents in the 1990s: Implications for promoting healthy growth and development.* Chapel Hill, NC: Center for Early Adolescence.

Sullivan, H. S. (1953). *The interpersonal theory of psychiatry.* New York: Norton.

Udry, J. R., and Billy, J. (1987). Initiation of coitus in early adolescence. *American Sociological Review, 52*, 841–855.

Welsh, D. P., Rostosky, S. S., & Kawaguchi, M.C. (in press). A normative perspective of adolescent girls' developing sexuality. In C. B. Travis & J. S. White (Eds.), *Sex, culture, and feminism: Psychological perspectives on women.* Washington, DC: American Psychological Association.

See also: Adolescent pregnancy; Gender socialization; Sex education.

DEBORAH P. WELSH, MYRA C. KAWAGUCHI,
AND SHARON S. ROSTOSKY

Sexual offenders, youthful. Any male or female who uses coercion (i.e., manipulation or control) to force another person to engage in sexual behavior considered socially or developmentally inappropriate may be characterized as a *sexual offender*. Although *youthful sexual offenders* commonly range in age from 12 through 18, younger offenders (i.e., 4 years of age) have been identified. Sexual offenses perpetrated by youthful offenders include assaultive sexual behavior (e.g., oral and vaginal penetration or sexual touching and fondling) as well as so-called hands-off offenses (e.g., exhibitionism, voyeurism, and obscene telephone calls). Offenses may be heterosexual or homosexual and are more commonly perpetrated against youth younger than themselves. Though some variance by jurisdiction and research exists, it is common to believe that youth under the age of 18 cannot engage in "consensual" sexual behavior; thus, sexual interaction between an adolescent and a younger child is regarded as an offense regardless of whether coercion is involved.

Due to the number of victims, the frequency of assaults, and the long- and short-term consequences of sexual victimization, the issue of sexual perpetration has become an important and serious problem in modern Western society. Prior to 1970, only nine major papers addressed youthful sexual offending. Previous to 1980 the prevailing view of sexual offenses committed by youth was that "they constituted nuisance value only, reflecting a 'boys-will-be-boys,' attitude," thus perpetuating "a discounted estimate of the severity of harm produced" (Barbaree, Hudson, & Seto, 1993, p. 10). However, sexual offenses committed by youth range from 5 to 16 per 1000, with Knopp (1982) suggesting that 450,000 offenses were committed by youth in the United States in 1976. The seriousness of the problem is intensified when one considers that the average youthful sexual offender will, without treatment, commit 380 sexual crimes in his or her lifetime (Abel et al., 1984).

Research on the sex offenses among youth focuses on its biological and developmental origins. *Biological theories* suggest that the basis of the sexually aberrant behavior may be correlated with hormonal (e.g., testosterone) or brain anomalies (e.g., brain damage or dysfunction resulting from accidents, surgery, epilepsy, or toxic substances) that impede cognitive processing. Overall, research only modestly supports the assumption that there is a relationship between hormonal influences and sexually offensive behavior.

Developmental theories suggest the foundation for sexually offensive behavior lies in the formation of interpersonal relationship skills and self-reinforcing compulsive behaviors. Deficits in interpersonal skills, repertoire and/or behavioral, may promote intimacy issues such as lack of respect, inappropriate expectations, and distorted perceptions. Origins of sexually aberrant behaviors have been correlated with pathological family interaction, with individuals progressing through three levels (Schwartz, 1995). *Level One* incorporates a wide range of sexual behaviors including masturbation, heterosexual and homosexual relationships, pornography, and prostitution. *Level Two* is comprised of sexual activities for which individuals, if apprehended, will be prosecuted (e.g., voyeurism, exhibitionism, and obscene phone calls). *Level Three* is characterized by felony sex offenses—rape, child molestation, and incest. Carnes (1983) suggests that the aberrant cycle begins with distorted beliefs, followed by impaired thinking, and inclusion of acting-out patterns similar to substance abuse, gambling, and/or eating disorders. Thus, the behavior becomes self-reinforcing much the same as addictive or obsessive-compulsive behaviors.

Perry and Orchard (1992) suggest five broad goals important to treatment:

- fostering a sense of responsibility by working through distorted perceptions about the offenses and interpersonal relationships
- establishing an appropriate sense of empathy for victims, and generalizing this sense of respect and concern toward others
- identifying one's offense pattern and establishing strategies that interrupt the behavior when specific trigger signals are provided
- reeducating the offender in appropriate sexual knowledge and social interaction patterns while challenging stereotyped attitudes about sex roles and intimacy
- facilitating positive interpersonal relations by providing specific skills training according to diagnosed deficits (e.g., assertiveness or empathy training)

While the impact of perpetration by a family member on the family system is not well addressed, three factors enhance family resiliency while fostering a proactive response. First is *the lack of personal (psychopathology) and/or family dysfunction.* Healthy patterns of interpersonal interaction—for example, effective communication, appropriate generational boundaries, coparental stability, and empathy for others—increase the likelihood that sexually offensive behavior will be appropriately addressed. Second is *victimization status*, which refers to whether the youth has been victimized, the length of time victimization occurred, and the relationship of the victim to his perpetrator. While current research suggests that a majority of physically and sexually abused male youth perpetrate, not all abused youth become perpetrators! Impact on the family is lessened when the abuse of a child is recognized, with intervention instigated prior to the first offense. Finally, *community support* (e.g., religious or social organizations, or neighbors) provides the family with a system they can turn to through the difficult times of restructuring and intervention. Effective utilization of community resources can provide temporary stability for the family during a period of crisis.

References
Able, G. G., Becker, J. V., Cunningham-Rathner, J., Rouleau, J., Kaplan, M., & Reich, J. (1984). *Treatment manual: The treatment of child molesters*. Tuscaloosa, AL: Emory University Clinic, Department of Psychiatry.
Barbaree, H. E., Hudson, S. M., & Seto, M. C. (1993). Sexual assault in society: The role of the juvenile offender. In H. E. Barbaree, W. L. Marshall, & S. M. Hudson (Eds.), *The juvenile sex offender* (pp. 1-24). New York: Guilford Press.
Carnes, P. (1983). *Out of the shadows*. Minneapolis, MN: CompCare.
Knopp, F. H. (1982). *Remedial intervention in adolescent sex offenses: Nine program descriptions*. Syracuse, NY: Safer Society Press.
Perry, G. P., & Orchard, J. (1992). *Assessment & treatment of adolescent sex offenders*. Sarasota, FL: Professional Resource Press.
Schwartz, B. K. (1995) Theories of sex offenses. In B. K. Schwartz & H. R. Cellini (Eds.), *The sex offender: Corrections, treatment and legal practice*. Kingston, NJ: Civic Research Institute.

See also: Abuse, child; Aggression, chilhood; Delinquency, juvenile; Sexuality, adolescent.

D. KIM OPENSHAW

Shame. Shame is a global evaluation that one's central, personal inadequacies have been exposed. To feel shame is to feel seen in a painfully diminished sense. The self feels exposed to both itself and anyone else present. This sudden, unexpected feeling of exposure and accompanying self-consciousness characterizes the essential nature of the affect of shame.

According to Lewis (1992), shame is a negative judgment that one makes about one's self as a whole. Shame results in the disruption of ongoing behavior, confusion in thought, and a withdrawal from contact. The physical reaction involves a shrinking of the body, as though to disappear from the eye of the self or other. Signs of shame also include lowering the eyes, hanging the head, or blushing. Because it is a global evaluation, shame tends to persist over time.

Shame has critical functions for the development of conscience (Barrett, 1995). The intensity of the feeling has an impact on behavior and its display serves to communicate deference and submission. Shame makes it painful to "do wrong." Shame helps the child in acquiring knowledge of the self as an object by highlighting how the self appears to others (or the internalized others). Shame highlights standards and their importance. The emotion amplifies awareness of wrongdoing, connecting whatever event activated shame with any responses that follow it. Shame is crucial to the development of identity, conscience, and personal dignity. Shame is equally central to the development of self-esteem and intimacy. It also serves to maintain the other's respect and/or affection and preserve self-regard. Excessive shame, however, is associated with worthlessness, incompetence, and helplessness.

Research on self-referencing ability illustrates the developmental progression of a child's capacity for feeling shame (Lewis, 1992). By the end of their second year, children have objective self-awareness in a mirror. They will recognize by their reflection that they have a smudge on their nose, for example. In the middle of the second year of life, children seem to be capable of recognizing their own pictures on the basis of feature differences alone. They will label their own pictures by the end of their second year. Personal pronouns appear at this time but are not used by a majority until 36 months of age. During the middle of their third year, children develop the ability to abstract. They can create representations of representations—for example, use a toy block to represent a toy car. This representational ability is important for children to develop representations of themselves based on experience and memory. Also at this time, children will look up at an adult after achieving some goal and call his or her attention to the achievement.

The understanding of shame becomes more sophisticated as children grow older (Ferguson, Stegge, & Damhuis, 1990). Elementary school children can differentiate between shame and guilt. Social-cognitive, physical, and interpersonal changes during early adolescence may be associated with normative increases in shame.

What impact do parents have on the development of shame? Parental reactions of shame to a child's behavior through what Lewis (1992) calls a "disgusted, contemptuous face" are influential. Love withdrawal (e.g., "I don't what to be near you when you are like that!") can trigger shame. There are also intriguing sex differences in the acquisition of shame and guilt. Girls are generally socialized to place responsibility on themselves for failure while attributing success to something outside of themeselves. Consequently, girls are more likely to feel shame when they fail than boys.

Parents who have long-term heightened emotionality can also affect the extent of shame in children. Depressed mothers are likely to blame themselves for their problems. These women tend to make global evaluations of failure about themselves and about their children. Moreover, the children of depressed mothers receive more love withdrawal punishment and are likely to assume blame for their parents' distress.

A global feeling of self-worth moderates shame. Forming a personal relationship where one feels deeply affirmed and valued will strengthen the child's capacity for integrating shame into a healthy conscience.

References

Barrett, K. C. (1995). A functionalist approach to shame and guilt. In J. Tangney & K. Fischer (Eds.), *Self-conscious emotions: The psychology of shame, guilt, embarrassment, and pride* (pp. 25–63). New York: Guilford Press.

Ferguson, T., Stegge, H., & Damhuis, I. (1990). Guilt and shame experiences in elementary school-age children. In P. D. Drenth, J. A. Sergeant, & R. J. Takens (Eds.),

European perspectives in psychology (Vol. 1, pp. 195–218). New York: John Wiley
& Sons.
Lewis, M. (1992). *Shame: The exposed self.* New York: Free Press.

See also: Guilt; Limit setting; Moral development; Rules, implicit; Self-esteem.

CHARLES A. SMITH

Shyness. Theories concerning the origins of shyness vary depending on the
theoretical background of related research. They range from inherited personality traits to symptoms of unconscious conflicts, to the programming of society,
to the lack of learned social skills, to the concept of labeling one as "shy." The
concept of social fear is present in some way in all perspectives on shyness.

Shyness shares the physiological characteristics of other types of fear including pounding heart, sweaty palms, and the cognitive perception of threat.
What makes shyness different from other forms of fear is that the perceived
threat involves fear of people and social situations. Shy children tend to feel
very anxious and distressed during interpersonal encounters. These feelings stem
from being emotionally threatened by those around them (see Zimbardo, 1977).

Shy children are more vulnerable than "nonshy" children in their need for
acceptance and approval by others. This vulnerability leads to fears of rejection
and nonacceptance by the shy child's peers. The conflict that shy children face
involves wanting to *approach* others and gain acceptance, coupled with the
overwhelming fear of wanting to *avoid* social rejection (Asendorpf, 1993). Shyness can be manifested anywhere on a continuum from feeling awkward and
embarrassed to traumatic episodes of withdrawal and depression. Two types of
shyness, *fearful* shyness and *self-conscious* shyness, have been explored in depth
by Arnold H. Buss (1980). Parenting styles influence both types of shyness.

Fearful shyness is developed in the first year of life, mainly in response to
unfamiliar adults. Infants seek the comfort and security of their parents when
they experience stranger anxiety. If this security is provided along with continued exposure to other adults who are non-threatening, this fearful shyness diminishes over time. In some children, this type of shyness persists and is exacerbated not only by stranger anxiety but by intrusiveness of others on both
physical and psychological levels. This fear of being intruded on can lead to inhibition and withdrawal in older children and adults. Respect for individual
space and privacy is vital in helping children overcome this sense of invasion.
The third cause of fearful shyness is social evaluation. When children perceive
themselves as rejected by others or making social mistakes, those prone to shyness withdraw and become extremely cautious. Parents must be aware of the
dangers of negative evaluations on the self-esteem of their children and work
hard to not become evaluators themselves.

Self-conscious shyness develops only after children become aware of themselves as social objects. Parents become extremely influential in the development of this shyness. Although it is very fitting to teach children socially appropriate behaviors, parents can foster self-conscious shyness by constantly reminding children that they are being observed and judged by others. For exam-

ple, parents who feel that others are scrutinizing them may pass their own sense of self-consciousness onto their children by focusing on the acceptability of children's manners, behaviors, and personal styles. When parents constantly demand that children pay attention to the way others perceive and accept them, children who are afraid of rejection withdraw even more to escape this pressure. Conversely, parents who demonstrate acceptance and support tend to foster healthier self-esteem and less shyness in their children.

Eastburg and Johnson (1990) examined the correlation between acceptance and support and shyness in a study involving female college students. Their study produced results indicating that the more acceptance the participants received from their mothers, the less shy they perceived themselves. Acceptance was measured by amounts of child centeredness, possessiveness, rejection, positive involvement, acceptance of individuation, and hostile detachment students felt their mothers demonstrated. Low amounts of hostile detachment and high amounts of the other variables correlated with nonshy behaviors and attitudes.

Family environment as well as genetics appeared to affect the shyness of children (Plomin & Daniels, 1986). Infants who were adopted appeared to develop a shyness level similar to that of their biological mothers. Adopted children's shyness also correlated with their adoptive parents' shyness and sociability. Though more research needs to be conducted to further examine the genetic variable, it is apparent that parents definitely have an effect on the amount of shyness their children develop.

There appears to be a correlation between shy parents and shy children. This is a particularly difficult situation requiring parents to overcome their own very real fears in order to help their children and prevent shyness from becoming a generational inhibitor. Teachers, researchers, and practitioners all play vital roles in helping those who are inhibited by social fears.

References
Asendorpf, J. B. (1993). Abnormal shyness in children. *Journal of Child Psychology and Psychiatry, 34* (7), 1069–1081.
Buss, A. H. (1980). *Self-consciousness and social anxiety.* New York: W. H. Freeman.
Eastburg, M., & Johnson, W. B. (1990). Shyness and perceptions of parental behavior. *Psychological Reports, 66,* 915–921.
Plomin, R., & Daniels, D. (1986). *Shyness: Perspectives on research and treatment.* New York & London: Plenum Press.
Zimbardo, P. G. (1977). *Shyness: What it is, what to do about it.* New York: Addison-Wesley.

See also: Peer influence; Social competence; Temperament.

                                                                                      JILL M. THORNGREN

Siblings. Empirical research has addressed a broad spectrum of questions about siblings from childhood through adolescence and in numerous cultural contexts (see, e.g., Brody, 1996; Cicirelli, 1995; Dunn & Plomin, 1990; Zukow, 1989). The majority of this research focuses on the relationship between brothers and sisters who share the same biological parents; little research has focused on stepbrothers, stepsisters, or adopted children.

Individual differences in sibling relationships in early childhood have been identified along two affective dimensions. Whether called prosocial and agonistic, affectionate and hostile, friendly and conflictual, or simply positive and negative, these two dimensions of opposite emotional valence surface repeatedly in the literature as the best way to conceptualize the quality of sibling interactions at a particular point in time. Recently, researchers have begun to investigate the organization of these dimensions into more complex patterns of positive and negative qualities, leading to characterizations of siblings as harmonious, hostile, intense, detached, ambivalent, and neutral (Rosen, 1997). The antecedents and consequences of these patterns, the factors that lead to their organization and relative stability over time, are issues to be addressed in future research.

Developmental changes in sibling relationships. Over the first year of the younger sibling's life, there is evidence of a mutually interactive relationship developing. This follows an initial period of adjustment for the older sibling, who may respond to the entrance of the new sibling with a combination of helpfulness, curiosity, and affection, as well as regressive behaviors (e.g., regression in toilet training, temper tantrums, withdrawal, and increased whining and clinging behavior). During the second and third years, younger siblings grow in their understanding of others' feelings. In the sibling relationship that knowledge can lead to greater empathy and concern, as well as teasing and mischievous rule breaking. Younger siblings also become more equal partners as language, imitation, and pretend play become more sophisticated. Conflict changes from physical aggression to more frequent use of verbal strategies.

Several cross-sectional studies show that as siblings move through childhood into adolescence, their relationships tend to become more egalitarian and less conflictual. Longitudinal studies reveal that with new individual and dyadic developmental challenges there is little continuity in discrete behaviors but marked stability in qualitative aspects of the sibling relationship. The processes that lead to this relative stability within a context of developmental change remain unclear and warrant further study.

Factors that influence the sibling relationship. Studies examining maternal behaviors, such as control, approval, and responsiveness, as well as security in the mother-child attachment relationship, have found correlations between these variables (high control, disapproval, low responsiveness, insecure attachments) and negative aspects of the sibling relationship (rivalry, hostility, control, competition, distress, aggression). But mothers' behaviors are also related to more positive aspects of sibling relationships. Mothers who talk more frequently to the older sibling about the younger one's feelings and attributes as a person later have children with friendlier sibling relationships. Infants who engage in longer social exchanges with their mothers are more likely to have longer turn-taking sequences with their older siblings. Older siblings with secure attachments to their mothers provide more caregiving to distressed younger siblings. Even when maternal behavior is not measured explicitly, but sibling behavior in her presence is compared to sibling behavior in her absence, siblings interact more negatively (but not less positively) when she is present. However, the processes leading to these associations, the influence of each child's temperament, and the role that fathers and other caregivers play in the patterns that develop between siblings have not been clarified.

The links between paternal behavior and aspects of sibling relationships may differ from those for maternal behavior; however, the paucity of research on fathers and siblings precludes definitive conclusions at this time. The few observational studies of young siblings that included both parents have found similarities and differences in maternal and paternal behaviors with young siblings. For example, mothers have been found to direct more positive behavior to both their children than do fathers. Both parents enact differential behavior with their children (unequal treatment of older versus younger siblings) to a similar degree, and both parents interact more with the younger (than older) sibling. Mothers report spending more time with their younger (and older) children than fathers; their interactions tend to be organized around nurturance and guidance, often incorporated into household activity, while father-child interactions tend to involve play, physical activity, and special outings.

Future research needs to incorporate multiple methods of assessing siblings in different contexts and over time. Contributions of each child to the patterns that emerge in the dyad need to be better understood. The influence of mothers and fathers, characteristics of each child, multiple attachments within the family, and the marital relationship on the sibling dyad all need to be clarified. The study of the developmental consequences of patterns of sibling relationships is an important new direction for research, theory, and clinical intervention.

References

Brody, G. H. (Ed.). (1996). *Sibling relationships: Their causes and consequences.* Norwood, NJ: Ablex Publishing Corporation.

Cicirelli, V. G. (1995). *Sibling relationships across the life span.* New York: Plenum Press.

Dunn, J., & Plomin, R. (1990). *Separate lives: Why siblings are so different.* New York: Basic Books.

Rosen, K. S. (1997). *Untangling the web of sibling connections.* Paper presented at The Mary Ingraham Bunting Institute of Radcliffe College. Cambridge, MA.

Zukow, P. G. (1989). *Sibling interaction across cultures: Theoretical and methodological issues.* New York: Springer-Verlag.

See also: Family systems; Temperament.

KAREN ROSEN AND PATRICIA B. BURKE

Single parents. Single parents are those who have primary responsibility for caring for their minor (under the age of 18 years) children living in their homes. About 50% to 60% of children will live in a single-parent family for some time before they reach the age of 18 (Martin & Bumpass, 1989). Thus, many children will spend some of their childhood being raised primarily by a single parent. Most (90%) single parents are women.

The majority of these parents become single parents following divorce (particularly for white Americans), but an increasing number of single parents have never been married to their children's other parent (particularly for African Americans). A smaller percentage become single parents when a parent in a two-parent family dies. Death was the most common pathway to becoming a single parent in the past but is now relatively rare because of the increased longevity of the population.

Challenges. Being a single parent poses numerous challenges for parents and children. First, because there is only one adult in the home rather than two, single parents have to perform a larger proportion of household maintenance and child-rearing responsibilities than they would in a two-parent family. Second, single parents, particularly single mothers, have fewer economic resources than parents in two-parent families (Huston, McLoyd, & Garcia Coll, 1994). This lack of resources places stress on the single parent's ability to meet family needs and has been implicated as leading to lower levels of child well-being, particularly academic achievement. Third, becoming a single parent either delays or halts the parent's educational progress. In either case, this lower educational attainment will likely lead to lower occupational achievement and a greater likelihood of poverty.

Potential benefits. First, if the single parent is divorced, there may be *less marital conflict* in the home. Reduced marital conflict may be beneficial for both parents and children. Marital conflict, particularly when it occurs in the presence of the children, undermines parent and child well-being (Fincham, Grych, & Osborne, 1994). Second, because they are asked to assume more household and child care (if they have siblings) responsibilities, children in single-parent families may *mature more quickly than children in two-parent families* (Weiss, 1979). Third, being a single parent may lead to *greater access to extended support* from family members and friends. If it is perceived as helpful (not always the case), this support can help relieve some of the burdens of being a single parent and can enhance the well-being of both parents and children. Fourth, as single parenthood has become more common in the last 30 years, the *stigma associated with it has diminished*. This is particularly the case in African American families, where single parenthood is more accepted as a viable family form than in white families.

Parenting by single parents. Single parents have more difficulty supervising/controlling their children than do parents in two-parent families. Because most single parents must work outside of the home, they are likely to find it difficult to monitor their children's behavior (Hetherington, Stanley-Hagan, & Anderson, 1989). Divorced single parents are more lenient and less restrictive than are parents in two-parent families, at least in the first two years following divorce (Hetherington, Stanley-Hagan, & Anderson, 1989).

Life course of single parents. For single parents who are divorced, and especially for white Americans, there is a high likelihood that the single parent will remarry. About 75% of divorced mothers and 83% of divorced fathers will remarry, most within five years following the divorce (Glick, 1989). Thus, these single parents and their children will experience life in a stepfamily. Consequently, a single-parent family can be a transitional stage into a stepfamily.

Single parents have several critical needs. First, they need access not only to child care services but to *high-quality child care*. Second, they need access to *greater economic resources*, including adequate child support. Single parents wish to be economically self-sufficient, but they cannot reach this goal unless structural barriers (such as inadequate child care or a lack of job training opportunities) to educational and occupational advancement are reduced. Finally, single parents need more *extrafamilial support* to meet the multiple needs of a family than many currently receive. Social support is needed to meet child rearing, housekeeping, and other responsibilities. Such support cannot be mandated by governmental programs but can be initiated by changing societal attitudes that single parents are unmotivated and unwilling to work outside the home to the reality that they would like to work toward economic self-sufficiency (Rank, 1994).

References

Fincham, F. D., Grych, J. H., & Osborne, L. N. (1994). Does marital conflict cause child maladjustment? Directions and challenges for longitudinal research. *Journal of Family Psychology, 8,* 128–140.

Glick, P. C. (1989). Remarried families, stepfamilies, and stepchildren: A brief demographic profile. *Family Relations, 38,* 24–27.

Hetherington, E. M., Stanley-Hagan, M., & Anderson, E. (1989). Marital transitions: A child's perspective. *American Psychologist, 44,* 303–312.

Huston, A. C., McLoyd, V. C., & Garcia Coll, C. (1994). Children and poverty: Issues in contemporary research. *Child Development, 65,* 275–282.

Martin, T. C., & Bumpass, L. L. (1989). Recent trends in marital disruption. *Demography, 26,* 37–51.

Rank, M. (1994). *Living on the edge: The realities of welfare in America.* New York: Columbia University Press.

Weiss, R. (1979). Growing up a little faster: The experience of growing up in a single-parent household. *Journal of Social Issues, 35,* 97–111.

See also: Conflict, interparental; Custody; Divorced families; Kinship care; Limit setting; Stepparents.

MARK FINE

Skinner, B. F. (1904-1990). B. F. Skinner was a behavioral psychologist who focused on the observable, scientific dimensions of human and environment interaction. Although many consider him to have been cold and calculating in his view of human nature, Skinner was committed to the improvement of the human condition through precise scientific understanding of the impact of external stimuli on human behavior.

Burrhus Frederick Skinner was born on March 20, 1904, and grew up in Susquehanna, Pennsylvania, where he spent the first 18 years of his life. He attended Hamilton College in Clinton, New York, where he majored in English. He received his doctorate from Harvard in 1931. He returned in 1948 to Harvard as a faculty member in the Department of Psychology, where he remained until his death in 1990.

As the major heir and advocate of behaviorism in the latter half of the twentieth century, Skinner expanded on the work of John B. Watson and Ivan Pavlov. The core of behaviorism is based on the assertion that the empirically demonstrable environment determines behavior rather than such inner constructs as values, self-esteem, or personal identity. This stimulus-response model is in dramatic contrast with psychoanalytic or cognitive-developmental theorists who insist that intervening variables, such as a person's mind, shapes the meaning of the stimuli and influences the consequent response. Skinner dismissed such thinking as wishful and naive. He believed that any objective observer with the right measurement tools would discover that all behavior was governed by the environment.

The key to behavior change, in Skinner's view, is *operant conditioning*. *Classical conditioning* involved learning through association. An originally neutral stimulus (e.g., a bell) is paired with an unconditioned stimulus (e.g., food), which produces an unconditioned response (e.g., salivation). If this association occurs a sufficient number of times, the now-conditioned stimulus (bell) will produce a conditioned response (salivating). Skinner broadened this view of conditioning to include more precise behavior *shaping* through *operant*, rather than classical (or respondant), conditioning. Responses followed by reinforcers are likely to be repeated. To change behavior, one has to change the reinforcement, making it more effectively contingent on the desired behavioral consequences. A child having a temper tantrum, for example, who is reinforced with a parent's attention is likely to repeat the temper tantrum in the future. Negative behavior can be *extinguished*, or eliminated, through the removal of such reinforcement or by reinforcing a response incompatible with the negative behavior (see Todd & Morris, 1995).

Skinner was never a proponent of aversive, manipulative control, preferring more positive methods and greater understanding by those involved of the underlying forces that affect their behavior. He created what has become known as the "Skinner Box" for his infant daughter who spent the first 2.5 years of her life in a controlled sleeping environment where temperature and humidity were kept at an ideal level and clothes were unnecessary. His book *Waldon 2* (1948) revealed how his principles of positive reinforcement might be implemented in a utopian community. The publication of *Beyond Freedom and Dignity* (1971) shocked a nation with its assertion that the pursuit of freedom was a dangerous illusion and that human nature was really behavior, verbal or otherwise, controlled by evolutionary history and the contingencies of the environment (Bjork, 1993). To behave as though this relationship did not exist was, in Skinner's view, dangerous because it made human beings more subject to manipulation.

Skinner's ideas, and behaviorism in general, had a powerful influence among academics attracted to the rigors of scientific control and measurement. Because of its scientific overtones, however, behaviorism never captured the public imagination, which was and is more easily threatened by the dangers of exploitation. Nevertheless, his ideas have found their way into common practice where they neatly coexist with other theoretical viewpoints (Rachlin, 1980). Parents who ignore a child's misbehavior that was originally strengthened with their attention or who reward a child with approval for small steps of progress toward a more difficult task are putting behaviorist principles into practice. Parents who insist that children are neither inherently good nor bad but are primarily the products of how they have been treated are behaviorists. Businesspeople, mental health professionals, and teachers have used Skinner's reinforcement techniques to improve worker productivity and morale, help clients overcome addiction, and control aggressive behavior in the classroom (Bjork, 1993).

B. F. Skinner died on August 18, 1990, of leukemia, eight days after delivering a 20-minute speech without notes to a standing room audience at the American Psychological Association convention in Boston.

In some ways, B. F. Skinner and the behaviorists he trained are great optimists. They insist that no human being is fated to act a certain way because of their past experiences or heritage. With controlled conditions and proper reinforcement, they tell us, any behavior can be changed.

References

Bjork, D. W. (1993). *B. F. Skinner: A life.* New York: Basic Books.
Rachlin, H. (1980). *Behaviorism in everyday life.* Englewood Cliffs, NJ: Prentice-Hall.
Skinner, B. F. (1971). *Beyond freedom and dignity.* New York: Alfred A. Knopf.
Skinner, B. F. (1948). *Waldon two.* New York: Macmillan.
Todd, J. T., & Morris, E. K. (Eds.). (1995). *Modern perspectives on B. F. Skinner and contemporary behaviorism.* Westport, CT: Greenwood Press.

See also: Consequences, natural and logical; Locke, John.

CHARLES A. SMITH

Smoking. Parents who choose to smoke have more to consider than the effects of smoking on their personal health. Children who are exposed to secondhand smoke have a greater frequency of related respiratory problems, and the legal issues involved are controversial and complicated (Time, 1993). Legally, many adults feel that it is their constitutional right to smoke in the privacy of their home; however, court child custody case rulings have included protective rulings to consider the child's best interest in the issue of exposure to smoking (Moorby, 1995).

Smoking is commonly believed to be a high-risk behavior for pregnant women. Prenatal exposure to cigarette smoking may be a risk factor for the likelihood of several different types of cancers in children, including acute lymphocytic leukemia, lymphoma, and brain cancer (John, Savitz, & Sandler, 1991).

The detrimental effects of prenatal exposure to smoking are ever present in the minds of educators, health care professionals, and advocates for children's health. The advice given to parents to stop smoking for the welfare of their children can be met with a variety of attitudes dependent on whether the parents are smokers or nonsmokers. Stacy and McIlvain (1994) found that less than half the parents believed that they could prevent their child from smoking and that the level of knowledge about smoking and health issues varied greatly. Parents who participated in the study lacked an understanding of the following:

- tobacco as a gateway drug
- of low tar and nicotine cigarettes
- the effects of parental smoking on the respiratory illness frequency in their children
- the effect of early smoking and difficulty in smoking cessation

Some believe that pediatricians are the first line of defense in educating perspective parents on smoking cessation. The opportunity to help families make lifestyle changes for the benefit of the new baby afford these physicians a unique teachable moment (Frankowski & Secker-Walker, 1989).

A longitudinal, cross-sectional study examining the influence of parents and friends on the initiation of smoking in children found that the influence of parents on their children's initiation of smoking may or may not decrease in adolescence, but the influence of peer pressure increases during the teen years. There was little evidence that children model or are motivated by their parents' behavior when it comes to smoking (Stanton & Silva, 1992). If so, other than keeping their children informed about the serious health risks associated with smoking, parents will have to depend on other institutions, primarily the school, to influence smoking behavior in their children.

The increase in the over-the-counter availability of nicotine addiction cessation products will perhaps address the needs of parents who wish to stop smoking. The best advice continues to urge abstention from smoking before addiction occurs and to stop smoking as soon as possible for the long-term benefit of the parent and child.

References
Frankowski, B. L., & Secker-Walker, R. H. (1989). Advising parents to stop smoking. *American Journal of Diseases of Children, 143* (9), 1091–1094.
John, E. M., Savitz, D. A., & Sandler, D. P. (1991). Prenatal exposure to parents' smoking and childhood cancer. *American Journal of Epidemiology, 133* (2), 123–132.
Moorby, M. S. (1995). Smoking parents, their children, and the home: Do the courts have the authority to clear the air? *Pace Environmental Law Review, 12* (2), 827.
Stacy, R. D., & McIlvain, H. E. (1994). Knowledge and attitudes of parents who smoke about the smoking behavior of their children. *Journal of Alcohol and Drug Education, 40* (1), 103–114.
Stanton, W. R., & Silva, P. A. (1992). A longitudinal study of the influence of parents and friends on children's initiation of smoking. *Journal of Applied Developmental Psychology, 13* (4), 423–434.
Time (1993, October). Law: Do parents abuse kids by smoking? The anti-tobacco crusade moves inside the home. *Time, 142* (17), 56.

See also: Abuse, child; Physical fitness.

DEBORAH J. THOMASON

Social competence. Traditionally, social competence is defined as an evaluative judgment made about a child's effectiveness in a given social situation. Judgments concerning a child's social competence are based, in part, on the behaviors displayed by the child in social situations and the effectiveness of those behaviors in achieving desired social goals. A socially competent child has the ability to interact with others in socially acceptable ways to the extent that the outcome of the interaction is mutually beneficial to all interacting participants.

The process of socialization begins in the home with parents serving as the primary trainers. Developing compliance lays the groundwork for the socialization process and the development of prosocial skills in children. Children who develop adequate levels of compliance early in life are primed for the socialization process because they will have learned the social skills necessary for success in school and in other social relationships outside of the home. The success or failure of compliance training largely determines the outcome of the socialization process (Patterson, Reid, & Dishion, 1992). The basic tenets identified as necessary for the training of compliance carry forward throughout the process of raising a socially competent child. These tenets include the delineation of effective parental management skills as well as the establishment of certain affective qualities necessary for setting the context within which behavior management techniques are successfully practiced and social competence developed.

Effective parent management skills: Crucial determinants in the development of social competence in children include the following (Patterson, 1982; Patterson, Reid, & Dishion, 1992; Putallaz & Heflin, 1990):

- *Ability to set clear limits and expectations for child behavior.* In order to set clear limits and reasonable expectations for child behavior, parents must be able to appropriately identify deviant behavior. Parents who see more "deviancy" in their children are more likely to use punishment and have more tension in their relationships with their children. Parents who view their children as problematic are likely to apply judgments of deviancy to behavior that parents of socially competent children would view as normal.
- *Use of effective parent disciplinary skills for inappropriate behavior and contingent positive reinforcement for appropriate behavior.* When necessary, discipline should be direct, concise, and followed up immediately by backup consequences for noncompliance.
- *Use of induction.* This process, also known as other-oriented discipline, involves the use of reasoning so that the child can understand the rationale underlying the parent's reason for engaging in certain actions.

Affective qualities and general parenting styles. Family management skills aimed at control of behavior cannot exist in isolation. Simply using the mechanics of management skills to train compliance and develop prosocial behaviors will not necessarily result in socially competent children. There are affective qualities and certain styles of parenting associated with these skills that set the context for the successful development of child competence (Grusec & Lytton, 1988; Patterson, Reid, & Dishion, 1992; Putallaz & Heflin, 1990; Wahler & Dumas, 1987). The display of parental warmth within a nurturant, caring, and responsive environment has been identified as a major determinant in the development of socially competent children. Research has differentiated between the *authoritarian* (high control, low warmth), *authoritative* (high control, high warmth), and *permissive* (low control, high warmth) parenting styles. The use of gentle parental control associated with the authoritative style appears to be the most successful in establishing social competent actions in the child. Too much control without warmth appears to reverse the desired effects. It is hypothesized that children reared within the high-control environment coupled with at least some level of warmth typically have positive relationships with their parents that help to develop a positive social orientation generalizing to other people and situations. Additionally, parental warmth increases the effectiveness of parents in serving as a model of positive social behavior for the child.

The relationship between appropriate management of child behavior and the development of social competence is complicated by the existence of external setting events that influence the parent-child relationship. Factors such as parental psychopathology, difficult child temperament, and lack of social support for the parent within a stressful environment can negatively influence the nature of parent-child interactions, thereby impeding the socialization process and the development of social competence. Consideration not only of the microsocial processes operating between parent and child but of extenuating individual characteristics of the participants as well as negative, stressful macrosocial variables affecting the home environment must be taken into consideration when seeking to understand the process of social competence development.

References

Grusec, J. E., & Lytton, H. (1988). *Social development*. New York: Springer-Verlag.

Patterson, G. R. (1982). *A social learning approach: Vol. 3. Coercive family process*. Eugene, OR: Castalia.

Patterson, G. R., Reid, J. B., & Dishion, T. J. (1992). *Antisocial boys*. Eugene, OR: Castalia.

Putallaz, M. & Heflin, A. (1990). Parent-child interaction. In S. R. Asher & J. D. Coie (Eds.), *Peer rejection in childhood*. Cambridge: Cambridge University Press.

Wahler, R. G., & Dumas, J. E. (1987). Family factors in childhood psychology. In T. Jacob (Ed.), *Family interaction and psychopathology*. New York: Plenum Press.

See also: Discipline; Limit setting; Prosocial behavior; Styles, parenting.

BETSY DAVIS

Social context. Social context refers to the combined influence of parenting styles (such as *authoritative, authoritarian,* and *neglectful*), *socioeconomic status* (i.e., social class), socialization *practices* (e.g., harsh discipline, violence in the home, parental warmth), parental *overcontrol* and *involvement* in decision making on child outcomes, and *ethnicity*. Such outcomes include academic performance, conduct problems, and peer overinvolvement.

Authoritative parenting fosters autonomy and competence. Baumrind's (1971) classic work on preschoolers shows that instrumental competence is fostered more by an authoritative parenting style. Parents with this style expect high standards of conduct and achievement of their children through the use of rewards and negotiated communication and support. Authoritarian parents are relatively more likely to use arbitrary unilateral discipline, which is inherently less supportive and less likely to promote social and academic success. Note that these styles are surprisingly similar to social class differences in child rearing characterized by Kohn (1963).

Class differences in parenting values reflect occupational requirements. Kohn (1963) integrated literature on social class and suggested that middle-class parents have unique parenting values. For instance, these parents are more likely to be responsive to child-rearing techniques espoused by experts and to read such material that agrees with their middle-class goals. Middle-class parents value curiosity, happiness, and consideration and most especially self-control and self-direction. On the other hand, working-class parents prefer to retain familiar methods that stress obedience to commands. Kohn reasoned that class differences in parents' values stem largely from occupational requirements, with middle-class parents stressing interpersonal relations and symbolic thought and therefore placing greater adaptive emphasis on their children's thoughts and feelings. Conversely, working-class parents are more apt to stress compliance because such behavior is adaptive to working-class occupations.

Working-class parenting practices encourage children's conduct problems. Dodge, Pettit, and Bates (1994) examined the effect of parents' social class on their offsprings' conduct problems from kindergarten to third grade. Social class predicted externalizing problems rated by teachers and aggressive problems rated by classmates. The lower the parents' social class, the more such problems occurred. Moreover, these social class effects were significantly mediated (greater than 50%) by socialization practices separate from the class label itself. Working-class designation increased the probability of such problems as harsh discipline, lack of social support, exposure to aggression, parental aggressive values, and lack of cognitive stimulation (i.e., books in the home). These issues independently contributed to such problems as life stressors (e.g., divorce), lack of maternal warmth, and peer group instability. Harsh discipline fosters antisocial behavior, which is contrary to parents' "urgent needs" to curtail it. Single-parent status itself did not contribute significantly to conduct problems.

Overcontrolling parents are at risk for exposing their early adolescent children to excessive (and negative) peer influence. Competition between parent and peers for control of children is heightened during early adolescence. Fuligni and Eccles (1993) examined this problem with children in grades 6 and 7, finding that overcontrolling parents who do not involve their children enough in decision making are more likely to encourage them to become overinvolved with their peers in making important life decisions. Parents who decreased decision-making opportunities with their children were more likely to encourage them to turn to their friends for personal (e.g., talking about personal problems) and instrumental support (e.g., talking about which courses to take). Those who viewed their parents as excessively strict, high in unilateral decision making, and high in parental monitoring were more likely to trade off parents' rules, homework, and even their talents in order to retain peer popularity.

Parenting style interacts with ethnicity in fostering academic achievement in adolescence. Steinberg, Dornbusch, and Brown (1992) found that high school achievement is connected to parenting styles in interaction with ethnicity. Caucasians' academic achievement is usually fostered by an authoritative parenting style (see Baumrind, 1971), whereas an authoritarian style may be more common with respect to African American and Asian parents. However, relative to their African American and Hispanic counterparts, Asian American students tend to provide one another with mutual support. This support helps to buffer them from authoritarian parenting and ill effects of being socially unaccepted by their classmates. Moreover, even with the benefits of authoritative parenting,

lack of such peer support places African American students at relatively more academic risk and leaves them facing the "glass ceiling."

References

Baumrind, D. (1971). Current patterns of parental authority. *Developmental Psychology Monographs, 4* (1, Pt. 2).

Dodge, K. A., Pettit, G. S., & Bates, J. E. (1994). Socialization mediators of the relation between socioeconomic status and child conduct problems. *Child Development, 65,* 649-665.

Epps, E. G., & Smith, S. F. (1984). School and children: The middle childhood years. In W. A. Collins (Ed.), *Development during middle childhood: The years from six to twelve* (pp. 283–334). Washington, DC: National Academy Press.

Fuligni, A. J., & Eccles, J. S. (1993). Perceived parent-child relationships and early adolescents' orientation toward peers. *Developmental Psychology, 29,* 622–632.

Kohn, M. L. (1963). Social class and parent-child relationships: An interpretation. *American Journal of Sociology, 68,* 471–480.

Steinberg, L., Dornbusch, S. M., & Brown, B. B. (1992). Ethnic differences in adolescent achievement: An ecological perspective. *American Psychologist, 47,* 723–729.

See also: Discipline; Styles, parenting.

BRIAN J. BIGELOW

Social support, informal. While formal support involves sponsored professional services, informal support involves a network of family, friends, and neighbors who provide resources to parents to help them deal with the pressures of child rearing. These resources include emotional reassurance, information, social participation, material aid, and physical assistance. Social support is embedded in a network, "a set of interconnected relationships among a group of people that provides enduring patterns of nurturance and provides contingent reinforcement for efforts to cope with life on a day-to-day basis" (Garbarino, 1983, p. 5).

The power of the social support network of family, friends, and neighbors for someone experiencing distress has been clearly documented (Cohen & Wills, 1985; Garbarino, 1983; House, Umberson, & Landis, 1988).

In their review of the research on social support and parents, Smith and Kuhn (1996) made the following conclusions:

Social isolation is a significant risk factor for child abuse. The maladaptive behavior of abusing parents is, in part, the result of the absence of stress- and anxiety-reducing mechanisms provided by strong, supportive social networks. Less support creates more anxiety and leads to fewer adaptive responses to stressful situations. Neglectful mothers tend to be lonely and isolated. Social networks provide parents with emotional support and assistance that improve their disposition and reduce the tendency to use coercive discipline. Social support also provides feedback about one's parenting and information about discipline alternatives (Moncher, 1995).

Social support for parents may be critical for families living in poverty. Neglectful mothers living in poverty were found to be significantly more isolated from family members and neighbors than those not living in poverty. Poor par-

ents are unable to purchase services (e.g., child care) that reduce stress on child rearing. Perceiving a lack of social support may intensify feelings of hopelessness, which in turn may influence the way poor parents interact with their children. Poor parents who reported few sources of assistance to draw upon in a crisis were especially likely to report that they yelled at or slapped their children "very often." Economic deprivation combined with a lack of social support creates a dangerous situation for children.

Parents experiencing stress may not feel empowered to reach out to others. Adversity tends to undermine a person's confidence in reaching out to others, especially if the problem is thought to elicit little sympathy. Feelings of inadequacy can be projected outward, and affected individuals may believe that others have little interest in helping them. They may misinterpret the efforts of others to help. Neglecting and maltreating mothers, although in much greater need of support than most other parents, were likely to avoid potential sources of help or act in ways that discouraged others from offering help. Those most in need of support often have to depend on others to take the initiative of reaching out.

Individuals in the community are often less responsive to offer help to parents experiencing chronic stress, especially when the conditions are stigmatizing. Parents who are too emotionally fragmented to be effective with their children may be shunned as undeserving by the community. For example, parents whose child rearing falls markedly below accepted norms, as evidenced by neglect, are likely to be distanced by their neighbors and others in the community. Parents who need the support the most may not appear very attractive to potential helpers. In addition, these parents may "burn out" the sources of support in the informal network by the intensity of their need and their inability to reciprocate support.

The failure of a community to respond effectively is not limited to families who deviate from acceptable norms for parenting behavior. The longer a child is ill, for example, the less support parents may receive from the informal network of family and friends. This support may be considerable during the early stages of a child's illness, but potential helpers may eventually become distracted by other demands on their time. They may feel powerless to make a difference or may not know what to do. Parents of handicapped children often experience social isolation. The social networks of parents of handicapped children are smaller than those of parents without handicapped children.

Social support increases parental self-confidence and moderates or buffers stress. Women who reported high levels of social support during prenatal assessment subsequently reported higher levels of self-confidence in the parenting role and less depression three months after delivery. Women who had other people on whom they could rely for a variety of social resources had more confidence in their ability to perform well as mothers. This confidence was also an effective deterrent to depression. Both friendship and community support consistently acted to moderate mothers' experiences of daily hassles on their relationships with others. Fathers, however, often lack emotional support and frequently feel lonely.

The social support of parents has an indirect positive effect on children. Women with higher-quality support had healthier babies and experienced less

postpartum depression. Mothers' satisfaction with their personal networks and the size of their maternal networks was related to a warmer and less intrusive style of interaction with their children. The availability of social support for parents is particularly critical when the family is under stress. Irritable infants, growing up in families characterized by low support for their mothers, experienced less responsive mothering. Under these conditions, infants developed insecure attachments.

The support of friends is significant and may be less stressful than support from relatives. Family members are more likely to offer instrumental help and some emotional support, while friends are the main sources of emotional and cognitive support, such as the need for approval, engaging others in discussion and opinion sharing, and seeking advice and information. Fathers were found to rely more on friends than relatives for emotional support.

Social support is a critical community-based variable that should be considered when developing intervention strategies for parent education.

References

Cohen, S., & Wills, T. A. (1985). Stress, social support, and the buffering hypothesis. *Psychological Bulletin, 98*, 310–357.

Garbarino, J. (1983). Social support networks: Rx for the helping professions. In J. K. Whittaker & J. Garbarino (Eds.), *Social support networks: Informal helping in the human services* (pp. 3–28). New York: Aldine Publishing.

House, J. S., Umberson, D., & Landis, K. R. (1988). Structures and processes of social support. *Annual Review of Sociology, 14*, 293–318.

Moncher, F. J. (1995, September). Social isolation and child-abuse risk. *Families in Society: The Journal of Contemporary Human Services*, pp. 421–433.

Simons, R. L., & Johnson, C. (1996). The impact of marital and social network support on quality of parenting. In G. R. Pierce, B. R. Sarason, & I. G. Sarason (Eds.), *Handbook of social support and the family* (pp. 269–287). New York: Plenum Press.

Smith, C. A., & Kuhn, K. (1996). *Introduction to ParentShare, the parent mentor program*. Manhattan, KS: Kansas State Research and Extension.

See also: Community; Stress.

CHARLES A. SMITH

Sociocultural background. Sociocultural background refers to certain environmental influences that impact the development of an individual. It includes other human beings, laws, language, neighborhoods, community organizations, values, and practices. Family structure and size, kinship connections, and family communication also are viewed as part of a person's sociocultural background as well as numerous influences from the larger society (Hildebrand et al., 1996).

There are several tiers of influence involved in an individual's sociocultural background or environment. The family is part of the sociocultural background closest to the individual and can be described conceptually as an *ecosystem*. Any ecosystem, whether large or small, is a group of associated species living and interacting within a specific habitat (Hook & Paolucci, 1970).

With any ecosystem the transactions are mutual and interactive. In the world of humans, the family impacts the individual, and the individual impacts the family. At the same time, an individual has an interdependent relationship with both visible and invisible sociocultural forces outside the family. For instance, a young parent employed outside the home is impacted by the availability of child care provided in the community. If the community has placed a high value on quality child care, the parent may have an employer who provides high-quality child care facilities at the job site. A young child's sociocultural background could be quite different if the family lived in a community that offers few options for quality day care.

What happens in the larger society also influences the sociocultural background of each individual. As we look at the history of race relations in our country today, we recognize the sociocultural legacy that allowed laws to enslave Africans for economic production over a century ago. Throughout the intervening years, a person's education, employment, housing, and interpersonal relationships may have been subject to this historical sociocultural influence.

Recognizing the interdependence of individuals with their environments has a long history implied in the works of Plato and Aristotle (Bubolz & Sontag, 1993). In more recent history, Urie Bronfenbrenner (1979) conceptualized the *human ecological model* for studying individual development. Besides the sociocultural environment, other environments generally described in ecological models are the biophysical environment (e.g., organic life cycle, water, land, other natural resources) and the technology or human-built environment (e.g., buildings, medicine, material goods).

The individual's interaction with these multiple environments is not one directional. A person interacts with each of the three different environments, and the environments are interactive as well. The introduction of the automobile into the human-built environment affected the sociocultural environment as well as the biophysical environment. Individuals and families had the option to become much more mobile and have subsequently put a high value on the independence the automobile affords, thus influencing the sociocultural environment. Simultaneously, the changes occurring in the human-built and sociocultural environments have required the use of natural resources from the biophysical environment in amounts unthinkable a century ago.

The example of the automobile demonstrates the interdependent nature of an individual and the family with their environments. People have the capacity to make decisions. They can act upon their environments at the same time that the environments can act upon them. Individuals and families can attempt to modify their sociocultural environment as well as the biophysical and human-made environments through constant interactions. This may be easiest to do at the individual and family tier. For instance, a parent might face unemployment through company layouts, having no input into this decision that profoundly affects the person's family. Yet the family's creative decision making in dealing with such a situation can have an impact on the family's ongoing sociocultural climate.

The sociocultural environment is never static, creating different sociocultural backgrounds for individuals even within the same family. For instance, a first-born in the family has a different sociocultural background than a younger sibling. Communication patterns are likely to differ among and between different family members. The patterns will change as children grow and parents become older. The family economic resources may change over time. How a family makes decisions may not remain static. Parental divorce and remarriage represent changes in an individual's sociocultural environment. How the community reacts to these familial changes also has an impact. As is evident, numerous variables make a difference in an individual's sociocultural background.

References

Bronfenbrenner, U. (1979). *The ecology of human development.* Cambridge, MA: Harvard University Press.

Bubolz, M. M., & Sontag, S. (1993). Human ecology theory. In P. G. Boss, W. J. Doherty, R. LaRossa, W. R. Schumm, & S. K. Steinmetz (Eds.), *Sourcebook of family theories and methods: A contextual approach* (pp. 419–448). New York: Plenum Press.

Hildebrand, V., Phenice, L. A., Gray, M. M., & Hines, R. P. (1996). *Knowing and serving diverse families.* Englewood Cliffs, NJ: Prentice-Hall.

Hook, N., & Paolucci, B. (1970). The family as an ecosystem. *Journal of Home Economics, 62* (5), 315–318.

See also: Cultural competence; Socioeconomic status.

CHARLOTTE SHOUP OLSEN

Socioeconomic status. Socioeconomic status (SES) is a multidimensional construct, often used interchangeably with the term *social class*. It is typically measured by some combination of the income, education, and occupation either of the head of the household or of the parents in a family (Hoff-Ginsberg & Tardif, 1995). Indexes commonly used to measure SES include the *Duncan Socioeconomic Index, United States Bureau of the Census* classification scheme, the *Hollingshead Two-Factor Index of Social Position,* the *Siegel Prestige Scale,* the *Standard International Occupational Prestige Scale,* and the *Green Three-Factor Index* (Mueller & Parcel, 1981).

In their review of developmental research, Mueller and Parcel (1981) found that SES indicators are typically used for the following purposes: as a criterion for selecting subjects into studies and as an explanatory and/or control variable in the analysis. Because SES is confounded with other background variables such as race, ethnicity, immigrant status, and family structure, it is often important that researchers measure and control its effects on family processes and child outcomes. However, all too often such background variables as SES are used as social address indicators, and there is little attempt to unpack the meaning of SES for the specific outcomes under study (Bronfenbrenner & Crouter, 1982). Asserting that a family's SES is related to a child's educational attainment describes an association but does not explain why it exists.

Differences in the socioeconomic status of families have been related to differences in a wide range of outcomes for children and adolescents. Outcomes such as birth weight or nutritional status can be directly connected to the financial resources of the family. However, family processes and parenting practices

have been found to vary by SES. For example, socioeconomic status is positively correlated with the use of reasoning and verbal explanations as disciplinary techniques, with a communication and decision-making style that respects
the autonomy of all family members, with parental aspirations for a child's educational and occupational attainment, and with parents' general beliefs about
developmentally appropriate competencies in children. The problem with much
of this comparative literature is that it is descriptive but not explanatory—that is,
it presents differences between parents, families, and children based on their socioeconomic status but fails to account for SES characteristics that explain those
differences. In addition, comparative research can often lead to inferences about
deficiency, that is, that the parenting practices or family processes in one SES
group are better than those in another.

Contextual models of family processes and child development provide an
alternative to a strictly comparative approach. When SES differences in family
processes are placed in the larger context of where the family resides and what
risks and stressors various socioeconomic groups encounter, it becomes clear
that parents are making decisions about raising children for optimal development in the settings where they live. For example, the more restrictive and less
democratic parenting styles of lower SES groups may be optimal for raising
children in dangerous neighborhoods.

Perhaps the closest links between occupational stratification and parenting
can be found in the work of Melvin Kohn (1977). Across three nations, Kohn
has shown that parents' child-rearing values are closely connected to the degree
of conformity and supervision the parents themselves experience on the job.
Parents from higher SES backgrounds tend to enjoy more autonomy and self-
direction in their work and, in turn, emphasize such values as independent
thinking and creativity in their child rearing. In contrast, parents in lower SES
groups tend to do repetitive jobs with a good deal of supervision and little opportunity for self-direction, and these parents tend to emphasize conformity and
obedience in their child-rearing values.

Coleman (1988) theorizes that a family's socioeconomic status reflects three
kinds of capital that families provide to children. *Financial capital* is a material
resource that determines a family's standard of living, including the size and location of housing and the opportunities and advantages parents can buy for their
children. The other two kinds of capital are nonmaterial but, nonetheless, reflect
the family's social status, information, and connections in the larger society—
advantages that accrue to children. *Human capital* is closely connected to the
educational resources and motivation a family can provide. If parents are
educated but do not have a high income, they can still provide academic
mentoring and cultural advantages to their children as well as motivate the
child's interest in learning and aspirations for educational attainment. *Social
capital* refers to the ways that family members make connections for the child to
the larger society. Adult family members can help link children to opportunities,
whether educational, occupational, cultural, or social, through the network of
relationships and information the adults themselves have formed. Two children
may come from families with similar incomes and even levels of parent
education. To the extent that one family can provide connections to job

opportunities or informational links to summer camp opportunities, that child will be more advantaged.

Entwisle and Astone (1994) use Coleman's theory as the foundation for their recommendations for measuring SES in research or programming for children and families. They recommend that SES be measured with indicators of family income (financial capital); mother's educational attainment (which is highly correlated with father's education and less subject to missing information in surveys) as a measure of human capital; and household structure (the number of adults in the household available to provide social resources to children as a measure of social capital).

References

Bronfenbrenner, U., & Crouter, A. (1982). Work and family through time and space. In S. B. Kamerman and C. D. Hayes (Eds.), *Families that work: Children in a changing world* (pp. 39-83). Washington, DC: National Academy Press.

Coleman, J. S. (1988). Social capital in the creation of human capital. *American Journal of Sociology*, *94* (Suppl.), S95–S120.

Entwisle, D.R., & Astone, N. M. (1994). Some practical guidelines for measuring youth's race/ethnicity and socioeconomic status. *Child Development*, *65*, 1521–1540.

Hoff-Ginsberg, E., & Tardif, T. (1995). Socioeconomic status and parenting. In M. H. Bornstein (Ed.), *Handbook of parenting: Vol. 2. Biology and ecology of parenting* (pp. 161–188). Mahwah, NJ: Lawrence Erlbaum Associates.

Kohn, M. (1977). *Class and conformity, a study in values, with a reassessment* (2nd ed.). Chicago: University of Chicago Press.

Mueller, C. W., & Parcel, T. L. (1981). Measures of socioeconomic status: Alternatives and recommendations. *Child Development*, *52*, 13–30.

See also: Poverty; Sociocultural background.

CONNIE FLANAGAN AND GWEN LAYFIELD

Spirituality. Nourishing a child's spiritual development is an essential parenting skill. As with physical, intellectual, and social development, opportunities for fostering spirituality during childhood and adolescence are abundant.

By its very nature spirituality is difficult to quantify or define. The word *spirit* derives from the Latin *spirare*, meaning "to breathe." Just as we feel the invisible air we breathe and know its importance, so also the sustaining essence of spirit is within us and around us although we cannot see it.

Spirituality refers to a sacred, unifying principle that expresses itself in a sense of wonder and inspiration, a feeling of connectedness with people and nature, and a reverence for life. Also central to spirituality is attunement with a universal guiding force, compassion for those in pain, and the giving and receiving of love.

Spiritual experiences occur frequently in childhood and adolescence (Tamminen, 1994). Common among these experiences are an awareness of a divine presence and a sense of being guided by God or a higher power. Parental acknowledgment and nurturance of healthy spirituality appears to strengthen a child's serenity, competence, and kindness. Whether they have been taught to believe in God or not, children speculate about a higher power and show a natural curiosity about the spiritual dimensions of life. They do more than echo their parents' beliefs; they think for themselves when given the opportunity (Coles, 1990).

Yet children's spiritual development and their conception of a higher power are strongly influenced by the parent-child relationship. For example, in a nationwide sample of more than 3,400 mother-father-youth triads, researchers found that: (1) the greater the tendency of parents to view God as loving, the greater the tendency of the children to view their parents as loving; (2) children's reports of loving or authoritarian parenting styles correlate with the children's images of God; and (3) children's loving or authoritarian God images correspond with their parents' images of God (Hertel & Donahue, 1995).

To better assist parents in supporting the spiritual growth of their children, researchers, educators, and practitioners need to address three critical issues.

Inadequate research base. Although experiences of spirituality are common throughout childhood and adolescence, research on spirituality during these critical years has been sparse. Well-designed studies are needed that provide practical guidance for parents on questions such as: How does spirituality develop during the various stages from infancy to late adolescence? How can parents best foster the awakening of a child's spirituality? What hinders spiritual development?

Insufficient treatment of spirituality in textbooks. The topic of spirituality typically has received little attention in child development and parenting textbooks. Thus, both the general student body and those preparing for parenting-related careers receive at best a minimal exposure to spiritual development. Given the important role that spirituality plays among the vast majority of the population, this oversight and the avoidance message it sends need to be corrected.

Need for more integration of spirituality in educational and therapeutic interventions. Despite its importance to their clientele, parent educators and family therapists often avoid the spiritual dimension in their work with parents and children (Prest & Keller, 1993). In workshop settings and parenting classes where people from a variety of spiritual orientations and belief systems are present, spirituality can be addressed in diverse and sensitive ways.

- Recognize children as spiritual beings. Respect and trust them. Allow their spirituality to unfold according to their unique nature and developmental cycles.
- Share spiritual beliefs in developmentally appropriate ways but realize that adults teach spirituality primarily by the example of their daily lives.
- Permit each child to teach us about his or her spiritual nature, perceptions, and experiences. This requires parents and other interested adults be with children in fresh, open-minded, deeply receptive ways.
- Listen well and generally give simple, straightforward answers, particularly with younger children. Gently explore emotions that seem unusually pronounced—both feelings of joy and discomfort.
- Arrange for frequent periods of quiet and calmness. Inner peace and times of reflection feed spiritual growth.
- Nourish the development of intuitive inner guidance. Support children in learning to trust their own inner sense of what is best.

- Help children develop spiritually through direct experience. Join with them in a community service project, in reaching out to a neighbor who needs assistance, in community worship, in daily prayer and meditation, or in helping to heal our environment.
- Teach tolerance, understanding, and respect for different viewpoints and practices that represent healthy spirituality.
- Encourage a sense of appreciation, wonder, and unity—whether in the beauty of a flower, the joy of friendship, the presence and guidance of God, or feelings of oneness with nature and people.

References

Coles, R. (1990). *The spiritual life of children*. Boston, MA: Houghton Mifflin.

Hertel, B., & Donahue, M. (1995). Parental influences on God images among children: Testing Durkheim's metaphoric parallelism. *Journal for the Scientific Study of Religion, 34* (2), 186–199.

Prest, L., & Keller, J. (1993). Spirituality and family therapy: Spiritual beliefs, myths, and metaphors. *Journal of Marital and Family Therapy, 19* (2), 137–148.

Tamminen, K. (1994). Religious experiences in childhood and adolescence: A viewpoint of religious development between the ages of 7 and 20. *International Journal for the Psychology of Religion, 4* (2), 61–85.

See also: Guilt; Moral development; Religious development; Conscience; Prosocial behavior; Shame.

SAM QUICK

Spock, Benjamin (1903–1998). American pediatrician, Benjamin McLane Spock, was born on May 3, 1903, received a B. A. from Yale in 1925 and obtained an M.D. at Columbia in 1929. While at Yale, he was a star oarsman and competitor in the 1924 Olympics. In addition to medical internships and residencies in pediatrics and psychiatry, he completed six years of training at the New York Psychoanalytic Institute. While on active duty in the United States Naval Reserve, he completed one of the all-time best selling books, *The Common Sense Book of Baby and Child Care* (1946). Exhibiting an attitude toward child rearing that was kindly and understanding, he urged parents to "Trust yourself. You know more than you think you do. . . . Don't take too seriously all that the neighbors say. Don't be overawed by what the experts say. Don't be afraid to trust your own common sense." He emphasized the fact that babies' personalities differ and that parental flexibility in addition to affectionate firmness is a necessary requisite to successful child rearing. His text became the child-rearing manual of choice for a generation of parents dissatisfied with the prevailing standard of authority on child rearing, *Psychological Care of Infant and Child* (1928), written by behaviorist John B. Watson. Spock's book, later renamed *Baby and Child Care* has been translated into more than 32 languages and has sold more than 46 million copies to date. The 7th edition of his book, with updated advice on diseases and vaccinations, diet, and drugs but no change to his basic approach to child rearing, was released in 1998.

Believing that modern warfare is a serious public health problem, Dr. Spock became publicly identified with the opposition to the Vietnam War, appearing at numerous protest rallies and marches throughout the United States. To devote himself to pacifism, he retired from his psychiatry and child development work at Western Reserve in 1967. Found guilty of conspiring to violate selective service laws, he was fined and given a two-year prison sentence. The appellate court, however, reversed the conviction. From this controversy, he wrote *Decent and Indecent: Our Personal and Political Behavior* (1969) in which he clarified his concerns for the fate of adults and the country at large. In 1972, Spock was the pacifist People's Party candidate for president.

During the past three decades, Dr. Spock continued to impact child rearing by authoring several books and regular articles in magazines such as *Redbook* and *Parenting*. In his most recent book, A *Better World for Our Children: Rebuilding American Family Values* (1994), he laments the world of heightened materialism. Spock believes that American children are suffering because of marital instability, lack of religious values, poor quality day care, and excessive regimentation in daily life. To remedy social ills, Dr. Spock advocates an effort "to cultivate serenity" and a return to tradition: "We must all face up to our responsibilities, embrace our heritage, and 'remember who we are.'"

References
Link, E. P. (1996). Spock, Benjamin McLane. In J. A. Garrity & J. L. Sternstein (Eds.), *Encyclopedia of American biography* (2nd ed., pp. 1044–1046). New York: Harper-Collins, Publishers.

Spock, B. (1946). *The common sense book of baby and child care.* New York: Duell, Sloan, and Pearce.

Spock, B. (1994). *A better world for our children: Rebuilding Amerian family values.* Bethesda, MD: National Press Books.

Watson, J. B. (1926). *Psychological care of infant and child.* New York: Norton.

See also: Brazelton, T. Berry; Developmentally Appropriate Practice.

MARY DELUCCIE

Spoiling. *Spoiling* is a term used to describe children's behavior in relation to their interactions with their parents. Spoiling is typically viewed as originating during infancy and toddlerhood and then appearing later in the child's life. A spoiled child is seen as having an impaired character as a result of overindulgence.

There is no consensus among parents regarding the issue of spoiling. Not all parents believe that a parent can spoil a child. In a study done of 303 parents, researchers found that 45% of parents believe that a child can be spoiled. Parents fall into three categories in their beliefs about spoiling (Solomon, Martin, & Cottington, 1993). Parents were asked if they agreed with the statement that spoiling is "to damage the disposition of by pampering" (p. 175).

- *Type 1 parents* do not feel children can be spoiled and do not agree with the definition.
- *Type 2 parents* believe a child can be spoiled, but that spoiling is good. In terms of the definition, these parents agree but feel the spoiled behaviors exhibited by the child would be positive.

- *Type 3 parents* believe a child can be spoiled but that spoiling is not beneficial to the child and agree with the definition but feel the outcomes are negative.

Wilson, Witzke, and Volin (1981) questioned 531 parents and found that 66% of mothers and 79% of fathers felt a baby could be spoiled. These parents believed that children who received too much rocking, holding, receiving affection, and/or attention might become spoiled. The investigators also found that parents associated spoiling with buying material things for and not setting limits for children.

Parents viewed spoiled children as being difficult to control, demanding, and obnoxious. About 60% of mothers and 79% of fathers felt that spoiling a child would negatively affect the child in the future (Wilson, Witzke, & Volin, 1981).

Parents view spoiling in many different ways, and since parenting styles differ, spoiling will be thought of in different terms by each parent. For instance, Rogers (1985) found that parents may be overly permissive due to lack of confidence and a lack of flexibility.

References

Rogers, R. (1985). Overpermissive parenting. *Medical Aspects of Human Sexuality, 19,* 58–72.

Solomon, R., Martin, K., & Cottington, E. (1993). Spoiling an infant: further support for the construct. *Topics in Early Childhood Education, 13,* 175–183.

Wilson, A., Witzke, D., & Volin, A. (1981). What it means to "spoil" a baby. *Clinical Pediatrics, 20,* 798–802.

See also: Discipline; Temper tantrums; Whining.

MARCI R. AARSTAD

Sport. Many children and adolescents are involved in competitive sport programs, sponsored by schools or community agencies. One of the major questions that parents might ask is, "Should my child become involved in a competitive sports program?" In deciding whether they should enroll their children in sport programs or have them continue for another year, parents should consider the benefits and costs (pros and cons) of participation. Competitive sports can contribute to children's growth and development in several important areas: *physical fitness, motor skill development, social development, psychological development* (enhancement of self-esteem, perceptions of competence, perseverance), and *cognitive development* (decision making, problem solving) (Seefeldt and Ewing, 1997). Sport experiences are equally as valuable for girls as for boys (Bunker, 1998). There are also some costs and concerns with any sport experience: financial costs for equipment, fees, travel, and time commitments for the family that can disrupt family life. Frequently, an overemphasis on winning can produce excessive stress and anxiety and lower self-esteem. This might lead to early withdrawal from competition.

Parents should also consider their own child's characteristics when deciding whether to have them participate in a sport program. Their interests and temperament are important. Are children really interested in sporting activities, and do they enjoy/react well in a competitive situation? Competitive sports are not for every child. There are many forms of physical activity (e.g., outdoor pursuits, fitness activities) that offer many of the same benefits as sport programs and contribute to children's health and well-being.

Physical attributes and abilities should also be considered. Some children have physiques and motor skills that enable them to be more successful. Maturity rate, which is genetically determined, is a particularly important factor. Before puberty, early maturing children will have an advantage. However, after puberty, late maturers often excel because, on average, they end up taller due to their longer growth period.

Most sports are appropriate for both girls and boys at about age 6 or later if they are led in a manner appropriate to the children's level of development. At young ages, children should have good instruction in the sport and have the opportunity to develop skill before they are put into competitive situations. As their age and skill level increases, the amount of competition can increase.

The effectiveness of the coach makes a significant impact on the quality of a child's sport experience. Before enrolling a child in a program, parents should inquire about the prospective coach's training and about his or her philosophy on winning and participation. There are national training programs in both the United States (e.g., *Coaching Effectiveness Training* or CET), and Canada (e.g., the *National Coaching Certification Program* or NCCP) designed to educate and sensitize coaches. The CET program encourages coaches to emphasize "doing your best," "getting better," and "having fun" as opposed to a "win at all costs" orientation (Smoll & Smith, 1996).

A recent survey asked grades 7 through 12 school participants what their main reasons were for participating in competitive sport (Athletic Footwear Association, 1990). The top three reasons were to have fun, to improve my skills, and to stay in shape. Thus, parents should ensure that their children are indeed deriving enjoyment from their competitive sport experience and are having the opportunity to improve their skills. This survey also found that the three most important reasons for quitting a sport were losing interest, not having fun, and taking too much time. For older athletes there is also a concern with violence and the use of illegal drugs.

There are several guidebooks available to assist parents (e.g., American Sport Education Program, 1994). The topic has also received considerable research attention in recent years with several excellent resources available (Bar-Or, 1996; Smoll & Smith, 1996).

References

American Sport Education Program. (1994). *Sport parent*. Champaign, IL: Human Kinetics.

Athletic Footwear Association. (1990). *American youth and sports participation*. North Palm Beach, FL: Author.

Bar-Or, O. (Ed.). (1996). *The child and adolescent athlete: The encyclopedia of sports medicine* (Vol. 5). Oxford: Blackwell Scientific.

Bunker, L. K. (1998) Psycho-physiological contributions of physical activity and sports for girls. *Physical Activity and Fitness Reasearch Digest, 3* (1), 1-8.

Seefeldt, V. D., & Ewing, M. E. (1997). Youth sports in America: An overview. *Physical Activity and Fitness Research Digest, 2* (11), 1-12.

Smoll, F. L., & Smith, R. E. (Eds.). (1996). *Children and youth in sport: A biopsychosocial perspective*. Dubuque, IA: Brown & Benchmark.

See also: Competition; Physical activity; Physical fitness.

JANICE BUTCHER

Standards of care, minimum. Throughout history, the rights of the parents have been paramount to the rights of the child. In the last 50 years, the rights of children and ethical child protection concerns have emerged as a topic of debate (Doxiadis, 1989). Child abuse became a legal and clinical issue with the identification of the *Battered Child Syndrome* (Kempe et al., 1962). The evolving family presents new social, moral, and psychological issues in the area of child rearing and protection.

With the enactment of child protective laws such as PL 88-164, the Community Mental Health and Mental Retardation Centers Act of 1963, the Juvenile Justice and Delinquency Prevention Act of 1974, and PL 93-247, the Child Abuse Prevention and Treatment Act of 1974, the interests of children and families became a state issue. Agencies established during this interval included the Children's Defense Fund and the Children's Bureau of the Office of Human Development (Morton, 1993).

Public Law 96-272, the Adoption Assistance and Child Welfare Act of 1980, is considered the impetus for the renewed emphasis of the child welfare system on strengthening families as a means for providing protection for children. A direct result of the increasing numbers of children entering foster care and experiencing multiple placements while the family deteriorated, these mandates focused on resolving the problem with the family intact, to ensure that children are not unnecessarily removed from their families and that parents are given the opportunity to correct difficulties that led to the involvement of social control agents.

Increased emphasis of public policy on family preservation and mandated reporting laws for suspected child abuse and/or neglect (resulting in an increased number of child abuse and neglect reports), along with confidentiality laws, have sparked debate as to the responsibility of the state, the sanctity of the family, definition of protection, parental rights and child rights, concerns as to appropriate protective roles and interventions, and the interpretation of the "best interests of the child." Balancing parental rights with child protection continues to be a matter of contention within the helping professions.

The identification of a minimum standard of care has established a guiding standard in the child welfare system. This standard, although subjective, has been used to establish the boundary determining such protective issues as removal from the home, level of legal and clinical intervention, and whether services are provided. Minimum standards of care are theoretically based upon the identified level of care that can be provided to the child that does not place the child at undue risk for physical harm. Risk of physical harm includes physical and sexual abuse, neglect, unmet health needs, and such environmental hazards as drugs, guns, and unsanitary living conditions. It does not include "dirty houses," poverty, use of corporal punishment, and religious and moral values in and of themselves. Further, this standard is predicated on the belief that it is not the job of the state to raise a child, except in extreme circumstances and that the parents have a right and responsibility to raise their child without interference from the state.

The issue of individual maximization versus minimum standard of care has become controversial. Increased referrals and publicity of extreme cases have resulted in increased pressure for child protection agencies to provide the "best" environment for the child, whether or not that environment is the child's birth family. Specht and Courtney (1994) suggest that middle-class values and the denigration of alternative values and lifestyles, particularly those of the lower-class service users, convolute the child protection efforts through the imposition of the "therapeutic ideal" of what a family should look like, how a family should behave, and what type of lifestyle a child is entitled to have.

Operational definitions are needed to help establish clarity and consistency in decision making and criteria for reporting and intervention (Roberts, 1991). Standardized risk assessment documents are being considered in many states. These documents are designed to assess both the risks and strengths of families referred to child protective services and involve a complex formula to determine actual risk to the child. With the assignment of an objective risk level, better decisions can theoretically be made as to whether the family can provide the minimum standard of care for a child without the assistance of the state—that is, the child is not at risk for physical harm (abuse, malnutrition, and unsafe environment). This type of assessment would also open doors for preventive efforts through the identification of potential risk factors. Identification of community resources that can be voluntarily accessed by families as a result of the assessment could provide opportunities for families to resolve their own problems without intrusive court orders.

References

Doxiadis, S. A. (1989). Children, society and ethics. Seventh International Congress of the International Society for Prevention of Child Abuse and Neglect. *Child Abuse and Neglect, 13*, 11–17.

Kempe, C. H., Silverman, F. N., Steele, B. F., Droegmueller, W., & Silver, H. K. (1962). The Battered-Child Syndrome. *Journal of the American Medical Association, 181*, 17–24.

Morton, E. S. (1993). The evolution of family preservation. In E. S. Morton & R. K. Grigsby (Eds.), *Advancing family preservation practice* (pp. 39–55). Newbury Park, CA: Sage Publications.

Roberts, D. (1991). Child protection in the 21st century. *Child Abuse and Neglect, 15*, 25–30.

Specht, H., & Courtney, M. E. (1994). *Unfaithful angels*. New York: Free Press.

See also: Developmentally Appropriate Practice.

                                                                         VICKY PRIMER

Stepparents. Stepfamilies consist of at least one child under the age of 18 years who is living with a biological parent and a stepparent who is the spouse of the child's biological parent. In the United States, it has been estimated that 17% of all married-couple families with children are stepfamilies and that 19% of all minor children live in stepfamilies (Glick, 1989).

Stepfamilies can be categorized on the basis of the stepparent's gender (stepfather versus stepmother) and if children are living in the home. A *complex* stepfamily is composed of stepparents who each have their own children living in the home. A *simple* stepfamily includes children from one parent.

Because mothers are more likely to receive custody of their children following divorce than are fathers, there are more stepfathers than there are stepmothers. There are also more stepparents in simple stepfamilies than complex stepfamilies.

Challenges. Stepparenting poses numerous challenges. First, stepparents are entering an already existing, single-parent family system, with its own history and routines. Unlike first-marriage families, in which the parents typically have an established relationship before children are born, in stepfamilies the parent-child relationship predates the relationship between the parent and the stepparent. Thus, stepparents must cope with the stresses inherent in being an outsider trying to become an integral member of an already existing family subsystem.

Second, the role of the stepparent is ambiguous (Fine, 1995). This ambiguity and confusion are evident in the number of plausible ways that stepparents might relate to their stepchildren: (1) as a "parent" to the child, (2) as a supportive friend to the stepchild, (3) as an adult who supports the disciplinary practices of the biological parent without independently establishing his or her own rules, or (4) as a detached adult who is not involved in the stepchild's life.

Third, stepparents may have unrealistic expectations about their families (Visher & Visher, 1996), including the following: (1) Stepfamily members will instantly love each other, (2) stepfamilies will immediately be cohesive, (3) stepfamily adjustment will occur immediately, and (4) stepfamilies are functionally equivalent to first-marriage families. These beliefs are considered unrealistic because they are inconsistent with the experiences of most stepfamily members. Holding these unrealistic expectations may lead to disappointment, as most stepparents' experiences are unlikely to meet these expectations.

Relationships. Stepparents generally believe that they should be less active in parenting stepchildren than are biological parents. Most also report that they are actually less active than are biological parents (Fine, Voydanoff, & Donnelly, 1993). This approach is adaptive given that numerous studies have suggested that it is best if stepparents do not actively discipline their stepchildren, particularly early in their relationship (Fine, 1995). The available evidence indicates that the quality of the stepparent-stepchild relationship is fostered when stepparents initially play the role of a supportive, adult friend and do not independently set or enforce household rules. As the relationship develops, and depending on a host of other familial factors, some stepparents are able to play an increasingly active disciplinary role. Effective stepparents follow the lead of the child and allow the child to establish the pace at which cohesion develops within the relationship. Above all, stepparents need to realize that change occurs slowly and that patience is an important virtue in stepparenting.

Effectiveness. Recent attention has been devoted to identifying factors that appear to help stepparents and stepfamilies function more effectively (Ganong, Coleman, & Fine, 1995). First, a *strong marital relationship* is the foundation of a successful stepparent-stepchild relationship and stepfamily. The biological parent and stepparent show a united front in their interactions with children.

Second, successful stepparents help *establish new traditions* while respecting those that existed before the new family. Establishing new traditions builds cohesion by integrating all members into the new family.

Third, successful stepparents have *realistic expectations* regarding establishing affection, family cohesiveness, and the challenges of forming a new group with its own uniqueness.

Fourth, successful stepparents are *flexible*. Because of the complexity of such issues as household and family membership, relationships, and roles, stepparents may need to be more flexible than parents in first-marriage families if they are to function effectively. In addition, because children may move in and out of the household, family structure in stepfamilies may be more fluid than that in first-marriage families. Because of this potential fluidity, stepparents need to be more flexible in how household and child-rearing responsibilities are met.

Finally, successful stepparents tend to have a clear sense of their roles as stepparents. They feel reasonably confident about how they should behave toward their stepchildren while recognizing that their role may change over the life span of the stepfamily.

References

Fine, M. A. (1995). The clarity and content of the stepparent role: A review of the literature. *Journal of Divorce and Remarriage, 24*, 19–34.

Fine, M. A., Voydanoff, P., & Donnelly, B. W. (1993). Relations between parental control and warmth and child well-being in stepfamilies. *Journal of Family Psychology, 7*, 222–232.

Ganong, L. H., Coleman, M., & Fine, M. A. (1995). Remarriage and stepfamilies. In R. D. Day, K. R. Gilbert, B. H. Settles, & W. R. Burr (Eds.), *Research and theory in family science* (pp. 287–303). Pacific Grove, CA: Brooks/Cole.

Glick, P. C. (1989). Remarried couples, stepfamilies, and stepchildren: A demographic profile. *Family Relations, 38*, 24–27.

Visher, E., & Visher, J. (1996). *Therapy with stepfamilies*. New York: Brunner/Mazel.

See also: Divorced families; Paradigms, parenting; Single parents; Styles, parenting.

MARK FINE

Stress, parental. Stress refers to the problems and hardships that people face. Stress can take many different forms and can arise out of many different kinds of situations and experiences. Research has focused on three types of stress and stressors.

- *Chronic or environmental stressors* are persistent life conditions such as poverty, inadequate housing, unsafe neighborhoods, and family disturbance such as that caused by one member's alcoholism. These stressors are ongoing and continuously tax coping resources.

- *Major life events* are discrete occurrences such as the birth of a child, parental separation or divorce, death of a family member, and moving to a new home. They are relatively infrequent compared to other kinds of stressors.
- *Daily hassles* are the annoying, irritating, and frustrating realities and demands of day-to-day life that may be stressful. Examples of hassles include traffic jams, arguments, noisy neighbors, and bad weather. Some hassles occur regularly, whereas others may be infrequent.

Chronic stress and major life events may exert their influence on psychological functioning by creating new daily hassles or intensifying those that already are being experienced. For example, the persistent stress of poverty may cause hassles such as a lack of reliable transportation to work. A major life event such as father death may lead to role changes within the family that can cause new hassles, such as mother starting to work and having to deal with child care issues or mother having to start dealing with car repairs.

Stress can affect parents psychologically and emotionally. Parents who are stressed are more likely to experience depressed mood, anxiety, and irritability. These feelings, when persistent, can lead to changes in parental behavior, including the use of harsh and inconsistent discipline, greater use of physical discipline, hostile or coercive interactions with other family members, rejection of children, less reasoning and less sensitivity in dealing with children, less monitoring of children's activities, and more control of children so that they are allowed less self-direction and autonomy. Stressed parents exhibit fewer positive behaviors, such as hugging and praising, and more negative behaviors, such as threats and derogatory statements (Ge et al., 1994; McLoyd, 1990). Psychological changes in parents caused by stress also can lead to changes in how a parent views his or her children and to negative parental attitudes. As stress increases, children's characteristics may be perceived in an increasingly negative way (Patterson, 1982), and children's behavior may be perceived as more deviant (Krech & Johnston, 1992). Both these factors may play a role in the disruption of parenting practices that is linked with stress.

Stress also may lead to changes in behavior with one's spouse. For example, fathers experiencing economic hardship have been reported to be more withdrawn, irritable, and explosive in their interactions with their wives (Conger et al., 1992). This creates a negative environment for everyone in the family.

Children are sensitive to their parents' interactions with them and to the negative emotional tone of a home environment influenced by parents' psychological distress. When parents are stressed and their parenting practices become negative, children may respond with maladjustment. Children may evidence problems in their social, emotional, behavioral, and academic functioning. The negative home environment created by stress is linked with children's depression, anxiety, moodiness, withdrawal, poorer self-esteem, less social competence with peers, behavior problems, delinquency, drug use, and learning problems in school.

Parents and children react individually to stress. Some people who experience stressful situations and circumstances do not experience psychological problems or distress. These differences are explained by variables that act to buffer the effects of stress. *Social support* is one buffering variable. Parents and children who feel that they receive emotional or instrumental support from others, either inside or outside the home, often handle stress better than those who do not have support systems available. Social support serves to make psychological distress less likely, which in turn lessens the likelihood of a disrupted home environment. Well-developed *coping* strategies represent another variable that may lessen the impact of stress. Parents and children who use problem-focused or emotion-focused coping fare better in the long term when dealing with stressful situations than people who use less successful forms of coping such as avoidance. *Personal characteristics* such as an easygoing temperament and high self-esteem also serve to protect some people from the negative effects of stress.

References

Conger, R. D., Conger, K. J., Elder, G. H., Jr., Lorenz, F. O., Simons, R. L., & Whitbeck, L. B. (1992). A family process model of economic hardship and adjustment of early adolescent boys. *Child Development, 62,* 526–541.

Ge, X., Conger, R. D., Lorenz, F. O., & Simons, R. L. (1994). Parents' stressful life events and adolescent depressed mood. *Journal of Health and Social Behavior, 35,* 28–44.

Krech, K. H., & Johnston, C. (1992). The relationship of depressed mood and life stress to maternal perceptions of child behavior. *Journal of Clinical Child Psychology, 21,* 115–122.

McLoyd, V. C. (1990). The impact of economic hardship on black families and children: Psychological distress, parenting, and socioemotional development. *Child Development, 61,* 311–346.

Patterson, G. R. (1982). *Coercive family process.* Eugene, OR: Castalia.

See also: Conflict, interparental; Consistency; Depression in parents; Discipline; Social support, informal.

KIM M. PIERCE

Styles, parenting. Parenting style is defined as "a constellation of attitudes toward the child that are communicated to the child and that, taken together, create an emotional climate in which the parents' behaviors are expressed" (Darling & Steinberg, 1993, p. 493). These attitudes are present across a variety of contexts as well as a variety of parent-child interactions. Parenting styles are perceived as conveying an attitude toward the child, not an attitude toward the child's behavior. They are influenced by the goals and values held by the parent, which creates an emotional climate in which the child develops.

Early classification of parenting styles included three categories: authoritative, authoritarian, and permissive (Baumrind, 1989). This system classifies parents based on certain characteristics. *Authoritative* parents exhibit high parental control and encourage the child's independence. They attempt to direct their children's behaviors in a rational manner. They affirm their child's uniqueness while also setting standards for conduct. Emotionally detached and controlling parents are classified as *authoritarian*. These parents value obedience and attempt to shape and control their child's behavior in accordance with a set standard of conduct. They are less warm than other parents. Finally, noncontrolling, nondemanding, and relatively warm parents are classified as *permissive*. These parents are nonpunitive and accepting toward their children. They allow their children to regulate their own behavior and do not insist they obey external standards of conduct.

Later research has emphasized the presence of two dimensions in parenting styles: *responsiveness* and *demandingness*. Responsiveness, according to Baumrind, includes both affective warmth and cognitive responsiveness. Parents are emotionally expressive and children are encouraged to express their point of view and negotiate differences even in the case of conflict. Demandingness consists of clear, rational guidelines for child behavior as well as the monitoring and supervision of children's behavior to ensure that they meet these guidelines (Baumrind, 1989).

As discussed above, different parenting styles are associated with different parent-child interactions. More important, there are significant differences in child outcomes for children raised with different parenting styles. Research looking at the two-dimensional approach to parenting style has found that the presence of both demandingness and responsiveness leads to the most optimal adolescent outcomes, regardless of ethnicity, socioeconomic status, and family structure (Steinberg et al., 1991). Regardless of their ethnicity, class, or parents' marital status, adolescents whose parents were perceived as being firm, accepting, and democratic earned high grades in school and behaved in socially appropriate ways.

The optimal parent-child relationship consists of a balance between demandingness and responsiveness (Baumrind, 1989). Specifically, in the optimal relationship, the parent is knowledgeable about the child's development and provides appropriate structure and control. This balance is sensitive to the child's development. For example, while a preschool child may require a parent to be more demanding, in adolescence, the optimal balance may shift toward a focus on the individuality of the adolescent.

In using this information when working with parents, it is crucial for practitioners to realize that no parent uses a "pure" style all the time. In other words, a parent's style may vary from situation to situation (Grusec & Goodnow, 1994). While parents may generally use a particular style, there are variations depending on the environmental stresses or circumstances families face. We do not currently understand how these styles develop and change over time. Future research needs to consider the antecedents of and changes in the style of parenting used by individuals. Furthermore, research will be most effective if it is longitudinal and developmental in nature and gathers information from multiple sources.

Distinguishing between parenting *practices* and parenting *styles* is important. Darling and Steinberg (1993) explain that while both practices and styles result from the goals and values held by parents, they influence outcomes for the child through different mechanisms. Parenting practices have a direct effect on the child's behavior, while parenting styles indirectly influence child development. In this sense, parenting styles mediate the influence of specific parenting techniques (such as punishment and discipline) on child development. Thus, a particular parenting style can enhance or inhibit the effectiveness of specific parent practices.

Also, the context in which the family lives, or the different realities that families face, must be considered when determining the effectiveness of a particular parenting style. For example, socialization methods that a white, middle-class family might consider punitive or excessive may be adaptive for an African American adolescent trying to deal with the hazards of ghetto life (Baumrind, 1991). Thus, while the dimensions of demandingness and responsiveness are important across contexts, the reality a family faces may influence the adaptation of one parenting style over another.

References

Baumrind, D. (1989). Rearing competent children. In W. Damon (Ed.), *Child development today and tomorrow* (pp. 349–378). San Francisco: Jossey-Bass.

Baumrind, D. (1991). The influence of parenting style on adolescent competence and substance use. *Journal of Early Adolescence, 11,* 56–95.

Darling, N., & Steinberg, L. (1993). Parenting style as context: An integrative model. *Psychological Bulletin, 113,* 487–496.

Grusec, J., & Goodnow, J. J. (1994). The impact of parental discipline methods on the child's internalization of values: A reconceptualization of current points of view. *Developmental Psychology, 30,* 4–19.

Steinberg, L., Mounts, N. S., Lamborn, S. D., & Dornbusch, S. M. (1991). Authoritative parenting and adolescent adjustment across varied ecological niches. *Journal of Research on Adolescence, 1* (1), 19–36.

See also: Discipline; Goodness of fit model; Temperament.

TARA THOMAS SCHLUESCHE, JUANITA LARAMIE,
AND SANDRA L. CHRISTENSON

Substance abuse, parents. Substance abuse refers to the problem use of or dependence on alcohol, marijuana, cocaine, amphetamines, or other legal or illegal substances. Most of the research has been conducted with children of alcoholics and their parents. Although the results of a majority of these studies are generalizable across substances, the abuse of different substances may have a different impact on the child. For example, the child may be removed from the home if the parent is arrested for criminal activity associated with his or her drug use.

Reviews suggest that parental substance abuse affects children in several ways (Mayes, 1995; Sher, 1993). First, substance abuse by parents increases the probability that children will become substance users and abusers. This intergenerational transmission of parental substance abuse may have a genetic component. Second, substance abuse by parents has a harmful impact on parenting and on the family environment. Third, substance abuse by mothers has a harmful effect on the fetus, resulting in subsequent cognitive dysfunction as the child develops.

Intergenerational transmission. A recent meta-analysis (Pollock et al., 1987) suggested that sons and daughters of male alcoholics and daughters of female alcoholics are more likely than children of nonalcoholics to become alcoholic at some point in their lives. Parent alcoholism also raises the risk of alcohol and drug use in adolescence. Reviews suggest the possibility of genetic determinants of alcohol abuse and dependence, but the extent of genetic influence appears to be modest. Multiple mechanisms are most likely responsible.

One important causal pathway for children of substance abusers to become substance users or abusers may be modeling of parents' behavior. Use of substances by adolescents is related to the use of substances by their parents (see Andrews, Hops, & Duncan, 1997). Children emulate their parents' behavior, particularly if they have a good relationship with that parent.

However, in addition to affecting children's substance use directly, it is likely that the use and abuse of substances by parents exerts an indirect effect on children's substance use. This indirect effect may be through the impact of parental substance abuse on the family environment and parenting practices and on the resulting psychological functioning of the child. For example, Chassin et al. (1996) showed that in addition to affecting the substance use of their adolescent children directly paternal alcoholism was associated with the adolescent's stress and negative affect. Furthermore, the adolescent's stress and negative affect was also associated with their substance use.

Effect on family environment and parenting. Families with alcohol-abusing parents are less cohesive and less expressive and have less intellectual-cultural orientation and less recreational orientation and more conflict than do families without alcohol-abusing parents (Sher, 1993). Direct observations of alcoholic families have also shown that they have more impaired problem solving, more negative and hostile communication, and less congeniality than do non-alcoholic families.

An impaired parenting style is characteristic of the abuser of alcohol and other substances. Impaired parenting not only may be the direct result of substance abuse but also may be due to preexisting psychological and psychiatric conditions that may contribute to the individuals addiction (Mayes, 1995). The parenting style of substance-abusing parents is generally either *autocratic*— placing expectations and conditions on children but not being responsive to their needs—or *unengaged*—neither demanding of their children nor responsive to their needs. Adolescents from homes with parents who are autocratic tend not to be self-reliant and achieving. Adolescents from homes with parents who are unengaged have a high incidence of problem behavior, including illicit drug use and problem alcohol use.

Parent drug abuse is also associated with impaired monitoring of their children's behavior. Adolescents with parents who do not monitor or supervise their behavior are more likely to associate with an antisocial peer group who uses substances.

Prenatal exposure. Prenatal exposure to alcohol, cocaine, or heroin may contribute to specific short- and long-term impairments in arousal modulation, activity level, or attentional regulation. Children of substance abusers tend to have poor impulse control and thus be more likely to engage in antisocial activities. These childhood characteristics may make it difficult for an adult to parent the child. When that adult is involved in substance use, his or her addiction and the associated effects may further impair the interactions between the child and parent.

References
Andrews, J. A., Hops, H., & Duncan, S. D. (1997). Adolescent modeling of parent substance use: The moderating effect of the relationship with the parent. *Journal of Family Psychology, 11,* 259-270.
Chassin, L., Curran, P. J., Hussong, A. M., Colder, C. R. (1996). The relation of parent alcoholism to adolescent substance use: A longitudinal follow-up study. *Journal of Abnormal Psychology, 105,* 70–80.
Mayes, L. C. (1995). Substance abuse and parenting. In M. H. Bornstein (Ed.), *Handbook of parenting: Vol. 4. Applied and practical parenting* (pp. 101–125). Hillsdale, NJ: Lawrence Erlbaum Associates.
Pollock, V. E., Schneider, L. S., Gabrielli, W. F., & Goodwin, D. W. (1987). Sex of parent and offspring in the transmission of alcoholism: A meta-analysis. *Journal of Nervous and Mental Disease, 173,* 668–673.
Sher, K. J. (1993). Children of alcoholics and the intergenerational transmission of alcoholism: A biopsychosocial perspective. In J. S. Baer, G. A. Marlatt & R. J. McMahon, *Addictive behaviors across the life span: Prevention treatment and policy issues* (pp. 3–33). Newbury Park, CA: Sage Publications.

See also: Abuse, child; Smoking; Substance use, children.

JUDY A. ANDREWS

Substance use, children. Substance use refers to the use of alcohol, tobacco (cigarettes and smokeless tobacco), marijuana, inhalants, as well as other illicit drugs. According to the 1994 Monitoring the Future Study, the prevalence of substance use is high among the youth of today and has recently increased (Johnston, O'Malley, & Bachman, 1996). By eighth grade, 54.5% of students have tried alcohol, with 25.3% reporting that they have been drunk, 46.4% have tried cigarettes, and 20%, 19.9%, and 21.6% have tried smokeless tobacco, marijuana, and inhalants, respectively. Recent studies suggest that children across the United States begin initiating substance use early, some as early first grade, with increasing prevalence throughout childhood. By fourth grade, a substantial proportion (30% to 50%) has tried alcohol. This is particularly problematic since early initiation of the use of alcohol and other drugs is a key risk factor associated with the development of problem substance use later in adolescence or young adulthood.

Parent and peer substance use. Several reviews (e.g., Petraitis, Flay, & Miller, 1995) suggest that the use of substances is learned, either from parents or from peers. If parents use drugs or have a positive attitude toward the use of drugs, adolescents are more likely to use drugs (Andrews et al., 1993). Thus, adolescents model or imitate the use of drugs by parents and learn parents' beliefs regarding the use of these drugs. Furthermore, this effect appears to generalize beyond the specific drug used by parents. Thus, if parents smoke cigarettes, adolescents are more likely to drink alcohol. Conversely, parents' negative attitude toward drugs may protect the child from using a substance.

Reviewers note that the association with drug-using peers is one of the strongest predictors of adolescent substance use (Dishion et al., 1995). The substance use of younger children is also strongly influenced by peer drug use. Parental awareness of the child's peer group along with supervision and monitoring of activities with peers are powerful predictors of the initiation and use of drugs by children and adolescents (Dishion et al., 1995). Adolescents with parents who know what they are doing and whom they are spending their time with are less likely to use substances. Without parental monitoring, children are free to choose peers who engage in substance use.

Relationship with parents and parenting practices. Lack of attachment to parents and conflictual relationships with parents have been identified as a risk factor for adolescent substance use in multiple theories (see Petraitis, Flay, & Miller, 1995). The patterns of interaction learned in a conflictual family (e.g., coercion, lack of problem solving) are most likely practiced with peers, leading to rejection by conventional peers and subsequent association with antisocial peers, who may be more likely to use substances. Alternatively, high levels of conflict between the child and parents could result in low levels of monitoring and poor discipline techniques, which, in turn, could affect the child's association with antisocial peers. Conversely, family cohesion has been shown to be protective, buffering the effect of other risk factors.

Parenting practices in early and middle childhood affect the substance use of adolescents. For example, coercive parent-child exchanges along with poor family management practices in middle childhood are associated with high levels of antisocial behavior in adolescence (Dishion et al., 1995). Furthermore, children from homes with parents who are unengaged, neither demanding of their child nor responsive to their child's needs, have a high incidence of problem behavior in adolescence, including illicit drug use and problem alcohol use (Baumrind, 1991). Authoritative parents, who are highly demanding (strict control with many rules), yet highly responsive to their child's needs (with mutual discussion of rules), help to protect their child from problem drug use (Baumrind, 1991).

Several studies suggest (e.g., Andrews et al., 1993) that an attempt by parents to control the substance use of their adolescent through rules and punishment may backfire. In adolescence, youths may react to a heightened sense of parental restriction by rebelling and engaging in the behavior that the parent is trying to prohibit. Thus, rules and expectations regarding drug use need to be in place prior to adolescence, perhaps in early and middle childhood.

The environment of both the family and the peer group must be considered jointly in determining the etiology of youth substance use. Attitudes and values of parents regarding substance use, a lack of parental monitoring, conflict within the family, and an unengaged parenting style, along with association with drug-using peers, all put the adolescent at risk for substance use.

References

Andrews, J. A., Hops, H., Ary, D., Tildesley, E., & Harris, J. (1993). Parental influence on early adolescent substance use: Specific and nonspecific effects. *Journal of Early Adolescence, 13,* 285–310.

Baumrind, D. (1991). The influence of parenting style on adolescent competence and substance use. *Journal of Early Adolescence, 11*, 56–95.

Dishion, T. J., Capaldi, D., Spracklen, K. M. & Li, F. (1995). Peer ecology of male adolescent drug use. *Development and Psychopathology, 7*, 803–824.

Johnston, L. D., O'Malley, P. M., & Bachman, J. G. (1996). *National survey results on drug use from the Monitoring the Future Study, 1975-1995*. Washington, DC: National Institute of Drug Abuse.

Petraitis, J., Flay, B. R., & Miller, T. Q. (1995). Reviewing theories of adolescent substance use: Organizing pieces in the puzzle. *Psychological Bulletin, 117*, 67–86.

See also: Delinquency, juvenile; Physical fitness; Styles, parenting.

JUDY A. ANDREWS

Sudden Infant Death Syndrome. Sudden Infant Death Syndrome (SIDS) is the sudden death of an infant under 1 year of age that remains unexplained after the performance of a complete postmortem investigation, including an autopsy, an examination of the scene of death, and a review of the case history. Babies, usually between 2 and 4 months of age, stop breathing and die in their sleep. SIDS is the leading cause of death in infants between 1 month and 1 year of age, accounting for approximately 40% of infant deaths in the United States. In the United States it occurs in about 1 in 700 babies (Sears, 1995).

Risk factors for SIDS include the following (Carolan, 1993; Sears, 1995; Thomas, 1992):

- mother less than 20 years old
- prematurity (less than 37 weeks)
- birth weight less than 2,500 grams
- maternal smoking or illegal drug use during pregnancy
- exposure to smoke after birth
- sleeping on the stomach
- bottle feeding
- recent respiratory tract infection
- apparent life-threatening events (ALTEs) such as a stop-breathing episode in which the baby was pale, blue, and limp
- lack of prenatal care and poverty
- siblings of a previous SIDS baby
- cold weather months

Presence of these risk factors does not ensure SIDS. Even babies with all these risk factors have less than a 1% chance of death. This risk is still associated with a sevenfold increase in the overall death rate. Not all SIDS infants are from families that fit this profile.

There is no guaranteed method of preventing SIDS. Parents can, however, reduce most of the risk factors by taking the following actions:

- Use firm and flat bedding. Avoid soft, synthetic foam-filled cushions.
- Place the baby on his or her back or side—unless the physician recommends otherwise.

- Eliminate all smoking by those living in the home during pregnancy and after the birth.
- Keep the infant comfortably warm while avoiding overheating.
- Choose to breastfeed the infant if possible.

The devastating impact SIDS has on the thousands of families it touches each year is heartbreaking (Byard, 1996). Support groups have emerged as a vehicle to help families heal after the loss of a child to SIDS. The fact that the infant seems healthy and normal prior to death makes the untimely loss even more difficult to accept. Comforting the parents becomes the primary focus (Thomas, 1992).

Parents will show grief and shock differently when experiencing the loss of a child to SIDS. They may blame themselves, the spouse, sitter, or even the medical personnel who fail to save the child (Thomas, 1992). Parents may be afraid to have another baby, feel afraid and vulnerable, and become overprotective of other children. They may even experience hallucinations, waking up to hear their baby crying, for example (Sears, 1995). DeFrain, Taylor, and Ernst (1987) estimate that it takes an average of 8 months for a family to regain the level of family organization that they had prior to the death and an average of 16 months to approach the former level of personal happiness. The sudden loss, guilt, and lack of adequate support are the main conditions that can lead to additional complications with marital relationships, subsequent children, and siblings (Carlson, 1993).

Support for the families of SIDS victims is available from various local community agencies. In addition, there are several national sources for information. Contact: the National SIDS Resource Center, Health Resources, and Services Administration, Clearinghouse Staff, Tycon Courthouse, 2070 Chain Bridge Road, Suite 450, Vienna, VA 22182. Parents can also contact the Sudden Infant Death Syndrome Alliance, 1314 Bedford Avenue, Suite 210, Baltimore, MD 21208, 800-221-7437. Information is also available from the World Wide Web (http://sids-network.org/).

References

Byard, R. W. (1996, February). Sudden Infant Death Syndrome—The mystery continues. *Australian Family Physician*, p. 210.

Carlson, J. (1993). The psychological effects of Sudden Infant Death Syndrome on parents. *Journal of Pediatric Health Care*, 7 (2), 77.

Carolan, P. (1993, June). Can risk factor intervention lower SIDS risk? *Minnesota Sudden Infant Death Center Newsletter*.

DeFrain, J., Taylor, J., & Ernst, L. (1987). *Coping with sudden infant death*. Lexington, MA: Lexington Books.

Sears, W. (1995). *SIDS: A parent's guide to understanding and preventing Sudden Infant Death Syndrome*. Boston: Little, Brown.

Thomas, D. O. (1992, September). Every parent's nightmare. *RN*, p. 34.

See also: Blaming, parent; Death of a child; Stress.

DEBORAH J. THOMASON

Suicide in children. Suicide is the third leading cause of death for children and young adults between ages 10 and 24. Ranked behind accidents and homicides, suicide accounts for 5000 childhood deaths annually, 14 per day. In 1994 (Centers for Disease Control, 1997), 318 deaths of children ages 10 to 14 were reported as suicide. During the same year, for the 15 to 24 age group, deaths by suicide were 4,956. Furthermore, the reported numbers probably underestimate the total suicides since, due to social stigma, suicide may be mislabeled as an accident-caused death (Henry et al., 1993).

Suicide is particularly troubling as a cause of death among children because it is unexpected. Additionally, it is all too often a constant reminder of lost opportunities and possibilities for the victim's family and friends (Zastrow, 1996). Feelings of guilt can compound the sense of loss when family members and friends blame themselves for not recognizing the symptoms or doing more to help prevent the suicide. In reality, however, while family and friends may play a significant role in preventing a suicide or suicide attempt, their role may be only one of many among the variety of causes and interventions related to suicide.

According to Zastrow (1996), there are five important variables related to adolescent suicide:

Feeling helpless and hopeless. Beginning around age 10, young people are expected to strive to develop their own personal identity and ways of behaving. However, they must develop that identity and those behaviors while conforming to the rules of the family, the school, their peer group, and the community. In other words, they often lack the power and opportunity to direct their own identity and behavioral development. When young people feel that their own personal being or "self" has little power to direct their own choices concerning friends, time allocation, activities, dress, and other behaviors, they may feel helpless and without hope of anything ever changing.

Loneliness and social isolation. The lack of close personal ties to other human beings often characterizes young people who either attempt or complete the suicide act. Among factors that can contribute to loneliness are the loss of a close relative (especially a parent) or friend and feeling ignored or rejected by a parent. In addition, when multiple problems of long duration (over a year) in a variety of social relationships occurs, the child's ability to cope with the associated stress is lowered. Consequently, the child then withdraws from relationships to avoid stress.

Lack of a stable environment. This can be the result of divorce, parental alcohol abuse, economic insecurity, depression or suicide attempts by other family members, poor conflict resolution within the family, child abuse and neglect, and/or ineffective parental communication. The lack of a stable environment also contributes to feelings of loneliness and isolation mentioned above.

Increased pressures. In the interest of success and achievement, young people today are expected to grow up faster than previous generations and adopt mature identities and behaviors without the appropriate opportunities and resources to develop these behaviors (Elkind, 1984). In other words the pressure to succeed is great (Zastrow, 1986). The most serious suicide attempts are likely to occur among the most successful students (Henry et al., 1993).

Research (Henry et al., 1993) also shows increased suicide rates among pregnant (an adult role) adolescent females, new mothers (another adult role) who are adolescents, and adolescents who have had abortions as well as married adolescents (again, an adult role requiring maturity).

Impulsivity. When a logical "well-thought-out" planned approach to behavior seems impossible due to lack of time or seems ineffective due to prior results of such planning, then impulsivity may be the alternative. Lack of power to implement the preferred decision or lack of socially significant others to show alternatives can also result in impulsive behavior. Confused shortsighted decision making, feelings of powerlessness, and social isolation can lead to an impulsive decision to commit suicide. Indeed, the completion of a suicide or media focus on suicides can precipitate additional attempts or actual suicide completions (Henry et al., 1993).

Preventions and interventions supported by research (Henry et al., 1993) include understanding and subsequent treatment for depression since it also is correlated with feelings of helplessness and loneliness. Family therapy to improve child-parent interactions and reduce child and/or parent alcohol and drug dependence and therapies that improve a child's ability to cope with stress are helpful. In cases of isolation, assistance in integrating into peer groups or establishing friendships is helpful. This can be after moving to a new area, for example, or changing schools. After a completed suicide, both school and family educational and therapeutic (in the case of a family member) interventions can aid in reducing the likelihood of future occurrences. Research evidence (Boehm & Campbell 1995) also points to the effectiveness of community suicide hotlines in identifying suicide-related problems among young people, which, in turn, may prevent suicides.

References

Boehm, K. E., & Campbell, N. B. (1995). Suicide: A review of calls to an adolescent peer listening phone service. *Child Psychiatry and Human Development, 26* (1), 61–66.

Centers for Disease Control. (1997). *Ten leading causes of death—1994* [On-line]. Available: http://www.cdc.gov/ncipc/pub-res/smalmap.htm.

Elkind, D. (1984). *All grown up and no place to go: Teenagers in crisis.* Reading, MA: Addison-Wesley.

Henry, C. S., Stephenson, A. L., Fryer, M., Hanson, M. F., & Hargett, W. (1993). Adolescent suicide and families: An ecological approach. *Adolescence, 28* (110), 291–308.

Zastrow, C. (1996). *Social problems: Issues and solutions* (4th ed.). Chicago: Nelson-Hall.

See also: Death of a child; Resiliency in children; Resiliency in parents, Stress, parental.

LEE HAMILTON

Surrogate motherhood. For some infertile couples, traditional adoption is not a viable option because they want biological offspring. Also, the supply of adoptable babies has shrunk considerably as more single mothers rear their own children. One alternative is surrogacy, where a woman contracts with a man for artificial insemination, carries the child to term, and relinquishes the baby and parental rights to the biological father and his wife. In return, the contracting parents pay more than $30,000 to cover program costs and the surrogate's fee.

Surrogate mothers have been used since biblical times, but contractual surrogacy did not begin until 1976. Approximately 600 surrogate pregnancies were completed in the following decade, but the practice has waned as state legislatures restricted or prohibited it. Currently, there are seven commercial surrogate mother programs plus various freelance brokers.

Several court cases crystallized ethical and legal issues associated with reproductive technologies (Garrison, 1988). In one high-profile case, the surrogate mother, Mary Beth Whitehead, refused to relinquish "Baby M" to William and Elizabeth Stern. The New Jersey Supreme Court invalidated the Whitehead-Stern contract, ruling that it constituted baby selling because money was exchanged for waiver of parental rights rather than for services rendered. The Baby M case also highlights ambiguities in who gains custody, should the surrogate mother change her mind. Is a surrogate akin to a foster mother, as some courts have upheld in cases of embryo transfers? Or is she the "real mother" because of her biological contribution? What claim does the father have, because he contributed genes as well as financial support? In the few cases where custody has been disputed, courts tend to award shared custody or grant visitation rights to the surrogate (as in Baby M).

Surrogacy also raises the specter of exploitation of women. Rothman (1989) argues that surrogacy substitutes a genetic definition of parenthood for one based on nurturance and social relationships. In this line of reasoning, paying for an ovum and a "womb for rent" creates a commodity out of parenthood. Indeed, when programs emphasize surrogacy as a business transaction, women *are* treated as a commodity: Minimal attention is given to screening, informed consent, and the psychological needs of the surrogate (see Ragone, 1994). As well, low-income women who are motivated by surrogacy fees are most vulnerable to exploitation. A final but uncommon instance of exploitation is when a fertile couple hires a surrogate in order to circumvent the "inconveniences" of pregnancy.

Critics also contend that surrogacy creates one family bond only by destroying another. This concern rests on the assumption that the surrogate "bonds" with the fetus or newborn. Although prenatal attachment is common among pregnant women, research shows that surrogate mothers are less likely to form such bonds (Fischer & Gillman, 1991). Also, careful studies indicate that bonding immediately after birth is a myth. These results partly explain why surrogate mothers usually do not experience much grief after relinquishment. Many surrogate mothers also minimize their genetic contribution to the child, which helps to alleviate a sense of loss. Most also say that they would be willing to be surrogates again, although this sentiment depends on the supportiveness of the program and the nature of the relationship forged with the social parents.

The perception of surrogacy shaped by the Baby M case is that there is an adversarial relationship between the surrogate and social parents. In fact, most surrogates develop rewarding relationships with the social parents and are distressed if this bond is severed after the child's birth (MacPhee & Forest, 1990).

For this reason, some surrogacy programs require an open adoption, where both sets of parents are known to each other and to the child.

Why would a woman wish to become a surrogate mother? Most surrogates minimize the importance of the money, focusing instead on an altruistic wish to help infertile couples become parents. Many surrogates also enjoy pregnancy as well as the attention it brings to them. Finally, Ragone (1994) suggests that many are traditional women who see surrogacy as a way to affirm the importance of motherhood without actually rearing the child.

Surrogacy has prompted a redefinition of motherhood—or at least brought its ambiguous meanings into focus in this age of reproductive technology. As Rothman (1989) suggests, "[M]othering was not something women *did*, it was something women *were*" (p. 313). She rues the increasing emphasis on mothering as an activity or service, especially when it is reduced to a genetic contribution. In an era when biological and social ties are often divorced from each other, courts view genetics and gestation as having a stronger claim on to whom a child belongs (Annas, 1988). In contrast, social scientists are prone to define kinship in terms of the nurturance that rearing a child entails. Thus, by fragmenting motherhood into genetics, gestation, and nurturance, surrogacy is modifying definitions of family and kinship.

References

Annas, G. J. (1988). Death without dignity for commercial surrogacy: The case of Baby M. *Hastings Center Report, 18*, 21–24.

Fischer, S., & Gillman, I. (1991). Surrogate motherhood: Attachment, attitudes and social support. *Psychiatry, 54*, 13–20.

Garrison, M. (1988). Surrogate parenting: What should legislatures do? *Family Law Quarterly, 22*, 149–172.

MacPhee, D., & Forest, K. (1990). Surrogacy: Program comparisons and policy implications. *International Journal of Law and the Family, 4*, 308–317.

Ragone, H. (1994). *Surrogate motherhood: Conception in the heart*. Boulder, CO: Westview.

Rothman, B. K. (1989). *Recreating motherhood: Ideology and technology in a patriarchal society*. New York: Norton.

See also: Donor insemination; Fertilization, in vitro; Infertility; Reproductive technology, assisted.

DAVID MACPHEE

Synchrony. Synchrony is defined by Rothbaum and Weisz (1994, p. 58) as "parental behavior that is congruent with the child's preceding behavior. It consists of attending and listening to the child's signals, acknowledging the child's verbalizations and needs, cooperating with the child's requests, and following and participating in the child's initiatives." Concepts related to synchrony include attunement, availability, empathy, involvement, mutuality, openness, participation, and sensitivity.

Parents and even some professionals may have defined effective parenting as providing adequate stimulation for infants and children. Synchrony challenges and extends this thinking by showing the importance of interactional sensitivity in responding. It is clearly not enough to provide some predetermined level of stimulation. The best parental behavior must be sensitive to the changing and subtle cues from the child.

Recent theories, which emphasize parent-child reciprocity, suggest that "the quality of the parents' responsiveness to children's needs, more than specific behaviors or characteristics of parents, fosters children's responsiveness to the expectations and desires of their parents" (Rothbaum & Weisz, 1994, p. 69).

Harrist et al. (1994) have discussed three kinds of synchrony: *positive synchrony*, in which the parent and child are connected in an extended exchange that is not negative; *negative synchrony*, which also involves an extended exchange but one that is negative; and *nonsynchrony* which involves imbalanced or disconnected exchanges. They conclude that "it is not simply the absence of a negative interactional style in the family that prevents or reduces child aggression (as is implicit in traditional behavior management parent training approaches) but also the frequent experience of positively synchronous interactions" (pp. 422-423).

The important contribution of synchrony to parent education is the understanding that parents must be more than positive. They must be sensitively connected to their children in ways that may be best described as synchronous.

References
Harrist, A. W., Pettit, G. S., Dodge, K. A., & Bates, J. E. (1994). Dyadic synchrony in mother-child interaction: Relation with children's subsequent kindergarten adjustment. *Family Relations, 43*, 417–424.
Rothbaum, F., & Weisz, J. R. (1994). Parental caregiving and child externalizing behavior in nonclinical samples: A meta-analysis. *Psychological Bulletin, 116*, 55–74.

See also: Attachment, secure; Communication; Mutuality; Play.

H. WALLACE GODDARD

T

Teacher training. Teacher training refers to the preservice or in-service training that takes place for K–12 teachers in our educational system. Concerning parenting and parent-child relations, teacher training refers to preparing teachers to work with families, specifically the parent. As research continues to recognize the influence that teachers and school environments have on the development and competence of children, more attention has been given to the role teachers play in working with the family in raising the child. Despite the consensus that future improvement of education relies on family involvement, few have seriously addressed the logistical barriers to this agreed-upon school reform strategy (Weiss, 1996). Little work has been done in preparing teachers to work with parents.

Although limited attention has been given to preparing teachers to work with parents and support them in their parental challenges and responsibilities, there are theoretical frameworks that suggest researchers and practitioners need to increase their attention to this issue. For example, Bronfenbrenner's (1979) use of the ecological theory in human behavior provides a framework for considering ways in which parenting behaviors and practices within a family are influenced by extrafamilial conditions and environments (Bubolz & Sontag, 1993) such as schools and educators.

As the relationship between parenting and other settings is acknowledged and studied, the application of Bronfenbrenner's model would mean that it is necessary to consider not only how children are influenced by parents and by teachers but also the influence of the relationship between the parent and teacher. Developmental as well as parental potential can be enhanced when researchers and practitioners attend to relational processes between different settings that include the parent (Bretherton, 1993). Thus, the shared meanings, values, and goals and nature of the relationship between parents and teachers will also influence the parental behaviors and patterns. The application of the ecological perspective in parenting also points to the need of considering the direct and indirect impact teachers have on parent-child interactions.

Because of the role or influence teachers have in parent-child relations, helping teachers become aware of this and preparing them to work with parents so that goals, behaviors, patterns, and attitudes are shared between settings becomes an important issue for practitioners and researchers. Weiss (1996) makes the following suggestions for developing programs that prepare or train teachers to become involved in families and work with parents. They include:

- giving prospective teachers more direct experiences with families and communities
- ensuring that teacher education coincides with education for other contributors to children's education
- emphasizing the benefits of partnership for the school and the teacher
- making school conditions conducive to family involvement
- identifying schools, human service agencies, and community programs that exemplify good relationships with families
- hiring more experts in family and community involvement

In addition, Korth (1996) suggests that there is a need to conduct a systematic analysis of the concept of teacher training and recommends teacher preservice and in-service training programs that can prepare teachers to address familial issues and work with parents. These training programs need to be guided by a familial or relational perspective that emphasizes processes and dynamics that are unique to the family relationships. This relational perspective views teachers' experience, relationships, and humanity as fundamental to quality education. Programs that are based on this perspective would invite teachers to critically reflect on and analyze their educational philosophies and personal behaviors that empower or impede effective work with parents. Teacher training regarding parental and family issues might benefit from moving beyond the traditional concept of teaching strategies and skills as well as introducing a specific curriculum.

References

Bretherton, I. (1993). Theoretical contributions from developmental psychology. In P. B. Boss, W. J. Doherty, R. LaRosa, W. R. Schumm, & S. K. Steinmetz (Eds.), *Sourcebook of family theories and methods: A contextual approach* (pp. 275–297). New York: Plenum Press.

Bronfenbrenner, U. (1979). *The ecology of human development*. Cambridge, MA: Harvard University Press.

Bubolz, M. M., & Sontag, M. S. (1993). Human ecology theory. In P. B. Boss, W. J. Doherty, R. LaRosa, W. R. Schumm, & S. K. Steinmetz (Eds.), *Sourcebook of family theories and methods: A contextual approach* (pp. 419–448). New York: Plenum Press.

Korth, B. B. (1996). *A narrative study of teachers' responses to a relational in-service.* Unpublished master's thesis, Brigham Young University.

Weiss, H. (1996). *Preparing teachers for family involvement*. New York: National Conference of the Family Involvement Partnership for Learning. (ERIC Document Reproduction Service No. ED 396 823)

See also: Academic achievement; Child care; Family-school partnerships; School.

BYRAN B. KORTH

Television viewing. By the time children graduate from high school, they will have spent about 11,000 hours in school but more than 15,000 hours watching television. To say that television is an electronic teacher that rivals the instruction of a classroom teacher is to underestimate television's power and influence (Murray, 1997).

The amount of time spent with television is usually time taken away from other activities such as playing with friends, hobbies, sleep, or school-related reading and homework (Huston et al., 1992; Singer, Singer, & Zuckerman, 1981). Also, large amounts of time spent viewing television means that children are likely to see more violence and more advertising, which may be harmful to their social development and increase their consumer needs.

However, there are many strategies that parents can employ to focus or limit both the nature and amount of television viewed by their children. To limit the amount of time spent with TV, parents can set weekly or daily restrictions on the number of hours viewed, or they can set particular time periods when viewing is prohibited. It is best to keep the limits clear and concise in order to avoid confusion on the part of either parents or children.

For example, the family might set a rule that there is no television viewing on school nights after dinner or no TV in the morning before going to school. These are clear prohibited times, and the reasons for these limits (e.g., need to complete homework and hobbies or prepare for school) can be clearly communicated.

Another approach to setting television viewing limits is to discuss programming choices and options with the youngster by reviewing a weekly program guide from the newspaper or magazine. In this setting, children are asked to select the programs that they want to watch during the coming week. Contrary to expectations, children can be selective in their viewing choices. The total amount of viewing declines because the "random" or "carryover" viewing is eliminated by a decline in "channel surfing" or turning the TV set on just to see what is on. Children watch only those programs that they have selected in advance and turn the set off when a program choice is completed. One additional advantage of this approach is the enhanced autonomy given to the youngster to set a reasonable viewing "diet" and time schedule. In this way, parents can use television-viewing choices to talk about "budgeting time" or setting schedules and making choices among competing alternatives. If parents are still concerned about the amount of time scheduled for TV viewing or the nature of the program choices, this issue can be addressed as a topic of discussion in developing the weekly viewing guide.

Finally, television viewing should be considered in the context of all the other activities that a youngster might engage in daily, weekly, or throughout the year (Kuby, 1996; Murray & Lonnborg, 1995). Like a balanced food diet, the television diet should be balanced for entertainment and education. Television is a window on the world, and while it is exciting and entertaining, TV can be used to expand the child's horizons and enhance knowledge and understanding—a clearer view through the electronic window.

References

Huston, A. C., Donnerstein, E., Fairchild, H., Feshbach, N. D., Katz, P. A., Murray, J. P., Rubinstein, E. A., Wilcox, B., & Zuckerman, D. (1992). *Big world, small screen: The role of television in American society*. Lincoln: University of Nebraska Press.

Kuby, R. W. (1996). Television dependence, diagnosis, and prevention: With commentary on video games, pornography, and media education. In T. M. MacBeth (Ed.), *Tuning in to young viewers: Social science perspectives on television* (pp. 221-260). Thousand Oaks, CA: Sage Publications.

Murray, J. P. (1997). Media violence and youth. In J. Osofsky (Ed.), *Children in a violent society* (pp. 72-96). New York: Guilford Press.

Murray, J. P., & Lonnborg, B. (1995). *Children and television: Using TV sensibly*. [Online]. Manhattan: Kansas Research and Extension. Available: http://www.ksu.edu/humec/fshs/c&t.htm.

Singer, D. G., Singer, J. L., & Zuckerman, D. M. (1981). *Teaching television: How to use TV to your child's advantage*. New York: Dial Press.

See also: Aggression, children; Television violence.

JOHN P. MURRAY

Television violence. Television broadcasting began in the United States in 1941, and concern about TV violence surfaced in congressional hearings in 1952 and 1954. Since that time, various public reviews and commissions have summarized the research evidence on the harmful effects of televised violence, for example, the 1969 *National Commission on the Causes and Prevention of Violence*; 1972 surgeon general's *Scientific Advisory Committee on Television and Social Behavior*; 1982 *National Institute of Mental Health Television and Behavior Report*; and the 1992 *American Psychological Association Task Force on Television and Society*. All of these reviews have concluded that televised violence can lead to increases in aggressive behavior and changes in attitudes and values about the role of violence in society (see Murray, 1997).

Studies tracking the level of violence over the past three decades on primetime, evening television and Saturday morning children's television have found consistently high levels of violence. On average, 5 violent acts occur during each hour of evening television, and 20 to 25 violent acts occur during each hour of children's programming (see Gerbner et al., 1994). A study conducted for the National Cable Television Association (Mediascope, 1996) monitored 2,693 programs, shown on 23 channels, over a 20-week period in 1994-1995. The study found that the percentage of programs containing violence varied across the types of broadcast or cable systems. Only 18% of programs on Public Broadcasting contained violence compared to 44% on broadcast network TV;

55% on broadcast independent stations; 59% on basic cable stations; and 85% on premium subscription cable channels. The typical perpetrator of violence is adult (76%), male (78%), and Caucasian (76%) and the victims of violence are likely to be female, elderly, nonwhite, or foreign-born. The violence in children's programming is likely to be shown in a humorous context (67%), and only 5% of the violence in kids fare shows any long-term negative consequences of the violent acts. As a result of this viewing, studies by Gerbner et al. (1994) show that heavy viewers (more than five hours per day) as compared to lighter viewers (less than three hours per day) are more fearful of the world and view it as a mean and dangerous place where most people "cannot be trusted" and most people are "just looking out for themselves."

Experimental studies conducted with preschool children, school-age youngsters and college students demonstrate that viewing violence leads to increases in aggressive behavior in the short time following viewing and can lead to long-term changes in values and behavior (Huston et al., 1992). One study demonstrated that there was a relationship between violence viewing at age 8 and aggressive behavior at age 18. Researchers found a relationship between 8-year-old violence viewing and arrest and conviction for serious interpersonal violence (spouse abuse, child abuse, assault, murder, rape) at age 30 (see Eron, 1995; Huesmann et al., 1984).

Proposals to reduce violence on television, mitigate the effects of violence, or enable parents to screen and monitor television violence have led to the development of ratings systems for television programming, the installation of an electronic blocking device (V-Chip) in new television sets after 1998, and suggestions for helping children understand the meaning and import of television violence. Actions taken by parents and community groups, in concert with ratings systems for programs and blocking devices for parental lock-out and screening of viewing, can lead to changes in the viewing patterns and moderation of the effects of viewing on young children (see Eron, 1995; Murray, 1997; Murray & Lonnborg, 1995).

References

Eron, L. D. (1995). Media violence. *Pediatric Annals, 24* (2), 1–3.

Gerbner, G., Gross, L., Morgan, M., & Signorielli, N. (1994). Growing up with television: The cultivation perspective. In J. Bryant & D. Zillmann (Eds.), *Media effects: Advances in theory and research* (pp. 17-41). Hillsdale, NJ: Erlbaum.

Huesmann, L. R., Eron, L. D., Lefkowitz, M. M., & Walder, L. O. (1984). Stability of aggression over time and generations. *Developmental Psychology, 20*, 1120–1134.

Huston, A. C., Donnerstein, E., Farichild, H., Feshbach, N. D., Katz, P. A., Murray, J. P., Rubinstein, E. A., Wilcox, B., & Zuckerman, D. (1992). *Big world, small screen: The role of television in American society*. Lincoln: University of Nebraska Press.

Mediascope. (1996). *National television violence study—Executive summary, 1994–95*. Thousand Oaks, CA: Sage Publications.

Murray, J. P. (1998). Studying television violence: A research agenda for the 21st century. In J. K. Asamen & G. L. Berry (Eds.), *Research paradigms in the study of television and social behavior*. Thousand Oaks, CA: Sage Publications.

Murray, J. P., & Lonnborg, B. (1995). *Children and television: Using TV sensibly*. [Online]. Manhattan: Kansas Research and Extension. Available: http://www.ksu.edu/humec/fshs/c&t.htm.

See also: Aggression, childhood; Delinquency, juvenile; Television viewing.

JOHN P. MURRAY

Temperament. McCall, in a roundtable discussion with temperament researchers (Goldsmith et al., 1987, p. 523), defined temperament as a "relatively consistent, basic dispositions inherent in the person that underlie and modulate the expression of activity, reactivity, emotionality, and sociability." Recognizing that a biological component exists, he also notes influence of the environment.

Thomas and Chess (see Chess & Thomas, 1986; Thomas & Chess, 1977) conducted a study of temperament, the *New York Longitudinal Study* (NYLS), and followed 141 subjects from infancy to adulthood. They identified nine temperament traits: activity level, rhythmicity, distractibility, approach/withdrawal, adaptability, attention span and persistence, intensity of reaction, threshold of responsiveness, and quality of mood. *Activity level* involves the motor component present in a given child's functioning and the proportion of active and inactive periods. *Rhythmicity* refers to the predictability or unpredictability of bodily functions, such as the sleep-wake cycle, feeding, and elimination schedule. *Distractibility* involves the effectiveness of extraneous environmental stimuli in interfering with or in altering the direction of the ongoing behavior. *Approach/withdrawal* is the nature of the initial response to a new stimulus (i.e., food, toy, and person). *Adaptability* is the response to new or altered situations. *Attention span and persistence* refer to the length of time a particular activity is pursued by the child and the continuation of the activity in the face of obstacles to the maintenance of the activity direction. *Intensity of reaction* is the energy level of a response. *Threshold of responsiveness* is the intensity level of stimulation that is necessary to evoke a discernible response. *Quality of mood* is the amount of pleasant, joyful, and friendly behavior, as contrasted with unpleasant, crying, and unfriendly behavior.

From the nine temperament traits, the researchers noted three temperamental styles of children: the easy child, the difficult child, and the slow-to-warm-up child (Chess & Thomas, 1986). The *easy* child is characterized by regularity, positive approach responses to new stimuli, high adaptability to change, and mild or moderately intense mood that is generally positive. In contrast to the easy child is the *difficult* child. This child is characterized by irregularity in biological functions, negative withdrawal responses to new stimuli, nonadaptability or slow adaptability to change, and intense mood expressions that are frequently negative. The *slow-to-warm-up* child has a combination of negative responses of mild intensity to new stimuli with slow adaptability after repeated contact. Mild intensity of reactions and less irregularity of biological functions distinguish the slow-to-warm-up child from the difficult child.

The notion of goodness of fit involves an effective match between a child's temperament and environmental factors, such as the parent's child-rearing practices and the parent's temperament. Thomas and Chess concluded that this was the major determinant of children's adjustment. Children need to be treated as individuals, with different child-rearing needs. A child who is slow to warm up has a different way of approaching the world than does an easy child. Parents must be aware of this and must be sensitive to each child's individual needs. Goodness of fit remains an important concept from infancy through adulthood.

Chess and Thomas (1986) cite their NYLS as the first systematic exploration of the active influence of the child's own characteristics on the parents and other influential persons in the child's environment. They further report that data from the NYLS confirmed their hypothesis that the parent-child interaction is a two-way process: The child's behavioral style influences parental attitudes and practices, and the parents' attitudes and practices influence the child. Gearing child-rearing practices to the child's temperament can facilitate favorable adjustment.

Goldsmith et al. (1987) report that temperament research receives input from diverse disciplines. The research literature provides interesting studies of temperament and its impact on many variables, such as school adjustment, cognition, attachment, social interaction, aggression, peer rejection, and maternal teaching (Bomba, Goble, & Moran, 1994; Lamb, Ketterlinus, & Fracasso, 1992; Rubin & Coplan, 1992).

As Chess and Thomas (1986) note, temperament affects parent-child interactions. They also note that the child's way of approaching situations remains relatively stable across time (in their NYLS study, approximately 30 years). Parents should determine their child's temperamental style and identify parenting strategies that are respectful of the child's and the parents' temperament. Consideration of these issues should facilitate the child's adjustment.

References

Bomba, A. K., Goble, C. B., & Moran, J. D. III (1994). Maternal teaching behaviors and temperament in preschool children. *Perceptual and Motor Skills, 78*, 403-406.

Chess, S., & Thomas, A. (1986). *Temperament in clinical practice.* New York: Guilford.

Goldsmith, H. H., Buss, A. H., Plomin, R., Rothbart, M. K., Thomas, A., Chess, S., Hinde, R. A., & McCall, R. B. (1987). Roundtable: What is temperament? Four approaches. *Child Development, 58*, 505–529.

Lamb, M. E., Ketterlinus, R. D., & Fracasso, M. P. (1992). Parent-child relationships. In M. H. Bornstein, & M. E. Lamb (Eds.), *Developmental psychology: An advanced textbook* (3rd ed., pp. 465–518). Hillsdale, NJ: Lawrence Erlbaum.

Rubin, K. H., & Coplan, R. J. (1992). Peer relationships in childhood. In M. H. Bornstein & M. E. Lamb (Eds.), *Developmental psychology: An advanced textbook* (3rd ed., pp. 519–578). Hillsdale, NJ: Lawrence Erlbaum.

Thomas, A., & Chess, S. (1977). *Temperament and development.* New York: Brunner/Mazel.

See also: Affectivity, positive and negative; Dimensions of Temperament Survey–Revised (DOTS–R); Emotion language; Goodness of fit model; Identity development.

ANNE K. BOMBA

Temper tantrums. Temper tantrums are a common behavior problem in preschool children who may express their anger by lying on the floor, kicking, screaming, and occasionally holding their breath (Geelard, 1945). They are natural, especially in children who are not yet able to use words to express their frustrations.

Tantrums typically occur at age 2 to 3 years when children are forming a sense of self. The toddler is old enough to have a sense of "me" and "my wants" but is too young to know how to satisfy the want. Tantrums are the result of high energy and low ability to use words to get needs or wants met.

Tantrums typically peak between ages 2 and 3 and start to decline by 4. They typically run their course within a year. About 23% to 83% of all 2- to 4-year-olds have temper tantrums at least occasionally (Bhatia et al., 1990; Fetsch & Jacobson, 1996).

Most children throw tantrums in a particular place with a particular person. They are usually a public display after the child has been told "no" to something he or she wants to do. The tantrum usually stops when the child gets his or her wish. What happens with the temper tantrum depends on the child's level of energy and the parent's level of patience and parenting skill.

Some of the causes of temper tantrums include family problems like inconsistent discipline, problems with the marriage, interference with play, emotional problems for either parent, meeting a stranger, rivalry with brothers or sisters, having problems with speech, and illness (Bhatia et al., 1990). Other common causes of temper tantrums not indicating family problems include being hungry or tired. Children who have temper tantrums often have other problems like thumb sucking, head banging, bed-wetting, and sleeping problems. If these behaviors occur, or if a child has temper tantrums that last more than 15 minutes or occur three or more times a day at younger than 1 or older than 4, parents should seek help from a family physician, psychologist, or marriage and family therapist. Parents might be advised to seek more than an exclusively behavior therapy approach, for results have been reported to be about equally effective and ineffective (Fetsch & Jacobson, 1996). The best strategy might be to combine the best of behavior modification, family systems thinking, and other approaches like paradoxical intervention (Fetsch & Jacobson, 1996).

Inconsistent parenting contributes to temper tantrum problems. One solution lies in stopping the shouting, scolding, spanking; in getting oneself calm; stating clear rules and requiring compliance; noticing and complimenting appropriate behavior; and following through with logical consequences.

Parents can learn how to nurture and discipline effectively. Overly *authoritarian* parents who are exercising too much power and using discipline punitively can learn more effective authoritative parenting. Overly *permissive* parents who are exercising too little power and using too little discipline can also learn to be authoritative parents. Balance is important. *Authoritative* parents learn daily when and how to discipline their children effectively by setting standards, enforcing rules, exercising authority when necessary, and yet recognizing children's rights (Maccoby & Martin, 1983).

Most tantrums and angry outbursts come and go as children and youth grow in their ability to use language and learn to solve problems using words. Sometimes temper tantrums in preschool children are the beginning of patterns that lead to children becoming increasingly disobedient, rebellious, and aggressive as they grow older. Sometimes biological sources of anger require diagnosis by a physician or psychologist. If someone is getting hurt or if parents use the suggestions listed and nothing seems to work, it is time to get professional help.

Physicians, school guidance counselors, or psychologists can provide the names of those skilled in working with children with anger issues. One can also check the yellow pages, under *counselors*, for psychologists and marriage and family therapists who specialize in child behavioral problems.

References

Bhatia, M. S., Dhar, N. K., Singhal, P. K., Nigam, V. R., Malik, S. C., & Mullick, D. N. (1990). Temper tantrums: Prevalence and etiology in a non-referral outpatient setting. *Clinical Pediatrics, 29*, 311–315.

Fetsch, R. J., & Jacobson, B. (1996). *Children's anger and temper tantrums* (Fact Sheet #10.248). Fort Collins: Colorado State Cooperative Extension.

Geelard, E. R. (1945). Observations on temper tantrums in children. *American Journal of Orthopsychiatry, 15*, 238–241.

Maccoby, E. E., & Martin, J. A. (1983). Socialization in the context of the family: Parent-child interaction. In P. H. Mussen (Ed.), *Handbook of child psychology* (Vol. 4, pp. 1–101). New York: John Wiley & Sons.

See also: Authority, parental; Limit setting; Misbehavior; Whining.

ROBERT J. FETSCH

Throwaway children. Throwaway children, also known as *pushaways* and *fallaways* (Payne, 1995), are adolescents who have been "thrown out" of their homes. Kurtz, Jarvis, and Kurtz (1991) have noted a subgroup of throwaway youth. Specifically, these adolescents have been "removed" from their homes, placed in state custody, and subsequently placed in unsuitable settings from which they run away.

In general, throwaway youth do not differ from other homeless teens, particularly relative to family experiences (e.g., parent-child conflict, physical violence, abuse, neglect, social isolation, parental psychopathology) and the risks and dangers associated with living on the streets and in shelters (e.g., prostitution, substance abuse, victimization). However, there is some evidence that there are some minor differences between subgroups. For example, throwaway youth are more inclined to believe that their parents want them to leave home and perceive their parents' interpersonal relationships as more stressed (Adams, Gullotta, & Clancy, 1985). Further, Peretti and Purham (1991) compared youth who ran away from home with those who had been thrown out of their homes on measures of self-worth, self-confidence, motivation, self-reliance, depression, and self-acceptance. While there was no difference between the groups on self-reliance, the throwaway youth had greater self-reported depression and self-acceptance, and the runaway youth reported higher levels of self-confidence and motivation.

Services available to homeless youth range from shelter programs to home-based interventions. Throwaway youth present a unique opportunity therapeutically due to the fact that parents generally play a significant role in the child's homelessness. Therefore, interventions designed to ameliorate throwaway youth must include at least the parents, if not the entire family. Short-term family therapy designed to allow the youth to return home in concert with longer-term follow-up seems necessary to protect throwaway children from the dangers on the street and ensure that they can remain in their homes. While the impetus for throwaway youth to leave home seems to lie with the parents, in general, there is a history of problematic behavior on the part of both parents and child. Consequently, clinicians must strive to understand the context in which the acting out behavior occurs in the family. Often it is necessary for clinicians to negotiate with the rules and behavior that are acceptable and unacceptable to all involved. This negotiation, if successful, can allow the youth to return home and lay the groundwork for further intervention. The future interventions can include outpatient counseling, in-home family preservation, advocate services, or some combination of these services.

Generally, throwaway youth are stuck in a precarious position relative to the societal institutions designed to help children in trouble. This is particularly true in states where the child protective and juvenile justice services are separate entities. Given the myriad number of problems that cause children to be thrown out of their homes, the jurisdiction and/or responsibility for the throwaway youth may be contested depending on the perspective of the institution. For example, when referring a throwaway child who has previous involvement with the juvenile court to child protective services, no action may be taken because child protective services will consider the child the jurisdiction of juvenile services. Similarly, if a report is made to juvenile services and the child has not committed another delinquent act, the child will be considered under the jurisdiction of child protective services. These responses are more common in locales where there are limited resources available to provide services. Without collaborative multisystem interventions, it is likely that these throwaway children will not receive the services they need.

Legally, both parents and throwaway children run the risk of being held responsible for the runaway behavior. Youth who run away, regardless of the reason, are considered status offenders and can be adjudicated by the juvenile justice system. Likewise, parents who refuse to allow their child to return home can be charged with "child abandonment" in most states. Legal responses to throwaway children are least desirable and counterproductive to reunification of families but must be considered when attempting to provide effective services.

References

Adams, G. R., Gullotta, T., & Clancy, M. A. (1985). Homeless adolescents: A descriptive study of similarities and differences between runaways and throwaways. *Adolescence, 20,* 715–724.

Kurtz, P. D., Jarvis, S. V., & Kurtz, G. L. (1991). Problems of homeless youths: Empirical findings and human services issues. *Social Work, 36,* 309–314.

Payne, M. (1995). Understanding "going missing": Issues for social work and social services. *British Journal of Social Work, 25,* 333–348.

Peretti, P. O., & Purham, C. (1991). Escapist and throwaway runaways' perceived self-image. *Indian Journal of Clinical Psychology, 18,* 3–6.

See also: Abuse, child; Attachment, secure; Mediation, parent-child; Runaway children.

WILLIAM F. NORTHEY, JR.

Thumb sucking. Thumb sucking is a common behavior of infancy, early childhood, and preadolescence. This type of nonnutritive sucking is generally thought to be harmless until the age of 4, after which persistent, chronic thumb sucking is of concern due to physical and psychological risk factors. Thumb sucking is considered chronic if it occurs in the daytime and nighttime and across two or more contexts (Friman & Schmitt, 1989).

Studies on the prevalence of thumb sucking have failed to produce uniform findings. However, a recent review (Peterson, Campise & Azrin, 1994) suggests that incidence rates are between 30% to 40% in preschoolers and 10% to 20% in children over 6 years.

Theories regarding parent-child interactions that elicit thumb sucking include both a developmental, and an environmental/situational perspective. The developmentalists suggest that the child's use of a transitional object usually occurs in the second half of the first year of life and reflects a stage of development when the child begins to distinguish their internal experience from external reality. During this transitional time, they claim that the use of an object promotes a facilitative environment that is a good substitute for mother. This is a normal, healthy part of emotional development; but if the thumb sucking continues beyond the transitional period, they claim it may be an indicator of an emotional disturbance in the child (Winnicott, 1953).

Conversely, the environmental/situational hypothesis states that the use of an object represents the child's redirection of attachment behavior when the mother is not available. They question the universality of attachment to an object and emphasize their association with the continual or habitual emotional and physical distance of mothers from their children (Bowlby, 1969).

Few research studies on parent-child interactions that foster thumb sucking exist. To limit this behavior, available studies support the need for parent-child contact during the passage to sleep and a pattern of positive parental interactions (stimulation, nurturance, attention) during feeding and others periods of daily contact (Wolf & Lozoff, 1989). After the age of 4 physical and psychological risk factors are associated with chronic thumb sucking. The most prevalent physical risks are associated with dental care: malocclusion (abnormality in the coming together of teeth), open bite, and overjet as well as facial malformations and jaw imbalance. Other physical risks include accidental poisoning and alopecia (hair pulling and twisting associated with sucking) (Friman & Schmitt, 1989).

Associated psychological risks pertain to the educational, social, emotional, and relational development of the child. Thumb sucking may prevent children from responding to questions during formal educational activities, may inhibit their use of materials in manipulative play, and may lessen their attention to planned activities. The potential for peer social acceptance lessens for thumb sucking children. They are viewed by peers as less fun, happy, intelligent, and attractive, and thus less desirable (Peterson, Campise, & Azrin, 1994). In addition, a longitudinal study indicated that thumb sucking at 5 and 7 years predicted behavior problems at 7, 9, and 11 years (Mahalski & Stanton, 1992).

Parental response can also be detrimental to children with a thumb sucking habit. Friman and Schmitt (1989) suggest that parents often resort to methods like ridicule, criticism, and nagging that appear to increase the behavior and worsen parent-child relationships. This negative pattern along with the child's dislike of their thumb sucking often fosters a negative self-image. Treatment for thumb sucking is rarely considered before the age of 4 and may not be needed even after the child reaches that age. Due to possibility of negative side effects like bed-wetting, spitting, or oppositional behaviors, a parent's decision to professionally treat chronic thumb sucking should be made carefully through considering the balance between potential risks and benefits.

A good parental checklist includes assessing the frequency of the sucking, the context in which it occurs, and any other life circumstance in the child or parent-child relationship that may relate to the use of thumb sucking as a coping behavior. For example, sucking briefly at night is not likely to cause physical or psychological damage even in older children. In addition, if a child has experienced a substantial loss or is fearful or in pain, the thumb sucking may be a temporary coping mechanism. Within parent-child relationships the intensity of negative interactions between the child and parent or the presence of excessive parental reactions may be an indicator of the need for professional interventions (Friman & Schmitt, 1989).

Treatment for thumb sucking varies depending on the nature of the problems associated with its occurrence. The most frequent indicator for treatment is the need for orthodontic care that is clearly related to thumb sucking. Treatment is also indicated if a child specifically requests help in quitting for social or other reasons. Interventions that relate to parent-child interactions need to begin with a "wait and see" and "planned ignorance" attitude for a period of at least one month. It is likely that the thumb sucking may cease when parental reactions to the behavior stop and do not provide the potentially reinforcing attention (Friman & Schmitt, 1989).

If further treatment is necessary, research reviews indicate that the most effective treatment includes the use of an aversive tasting substance applied to the thumb and the simultaneous use of a reward system. This method has been shown to eliminate thumb sucking in 95% of the cases as compared to 30% to 50% of the cases that utilized habit reversal (Peterson, Campise, & Azrin, 1994).

References

Bowlby, J. (1969). *Attachment and loss: Vol. 1. Attachment*. London: Hogarth Press.

Friman, P. C., & Schmitt, B. D. (1989). Thumb sucking: Pediatricians' guidelines. *Clinical Pediatrics*, *28* (10), 438–440.

Mahalski, P. A., & Stanton, W. R. (1992). The relationship between digit sucking and behaviour problems: A longitudinal study over 10 years. *Journal of Child Psychology and Psychiatry*, *33* (5), 913–923.

Peterson, A. L., Campise, R. L., & Azrin, N. H. (1994). Behavioral and pharmacological treatments for tic and habit disorders: A review. *Developmental and Behavioral Pediatrics*, *15* (6), 430–441.

Wolf, A. W., & Lozoff, B. (1989). Object attachment, thumb sucking and the passage to sleep. *Journal of the American Academy of Child and Adolescent Psychiatry*, *28* (2), 287–292.

Winnicott, D. W. (1953). Transitional objects and transitional phenomena. *International Journal of Psychoanalysis*, *34*, 89–97.

See also: Attachment, secure; Fear; Touching.

FAYE SPRUNGER KOOP

Toilet learning. In the traditional approach to toilet *training*, parents simply undressed the child and sat them in a potty-chair for extended periods until the child eliminated. A more recent perspective emphasizing toilet *learning* recognizes the child as an active participant in the toileting process (Furman, 1992).

Toilet learning is a developmental process of learning to use the toilet appropriately. As in many areas of child development, children must reach a certain age or be in the proper setting or situation before they are ready to learn. Children are ready to learn when they are healthy, well nourished, and not pressured to achieve at a level above their capability.

Toilet learning generally is initiated in early childhood, a potentially challenging period. Children are exploring their growing sense of independence while parents are experiencing the sensitive balance between helping the child search for independence while avoiding a developed sense of shame or doubt.

With encouragement, children are able to provide parents with clues of their toilet readiness. If children are pressured to learn toileting before they are physically and intellectually able, then there will be unavoidable accidents. Accidental embarrassment combined with parental disapproval increases the child's sense of shame and slows the natural sense of independence. Punishing accidents by taking away toys can lead to an unhealthy and intense struggle (Durrell, 1984).

Many young children are frightened by or curious about toilets. The size, noise, and rapid water movement are alarming to them. Allow children to ask questions such as "Where does it go?" and "Will I fall in (and disappear)?" Give simple answers without scorning the child for asking.

Some parents find children who are curious playing in the water or clogging the plumbing by throwing objects in the toilet to see what happens. Adults may have to be very clear about why nothing else may be put in the toilet. Parents should make sure they know where the valve is located to turn off water, just in case.

In general, children learn about bowel needs before urine needs. This is because children can generally control the sphincter muscle at an earlier age than they are able to recognize and control urination muscles.

Parents can recognize some signs of readiness. These responses may be helpful during the toilet learning process.

- Children know names for body parts and can dress and undress themselves.
- Children acquire the desire to be clean.
- Children who urinate a larger amount at one time as opposed to dribbling throughout the day may be ready to begin toilet learning.
- Parents may be able to recognize some signs that the child is ready to have a bowel movement, and respond.
- As soon as signs of pushing and concentration are noticed, the parent may take the child to the toilet to finish.

- Children who can walk steadily from room to room and have the coordination to stoop and pick up things and can pull their pants up and down may have the physical ability to complete toileting tasks.
- Daytime training occurs before nighttime training. Children who show an interest in and are motivated by wearing "real" underwear may be ready to learn toileting.
- The child needs to be old enough to learn to gage their own body signals and attend to them. Children who stay dry for several hours and feel the need to urinate (posture, gestures, verbal or facial expressions) may be ready to begin the process.
- Girls usually learn toileting before boys. For girls, toilet learning may occur as early as 18 months; around 22 months for boys.

Problems in toilet learning often can be traced to parental stress or other struggles between parent and child. For example, if both parents work away from the home, the process may need to be started on the weekend. Or if there is a family crisis or other major family or child task that requires the child's or adults attention at present, the timing may be wrong (Azrin & Foxx, 1974). The process should be discussed and procedures agreed upon with child care providers, family members, and friends. Parents should be prepared with extra supplies such as training underwear, clean-up supplies, and a child-sized toilet or toilet chair.

In general, the learning process is least stressful when parents think through the process and give the child strategies and reinforcement to begin work on this special growing step.

- Teach children words needed to talk about elimination.
- Begin the process when an interest is shown, without pushing.
- Gently ask the child several times throughout the day if they need to go to the bathroom.
- Monitor fluid intake at nighttime.
- Teach routine handwashing at the same time as toileting.
- Postpone the process if the child does not seem to catch on or loses interest.
- Do not blame or demoralize the child.
- Expect accidents, remain calm, enlist child's help with clean-up, and do not punish harshly.
- Involve the child in clean-up, dressing, flushing, emptying potty chair.
- Use same-sex modeling.
- With success, use praise (hand clapping, positive words).
- Do not insist the child remain seated on the toileting chair for longer than 5 to 7 minutes. An unpleasant association with the bathroom or toilet seat may result.

References

Azrin, N., & Foxx, R. (1974). *Toilet training in less than a day*. New York: Simon & Schuster.

Durrell, D. (1984). *The critical years:A guide for dedicated parents*. Oakland, CA: New Harbinger Publications.

Furman, E. (1992). *Toddlers and their mothers*. Madison, CT: International Universities Press.

See also: Sex education.

KAREN B. DEBORD

Touching. The greatest impact parents may have on their children's lives is through the direct physical contact of touch. Touching can be a soothing expression of love and affirmation, setting the grounds for a lifelong secure attachment. Painful forms of touching in the form of beatings and sexual abuse can bring about a lifetime of anguish. Touch defines the child's relationship to the rest of humanity.

The classical monkey experiments of Harry Harlow (1971) clearly established the importance of physical contact for the young. Monkey infants clearly prefer a "mother" made of cloth to one made of wire. Monkey infants reared by a cloth mother would first cling to the device when frightened by a stuffed bear and then venture forth to explore. Those reared by the wire mother shoved the stuffed bear away and then would clutch themselves and rock back and forth, or they would throw themselves on the floor or rub against the side of the cage. When frightened, they sought the security of being touched. The critical variable Harlow isolated in his series of experiments was the opportunity for the infant to have comforting physical contact with a soft object. Monkeys raised in complete isolation expressed their trauma through withdrawal and self-stimulation. Monkeys isolated for three or six months would substantially recover when returned to a more normal setting. Those isolated for one year showed no signs of improvement.

The most passionate defense of the importance of touch can be found in *Touching* (1971) by Ashley Montagu. By citing studies from a variety of disciplines and cultures, Mantagu builds a case for the physical and emotional consequences of being touched. Tactile stimulation is a universal, fundamental need necessary for survival. Tactile deprivation in infancy usually results in poor health, if not death, and behavioral inadequacies later in life. In a definitive work on institutionalization, Provence and Lipton (1962) found that infant apathy and withdrawal were associated with the failure to receive consistent and appropriate sensory stimulation.

Children who are deprived of touch, movement, sound, and other normal sensory input may experience Sensory Integration Dysfunction (SID), a neurological disorder that results in inefficient organization of sensory input received by the nervous system (Ayres, 1979).

Children with Sensory Integration Dysfunction may

- be overly sensitive or underreactive to touch, movement, sights, or sounds
- seek out intense self-stimulation (e.g., body whirling)
- have problems with coordination
- experience speech and language delays

The infant's reaching out constitutes a call, a state, a form of cognitive anticipation (anticipation of the unfolding of the action of being lifted up and held in someone's arms). The baby reaches out for joy in uniting and closeness as well as in distress and fear. At about 2 years of age, kissing (as opposed to mouthing) appears as a deliberate and intentional expression of affection. Real, emotionally satisfying attachment occurs when these tactile behaviors become incorporated into an emotional exchange and accommodation with a parent (Casati, 1991). "Tender gestures, woven tightly into the to-and-fro of tonic and postural dialogues gradually take on form and meaning and can serve to elicit and provide physical closeness, abolish distances magically, make social gestures such as greetings, and express feelings that the small child progressively learns to construct—the gestures of mutual love" (Casati, 1991, p. 14).

The child who is not touched in a loving and supportive manner will be disenfranchised from the human community. The current preoccupation with associating any kind of affectionate touch with sexuality may deprive children of an experience that is fundamentally critical for their long-term welfare.

References

Ayres, J. (1979). *Sensory integration and the child*. Los Angeles, CA: Western Psychological Services.

Casati, I. (1991). Hugging and embracing; kisses given, kisses received. Preludes to tenderness between infant and adult. *Early Child Development and Care, 67*, 1–15.

Harlow, H. (1971). *Learning to love*. New York: Ballantine Books.

Montagu, A. (1971). *Touching: The human significance of the skin*. New York: Columbia University Press.

Provence, S., & Lipton, R. C. (1962). *Infants in institutions*. New York: International Universities Press.

See also: Attachment, secure; Nurturance; Synchrony.

CHARLES A. SMITH

Toys. Toys provide children the experience of mastery that helps them to learn about the world and how to function as an adult later in life. When children master a certain toy, they then use it as a means of self-expression, the basis for play (Sutton-Smith, 1981). Many young children have toy preferences that appear as early as 12 months and are well established by the age of 3. Children tend to prefer toys that are viewed as stereotypical or gender appropriate, meaning that children of one sex typically choose to play with it, while children of the other sex do not.

Girls tend to play more frequently and longer with dolls and art materials, while boys prefer to play with blocks and transportation toys. Other common toys and activities preferred by girls are stuffed animals and bead bracelets, as well as dressing up, dancing, and quiet indoor play. Boys prefer outdoor active play and spend more time playing with manipulation objects and guns than do girls (Liss, 1986).

Caldera, Huston, and O'Brien (1989) examined whether parents encouraged involvement with sex-stereotyped toys or avoidance of cross-sex-stereotyped toys to determine if masculine and feminine toys lead to different patterns of parent-child interaction. After mothers, fathers, and their toddlers played in a room with male, female, or neutral toys, they found that parents showed subtle tendencies to respond more positively to and be more involved with child-same-sex toys.

Some researchers suggest that parents might even reward aggressive, assertive behaviors with their sons and punish aggressive behavior in daughters. Daughters are consistently reinforced for behaviors such as dancing, dressing-up, following parents around, asking for help, and playing with dolls. They are likely to be discouraged from manipulating objects, running, jumping, and climbing. In contrast, sons are often punished for these feminine behaviors while being encouraged to play with blocks, trucks, and toys that require large muscle activity (Shaffer, 1994). This shows that through reinforcement and modeling parents have an influence on the toy choices and play behavior of young children.

According to Bronson (1995), children's toy preferences are important to parents and teachers because if a toy does not attract their attention, children will not play with it at all. What children prefer, however, is not necessarily in their best interest. Social-linguistic, perceptual-cognitive, and gross/fine motor development skills should be considered when selecting toys. Play materials should nourish a growing imagination and encourage mental representation; extend children's knowledge and interest in the physical world; support the development of creative expression; and foster large muscle development (Bronson, 1995).

Age range and developmental level of the child are also important considerations when selecting toys. Appropriate play materials should be appealing and interesting to the child, matched to the child's capabilities, durable, and safe for the intended age of the child (Bronson, 1995).

Different kinds of toys are appropriate for children at different developmental levels. For example, play materials for young infants are primarily for looking, listening, sucking, grasping, or fingering. Older infants need materials that provide active exploration (Bronson, 1995). A baby's discovery that rattles make different sounds depending upon the way they are held is an early form of reasoning (Sutton-Smith, 1981).

Toddlers and preschool children need toys that not only allow them to enhance their large and fine motor skills but also to manipulate the object world. Parents usually give their girls dolls, whereas they give their sons varied types of manipulative toys. Girls should also be given the opportunity to gain from play with stores, gas stations, blocks, and other manipulative materials. These toy experiences give children an opportunity to control models of the adult world, which in turn gives the child a sense of mastery. Also, art materials give this age group a sense of innovation and creativity. Children from age 6 onward enjoy board games that encourage decision making and opportunities for success and failure. Children this age also enjoy doctor kits, tea sets, stamps, paint sets, and more complex trucks and trains (Sutton-Smith, 1981).

Parents and teachers are important resources for children's play and learning. Sutton-Smith (1981) maintains that parents should join in with their children's toy play by first watching how the child plays with a toy and then playing with it themselves. Parents can also model play to their child. Regardless of the gender of the child, toys should facilitate growth and development and allow the opportunity for both mastery and novelty. Some toys will enhance motor learning (tricycles), some will enhance cognitive learning (puzzles), and other toys will enhance social learning (strategic games and drama props). Toys should be realistic and working models of some aspect of the world that can be easily managed by the child. These qualities are the steps that lead from playfulness to mastery (Sutton-Smith, 1981).

References
Bronson, M. B. (1995). *The right stuff for children birth to 8: Selecting play materials to support development*. Washington, DC: National Association for the Education of Young Children.
Caldera, Y. M., Huston, A. C., & O'Brien, M. (1989). Social interactions and play patterns of parents and toddlers with feminine, masculine, and neutral toys. *Child Development, 60*, 70–76.
Liss, M. B. (1986). The play of boys and girls. In G. Fein & M. Rivkin (Eds.), *The young child at play* (pp. 127–139). Washington, DC: National Association for the Education of Young Children.
Shaffer, D. R. (1994). *Social and personality development* (3rd ed.). Pacific Grove, CA: Brooks/Cole.
Sutton-Smith, B. (1981). Toys that reach and teach kids of all ages. In R. Strom (Ed.), *Growing through play: Readings for parents and teachers* (pp. 199–203). Monterey, CA: Brooks/Cole.

See also: Play; Sex roles.

TRICIA K. NEPPL

Traditions. Certain experiences in the lives of families are especially potent, not only because they are shared but because they provide solidarity and a sense of family identity. These experiences are the raw materials of family life and are often recalled or reenacted because they are important to a particular family (Meredith, 1985). The collection of family routines, rituals, customs, myths, and beliefs that each family passes on to the next generation, including those by word of mouth and practice, comprise family traditions.

Traditions are familiar events that bring family members together. Family traditions include special events, stories, songs, customs, values, and expressions. In this sense they are similar to rituals; however, the key difference is the fact that traditions have or intend to be transmitted from generation to generation. Past cultural, ethnic, and religious practices tend to maintain significance and influence decisions regarding family interaction patterns based on the traditions established across the generations.

Traditions are characterized by regularity, commitment, and predictable behavior or activity. While the culture may influence the occasion and define the events observed, individual families put their own mark on the way they participate, developing very specific practices that are unique to their families. Since traditions have a beginning, contemporary families can be originators of new rituals that can be added to the family's canon for future use.

Family traditions are not only a means to pass values, behavior, and social tools from one generation to the next. They are also powerful processes of family interaction that serve many sundry functions. For example, traditions can reinforce cohesion and closeness, reveal family rules and statuses, recognize family milestones, maintain family values, and delineate appropriate behavior for special occasions (Meredith et al., 1989; Rosenthal & Marshall, 1988).

The observance of traditions has been identified as a characteristic of strong families (Curran, 1983; Meredith, 1985). Passed along from one generation to the next, traditions establish continuity with the past, identity with the present, and predictability toward the future. In other words, traditions can give a sense of connection by helping anchor families securely in the present while building a bridge between the past and the future (Fiese, 1992; Rosenthal & Marshall, 1988).

Family traditions are designed to foster a sense of continuity, security, and stability in families (Curran, 1983). As families keep this in mind, they can repeat, modify, and develop their traditions to accomplish this end. Some traditions can be repeated from the past with almost no change, whereas others may need to be modified to fit contemporary tastes and lifestyles. Some may be discarded, others invented, but there is always a fundamental family value at the core of the tradition regardless of any modifications to it. In this way, traditions can be used to strengthen families by maintaining a sense of stability over time.

There is a contemporary, as well as historical, dimension to family traditions. Current families often fashion inherited ritual according to their own circumstances and thus add their generational layer of meaning to the body of tradition to be handed down to subsequent cohorts. Whatever else it is or does, tradition communicates collective wisdom and prepares family members to receive relevant messages about their lives together with clarity and affective impact. Thus, traditions are built on ritualized behavior that associates meaning with certain activities and is passed from one generation to the next in some recognizable form.

References

Curran, D. (1983). *Traits of a healthy family*. Minneapolis, MN: Winston.

Fiese, B. (1992). Dimensions of family rituals across two generations: Relation to adolescent identity. *Family Process, 31*, 131–162.

Meredith, W. (1985). The importance of family traditions. *Wellness Perspectives, 2* (2), 17–19.

Meredith, W., Abbott, D., Lamanna, M., & Saunders, G. (1989). Rituals and family strengths: A three generation study. *Family Perspective, 23*, 75–83.

Rosenthal, C., & Marshall, V. (1988). Generational transmission of family ritual. *American Behavioral Scientist, 31*, 669–684.

See also: Family loyalty; Rituals; Routines.

JAMES J. PONZETTI, JR.

Transition to parenthood. The transition to parenthood has received a considerable amount of attention from researchers interested in the development of the family and social transitions (for extensive reviews, see Belsky & Kelly, 1994; Cowan & Cowan, 1992). Early studies characterized the transition to parenthood as a crisis point, especially in the marital relationships of new parents. Later studies reported data that reversed this characterization and suggested that while stressful, becoming a parent was certainly not a crisis but a manageable and normative transition. The controversy continued into and through the 1980s as researchers instigated longitudinal studies that followed couples from pregnancy into the child-rearing years (e.g., Belsky & Rovine, 1990; Cowan et al., 1985).

These more recent longitudinal studies have shown that one third to one half of men and women experience some decline in marital quality after the birth of a child. In general, the degree of decline in marital satisfaction is modest, but in some couples, the decline puts the relationship in what marital therapists would characterize as distress. The ranking of individual couples remains relatively stable from pre- to post birth. That is, within a group, couples that reported highest levels of satisfaction before parenthood were likely to exhibit highest levels of marital satisfaction after the birth of their child. Consequently, the arrival of a child is not thought to be likely to destroy successful marriages or salvage a troubled one. The marital change that takes place with the birth of a first child has been characterized in several ways. Belsky and Pensky (1988) organized the changes in the marital relationship into the following categories: (1) activities and interactions and (2) subjective feelings.

Activities and interactions. The sharing of household tasks becomes more traditional after the birth of the first child, with the wife taking on more household tasks (both child related and non–child related). Household tasks may increase for both husbands and wives, but the increase for women is larger. Couples experience a decrease in joint leisure activity. Parents do not spend less time together, but joint activity more often centers around household and child care tasks. Both husbands and wives report a decrease in positive interactions and an increase in conflict. At the same time, both husbands and wives report an increasing desire for positive interactions. It is important to note that non parent couples also experience a decline in positive interactions, but it is not as severe as that experienced by new parents.

Subjective feelings. To investigate the changes in a couple's marital satisfaction as a result of the changes described above, standardized measures of overall marital quality are typically used. The results of these analyses suggest that marital satisfaction tends to decline over the transition to parenthood for both husbands and wives. These results suggest that women experience this decline more severely than do men, and they experience it earlier during the transition to parenthood than do men.

References

Belsky, J., & Kelly, J. (1994). *Transition to parenthood.* New York: Delacorte Press.

Belsky, J., & Pensky, E. (1988). Marital change across the transition to parenthood. *Marriage and Family Review, 12* (3–4), 133–156.

Belsky, J., & Rovine, M. (1990). Patterns of marital change across the transition to parenthood. *Journal of Marriage and the Family, 52,* 109–123.

Cowan, C. P., & Cowan, P. A. (1992). *When partners become parents: The big life change for couples.* New York: Basic Books.

Cowan, C. P., Cowan, P. A., Heming, G., Garrett, E., Coysh, W. S., Curtis-Boles, H., & Boles, A. J. (1985). Transitions to parenthood: His, hers, and theirs. *Journal of Family Issues, 6,* 451–481.

See also: Conflict, interparental; Marital interaction; Styles, parenting.

BRENDA J. BOYD

Transition to school. The transition to school refers to the time point at which a child enters formal schooling, typically in kindergarten or first grade. The transition is marked by a period of adjustment in which children must meet new academic and social challenges. Social challenges include taking on a new role as student, becoming acquainted with a new peer group and teacher, and adjusting to a larger and less personal setting than the family, day care, and nursery school. Academically, children must adjust to harsher evaluations of work and come to understand teachers' performance expectations. Successfully negotiating these challenges is important because early academic performance and classroom social behavior are highly predictive of later performance (Alexander & Entwisle, 1988). Furthermore, during the transition to school, individual differences become more apparent as children stretch to meet these new challenges (Alexander & Entwisle, 1988). Approximately 13% to 15% of children have difficulties with the initial transition to school.

Typically the transition to school is studied as a yearlong adjustment process and is evaluated through achievement tests, school marks, social acceptance, and behavior problems at the end of the school year. The first few days and weeks of school are seen as an acute stressful event with the predominant task being coping with separation from parents. Parents and families are seen as particularly influential during this time because young children rely heavily on parents for social support and self-evaluation. Parents can influence the initial adjustment through their cognitions (beliefs and expectations), personal interactions and relationships, and direct involvement in school-related activities.

Parent cognitions. While parent expectations and beliefs influence children's behavior in school, the nature of the relation is complex and may involve mediating variables (Christenson, Rounds, & Gorney, 1992). Parents who hold high academic expectations may provide more support and encouragement for academic activities and help children develop a competent school self-image. Relations between parent expectations and children's school adjustment in kindergarten and first grade may be weaker than at other time points, perhaps because parental school expectations are still developing. The racial and cultural background of the family may also impact on these relations because the social distance between schools and nonwhite lower-class families may be greater than for others (Alexander & Entwisle, 1988).

Parent-child relationship qualities. There is remarkable consistency across different studies in the parent-child relationship qualities that are associated with academic and social competence during the early school years (Barth & Parke, 1996). Better academic performance and social relations in the classroom are associated with a positive affective home environment that includes children's positive emotional expressions and parental acceptance, warmth, nurturance, encouragement, engagement, and responsivity. The quality of instruction that parents provide, their communicative skills, and their ability to structure tasks for children are also related to better academic performance. Poor school adjustment is linked to high parental control, parents' lack of respect for the child's autonomy, child negativity, and child control behaviors. Global measures of the parent-child relationship such as parent-infant attachment have shown less consistent relations with early school behaviors.

Some evidence suggests that how parent-child relationship qualities are related to children's adjustment may depend in part on when a child's school behavior is measured during the transition period. For example, parental control and child negativity are related to dependency on the teacher early in the school year and hostility with peers later in the school year (Barth & Parke, 1996).

Parental involvement. High parental involvement in education is characteristic of successful schools. Parental involvement includes a number of tasks such as volunteering in the classroom, participating in school organizations such as parent-teacher associations, and monitoring and assisting children with homework. Parental involvement may benefit children because it promotes improvement in the quality of instruction in the classroom, creates consistency between the values expressed at home and at school, and increases children's motivation to do well in school (Barth & Parke, 1996; Christenson, Rounds, & Gorney, 1992). Parental education level, economic status, work patterns, and marital status have each been hypothesized to influence the nature and degree of involvement. During the early school years while children are making the transition to school, parental involvement is typically higher than at other time points. However, there has been little focus on the specific effects of parental involvement on kindergarten and first-grade children's school adjustment. Parents and teachers differ somewhat in their sense of priorities for preparing children for school, with parents emphasizing reading and math skills more than teachers, and teachers emphasizing problem-solving skills and small muscle development (Harris & Lindauer, 1988).

Parent cognitions, parent-child relationship qualities, and parental involvement have each shown independent relations to children's early school adjustment, and it is likely that these aspects of parenting are interrelated. A specific research focus on the transition to school is rare, which limits our knowledge of how parental influences on school behavior differ for this critical period compared to other time points. Research does tell us that parental cognition, parent-child relationship qualities, and parental involvement are different in the early school years and vary somewhat by race and socioeconomic status. Furthermore, educational goals are also different for this age group. Thus, professionals should be cautious about generalizing findings from studies with older children and predominantly white middle-class samples. In addition to this concern, it is important to recognize that most studies of "parents" have actually been studies of mothers, despite evidence that fathers make unique and important contributions to children's early social and academic adjustment (Barth & Parke, 1996). Nevertheless, preschool intervention programs that heavily involve parents tend to promote academic achievement in children (Campbell & Ramey, 1994).

References

Alexander, K. L., & Entwisle, D. R. (1988). Achievement in the first 2 years of school: Patterns and processes. *Monographs of the Society for Research in Child Development, 53* (2, Serial No. 218).

Barth, J. M., & Parke R. D. (1996). The impact of the family on children's early school social adjustment. In A. J. Sameroff & M. M. Haith (Eds.), *The five to seven shift* (pp. 329–361). Chicago: University of Chicago Press.

Campbell, F. A., & Ramey, C. T. (1994). Effects of early intervention on intellectual and academic achievement: A follow-up study of children from low income families. *Child Development, 65,* 684–698.

Christenson, S. L., Rounds, T., & Gorney, D. (1992). Family factors and student achievement: An avenue to increase students' school success. *School Psychology Quarterly, 7,* 178–206.

Harris, K., & Lindauer, S. L. K. (1988). Parental and teacher priorities for kindergarten preparation. *Child Study Journal, 18,* 61–73.

See also: Attachment, secure; Family-school partnerships; Fear; School.

JOAN M. BARTH

Triangulation. Triangulation refers to the inappropriate involvement of a third party in the relationship between two persons. The use of the term in the family literature can be dated from Bowen's (1978) work, in which he pointed out that the triangle was the most stable geometric form and, by analogy, a kind of family relationship both highly likely to develop and highly resistant to change. In particular, family systems theorists point to the child's triangulation in interparental conflicts as a key to understanding the development of emotional problems in childhood. As Framo (1975) stated, "[W]henever you have a disturbed child, you have a disturbed marriage" (p. 22).

Minuchin (1974) articulated the concept of triangulation in his work on structural family theory. Minuchin emphasized the importance of the maintenance of appropriate boundaries between the subsystems of the family, particularly the couple subsystem and the child subsystem. He proposed that the origins of emotional problems derive from cross-generational boundary violations, such as when a parent relies on a child rather than the spouse for the fulfillment of his or her emotional needs. Through his work with children suffering from psychosomatic illnesses and eating disorders, Minuchin discerned three forms of triangular family relationships that lead to individual and family distress.

Parent-child coalition. One parent involves the child in a cross-generational coalition that excludes the other parent. Such a relationship may take the form of an overly intimate relationship between one parent and the child or a parent encouraging the child to reject or disrespect the other parent. This family dynamic may create a *parentalized child* who is burdened by the assumption of developmentally inappropriate tasks such as offering emotional support and intimacy to his or her parent. This is a family form often described in clinical work with children of alcoholics.

Rigid triangle. In this family form, the child attempts to maintain a coalition with each parent, whether because of the child's wish to be a "peacemaker" or "go-between" or due to pressure exerted by each parent for the child to side with one against the other. Minuchin described this as the most distressing family dynamic for the child, whose attempts to maintain closeness to either parent may be interpreted as disloyalty by the other parent, thus causing further stress. This family form may be particularly evident during conflictual divorces and disagreements over child custody (e.g., Buchanan, Maccoby, & Dornbusch, 1991).

Detouring. This is the subtlest of triangular family forms, in that there may be no apparent conflict between the parents. While the marital relationship in such families is unhappy, the couple avoids acknowledging their marital problems, or detours around them, by displacing their concerns onto their child. Deviant behavior on the part of the child meets a need in the family by providing the parents with a problem external to their relationship on which they can focus their attention. Because they are united when attempting to respond to their "problem child," detouring allows the couple to maintain an illusion of harmony. Therefore, detouring couples are motivated to covertly reinforce children's behavior problems in order to maintain the homeostasis in the family system. The child in this family triangle may be known as the *identified patient* because he or she is the only one in the family who is overtly symptomatic and brings the family to the attention of the therapist.

The concept of triangulation has been empirically validated through both observational and self-report data. For example, Christensen and Margolin (1988) compared the interactions of distressed families, in which both marital discord and child conduct problems were present, to those of nondistressed families. Using observational ratings, they found that distressed families evidenced weaker marital alliances and more frequent cross-generational coalitions between parents and target children. Further, they found that in distressed families conflicts that originated between husband and wife were more likely to spill over onto relationships between parents and children. In another study, Kerig (1995) asked mothers, fathers, and their school-aged children to describe their family structure with the *Family Cohesion Index*, which classified families according to Minuchin's typology. Families in which there was a parent-child coalition were higher in marital conflict, and children in rigid triangle families reported more negative affect in the family. Children in detouring families were more likely to blame themselves for their parents' conflicts, and their parents rated them as higher in internalizing problems such as anxiety and depression.

Triangular family forms such as detouring help families to maintain their equilibrium and to avoid confronting issues that might threaten the stability of the family, such as marital unhappiness. Therefore, such dynamics may be difficult for family members to acknowledge and difficult to change. Structural therapists such as Minuchin use techniques such as *blocking* the interference of a child in marital issues in order to reinforce the couple coalition, or assigning activities that will increase the involvement of a parent and child who have been alienated from one another by a parent-child coalition. Strategic family therapists such as Papp (1983) use paradoxical techniques that motivate resistant families to change by prescribing that they stay the same, such as recommending that a child continue to misbehave because it is his way of bringing his parents closer together.

References

Bowen, M. (1978). *Family therapy in clinical practice*. New York: Jason Aronson.

Buchanan, C. M., Maccoby, E. E., & Dornbusch, S. M. (1991). Caught between parents: Adolescents' experience in divorced homes. *Child Development, 62*, 1008–1029.

Christensen, A., & Margolin, G. (1988). Conflict and alliance in distressed and nondistressed families. In R. Hinde & J. Stevenson-Hinde (Eds.), *Relationships within families* (pp. 263–282). Oxford: Clarendon.

Framo, J. L. (1975). Personal reflections of a family therapist. *Journal of Marriage and Family Counseling*, *1*, 15–28.

Kerig, P. K. (1995). Triangles in the family circle: Effects of family structure on marriage, parenting, and child adjustment. *Journal of Family Psychology*, *9*, 28–43.

Minuchin, S. (1974). *Families and family therapy*. Cambridge, MA: Harvard University Press.

Papp, P. (1983). *The process of change*. New York: Guilford.

See also: Alliance, parenting; Conflict, interparental; Divorced families; Family systems; Marital interaction.

PATRICIA K. KERIG

U

Urban parenting. *Webster's Third New International Dictionary* (1993) defines urban as "relating to, characteristic of, or taking place in a city" (p. 2520). The parent-child relationship is markedly different for urban parents than for suburban or rural parents. Urban parents represent all social classes, yet they share common concerns about parenting in a city environment.

Unique issues related to urban parenting include neighborhood dangers (such as gangs, gun violence, and drugs), child supervision, increasing numbers of younger mothers, and intergenerational raising of the children and the need for social supports.

Gangs are an active force in the urban environment. With gangs comes increased violence, especially gun violence, and drug trafficking. Parents in the urban setting are acutely aware of gangs and the trouble they pose to children's safety. Parents report that they often need to plan the children's outdoor activities in the morning or early afternoon. This schedule keeps the children out of the path of the gangs and random violence. The gang members and drug traffickers generally appear on the streets in the late afternoon and night. Parents may be prevented from using neighborhood services such as public parks and libraries if the service is in a different gang territory or a gang-infested building.

Parents also cannot safely leave children to play unsupervised. Children may find dangerous items, such as drug paraphernalia, broken bottles, and discarded trash in and around play lots and on private lawns. Unsupervised children are also likely to be approached by untrustworthy people. Many parents do not involve themselves with their immediate neighbors but instead become active within their church or community organization. As a result, many children do not socialize with people in their immediate surroundings but only with people from their church.

The Children's Defense Fund (1996) reported that many families, of all races, are affected by gun violence. In 1993 (the most recent data available), 5,751 American children were killed by guns. This number is rising annually and accounts for the majority of youth deaths, of which the majority of the victims are between the ages of 15 and 19. Furthermore, of those children killed by guns, 1,460 were the result of suicide (Children's Defense Fund, 1996).

Drug use (including alcohol and tobacco) also negatively affects the developing child in utero. Drug use can be an underlying cause of premature births. Children born prematurely are at high risk for physical and cognitive delays and disabilities. A high incidence of drug use in the urban environment directly influences the high rate of premature infants who may require expensive and long-term medical, developmental, and social interventions. Young parents as well as older parents require increased social supports. Young parents benefit from parenting programs. Myers et al. (1992) and Brown (1993) concur that effective parental functioning results in high self-esteem for the child and social and academic competence. Parenting programs should focus on teaching acceptance and promote a variety of positive child outcomes.

References

Brown, E. (1993). Black mothers and their children: Competent parenting and the promotion of childhood social skills. *Dissertation Abstracts International, 53* (9), 4973B–4974B.

Children's Defense Fund. (1996, April). *Special report: Gun violence* (CDF Reports), pp. 5–9.

Myers, H. F., Alvy, K. T., Arrington. A., Richardson, M. A., Marigna, M., Huff, R., Main, M., & Newcomb, M. D. (1992). The impact of a parent training program on inner-city African-American families. *Journal of Community Psychology, 20,* 132–147.

Webster's Third New International Dictionary. (1993). Springfield, MA: Merriam-Webster.

See also: Community; Social support, informal; Violence, community.

ROBERTA O'SHEA, JAMES V. KAHN, AND ABIGAIL BAXTER

V

Victim-centered discipline. Victim-centered discipline is any discipline that draws the attention of the child to the effects of his or her behavior on the victim. For example, when Johnny knocks over his friend's tower of blocks, a wise parent might kneel in front of Johnny and say, "Johnny, I think your friend feels very sad. He worked hard to build his tower. I wonder if you might want to comfort your friend." It might also be appropriate to point out to Johnny that when he treats other people unkindly, it makes them less likely to want to play with him.

Victim-centered discipline is similar to *induction*, control behavior that includes reasoning with children and helping them to understand the effects of their behavior on others. In this discussion, *victim-centered discipline* and *induction* will be used interchangeably.

Induction is one of three categories of control behavior described by Rollins and Thomas (1979). Unlike the other two control techniques of *love withdrawal* and *power assertion*, parental use of induction is consistently associated with positive outcomes for children, including greater social competence and moral internalization.

Effective use of victim-centered discipline is different from *guilt-inducing* techniques, which are more likely to attack and blame the child. In contrast, induction is intended to inform children and to activate empathy for victims.

Hoffman (1983) has theorized on why induction may be more effective than other control techniques. He suggests that induction, unlike anger that overloads children or soft requests that do not get their attention, provides just enough activation to get their attention. It provides information that will be stored in the child's mind: "If I hurt other people, they will not want to be my friends." In addition, effective induction activates children's empathy: "I am sorry that my friend was hurt." Hoffman suggests that effective use of induction results in an internalized concern for others, which is the basis for moral development.

Induction shows respect for children and helps them better understand the needs and feelings of people in the social environment. It also allows children to be more active agents in their own lives than when coercive control techniques are used.

Helping parents and other caregivers to understand victim-centered discipline and become skillful in its use can make a substantial contribution to children's development.

References
Hoffman, M. L. (1983). Affective and cognitive processes in moral internalization. In E. T. Higgins, D. N. Ruble, & W. W. Hartup (Eds.), *Social cognition and social development: A sociocultural perspective* (pp. 236–275). New York: Cambridge University Press.

Rollins, B. C., & Thomas, D. L. (1979). Parental support, power, and control techniques in the socialization of children. In W. R. Burr, R. Hill, F. I. Nye, & I. L. Reiss (Eds.), *Contemporary theories about the family* (Vol. 1, pp. 317–364). New York: Free Press.

See also: Conscience; Consequences, natural and logical; Control strategies; Discipline; Empathy.

H. WALLACE GODDARD

Violence, community. The United States is the most violent country in the industrialized world, particularly for young people. Homicide in the United States ranks as the second leading cause of death between 15 and 24 years of age. Statistics that were available between 1986 and 1987 indicate that young males were 4 times more likely to be murdered than their counterparts in the next-highest country, Scotland; 21 times more likely than those in West Germany; and 40 times more likely than same-age males in Japan. Class, race, and gender exert important influences on exposure to community violence. The United States homicide rate for young African American males was more than 7 times the homicide rate for white males in this age range. These figures are more alarming in light of the fact that homicide rates for young people in the major United States cities are on the rise since these data were recorded (Osofsky, 1995).

Recent research has focused on elementary school–age and younger children who are exposed to chronic community violence (see Osofsky, 1995 for a review). Exposure to chronic community violence is defined as "frequent and continual exposure to the use of guns, knives, and drugs, and random violence" (Osofsky, 1995, p. 782). A survey in New Haven in 1992 reported that 40% of 6th, 8th, and 10th graders had witnessed at least one violent crime in the past year (Marans & Cohen, 1993).

Reports of even younger children's exposure to violence indicate that 1 out of 10 children under the age of 6 reported having witnessed a shooting or stabbing (Marans & Cohen, 1993). When 3rd and 5th graders living in violent neighborhoods in New Orleans were asked to draw pictures of "what happens" in their neighborhoods (Osofsky & Fenichel, 1994), children drew in graphic detail pictures of shootings, stabbings, drug deals, fighting, and funerals. They also reported being scared of the violence and of something happening to them.

The mothers in several studies (Osofsky, 1995) provided anecdotal data related to their feelings about their children's exposure to violence and the ways in which they tried to handle the problem. A nonemotional and matter-of-fact quality permeated their reports, likely related to the extent of living with so much violence. Interpretations from these maternal reports seemed to suggest that from very early in their lives these children and their parents must learn to deal with loss and cope with grieving for family members and friends who have been killed.

Developmental issues. Adolescent problems related to violence exposure have been most visible in literature and in media. Less well known are the problems that are frequently seen in younger children exposed to violence. Many people assume that very young children are not affected at all, erroneously believing that they are too young to know or remember what has happened. However, even in the earliest phases of infant and toddler development, clear associations have been found between exposure to violence and posttraumatic symptoms and disorders (see Osofsky, 1995 for a review).

Infants show increased irritability and sleep disturbances as well as fears of being alone. Exposure of trauma interferes with their sense of trust and with their later emergence of autonomy through exploration. These infants also show signs of regressed developmental achievements, such as in toileting and language (Osofsky & Fenichel, 1994).

School-age children often experience increases in anxiety and sleep disturbances with exposure to violence. They may have difficulty paying attention and concentrating because they often experience intrusive thoughts. Preschool as well as school-age children are less likely to explore their physical environment and play freely, showing less motivation to master their environment. Autonomous striving may be subverted, and trauma-generated adventuresome pursuits beyond the child's developmental capabilities may be accelerated (Osofsky, 1995).

Effects on children. Studies (Osofsky, 1995) with a clinical focus have stressed three different effects on children exposed to violence:

- *Development of aggressive behavior and negative emotions following violence exposure.* Generation of intense negative affect interferes with the normal course of development, thus increasing self-attributions of shame, ineffectiveness, or self-blame. This can lead to negative self-image. Feelings of desensitization and addiction to violence may also be problematic in helping children regulate their emotions.
- *Post-traumatic Stress Disorder* (PTSD). Children who are exposed to violent environments generally show signs of PTSD. Disrupted patterns of eating and sleeping,

- difficulties in attending and relating, anxious reactions, fearfulness, and reexperiencing the trauma are common to these children.
- *Problems with early relationships.* Although no studies directly link violence exposure with child-caregiver, studies that have compared maltreated infants with non-maltreated infants provide clues. Maltreated infants often form insecure attachments, characterized by avoidance and resistance to be comforted by the caregiver or a pattern of disorganization and disorientation. This state of affairs is characterized by a combination of avoidance, resistance, apprehension, aggression, apathy, freezing, and stilling (abrupt freezing gestures by a child resisting or avoiding contact).

Accumulation of risk factors. Researchers such as Garbarino (1995) believe that there is a direct correlation between the number of risk factors that children encounter and the resulting developmental damage. Children are capable of coping with one or two major risk factors. When risk accumulates, however, there is a dramatic increase in developmental damage.

Garbarino (1995) applied the "risk model" to children exposed to community violence: They often are poor, live in father-absent families, contend with parental incapacity due to depression or substance abuse, are raised by parents with little education or employment prospects, and are exposed to domestic violence. Bearing in mind that approximately 20% of American children live with this sort of accumulation of risk, the problem of violence is clearly a national problem with far-reaching implications for child development.

Miller (1996) suggests that parents can play an important role in helping their children cope with these violent circumstances by reaching out to others for *social support* as a personal resource that will help them focus on their children's needs. Parents can also *reaffirm family bonds*, making a commitment of extra time for children to affirm their love and care. Finally, parents, working alone or in concert with others, can *become advocates* in their communities for making that environment safe for families.

References

Garbarino, J. (1995). The American war zone: What children can tell us about living with violence. *Developmental and Behavioral Pediatrics, 16* (6), 431–435.

Marans, S., & Cohen, D. (1993). Children and inner-city violence: Strategies for intervention. In L. Leavitt & N. Fox (Eds.), *Psychological effects of war and violence on children* (pp. 281–302). Hillsdale, NJ: Erlbaum.

Miller, K. (1996). *The crisis manual for early childhood teachers: How to handle the really difficult problems.* Beltsville, MD: Gryphon House.

Osofsky, J. D. (1995). The effects of exposure to violence on young children. *American Psychologist, 50* (9), 782–788.

Osofsky, J. D., & Fenichel, E. (1994). *Caring for infants and toddlers in violent environments: Hurt, healing, and hope.* Arlington, VA: Zero to Three/National Center for Clinical Infant Programs.

See also: Advocacy; Aggression, childhood; Community.

HIRA NAIR

Vulnerable Child Syndrome. The term *vulnerable child* has been used when parental expectations of a child's susceptibility to medical or developmental problems are unrealistically high relative to the child's actual health status. The *Vulnerable Child Syndrome* (VCS) refers to a constellation of behaviors stemming from both parental expectations and anxiety, usually precipitated by a child being labeled early on as vulnerable in some way. In their landmark paper, Green and Solnit (1964) defined the syndrome in terms of its clinical features or outcomes: difficulties with separation in both parent and child, overprotection of the child, bodily concerns, and school underachievement.

Common precipitating factors associated with the development of the VCS include, but are not limited to, the following: prematurity, perinatal congenital heart disease, infant jaundice, prior loss during pregnancy, and hospitalization of other children. Although the event that might promote the development of the VCS is initially real and often life-threatening, the VCS becomes problematic when the label of vulnerability persists over time, despite the child showing no lingering objective evidence of being vulnerable. This syndrome is thought to develop and is perpetuated through the operation of a self-fulfilling prophecy whereby parents subsequently treat the child as vulnerable, often overprotecting them and thereby producing a child who adopts a self-concept and behaviors in line with the parents' initial expectations (Stern & Karraker, 1990).

The two most important factors thought to contribute to perceived vulnerability on the part of the parent include an actual vulnerability in the child due to illness and/or a past belief that the child might die (Forsyth et al., 1996). In a study that examined the relative influence of sociodemographic status, maternal reproductive and child-rearing experience, and the infant's actual health status on parental expectations, infant health status was found to be the main determinant of parental expectations (McCormick, Shapiro, & Starfield, 1982). Most research on the VCS has focused on children who were medically fragile as infants, and a great deal of this research has examined the influence of prematurity as a factor influencing parental expectations, reactions, and behaviors.

Further evidence for the VCS comes from research that has suggested that some mothers of premature infants continue to interact differently with their infants despite evidence that their infants are actually capable and competent, and long after differences observed in premature and full-term infant behavior have declined (Barnard, Bee, & Hammond, 1984). Indeed, most differences between premature and full-term infants diminish or disappear in later infancy and childhood, with only a small proportion of premature infants having long-term serious problems. Further, a persistent relationship between the early interactions of mothers and their premature infants and later child cognitive and social competence has been documented (e.g., Beckwith, Rodning & Cohen, 1992). Taken together, these observations suggest that lowered expectations for the competence of premature infants may be influencing parent behavior independent of actual infant behavior and that parental reactions to premature infants are based at least in part on a stereotype associated with the label of prematurity, promoting the development of the VCS. Therefore, the social or cognitive deficits manifested in some children born prematurely may more accurately be attributable to their social experiences, rather than to damage resulting directly from the premature birth (Sameroff & Seifer, 1983).

Discerning the effects of such a *vulnerability stereotype* in the natural environment is clearly difficult because premature infants may emit behavioral cues of vulnerability that elicit negative reactions from their caregivers. One line of research (Stern & Karraker, 1990) has attempted to provide empirical documentation for the existence and impact of a vulnerability stereotype by comparing adult responses to the same infants described as either full-term or premature. Collectively, these studies indicate that adults hold a negative set of beliefs about premature infants and that these beliefs may be associated with nonoptimal adult behaviors and infant outcomes.

Because negative expectations on the part of parents and health care professionals may lead to the Vulnerable Child Syndrome, it is important to explore factors that may mitigate these expectations. For example, depressed mothers with a lower sense of self-efficacy have been shown to view their children as more vulnerable than nondepressed mothers (Bendell et al., 1994). Self-efficacy may therefore be an important determinant of expectations and can potentially explain to an extent why some children continue to be perceived as vulnerable over time. An understanding and recognition of the operation of stereotypes are clearly required. Practitioners can help to mitigate this process by providing accurate information to parents that attempts to discredit inaccurate beliefs and thereby reduce the possibility of a self-fulfilling process in which parent-child relationships are significantly harmed.

References
Barnard, K., Bee, H., & Hammond, M. (1984). Developmental changes in maternal interactions with term and preterm infants. *Infant Behavior and Development, 7,* 101–113.
Beckwith, L., Rodning, C., & Cohen, S. (1992). Preterm children at early adolescence and continuity and discontinuity in maternal responsiveness from infancy. *Child Development, 63,* 1198–1208.
Bendell, D., Field, T., Yando, R., Lang, C., Martinez, A., & Pickens, J. (1994). Depressed mothers' perceptions of their preschool children's vulnerability. *Child Psychiatry and Human Development, 24* (3), 183–190.
Forsyth, B. W. C., Horowitz, S. M., Leventhal, J. M., Burger, J., & Leaf, P. (1996). The child vulnerability scale: An instrument to measure parental perceptions of child vulnerability. *Journal of Pediatric Psychology, 21* (1), 89–101.
Green, M., & Solnit, A. J. (1964). Reactions to the threatened loss of a child: A vulnerable child syndrome. *Pediatrics, 34,* 58-66.
McCormick, M. C., Shapiro, S. & Starfield, B. (1982). Factors associated with maternal opinion of infant development—clues to the vulnerable child? *Pediatrics, 69* (5), 537–543.
Sameroff, A., & Seifer, R (1983). Familial risk and child competence. *Child Development, 54,* 1254–1268.
Stern, M., & Karraker, K. (1990). The prematurity stereotype: Empirical evidence and implications for practice. *Infant Mental Health Journal, 11,* 3–11.

See also: Attachment, secure; Premature birth; Self-fulfilling prophecy.

MICHELLE OLEXA AND MARILYN STERN

Vygotsky, Lev Semenovich (1896–1934). Lev Semenovich Vygotsky was a Russian educational psychologist who was born near Minsk in 1896 and died of tuberculosis in 1934 at the early age of 38. Although his professional activities only spanned 10 years (1924–1934), his work on developmental processes continues to have an impact among scientists and educators today. Vygotsky's ideas were formed during a period of major intellectual upheaval after the Russian revolution in 1917. Vygotsky has been described as a humanist whose work was interdisciplinary and comprised a dazzling range of interests from literary analysis of Shakespeare to the rehabilitation of deaf children (Kozulin, 1990). During his productive years, he conducted research on the development of children, wrote at a frenetic pace, and gave electrifying lectures to packed auditoriums in Moscow and in other intellectual centers in Russia (Wertsch, 1985). Until recently, Vygotsky was little known in the West as his writings were suppressed in 1936 under the dictatorship of Stalin. It was not until the 1960s that Vygotsky's works began to be translated into English and became known to psychologists in the West.

Of interest to parents and educators is Vygotsky's claim that higher mental processes have their origin in social processes (Wertsch, 1985). Unlike Piaget, who deemphasized the role of culture, Vygotsky argued that development can only be understood with reference to social and cultural influences on the thinking process (Wertsch, 1985). For Vygotsky, mastering the tools of the culture (e.g., reading, writing, numeracy) does not occur in a vacuum but through extensive interaction with others who have knowledge of the culture's symbol systems.

To describe the teaching-learning process, Vygotsky developed the concept of the *zone of proximal development* (ZPD) (Rieber & Carton, 1987). The ZPD is the difference between the child's actual and potential levels of development. A good teacher, according to Vygotsky, operates in this zone by providing material slightly ahead of the child's development while scaffolding or supporting their responses to a higher level. As a child becomes more proficient, the teacher gradually withdraws the supports until the child can perform the task successfully without help. During this process, the dialogue that occurs externally between teachers and learners becomes internalized and is subsequently used as inner speech by children to guide their own actions.

The ZPD illustrates Vygotsky's claim that higher mental processes originate in social interaction, and the concept applies equally well to parents and teachers interacting with children. In this way, children progress from more elementary biologically based forms of behavior to the higher mental functions that are mediated by the tools or symbol systems of the culture. Cultural tools such as language, reading, writing, and mathematical reasoning are not seen by Vygotsky as derivatives of intelligence but rather as central functions that, when internalized, shape the mind (Kozulin, 1990). According to Vygotsky, biological evolution has been replaced by cultural evolution through the transmission of increasingly complex symbol systems (Wertsch, 1985).

Vygotsky's concepts have important implications for parenting and teaching. Children of all ages learn best through individualized instruction that is both tailored to their level of understanding and challenges their development at the leading edge of their capabilities. However, even as toddlers many children receive too little of the verbal interaction that is necessary to stimulate the development of higher levels of thinking (Hart & Risley, 1995). This suggests the need for more one-to-one interaction or guided assistance by adults during the teaching-learning process, especially in the early stages of the mastery of skills and concepts. For teachers, Vygotsky's theory argues for an apprenticeship style of teaching rather than the large group instruction that is common in our school systems (Tharp & Gallimore, 1989). For parents, Vygotsky's theory argues for more awareness of and support for the critical role that parents play in transmitting cultural tools to their children (e.g., language, preliteracy, and prenumeracy skills) during early childhood before formal schooling.

References
Hart, B., & Risley, T. (1995). *Meaningful differences in the everyday experience of young American children.* New York: Paul H. Brooks.
Kozulin, A. (1990). *Vygotsky's psychology.* Cambridge, MA: Harvard University Press.
Rieber, R., & Carton, A. (Eds.). (1987). *The collected works of L. S. Vygotsky: Vol. 1. Problems in general psychology.* New York: Plenum.
Tharp, R., & Gallimore, R. (1989). *Rousing minds to life.* Cambridge: Cambridge University Press.
Wertsch, J. (1985). *Vygotsky and the social formation of mind.* Cambridge, MA: Harvard University Press.

See also: Communication; Scaffolding; Social context.

ANN D. MURRAY

Whining. We can all recognize a whine when we hear one, although defining whining is somewhat harder. Whines are complaints or demands accompanied by high-pitched plaintive or distressed cries. Yet it is often less the nature of the sound and more the repetitive, drawn-out nagging nature of the plea that makes it a whine.

Children's whining has not been well studied (Endo et al., 1991) and has been considered an annoyance problem. Yet for many families it is these irritating daily behaviors that are most troublesome. Whining is among the most common concerns expressed by parents of both normal and referred children. Achenbach and Edelbrock (1981) noted that approximately 50% of normal 4-year-olds and 25% of 8-year-olds were reported to whine by their parents (figures are higher for referred children). While whining was reported for less than 10% of children older than 10, some do continue to whine into adolescence and beyond. Whining typically begins in earnest during the preschool years (Whitham, 1991) when children first acquire the level of verbal skills needed to whine and is a means of communication. Because others find it irritating, parents need to teach their children more appropriate communication strategies.

Occasional whining due to illness or fatigue can be dealt with differently than when a child whines chronically as a daily habit. If parents notice that their children habitually whine in the half-hour before supper because of hunger, for example, this may warrant a modification in the dinnertime routine. Whining typically occurs to get a parent's attention (Whitham, 1991). Whining to interrupt a phone call is a common example. Whining in public, because of a parent's fear of humiliation, is most likely to lead a parent to give in despite not wanting to or to become frustrated and angry. Parents may inadvertently encourage whining in their children by giving in to the whine. If parents, having made a decision not to reward the whine, then cave in to the pressures of a child's whining, the child will be encouraged to whine more frequently, having discovered that whining is an effective strategy (Whitham, 1991). Always or frequently giving in to a child's whining sets the stage for the development of a spoiled child who may later have difficulty not only at home but also at school and with friends.

Programs to reduce whining are typically based on behavior modification principles (e.g., Webster-Stratton, 1992; Whitham, 1991). To reduce whining, parents and other key caretakers must cooperate to establish and consistently maintain a "no whining" policy. This means ignoring the whining and focusing on teaching children more appropriate forms of communication. If children avoid whining when making a request or protest, parents might then respond more attentively in order to strengthen the more appropriate behavior.

References

Achenbach, T., & Edelbrock, C. (1981). Behavioral problems and competencies reported by parents of normal and disturbed children aged four through sixteen. *Monographs of the Society for Research in Child Development, 46* (1).

Endo, G., Sloane, H., Hawkes, T., & Jenson, W. (1991). Reducing child whining through self-instructional parent training materials. *Child and Family Behavior Therapy, 13* (3) 41–58.

Webster-Stratton, C. (1992). *The incredible years: A trouble-shooting guide for parents of children aged 3-8*. Toronto, Ontario: Umbrella.

Whitham, C. (1991). *Win the whining war & other skirmishes: A family peace plan*. Chicago: Perspective.

See also: Authority, parental; Discipline; Limit setting; Temper tantrums.

ELIZABETH A. LEVIN

Bibliography

Ainsworth, M. D. S., Blehar, M., Waters, E., & Wall (1978). *Patterns of attachment.* Hillsdale, NJ: Erlbaum.

Bornstein, M. (Ed.). (1994). *Handbook of parenting*. Mahwah, NJ and Hove, UK: Lawrence Erlbaum.

Boss, P. G., Doherty, W. J., LaRossa, R., Schumm, W. R., & Steinmetz, S. K. (Eds.). (1993). *Sourcebook of family theories and methods: A contextual approach* (pp. 591-625). New York: Plenum.

Brazelton, T. B., & Cramer, B. (1990). *The earliest relationship*. New York: Addison-Wesley.

Broderick, C. B. (1993). *Understanding family processes: Basics of family systems theory*. Newbury Park, CA: Sage Publications.

Bronfenbrenner, U. (1979). *The ecology of human development: Experiments by nature and design*. Cambridge, MA: Harvard University Press.

Carter, N. (1996). *See how we grow: A report on the status of parenting education in the U.S.* Philadelphia: The Pew Charitable Trusts.

Cowan, P. A., & Hetherington, E. M. (Eds.). (1991). *Family transitions*. Hillsdale, NJ: Erlbaum.

Cummings, E. M., & Davies, P. (1994). *Children and marital conflict: The impact of family dispute and resolution*. New York: Guilford.

Damon, W. (Ed.). (1998). *Handbook of child psychology* (5th ed.). New York: Wiley.

Day, R. D., Gilbert, K. R., Settles, B. H., & Burr, W. R. (Eds.). (1995). *Research and theory in family science*. Pacific Grove, CA: Brooks/Cole.

Eshelman, J. R. (1997). *The family* (8th edition). Boston: Allyn & Bacon.

Gottman, J. M., Katz, L. F., & Hooven, C. (1997). *Meta-emotion: How families communicate emotionally*. Mahwah, N.J.: Lawrence Erlbaum

Hamner, T. J., & Turner, P. H. (1996). *Parenting in contemporary society*. Boston: Allyn & Bacon.

Holden, G. W. (1997). *Parents and the dynamics of childrearing*. Boulder, CO: Westview Press.

Kagan, S., & Weissbourd, B. (1994). *Putting families first*. San Francisco: Jossey Bass.

Levinson, D. (Ed.). (1995). *Encyclopedia of marriage and the family*. New York: Macmillan.

Luster, T., & Okagaki, L. (Eds.). (1993). *Parenting: An ecological perspective*. Hillsdale,
N. J.: Lawrence Earlbaum.

Manony, R. (1995). *Kidding ourselves: Breadwinning, babies, and bargaining power*.
New York: Basic Books.

Mindel, C. H., Habenstein, R. W., & Wright, R. (Eds.). (1988). *Ethnic families in America: Patterns and variations* (3rd ed.). New York: Elsevier Science Publishing.

Olson, R.A. Mullens, L. L., Gillman, J. B., & Chaney, J. M. (Eds.) (1994). *The sourcebook of pediatric psychology*. Boston: Allyn & Bacon.

Powell, D. R. (Ed.). (1988). *Parent education as early childhood intervention: Emerging
directions in theory, research, and practice*. Norwood, NJ: Ablex Publishing.

Roberts, T. W. (1994). *A systems perspective of parenting: The individual, the family,
and the social network*. Pacific Grove, CA: Brooks/Cole.

Smith, C. A., Cudaback, D., Goddard, H. W., and Myers- Walls, J. A. (1994). *National
Extension Parent Education Model of critical parenting practices*. Manhattan, KS:
Kansas State Research and Extension.

Zeanah, C. H. (Ed.) (1993), *Handbook of infant mental health*. New York: Guilford
Press.

Index

About the Contributors

Marci R. Aarstad, School of Family Studies and Human Services, Kansas State University, Manhattan, KS. *Spoiling*

Edward "Abe" Abelson, Private Practice and faculty of the Rudolf Dreikurs Summer Institute, Ithaca, NY. *Dreikurs, Rudolf*

Vivienne Adair, Education Department, University of Aukland, Aukland, New Zealand. *Donor insemination; Fertilization, in vitro; Infertility; Reproductive technology, assisted*

Steven M. Alessandri, Division of Child and Adolescent Psychiatry, Medical College of PA, Philadelphia PA. *Autism; Genetic disorders; Rousseau, Jean Jacques*

Mary Sue Ammon, Family Development and Education, University of California, Orinda, CA. *Literacy*

Judy A. Andrews, Oregon Research Institute, Eugene, OR. *Academic achievement; Substance abuse, parents; Substance use, children*

Carol Ford Arkin, Department of Department of Human Development and Family Science, The Ohio State University, Columbus, OH. *Conflict resolution*

Julia Reguero de Atiles, Child and Family Development, University of Georgia, Athens, GA. *Hispanic/Latino parents*

David E. Balk, Family Relations and Child Development, Oklahoma State University, Stillwater, OK. *Death of a child; Death of a parent*

Sheila A. Balog, Department of Psychology, St. Louis Children's Hospital, St. Louis, MO. *Disability, learning; Gifted children*

Joan M. Barth, Psychology Department, Massachusetts College of Liberal Arts, North Adams, MA. *Transition to school*

Abigail Baxter, Department of Special Education, University of South Alabama, Mobile, AL. *Disability, physical; Empowerment; Mental retardation; Urban parenting*

Marcia M. Bell, Marriage and Family Therapist, Lexington, KY. *Prison, parents in*

M. Betsy Bergen, School of Family Studies and Human Services, Kansas State University, Manhattan, KS. *Sex education; Sex roles*

Betty Lou Bettner, Psychotherapist and author, Media, PA. *Adler, Alfred*

Brian J. Bigelow, Department of Psychology, Laurentian University, Sudbury, Ontario, Canada. *Rules, implicit; Scaffolding; Social context*

Jerry J. Bigner, Department of Human Development and Family Studies, Colorado State University, Ft. Collins, CO. *Gay fathers; Lesbian mothers*

Jennifer Birckmayer, Department of Human Development and Family Studies, Cornell University, Ithaca, NY. *Discipline*

Belinda Blevins-Knabe, Department of Psychology, University of Arkansas at Little Rock, Little Rock, AR. *Mathematics*

Anne K. Bomba, Family and Consumer Sciences, University of Mississippi, University, MS. *Temperament*

Brenda J. Boyd, Department of Human Development, Washington State University, Pullman, WA. *Consequences, natural and logical; Developmentally Appropriate Practice; Goodness of fit model; Transition to parenthood*

Michael Bradshaw, School of Family Studies and Human Services, Kansas State University, Manhattan, KS. *Immunization*

Ronald T. Brown, Department of Pediatrics, Medical University of South Carolina, Children's Hospital, Charleston, SC. *Enuresis; Munchausen Syndrome by Proxy*

Patricia B. Burke, The Institute for Child and Adolescent Development, Wellesley, MA. *Siblings*

Janice Butcher, Faculty of Physical Education and Recreation Studies, University of Manitoba, Winnipeg, MB, Canada. *Motor development; Physical activity; Physical fitness; Playground skills; Sport*

Kelly C. Byars, Kennedy Kriedger Institute, Baltimore, MD. *Munchausen Syndrome by Proxy*

Stacy L. Koser Carmichael, Center for Pediatric Psychology and Family Studies, University of Florida, Gainsville, FL. *Illness, chronic, in children*

Michelle G. Carro, Human Behavior Institute, Las Vegas, NV. *Depression, postpartum*

Nick Carter, Targeted Marketing Solutions, Inc. (TMSI), Newton Upper Falls, MA. *Education, parenting*

Sandra L. Christenson, Department of Educational Psychology, University of Minnesota, Minneapolis, MN. *Family-school partnerships; Styles, parenting*

Jennifer Clark, Department of Human Development and Family Studies, The Pennsylvania State University, University Park, PA. *Family support; Kinship care*

Lindsey L. Cohen, Department of Psychology, University of Georgia, Athens, GA. *Enuresis*

Bruce E. Compas, Psychology Department, University of Vermont, Burlington, VT. *Depression, postpartum*

Helen Cowie, School of Psychology and Counselling, Roehampton Institute London, West Hill, London, England. *Freud, Anna*

Betsy Davis, Oregon Research Institute, Eugene, OR. *Social competence*

Karen B. DeBord, Department of Family and Consumer Sciences, North Carolina State University, Raleigh, NC. *Community; Toilet learning*

Mary DeLuccie, School of Family Studies and Human Services, Kansas State University, Manhattan, KS. *Fathering; Spock, Benjamin*

Susanne A. Denham, Department of Psychology, George Mason University, Fairfax, VA. *Affectivity, positive and negative; Emotion language; Separation anxiety*

Shannon Dermer, School of Family Studies and Human Services, Kansas State University, Manhattan, KS. *Compliance; Feminism; Limit setting*

Elisa Doebler-Irvine, Homestead Youth Lodge, Pendleton, OR. *Attachment, secure; Eating disorders*

Mary B. Eberly, Department of Psychology, Oakland University, Rochester, MI. *Chores*

Nancy Eisenberg, Department of Psychology, Arizona State University, Tempe, AZ. *Empathy; Prosocial behavior*

Robert J. Fetsch, Department of Human Development and Family Studies, Colorado State University, Ft. Collins, CO. *Family council; Temper tantrums*

Mark Fine, Department of Human Development and Family Studies, University of Missouri, Columbia, MO. *Single parents; Stepparents*

Connie Flanagan, Department of Agricultural and Extension Education, Pennsylvania State University, University Park, PA. *Socioeconomic status*

Gary R. Geffken, Department of Psychiatry, University of Florida HSC, Gainsville, FL. *Illness, chronic, in children; Pain, children and adolescents with*

Sandra Glasner, Early Childhood Department, North Georgia College and State University, Dahlonega, GA. *Hispanic/Latino parents*

Virginia Gobeli, Families, 4-H and Nutrition, Cooperative State Research, Education and Extension Service, USDA, Washington, DC. *Cooperative Extension Service; Recognition/encouragement*

H. Wallace Goddard, Home and Family, Franklin-Covey Co., Provo, UT. *Control strategies; Ginott, Haim; Moral development; Nature versus nurture; Nurturance; Synchrony; Victim-centered discipline*

Sam Goldstein, Neurology, Learning and Behavior Center, Salt Lake City, UT. *Attention Deficit Hyperactivity Disorder*

Ian H. Gotlib, Department of Psychology, Stanford University, Stanford, CA. *Depression, postpartum*

Theodore N. Greenstein, Department of Sociology and Anthropology, North Carolina State University, Raleigh, NC. *Employment, early maternal*

Wendy Haight, School of Social Work, University of Illinois at Urbana-Champaign, Urbana, IL. *Religious development*

Lee Hamilton, Department of Sociology and Anthropology, New Mexico State University, Las Cruces, NM. *Suicide in children*

Wendy Hamilton, 4H and Family Department, New Mexico State University, Las Cruces, NM. *Dual-earner families*

Gary L. Hansen, Department of Sociology, University of Kentucky, Lexington, KY. *Gender socialization; Jealousy*

Chryse Hatzichristou, Department of Education, University of Thessaly, Athens, Greece. *Cultural context; Divorced families; Peer influence; School*

Crystal Wilhite Hemesath, School of Family Studies and Human Services, Kansas State University, Manhattan, KS. *Feminism*

C. C. Herbison, School of Education, University of Kansas, Lawrence, KS. *Asian American parents*

Mindi R. Higgins-Kessler, Marriage and Family Therapist in Private Practice, Wichita, KS. *Runaway children; Scapegoating*

Nuran Hortaçsu, Department of Psychology, Middle East Technical University, Ankara, Turkey. *Paradigms, parenting; Popularity*

Jennifer B. Hutchings, Galacia Institute, Kansas State University, Manhattan, KS. *Self-fulfilling prophecy*

Carolyn Ievers, Department of Pediatrics, Rainbow Babies & Children's Hospital, Cleveland, OH. *Role strain*

James V. Kahn, Early Childhood Research and Intervention Program, Chicago, IL. *Disability, physical; Empowerment; Mental retardation; Urban parenting*

Carol Kauppi, Centre for Research in Human Development, Laurentian University, Sudbury, Ontario, Canada. *Paradigms, parenting; Reconstituted families*

Myra C. Kawaguchi, Department of Psychology, University of Tennessee, Knoxville, TN. *Dimensions of Temperament Survey–Revised; Identity development; Sexuality, adolescent*

Michelle L. Kelley, Department of Psychology, Old Dominion University, Norfolk, VA. *Military families*

Patricia K. Kerig, Department of Psychology, Simon Fraser University, Burnaby, BC, Canada. *Alliance, parenting; Conflict, interparental; Triangulation*

Jacqueline J. Kirby, Department of Human Development and Family Science, The Ohio State University, Columbus, OH. *Multiples*

Danielle Knafo, Department of Psychology, Bar Ilan University, Ramat Gan, Israel. *Puberty*

Lynne Sanford Koester, Department of Psychology, University of Montana, Missoula, MT. *Deaf children, parenting; Intuitive parenting*

Helma M. Y. Koomen, Faculty of Psychology and Pedagogical Sciences, Vrije Universiteit, Amsterdam, The Netherlands. *Cleft lip and palate; Hospitalization*

Faye Sprunger Koop, Department of Psychology, Hesston College, Hesston, KS. *Failure to thrive; Thumbsucking*

Byran B. Korth, Department of Human Development and Family Studies, Auburn University, Auburn, AL. *Deaf parents; Teacher training*

Wendy Rodenberger Kuppenheimer, Children's Hospital of Cincinnati, Cincinnati, OH. *Munchausen Syndrome by Proxy*

Juanita Laramie, School Psychologist, Mapleton Public Schools, Denver, CO. *Family-school partnerships; Styles, parenting*

Lucille Larney, Department of Counseling Psychology, University at Albany, State University of New York, Albany, NY. *Premature birth*

Gwen Layfield, Department of Agricultural and Extension Education, Pennsylvania State University, University Park, PA. *Head Start; Socioeconomic status*

Elizabeth A. Levin, Department of Psychology, Laurentian University, Sudbury, Ontario, Canada. *Money and children; Whining*

Kathleen L. MacNaughton, Department of Clinical and Health Psychology, University of Florida Health Center, Gainsville, FL. *Pain, children and adolescents with*

David MacPhee, Department of Human Development and Family Studies, Colorado State University, Fort Collins, CO. *Domestic labor; HOME Inventory; Poverty; Prevention; Surrogate motherhood*

Sarah P. McCamman, Child Development Unit/University Affiliated Program, University of Kansas Medical Center, Kansas City, KS. *Breastfeeding*

Kier Maxwell, School of Family Studies and Human Services, Kansas State University, Manhattan, KS. *Locke, John; Parents Anonymous*

Richard B. Miller, School of Family Studies and Human Services, Kansas State University, Manhattan, KS. *Adult children; Illness, chronic, in children*

Raymond Montemayor, Department of Psychology, Ohio State University, Columbus, OH. *Chores*

Christine Irish Motley, Department of Family Relations and Child Development, Oklahoma State University, Stillwater, OK. *Death, understanding of; Eating behavior, children and*

Miriam Mulsow, Human Development and Family Studies, Texas Tech University, Lubbock, TX. *Physical punishment*

Megan J. Murphy, Department of Child and Family Development, University of Georgia, Athens, GA. *Distancing strategies; Instrumental versus expressive functions; Marital boundaries*

Ann D. Murray, School of Family Studies and Human Services, Kansas State University, Manhattan, KS. *Brazelton, T. Berry; Critical periods; Crying; Floortime; Mutuality; Vygotsky, Lev Semenovich*

John P. Murray, School of Family Studies and Human Services, Kansas State University, Manhattan, KS. *Captain Kangaroo; Rogers, Fred; Television viewing; Television violence*

Velma McBride Murry, Department of Child and Family Development, University of Georgia, Athens, GA. *African American parents; Physical punishment*

Linda Musun-Miller, Psychology Department, University of Arkansas at Little Rock, Little Rock, AR. *Birth order*

Judith A. Myers-Walls, Child Development and Family Studies, Purdue University, W. Lafayette, IN. *Abuse, child; Adolescent parenthood; Adolescent pregnancy; Advocacy; Biting; Home visitation; Peace education*

Rowan R. Myron-Wilson, Department of Psychology, University of London, New Cross, London, England. *Bullying*

Hira Nair, Social Sciences Division, Kansas City Kansas Community College, Overland Park, KS. *Violence, community*

Tricia K. Neppl, Department of Human Development and Family Studies, Iowa State University, Ames, IA. *Play; Toys*

William F. Northey, Jr. Department of Family and Consumer Sciences, Bowling Green State University, Bowling Green, OH. *Foster parenting; Throwaway children*

Mary J. O'Connor, Department of Psychiatry, UCLA School of Medicine, Los Angeles, CA. *Fetal Alcohol Syndrome*

Michelle Olexa, Department of Counseling Psychology, University at Albany, Albany, NY. *Vulnerable Child Syndrome*

Charlotte Shoup Olsen, School of Family Studies and Human Services, Kansas State University, Manhattan, KS. *Communication; Cultural competence; Racial identity; Sociocultural background*

D. Kim Openshaw, Department of Family and Human Development, Utah State University, Logan, UT. *AIDS/HIV; AIDS/HIV, adolescent; AIDS/HIV, pediatric; Custody; Resiliency in children; Sexual offenders, youthful*

Roberta O'Shea, Early Childhood Research and Intervention Program at the University of Illinois at Chicago, Chicago, IL. *Mental retardation; Urban parenting*

Rick L. Peterson, Virginia Cooperative Extension Service, Virginia Polytechnic Institute and State University, Blacksburg, VA. *Family loyalty*

Christopher G. Petr, University of Kansas School of Social Welfare, Lawrence, KS. *Family-centered services*

Scott Phillips, School of Family Studies and Human Services, Kansas State University, Manhattan, KS. *Locke, John; Mental illness, children; Parents Anonymous*

Kim M. Pierce, Wisconsin Center for Education Research, University of Wisconsin at Madison, Madison, WI. *After-school child care; Self-care; Stress, parental*

Karen Lynn Poff, Virginia Cooperative Extension, Woodstock, VA. *Aggression, childhood*

James J. Ponzetti, Jr., Associate Professor, Warner Pacific College, Portland, OR. *Home schooling; Rituals; Routines; Traditions*

Elaine G. Porter, Department of Sociology and Anthropology, Laurentian University, Sudbury, Ontario, Canada. *Blaming, parent; Family size*

Vicky Primer, St. Anthony Villa/Boysville, Toledo, OH. *Family preservation; Foster parenting; Intergenerational parenting; Standards of care, minimum*

Kristin Pruett, School of Family Studies and Human Services, Kansas State University, Manhattan, KS. *Limit setting*

Sam Quick, Department of Family Studies, University of Kentucky, Lexington, KY. *Prison, parents in; Spirituality*

Andrew G. Renouf, Department of Psychology, St. Louis Children's Hospital, St. Louis, MO. *Depression in children; Depression in parents*

James R. Rodrigue, Department of Clinical and Health Psychology, University of Florida, Gainsville, FL. *Illness, chronic, in children; Pain, children and adolescents with*

Karen Rosen, Department of Psychology, Boston College, Chestnut Hill, MA. *Acceptance, parental; Siblings*

Sharon S. Rostosky, Department of Psychology, University of Tennessee, Knoxville, TN. *Dimensions of Temperament Survey–Revised; Identity development; Sexuality, adolescent*

Fred Rothbaum, Department of Child Development, Tufts University, Medford, MA. *Acceptance, parental*

Anna Rumball, Elleslie, Auckland, New Zealand. *Donor insemination*

Candyce S. Russell, School of Family Studies and Human Services, Kansas State University, Manhattan, KS. *Family systems*

Elizabeth J. Sandell, MELD, Minneapolis, MN. *MELD*

Tara Thomas Schluesche, Department of Educational Psychology, University of Minnesota, Minneapolis, MN. *Family-school partnerships; Styles, parenting*

James M. Seibold, School of Family Studies and Human Services, Kansas State University, Manhattan, KS. *Consistency; Mental illness, children*

Shmuel Shulman, Department of Psychology, Bar Ilan University, Ramat Gan, Israel. *Adolescent separation; Puberty*

Myrna B. Shure, Child Development/Family, Allegheny University of the Health Sciences, Philadelphia, PA. *Problem solving*

Benjamin Silliman, Department of Family and Consumer Sciences, University of Wyoming, Laramie, WY. *Marital interaction; Resiliency in parents*

A. Rae Simpson, Family Resource Center, Massachusetts Institute of Technology, Cambridge, MA. *Media, mass*

Charles A. Smith, School of Family Studies and Human Services, Kansas State University, Manhattan, KS. *Authority, parental; Competition; Conscience; Delinquency, juvenile; Fear; Guilt; Imagination; Narratives, personal; National Extension Parent Education Model; Self-esteem; Shame; Skinner, B. F.; Social support, informal; Touching*

Peter K. Smith, Department of Psychology, Goldsmiths College, New Cross, London, England. *Grandparenting*

Tracy Spinrad, Department of Psychology, Arizona State University, Tempe, AZ. *Colic; Mothering*

Marilyn Stern, Department of Counseling Psychology, University at Albany, State University of New York, Albany, NY. *Mediation, parent-child; Premature birth; Vulnerable Child Syndrome*

Cynthia Stifter, Human Development and Family Studies, Pennsylvania State University, University Park, PA. *Colic; Mothering*

Anne Dopkins Stright, Department of Counseling and Educational Psychology, Indiana University, Bloomington, IN. *Child care*

Deborah J. Thomason, Department of Family and Youth Development, Clemson University, Clemson, SC. *Parents Without Partners; Pets and children; Smoking; Sudden Infant Death Syndrome*

Suzanne M. Thompson, Department of Psychology, St. Louis Children's Hospital, St. Louis, MO. *Nightmares; Night terrors; Nighttime fears; Night wakings; Obesity*

Jill M. Thorngren, Department of Counseling, Idaho State University, Pocatello, ID. *Shyness*

Joseph G. Turner, Department of Human Development and Family Studies, Colorado State University, Ft. Collins, CO. *Listening; Misbehavior*

Michael R. Van Slyck, Research Institute for Dispute Resolution, Albany, NY. *Mediation, parent-child*

Susan Ruth Waddington, Kingsborough Community College, Brooklyn, NY. *Psychological testing*

Deborah Wasserman, Department of Human Development and Family Science, The Ohio State University, Columbus, OH. *Conflict resolution*

Deborah P. Welsh, Department of Psychology, University of Tennessee, Knoxville, TN. *Dimensions of Temperament Survey–Revised; Identity development; Sexuality, adolescent*

Ronald Jay Werner-Wilson, Department of Human Development and Family Studies, Iowa State University, Ames, IA. *Distancing strategies; Instrumental versus expressive functions; Marital boundaries; Runaway children; Scapegoating*

Carmel Parker White, Department of Human Development and Family Studies, Auburn University, AL *Language development*

Mark B. White, Department of Human Development and Family Studies, Auburn University, AL. *Family therapy*

Michael Yellow Bird, School of Social Welfare, University of Kansas, Lawrence, KS. *Indigenous Peoples parent roles*

Martha York, Special Education Department, Kansas State University, Manhattan, KS. *Adoption*

ISBN 0-313-29699-5

90000>

EAN

9 780313 296994

HARDCOVER BAR CODE